Subaru Legacy
and Forester Automotive Repair Manual

by Jeff Killingsworth
and John H Haynes
Member of the Guild of Motoring Writers

Models covered:
Subaru Legacy 2010 through 2016
Forester 2009 through 2016
*Does not include information specific to six-cylinder
and diesel engine models*

ABCDE
FGHIJ
KLMNO
PQRST

Haynes Publishing Group
Sparkford Nr Yeovil
Somerset BA22 7JJ England

Haynes North America, Inc
859 Lawrence Drive
Newbury Park
California 91320 USA
www.haynes.com

Acknowledgements

Technical writers who contributed to this project include Demian Hurst and Scott "Gonzo" Weaver.

© **Haynes North America, Inc. 2017**

With permission from J.H. Haynes & Co. Ltd.

A book in the Haynes Automotive Repair Manual Series

Printed in Malaysia

ISBN-13: 978-1-62092-257-6
ISBN-10: 1-62092-257-6

Library of Congress Control Number: 2017933576

Contents

Haynes mechanic and photographer with a 2013 Subaru Legacy

About this manual

Its purpose

The purpose of this manual is to help you get the best value from your vehicle. It can do so in several ways. It can help you decide what work must be done, even if you choose to have it done by a dealer service department or a repair shop; it provides information and procedures for routine maintenance and servicing; and it offers diagnostic and repair procedures to follow when trouble occurs.

We hope you use the manual to tackle the work yourself. For many simpler jobs, doing it yourself may be quicker than arranging an appointment to get the vehicle into a shop and making the trips to leave it and pick it up. More importantly, a lot of money can be saved by avoiding the expense the shop must pass on to you to cover its labor and overhead costs. An added benefit is the sense of satisfaction and accomplishment that you feel after doing the job yourself.

Using the manual

The manual is divided into Chapters. Each Chapter is divided into numbered Sections, which are headed in bold type between horizontal lines. Each Section consists of consecutively numbered paragraphs.

The reference numbers used in illustration captions pinpoint the pertinent Section and the Step within that Section. That is, illustration 3.2 means the illustration refers to Section 3 and Step (or paragraph) 2 within that Section.

Procedures, once described in the text, are not normally repeated. When it's necessary to refer to another Chapter, the reference will be given as Chapter and Section number. Cross references given without use of the word "Chapter" apply to Sections and/or paragraphs in the same Chapter. For example, "see Section 8" means in the same Chapter.

References to the left or right side of the vehicle assume you are sitting in the driver's seat, facing forward.

Even though we have prepared this manual with extreme care, neither the publisher nor the author can accept responsibility for any errors in, or omissions from, the information given.

NOTE

A **Note** provides information necessary to properly complete a procedure or information which will make the procedure easier to understand.

CAUTION

A **Caution** provides a special procedure or special steps which must be taken while completing the procedure where the Caution is found. Not heeding a Caution can result in damage to the assembly being worked on.

WARNING

A **Warning** provides a special procedure or special steps which must be taken while completing the procedure where the Warning is found. Not heeding a Warning can result in personal injury.

Introduction

Legacy models are available in four-door sedan and Forester models are available in a wagon body style.

Engines available on these models are: a four-cylinder 2.0L DOHC turbocharged engine, a four-cylinder 2.5L SOHC engine, a four-cylinder 2.5L DOHC non-turbocharged engine, or a four-cylinder 2.5L DOHC turbocharged engine. All engines use 8 valves per cylinder head and are equipped with Multipoint fuel injection systems.

Power from the engine is transferred through a five-speed manual, a six-speed manual, 4-speed automatic, 5-speed automatic, or a continuously variable transmission (CVT), then through a pair of driveaxles to the front wheels. Power is also transferred through a driveshaft and a rear differential which drives the rear wheels through another pair of driveaxles.

Suspension is fully independent, utilizing MacPherson struts at the front end, with steering knuckles bolted to the lower ends of the struts and connected to control arms with a balljoint. The rear suspension consists of coil-over shock absorber assemblies, trailing arms, knuckles, an upper control arm and two lower lateral links on each side. Front and rear stabilizer bars reduce vehicle roll.

The steering gear is a power assisted rack-and-pinion type that is mounted to the front crossmember with rubber insulators. 2014 and earlier Legacy models/2013 and earlier Forester models use hydraulic power steering, while 2015 and later Legacy models/2014 and later Forester models use electric power steering.

The brakes are disc at the front and at the rear, with power assist and an Anti-lock Braking System (ABS) as standard equipment.

Most models have a power assisted disc-type front and rear brake system with an Anti-lock Brake System (ABS) as standard equipment.

Vehicle identification numbers

1   Modifications are a continuing and unpublicized process in vehicle manufacturing. Since spare parts lists and manuals are compiled on a numerical basis, the individual vehicle numbers are necessary to correctly identify the component required.

Vehicle Identification Number (VIN)

2   This very important identification number is stamped on a plate attached to the dashboard inside the windshield on the driver's side of the vehicle and on the engine compartment firewall (see illustration). The VIN also appears on the Vehicle Certificate of Title and Registration. It contains information such as where and when the vehicle was manufactured, the model year and the body style.

VIN engine and model year codes

3   Two particularly important pieces of information found in the VIN are the engine code and the model year code. Counting from the left, the engine code letter designation is the 6th digit and the model year code letter designation is the 10th digit.

On the models covered by this manual the engine codes are:

Legacy models

2014 and earlier
  A   2.5L (SOHC) non-turbocharged (U4)
  B   2.5L (DOHC) non-turbocharged (U5)
  C   2.5L (DOHC) non-turbocharged (U6)
  F   2.5L (DOHC) turbocharged (U4)
2015 and later
  A   2.5L (DOHC) non-turbocharged (U5)
  B   2.5L (DOHC) non-turbocharged (U6)

Forester models

  A   2.5L (DOHC) non-turbocharged (U5)
  B   2.5L (DOHC) non-turbocharged (U6)
  G   2.0L (DOHC) turbocharged (U4)

On the models covered by this manual the model year codes are:

  9   2009
  A   2010
  B   2011
  C   2012
  D   2013
  E   2014
  F   2015
  G   2016

Vehicle Certification Label

4   The Vehicle Certification Label is attached to the driver's side door pillar (see illustration). Information on this label includes the name of the manufacturer, the month and year of production, and the Vehicle Identification Number.

Engine identification number

5   The engine identification number (see illustration) is stamped onto a machined pad on the top of the engine block.

3.2 The VIN number is visible through the driver's side window

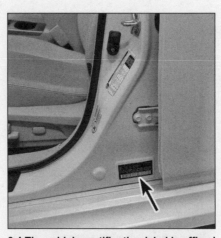

3.4 The vehicle certification label is affixed to the driver's side door pillar

3.5 The engine identification number is located on top of the block, near the transaxle

3.6 On automatic and manual transaxles, the transaxle identification number is located on the top of the bellhousing

3.7 The rear differential identification tag is affixed to the differential cover

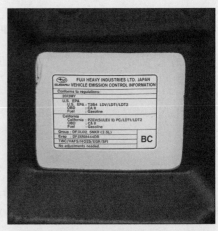

3.8 The vehicle emissions label is affixed to the underside of the hood in the engine compartment

Transaxle identification number(s)

6 The transaxle identification number is located on the top of the bellhousing (see illustration).

Rear differential identification number

7 The rear differential identification number is stamped on a tag affixed to the differential cover (see illustration).

Vehicle Emissions Control Information label

8 This label is found on the underside of the hood in the engine compartment (see illustration).

Recall information

Vehicle recalls are carried out by the manufacturer in the rare event of a possible safety-related defect. The vehicle's registered owner is contacted at the address on file at the Department of Motor Vehicles and given the details of the recall. Remedial work is carried out free of charge at a dealer service department.

If you are the new owner of a used vehicle which was subject to a recall and you want to be sure that the work has been carried out, it's best to contact a dealer service department and ask about your individual vehicle - you'll need to furnish them your Vehicle Identification Number (VIN).

The table below is based on informa-tion provided by the National Highway Traffic Safety Administration (NHTSA), the body which oversees vehicle recalls in the United States. The recall database is updated constantly. For the latest information on vehicle recalls, check the NHTSA website at www. nhtsa.gov, www.safercar.gov, or call the NHTSA hotline at 1-888-327-4236.

Recall date	Recall campaign number	Model(s) affected	Concern
May 07, 2010	10V196000	2010 Legacy	On some models equipped with CVT automatic transaxles, a crack or split can occur in the CVT cooler hose resulting in a fluid leak. If the fluid is completely leaked during driving, the vehicle will come to a stop, possibly resulting in a crash.
June 24, 2010	10V283000	2010 Legacy	On certain models, the wiring in the airbag clockspring connector located behind the vehicle's steering wheel may develop stress cracks and eventually break. If this were to happen certain electrical components may not operate as intended. The possible circuits affected are the driver's frontal airbag, paddle shifter function, cruise control, horn control and radio functions increasing the risk of a crash.

Recall date	Recall campaign number	Model(s) affected	Concern
July 20, 2010	10V326000	2010, 2011 Legacy	On some models, a programming error occurred and a lubrication hole within the 6-speed manual transmission was omitted. If the transmission gears are not properly lubricated, a groaning sound may begin to develop alerting the driver of a problem. If the sound is ignored and no action is taken, the gears will eventually break and this condition will lead to vehicle power loss, possibly resulting in a crash.
Sept. 07, 2011	11V467000	2011 Legacy	On certain models, the moonroof glass may come loose or detach. The amount and position of the adhesive between the glass and retainer was inadequately applied. The moonroof glass can loosen and detach from the vehicle during driving, resulting in a potential road hazard for other vehicles, increasing the risk of a crash.
Nov. 29, 2011	11V562000	2011 Legacy	Certain models may be equipped with a brake master cylinder that could malfunction and cause an increase in the amount of brake pedal travel distance required to slow or stop the vehicle. The driver might misjudge the amount of brake pedal travel required to achieve the desired stopping distance. This could occur unexpectedly and without prior warning, increasing the risk of a crash.
February 09, 2012	12V047000	2012 Legacy	Some vehicles may be equipped with side curtain air bags that contain an incorrect propellant mixture for the initiator component used, resulting in insufficient output of compressed gas. The side curtain air bags may not deploy, increasing the risk of injury.
March 13, 2012	12V099000	2012 Forester	On certain models the automatic locking retractor in the seat belt assemblies, located in the rear center seating of the affected vehicles do not meet lockability requirements. Specifically, the assemblies may not permit proper installation and secure attachment of a child restraint in that seating position. An insecure installation of a child restraint can increase the risk of injury to a child during a crash.
Dec. 26, 2012	12V602000	2010, 2011 Legacy, 2012 Forester	On some models equipped with accessory puddle lights, a short circuit can develop when either the puddle light or connector are exposed to an electrolytic moisture source (such as road spray that has road salt in it) and it penetrates the circuit board of the puddle light or the pins of the puddle light connector(s). Over time, migration of the moisture into the circuit board and/or into the connector cavity may result in a short circuit of the puddle light system. This may generate heat which may melt the plastic resulting in smoke or fire.

Recall date	Recall campaign number	Model(s) affected	Concern
February 25, 2013	13V061000	2010, 2011, 2012, 2013 Legacy	On some models, equipped with an automatic or CVT transmission and an Audiovox remote engine starter (RES), if the RES fob is dropped, the fob may malfunction and randomly transmit an engine start request without pressing the button. The engine may inadvertently start and run for up to fifteen minutes. The engine may continue to start and stop until the fob battery is depleted, or until the vehicle runs out of fuel. If the vehicle is parked in an enclosed area, there is a risk of carbon monoxide build-up which may cause headaches, dizziness or, in extreme cases, unconsciousness and/or asphyxiation.
March 05, 2013	13V077000	2012 Legacy	On certain models, the moonroof glass may come loose or detach. The amount and position of the adhesive between the glass and retainer was inadequately applied. The moonroof glass can loosen and detach from the vehicle during driving, resulting in a potential road hazard for other vehicles, increasing the risk of a crash.
April 24, 2013	13V159000	2014 Forester	On certain models, the backing for the carpeted floor mats was not manufactured to specification. As a result, the floor mats may curl when exposed to heat. Curling of the driver side floor mat could distract the driver and/or interfere with proper operation of one or a combination of, the vehicle's clutch, brake, and accelerator pedals. Brake or accelerator pedal interference may result in very high vehicle speeds and make it difficult to stop the vehicle, which could cause a crash.
May 13, 2013	13V194000	2013 Legacy	On certain models, the inner and outer shafts of the steering column assembly may become disengaged from one another. If the shafts become disengaged, the driver would lose the ability to steer the vehicle, increasing the risk of a crash.
August 01, 2013	13V336000	2014 Legacy	On some models equipped with 5-speed automatic transmissions, the parking rod may come loose inside the transmission. As a result of the parking rod detaching, the transmission may not be able to be moved from the "park" position, preventing the vehicle from being moved or driven. Furthermore, even with the transmission shifted into the 'park' position, the parking mechanism may not engage, and the vehicle may roll away while in the "park" position, increasing the risk of a crash.
June 10, 2014	14V311000	2010, 2011 Legacy, 2012, 2013 Forester	On some models, salt water could splash on the brake lines through a gap in the fuel tank protector, resulting in excessive corrosion of the brake lines. Brake line corrosion may result in brake fluid leakage. Fluid leakage may result in longer distances being required to slow or stop the vehicle, increasing the risk of a crash.

Recall date	Recall campaign number	Model(s) affected	Concern
Dec. 31, 2014	14V830000	2012, 2013 Forester	On some models that were remedied under recall 14V-311 prior to December 23, 2014, the brake lines may experience brake line corrosion due to salt water splashing on the brake lines through a gap in the fuel tank protector. Brake fluid may leak due to the brake line corrosion and may result in longer distances being required to slow or stop the vehicle, increasing the risk of a crash.
June 12, 2015	15V336000	2015 Legacy	On certain models equipped with the Eyesight Driver Assist System, if the switch that activates the brake lights fails, the automatic pre-collision braking component of the driver assist system will not function. If the automatic pre-collision braking system does not function as intended, the vehicle will not react to an obstacle in its path, increasing the risk of a crash.
August 10, 2015	15V502000	2015, 2016 Legacy	On certain models, transmission oil may leak from a deformed seal cap on the propeller shaft yoke. If the transmission oil leaks onto the exhaust pipe, there is a possible risk of fire.
Nov. 24, 2015	15V794000	2016 Legacy	On certain models, due to the improper tightening of the securing nuts, the drive shaft may separate from the rear differential. If the drive shaft detaches from the rear differential, it may strike the fuel tank and result in a fuel leak, increasing the risk of a fire.
March 21, 2016	16V162000	2015, 2016 Forester	On some models, the turbocharger air intake duct may crack and possibly result in an engine stall. An engine stall increases the risk of a crash.
April 27, 2016	16V251000	2015 Legacy	On certain models, the brake fluid used in these vehicles may contain excess moisture which may adversely affect the performance of the electronic stability control system. Poor performance of the electronic stability control system, may result in a loss of vehicle control, increasing the risk of a crash.
May 11, 2016	16V292000	2016 Legacy	On certain models, the steering column may have been improperly machined, and as a result, turning the steering wheel may have no effect on the direction of the wheels. The loss of steering ability would increase the risk of a crash.
May 25, 2016	16V358000	2010, 2011 Legacy	Some models may be equipped with certain air bag inflators assembled as part of the passenger frontal airbag modules, and used as original equipment or replacement equipment. In the event of a crash necessitating deployment of the front airbags, these inflators may rupture due to propellant degradation occurring after long-term exposure to absolute humidity and temperature cycling. An inflator rupture may result in metal fragments striking the vehicle occupants resulting in serious injury or death.

Recall date	Recall campaign number	Model(s) affected	Concern
Sept. 27, 2016	16V694000	2010, 2011, 2012, 2013, 2014 Legacy	On some models, components within the windshield wiper motor bottom cover may interfere with each other. If an obstruction, such as a buildup of snow or ice prevents the wiper arms from being able to stop in the parked position, the wiper motor may overheat and the bottom cover may melt. If the windshield wiper motor overheats, the wipers may fail, reducing driver visibility and increasing the risk of a crash. Additionally, the wiper motor cover may melt, increasing the risk of a fire.
October 13, 2016	16V738000	2012, 2013 Forester	On some models equipped with turbo-charged engines, the relay that controls the secondary air injection pump may fail, causing the pump to continuously operate and overheat. If the air injection pump overheats, it may melt and increase the risk of a fire.

Buying parts

Replacement parts are available from many sources, which generally fall into one of two categories - authorized dealer parts departments and independent retail auto parts stores. Our advice concerning these parts is as follows:

Retail auto parts stores: Good auto parts stores will stock frequently needed components which wear out relatively fast, such as clutch components, exhaust systems, brake parts, tune-up parts, etc. These stores often supply new or reconditioned parts on an exchange basis, which can save a considerable amount of money. Discount auto parts stores are often very good places to buy materials and parts needed for general vehicle maintenance such as oil, grease, filters, spark plugs, belts, touch-up paint, bulbs, etc. They also usually sell tools and general accessories, have convenient hours, charge lower prices and can often be found not far from home.

Authorized dealer parts department: This is the best source for parts which are unique to the vehicle and not generally available elsewhere (such as major engine parts, transmission parts, trim pieces, etc.).

Warranty information: If the vehicle is still covered under warranty, be sure that any replacement parts purchased - regardless of the source - do not invalidate the warranty!

To be sure of obtaining the correct parts, have engine and chassis numbers available and, if possible, take the old parts along for positive identification.

Maintenance techniques, tools and working facilities

Maintenance techniques

There are a number of techniques involved in maintenance and repair that will be referred to throughout this manual. Application of these techniques will enable the home mechanic to be more efficient, better organized and capable of performing the various tasks properly, which will ensure that the repair job is thorough and complete.

Fasteners

Fasteners are nuts, bolts, studs and screws used to hold two or more parts together. There are a few things to keep in mind when working with fasteners. Almost all of them use a locking device of some type, either a lockwasher, locknut, locking tab or thread adhesive. All threaded fasteners should be clean and straight, with undamaged threads and undamaged corners on the hex head where the wrench fits. Develop the habit of replacing all damaged nuts and bolts with new ones. Special locknuts with nylon or fiber inserts can only be used once. If they are removed, they lose their locking ability and must be replaced with new ones.

Rusted nuts and bolts should be treated with a penetrating fluid to ease removal and prevent breakage. Some mechanics use turpentine in a spout-type oil can, which works quite well. After applying the rust penetrant, let it work for a few minutes before trying to loosen the nut or bolt. Badly rusted fasteners may have to be chiseled or sawed off or removed with a special nut breaker, available at tool stores.

If a bolt or stud breaks off in an assembly, it can be drilled and removed with a special tool commonly available for this purpose. Most automotive machine shops can perform this task, as well as other repair procedures, such as the repair of threaded holes that have been stripped out.

Flat washers and lockwashers, when removed from an assembly, should always be replaced exactly as removed. Replace any damaged washers with new ones. Never use a lockwasher on any soft metal surface (such as aluminum), thin sheet metal or plastic.

Fastener sizes

For a number of reasons, automobile manufacturers are making wider and wider use of metric fasteners. Therefore, it is important to be able to tell the difference between standard (sometimes called U.S. or SAE) and metric hardware, since they cannot be interchanged.

All bolts, whether standard or metric, are sized according to diameter, thread pitch and length. For example, a standard 1/2 - 13 x 1 bolt is 1/2 inch in diameter, has 13 threads per inch and is 1 inch long. An M12 - 1.75 x 25 metric bolt is 12 mm in diameter, has a thread pitch of 1.75 mm (the distance between threads) and is 25 mm long. The two bolts are nearly identical, and easily confused, but they are not interchangeable.

In addition to the differences in diameter, thread pitch and length, metric and standard bolts can also be distinguished by examining the bolt heads. To begin with, the distance across the flats on a standard bolt head is measured in inches, while the same dimension on a metric bolt is sized in millimeters (the same is true for nuts). As a result, a standard wrench should not be used on a metric bolt and a metric wrench should not be used on a standard bolt. Also, most standard bolts have slashes radiating out from the center of the head to denote the grade or strength of the bolt, which is an indication of the amount of torque that can be applied to it. The greater the number of slashes, the greater the strength of the bolt. Grades 0 through 5 are commonly used on automobiles. Metric bolts have a property class (grade) number, rather than a slash, molded into their heads to indicate bolt strength. In this case, the higher the number, the stronger the bolt. Property class numbers 8.8, 9.8 and 10.9 are commonly used on automobiles.

Strength markings can also be used to distinguish standard hex nuts from metric hex nuts. Many standard nuts have dots stamped into one side, while metric nuts are marked with a number. The greater the number of

dots, or the higher the number, the greater the strength of the nut.

Metric studs are also marked on their ends according to property class (grade). Larger studs are numbered (the same as metric bolts), while smaller studs carry a geometric code to denote grade.

It should be noted that many fasteners, especially Grades 0 through 2, have no distinguishing marks on them. When such is the case, the only way to determine whether it is standard or metric is to measure the thread pitch or compare it to a known fastener of the same size.

Standard fasteners are often referred to as SAE, as opposed to metric. However, it should be noted that SAE technically refers to a non-metric fine thread fastener only. Coarse thread non-metric fasteners are referred to as USS sizes.

Since fasteners of the same size (both standard and metric) may have different

strength ratings, be sure to reinstall any bolts, studs or nuts removed from your vehicle in their original locations. Also, when replacing a fastener with a new one, make sure that the new one has a strength rating equal to or greater than the original.

Tightening sequences and procedures

Most threaded fasteners should be tightened to a specific torque value (torque is the twisting force applied to a threaded component such as a nut or bolt). Overtightening the fastener can weaken it and cause it to break, while undertightening can cause it to eventually come loose. Bolts, screws and studs, depending on the material they are made of and their thread diameters, have specific torque values, many of which are noted in the Specifications at the beginning of each Chapter. Be sure to follow the torque recommen-

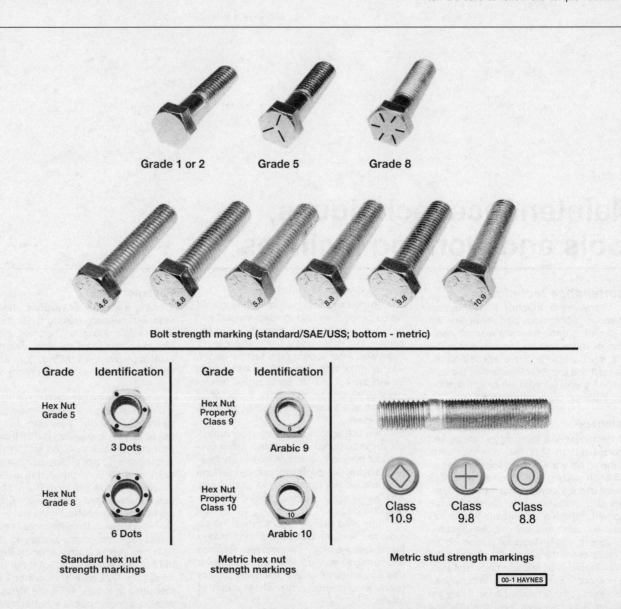

Grade 1 or 2   Grade 5   Grade 8

Bolt strength marking (standard/SAE/USS; bottom - metric)

Grade	Identification	Grade	Identification
Hex Nut Grade 5	3 Dots	Hex Nut Property Class 9	Arabic 9
Hex Nut Grade 8	6 Dots	Hex Nut Property Class 10	Arabic 10

Standard hex nut strength markings

Metric hex nut strength markings

Class 10.9   Class 9.8   Class 8.8

Metric stud strength markings

dations closely. For fasteners not assigned a specific torque, a general torque value chart is presented here as a guide. These torque values are for dry (unlubricated) fasteners threaded into steel or cast iron (not aluminum). As was previously mentioned, the size and grade of a fastener determine the amount of torque that can safely be applied to it. The figures listed here are approximate for Grade 2 and Grade 3 fasteners. Higher grades can tolerate higher torque values.

Fasteners laid out in a pattern, such as cylinder head bolts, oil pan bolts, differential cover bolts, etc., must be loosened or tightened in sequence to avoid warping the component. This sequence will normally be shown in the appropriate Chapter. If a specific pattern is not given, the following procedures can be used to prevent warping.

Initially, the bolts or nuts should be assembled finger-tight only. Next, they should be tightened one full turn each, in a criss-cross or diagonal pattern. After each one has been tightened one full turn, return to the first one and tighten them all one-half turn, following the same pattern. Finally, tighten each of them one-quarter turn at a time until each fastener has been tightened to the proper torque. To loosen and remove the fasteners, the procedure would be reversed.

Metric thread sizes

	Ft-lbs	Nm
M-6	6 to 9	9 to 12
M-8	14 to 21	19 to 28
M-10	28 to 40	38 to 54
M-12	50 to 71	68 to 96
M-14	80 to 140	109 to 154

Pipe thread sizes

1/8	5 to 8	7 to 10
1/4	12 to 18	17 to 24
3/8	22 to 33	30 to 44
1/2	25 to 35	34 to 47

U.S. thread sizes

1/4 - 20	6 to 9	9 to 12
5/16 - 18	12 to 18	17 to 24
5/16 - 24	14 to 20	19 to 27
3/8 - 16	22 to 32	30 to 43
3/8 - 24	27 to 38	37 to 51
7/16 - 14	40 to 55	55 to 74
7/16 - 20	40 to 60	55 to 81
1/2 - 13	55 to 80	75 to 108

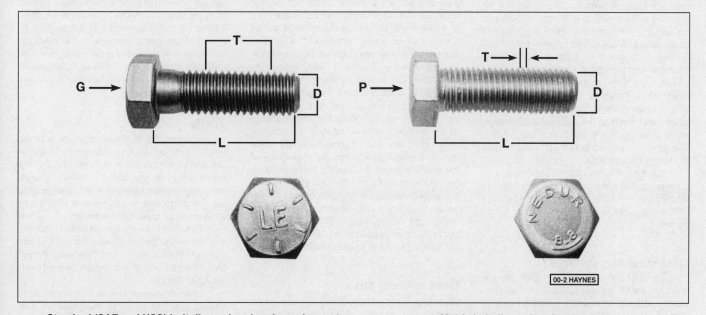

Standard (SAE and USS) bolt dimensions/grade marks

G   Grade marks (bolt strength)
L   Length (in inches)
T   Thread pitch (number of threads per inch)
D   Nominal diameter (in inches)

Metric bolt dimensions/grade marks

P   Property class (bolt strength)
L   Length (in millimeters)
T   Thread pitch (distance between threads in millimeters)
D   Diameter

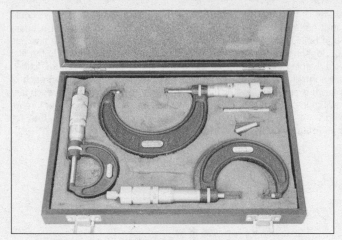

Micrometer set

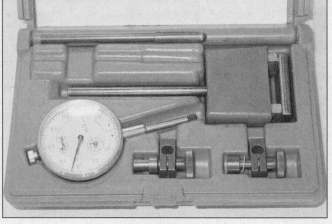

Dial indicator set

Component disassembly

Component disassembly should be done with care and purpose to help ensure that the parts go back together properly. Always keep track of the sequence in which parts are removed. Make note of special characteristics or marks on parts that can be installed more than one way, such as a grooved thrust washer on a shaft. It is a good idea to lay the disassembled parts out on a clean surface in the order that they were removed. It may also be helpful to make sketches or take instant photos of components before removal.

When removing fasteners from a component, keep track of their locations. Sometimes threading a bolt back in a part, or putting the washers and nut back on a stud, can prevent mix-ups later. If nuts and bolts cannot be returned to their original locations, they should be kept in a compartmented box or a series of small boxes. A cupcake or muffin tin is ideal for this purpose, since each cavity can hold the bolts and nuts from a particular area (i.e. oil pan bolts, valve cover bolts, engine mount bolts, etc.). A pan of this type is especially helpful when working on assemblies with very small parts, such as the carburetor, alternator, valve train or interior dash and trim pieces. The cavities can be marked with paint or tape to identify the contents.

Whenever wiring looms, harnesses or connectors are separated, it is a good idea to identify the two halves with numbered pieces of masking tape so they can be easily reconnected.

Gasket sealing surfaces

Throughout any vehicle, gaskets are used to seal the mating surfaces between two parts and keep lubricants, fluids, vacuum or pressure contained in an assembly.

Many times these gaskets are coated with a liquid or paste-type gasket sealing compound before assembly. Age, heat and pressure can sometimes cause the two parts to stick together so tightly that they are very difficult to separate. Often, the assembly can

be loosened by striking it with a soft-face hammer near the mating surfaces. A regular hammer can be used if a block of wood is placed between the hammer and the part. Do not hammer on cast parts or parts that could be easily damaged. With any particularly stubborn part, always recheck to make sure that every fastener has been removed.

Avoid using a screwdriver or bar to pry apart an assembly, as they can easily mar the gasket sealing surfaces of the parts, which must remain smooth. If prying is absolutely necessary, use an old broom handle, but keep in mind that extra clean up will be necessary if the wood splinters.

After the parts are separated, the old gasket must be carefully scraped off and the gasket surfaces cleaned. Stubborn gasket material can be soaked with rust penetrant or treated with a special chemical to soften it so it can be easily scraped off. **Caution:** *Never use gasket removal solutions or caustic chemicals on plastic or other composite components.* A scraper can be fashioned from a piece of copper tubing by flattening and sharpening one end. Copper is recommended because it is usually softer than the surfaces to be scraped, which reduces the chance of gouging the part. Some gaskets can be removed with a wire brush, but regardless of the method used, the mating surfaces must be left clean and smooth. If for some reason the gasket surface is gouged, then a gasket sealer thick enough to fill scratches will have to be used during reassembly of the components. For most applications, a non-drying (or semi-drying) gasket sealer should be used.

Hose removal tips

Warning: *If the vehicle is equipped with air conditioning, do not disconnect any of the A/C hoses without first having the system depressurized by a dealer service department or a service station.*

Hose removal precautions closely parallel gasket removal precautions. Avoid scratching or gouging the surface that the

hose mates against or the connection may leak. This is especially true for radiator hoses. Because of various chemical reactions, the rubber in hoses can bond itself to the metal spigot that the hose fits over. To remove a hose, first loosen the hose clamps that secure it to the spigot. Then, with slip-joint pliers, grab the hose at the clamp and rotate it around the spigot. Work it back and forth until it is completely free, then pull it off. Silicone or other lubricants will ease removal if they can be applied between the hose and the outside of the spigot. Apply the same lubricant to the inside of the hose and the outside of the spigot to simplify installation.

As a last resort (and if the hose is to be replaced with a new one anyway), the rubber can be slit with a knife and the hose peeled from the spigot. If this must be done, be careful that the metal connection is not damaged.

If a hose clamp is broken or damaged, do not reuse it. Wire-type clamps usually weaken with age, so it is a good idea to replace them with screw-type clamps whenever a hose is removed.

Tools

A selection of good tools is a basic requirement for anyone who plans to maintain and repair his or her own vehicle. For the owner who has few tools, the initial investment might seem high, but when compared to the spiraling costs of professional auto maintenance and repair, it is a wise one.

To help the owner decide which tools are needed to perform the tasks detailed in this manual, the following tool lists are offered: *Maintenance and minor repair, Repair/overhaul* and *Special.*

The newcomer to practical mechanics should start off with the *maintenance and minor repair* tool kit, which is adequate for the simpler jobs performed on a vehicle. Then, as confidence and experience grow, the owner can tackle more difficult tasks, buying additional tools as they are needed. Eventually the basic kit will be expanded into the *repair and overhaul* tool set. Over a period of time, the

Dial caliper

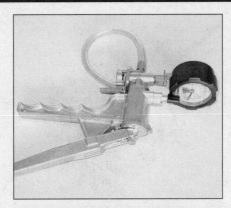

Hand-operated vacuum pump

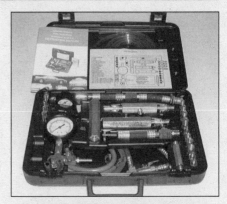

Fuel pressure gauge set

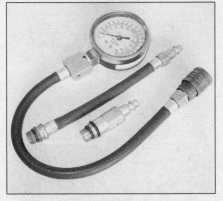

Compression gauge with spark plug
hole adapter

Damper/steering wheel puller

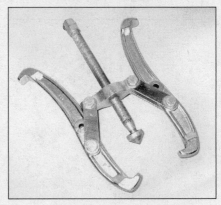

General purpose puller

Hydraulic lifter removal tool

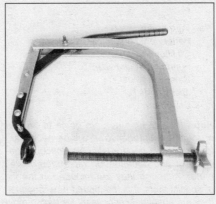

Valve spring compressor

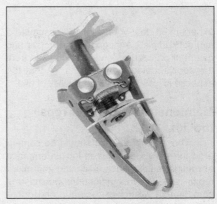

Valve spring compressor

Ridge reamer

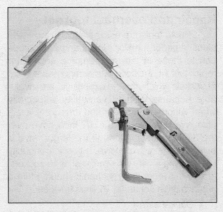

Piston ring groove cleaning tool

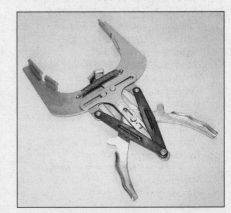

Ring removal/installation tool

Ring compressor

Cylinder hone

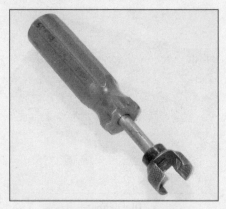

Brake hold-down spring tool

Torque angle gauge

Clutch plate alignment tool

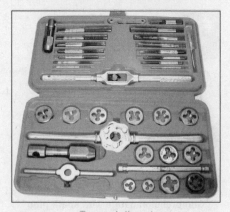

Tap and die set

experienced do-it-yourselfer will assemble a tool set complete enough for most repair and overhaul procedures and will add tools from the special category when it is felt that the expense is justified by the frequency of use.

Maintenance and minor repair tool kit

The tools in this list should be considered the minimum required for performance of routine maintenance, servicing and minor repair work. We recommend the purchase of combination wrenches (box-end and open-end combined in one wrench). While more expensive than open end wrenches, they offer the advantages of both types of wrench.

> *Combination wrench set (1/4-inch to 1 inch or 6 mm to 19 mm)*
> *Adjustable wrench, 8 inch*
> *Spark plug wrench with rubber insert*
> *Spark plug gap adjusting tool*
> *Feeler gauge set*
> *Brake bleeder wrench*
> *Standard screwdriver (5/16-inch x 6 inch)*
> *Phillips screwdriver (No. 2 x 6 inch)*
> *Combination pliers - 6 inch*
> *Hacksaw and assortment of blades*
> *Tire pressure gauge*
> *Grease gun*
> *Oil can*
> *Fine emery cloth*

> *Wire brush*
> *Battery post and cable cleaning tool*
> *Oil filter wrench*
> *Funnel (medium size)*
> *Safety goggles*
> *Jackstands (2)*
> *Drain pan*

Note: *If basic tune-ups are going to be part of routine maintenance, it will be necessary to purchase a good quality stroboscopic timing light and combination tachometer/dwell meter. Although they are included in the list of special tools, it is mentioned here because they are absolutely necessary for tuning most vehicles properly.*

Repair and overhaul tool set

These tools are essential for anyone who plans to perform major repairs and are in addition to those in the maintenance and minor repair tool kit. Included is a comprehensive set of sockets which, though expensive, are invaluable because of their versatility, especially when various extensions and drives are available. We recommend the 1/2-inch drive over the 3/8-inch drive. Although the larger drive is bulky and more expensive, it has the capacity of accepting a very wide range of large sockets. Ideally, however, the mechanic should have a 3/8-inch drive set and a 1/2-inch drive set.

> *Socket set(s)*
> *Reversible ratchet*

> *Extension - 10 inch*
> *Universal joint*
> *Torque wrench (same size drive as sockets)*
> *Ball peen hammer - 8 ounce*
> *Soft-face hammer (plastic/rubber)*
> *Standard screwdriver (1/4-inch x 6 inch)*
> *Standard screwdriver (stubby - 5/16-inch)*
> *Phillips screwdriver (No. 3 x 8 inch)*
> *Phillips screwdriver (stubby - No. 2)*
> *Pliers - vise grip*
> *Pliers - lineman's*
> *Pliers - needle nose*
> *Pliers - snap-ring (internal and external)*
> *Cold chisel - 1/2-inch*
> *Scribe*
> *Scraper (made from flattened copper tubing)*
> *Centerpunch*
> *Pin punches (1/16, 1/8, 3/16-inch)*
> *Steel rule/straightedge - 12 inch*
> *Allen wrench set (1/8 to 3/8-inch or 4 mm to 10 mm)*
> *A selection of files*
> *Wire brush (large)*
> *Jackstands (second set)*
> *Jack (scissor or hydraulic type)*

Note: *Another tool which is often useful is an electric drill with a chuck capacity of 3/8-inch and a set of good quality drill bits.*

Special tools

The tools in this list include those which are not used regularly, are expensive to buy, or which need to be used in accordance with their manufacturer's instructions. Unless these tools will be used frequently, it is not very economical to purchase many of them. A consideration would be to split the cost and use between yourself and a friend or friends. In addition, most of these tools can be obtained from a tool rental shop on a temporary basis.

This list primarily contains only those tools and instruments widely available to the public, and not those special tools produced by the vehicle manufacturer for distribution to dealer service departments. Occasionally, references to the manufacturer's special tools are included in the text of this manual. Generally, an alternative method of doing the job without the special tool is offered. However, sometimes there is no alternative to their use. Where this is the case, and the tool cannot be purchased or borrowed, the work should be turned over to the dealer service department or an automotive repair shop.

Valve spring compressor
Piston ring groove cleaning tool
Piston ring compressor
Piston ring installation tool
Cylinder compression gauge
Cylinder ridge reamer
Cylinder surfacing hone
Cylinder bore gauge
Micrometers and/or dial calipers
Hydraulic lifter removal tool
Balljoint separator
Universal-type puller
Impact screwdriver
Dial indicator set
Stroboscopic timing light (inductive pick-up)
Hand operated vacuum/pressure pump
Tachometer/dwell meter
Universal electrical multimeter
Cable hoist
Brake spring removal and installation tools
Floor jack

Buying tools

For the do-it-yourselfer who is just starting to get involved in vehicle maintenance and repair, there are a number of options available when purchasing tools. If maintenance and minor repair is the extent of the work to be done, the purchase of individual tools is satisfactory. If, on the other hand, extensive work is planned, it would be a good idea to purchase a modest tool set from one of the large retail chain stores. A set can usually be bought at a substantial savings over the individual tool prices, and they often come with a tool box. As additional tools are needed, add-on sets, individual tools and a larger tool box can be purchased to expand the tool selection. Building a tool set gradually allows the cost of the

tools to be spread over a longer period of time and gives the mechanic the freedom to choose only those tools that will actually be used.

Tool stores will often be the only source of some of the special tools that are needed, but regardless of where tools are bought, try to avoid cheap ones, especially when buying screwdrivers and sockets, because they won't last very long. The expense involved in replacing cheap tools will eventually be greater than the initial cost of quality tools.

Care and maintenance of tools

Good tools are expensive, so it makes sense to treat them with respect. Keep them clean and in usable condition and store them properly when not in use. Always wipe off any dirt, grease or metal chips before putting them away. Never leave tools lying around in the work area. Upon completion of a job, always check closely under the hood for tools that may have been left there so they won't get lost during a test drive.

Some tools, such as screwdrivers, pliers, wrenches and sockets, can be hung on a panel mounted on the garage or workshop wall, while others should be kept in a tool box or tray. Measuring instruments, gauges, meters, etc. must be carefully stored where they cannot be damaged by weather or impact from other tools.

When tools are used with care and stored properly, they will last a very long time. Even with the best of care, though, tools will wear out if used frequently. When a tool is damaged or worn out, replace it. Subsequent jobs will be safer and more enjoyable if you do.

How to repair damaged threads

Sometimes, the internal threads of a nut or bolt hole can become stripped, usually from overtightening. Stripping threads is an all-too-common occurrence, especially when working with aluminum parts, because aluminum is so soft that it easily strips out.

Usually, external or internal threads are only partially stripped. After they've been cleaned up with a tap or die, they'll still work. Sometimes, however, threads are badly damaged. When this happens, you've got three choices:

1) *Drill and tap the hole to the next suitable oversize and install a larger diameter bolt, screw or stud.*

2) *Drill and tap the hole to accept a threaded plug, then drill and tap the plug to the original screw size. You can also buy a plug already threaded to the original size. Then you simply drill a hole to the specified size, then run the threaded plug into the hole with a bolt and jam nut. Once the plug is fully seated, remove the jam nut and bolt.*

3) *The third method uses a patented thread repair kit like Heli-Coil or Slimsert. These easy-to-use kits are designed to repair damaged threads in straight-through holes and blind holes. Both are available as kits which can handle a variety of sizes and thread patterns. Drill the hole, then tap it with the special included tap. Install the Heli-Coil and the hole is back to its original diameter and thread pitch.*

Regardless of which method you use, be sure to proceed calmly and carefully. A little impatience or carelessness during one of these relatively simple procedures can ruin your whole day's work and cost you a bundle if you wreck an expensive part.

Working facilities

Not to be overlooked when discussing tools is the workshop. If anything more than routine maintenance is to be carried out, some sort of suitable work area is essential.

It is understood, and appreciated, that many home mechanics do not have a good workshop or garage available, and end up removing an engine or doing major repairs outside. It is recommended, however, that the overhaul or repair be completed under the cover of a roof.

A clean, flat workbench or table of comfortable working height is an absolute necessity. The workbench should be equipped with a vise that has a jaw opening of at least four inches.

As mentioned previously, some clean, dry storage space is also required for tools, as well as the lubricants, fluids, cleaning solvents, etc. which soon become necessary.

Sometimes waste oil and fluids, drained from the engine or cooling system during normal maintenance or repairs, present a disposal problem. To avoid pouring them on the ground or into a sewage system, pour the used fluids into large containers, seal them with caps and take them to an authorized disposal site or recycling center. Plastic jugs, such as old antifreeze containers, are ideal for this purpose.

Always keep a supply of old newspapers and clean rags available. Old towels are excellent for mopping up spills. Many mechanics use rolls of paper towels for most work because they are readily available and disposable. To help keep the area under the vehicle clean, a large cardboard box can be cut open and flattened to protect the garage or shop floor.

Whenever working over a painted surface, such as when leaning over a fender to service something under the hood, always cover it with an old blanket or bedspread to protect the finish. Vinyl covered pads, made especially for this purpose, are available at auto parts stores.

Booster battery (jump) starting

1   Observe the following precautions when using a booster battery to start a vehicle:

a) *Before connecting the booster battery, make sure the ignition switch is in the Off position.*

b) *Turn off the lights, heater and other electrical loads.*

c) *Your eyes should be shielded. Safety goggles are a good idea.*

d) *Make sure the booster battery is the same voltage as the dead one in the vehicle.*

e) *The two vehicles MUST NOT TOUCH each other.*

f) *Make sure the transaxle is in Park.*

g) *If the booster battery is not a maintenance-free type, remove the vent caps and lay a cloth over the vent holes.*

2   Connect the red jumper cable to the positive (+) terminals of each battery.

3   Connect one end of the black cable to the negative (-) terminal of the booster battery. The other end of this cable should be connected to a good grounding point, such as a bolt or bracket (see illustration). Make sure the cable will not come into contact with the fan, drivebelts or other moving parts of the engine.

4   Start the engine using the booster battery, then, with the engine running at idle speed, disconnect the jumper cables in the reverse order of connection

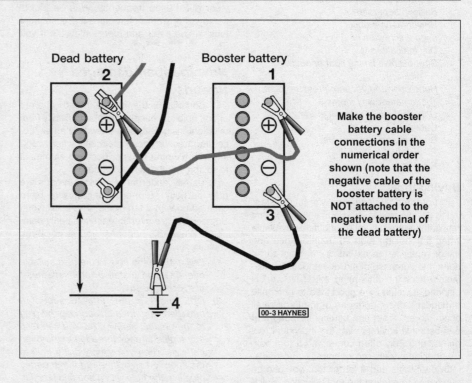

Dead battery   Booster battery

Make the booster battery cable connections in the numerical order shown (note that the negative cable of the booster battery is NOT attached to the negative terminal of the dead battery)

00-3 HAYNES

Jacking and towing

Jacking

Warning: *The jack supplied with the vehicle should only be used for changing a tire or placing jackstands under the frame. Never work under the vehicle or start the engine while this jack is being used as the only means of support.*

1   The vehicle should be on level ground. Place the shift lever in Park (automatic) or Reverse (manual). Block the wheel diagonally opposite the wheel being changed. Set the parking brake.

2   Remove the spare tire and jack from stowage. Remove the wheel cover and trim ring (if so equipped) with the tapered end of the lug nut wrench by inserting and twisting the handle and then prying against the back of the wheel cover. Loosen the wheel lug nuts about 1/4-to-1/2 turn each.

3   Place the scissors-type jack under the side of the vehicle and adjust the jack height until it fits over the vertical rocker panel flange nearest the wheel to be changed. There is a front and rear jacking point on each side of the vehicle (see illustration).

4   Turn the jack handle clockwise until the tire clears the ground. Remove the lug nuts and pull the wheel off. Replace it with the spare.

5   Install the lug nuts with the beveled edges facing in. Tighten them snugly. Don't attempt to tighten them completely until the vehicle is lowered or it could slip off the jack. Turn the jack handle counterclockwise to lower the vehicle. Remove the jack and tighten the lug nuts in a diagonal pattern.

6   Install the wheel cover (and trim ring, if used) and be sure it's snapped into place all the way around.

7   Stow the tire, jack and wrench. Unblock the wheels.

Towing

8   The vehicle can be towed with all four wheels on the ground, as long as speeds do not exceed 20 mph and the distance is not over six miles.

9   For distances exceeding six miles, the preferred method for towing these models is on a flat-bed tow truck. Tow trucks that use wheel-lift or sling-type equipment cannot be used.

10   While towing, the parking brake should be fully released and the transaxle should be in Neutral. The steering must be unlocked (ignition switch in the Off position). Remember that power steering and power brakes will not work with engine off and never use the tie-down tabs to tow another vehicle.

11   Safety is a major consideration when

8.3 Front jacking point - place the jack so it engages the notch in the rocker panel (the rear jacking point, which is located just in front of the rear wheels, has a similar notch)

towing and all applicable state and local laws must be obeyed. A safety chain system must be used at all times. Remember that power steering and power brakes will not work with the engine off.

Automotive chemicals and lubricants

A number of automotive chemicals and lubricants are available for use during vehicle maintenance and repair. They include a wide variety of products ranging from cleaning solvents and degreasers to lubricants and protective sprays for rubber, plastic and vinyl.

Cleaners

Carburetor cleaner and choke cleaner is a strong solvent for gum, varnish and carbon. Most carburetor cleaners leave a dry-type lubricant film which will not harden or gum up. Because of this film it is not recommended for use on electrical components.

Brake system cleaner is used to remove brake dust, grease and brake fluid from the brake system, where clean surfaces are absolutely necessary. It leaves no residue and often eliminates brake squeal caused by contaminants.

Electrical cleaner removes oxidation, corrosion and carbon deposits from electrical contacts, restoring full current flow. It can also be used to clean spark plugs, carburetor jets, voltage regulators and other parts where an oil-free surface is desired.

Demoisturants remove water and moisture from electrical components such as alternators, voltage regulators, electrical connectors and fuse blocks. They are non-conductive and non-corrosive.

Degreasers are heavy-duty solvents used to remove grease from the outside of the engine and from chassis components. They can be sprayed or brushed on and, depending on the type, are rinsed off either with water or solvent.

Lubricants

Motor oil is the lubricant formulated for use in engines. It normally contains a wide variety of additives to prevent corrosion and reduce foaming and wear. Motor oil comes in various weights (viscosity ratings) from 0 to 50. The recommended weight of the oil depends on the season, temperature and the demands on the engine. Light oil is used in cold climates and under light load conditions. Heavy oil is used in hot climates and where high loads are encountered. Multi-viscosity oils are designed to have characteristics of both light and heavy oils and are available in a number of weights from 0W-20 to 20W-50.

Gear oil is designed to be used in differentials, manual transmissions and other areas where high-temperature lubrication is required.

Chassis and wheel bearing grease is a heavy grease used where increased loads and friction are encountered, such as for wheel bearings, balljoints, tie-rod ends and universal joints.

High-temperature wheel bearing grease is designed to withstand the extreme temperatures encountered by wheel bearings in disc brake equipped vehicles. It usually contains molybdenum disulfide (moly), which is a dry-type lubricant.

White grease is a heavy grease for metal-to-metal applications where water is a problem. White grease stays soft under both low and high temperatures (usually from -100 to +190-degrees F), and will not wash off or dilute in the presence of water.

Assembly lube is a special extreme pressure lubricant, usually containing moly, used to lubricate high-load parts (such as main and rod bearings and cam lobes) for initial start-up of a new engine. The assembly lube lubricates the parts without being squeezed out or washed away until the engine oiling system begins to function.

Silicone lubricants are used to protect rubber, plastic, vinyl and nylon parts.

Graphite lubricants are used where oils cannot be used due to contamination problems, such as in locks. The dry graphite will lubricate metal parts while remaining uncontaminated by dirt, water, oil or acids. It is electrically conductive and will not foul electrical contacts in locks such as the ignition switch.

Moly penetrants loosen and lubricate frozen, rusted and corroded fasteners and prevent future rusting or freezing.

Heat-sink grease is a special electrically non-conductive grease that is used for mounting electronic ignition modules where it is essential that heat is transferred away from the module.

Sealants

RTV sealant is one of the most widely used gasket compounds. Made from silicone, RTV is air curing, it seals, bonds, waterproofs, fills surface irregularities, remains flexible, doesn't shrink, is relatively easy to remove, and is used as a supplementary sealer with almost all low and medium temperature gaskets.

Anaerobic sealant is much like RTV in that it can be used either to seal gaskets or to form gaskets by itself. It remains flexible, is solvent resistant and fills surface imperfections. The difference between an anaerobic sealant and an RTV-type sealant is in the curing. RTV cures when exposed to air, while an anaerobic sealant cures only in the absence of air. This means that an anaerobic sealant cures only after the assembly of parts, sealing them together.

Thread and pipe sealant is used for sealing hydraulic and pneumatic fittings and vacuum lines. It is usually made from a Teflon compound, and comes in a spray, a paint-on liquid and as a wrap-around tape.

Chemicals

Anti-seize compound prevents seizing, galling, cold welding, rust and corrosion in fasteners. High-temperature ant-seize, usually made with copper and graphite lubricants, is used for exhaust system and exhaust manifold bolts.

Anaerobic locking compounds are used to keep fasteners from vibrating or working loose and cure only after installation, in the absence of air. Medium strength locking compound is used for small nuts, bolts and screws that may be removed later. High-strength locking compound is for large nuts, bolts and studs which aren't removed on a regular basis.

Oil additives range from viscosity index improvers to chemical treatments that claim to reduce internal engine friction. It should be noted that most oil manufacturers caution against using additives with their oils.

Gas additives perform several functions, depending on their chemical makeup. They usually contain solvents that help dissolve gum and varnish that build up on carburetor, fuel injection and intake parts. They also serve to break down carbon deposits that form on the inside surfaces of the combustion chambers. Some additives contain upper cylinder lubricants for valves and piston rings, and others contain chemicals to remove condensation from the gas tank.

Miscellaneous

Brake fluid is specially formulated hydraulic fluid that can withstand the heat and pressure encountered in brake systems. Care must be taken so this fluid does not come in contact with painted surfaces or plastics. An opened container should always be resealed to prevent contamination by water or dirt.

Weatherstrip adhesive is used to bond weatherstripping around doors, windows and trunk lids. It is sometimes used to attach trim pieces.

Undercoating is a petroleum-based, tar-like substance that is designed to protect metal surfaces on the underside of the vehicle from corrosion. It also acts as a sound-deadening agent by insulating the bottom of the vehicle.

Waxes and polishes are used to help protect painted and plated surfaces from the weather. Different types of paint may require the use of different types of wax and polish. Some polishes utilize a chemical or abrasive cleaner to help remove the top layer of oxidized (dull) paint on older vehicles. In recent years many non-wax polishes that contain a wide variety of chemicals such as polymers and silicones have been introduced. These non-wax polishes are usually easier to apply and last longer than conventional waxes and polishes.

Conversion factors

Length (distance)
Inches (in)	X	25.4 = Millimeters (mm)	X	0.0394	= Inches (in)
Feet (ft)	X	0.305 = Meters (m)	X	3.281	= Feet (ft)
Miles	X	1.609 = Kilometers (km)	X	0.621	= Miles

Volume (capacity)
Cubic inches (cu in; in³)	X	16.387 = Cubic centimeters (cc; cm³)	X	0.061	= Cubic inches (cu in; in³)
Imperial pints (Imp pt)	X	0.568 = Liters (l)	X	1.76	= Imperial pints (Imp pt)
Imperial quarts (Imp qt)	X	1.137 = Liters (l)	X	0.88	= Imperial quarts (Imp qt)
Imperial quarts (Imp qt)	X	1.201 = US quarts (US qt)	X	0.833	= Imperial quarts (Imp qt)
US quarts (US qt)	X	0.946 = Liters (l)	X	1.057	= US quarts (US qt)
Imperial gallons (Imp gal)	X	4.546 = Liters (l)	X	0.22	= Imperial gallons (Imp gal)
Imperial gallons (Imp gal)	X	1.201 = US gallons (US gal)	X	0.833	= Imperial gallons (Imp gal)
US gallons (US gal)	X	3.785 = Liters (l)	X	0.264	= US gallons (US gal)

Mass (weight)
Ounces (oz)	X	28.35 = Grams (g)	X	0.035	= Ounces (oz)
Pounds (lb)	X	0.454 = Kilograms (kg)	X	2.205	= Pounds (lb)

Force
Ounces-force (ozf; oz)	X	0.278 = Newtons (N)	X	3.6	= Ounces-force (ozf; oz)
Pounds-force (lbf; lb)	X	4.448 = Newtons (N)	X	0.225	= Pounds-force (lbf; lb)
Newtons (N)	X	0.1 = Kilograms-force (kgf; kg)	X	9.81	= Newtons (N)

Pressure
Pounds-force per square inch (psi; lbf/in²; lb/in²)	X	0.070 = Kilograms-force per square centimeter (kgf/cm²; kg/cm²)	X	14.223	= Pounds-force per square inch (psi; lbf/in²; lb/in²)
Pounds-force per square inch (psi; lbf/in²; lb/in²)	X	0.068 = Atmospheres (atm)	X	14.696	= Pounds-force per square inch (psi; lbf/in²; lb/in²)
Pounds-force per square inch (psi; lbf/in²; lb/in²)	X	0.069 = Bars	X	14.5	= Pounds-force per square inch (psi; lbf/in²; lb/in²)
Pounds-force per square inch (psi; lbf/in²; lb/in²)	X	6.895 = Kilopascals (kPa)	X	0.145	= Pounds-force per square inch (psi; lbf/in²; lb/in²)
Kilopascals (kPa)	X	0.01 = Kilograms-force per square centimeter (kgf/cm²; kg/cm²)	X	98.1	= Kilopascals (kPa)

Torque (moment of force)
Pounds-force inches (lbf in; lb in)	X	1.152 = Kilograms-force centimeter (kgf cm; kg cm)	X	0.868	= Pounds-force inches (lbf in; lb in)
Pounds-force inches (lbf in; lb in)	X	0.113 = Newton meters (Nm)	X	8.85	= Pounds-force inches (lbf in; lb in)
Pounds-force inches (lbf in; lb in)	X	0.083 = Pounds-force feet (lbf ft; lb ft)	X	12	= Pounds-force inches (lbf in; lb in)
Pounds-force feet (lbf ft; lb ft)	X	0.138 = Kilograms-force meters (kgf m; kg m)	X	7.233	= Pounds-force feet (lbf ft; lb ft)
Pounds-force feet (lbf ft; lb ft)	X	1.356 = Newton meters (Nm)	X	0.738	= Pounds-force feet (lbf ft; lb ft)
Newton meters (Nm)	X	0.102 = Kilograms-force meters (kgf m; kg m)	X	9.804	= Newton meters (Nm)

Vacuum
Inches mercury (in. Hg)	X	3.377 = Kilopascals (kPa)	X	0.2961	= Inches mercury
Inches mercury (in. Hg)	X	25.4 = Millimeters mercury (mm Hg)	X	0.0394	= Inches mercury

Power
Horsepower (hp)	X	745.7 = Watts (W)	X	0.0013	= Horsepower (hp)

Velocity (speed)
Miles per hour (miles/hr; mph)	X	1.609 = Kilometers per hour (km/hr; kph)	X	0.621	= Miles per hour (miles/hr; mph)

Fuel consumption*
Miles per gallon, Imperial (mpg)	X	0.354 = Kilometers per liter (km/l)	X	2.825	= Miles per gallon, Imperial (mpg)
Miles per gallon, US (mpg)	X	0.425 = Kilometers per liter (km/l)	X	2.352	= Miles per gallon, US (mpg)

Temperature
Degrees Fahrenheit = (°C x 1.8) + 32

Degrees Celsius (Degrees Centigrade; °C) = (°F - 32) x 0.56

*It is common practice to convert from miles per gallon (mpg) to liters/100 kilometers (l/100km),
where mpg (Imperial) x l/100 km = 282 and mpg (US) x l/100 km = 235

DECIMALS to MILLIMETERS

Decimal	mm	Decimal	mm
0.001	0.0254	0.500	12.7000
0.002	0.0508	0.510	12.9540
0.003	0.0762	0.520	13.2080
0.004	0.1016	0.530	13.4620
0.005	0.1270	0.540	13.7160
0.006	0.1524	0.550	13.9700
0.007	0.1778	0.560	14.2240
0.008	0.2032	0.570	14.4780
0.009	0.2286	0.580	14.7320
0.010	0.2540	0.590	14.9860
0.020	0.5080	0.600	15.2400
0.030	0.7620	0.610	15.4940
0.040	1.0160	0.620	15.7480
0.050	1.2700	0.630	16.0020
0.060	1.5240	0.640	16.2560
0.070	1.7780	0.650	16.5100
0.080	2.0320	0.660	16.7640
0.090	2.2860	0.670	17.0180
0.100	2.5400	0.680	17.2720
0.110	2.7940	0.690	17.5260
0.120	3.0480	0.700	17.7800
0.130	3.3020	0.710	18.0340
0.140	3.5560	0.720	18.2880
0.150	3.8100	0.730	18.5420
0.160	4.0640	0.740	18.7960
0.170	4.3180	0.750	19.0500
0.180	4.5720	0.760	19.3040
0.190	4.8260	0.770	19.5580
0.200	5.0800	0.780	19.8120
0.210	5.3340	0.790	20.0660
0.220	5.5880	0.800	20.3200
0.230	5.8420	0.810	20.5740
0.240	6.0960	0.820	21.8280
0.250	6.3500	0.830	21.0820
0.260	6.6040	0.840	21.3360
0.270	6.8580	0.850	21.5900
0.280	7.1120	0.860	21.8440
0.290	7.3660	0.870	22.0980
0.300	7.6200	0.880	22.3520
0.310	7.8740	0.890	22.6060
0.320	8.1280	0.900	22.8600
0.330	8.3820	0.910	23.1140
0.340	8.6360	0.920	23.3680
0.350	8.8900	0.930	23.6220
0.360	9.1440	0.940	23.8760
0.370	9.3980	0.950	24.1300
0.380	9.6520	0.960	24.3840
0.390	9.9060	0.970	24.6380
0.400	10.1600	0.980	24.8920
0.410	10.4140	0.990	25.1460
0.420	10.6680	1.000	25.4000
0.430	10.9220		
0.440	11.1760		
0.450	11.4300		
0.460	11.6840		
0.470	11.9380		
0.480	12.1920		
0.490	12.4460		

FRACTIONS to DECIMALS to MILLIMETERS

Fraction	Decimal	mm	Fraction	Decimal	mm
1/64	0.0156	0.3969	33/64	0.5156	13.0969
1/32	0.0312	0.7938	17/32	0.5312	13.4938
3/64	0.0469	1.1906	35/64	0.5469	13.8906
1/16	0.0625	1.5875	9/16	0.5625	14.2875
5/64	0.0781	1.9844	37/64	0.5781	14.6844
3/32	0.0938	2.3812	19/32	0.5938	15.0812
7/64	0.1094	2.7781	39/64	0.6094	15.4781
1/8	0.1250	3.1750	5/8	0.6250	15.8750
9/64	0.1406	3.5719	41/64	0.6406	16.2719
5/32	0.1562	3.9688	21/32	0.6562	16.6688
11/64	0.1719	4.3656	43/64	0.6719	17.0656
3/16	0.1875	4.7625	11/16	0.6875	17.4625
13/64	0.2031	5.1594	45/64	0.7031	17.8594
7/32	0.2188	5.5562	23/32	0.7188	18.2562
15/64	0.2344	5.9531	47/64	0.7344	18.6531
1/4	0.2500	6.3500	3/4	0.7500	19.0500
17/64	0.2656	6.7469	49/64	0.7656	19.4469
9/32	0.2812	7.1438	25/32	0.7812	19.8438
19/64	0.2969	7.5406	51/64	0.7969	20.2406
5/16	0.3125	7.9375	13/16	0.8125	20.6375
21/64	0.3281	8.3344	53/64	0.8281	21.0344
11/32	0.3438	8.7312	27/32	0.8438	21.4312
23/64	0.3594	9.1281	55/64	0.8594	21.8281
3/8	0.3750	9.5250	7/8	0.8750	22.2250
25/64	0.3906	9.9219	57/64	0.8906	22.6219
13/32	0.4062	10.3188	29/32	0.9062	23.0188
27/64	0.4219	10.7156	59/64	0.9219	23.4156
7/16	0.4375	11.1125	15/16	0.9375	23.8125
29/64	0.4531	11.5094	61/64	0.9531	24.2094
15/32	0.4688	11.9062	31/32	0.9688	24.6062
31/64	0.4844	12.3031	63/64	0.9844	25.0031
1/2	0.5000	12.7000	1	1.0000	25.4000

Safety first!

Regardless of how enthusiastic you may be about getting on with the job at hand, take the time to ensure that your safety is not jeopardized. A moment's lack of attention can result in an accident, as can failure to observe certain simple safety precautions. The possibility of an accident will always exist, and the following points should not be considered a comprehensive list of all dangers. Rather, they are intended to make you aware of the risks and to encourage a safety conscious approach to all work you carry out on your vehicle.

Essential DOs and DON'Ts

DON'T rely on a jack when working under the vehicle. Always use approved jackstands to support the weight of the vehicle and place them under the recommended lift or support points.

DON'T attempt to loosen extremely tight fasteners (i.e. wheel lug nuts) while the vehicle is on a jack - it may fall.

DON'T start the engine without first making sure that the transmission is in Neutral (or Park where applicable) and the parking brake is set.

DON'T remove the radiator cap from a hot cooling system - let it cool or cover it with a cloth and release the pressure gradually.

DON'T attempt to drain the engine oil until you are sure it has cooled to the point that it will not burn you.

DON'T touch any part of the engine or exhaust system until it has cooled sufficiently to avoid burns.

DON'T siphon toxic liquids such as gasoline, antifreeze and brake fluid by mouth, or allow them to remain on your skin.

DON'T inhale brake lining dust - it is potentially hazardous (see *Asbestos* below).

DON'T allow spilled oil or grease to remain on the floor - wipe it up before someone slips on it.

DON'T use loose fitting wrenches or other tools which may slip and cause injury.

DON'T push on wrenches when loosening or tightening nuts or bolts. Always try to pull the wrench toward you. If the situation calls for pushing the wrench away, push with an open hand to avoid scraped knuckles if the wrench should slip.

DON'T attempt to lift a heavy component alone - get someone to help you.

DON'T rush or take unsafe shortcuts to finish a job.

DON'T allow children or animals in or around the vehicle while you are working on it.

DO wear eye protection when using power tools such as a drill, sander, bench grinder, etc. and when working under a vehicle.

DO keep loose clothing and long hair well out of the way of moving parts.

DO make sure that any hoist used has a safe working load rating adequate for the job.

DO get someone to check on you periodically when working alone on a vehicle.

DO carry out work in a logical sequence and make sure that everything is correctly assembled and tightened.

DO keep chemicals and fluids tightly capped and out of the reach of children and pets.

DO remember that your vehicle's safety affects that of yourself and others. If in doubt on any point, get professional advice.

Steering, suspension and brakes

These systems are essential to driving safety, so make sure you have a qualified shop or individual check your work. Also, compressed suspension springs can cause injury if released suddenly - be sure to use a spring compressor.

Airbags

Airbags are explosive devices that can **CAUSE** injury if they deploy while you're working on the vehicle. Follow the manufacturer's instructions to disable the airbag whenever you're working in the vicinity of airbag components.

Asbestos

Certain friction, insulating, sealing, and other products - such as brake linings, brake bands, clutch linings, torque converters, gaskets, etc. - may contain asbestos or other hazardous friction material. Extreme care must be taken to avoid inhalation of dust from such products, since it is hazardous to health. If in doubt, assume that they do contain asbestos.

Fire

Remember at all times that gasoline is highly flammable. Never smoke or have any kind of open flame around when working on a vehicle. But the risk does not end there. A spark caused by an electrical short circuit, by two metal surfaces contacting each other, or even by static electricity built up in your body under certain conditions, can ignite gasoline vapors, which in a confined space are highly explosive. Do not, under any circumstances, use gasoline for cleaning parts. Use an approved safety solvent.

Always disconnect the battery ground (-) cable at the battery before working on any part of the fuel system or electrical system. Never risk spilling fuel on a hot engine or exhaust component. It is strongly recommended that a fire extinguisher suitable for use on fuel and electrical fires be kept handy in the garage or workshop at all times. Never try to extinguish a fuel or electrical fire with water.

Fumes

Certain fumes are highly toxic and can quickly cause unconsciousness and even death if inhaled to any extent. Gasoline vapor falls into this category, as do the vapors from some cleaning solvents. Any draining or pouring of such volatile fluids should be done in a well ventilated area.

When using cleaning fluids and solvents, read the instructions on the container carefully. Never use materials from unmarked containers.

Never run the engine in an enclosed space, such as a garage. Exhaust fumes contain carbon monoxide, which is extremely poisonous. If you need to run the engine, always do so in the open air, or at least have the rear of the vehicle outside the work area.

The battery

Never create a spark or allow a bare light bulb near a battery. They normally give off a certain amount of hydrogen gas, which is highly explosive.

Always disconnect the battery ground (-) cable at the battery before working on the fuel or electrical systems.

If possible, loosen the filler caps or cover when charging the battery from an external source (this does not apply to sealed or maintenance-free batteries). Do not charge at an excessive rate or the battery may burst.

Take care when adding water to a non maintenance-free battery and when carrying a battery. The electrolyte, even when diluted, is very corrosive and should not be allowed to contact clothing or skin.

Always wear eye protection when cleaning the battery to prevent the caustic deposits from entering your eyes.

Household current

When using an electric power tool, inspection light, etc., which operates on household current, always make sure that the tool is correctly connected to its plug and that, where necessary, it is properly grounded. Do not use such items in damp conditions and, again, do not create a spark or apply excessive heat in the vicinity of fuel or fuel vapor.

Secondary ignition system voltage

A severe electric shock can result from touching certain parts of the ignition system (such as the spark plug wires) when the engine is running or being cranked, particularly if components are damp or the insulation is defective. In the case of an electronic ignition system, the secondary system voltage is much higher and could prove fatal.

Hydrofluoric acid

This extremely corrosive acid is formed when certain types of synthetic rubber, found in some O-rings, oil seals, fuel hoses, etc. are exposed to temperatures above 750-degrees F (400-degrees C). The rubber changes into a charred or sticky substance containing the acid. *Once formed, the acid remains dangerous for years. If it gets onto the skin, it may be necessary to amputate the limb concerned.*

When dealing with a vehicle which has suffered a fire, or with components salvaged from such a vehicle, wear protective gloves and discard them after use.

Troubleshooting

Contents

This section provides an easy reference guide to the more common problems which may occur during the operation of your vehicle. These problems and their possible causes are grouped under headings denoting various components or systems, such as Engine, Cooling system, etc. They also refer you to the chapter and/or section which deals with the problem.

Remember that successful troubleshooting is not a mysterious black art practiced only by professional mechanics. It is simply the result of the right knowledge combined with an intelligent, systematic approach to the problem. Always work by a process of elimination, starting with the simplest solution and working through to the most complex - and never overlook the obvious. Anyone can run the gas tank dry or leave the lights on overnight, so don't assume that you are exempt from such oversights.

Finally, always establish a clear idea of why a problem has occurred and take steps to ensure that it doesn't happen again. If the electrical system fails because of a poor connection, check the other connections in the system to make sure that they don't fail as well. If a particular fuse continues to blow, find out why - don't just replace one fuse after another. Remember, failure of a small component can often be indicative of potential failure or incorrect functioning of a more important component or system.

Engine

1   Engine will not rotate when attempting to start

1   Battery terminal connections loose or corroded (Chapter 1).
2   Battery discharged or faulty (Chapter 1).
3   Automatic transaxle not completely engaged in Park (Chapter 7B) or clutch pedal not completely depressed (Chapter 8).
4   Broken, loose or disconnected wiring in the starting circuit (Chapters 5 and 12).
5   Starter motor pinion jammed in flywheel ring gear (Chapter 5).
6   Starter solenoid faulty (Chapter 5).
7   Starter motor faulty (Chapter 5).
8   Ignition switch faulty (Chapter 12).
9   Starter pinion or flywheel teeth worn or broken (Chapter 5).

2   Engine rotates but will not start

1   Fuel tank empty.
2   Battery discharged (engine rotates slowly) (Chapter 5).
3   Battery terminal connections loose or corroded (Chapter 1).
4   Leaking fuel injector(s), faulty fuel pump, pressure regulator, etc. (Chapter 4).
5   Broken or stripped timing belt (Chapter 2A).
6   Ignition components damp or damaged (Chapter 5).
7   Worn, faulty or incorrectly gapped spark plugs (Chapter 1).
8   Broken, loose or disconnected wiring in the starting circuit (Chapter 5).
9   Broken, loose or disconnected wires at the ignition coil or faulty coil (Chapter 5).

3   Engine hard to start when cold

1   Battery discharged or low (Chapter 1).
2   Malfunctioning fuel system (Chapter 4).
3   Faulty coolant temperature sensor (Chapter 6).
4   Injector(s) leaking (Chapter 4)
5   Faulty ignition system (Chapter 5).

4   Engine hard to start when hot

1   Air filter clogged (Chapter 1).
2   Fuel not reaching the fuel injection system (Chapter 4).
3   Corroded battery connections, especially ground (Chapter 1).
4   Faulty coolant temperature sensor (Chapter 6).

5   Starter motor noisy or excessively rough in engagement

1   Pinion or flywheel gear teeth worn or broken (Chapter 5).
2   Starter motor mounting bolts loose or missing (Chapter 5).

6   Engine starts but stops immediately

1   Loose or faulty electrical connections at coil or alternator (Chapter 5).
2   Insufficient fuel reaching the fuel injectors (Chapters 1 and 4).
3   Vacuum leak at the gasket between the intake manifold/plenum (Chapters 1, 4).

7   Oil puddle under engine

1   Oil pan gasket and/or oil pan drain bolt washer leaking (Chapter 2A).
2   Oil pressure sending unit leaking (Chapter 2B).
3   Valve covers leaking (Chapter 2A).
4   Engine oil seals leaking (Chapter 2A).
5   Oil pump housing leaking (Chapter 2A).

8   Engine lopes while idling or idles erratically

1   Vacuum leakage (Chapters 2B and 4).
2   Leaking EGR valve (Chapter 6).
3   Air filter clogged (Chapter 1).
4   Fuel pump not delivering sufficient fuel to the fuel injection system (Chapter 4).
5   Leaking head gasket (Chapter 2A).

6   Timing belt and/or pulleys worn (Chapter 2A).
7   Camshaft lobes worn (Chapter 2A).

9   Engine misses at idle speed

1   Spark plugs worn or not gapped properly (Chapter 1).
2   Faulty spark plug wires (Chapter 1).
3   Vacuum leaks (Chapter 1).
4   Incorrect ignition timing (Chapter 5).
5   Uneven or low cylinder compression (Chapter 2B).
6   Problem with the fuel injection system (Chapter 4).

10   Engine misses throughout driving speed range

1   Fuel filter clogged and/or impurities in the fuel system (Chapter 1).
2   Low fuel output at the injectors (Chapter 4).
3   Faulty or incorrectly gapped spark plugs (Chapter 1).
4   Incorrect ignition timing (Chapter 5).
5   Cracked coil (Chapters 1 and 5).
6   Leaking spark plug wires (Chapters 1 and 5).
7   Faulty emission system components (Chapter 6).
8   Low or uneven cylinder compression pressures (Chapter 2B).
9   Weak or faulty ignition system (Chapter 5).
10   Vacuum leak around fuel injector(s), intake manifold or vacuum hoses (Chapters 2A, 4).

11   Engine stumbles on acceleration

1   Spark plugs fouled (Chapter 1).
2   Problem with fuel injection system (Chapter 4).
3   Fuel filter clogged (Chapters 1 and 4).
4   Incorrect ignition timing (Chapter 5).
5   Intake manifold air leak (Chapters 2A and 4).
6   Problem with the emissions control system (Chapter 6).

12 Engine surges while holding accelerator steady

1   Intake air leak (Chapter 4).
2   Fuel pump or fuel pressure regulator faulty (Chapter 4).
3   Problem with fuel injection system (Chapter 4).
4   Problem with the emissions control system (Chapter 6).

13 Engine stalls

1   Fuel filter clogged and/or water and impurities in the fuel system (Chapters 1 and 4).
2   Ignition components damp or damaged (Chapter 5).
3   Faulty emissions system components (Chapter 6).
4   Faulty or incorrectly gapped spark plugs (Chapter 1).
5   Faulty spark plug wires (Chapter 1).
6   Vacuum leak in the fuel injection system, intake manifold or vacuum hoses (Chapters 2A and 4).
7   Valve clearances incorrectly set (Chapter 2A).

14 Engine lacks power

1   Faulty spark plug wires or coil (Chapters 1 and 5).
2   Faulty or incorrectly gapped spark plugs (Chapter 1).
3   Problem with the fuel injection system (Chapter 4).
4   Plugged air filter (Chapter 1).
5   Brakes binding (Chapter 9).
6   Automatic transaxle fluid level incorrect (Chapter 1).
7   Clutch slipping (Chapter 8).
8   Fuel filter clogged and/or impurities in the fuel system (Chapters 1 and 4).
9   Emission control system not functioning properly (Chapter 6).
10 Low or uneven cylinder compression pressures (Chapter 2B).
11 Obstructed exhaust system (Chapter 4).

15 Engine backfires

1   Emission control system not functioning properly (Chapter 6).
2   Faulty secondary ignition system (cracked spark plug insulator, faulty plug wires) (Chapters 1 and 5).
3   Problem with the fuel injection system (Chapter 4).
4   Vacuum leak at fuel injector(s), intake manifold or vacuum hoses (Chapters 2A and 4).
5   Valve clearances incorrectly set and/or valves sticking (Chapter 2A).

16 Pinging or knocking engine sounds during acceleration or uphill

1   Incorrect grade of fuel.
2   Fuel injection system faulty (Chapter 4).
3   Improper or damaged spark plugs or wires (Chapter 1).
4   Knock sensor defective (Chapter 6).
5   EGR valve not functioning (Chapter 6).
6   Vacuum leak (Chapters 2A and 4).

17 Engine runs with oil pressure light on

1   Low oil level (Chapter 1).
2   Idle rpm below specification (Chapter 1).
3   Short in wiring circuit (Chapter 12).
4   Faulty oil pressure sender (Chapter 2A).
5   Worn engine bearings and/or oil pump (Chapter 2A).

18 Engine continues to run after switching off

Excessive engine operating temperature (Chapter 3).

Engine electrical system

19 Battery will not hold a charge

1   Alternator drivebelt defective or not adjusted properly (Chapter 1).
2   Battery electrolyte level low (Chapter 1).
3   Battery terminals loose or corroded (Chapter 1).
4   Alternator not charging properly (Chapter 5).
5   Loose, broken or faulty wiring in the charging circuit (Chapter 5).
6   Short in vehicle wiring (Chapter 12).
7   Internally defective battery (Chapters 1 and 5).

20 Alternator light fails to go out

1   Faulty alternator or charging circuit (Chapter 5).
2   Alternator drivebelt defective or out of adjustment (Chapter 1).
3   Alternator voltage regulator inoperative (Chapter 5).

21 Alternator light fails to come on when key is turned on

1   Warning light bulb defective (Chapter 12).
2   Fault in the printed circuit, dash wiring or bulb holder (Chapter 12).

Fuel system

22 Excessive fuel consumption

1   Dirty or clogged air filter element (Chapter 1).
2   Emissions system not functioning properly (Chapter 6).
3   Fuel injection system not functioning properly (Chapter 4).
4   Low tire pressure or incorrect tire size (Chapter 1).

23 Fuel leakage and/or fuel odor

1   Leaking fuel feed or return line (Chapters 1 and 4).
2   Tank overfilled.
3   Evaporative canister filter clogged (Chapter 6).
4   Problem with fuel injection system (Chapter 4).

Cooling system

24 Overheating

1   Insufficient coolant in system (Chapter 1).
2   Water pump defective (Chapter 3).
3   Radiator core blocked or grille restricted (Chapter 3).
4   Thermostat faulty (Chapter 3).
5   Electric coolant fan inoperative or blades broken (Chapter 3).
6   Radiator cap not maintaining proper pressure (Chapter 3).

25 Overcooling

1   Faulty thermostat (Chapter 3).
2   Inaccurate temperature gauge sending unit (Chapter 3).
3   Cooling fan runs continuously.

26 External coolant leakage

1   Deteriorated/damaged hoses; loose clamps (Chapters 1 and 3).
2   Water pump defective (Chapter 3).
3   Leakage from radiator core or coolant reservoir bottle (Chapter 3).
4   Engine drain or water jacket core plugs leaking (Chapter 2A).

27 Internal coolant leakage

1   Leaking cylinder head gasket (Chapter 2A).
2   Cracked cylinder bore or cylinder head (Chapter 2A).

28 Coolant loss

1 Too much coolant in system (Chapter 1).
2 Coolant boiling away because of over-heating (Chapter 3).
3 Internal or external leakage (Chapter 3).
4 Faulty radiator cap (Chapter 3).

29 Poor coolant circulation

1 Inoperative water pump (Chapter 3).
2 Restriction in cooling system (Chapters 1 and 3).
3 Water pump drivebelt defective/out of adjustment (Chapter 1).
4 Thermostat sticking (Chapter 3).

Clutch

30 Fails to release (pedal pressed to the floor-shift lever does not move freely in and out of gear)

Note: *All clutch-related service information is located in Chapter 8, unless otherwise noted.*
5 Freeplay incorrectly adjusted.
6 Clutch contaminated with oil. Remove clutch disc and inspect.
7 Clutch disc warped, distorted or otherwise damaged.
8 Diaphragm spring fatigued. Remove clutch cover/pressure plate assembly and inspect.
9 Leakage of fluid from clutch hydraulic system. Inspect master cylinder, operating cylinder and connecting lines.
10 Air in clutch hydraulic system. Bleed the system.
11 Insufficient pedal stroke. Check and adjust as necessary.
12 Piston seal in master or release cylinder deformed or damaged.
13 Lack of grease on pilot bearing.

31 Clutch slips (engine speed increase with no increase in vehicle speed)

1 Worn or oil-soaked clutch disc.
2 Clutch disc not broken in. It may take 30 or 40 starts for a new clutch to seat.
3 Diaphragm spring weak or damaged. Remove clutch cover/pressure plate assembly and inspect.
4 Debris in master cylinder preventing the piston from returning to its normal position.
5 Clutch hydraulic line damaged internally (not allowing fluid to return to the clutch master cylinder).
6 Binding in the release mechanism.

32 Grabbing (chattering) as clutch is engaged

1 Oil on clutch disc. Remove and inspect. Repair any leaks.
2 Worn or loose engine or transaxle mounts. These units may move slightly when clutch is released. Inspect mounts and bolts.
3 Worn splines on clutch disc. Remove clutch components and inspect.
4 Warped pressure plate or flywheel. Remove clutch components and inspect.
5 Diaphragm spring fatigued. Remove clutch cover/pressure plate assembly and inspect.
6 Clutch linings hardened or warped.
7 Clutch lining rivets loose.

33 Squeal or rumble with clutch fully engaged (pedal released)

1 Improper pedal adjustment. Adjust pedal freeplay.
2 Release bearing binding on transaxle input shaft. Remove clutch components and check bearing. Remove any burrs or nicks, clean and relubricate before reinstallation.
3 Pilot bearing worn or damaged.
4 Clutch rivets loose.
5 Clutch disc cracked.
6 Fatigued clutch disc torsion springs. Replace clutch disc.
7 Weak pedal return spring. Replace the spring.

34 Squeal or rumble with clutch fully disengaged (pedal depressed)

1 Worn, faulty or broken release bearing.
2 Worn or broken pressure plate diaphragm fingers.

35 Clutch pedal stays on floor when disengaged

1 Bind in cable or release bearing. Inspect cable or remove clutch components as necessary.
2 Clutch pressure plate weak or broken. Remove and inspect clutch pressure plate.

Manual transaxle

36 Noisy in Neutral with engine running

1 Mainshaft bearing worn.
2 Damaged pinion shaft bearing.

3 Insufficient transaxle lubricant (Chapter 1).
4 Transaxle lubricant in poor condition. Drain and fill with proper grade (Chapter 1). Inspect old lubricant for water and debris.

37 Noisy in all gears

1 Mainshaft bearing worn.
2 Damaged pinion shaft bearing.
3 Insufficient transaxle lubricant (Chapter 1).

38 Noisy in one particular gear

1 Worn, damaged or chipped gear teeth for that particular gear.
2 Worn or damaged synchronizer for that particular gear.

39 Slips out of high gear

1 Transaxle mounting bolts loose.
2 Shift mechanism not working freely.
3 Damaged pilot bearing.
4 Worn or improperly adjusted linkage (Chapter 8).

40 Difficulty in engaging gears

1 Clutch not releasing (Chapter 8).
2 Loose, damaged or misadjusted shift linkage. Make a thorough inspection, replacing parts as necessary. Adjust as described in Chapter 8.

41 Oil leakage

1 Excessive amount of lubricant in transaxle (Chapter 1). Drain lubricant as required.
2 Driveaxle oil seals defective.
3 Extension housing seal or speedometer driven-gear O-ring defective.

Automatic transaxle

42 Fluid leakage

1 Automatic transaxle fluid is a deep red color; fluid in CVT transaxles is a transparent green color. Fluid leaks should not be confused with engine oil which can easily be blown by airflow to the transaxle.
2 To pinpoint a leak, first remove all built-up dirt and grime from around the transaxle. Degreasing agents and/or steam cleaning will

achieve this. With the underside clean, drive the vehicle at low speeds so that air flow will not blow the leak far from its source. Raise the vehicle and determine where the leak is coming from. Common areas of leakage are:

a) *Fluid pan: tighten mounting bolts and/or replace pan gasket as necessary (Chapter 1)*
b) *Extension housing seal: replace seal as necessary (Chapter 7B)*
c) *Vent pipe: transaxle over-filled and/or water in fluid (see checking procedures, Chapter 1)*
d) *Speedometer driven gear O-ring defective.*

43　General shift mechanism problems

1   Chapter 7B deals with checking and adjusting the shift linkage on automatic transaxles. Common problems which may be attributed to out-of-adjustment linkage are:

a) *Engine starts in gears other than P (Park) or N (Neutral)*
b) *Gear position indicator points to a gear other than the one the transaxle is actually in*
c) *Vehicle will not hold firm when in P (Park) position*

44　Transaxle will not downshift with the accelerator pedal pressed to the floor

Faulty electronics in the transaxle control system. Take the vehicle to a dealer or other qualified repair shop.

45　Engine will start in gears other than P (Park) or N (Neutral)

Check the Transmission Range (TR) sensor (Chapter 6).

46　Transaxle slips, shifts rough, is noisy or has no drive in forward or reverse gears

1   There are many probable causes for the above problems, but the home mechanic should concern himself only with one possibility: fluid level.
2   Before taking the vehicle to a repair shop, check the level of the fluid and condition of the fluid as described in Chapter 1. Correct fluid level as necessary or change the fluid and filter if needed. If problem persists, have a professional diagnose the probable cause.

Driveshaft

47　Leakage of fluid at front of driveshaft

Defective extension housing seal (Chapter 7A). Also, inspect the splined yoke for burrs or a rough condition which may be damaging the seal. If found, these can be dressed with crocus cloth or a fine whetstone.

48　Knock or clunk when the transaxle is under initial load (just after transaxle is put into gear)

1   Loose or disconnected rear suspension components. Check all mounting bolts and bushings (Chapters 1 and 10).
2   Loose driveshaft bolts. Inspect all bolts and nuts and tighten to the specified torque (Chapter 8).
3   Worn or damaged universal joint bearings. Replace the driveshaft (Chapter 8).
4   Worn sleeve yoke and mainshaft splines (Chapter 8).

49　Metallic grating sound consistent with vehicle speed

Pronounced wear in the universal joint bearings. Replace the driveshaft (Chapter 8).

50　Vibration

1   Before performing this test, have the wheels professionally balanced.
2   Install a tachometer inside the vehicle to monitor engine speed as it is driven. Drive the vehicle and note the engine speed at which the vibration (roughness) is most pronounced. Now shift the transaxle to a different gear and bring the engine speed to the same point.
3   If the vibration occurs at the same engine speed (rpm) regardless of which gear the transaxle is in, the driveshaft is NOT at fault since the driveshaft speed varies.
4   If the vibration decreases or is eliminated when the transaxle is in a different gear at the same engine speed, refer to the following probable causes.
5   Bent or dented driveshaft. Inspect and replace as necessary (Chapter 8).
6   Undercoating or built-up dirt, etc. on the driveshaft. Clean the shaft thoroughly and test.
7   Worn universal joint bearings (Chapter 8).

Front differential

51　Gear noise when driving

If noise increases as vehicle speed increases, it may be due to insufficient gear oil (Chapter 1), incorrect gear engagement or damaged gears. Remove the transaxle/differential unit and have it checked and repaired by a dealer service department or other qualified repair shop.

52　Gear noise when coasting

Damaged gears caused by bearings and shims that are worn or out of adjustment.

53　Bearing noise

Usually caused by cracked, broken or otherwise damaged bearings (see Section 48)

54　Noise when turning

Damaged or worn differential side gear, pinion gear or pinion shaft (see Section 51).

Rear differential

55　Oil leakage

1   Worn or incorrectly installed pinion seal or axleshaft oil seal.
2   Scored or excessively worn sliding surface of companion flange.
3   Clogged air vent.
4   Loose rear cover attaching bolts or damaged gasket.
5   Loose oil fill or drain plug.

56　Noise when starting or shifting gears

1   Excessive gear backlash.
2   Insufficient bearing preload.
3   Loose drive pinion nut.

57　Noise when turning

1   Damaged or worn side gears or bearings.
2   Broken or seized spider gear shaft.
3   Excessively worn side gear thrust washer.
4   Broken teeth on differential hypoid gears.

Driveaxles

58 Clicking noise in turns

Worn or damaged outer CV joint. Check for cut or damaged boots. Repair as necessary.

59 Knock or clunk when accelerating after coasting

Worn or damaged inner CV joint. Check for cut or damaged boots. Repair as necessary.

60 Shudder or vibration during acceleration

1   Worn or damaged inner or outer CV joints. Repair or replace as necessary.
2   Sticking inner CV joint assembly. Correct or replace as necessary.

Brakes

61 Vehicle pulls to one side during braking

1   Defective, damaged or oil-contaminated disc pad on one side. Inspect as described in Chapter 1. Replace as necessary.
2   Excessive wear of brake pad material or disc on one side. Inspect and correct as necessary.
3   Loose or disconnected front suspension components. Inspect and tighten all bolts to the torque listed in the Chapter 10 Specifications.
4   Defective caliper assembly. Remove caliper and inspect for stuck piston or damage.

62 Noise (high-pitched squeal without brake applied)

Brake pads worn out. Replace pads with new ones immediately.

63 Excessive brake pedal travel

1   Partial brake system failure. Inspect entire system (Chapter 1) and correct as required.
2   Insufficient fluid in master cylinder. Check (Chapter 1), add fluid and bleed system if necessary.

64 Brake pedal feels spongy when depressed

1   Air in hydraulic lines. Bleed the brake system.
2   Faulty flexible hoses. Inspect all system hoses and lines. Replace parts as necessary.
3   Master cylinder mount loose. Inspect master cylinder bolts (nuts) and tighten to the torque listed in the Chapter 9 Specifications.
4   Master cylinder faulty.

65 Excessive effort required to stop vehicle

1   Power brake booster not operating properly.
2   Excessively worn pads. Inspect (Chapter 1) and replace if necessary.
3   One or more caliper pistons seized. Inspect and replace as required.
4   Brake pads contaminated with oil or grease. Inspect and replace as required (Chapter 1).
5   New pads installed and not yet seated. It will take awhile for the new material to seat against the disc.

66 Pedal travels to floor with little resistance

Little or no fluid in the master cylinder reservoir (caused by leaking wheel cylinder(s), leaking caliper piston(s), loose, damaged or disconnected brake lines). Inspect entire system and correct as necessary.

67 Brake pedal pulsates during brake application

1   Wheel bearings worn (Chapter 10).
2   Disc not within specifications. Remove the disc and check for excessive lateral run-out and parallelism. Have the disc machined or replace it with a new one.
3   Out-of-round rear brake drums. Remove the drums and have them machined, or replace them.

68 Hill-holder fails to hold

1   Incline of hill may be too gentle to activate holder.
2   Pressure holder valve in need of adjustment.

Suspension and steering

69 Excessive tire wear (not specific to one area)

1   Incorrect tire pressures (Chapter 1).
2   Tires out of balance. Have professionally balanced.
3   Wheel damaged. Inspect and replace as necessary.
4   Suspension or steering components excessively worn (Chapter 1).

70 Excessive tire wear on outside edge

1   Inflation pressures incorrect (Chapter 1).
2   Excessive speed on turns.
3   Front end alignment incorrect (excessive toe-in). Have professionally aligned.
4   Suspension arm bent or twisted.

71 Excessive tire wear on inside edge

1   Inflation pressures incorrect (Chapter 1).
2   Front or rear toe incorrect. Have wheels aligned.
3   Loose or damaged steering components (Chapter 1).

72 Tire tread worn in one place

1   Tires out of balance. Balance tires professionally.
2   Damaged wheel. Inspect and replace if necessary.
3   Defective tire.

73 General vibration at highway speeds

1   Out-of-balance front wheels or tires. Have them professionally balanced.
2   Front or rear wheel bearings loose or worn. Check and replace as necessary (Chapter 10).
3   Defective tire or wheel. Have them checked and replaced if necessary.

74 Noise whether coasting or in drive

1   Road noise. No corrective procedures available.

2   Tire noise. Inspect tires and tire pressures (Chapter 1).
3   Front wheel bearings worn or damaged. Check (Chapter 10) and replace if necessary.
4   Damaged shock absorbers or mounts (Chapter 1).
5   Loose wheel lug nuts. Check and tighten as necessary (Chapter 1).

75   Vehicle pulls to one side

1   Tire pressures uneven (Chapter 1).
2   Defective tire (Chapter 1).
3   Excessive wear in suspension or steering components (Chapter 1).
4   Front end in need of alignment.
5   Front brakes dragging. Inspect brakes as described in Chapter 1.

76   Shimmy, shake or vibration

1   Tire or wheel out of balance or out of round. Have professionally balanced.

2   Worn wheel bearings. Replace as necessary (Chapter 10).
3   Struts and/or suspension components worn or damaged.

77   Excessive pitching and/or rolling around corners or during braking

1   Defective struts. Replace as a set.
2   Broken or weak coil springs and/or suspension components. Inspect as described in Chapter 11.

78   Excessively stiff steering

1   Lack of fluid in power steering fluid reservoir (Chapter 1).
2   Incorrect tire pressures (Chapter 1).
3   Lack of lubrication at balljoints (Chapter 1).
4   Front end out of alignment.

79   Excessive play in steering

1   Worn wheel bearings (Chapter 10).
2   Excessive wear in suspension or steering components.

80   Lack of power assistance

1   Steering pump drivebelt faulty, broken or not adjusted properly (Chapter 1).
2   Fluid level low (Chapter 1).
3   Hoses or lines restricting the flow. Inspect and replace parts as necessary.
4   Air in power steering system. Bleed system.

Chapter 1
Tune-up and routine maintenance

Contents

Specifications

Recommended lubricants and fluids

Note: *Listed here are manufacturer recommendations at the time this manual was written. Manufacturers occasionally upgrade their fluid and lubricant specifications, so check with your auto parts store for current recommendations.*

Engine oil
  Type .... API "Certified for gasoline engines"
  Viscosity
    Non-turbocharged engine
      2012 and earlier models .... SAE 5W-30 synthetic
      2013 and later models .... SAE 0W-30 synthetic
    Turbocharged engine .... SAE 5W-30 synthetic
Coolant .... Genuine Subaru coolant or equivalent anti-corrosive, ethylene glycol-based antifreeze, 50/50 mixture*

Brake fluid .... DOT 3 or DOT 4
Clutch fluid .... DOT 3 or DOT 4
Power steering fluid .... DEXRON III ATF
Automatic transaxle fluid .... Subaru ATF, Type-HP (or equivalent)
Continuously Variable Transmission (CVT) .... Subaru CVT oil for Lineartronic (or equivalent)
Manual transaxle lubricant .... API GL-5 SAE 75W-90 gear oil
Differential lubricant .... API GL-5 SAE 75W-90 gear oil
  Front (automatic transaxle) .... API GL-5 SAE 75W-90 gear oil
  Rear .... API GL-5 SAE 75W-90 gear oil

* If the coolant purchased is pre-diluted, do not add water to it.

Capacities*

Engine oil (with filter change)
  Turbocharged engines
    2.0L turbocharged engines .... 5.4 quarts   5.1 liters
    2.5L turbocharged engines
      2011 and earlier models .... 4.4 quarts   4.2 liters
      2012 and later models... 4.5 quarts   4.3 liters
  Non-turbocharged engines
    2012 and earlier models
      SOHC engines .... 4.4 quarts   4.2 liters
      DOHC engines .... 5.5 quarts   5.2 liters
    2013 and later models.. 5.1 quarts   4.8 liters
Cooling system
  Legacy models
    2011 and earlier models
      2.5L (SOHC) engines .... 6.9 quarts   6.5 liters
      2.5L (DOHC) turbocharged engines............................ 7.0 quarts   6.6 liters
    2012 models
      2.5L (SOHC) engines
        Automatic transaxle .... 6.8 quarts   6.4 liters
        Manual transaxle .... 6.9 quarts   6.5 liters
      2.5L (DOHC) turbocharged engines............................ 6.9 quarts   6.5 liters
    2013 and 2014 models
      CVT transaxle... 7.9 quarts   7.5 liters
      Manual transaxle .... 8.0 quarts   7.6 liters
    2015 and later models
      CVT transaxle... 8.2 quarts   7.8 liters
      Manual transaxle .... 8.0 quarts   7.6 liters
  Forester models
    2.0L (DOHC) turbocharged engines .... 9.4 quarts   8.9 liters
    2013 and earlier models
      2.5L (DOHC) Non-turbocharged
        Automatic transaxle .... 7.4 quarts   7.0 liters
        Manual transaxle .... 7.5 quarts   7.1 liters
      2.5L (DOHC) Turbocharged .... 8.5 quarts   8.0 liters
    2014 and later models
      2.5L (DOHC) Non-turbocharged
        CVT transaxle.. 8.0 quarts   7.6 liters
        Manual transaxle .... 7.8 quarts   7.4 liters
Automatic transaxle... 10 quarts   9.6 liters
Continuously variable transmission (CVT) .... 13.1 quarts 12.43 liters
Manual transaxle
  5-Speed.. 3.7 quarts   3.5 liters
  6-Speed
    2012 and earlier models .... 3.9 quarts   3.7 liters
    2013 and later models .... 3.5 quarts   3.3 liters
Differential
  Front (automatic transaxle) .... 1.5 quarts   1.3 liters
  Rear   0.8 quarts .... 0.8 liter

All capacities approximate. Add as necessary to bring to appropriate level.

Ignition system

Spark plug type
  2012 and earlier 2.5L non-turbocharged (SOHC) models .... NGK - SILFR6A11
  2012 and earlier 2.5L turbocharged (DOHC) models .... NGK - SILFR6B8
  2013 and later 2.5L non-turbocharged (DOHC) models .... NGK - SILZKAR7B11
  2.0L turbocharged engines .... NGK - ILKAR8H6
Spark plug gap
  Non-turbo engine .... 0.039 to 0.043 inch   1.0 to 1.1 mm
  Turbocharged engines
    2.0L engine .... 0.020 to 0.022 inch   0.50 to 0.55 mm
    2.5L engine .... 0.028 to 0.031 inch   0.7 to 0.8 mm
Firing order 1-3-2-4

Cylinder locations (and SOHC coil terminal locations)

Brakes and clutch

Disc brake pad lining thickness (minimum)	1/16 inch	1.6 mm
Clutch pedal free play		
5-speed models..	0.197 inch or less	5.0 mm or less
6-speed models..	0.157 inch or less	4.0 mm or less
Brake pedal freeplay...	See Chapter 9	
Disc minimum thickness	Refer to the dimension marked on the disc	
Wheel bearing freeplay limit	0.002 inch	0.05 mm

Torque specifications

Note: *One foot-pound (ft-lb) of torque is equivalent to 12 inch-pounds (in-lbs) of torque. Torque values below approximately 15 ft-lbs are expressed in inch-pounds, because most foot-pound torque wrenches are not accurate at these smaller values.*

	Ft-lbs (unless otherwise indicated)	Nm
Automatic transaxle drain plug	18.5	25
Manual transaxle drain plug		
5-speed models		
Aluminum gasket...	32	44
Copper gasket	51	70
6-speed models		
Oil pan drain plug...	31	41
Clutch housing side plug...	51	70
Manual transaxle fill plug (6-speed models).............................	37	50
Front differential drain plug (automatic transaxle)		
Aluminum gasket..	32	44
Copper gasket...	51	70
Metal gasket...	51	70
Rear differential check/fill and drain plugs............................	36	49
Engine oil drain plug	32	44
Spark plugs...	155 in-lbs	17.5
Wheel lug nuts..	88.5	120

Typical DOHC engine compartment component locations - non-turbo engine

1	Brake fluid reservoir	5	Battery	9	Drivebelt
2	Underhood fuse/relay block	6	Windshield washer fluid reservoir	10	Engine oil dipstick
3	Engine oil filter	7	Coolant reservoir	11	Air filter housing
4	Engine oil filler cap	8	Radiator cap	12	Power steering fluid reservoir

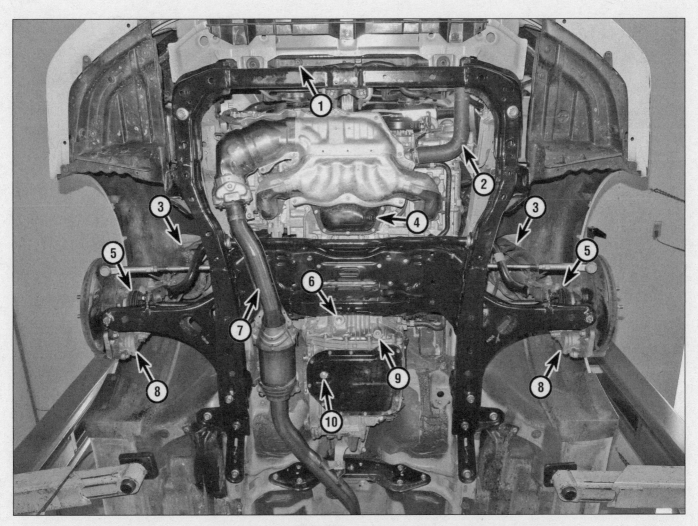

Typical engine compartment underside component locations

1	Radiator drain	5	Driveaxle boot	8	Brake caliper
2	Lower radiator hose	6	Differential drain and fill plug	9	Differential check plug
3	Strut and coil spring assembly		(automatic transaxle models)		(automatic transaxle models)
4	Engine oil drain plug	7	Exhaust pipe	10	Automatic transaxle fluid drain plug

Typical rear underside component locations

1	Driveshaft	3	Outer driveaxle boot
2	Inner driveaxle boot	4	Shock absorber and coil spring

5	Rear differential
6	Muffler

1 Maintenance schedule

The following maintenance intervals are based on the assumption that the vehicle owner will be doing the maintenance or service work, as opposed to having a dealer service department do the work. Although the time/ mileage intervals are loosely based on factory recommendations, most have been shortened to ensure, for example, that such items as lubricants and fluids are checked/changed at intervals that promote maximum engine/driveline service life. Also, subject to the preference of the individual owner interested in keeping his or her vehicle in peak condition at all times, and with the vehicle's ultimate resale in mind, many of the maintenance procedures may be performed more often than recommended in the following schedule. We encourage such owner initiative.

When the vehicle is new it should be serviced initially by a factory authorized dealer service department to protect the factory warranty. In many cases the initial maintenance check is done at no cost to the owner (check with your dealer service department for more information).

Every 250 miles or weekly, whichever comes first

Check the engine oil level (see Section 4)
Check the engine coolant level (see Section 4)
Check the brake and clutch fluid level (see Section 4)
Check the windshield washer fluid level (see Section 4)
Check the power steering fluid level (see Section 4)
Check the automatic transaxle fluid level or manual transaxle/front differential lubricant and the rear differential lubricant level (see Section 4)
Check the tires and tire pressures (see Section 5)

Every 3000 miles or 3 months, whichever comes first

All items listed above, plus . . .
Change the engine oil and filter (see Section 6)

Every 7500 miles or 6 months, whichever comes first

All items listed above, plus . . .
Check and service the battery (see Section 7)
Rotate the tires (see Section 8)
Inspect and replace, if necessary, the windshield wiper blades (see Section 9)
Inspect the exhaust system (see Section 10)
Check the seat belts (see Section 11)
Inspect and replace, if necessary, all underhood hoses (see Section 12)
Check the cooling system (see Section 13)
Replace the cabin air filter (Section 28)

Every 15,000 miles or 12 months, whichever comes first

All items listed above, plus . . .
Inspect the fuel system (see Section 14)
Check the brakes (see Section 15)
Inspect the suspension and steering components (see Section 16)
Inspect and replace, if necessary, the air filter (see Section 17)
Check the clutch pedal height (see Chapter 8)
Check the brake pedal height and hill holder adjustment (see Chapter 9)

Every 30,000 miles or 30 months, whichever comes first

All items listed above, plus . . .
Change the brake fluid (see Section 18)
Check the engine drivebelts (see Section 19)
Replace the fuel filter (see Section 20)
Service the cooling system (drain, flush and refill) (see Section 21)
Replace the spark plugs (non-platinum type plugs) (see Section 22)
Inspect the ignition coils (turbo engines) (see Section 23)
Inspect the spark plug wires (2009 SOHC Legacy/2009 and 2010 SOHC Forester (see Section 29)
Change the automatic transaxle fluid (see Section 24)**
Change the manual transaxle lubricant (see Section 25)
Change the differential lubricant (see Section 26)
Inspect the timing belt (see Chapter 2A)
Replace the air filter (see Section 17)*

Every 60,000 miles or 48 months, whichever comes first

All items listed above, plus . . .
Replace the spark plugs (platinum-type plugs) (see Section 22)
Inspect the front and rear wheel bearings (see Section 27)

Every 105,000 miles or 105 months, whichever comes first

Replace the engine drivebelts (see Section 19)
Replace the timing belt (see Chapter 2A)

This item is affected by "severe" operating conditions, as described below. If the vehicle is operated under severe conditions, perform all maintenance indicated with an asterisk (*) at 7500 mile/six-month intervals. Severe conditions exist if you mainly operate the vehicle . . .

a) In dusty areas
b) Towing a trailer
c) Idling for extended periods and/or driving at low speeds when outside temperatures remain below freezing and most trips are less than four miles long

**If operated under one or more of the following conditions, change the automatic transaxle fluid every 15,000 miles:*

a) In heavy city traffic where the outside temperature regularly reaches 90-degrees F or higher
b) In hilly or mountainous terrain
c) Frequent trailer pulling

2   Introduction

1   This Chapter is designed to help the home mechanic maintain his or her vehicle for peak performance, economy, safety and long life.

2   On the following pages is a master maintenance schedule, followed by Sections dealing specifically with each item on the schedule. Visual checks, adjustments, component replacement and other helpful items are included. Refer to the accompanying illustrations of the engine compartment and the underside of the vehicle for the location of various components.

3   Servicing your vehicle in accordance with the mileage/time maintenance schedule and the following Sections will provide it with a planned maintenance program that should result in a long and reliable service life. This is a comprehensive plan, so maintaining some items but not others at the specified service intervals will not produce the same results.

4   As you service your vehicle, you will discover that many of the procedures can, and should, be grouped together because of the nature of the particular procedure you're performing or because of the close proximity of two otherwise unrelated components to one another.

5   For example, if the vehicle is raised for any reason, you should inspect the exhaust, suspension, steering and fuel systems while you're under the vehicle. When you're rotating the tires, it makes good sense to check the brakes and wheel bearings since the wheels are already removed.

6   Finally, let's suppose you have to borrow or rent a torque wrench. Even if you only need to tighten the spark plugs, you might as well check the torque of as many critical fasteners as time allows.

7   The first step of this maintenance program is to prepare yourself before the actual work begins. Read through all Sections pertinent to the procedures you're planning to do, then make a list of and gather together all the parts and tools you will need to do the job. If it looks as if you might run into problems during a particular segment of some procedure, seek advice from your local parts man or dealer service department.

Owner's Manual and VECI label information

8   Your vehicle owner's manual was written for your year and model and contains very specific information on component locations, specifications, fuse ratings, part numbers, etc. The owner's manual is an important resource for the do-it-yourselfer to have; if one was not supplied with your vehicle, it can generally be ordered from a dealer parts department.

9   Among other important information, the Vehicle Emissions Control Information (VECI) label contains specifications and procedures for applicable tune-up adjustments and, in some instances, spark plugs. The information on this label is the exact maintenance data

recommended by the manufacturer. This data often varies by intended operating altitude, local emissions regulations, month of manufacture, etc.

10   This Chapter contains procedural details, safety information and more ambitious maintenance intervals than you might find in manufacturer's literature. However, you may also find procedures or specifications in your owner's manual or VECI label that differ with what's printed here. In these cases, the owner's manual or VECI label can be considered correct, since it is specific to your particular vehicle.

3   Tune-up general information

1   The term tune-up is used in this manual to represent a combination of individual operations rather than one specific procedure.

2   If, from the time the vehicle is new, the routine maintenance schedule is followed closely and frequent checks are made of fluid levels and high wear items, as suggested throughout this manual, the engine will be kept in relatively good running condition and the need for additional work will be minimized.

3   More likely than not, however, there will be times when the engine is running poorly due to lack of regular maintenance. This is even more likely if a used vehicle, which has not received regular and frequent maintenance checks, is purchased. In such cases, an engine tune-up will be needed outside of the regular routine maintenance intervals.

4   The first step in any tune-up or diagnostic procedure to help correct a poor running engine is a cylinder compression check. A cylinder compression check (see Chapter 2B) will help determine the condition of internal engine components and should be used as a guide for tune-up and repair procedures. If, for instance, the compression check indicates serious internal engine wear, a conventional tune-up won't improve the performance of the engine and would be a waste of time and money. Because of its importance, the compression check should be done by someone with the right equipment and the knowledge to use it properly.

5   The following procedures are those most often needed to bring a generally poor running engine back into a proper state of tune.

Minor tune-up

Check all engine related fluids
    (see Section 4)
Clean, inspect and test the battery
    (see Section 7)
Check the cooling system (see Section 13)
Check all underhood hoses (see Section 12)
Check and adjust the drivebelts
    (see Section 19)
Inspect the spark plug wires (2009 SOHC
    Legacy/2009 and 2010 SOHC
    Forester models) (see Section 29)
Check the air filter (see Section 17)

Major tune-up

All items listed under Minor tune-up, plus . . .
    Check the fuel system (see Section 14)
    Replace the fuel filter (see Section 20)
    Replace the spark plugs (see Section 22)
    Replace the spark plug wires
        (2009 SOHC Legacy/2009 and 2010
        SOHC Forester models) (see Section 29)
    Replace the air filter (see Section 17)
    Check the charging system (see Chapter 5)

4   Fluid level checks (every 250 miles or weekly)

Note: *The following are fluid level checks to be done on a 250 mile or weekly basis. Additional fluid level checks can be found in specific maintenance procedures which follow. Regardless of intervals, be alert to fluid leaks under the vehicle which would indicate a fault to be corrected immediately.*

1   Fluids are an essential part of the lubrication, cooling, brake and windshield washer systems. Because the fluids gradually become depleted and/or contaminated during normal operation of the vehicle, they must be periodically replenished. See *Recommended lubricants and fluids* in this Chapter's Specifications before adding fluid to any of the following components.

Note: *The vehicle must be on level ground when fluid levels are checked.*

Engine oil

2   The engine oil level is checked with a dipstick located on the right side of the engine compartment, near the air filter housing (see illustrations).

3   The oil level should be checked before the vehicle has been driven, or about 5 minutes after the engine has been shut off. If the oil is checked immediately after driving the vehicle, some of the oil will remain in the upper engine components, resulting in an inaccurate reading on the dipstick.

4   Pull the dipstick out of the tube and wipe all the oil from the end with a clean rag or paper towel. Insert the clean dipstick all the way back into the tube, then pull it out again. Note the oil at the end of the dipstick. Add oil as necessary to keep the level between the LOW and FULL marks on the dipstick (see illustration).

5   Do not overfill the engine by adding too much oil since this may result in oil-fouled spark plugs, oil foaming, oil leaks or oil seal failures.

6   Oil is added to the engine after removing the threaded cap from the oil filler tube (see illustration). A funnel may help to reduce spills.

7   Checking the oil level is an important preventive maintenance step. A consistently low oil level indicates oil leakage through damaged seals, defective gaskets or past worn rings or valve guides. If the oil looks milky or has water droplets in it, the cylinder

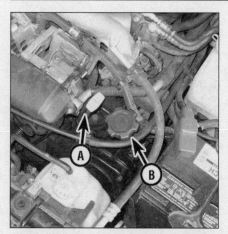

4.2a On timing belt engines, the engine oil dipstick (A) is located on the left side of the engine, near the oil filler cap (B)

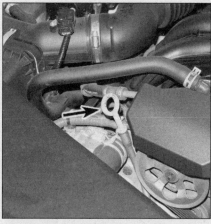

4.2b On timing chain engines, the engine oil dipstick is located on the right side

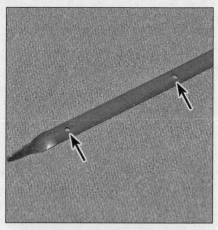

4.4 The oil level must be maintained between the marks at all times

head gasket(s) may be blown or the head(s) or block may be cracked. The engine should be checked immediately. The condition of the oil should also be checked. Whenever you check the oil level, slide your thumb and index finger up the dipstick before wiping off the oil. If you see small dirt or metal particles clinging to the dipstick, the oil should be changed (see Section 6).

Engine coolant

Warning: *Do not allow antifreeze to come in contact with your skin or painted surfaces of the vehicle. Flush contaminated areas immediately with plenty of water. Don't store new coolant or leave old coolant lying around where it's accessible to children or pets - they're attracted by its sweet smell. Ingestion of even a small amount of coolant can be fatal! Wipe up garage floor and drip pan spills immediately. Keep antifreeze containers covered and repair cooling system leaks as soon as they're noticed.*

Warning: *DO NOT remove the radiator cap or the coolant reservoir cap while the cooling system is hot, as escaping steam could cause serious injury.*

8   These models are equipped with a pressurized coolant recovery system. A white coolant reservoir, which is located by the radiator in the engine compartment, is connected by a hose to the base of the radiator cap (see illustration). If the coolant gets too hot during engine operation, coolant can escape from the radiator through a pressurized filler cap, then through a connecting hose into the reservoir. As the engine cools, the coolant is automatically drawn back into the cooling system to maintain the correct level.

9   The coolant level should be checked regularly. The coolant level should be between the FULL and LOW lines on the reservoir tank. The level will vary with the temperature of the engine. When the engine is cold, the coolant level should be at or slightly above the LOW mark on the tank. Once the engine has

4.6 Oil filler cap location

warmed up, the level should be at or near the FULL mark. If it isn't, allow the fluid in the tank to cool, then remove the cap from the reservoir and add coolant to bring the level up to the FULL line.

10   Use only ethylene-glycol type coolant and water in the mixture ratio recommended by your owner's manual. Do not use supplemental inhibitor additives. If only a small amount of coolant is required to bring the system up to the proper level, water can be used. However, repeated additions of water will dilute the recommended antifreeze and water solution. In order to maintain the proper ratio of antifreeze and water, it is advisable to top up the coolant level with the correct mixture. Refer to your owners' manual for the recommended ratio.

11   If the coolant level drops within a short time after replenishment, there may be a leak in the system. Inspect the radiator, hoses, engine coolant filler cap, drain plugs and water pump. If no leak is evident, have the radiator cap pressure tested by your dealer.

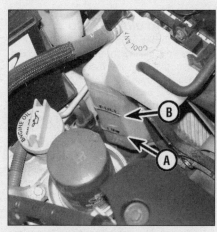

4.8 Coolant reservoir LOW (A) and FULL (B) marks

Warning: *Never remove the radiator cap or the coolant recovery reservoir cap when the engine is running or has just been shut down, because the cooling system is hot. Escaping steam and scalding liquid could cause serious injury.*

12   If it is necessary to open the radiator cap, wait until the system has cooled completely, then wrap a thick cloth around the cap and turn it to the first stop. If any steam escapes, wait until the system has cooled further, then remove the cap.

13   When checking the coolant level, always note its condition. It should be relatively clear. If it is brown or rust colored, the system should be drained, flushed and refilled. Even if the coolant appears to be normal, the corrosion inhibitors wear out with use, so it must be replaced at the specified intervals.

14   Do not allow antifreeze to come in contact with your skin or painted surfaces of the vehicle. Flush contacted areas immediately with plenty of water.

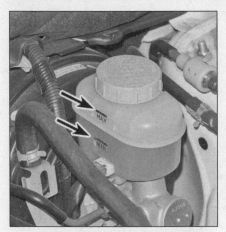

4.16 The fluid level inside the brake reservoir can easily be checked by observing the level from the outside

4.23 The windshield washer fluid reservoir is located at the left front of the engine compartment

4.26 The power steering fluid reservoir is located at the front of the engine compartment

Brake and clutch fluid

15   The brake and clutch fluid level is checked by looking through the plastic reservoir mounted on the master cylinder. The brake master cylinder is mounted on the front of the power booster unit in the driver's side rear corner of the engine compartment and the clutch master cylinder (if equipped) is mounted on the firewall.

16   The fluid level should be between the MAX and MIN lines on the side of the reservoir (see illustration).

17   If the fluid level is low, wipe the top of the reservoir and the cap with a clean rag to prevent contamination of the system as the cap is unscrewed.

18   Add only the specified brake fluid to the reservoir (refer to *Recommended lubricants and fluids* in this Chapter's Specifications, or your owner's manual). Mixing different types of brake fluid can damage the system. Fill the reservoir to the MAX line.

Warning: *Brake fluid can harm your eyes and damage painted surfaces, so use extreme caution when handling or pouring it. Do not use brake fluid that has been standing open or is more than one year old. Brake fluid absorbs moisture from the air, which can cause a dangerous loss of effectiveness.*

19   While the reservoir cap is off, check the master cylinder reservoir for contamination. If rust deposits, dirt particles or water droplets are present, the system should be bled repeatedly until clean brake fluid emerges from the bleeder valves (see Section 18). For clutch bleeding, see Chapter 8.

20   After filling the reservoir to the proper level, make sure the cap is seated to prevent fluid leakage and/or contamination.

21   The fluid level in the master cylinder will drop slightly as the brake shoes or pads at each wheel wear down during normal operation. If the brake fluid level drops consistently, check the entire system for leaks immediately. Examine all brake lines, hoses and connections, along with the calipers and master cyl-

inder (see Section 15). If the clutch master cylinder level drops, check the hoses and fittings of the clutch system (see Chapter 8).

22   When checking the fluid level, if you discover one or both reservoirs empty or nearly empty, the system(s) should be bled (see Chapter 8 or 9).

Windshield washer fluid

23   Fluid for the windshield washer system is stored in a plastic reservoir located on the left side of the engine compartment (see illustration).

24   In milder climates, plain water can be used in the reservoir, but it should be kept no more than 2/3 full to allow for expansion if the water freezes. In colder climates, use windshield washer system antifreeze, available at any auto parts store, to lower the freezing point of the fluid. Mix the antifreeze with water in accordance with the manufacturer's directions on the container.

Caution: *Do not use cooling system antifreeze - it will damage the vehicle's paint.*

Power steering fluid

25   Check the power steering fluid level periodically to avoid steering system problems, such as damage to the pump.

Caution: *DO NOT hold the steering wheel against either stop (extreme left or right turn) for more than five seconds. If you do, the power steering pump could be damaged.*

26   The power steering reservoir, located at the right side of the engine compartment (see illustration), has MIN and MAX fluid level marks on the side. The fluid level can be seen without removing the reservoir cap.

27   Park the vehicle on level ground and apply the parking brake.

28   Run the engine until it has reached normal operating temperature. With the engine at idle, turn the steering wheel back and forth about 10 times to get any air out of the steering system.

29   Shut the engine off with the wheels in the

straight-ahead position.

30   Note the fluid level on the side of the reservoir. It should be between the two marks (see illustration 4.26).

31   Add small amounts of fluid until the level is correct.

Caution: *Do not overfill the reservoir. If too much fluid is added, remove the excess with a clean syringe or suction pump.*

32   Check the power steering hoses and connections for leaks and wear.

Automatic transaxle fluid

33   All Legacy models and 2014 and later Forester models are equipped with CVT transaxles. On these models the transaxle fluid level check is not a routine maintenance item. Refer to Section 24 fluid level check (which would normally only be done if a leak is suspected or when the fluid is replaced).

2013 and earlier Forester models only

34   The level of the automatic transaxle fluid should be carefully maintained. Low fluid level can lead to slipping or loss of drive, while overfilling can cause foaming, loss of fluid and transaxle damage.

35   The transaxle fluid level should only be checked when the transaxle is hot (at its normal operating temperature). If the vehicle has just been driven over 10 miles (15 miles in a frigid climate), and the fluid temperature is 160 to 175-degrees F, the transaxle is hot.

Caution: *If the vehicle has just been driven for a long time at high speed or in city traffic in hot weather, or if it has been pulling a trailer, an accurate fluid level reading cannot be obtained. Allow the fluid to cool down for about 30 minutes.*

36   If the vehicle has not been driven, park the vehicle on level ground, set the parking brake, then start the engine and bring it to operating temperature. While the engine is idling, depress the brake pedal and move the selector lever through all the gear ranges,

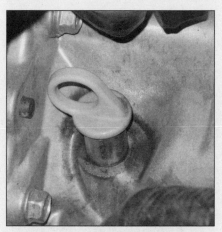

4.42 Manual transaxle dipstick location

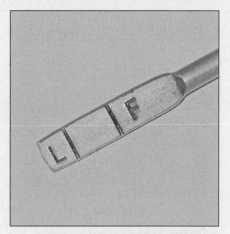

4.43 The lubricant level must be maintained between the marks at all times

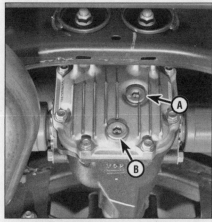

4.48 The rear differential check/fill plug (A) and drain plug (B) are located on the differential cover - use your finger as a dipstick to check the lubricant level

beginning and ending in Park.

37   With the engine still idling, remove the dipstick from its tube located towards the right side of the engine compartment. Check the level of the fluid on the dipstick and note its condition.

38   Wipe the fluid from the dipstick with a clean rag and reinsert it back into the filler tube until the cap seats.

39   Pull the dipstick out again and note the fluid level. If the transaxle is cold, the level should be in the COLD or COOL range on the dipstick. If it is hot, the fluid level should be in the HOT range. If the level is at the low side of either range, add the specified automatic transaxle fluid through the dipstick tube with a funnel.

40   Add just enough of the recommended fluid to fill the transaxle to the proper level. It takes about one pint to raise the level from the low mark to the high mark when the fluid is hot, so add the fluid a little at a time and keep checking the level until it is correct.

41   The condition of the fluid should also be checked along with the level. If the fluid at the end of the dipstick is black or a dark reddish brown color, or if it emits a burned smell, the fluid should be changed (see Section 24). If you are in doubt about the condition of the fluid, purchase some new fluid and compare the two for color and smell.

Manual transaxle lubricant/ automatic transaxle front differential lubricant

Manual transaxle lubricant

Note: *Vehicles equipped with a manual transaxle have an integral front differential (meaning they share the same lubricant). Vehicles equipped with an automatic transaxle have a non-integral front differential (meaning they DO NOT share the same lubricant). For the automatic transaxle front differential lubricant level check procedure, see Steps 45 and 46.*

42   All manual transaxles have a dipstick that extends through a small tube and into the transaxle (see illustration).

43   Pull the dipstick out of the tube and wipe all the lubricant from the end with a clean rag or paper towel. Insert the clean dipstick all the way back into the tube, then pull it out again. Note the lubricant at the end of the dipstick. Add lubricant as necessary to keep the level between the LOW and FULL marks on the dipstick (see illustration).

44   Lubricant is added to the transaxle through the dipstick tube. Use a funnel to prevent spills. Do not overfill the transaxle since this may result in lubricant leaks or lubricant seal failures.

45   After adding lubricant, be sure to reinstall the dipstick.

Front differential lubricant (automatic transaxle vehicles)

46   The front differential fluid level check is not a routine maintenance item. Refer to Section 26 for the fluid level check (which would normally only be done if a leak is suspected or when the fluid is replaced).

Note: *The front differential does not use a dipstick, the fluid level can only be accurately checked by adding lubricant to the front differential and allowing the excess to drain out of the check "overflow" plug (see Section 26).*

Rear differential lubricant level check

47   The rear differential has a check/fill plug which must be removed to check the lubricant level. If the vehicle must be raised to gain access to the plug, support it safely on jackstands - DO NOT crawl under the vehicle when it's supported only by the jack.

48   Remove the check/fill plug from the back of the rear differential (see illustration).

49   Use a finger to reach inside the housing to determine the lubricant level. The lubricant level should be at the bottom of the plug opening. If it isn't, use a hand pump (available

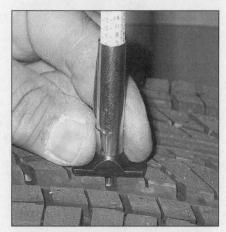

5.2 A tire tread depth indicator should be used to monitor tire wear - they are available at auto parts stores and service stations and cost very little

at auto parts stores) to add the specified lubricant until it just starts to run out of the opening.

50   Install the plug and tighten it to the torque listed in this Chapter's Specifications.

---

5   Tire and tire pressure checks (every 250 miles or weekly)

---

1   Periodic inspection of the tires may spare you the inconvenience of being stranded with a flat tire. It can also provide you with vital information regarding possible problems in the steering and suspension systems before major damage occurs.

2   The original tires on this vehicle are equipped with 1/2-inch wide wear bands that will appear when tread depth reaches 1/16-inch, at which time the tires can be considered worn out. Tread wear can be monitored with a simple, inexpensive device known as a tread depth indicator (see illustration).

UNDERINFLATION

CUPPING

OVERINFLATION

Cupping may be caused by:
- Underinflation and/or mechanical irregularities such as out-of-balance condition of wheel and/or tire, and bent or damaged wheel.
- Loose or worn steering tie-rod or steering idler arm.
- Loose, damaged or worn front suspension parts.

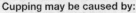

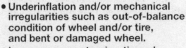
INCORRECT TOE-IN OR EXTREME CAMBER

FEATHERING DUE TO MISALIGNMENT

5.3 This chart will help you determine the condition of your tires, the probable cause(s) of abnormal wear and the corrective action necessary

3   Note any abnormal tread wear (see illustration). Tread pattern irregularities such as cupping, flat spots and more wear on one side than the other are indications of front end alignment and/or balance problems. If any of these conditions are noted, take the vehicle to a tire shop or service station to correct the problem.

4   Look closely for cuts, punctures and embedded nails or tacks. Sometimes a tire will hold air pressure for a short time or leak down very slowly after a nail has embedded itself in the tread. If a slow leak persists, check the valve stem core to make sure it's tight (see illustration). Examine the tread for an object that may have embedded itself in the tire or for a plug that may have begun to leak (radial tire punctures are repaired with a rubber plug that's installed in the hole). If a puncture is suspected, it can be easily verified by spraying a solution of soapy water onto the puncture area (see illustration). The soapy solution will bubble if there's a leak. Unless the puncture is unusually large, a tire shop or service station can usually repair the tire.

5   Carefully inspect the inner sidewall of each tire for evidence of brake fluid leakage. If you see any, inspect the brakes immediately (see Chapter 9).

6   Correct air pressure adds miles to the lifespan of the tires, improves mileage and enhances overall ride quality. Tire pressure cannot be accurately estimated by looking at

5.4a If a tire loses air on a steady basis, check the valve core first to make sure it's snug (special inexpensive wrenches are commonly available at auto parts stores)

5.4b If the valve core is tight, raise the corner of the vehicle with the low tire and spray a soapy water solution onto the tread as the tire is turned slowly - slow leaks will cause small bubbles to appear

a tire, especially if it's a radial. A tire pressure gauge is essential. Keep an accurate gauge in the vehicle. The pressure gauges attached to the nozzles of air hoses at gas stations are often inaccurate.

7   Always check tire pressure when the tires are cold. Cold, in this case, means the vehicle has not been driven over a mile in the three hours preceding a tire pressure check. A pressure rise of four to eight pounds is not uncommon once the tires are warm.

8   Unscrew the valve cap protruding from the wheel or hubcap and push the gauge firmly onto the valve stem (see illustration). Note the reading on the gauge and compare the figure to the recommended tire pressure shown on the placard on the driver's side door pillar. Reinstall the valve cap to keep dirt and moisture out of the valve stem mechanism. Check all four tires and, if necessary, add enough air to bring them up to the recommended pressure.

9   Don't forget to keep the spare tire inflated to the specified pressure (consult your owner's manual). Note that the air pressure specified for the compact spare is significantly higher than the pressure of the regular tires.

6   Engine oil and filter change (every 3000 miles or 3 months)

1   Frequent oil changes are the best preventive maintenance the home mechanic can give the engine, because aging oil becomes diluted and contaminated, which leads to premature engine wear.

2   Make sure that you have all the necessary tools before you begin this procedure (see illustration). You should also have plenty of rags or newspapers handy for mopping up any spills.

3   Access to the underside of the vehicle is greatly improved if the vehicle can be lifted on a hoist, driven onto ramps or supported

5.8 To extend the life of your tires, check the air pressure at least once a week with an accurate gauge (don't forget the spare!)

by jackstands.

4   Park the vehicle on a level spot. Start the engine and allow it to reach its normal operating temperature (the needle on the temperature gauge should be at least above the bottom mark). Warm oil and contaminants will flow out more easily. Turn off the engine when it's warmed up. Remove the oil filler cap.

5   Raise the vehicle and support it securely on jackstands.

Warning: *To avoid personal injury, never get beneath the vehicle when it is supported by only by a jack. The jack provided with your vehicle is designed solely for raising the vehicle to remove and install the wheels. Always use jackstands to support the vehicle when it becomes necessary to place your body underneath the vehicle.*

6   Remove the engine splash shield (see illustration).

7   Being careful not to touch the hot exhaust components, place the drain pan under the drain plug in the bottom of the pan

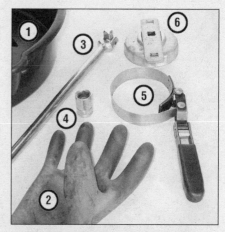

6.2 These tools are required when changing the engine oil and filter

*1   **Drain pan** - It should be fairly shallow in depth, but wide in order to prevent spills*

*2   **Rubber gloves** - When removing the drain plug and filter, it is inevitable that you will get oil on your hands (the gloves will prevent burns)*

*3   **Breaker bar** - Sometimes the oil drain plug is pretty tight and a long breaker bar is needed to loosen it*

*4   **Socket** - To be used with the breaker bar or a ratchet (must be the correct size to fit the drain plug)*

*5   **Filter wrench** - This is a metal band-type wrench, which requires clearance around the filter to be effective*

*6   **Filter wrench** - This type fits on the bottom of the filter and can be turned with a ratchet or beaker bar (different size wrenches are available for different types of filters)*

and remove the plug (see illustration). You may want to wear gloves while unscrewing the plug the final few turns if the engine is really hot.

6.6 Engine splash shield fastener locations

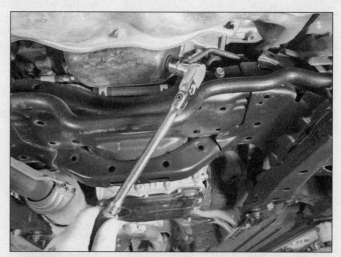

6.7 The engine oil drain plug is located on the bottom of the oil pan - it is usually very tight, so use the proper size box end wrench or socket to avoid rounding it off (engine cover removed for clarity)

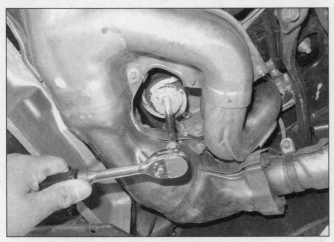

6.12a On models with the oil filter mounted under the engine, a filter wrench that grips the top of the filter must be used

6.12b On models with the oil filter mounted at the top of the engine, a standard filter wrench will work

8   Allow the old oil to drain into the pan. It may be necessary to move the pan farther under the engine as the oil flow slows to a trickle. Inspect the old oil for the presence of metal shavings and chips.

9   After all the oil has drained, wipe off the drain plug with a clean rag. Even minute metal particles clinging to the plug would immediately contaminate the new oil.

10   Clean the area around the drain plug opening, reinstall the plug and tighten it to the torque listed in this Chapter's Specifications. Do not strip the threads.

11   Move the drain pan into position under the oil filter.

12   Loosen the oil filter (see illustrations) by turning it counterclockwise with the filter wrench. Once the filter is loose, use your hands to unscrew it the rest of the way. The filter is located under the vehicle on some models, and at the top of the engine on others:

a)   *Underside of engine: Legacy - 2012 and earlier models/Forester - all 2009 and 2010 models, 2011-2013 turbocharged models.*

b)   *Top side of engine: Legacy - 2013 and later models/Forester - 2011 and later non-tubocharged models, 2014 and later turbocharged models.*

Warning: *The exhaust pipes may still be hot, so be careful.*

13   With a clean rag, wipe off the mounting surface on the oil filter adapter. If a residue of old oil is allowed to remain, it will smoke when the engine heats up. Also make sure that the none of the old gasket remains stuck to the mounting surface. It can be removed with a scraper if necessary.

14   Compare the old filter with the new one to make sure they are the same type. Smear some engine oil on the rubber gasket of the new filter and screw it into place (see illustration). Because over-tightening the filter will damage the gasket, do not use a filter wrench to tighten the filter. Tighten it by hand until the

gasket contacts the seating surface. Then seat the filter by giving it an additional 3/4-turn.

15   Remove all tools, rags, etc. from under the vehicle, being careful not to spill the oil in the drain pan, then lower the vehicle.

16   Remove the oil filler cap and add the new oil. Use a funnel to prevent oil from spilling onto the top of the engine. Pour three quarts of fresh oil into the engine. Wait a few minutes to allow the oil to drain into the pan, then check the level on the oil dipstick (see Section 4). If the oil level is at or near the FULL mark, install the filler cap hand tight, start the engine and allow the new oil to circulate.

17   Allow the engine to run for about a minute. While the engine is running, look under the vehicle and check for leaks at the oil pan drain plug and around the oil filter.

18   Wait a few minutes to allow the oil to trickle down into the pan, then recheck the level on the dipstick and, if necessary, add enough oil to bring the level to the H mark.

19   During the first few trips after an oil change, make it a point to check frequently for leaks and proper oil level.

20   The old oil drained from the engine can-

not be reused in its present state and should be discarded. Check with your local refuse disposal company, disposal facility or environmental agency to see if they will accept the oil for recycling. Don't pour used oil into drains or on the ground. After the oil has cooled, it can be drained into a suitable container (capped plastic jugs, topped bottles, milk cartons, etc.) for transport to one of these disposal sites.

7   Battery check, maintenance and charging (every 7500 miles or 6 months)

Warning: *Certain precautions must be followed when checking and servicing the battery. Hydrogen gas, which is highly flammable, is always present in the battery cells, so keep lighted tobacco and all other open flames and sparks away from the battery. The electrolyte inside the battery is actually dilute sulfuric acid, which will cause injury if splashed on your skin or in your eyes. It will also ruin clothes and painted surfaces. When removing the battery cables, always detach the negative cable first and hook it up last!*

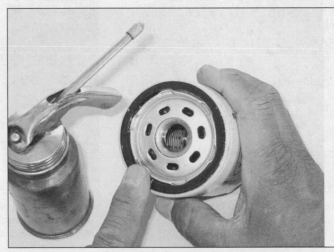

6.14 Lubricate the oil filter gasket with clean engine oil before installing the filter on the engine

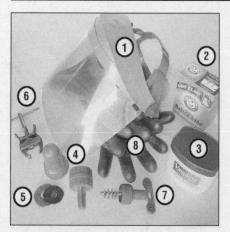

7.1 Tools and materials required for battery maintenance

7.6a Battery terminal corrosion usually appears as light, fluffy powder

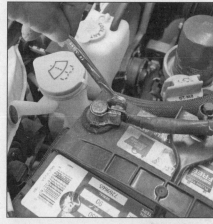

7.6b Removing a cable from the battery post with a wrench - sometimes a pair of special battery pliers are required for this procedure if corrosion has caused deterioration of the nut hex (always remove the ground (-) cable first and hook it up last!)

1   *Face shield/safety goggles* - *When removing corrosion with a brush, the acidic particles can easily fly up into your eyes*

2   *Baking soda* - *A solution of baking soda and water can be used to neutralize corrosion*

3   *Petroleum jelly* - *A layer of this on the battery posts will help prevent corrosion*

4   *Battery post/cable cleaner* - *This wire brush cleaning tool will remove all traces of corrosion from the battery posts and cable clamps*

5   *Treated felt washers* - *Placing one of these on each post, directly under the cable clamps, will help prevent corrosion*

6   *Puller* - *Sometimes the cable clamps are very difficult to pull off the posts, even after the nut/bolt has been completely loosened. This tool pulls the clamp straight up and off the post without damage*

7   *Battery post/cable cleaner* - *Here is another cleaning tool which is a slightly different version of number 4 above, but it does the same thing*

8   *Rubber gloves* - *Another safety item to consider when servicing the battery; remember that's acid inside the battery*

7.7a When cleaning the cable clamps, all corrosion must be removed (the inside of the clamp is tapered to match the taper on the post, so don't remove too much material)

7.7b Regardless of the type of tool used to clean the battery posts, a clean, shiny surface should be the result

Maintenance

1   A routine preventive maintenance program for the battery in your vehicle is the only way to ensure quick and reliable starts. But before performing any battery maintenance, make sure that you have the proper equipment necessary to work safely around the battery (see illustration).

2   There are also several precautions that should be taken whenever battery maintenance is performed. Before servicing the battery, always turn the engine and all accessories off and disconnect the cable from the negative terminal of the battery.

3   The battery produces hydrogen gas, which is both flammable and explosive. Never create a spark, smoke or light a match around the battery. Always charge the battery in a ventilated area.

4   Electrolyte contains poisonous and cor-

rosive sulfuric acid. Do not allow it to get in your eyes, on your skin on your clothes. Never ingest it. Wear protective safety glasses when working near the battery. Keep children away from the battery.

5   Note the external condition of the battery. If the positive terminal and cable clamp on your vehicle's battery is equipped with a rubber protector, make sure that it's not torn or damaged. It should completely cover the terminal. Look for any corroded or loose connections, cracks in the case or cover or loose hold-down clamps. Also check the entire length of each cable for cracks and frayed conductors.

6   If corrosion, which looks like white, fluffy deposits (see illustration) is evident, particularly around the terminals, the battery should be removed for cleaning. Loosen the cable clamp bolts with a wrench, being careful to remove the ground cable first, and slide them

off the terminals (see illustration). Then disconnect the hold-down clamp bolt and nut, remove the clamp and lift the battery from the engine compartment.

7   Clean the cable clamps thoroughly with a battery brush or a terminal cleaner and a solution of warm water and baking soda (see illustration). Wash the terminals and the top of the battery case with the same solution but make sure that the solution doesn't get into the battery. When cleaning the cables, terminals and battery top, wear safety goggles and rubber gloves to prevent any solution from coming in contact with your eyes or hands. Wear old clothes too - even diluted, sulfuric acid splashed onto clothes will burn holes in them. If the terminals have been extensively corroded, clean them up with a terminal cleaner (see illustration). Thoroughly wash all cleaned areas with plain water.

8   Make sure that the battery tray is in good condition and the hold-down clamp bolts are tight. If the battery is removed from the tray, make sure no parts remain in the bottom of the tray when the battery is reinstalled. When reinstalling the hold-down clamp bolts, do not overtighten them.

9   Any metal parts of the vehicle damaged by corrosion should be covered with a zinc-based primer, then painted.

10   Information on removing and installing the battery can be found in Chapter 5. See *Booster battery (jump) starting* at the front of this manual. For more detailed battery checking procedures, refer to the *Haynes Automotive Electrical Manual*.

Charging

Warning: *When batteries are being charged, hydrogen gas, which is very explosive and flammable, is produced. Do not smoke or allow open flames near a battery. Wear eye protection when near the battery during charging. Also, make sure the charger is unplugged before connecting or disconnecting the battery from the charger.*

Note: *The manufacturer recommends the battery be removed from the vehicle for charging because the gas that escapes during this procedure can damage the paint. Fast charging with the battery cables connected can result in damage to the electrical system.*

11   Slow-rate charging is the best way to restore a battery that's discharged to the point where it will not start the engine. It's also a good way to maintain the battery charge in a vehicle that's only driven a few miles between starts. Maintaining the battery charge is particularly important in the winter when the battery must work harder to start the engine and electrical accessories that drain the battery are in greater use.

12   It's best to use a one or two-amp battery charger (sometimes called a "trickle" charger). They are the safest and put the least strain on the battery. They are also the least expensive. For a faster charge, you can use a higher amperage charger, but don't use one rated more than 1/10th the amp/hour rating of the battery. Rapid boost charges that claim to restore the power of the battery in one to two hours are hardest on the battery and can damage batteries not in good condition. This type of charging should only be used in emergency situations.

13   The average time necessary to charge a battery should be listed in the instructions that come with the charger. As a general rule, a trickle charger will charge a battery in 12 to 16 hours.

14   Remove all the cell caps (if equipped) and cover the holes with a clean cloth to prevent spattering electrolyte. Disconnect the negative battery cable and hook the battery charger cable clamps up to the battery posts (positive to positive, negative to negative), then plug in the charger. Make sure it is set at 12-volts if it has a selector switch.

15   If you're using a charger with a rate

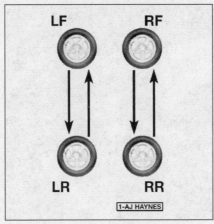

8.2 The recommended four-tire rotation pattern

higher than two amps, check the battery regularly during charging to make sure it doesn't overheat. If you're using a trickle charger, you can safely let the battery charge overnight after you've checked it regularly for the first couple of hours.

16   If the battery has removable cell caps, measure the specific gravity with a hydrometer every hour during the last few hours of the charging cycle. Hydrometers are available inexpensively from auto parts stores - follow the instructions that come with the hydrometer. Consider the battery charged when there's no change in the specific gravity reading for two hours and the electrolyte in the cells is gassing (bubbling) freely. The specific gravity reading from each cell should be very close to the others. If not, the battery probably has a bad cell(s).

17   Some batteries with sealed tops have built-in hydrometers on the top that indicate the state of charge by the color displayed in the hydrometer window. Normally, a bright-colored hydrometer indicates a full charge and a dark hydrometer indicates the battery still needs charging.

18   If the battery has a sealed top and no built-in hydrometer, you can hook up a voltmeter across the battery terminals to check the charge. A fully charged battery should read 12.6 volts or higher after the surface charge has been removed.

19   Further information on the battery can be found in Chapter 5. See *Booster battery (jump) starting* at the front of this manual.

8   Tire rotation (every 7500 miles or 6 months)

1   The tires should be rotated at the specified intervals and whenever uneven wear is noticed. Since the vehicle will be raised and the tires removed anyway, check the brakes (see Section 15) at this time.

2   Radial tires must be rotated in a specific pattern (see illustration).

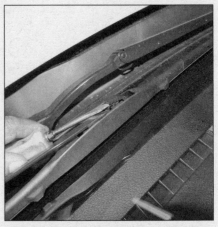

9.5a Use a screwdriver to pry the lock open . . .

3   Refer to the information in *Jacking and towing* at the front of this manual for the proper procedures to follow when raising the vehicle and changing a tire. If the brakes are to be checked, do not apply the parking brake as stated. Make sure the tires are blocked to prevent the vehicle from rolling.

4   Preferably, the entire vehicle should be raised at the same time. This can be done on a hoist or by jacking up each corner and then lowering the vehicle onto jackstands placed under the frame rails. Always use four jackstands and make sure the vehicle is firmly supported.

5   After rotation, check and adjust the tire pressures as necessary and tighten the lug nuts to the torque listed in this Chapter's Specifications.

6   For further information on the wheels and tires, refer to Chapter 10.

9   Windshield wiper blade inspection and replacement (every 7500 miles or 6 months)

1   The windshield wiper and blade assembly should be inspected periodically for damage, loose components and cracked or worn blade elements.

2   Road film can build up on the wiper blades and affect their efficiency, so they should be washed regularly with a mild detergent solution.

3   The action of the wiping mechanism can loosen bolts, nuts and fasteners, so they should be checked and tightened, as necessary, at the same time the wiper blades are checked.

4   If the wiper blade elements are cracked, worn or warped, or no longer clean adequately, they should be replaced with new ones.

5   Lift the arm assembly away from the glass for clearance, lift the lock up and off, then slide the wiper blade assembly out of the hook at the end of the arm (see illustrations).

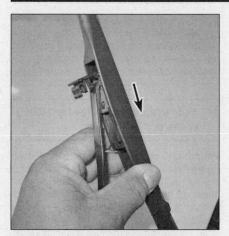

9.5b . . . and slide the wiper blade out of the hook in the end of the arm

6   Attach the new wiper to the arm. Connection can be confirmed by an audible click.

10 Exhaust system check (every 7500 miles or 6 months)

1   With the engine cold (at least three hours after the vehicle has been driven), check the complete exhaust system from the cylinder head to the end of the tailpipe. Be careful around the catalytic converter (if equipped), which may be hot even after three hours. The inspection should be done with the vehicle on a hoist to permit unrestricted access. If a hoist isn't available, raise the vehicle and support it securely on jackstands.
2   Check the exhaust pipes and connections for signs of leakage and/or corrosion indicating a potential failure. Make sure that all brackets and hangers are in good condition and tight (see illustrations).
3   Inspect the underside of the body for holes, corrosion, open seams, etc. which may allow exhaust gasses to enter the passenger

compartment. Seal all body openings with silicone sealant or body putty.
4   Rattles and other noises can often be traced to the exhaust system, especially the hangers, mounts and heat shields. Try to move the pipes, mufflers and catalytic converter. If the components can come in contact with the body or suspension parts, secure the exhaust system with new brackets and hangers.

11 Seat belt check (every 7500 miles or 6 months)

1   Check seat belts, buckles, latch plates and guide loops for obvious damage and signs of wear.
2   Where the seat belt receptacle bolts to the floor of the vehicle, check that the bolts are secure.
3   See if the seat belt reminder light comes on when the key is turned to the Run or Start position.

12 Underhood hose check and replacement (every 7500 miles or 6 months)

General

Caution: *Replacement of air conditioning hoses must be left to a dealer service department or air conditioning shop that has the equipment to depressurize the system safely and recover the refrigerant. Never remove air conditioning components or hoses until the system has been depressurized.*
1   High temperatures in the engine compartment can cause the deterioration of the rubber and plastic hoses used for engine, accessory and emission systems operation. Periodic inspection should be made for cracks, loose clamps, material hardening and leaks. Information specific to the cooling sys-

tem hoses can be found in Section 13.
2   Some, but not all, hoses are secured to their fittings with clamps. Where clamps are used, check to be sure they haven't lost their tension, allowing the hose to leak. If clamps aren't used, make sure the hose has not expanded and/or hardened where it slips over the fitting, allowing it to leak.

Vacuum hoses

3   It's quite common for vacuum hoses, especially those in the emissions system, to be color-coded or identified by colored stripes molded into them. Various systems require hoses with different wall thickness, collapse resistance and temperature resistance. When replacing hoses, be sure the new ones are made of the same material.
4   Often the only effective way to check a hose is to remove it completely from the vehicle. If more than one hose is removed, label the hoses and fittings to ensure correct installation.
5   When checking vacuum hoses, include any plastic T-fittings in the check. Inspect the fittings for cracks and the hose where it fits over the fitting for distortion, which could cause leakage.
6   A small piece of vacuum hose (1/4-inch inside diameter) can be used as a stethoscope to detect vacuum leaks. Hold one end of the hose to your ear and probe around vacuum hoses and fittings, listening for the hissing sound characteristic of a vacuum leak.
Warning: *When probing with the vacuum hose stethoscope, be very careful not to come into contact with moving engine components such as the drivebelt, cooling fan, etc.*

Fuel hose

Warning: *There are certain precautions that must be taken when inspecting or servicing fuel system components. Work in a well-ventilated area and do not allow open flames (cigarettes, appliances, etc.) or bare light bulbs near the work area. Mop up any spills immediately and do not store fuel soaked rags*

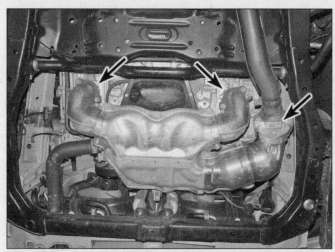

10.2a Check the exhaust pipes and connections for signs of leakage and corrosion

10.2b Check the exhaust system rubber hangers for cracks and damage

Check for a chafed area that could fail prematurely.

Check for a soft area indicating the hose has deteriorated inside.

Overtightening the clamp on a hardened hose will damage the hose and cause a leak.

Check each hose for swelling and oil-soaked ends. Cracks and breaks can be located by squeezing the hose.

13.4 Hoses, like drivebelts, have a habit of failing at the worst possible time - to prevent the inconvenience of a blown radiator or heater hose, inspect them carefully as shown here

where they could ignite. The fuel system is under high pressure, so if any fuel lines are to be disconnected, the pressure in the system must be relieved first (see Chapter 4 for more information).

7   Check all rubber fuel lines for deterioration and chafing. Check especially for cracks in areas where the hose bends and just before fittings, such as where a hose attaches to the fuel filter.

8   High quality fuel line, made specifically for high-pressure fuel injection systems, must be used for fuel line replacement. Never, under any circumstances, use unreinforced vacuum line, clear plastic tubing or water hose for fuel lines.

9   Spring-type clamps are commonly used on fuel lines. These clamps often lose their tension over a period of time, and can be

sprung during removal. Replace all spring-type clamps with screw clamps whenever a hose is replaced.

Metal lines

10   Sections of metal line are routed along the frame, between the fuel tank and the engine. Check carefully to be sure the line has not been bent or crimped and that cracks have not started in the line.

11   If a section of metal fuel line must be replaced, only seamless steel tubing should be used, since copper and aluminum tubing don't have the strength necessary to withstand normal engine vibration.

12   Check the metal brake lines where they enter the master cylinder and brake proportioning unit for cracks in the lines or loose fittings. Any sign of brake fluid leakage calls for an immediate and thorough inspection of the brake system.

13   Cooling system check (every 7500 miles or 6 months)

1   Many major engine failures can be attributed to a faulty cooling system. If the vehicle is equipped with an automatic transaxle, the cooling system also cools the transaxle fluid and thus plays an important role in prolonging transaxle life.

2   The cooling system should be checked with the engine cold. Do this before the vehicle is driven for the day or after it has been shut off for at least three hours.

3   Remove the cooling system pressure cap and thoroughly clean the cap, inside and out, with clean water. Also clean the filler neck on the radiator. All traces of corrosion should be removed. The coolant inside the radiator should be relatively transparent. If it is rust-colored, the system should be drained, flushed and refilled (see Section 21). If the coolant level is not up to the top, add additional antifreeze/coolant mixture (see Section 4).

4   Carefully check the large upper and lower radiator hoses along with the smaller diameter heater hoses that run from the engine to the firewall. Inspect each hose along its entire length, replacing any hose that is cracked, swollen or shows signs of deterioration. Cracks may become more apparent if the hose is squeezed (see illustration). Regardless of condition, it's a good idea to replace hoses with new ones every two years.

5   Make sure all hose connections are tight. A leak in the cooling system will usually show up as white or rust-colored deposits on the areas adjoining the leak. If wire-type clamps are used at the ends of the hoses, it may be a good idea to replace them with more secure screw-type clamps.

6   Use compressed air or a soft brush to remove bugs, leaves, etc. from the front of the radiator or air conditioning condenser. Be careful not to damage the delicate cooling fins or cut yourself on them.

7   Every other inspection, or at the first indication of cooling system problems, have the cap and system pressure tested. If you don't have a pressure tester, most repair shops will do this for a minimal charge.

14   Fuel system check (every 15,000 miles or 12 months)

Warning: *Gasoline is flammable, so take extra precautions when you work on any part of the fuel system. Don't smoke or allow open flames or bare light bulbs near the work area, and don't work in a garage where a gas-type appliance (such as a water heater or clothes dryer) is present. Since fuel is carcinogenic, wear fuel-resistant gloves when there's a possibility of being exposed to fuel, and, if you spill any fuel on your skin, rinse it off immediately with soap and water. Mop up any spills immediately and do not store fuel-soaked rags where they could ignite. When you perform any kind of work on the fuel system, wear safety glasses and have a Class B type fire extinguisher on hand. The fuel system is under constant pressure, so, before any lines are disconnected, the fuel system pressure must be relieved (see Chapter 4).*

1   If you smell fuel while driving or after the vehicle has been sitting in the sun, inspect the fuel system immediately.

2   Remove the fuel filler cap and inspect it for damage and corrosion. The gasket should have an unbroken sealing imprint. If the gasket is damaged or corroded, install a new cap.

3   Inspect the fuel feed line for cracks. Make sure that the connections between the fuel lines and the fuel injection system and between the fuel lines and the in-line fuel filter are tight.

Warning: *Your vehicle is fuel injected, so you must relieve the fuel system pressure before servicing fuel system components. The fuel system pressure relief procedure is outlined in Chapter 4.*

4   Since some components of the fuel system - the fuel tank and part of the fuel feed and return lines, for example - are underneath the vehicle, they can be inspected more easily with the vehicle raised on a hoist. If that's not possible, raise the vehicle and support it on jackstands.

5   With the vehicle raised and safely supported, inspect the fuel tank and filler neck for punctures, cracks and other damage. The connection between the filler neck and the tank is particularly critical. Sometimes a rubber filler neck will leak because of loose clamps or deteriorated rubber. Inspect all fuel tank mounting brackets and straps to be sure that the tank is securely attached to the vehicle.

Warning: *Do not, under any circumstances, try to repair a fuel tank (except rubber components). A welding torch or any open flame can easily cause fuel vapors inside the tank to explode.*

6   Carefully check all rubber hoses and metal lines leading away from the fuel tank. Check for loose connections, deteriorated hoses, crimped lines and other damage. Repair or replace damaged sections as necessary (see Chapter 4).

15   Brake system check (every 15,000 miles or 12 months)

Warning: *The dust created by the brake system is harmful to your health. Never blow it out with compressed air and don't inhale any of it. An approved filtering mask should be worn when working on the brakes. Do not, under any circumstances, use petroleum-based solvents to clean brake parts. Use brake system cleaner only!*
Note: *For detailed photographs of the brake system, refer to Chapter 9.*
1   In addition to the specified intervals, the brakes should be inspected every time the wheels are removed or whenever a defect is suspected.
2   Any of the following symptoms could indicate a potential brake system defect: The vehicle pulls to one side when the brake pedal is depressed; the brakes make squealing or dragging noises when applied; brake pedal travel is excessive; the pedal pulsates; or brake fluid leaks, usually onto the inside of the tire or wheel.
3   Loosen the wheel lug nuts.
4   Raise the vehicle and support it securely on jackstands.
5   Remove the wheels (see *Jacking and towing* at the front of this manual or your owner's manual, if necessary).

Disc brakes
6   There are two pads (an outer and an inner) in each caliper. The pads are visible with the wheels removed.
7   Check the pad thickness by looking at each end of the caliper and through the inspection window in the caliper body (see illustrations). If the lining material is less than the thickness listed in this Chapter's Specifications, replace the pads.
Note: *Keep in mind that the lining material is riveted or bonded to a metal backing plate and the metal portion is not included in this measurement.*
8   If it is difficult to determine the exact thickness of the remaining pad material by the above method, or if you are at all concerned about the condition of the pads, remove the caliper(s), then remove the pads from the calipers for further inspection (see Chapter 9).
9   Once the pads are removed from the calipers, clean them with brake cleaner and re-measure them with a ruler or a vernier caliper (see illustration).
10   Measure the disc thickness with a micrometer to make sure that it still has service life remaining. Refer to the dimension marked on the disc. If any disc is thinner than

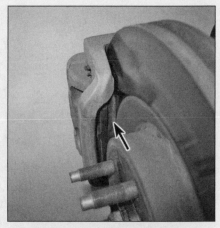

15.7a With the wheel off, check the thickness of the inner pad through the inspection hole (front brake shown, rear disc brake similar)

15.7b The outer pad is more easily checked at the edge of the caliper

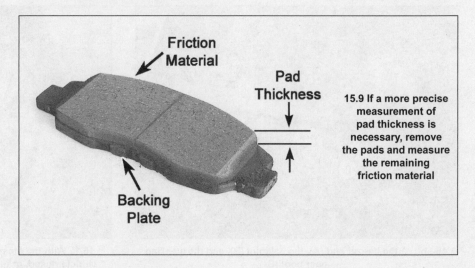

15.9 If a more precise measurement of pad thickness is necessary, remove the pads and measure the remaining friction material

the specified minimum thickness, replace it (see Chapter 9). Even if the disc has service life remaining, check its condition. Look for scoring, gouging and burned spots. If these conditions exist, remove the disc and have it resurfaced (see Chapter 9).
11   Before installing the wheels, check all brake lines and hoses for damage, wear, deformation, cracks, corrosion, leakage, bends and twists, particularly in the vicinity of the rubber hoses at the calipers. Check the clamps for tightness and the connections for leakage. Make sure that all hoses and lines are clear of sharp edges, moving parts and the exhaust system. If any of the above conditions are noted, repair, reroute or replace the lines and/or fittings as necessary (see Chapter 9). Make sure the lug nuts are tightened to the torque listed in this Chapter's Specifications.

Power brake booster check
12   Sit in the driver's seat and perform the following sequence of tests.
13   With the brake fully depressed, start the

engine - the pedal should move down a little when the engine starts.
14   With the engine running, depress the brake pedal several times - the travel distance should not change.
15   Depress the brake, stop the engine and hold the pedal in for about 30 seconds - the pedal should neither sink nor rise.
16   Restart the engine, run it for about a minute and turn it off. Then firmly depress the brake several times - the pedal travel should decrease with each application.
17   If your brakes do not operate as described, the power brake booster has failed. Refer to Chapter 9 for the replacement procedure.

Parking brake
18   One method of checking the parking brake is to park the vehicle on a steep hill with the parking brake set and the transaxle in Neutral (stay in the vehicle for this check!). If the parking brake cannot prevent the vehicle from rolling, it's in need of adjustment (see Chapter 9).

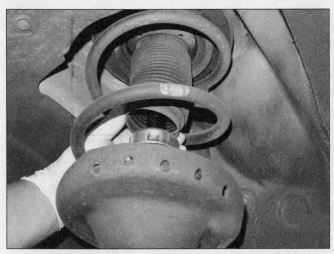

16.6 Check for signs of fluid leakage at this point on struts

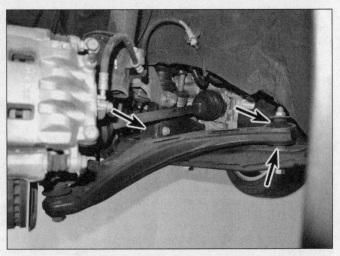

16.9a Examine the mounting points for the control arms . . .

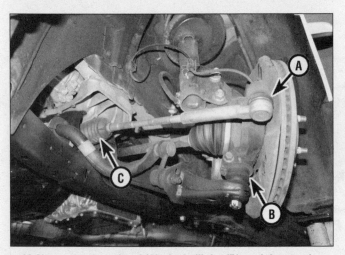

16.9b . . . the tie-rod end (A), the balljoint (B), and the steering gear boot (C)

16.11 With the steering wheel in the locked position and the vehicle raised, grasp the front tire as shown and try to move it back-and-forth - if any play is noted, check the steering gear mounts and tie-rod ends for looseness

16   Suspension, steering and driveaxle boot check (every 15,000 miles or 12 months)

Note: *The steering linkage and suspension components should be checked periodically. Worn or damaged suspension and steering linkage components can result in excessive and abnormal tire wear, poor ride quality and vehicle handling and reduced fuel economy. For detailed illustrations of the steering and suspension components, refer to Chapter 10.*

Shock absorber check

1   Park the vehicle on level ground, turn the engine off and set the parking brake. Check the tire pressures.
2   Push down at one corner of the vehicle, then release it while noting the movement of the body. It should stop moving and come to rest in a level position within one or two bounces.
3   If the vehicle continues to move up-and-down or if it fails to return to its original position, a worn or weak shock absorber is probably the reason.
4   Repeat the above check at each of the three remaining corners of the vehicle.
5   Raise the vehicle and support it securely on jackstands.
6   Check the struts for evidence of fluid leakage (see illustration). A light film of fluid is no cause for concern. Make sure that any fluid noted is from the shocks and not from some other source. If leakage is noted, replace the shocks as a set.
7   Check the shocks to be sure that they are securely mounted and undamaged. Check the upper mounts for damage and wear. If damage or wear is noted, replace the shocks as a set (front or rear).
8   If the shocks must be replaced, refer to Chapter 10 for the procedure.

Steering and suspension check

9   Visually inspect the steering and suspension components (front and rear) for damage and distortion. Look for damaged seals, bushings and leaks of any kind. Examine the bushings where the control arms meet the chassis (see illustrations).
10   Clean the lower end of the steering knuckle. Have an assistant grasp the lower edge of the tire and move the wheel in-and-out while you look for movement at the steering knuckle-to-control arm balljoint. If there is any movement the suspension balljoint(s) must be replaced (see Chapter 10).
11   Grasp each front tire at the front and rear edges, push in at the front, pull out at the rear and feel for play in the steering system components. If any freeplay is noted, check the idler arm and the tie-rod ends for looseness (see illustration).

12   Additional steering and suspension system information and illustrations can be found in Chapter 10.

Driveaxle boot check

13   The driveaxle boots are very important because they prevent dirt, water and foreign material from entering and damaging the constant velocity (CV) joints. Oil and grease can cause the boot material to deteriorate prematurely, so it's a good idea to wash the boots with soap and water. Because it constantly pivots back and forth following the steering action of the front hub, the outer CV boot wears out sooner and should be inspected regularly.

14   Inspect the boots for tears and cracks as well as loose clamps (see illustration). If there is any evidence of cracks or leaking lubricant, they must be replaced (see Chapter 8).

17   Air filter check and replacement (every 15,000 miles or 12 months)

1   The air filter is located inside a housing in the engine compartment. Separate the cover halves and remove the air filter element (see illustration).

2   Inspect the outer surface of the filter element. If it is dirty, replace it. If it is only moderately dusty, it can be reused by blowing it clean from the back to the front surface with compressed air. Because it is a pleated paper type filter, it cannot be washed or oiled. If it cannot be cleaned satisfactorily with compressed air, discard and replace it. While the cover is off, be careful not to drop anything down into the housing.

Caution: *Never drive the vehicle with the air filter removed. Excessive engine wear could result.*

3   Wipe out the inside of the air filter housing.

4   Place the new filter into the housing, making sure it seats properly.

5   The remainder of installation is the reverse of removal.

18   Brake fluid change (every 30,000 miles or 30 months)

Warning: *Brake fluid can harm your eyes and damage painted surfaces, so use extreme caution when handling or pouring it. Do not use brake fluid that has been standing open or is more than one year old. Brake fluid absorbs moisture from the air. Excess moisture can cause a dangerous loss of braking effectiveness.*

1   At the specified intervals, the brake fluid should be drained and replaced. Since the brake fluid may drip or splash when pouring it, place plenty of rags around the master cylinder to protect any surrounding painted surfaces.

2   Before beginning work, purchase the specified brake fluid as listed in this Chapter's Specifications.

3   Clean dirt and debris from the master cylinder reservoir cap. Remove the cap from the master cylinder reservoir.

4   Using a hand suction pump or similar device, withdraw the fluid from the master cylinder reservoir.

5   Add new fluid to the master cylinder until it rises to the base of the filler neck.

6   Bleed the brake system at all four brakes (see Chapter 9) until new and uncontaminated fluid is expelled from the bleeder screw. Maintain the fluid level in the master cylinder as you perform the bleeding process. If you allow the master cylinder to run dry, air will enter the system.

7   Refill the master cylinder with fluid and check the operation of the brakes. The pedal should feel solid when depressed, with no sponginess. Verify the brake fluid level before driving (see Section 4).

Warning: *Do not operate the vehicle if you are in doubt about the effectiveness of the brake system.*

19   Drivebelt check, adjustment and replacement (every 30,000 miles or 30 months)

Check

1   The drivebelts are located at the front of the engine and play an important role in the overall operation of the vehicle and its components. Due to their function and material make-up, the belts are prone to failure after a period of time and should be inspected and adjusted periodically to prevent major engine damage.

2   The number of belts used on a particular vehicle depends on the accessories installed. Drivebelts are used to turn the alternator, power steering pump and air conditioning compressor.

3   With the engine off, open the hood and locate the belts at the front of the engine. Using your fingers (and a flashlight, if nec-

essary), move along the belts checking for cracks and separation of the belt plies. Also check for fraying and glazing, which gives the belt a shiny appearance. Check the ribs on the underside of the belt. They should all be the same depth, with none of the surface uneven (see illustration).

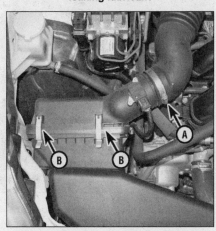

16.14 Inspect the inner and outer driveaxle boots for loose clamps, cracks or signs of leaking lubricant

17.1 Loosen the intake hose clamp (A), then unlatch the clips (B) to get to the air filter element

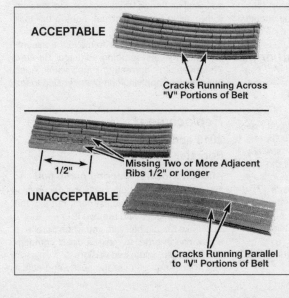

19.3 Here are some of the more common problems associated with drivebelts (check the belts very carefully to prevent an untimely breakdown)

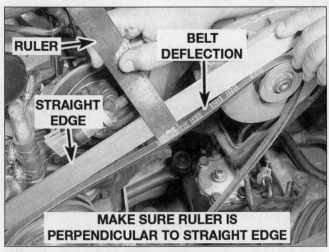

19.4 Measuring drivebelt deflection with a straightedge and ruler

19.7 Typical 2013 and earlier turbocharged Forester model alternator/power steering pump drivebelt adjustment tensioner bolt (A) and lock bolt (B) locations

19.16 Typical "stretchy belt" removal technique

4   On 2013 and earlier turbocharged Forester models, the tension of front (alternator/power steering pump) belt is checked by pushing on the belt at a distance halfway between the pulleys. Push firmly with your thumb and see how much the belt moves (deflects) (see illustration). As rule of thumb, the belt should deflect approximately 1/4-inch.

Adjustment (2013 and earlier turbocharged Forester models, alternator/power steering pump belt)

Note: *On 2013 and earlier turbocharged Forester models, the air conditioning compressor is of a unique design, called a "stretchy belt," which provides tension without the use of a mechanical tensioner; if the belt is loose it must be replaced (see Steps 13 through 17).*

5   The belt adjuster is located mid-way between the alternator and power steering pump pulleys and is equipped with a tensioner bolt and a lock bolt.

6   Remove the drivebelt cover mounting bolt(s) (see illustration 19.18).

7   To adjust tension on the belts, loosen the lock bolt and turn the tensioner bolt to loosen or tighten the belt tension (see illustration).

8   Hold the assembly in position and check the belt tension. If it is correct, tighten the lock bolt until just snug, then recheck the tension. If the tension is still correct, tighten the lock bolt.

9   Do not use a prybar to move the assembly while the belt is being adjusted. Be sure the drivebelt is correctly aligned within each pulley before applying complete tension to the drivebelt.

Replacement

2013 and earlier turbocharged Forester models

Alternator/power steering pump belt

10   To replace the belt, follow the above procedures for drivebelt adjustment, but slip the belt off the pulleys and remove it.

11   Take the old belt with you when purchase a new one in order to make a direct comparison for length, width and design.

12   Place the belt over the pulley and adjust

the belt as described in Steps 5 through 9.

Air conditioning compressor belt

13   The air conditioning drivebelt is of a unique design, called a "stretchy belt," which provides tension without the use of a mechanical tensioner.

14   Disconnect the cable from the negative terminal of the battery (see Chapter 5).

15   Remove the alternator/power steering pump drivebelt as described previously (see Steps 5 through 9).

16   Insert a long prybar behind the belt, using a bracket or solid casting as a prying point. Rotate the engine clockwise with a socket and breaker bar on the crankshaft pulley bolt while you lever the belt towards the front of the vehicle, forcing the belt up and off the air conditioning compressor pulley as it turns (see illustration).

Warning: *While performing this step, rotate the engine by hand only (do not use the starter).*

Caution: *Then belt can be easily damaged when prying it off, so work carefully.*

Note: *If the belt is not going to be re-used, you can simply cut it off.*

17   Route the new belt under the crankshaft pulley, then over the air conditioning compressor pulley and rotate the engine again; the belt should pop over the pulley on the compressor. Reinstall and adjust the alternator/power steering pump belt.

Caution: *Make sure the belt is centered properly on both pulleys.*

All models except 2013 and earlier turbocharged Forester models

18   Remove the drivebelt cover mounting bolt and detach the cover (see illustration).

19   Rotate the belt tensioner clockwise using a wrench on the pulley bolt to release tension on the drivebelt (see illustration).

Caution: *Do not loosen the drivebelt tensioner pulley bolt or it will be necessary to replace the entire tensioner with a new one.*

19.18 Remove the drivebelt cover bolt - 2.5L DOHC model shown, other models similar

19.19 Release the tension using a wrench, hold, then remove the belt and slowly release the tensioner

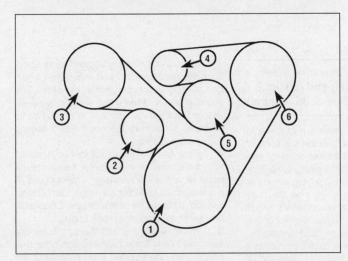

19.21a Drivebelt routing diagram - 2012 and earlier Legacy models

1	Crankshaft pulley	4	Alternator
2	Automatic tensioner pulley	5	Idler pulley
3	Power steering pump	6	Air conditioning compressor

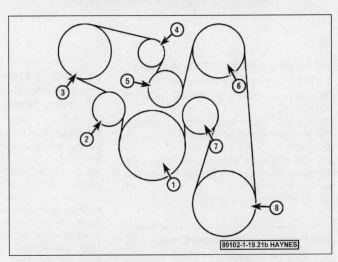

19.21b Drivebelt routing diagram - 2013, 2014 Legacy models and 2013 and earlier Forester non-turbocharged models

1	Crankshaft pulley	5	Idler pulley
2	Automatic tensioner pulley	6	Air conditioning compressor
3	Power steering pump	7	Idler pulley
4	Alternator	8	Water pump

20   Remove the drivebelt from the tensioner and all accessories.

21   Install the new drivebelt, making sure that it's properly routed (see illustrations).

Tensioner replacement

2013 and earlier turbocharged Forester models - alternator/power steering pump belt

22   Remove the belt cover (see illustration 19.18).

23   Remove the drivebelt (see Step 10).

24   Remove the tensioner bracket mounting bolts, remove the tensioner bolt, and unthread the tensioner from the adjustment rod.

25   Installation is the reverse of removal.

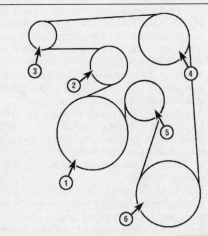

19.21c Drivebelt routing diagram - 2015 and later Legacy models and 2014 and later Forester models

1   Crankshaft pulley
2   Automatic tensioner pulley
3   Alternator
4   Air conditioning compressor
5   Idler pulley
6   Water pump pulley

19.28 On 2013 and later models, insert the Allen socket into the center of the tensioner and remove the bolt

21.3 Use a screwdriver to loosen the radiator drain plug

All models except 2013 and earlier turbocharged Forester models

26   Remove the drivebelt (see Steps 18 through 20).

27   On 2012 and earlier models, remove the tensioner mounting bolts and remove the tensioner.

28   On 2013 and later models remove the tensioner Allen head bolt (see illustration) and remove the tensioner.

29   Installation is the reverse of removal.

20   Fuel filter replacement (every 30,000 miles or 30 months)

Warning: *Gasoline is extremely flammable, so take extra precautions when you work on any part of the fuel system. Don't smoke or allow open flames or bare light bulbs near the work area, and don't work in a garage where a gas-type appliance (such as a water heater or clothes dryer) is present. Since gasoline is carcinogenic, wear fuel-resistant gloves when there's a possibility of being exposed to fuel, and, if you spill any fuel on your skin, rinse it off immediately with soap and water. Mop up any spills immediately and do not store fuel-soaked rags where they could ignite. The fuel system is under constant pressure, so, if any fuel lines are to be disconnected, the fuel pressure in the system must be relieved first (see Chapter 4). When you perform any kind of work on the fuel system, wear safety glasses and have a Class B type fire extinguisher on hand.*

Warning: *Relieve the fuel system pressure before removing the filter (see Chapter 4)!*

On these models there is no external fuel filter in the engine compartment. Instead, these models rely on the filter that's an integral part of the fuel pump/fuel level sending unit. See Chapter 4 for the replacement procedure.

21   Cooling system servicing (draining, flushing and refilling) (every 30,000 miles or 30 months)

Warning: *Do not allow antifreeze to come in contact with your skin or painted surfaces of the vehicle. Rinse off spills immediately with plenty of water. Antifreeze is highly toxic if ingested. Never leave antifreeze lying around in an open container or in puddles on the floor; children and pets are attracted by it's sweet smell and may drink it. Check with local authorities about disposing of used antifreeze. Many communities have collection centers which will see that antifreeze is disposed of safely.*

1   Periodically, the cooling system should be drained, flushed and refilled to replenish the antifreeze mixture and prevent formation of rust and corrosion, which can impair the performance of the cooling system and cause engine damage. When the cooling system is serviced, all hoses and the radiator cap should be checked and replaced if necessary.

2   Apply the parking brake and block the wheels. Raise the front of the vehicle and support it securely on jackstands, then remove the under-vehicle splash shield (see Section 6, illustration 6.6).

Warning: *If the vehicle has just been driven, wait several hours to allow the engine to cool down before beginning this procedure.*

3   Move a large container under the radiator drain to catch the coolant. The radiator drain plug is located at the bottom center of the radiator (see illustration).

4   Remove the radiator cap and allow the coolant to drain.

5   While the coolant is draining, check the condition of the radiator hoses, heater hoses and clamps (see Section 13).

6   Replace any damaged clamps or hoses.

7   Once the system is completely drained, flush the radiator with fresh water from a garden hose until it runs clear at the drain. The flushing action of the water will remove sediments from the radiator but will not remove rust and scale from the engine and cooling tube surfaces.

8   Rust and scale deposits can be removed with a chemical cleaner. Follow the procedure outlined in the manufacturer's instructions. If the radiator is severely corroded, damaged or leaking, it should be removed (see Chapter 3) and taken to a radiator repair shop.

9   Remove the cap and the overflow hose from the coolant reservoir and flush the reservoir with clean water, then reconnect the hose.

10   Close and tighten the radiator drain fitting.

11   Place the heater temperature control in the maximum heat position.

12   Slowly add new coolant (a 50/50 mixture of water and the antifreeze listed in this Chapter's Specifications) to the radiator (non-turbo models) or coolant filler tank (turbo models) until it's full. Add coolant to the reservoir up to the lower mark.

13   Install the radiator cap and, on turbo models the coolant filler tank cap, and run the engine in a well-ventilated area until the thermostat opens (coolant will begin flowing through the radiator and the upper radiator hose will become hot).

14   Turn the engine off and let it cool. Add more coolant mixture to bring the level back up to the lip on the radiator filler neck or coolant filler tank neck.

15   Squeeze the upper radiator hose to expel air, then add more coolant mixture if necessary. Reinstall the radiator cap.

16   Start the engine, allow it to reach normal operating temperature and check for leaks. Check the coolant level (see Section 4).

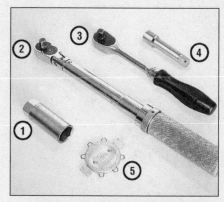

22.1 Tools required for changing spark plugs

1 **Spark plug socket** - *This will have special padding inside to protect the spark plug's porcelain insulator*
2 **Torque wrench** - *Although not mandatory, using this tool is the best way to ensure the plugs are tightened properly*
3 **Ratchet** - *Standard hand tool to fit the spark plug socket*
4 **Extension** - *Depending on model and accessories, you may need special extensions and universal joints to reach one or more of the plugs*
5 **Spark plug gap gauge** - *This gauge for checking the gap comes in a variety of styles. Make sure the gap for your engine is included*

22 Spark plug replacement (every 30,000 miles or 30 months)

1   In most cases, the tools necessary for spark plug replacement include a spark plug socket which fits onto a ratchet (spark plug sockets are padded inside to prevent damage to the porcelain insulators on the new plugs), various extensions and a gap gauge to check and adjust the gaps on the new plugs (see illustration). A torque wrench should be used to tighten the new plugs.
2   The best approach when replacing the spark plugs is to purchase the new ones in advance, adjust them to the proper gap and replace the plugs one at a time. When buying the new spark plugs, obtain the correct plug type for your particular engine. This information can be found in this Chapter's Specifications or in your owner's manual.
3   Allow the engine to cool completely before attempting to remove any of the plugs. These engines are equipped with aluminum cylinder heads, which can be damaged if the spark plugs are removed when the engine is hot. While you are waiting for the engine to cool, check the new plugs for defects and adjust the gaps.
4   The gap is checked by inserting the prop-

22.4a Spark plug manufacturers recommend using a wire-type gauge when checking the gap - if the wire does not slide between the electrodes with a slight drag, adjustment is required

22.8a Disconnect the electrical connector from the coil (1) then remove the mounting bolt (2) . . .

er-thickness gauge between the electrodes at the tip of the plug (see illustration). The gap between the electrodes should be the same as the one specified on the Emissions Control Information label or in this Chapter's Specifications. The gauge should just slide between the electrodes with a slight amount of drag. If the gap is incorrect, use the adjuster on the gauge body to bend the curved side electrode slightly until the proper gap is obtained (see illustration). If the side electrode is not exactly over the center electrode, bend it with the adjuster until it is. Check for cracks in the porcelain insulator (if any are found, the plug should not be used).
Caution: *When checking the gap on platinum or iridium-tipped plugs, don't force the gauge between the electrodes; doing so could scrape the thin coating from the electrodes and greatly reduce the spark plug's life.*
5   When working on the left-side spark plugs, remove the battery (see Chapter 5)

22.4b To change the gap, bend the side electrode only, as indicated by the arrows, and be very careful not to crack or chip the porcelain insulator surrounding the center electrode

22.8b . . . and remove the ignition coil

and secondary air pump (see Chapter 6), if equipped.
6   If equipped, remove the engine cover, then remove the air intake duct and, on models where it would interfere with access to the spark plugs, the resonator and/or the air filter housing (see Chapter 4).
7   On 2009 SOHC Legacy/2009 and 2010 SOHC Forester models, disconnect the spark plug wire from the spark plug, using a twisting motion.
Caution: *Pull only on the boot - not the wire.*
Note: *Replace one spark plug at a time to avoid mixing up the spark plug wires.*
8   On models equipped with individual ignition coils, remove the coils to access the spark plugs (see illustrations).
9   If compressed air is available, use it to blow any dirt or foreign material away from the spark plug hole. The idea here is to eliminate the possibility of debris falling into the cylinder as the spark plug is removed.

22.10 Use a socket and extension to unscrew the spark plugs

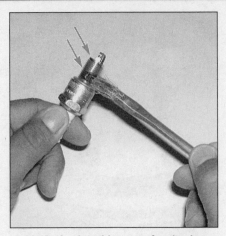

22.12a Apply a thin coat of anti-seize compound to the spark plug threads

22.12b A length of snug-fitting rubber hose will save time and prevent damaged threads when installing the spark plugs

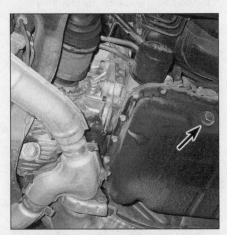

24.7 Location of the automatic transmission fluid drain plug

24.13 Automatic transaxle fluid drain plug

10   Place the spark plug socket over the plug and remove it from the engine by turning it in a counterclockwise direction (see illustration).
11   Compare the spark plug to those shown in the chart (see illustration) to get an indication of the general running condition of the engine.
12   Apply a small amount of anti-seize compound to the spark plug threads (see illustration). It is a good idea to slip a short length of rubber hose over the end of the plug to use as a tool to start threading it into place (see illustration). The hose will grip the plug well enough to turn it, but will start to slip if the plug begins to cross-thread in the hole - this will prevent damaged threads and the accompanying repair costs. Install one of the new plugs into the hole until you can no longer turn it with your fingers, then tighten it to the torque listed in this Chapter's Specifications.
13   Before reconnecting the spark plug wire or pushing the ignition coil onto the end of the plug, inspect the spark plug wire (see Section 29) or the ignition coil (see Section 23).
14   Repeat the procedure for the remaining spark plugs.

23   Ignition coil check (every 30,000 miles or 30 months)

1   Remove the ignition coil(s) (see Chapter 5). Clean the coil(s) with a dampened cloth and dry them thoroughly.
2   Inspect each coil, for cracks, damage and carbon tracking. If damage exists, replace the coil.

24   Automatic transaxle fluid change (every 30,000 miles or 30 months)

1   At the specified time intervals, the automatic transaxle fluid should be drained and replaced.
2   Before beginning work, purchase the transmission fluid listed in this Chapter's Specifications.
3   Other tools necessary for this job include jackstands to support the vehicle in a raised position, a wrench, a drain pan capable of holding at least 10 quarts, newspapers and clean rags.

4   The fluid should be drained after the vehicle has been driven and brought to operating temperature. Hot fluid is more effective than cold fluid at removing built up sediment. **Warning:** *Fluid temperature can exceed 350-degrees F in a hot transaxle. Wear protective gloves.*
5   Raise the vehicle and support it securely on jackstands. On CVT models, the vehicle must be raised to a level position.
6   Move the necessary equipment under the vehicle, being careful not to touch any of the hot exhaust components.

4- and 5-speed automatic transmission models

7   Place the drain pan under the drain plug in the transaxle housing or fluid pan and remove the drain plug (see illustration). Be sure the drain pan is in position, as fluid will come out with some force. Once the fluid is drained, reinstall the drain plug to the torque listed in this Chapter's Specifications.
8   Lower the vehicle.
9   With the engine off, add new fluid to the transaxle through the dipstick tube. Use a funnel to prevent spills. It is best to add a little fluid at a time, continually checking the level with the dipstick (see Section 4). Allow the fluid time to drain into the pan.
10   Once the fluid is at the correct level, start the engine and shift the selector into all positions from Park through Low then shift into Park and apply the parking brake.
11   With the engine idling, check the fluid level. Add fluid up to the lower level on the dipstick.

CVT transmission models

Note: *Failure to use the correct fluid will damage the transaxle and void the warranty.*
12   Move the necessary equipment under the vehicle, being careful not to touch any of the hot exhaust components.
13   Place the drain pan under the drain plug and remove the drain plug (see illustration).

24.14 CVT transmission fill plug location

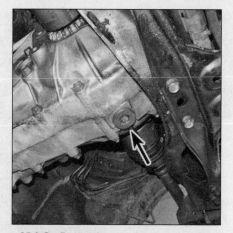

25.3 On 5-speed manual transaxles, the drain plug is located on the bottom of the transaxle case

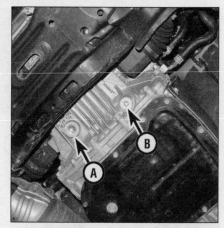

26.3 Front differential drain plug (A) and check (overflow) plug (B) - automatic transaxle models

Be sure the drain pan is in position, as fluid will come out with some force. Once the fluid is drained, reinstall the drain plug and tighten it to the torque listed in this Chapter's Specifications.

14 Remove the fill plug from the side of the transaxle (see illustration) and add fluid using a hand pump or syringe until the fluid level is even with the fill plug bottom threads, then temporarily install the plug hand tight.

15 Start the vehicle. With the engine idling, shift through the gears then place the transmission into Park.

16 With the engine running, remove the fill plug; the fluid level should be at the bottom of the plug hole. If it isn't, add fluid until the level is at the bottom of the hole.

17 Install the fill plug and tighten it to the torque listed in this Chapter's Specifications.

18 Lower the vehicle.

All models

19 The old fluid drained from the transaxle cannot be reused in its present state and should be discarded. Check with your local refuse disposal company, disposal facility or environmental agency to see if they will accept the fluid for recycling. Don't pour used fluid into drains or on the ground. After the fluid has cooled, it can be drained into a suitable container (capped plastic jugs, topped bottles, milk cartons, etc.) for transport to one of these disposal sites.

25 Manual transaxle lubricant change (every 30,000 miles or 30 months)

1 Drive the vehicle to warm the lubricant, then raise the vehicle and support it securely on jackstands.

2 Move a drain pan, rags, newspapers and wrenches under the transaxle.

3 Remove the transaxle drain plug(s) at

the bottom of the case and allow the lubricant to drain into the pan (see illustration). On 6-speed models there are two drain plugs - one at the bottom of the transaxle and one at the bottom of the clutch housing.

Warning: *Fluid will be extremely hot. Wear protective gloves.*

4 After the lubricant has drained completely, reinstall the plug(s) and tighten to the torque listed in this Chapter's Specifications.

5 Fill the transaxle with the recommended lubricant (see Section 4).

6 Lower the vehicle.

7 Drive the vehicle for a short distance, then check the drain plug(s) for leakage.

8 The old lubricant drained from the transaxle cannot be reused in its present state and should be discarded. Check with your local refuse disposal company, disposal facility or environmental agency to see if they will accept the oil for recycling. Don't pour used oil into drains or on the ground. After the oil has cooled, it can be drained into a suitable container (capped plastic jugs, topped bottles, milk cartons, etc.) for transport to one of these disposal sites.

26 Differential lubricant change (every 30,000 miles or 30 months)

Note: *The following procedure is used for the rear differential as well as the front differential on vehicles equipped with automatic transaxles.*

1 Drive the vehicle for several miles to warm up the differential oil, then raise the vehicle and support it securely on jackstands.

2 Move a drain pan, rags, newspapers and the proper tools under the vehicle.

3 With the drain pan under the differential, loosen the drain plug on the rear differential (see Section 4, illustration 4.49). On automatic transaxle models, also drain the front differential (see illustration).

4 Once the plug is loosened, carefully

unscrew it with your fingers until you can remove it from the case.

Warning: *Fluid will be extremely hot. Wear protective gloves.*

5 Allow all of the oil to drain into the pan, then reinstall the drain plug and tighten it securely.

6 Feel with your hands along the bottom of the drain pan for any metal bits that may have come out with the oil. If there are any, it's a sign of excessive wear.

7 Rear differential: Remove the rear differential check/fill plug (see Section 4). Using a hand pump, syringe or funnel, fill the differential with the correct amount and grade of oil (see this Chapter's Specifications) until the level is just at the bottom of the plug hole.

8 Reinstall the plug and tighten it to the torque listed in this Chapter's Specifications.

9 Front differential: Remove the fill plug from the side of the transaxle, using a hand pump, fill the differential with the correct amount and grade of lubricant (see this Chapter's Specifications) until the lubricant flows out of the check "overflow" plug hole (see illustration 26.3).

10 Allow the lubricant to flow out of the check "overflow" plug hole until it stops flowing then install the plug and tighten the fill plug and check hole plug to the torque listed in this Chapter's Specifications.

11 Lower the vehicle. Check for leaks at the fill and drain plugs after the first few miles of driving.

27 Wheel bearing check (every 60,000 miles or 48 months)

1 These models are equipped with sealed bearings in the front and rear hub assemblies. In most cases the wheel bearings will not need servicing. However, the bearings should be checked whenever the vehicle is raised for any reason. With the vehicle securely supported on jackstands, spin each wheel and

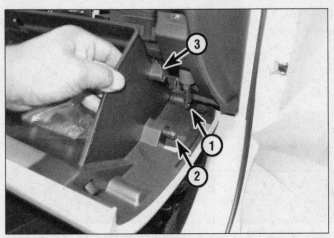

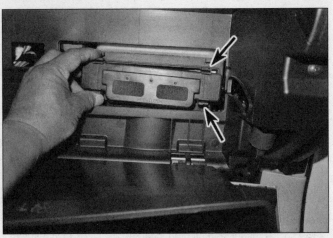

28.2 Disconnect the glove box damper (1) from the glove box door mount (2) and squeeze the glove box inwards until the stops (3) can clear the opening

28.3 Push the tabs together on each side of the cover and remove the cover

28.4 Install the filter with the arrow pointing up

check for noise, rolling resistance and free-play.

2   Grasp the top of each tire with one hand and the bottom with the other. Move the wheel in and out on the spindle. If there's any notice-able movement, remove the front wheel and check the freeplay using a dial indicator. Refer to the wheel bearing freeplay listed in this Chapter's Specifications.

3   Replace the bearing assembly if excess freeplay and bearing noise exists (see Chap-ter 10).

28   Cabin air filter - replacement (every 7500 miles or 6 months)

1   The manufacturer recommends replac-ing the cabin air filter at the specified intervals to maintain the performance of the HVAC sys-tem.

2   Open the glove box door, disconnect the glove box damper from the glove box door. Squeeze the glove box inwards to disengage the stops and lower the door (see illustration).

3   Depress the tabs on the cabin air filter cover and remove the cover (see illustration).
4   Remove the cabin air filter. If equipped, note that the arrow on the face of the cabin air filter faces up (see illustration).
5   Install a new cabin air filter with the arrow pointing UP.
6   The remainder of installation is the reverse of removal.

29   Spark plug wire check and replacement (2009 SOHC Legacy/2009 and 2010 SOHC Forester models) (every 30,000 miles or 30 months)

1   The spark plug wires should be checked at the recommended intervals or whenever new spark plugs are installed.
2   Begin this procedure by making a visual check of the spark plug wires while the engine is running. In a darkened garage (make sure there is adequate ventilation) or at night while using a flashlight, start the engine and observe each plug wire. Be careful not to come into contact with any moving engine parts. If possible, use an insulated or non-conductive object to wiggle each wire. If there is a break in the wire, you will see arcing or a small blue spark coming from the damaged area. Secondary ignition voltage increases with engine speed and sometimes a damaged wire will not produce an arc at idle speed. Have an assistant press the accelerator pedal to raise the engine speed to approximately 2000 rpm. Check the spark plug wires for arc-ing as stated previously. If arcing is noticed, replace all spark plug wires.
3   Perform the following checks with the engine OFF. The wires should be inspected one at a time to prevent mixing up the order that is essential for proper engine operation.
4   With the engine cool, disconnect the spark plug wire from the ignition coil pack. Pull only on the boot at the end of the wire; don't

pull on the wire itself. Special pliers area valu-able to help grip the cable boot securely. Use a twisting motion to free the boot/wire from the coil. Disconnect the same spark plug wire from the spark plug, using the same twisting method while pulling on the boot. Disconnect the spark plug wire from any retaining clips as necessary and remove it from the engine.
5   Check inside the boot for corrosion, which will look like a white, crusty powder (don't mistake the white dielectric grease used on some plug wire boots for corrosion protection).
6   Push the wire and boot back onto the end of the spark plug. It should be a tight fit on the plug end. If not, remove the wire and use a pair of pliers to carefully crimp the metal connector inside the wire boot until the fit is snug.
7   Push the wire and boot back into the end of the ignition coil terminal. It should be a tight fit in the terminal. If not, remove the wire and use a pair of pliers to carefully crimp the metal connector inside the wire boot until the fit is snug.
8   Now, using a cloth, clean each wire along its entire length. Remove all built-up dirt and grease. As this is done, inspect for burned areas, cracks and any other form of damage. Bend the wires in several places to ensure that the conductive material inside hasn't hardened. Repeat the procedure for the remaining wires.
9   If new spark plug wires are required, purchase a complete set for your particu-lar engine. The terminals and rubber boots should already be installed on the wires. Replace the wires one at a time to avoid mix-ing up the firing order and make sure the ter-minals are securely seated on the coil pack and the spark plugs.
10   Attach the plug wire to the new spark plug and to the ignition coil pack using a twist-ing motion on the boot until it is firmly seated. Attach the spark plug wire to any retaining clips to keep the wires in their proper location on the valve cover.

Chapter 2 Part A
Engines

Contents

Specifications

General

Firing order 1-3-2-4

Cylinder head gasket surface warpage limit

    2.5L (SOHC) engines and 2.5L (DOHC) turbocharged engines .... 0.0014 inch   0.035 mm

    2.5L (DOHC) non-turbocharged engines and

        2.0L turbocharged engines .... 0.00079 inch   0.020 mm

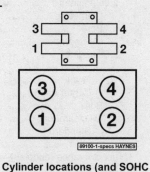

Cylinder locations (and SOHC coil terminal locations)

Camshaft

Non-turbocharged engines

Lobe height

  2.5L (SOHC) engine

    Intake .... 1.5778 to 1.5817 inches 40.075 to 40.175 mm

    Exhaust .... 1.5468 to 1.5507 inches 39.289 to 39.389 mm

  2.5L (DOHC) engine

    Legacy models

      2013 through 2015 models

        Intake .... 1.605 to 1.609 inches   40.77 to 40.87 mm

        Exhaust .... 1.581 to 1.585 inches   40.15 to 40.25 mm

      2016 models

        Intake .... 1.588 to 1.592 inches   40.34 to 40.44 mm

        Exhaust .... 1.561 to 1.565 inches   39.66 to 39.76 mm

    Forester models

      2014 and earlier models

        Intake camshaft .... 1.610 to 1.614 inches   40.89 to 40.99 mm

        Exhaust camshaft .... 1.581 to 1.585 inches   40.15 to 40.25 mm

      2015 and later models

        Intake camshaft .... 1.610 to 1.614 inches   40.89 to 40.99 mm

        Exhaust camshaft .... 1.581 to 1.585 inches   40.15 to 40.25 mm

Camshaft (continued)

Non-turbocharged engines (continued)

Journal		
2.5L (SOHC) engine		
Diameter	1.2570 to 1.2577 inches	31.928 to 31.946 mm
Bore	1.2598 to 1.2605 inches	31.999 to 32.017 mm
Oil clearance		
Standard	0.0022 to 0.0035 inch	0.056 to 0.089 mm
Limit	0.0039 inch	0.099 mm
2.5L (DOHC) engine		
Diameter	1.0215 to 1.0222 inch	25.946 to 25.963 mm
Standard oil clearance	0.0015 to 0.0028 inch	0.037 to 0.072 mm
Thrust clearance (endplay)		
2.5L (SOHC) engine		
Standard	0.0012 to 0.0035 inch	0.030 to 0.090 mm
Limit	0.0039 inch	0.099 mm
2.5L (DOHC) engine		
Standard	0.0027 to 0.0047 inch	0.068 to 0.116 mm

Turbocharged engines

Lobe height		
2.0L engines		
2014 models		
Intake		
Valve lobe	1.605 to 1.609 inches	40.77 to 40.87 mm
Fuel pump lobe	1.652 to 1.655 inches	41.97 to 42.03 mm
Exhaust	1.603 to 1.607 inches	40.72 to 40.82 mm
2015 and later models		
Intake		
Valve lobe	1.588 to 1.592 inches	40.34 to 40.44 mm
Fuel pump lobe	1.652 to 1.656 inches	41.95 to 42.05 mm
Exhaust	1.583 to 1.587 inches	40.20 to 40.30 mm
2.5L engines		
Intake	1.833 to 1.837 inches	46.56 to 46.66 mm
Exhaust	1.841 to 1.844 inches	46.76 to 46.84 mm
Journal		
2.0L engines		
Diameter	1.0215 to 1.0222 inches	25.946 to 25.963 mm
Bore	Not available	
Oil clearance	0.0015 to 0.0028 inch	0.037 to 0.072 mm
2.5L engines		
Diameter		
Front	1.4939 to 1.4946 inches	37.945 to 37.963 mm
Center and rear	1.1790 to 1.1796 inches	29.947 to 29.962 mm
Bore	Not available	
Oil clearance		
Standard	0.0015 to 0.0028 inch	0.038 to 0.071 mm
Limit	0.0039 inch	0.099 mm
Thrust clearance (endplay)		
Standard	0.0027 to 0.0047 inch	0.068 to 0.116 mm

Valve lifters (2.5L (DOHC) turbocharged engines)

Outer diameter	1.3763 to 1.3770 inch	34.958 to 34.976 mm
Lifter bore diameter	1.3777 to 1.3786 inch	34.994 to 35.016 mm
Lifter-to-bore clearance		
Standard	0.0007 to 0.0022 inch	0.018 to 0.056 mm
Service limit	0.0039 inch	0.099 mm

Valve clearances

2.5L (SOHC) non-turbocharged engines		
Intake	0.006 to 0.010 inch	0.16 to 0.24 mm
Exhaust	0.008 to 0.012 inch	0.21 to 0.29 mm
2.5L (DOHC) turbocharged engines		
Intake	0.006 to 0.010 inch	0.16 to 0.24 mm
Exhaust	0.012 to 0.017 inch	0.30 to 0.35 mm
2.5L (DOHC) non-turbocharged engines and 2.0L turbochrged engines		
Intake	0.0039 to 0.0059 inch	0.10 to 0.16 mm
Exhaust	0.0079 to 0.0095 inch	0.20 to 0.24 mm

Oil pump

Inner and outer rotor tip clearance		
Standard	0.0016 to 0.0055 inch	0.04 to 0.14 mm
Limit	0.0071 inch	0.18 mm
Outer rotor-to-pump housing clearance		
Standard	0.0039 to 0.0069 inch	0.099 to 0.175 mm
Limit	0.0079 inch	0.20 mm
Rotor-to-cover clearance (endplay)		
Standard	0.0008 to 0.0028 inch	0.02 to 0.07 mm
Limit	0.0047 inch	0.12 mm

Timing belt

Guide clearance	0.019 to 0.059 inch	0.5 to 1.5 mm
Tensioner rod protrusion (tip-to-body)	0.205 to 0.244 inch	5.2 to 6.2 mm

Torque specifications

Ft-lbs (unless otherwise indicated) **Nm**

Note: *One foot-pound (ft-lb) of torque is equivalent to 12 inch-pounds (in-lbs) of torque. Torque values below approximately 15 ft-lbs are expressed in inch-pounds, because most foot-pound torque wrenches are not accurate at these smaller values.*

	Ft-lbs	Nm
Crankshaft pulley bolt		
2.5L (DOHC) non-turbocharged and 2.0L turbocharged engines (illustration 12.42)		
Step 1	156 in-lbs	18
Step 2, bolts 1, 2, 3	Loosen bolts 180 degrees in sequence	
Step 3, bolts 1, 2, 3	156 in-lbs	18
Step 4, bolts 7, 8, 9	Loosen bolts 180 degrees in sequence	
Step 5, bolts 7, 8, 9	156-lbs	18
Step 6, 4, 8	Loosen bolts 180 degrees in sequence	
Step 7	156 in-lbs	18
2.5L (SOHC) engines		
Step 1	44.3	60
Step 2	Tighten an additional 55 to 65 degrees	
Camshaft cap bolts (2.5L (DOHC) turbocharged engines)		
Bolts 1 through 4	15	20
Bolts 5 through 8	86 in-lbs	9.5
Bolts 9 through 12	15	20
Camshaft end cap assembly mounting bolts		
Step 1, Bolts 1 through 4	Tighten lightly	
Step 2, Rocker arm bolts	Refer to rocker arm bolt torque specifications	
Step 3, Bolts 5 through 10	156 in-lbs	18
Step 4, Bolts 11 through 14, then 1 through 4	86 in-lbs	9.5
Step 5, Bolts 15 and 16	86 in-lbs	9.5
Cylinder head bolts		
2.5L (SOHC) non-turbocharged engines and 2.5L (DOHC) turbocharged engines (see illustration 13.18a)		
Step 1	30	40
Step 2	70	90
Step 3	Loosen all bolts 180 degrees in the reverse order of the tightening sequence	
Step 4	Loosen all bolts 180 degrees in the reverse order of the tightening sequence	
Step 5	96 in-lbs	10
Step 6	22	30
Step 7		
2.5L (SOHC) engines	44	60
2.5L (DOHC) turbocharged engines	51	70
Step 8	Tighten all bolts, in sequence, an additional 90 degrees	
Step 9	Tighten all bolts, in sequence, an additional 45 degrees	
Step 10, Bolts 1 and 2	Tighten and additional 45 degrees	
2.5L (DOHC) non-turbocharged engines and all 2.0L turbocharged engines		
Step 1, see illustration 13.18b		
2.0L engines	15	20
2.5L (DOHC) non-turbocharged engines	21.4	29
Step 2, see illustration 13.18b	73.8	100
Step 3, see illustration 13.18c	Loosen all bolts 360 degrees in the reverse order of the tightening sequence	
Step 4, see illustration 13.18b	15	20
Step 5, see illustration 13.18b	31	42
Step 6, see illustration 13.18b		
2.0L engines	Tighten all bolts, in numerical sequence, an additional 100 degrees	
2.5L (DOHC) non-turbocharged engines	Tighten all bolts, in numerical sequence, an additional 80 degrees	

Torque specifications (continued)   Ft-lbs (unless otherwise indicated)   Nm

Note: *One foot-pound (ft-lb) of torque is equivalent to 12 inch-pounds (in-lbs) of torque. Torque values below approximately 15 ft-lbs are expressed in inch-pounds, because most foot-pound torque wrenches are not accurate at these smaller values.*

	Ft-lbs	Nm
Cylinder head bolts (continued)		
2.5L (DOHC) non-turbocharged engines and all 2.0L turbocharged engines (continued)		
Step 7, see illustration 13.18d		
2.0L engines	Tighten bolts, in sequence, an additional 100 degrees	
2.5L (DOHC) non-turbocharged engines	Tighten bolts, in sequence, an additional 75 degrees	
Step 8, see illustration 13.18e		
2.0L engines	Tighten bolts, in sequence, an additional 50 degrees	
2.5L (DOHC) non-turbocharged engines	Tighten bolts, in sequence, an additional 30 degrees	
Engine mounts		
Forester models		
2.5L (SOHC) non-turbocharged and 2.5L turbocharged models		
Mount bracket-to-cylinder block bolts	26	35
Insulator-to-mount bracket nuts	31	42
Insulator-to-crossmember/frame nuts	63	85
2.5L (DOHC) non-turbocharged and 2.0L turbocharged models		
Mount bolts	26	35
Mount-to-crossmember nuts	33	45
Legacy models		
Front mount		
Mount bracket-to-engine bolts	22	30
Mount-to-engine bracket bolts	18	25
Mount bracket-to-body bolts	44	60
Mount through bolt/nut	33	45
Stopper mount		
Small bolt	16	22
Large bolts	26	36
Exhaust manifold-to-cylinder head bolts		
2.5L (SOHC) engines	22	30
2.5L (DOHC) non-turbocharged engines	22	30
2.0L turbocharged engines	31	42
2.5L (DOHC) turbocharged engines	24	33
Flywheel/driveplate-to-crankshaft bolts		
2.5L (SOHC) engines	53	72
2.5L (DOHC) non-turbocharged models		
Step 1	22	30
Step 2	Tighten an additional 35 degrees	
2.5L (DOHC) turbocharged models		
Step 1	29	40
Step 2	Tighten an additional 35 degrees	
2.0L engine models		
Step 1	22	30
Step 2	Tighten an additional 35 degrees	
Fuel rail protector mounting bolts	168 in-lbs	19
Intake manifold bolts		
Non-turbocharged engines		
2.5L (SOHC) engines	18.5	25
2.5L (DOHC) engines	74 in-lbs	8
Tumble generator valve assembly-to-cylinder head bolts	18.4	25
Turbocharged engines		
Intake manifold-to-tumble generator valve bolts		
2.0L engines	18.5	25
2.5L engines	74 in-lbs	8
Tumble generator valve assembly-to-cylinder head bolts	18	24
Lower oil pan bolts	44 in-lbs	5
Oil pressure sending unit	18	24
Oil pump housing mounting bolts	56 in-lbs	6
Oil pump cover mounting screws	44 in-lbs	5
Oil pump pickup tube mounting bolts	74 in-lbs	8
Upper oil pan	13	18
Rocker arm assembly bolts (non-turbocharged engines)		
2005 and earlier models	18	24
2006 and later models		
Step 1, Bolts 1 through 8	18	24
Step 2, Bolts 9 and 10	68 in-lbs	7.5
Timing belt cover bolts	44 in-lbs	5
Timing belt upper idler pulley	29	39

Torque specifications (continued)

	Ft-lbs (unless otherwise indicated)	Nm

Note: *One foot-pound (ft-lb) of torque is equivalent to 12 inch-pounds (in-lbs) of torque. Torque values below approximately 15 ft-lbs are expressed in inch-pounds, because most foot-pound torque wrenches are not accurate at these smaller values.*

	Ft-lbs (unless otherwise indicated)	Nm
Timing belt idler pulley number 1 bolt	29	39
Timing belt idler sprocket number 2 bolt	29	39
Timing belt tensioner		
Mounting bolt	29	39
Bracket bolts	18	24
Timing belt guide bolts (at crankshaft sprocket)	84 in-lbs	9.5
Camshaft sprocket bolts(s)		
2.5L (SOHC) engines	57	78
2.5L (DOHC) non-turbocharged engines	160 in-lbs	18
2.0L (DOHC) turbocharged engines	160 in-lbs	18
2.5L (DOHC) turbocharged engines		
Step 1	22	30
Step 2	Tighten an additional 45 degrees	
Timing chain cover bolts (see illustration 8.54)		
Bolts 1 through 5	89 in-lbs	10
Bolts 6 through 32	18.4	25
Timing chain tensioner bolts	56	6.4
Valve cover bolts	57-in-lbs	6.4

1   General information

1   The engines in these vehicles utilize a horizontally opposed, four-cylinder configuration. The crankcase is made of aluminum and is vertically split. The cylinder heads are also aluminum, while the crankshaft is made of steel and supported by five main bearings. The aluminum pistons have two compression rings and one combination-type oil control ring. Each cylinder is equipped with two intake valves and two exhaust valves, for a total of 16 valves.

2   There are two non-turbocharged engines, a 2.5L single overhead-cam (SOHC) design and a 2.5L (DOHC) design. The 2.5L single overhead-cam (SOHC) engines have camshafts (one mounted in each cylinder head) that operate the valves with rocker arms. The valves are adjusted with threaded adjuster screws on the rocker arms. The 2.5L (DOHC) engines are of a double overhead-cam (DOHC) design with four camshafts, two mounted on each cylinder head. The camshafts operate the valves by depressing roller rocker arm pivot (lash adjusters) and the roller rockers. Valve adjustment is carried out by replacing shims mounted to the bottom of the rocker arm pivots with ones of different thickness.

3   There are two turbocharged engines - a 2.0L and 2.5L; both are of a double overhead-cam (DOHC) design with four camshafts, two mounted on each cylinder head. The 2.0L (DOHC) engines are of a double overhead-cam (DOHC) design with four camshafts, two mounted on each cylinder head. The camshafts operate the valves by depressing roller rocker arm pivot (lash adjusters) and the roller rockers. Valve adjustment is carried out by replacing shims mounted to the bottom of the rocker arm pivots with ones of different thickness. The 2.5L engine camshafts operate the valves by depressing bucket-type valve lifters. Valve adjustment is carried out by replacing lifters with ones of different head thickness.

4   On 2.5L (SOHC) and 2012 and earlier 2.5L (DOHC) models the camshafts are driven by the crankshaft with a single timing belt. Timing belt tension is maintained by a tensioner mounted between the cylinder banks. The tensioner incorporates a compression spring that acts against a main spring and oil chamber to keep the tensioner balanced. The water pump is also driven by the timing belt. The timing belt is scheduled for replacement at prescribed service intervals (see Chapter 1).

5   On 2013 and later 2.5L (DOHC) models and all 2.0L models the camshafts are driven by two timing chains. Timing chain tension is maintained by spring loaded hydraulic tensioners. The oil pump on the 2.0L models driven by the crankshaft sprocket and is bolted on the front of the engine block. The oil pump on the 2013 and later 2.5L engine is an integral part of the timing cover and is not serviceable separately from the front cover. If there is a problem with the oil pump the the entire timing cover must be replaced.

6   On 2.5L (SOHC) and 2012 and earlier 2.5L (DOHC) models, the engine oil pump is driven by the crankshaft and it is mounted directly in the center of the engine behind the timing belt and covers.

2   Repair operations possible with the engine in the vehicle

1   Some major repair operations can be accomplished without removing the engine from the vehicle.

2   Clean the engine compartment and the exterior of the engine with some type of degreaser before any work is done. It will make the job easier and help keep dirt out of the internal areas of the engine.

3   Depending on the components involved, it may be helpful to remove the hood to improve access to the engine as repairs are performed (see Chapter 11). Cover the fenders to prevent damage to the paint. Special pads are available, but an old bedspread or blanket will also work.

4   If vacuum, exhaust, oil or coolant leaks develop, indicating a need for gasket or seal replacement, the repairs can generally be made with the engine in the vehicle. The intake and exhaust gaskets, oil pan gasket, and crankshaft oil seals are all accessible with the engine in place. On 2012 and earlier Legacy non-turbo/2010Legacy turbo and all 2010 and earlier Forester models the cylnider head gaskets are replaceable with the engine in the vehicle (all other models requre engine removal for camshaft and cylinder head removal/valve adjustment). However, cylinder head gasket replacement is easier with the engine out of the chassis.

5   Exterior engine components, such as the intake and exhaust, the oil pan (and the oil pump), the water pump, the starter motor, the alternator, the ignition system and fuel system components can be removed for repair with the engine in place.

6   On models where the cylinder heads can be removed without pulling the engine (although this is difficult), valve component servicing can also be accomplished with the engine in the vehicle. On those models, replacement of the camshafts, rocker arms and lifters can be accomplished with the engine in the chassis.

3   Top Dead Center (TDC) for number one piston - locating

1   Top Dead Center (TDC) is the highest point in the cylinder that each piston reaches as it travels up the cylinder bore. Each piston reaches TDC on the compression stroke and again on the exhaust stroke, but TDC generally refers to piston position on the compression stroke.

2   Positioning the piston(s) at TDC is an essential part of procedures such as valve adjustment, camshaft and timing belt/sprocket removal.

3   Before beginning this procedure, place the transaxle in Neutral and apply the parking brake or block the rear wheels. Disconnect the cable from the negative terminal of the battery (see Chapter 5), then remove the spark plugs (see Chapter 1).

4   To find TDC on the compression stroke for the number one cylinder, install a compression gauge in the number one spark plug hole (see Chapter 2B, Section 3).

5   Rotate the crankshaft (clockwise) using a socket and breaker bar on the crankshaft pulley while observing the compression gauge. When the compression stroke of number one cylinder is reached, compression pressure will begin to build and register on the gauge.

6   Continue rotating the crankshaft until the notch in the crankshaft pulley aligns with the "0" on the timing scale (see illustrations). If you go past the marks, release the gauge pressure and rotate the crankshaft two revolutions.

3.6a Typical TDC mark on the crankshaft pulley aligned with zero mark on the timing scale - timing belt engines

3.6b TDC mark on the crankshaft pulley aligned with zero mark on the front cover timing scale - timing chain engines

7   After the number one piston has been positioned at TDC on the compression stroke, TDC for any of the remaining pistons can be located by turning the crankshaft in its normal direction of rotation, in 180-degree (1/2-turn) increments, and following the firing order. Divide the crankshaft pulley into two equal sections with chalk marks at each point, each indicating 180-degrees of crankshaft rotation. Rotating the engine past TDC no. 1 to the next mark will place the engine at TDC for cylinder no. 3.

4   Valve covers - removal and installation

Removal

1   Disconnect the cable from the negative terminal of the battery (see Chapter 5).

Right (passenger's side) valve cover

2.5L (SOHC) non-turbocharged models and 2.5L (DOHC) turbocharged models

2   Remove the air intake ducts, the resonator and the air filter housing (see Chapter 4). **Note:** *Depending on the year and model of the vehicle, the air filter housing may not need to be removed.*

3   Disconnect the breather hose from the valve cover.

4   Raise the vehicle and support it securely on jackstands.

5   Remove the engine splash shield fasteners and remove the shield from under the vehicle (see Chapter 1, illustration 6.6).

2.5L (DOHC) non-turbocharged models

6   Remove the air filter housing and the air inlet to the throttle body (see Chapter 4).

7   Remove the front section of the exhaust pipe (see Section 6).

8   Remove the intake manifold shield bolts

and remove the shield.

2.0L (DOHC) turbocharged models

9   Remove the air filter housing (see Chapter 4).

All models

10   Disconnect the spark plug wires or remove the ignition coils from each cylinder.

11   Remove the bolts from the valve cover (see illustration) and separate the cover from the cylinder head. Depending on the tools you are using, it may be easier to remove the lower valve cover bolts from under the vehicle. If this is the case, raise the vehicle and support it securely on jackstands.

Left (driver's side) valve cover

2.5L (SOHC) non-turbocharged models and 2.5L (DOHC) turbocharged models

12   Raise the vehicle and support it securely on jackstands.

13   Remove the engine splash shield fasteners and remove the shield from under the vehicle.

14   Disconnect the breather hose from the valve cover.

2.5L (DOHC) non-turbocharged models

15   Remove the drivebelt cover and drivebelts (see Chapter 1).

16   With the engine at TDC (see illustration 3.6b) place a socket and ratchet on the crankshaft pulley and rotate the engine 180-degrees clockwise. **Note:** *The engine must be rotated to this position to allow the valve cover to clear the lobes of the camshaft.*

17   Remove the intake manifold shield bolts and remove the shield.

2.0L (DOHC) turbocharged models

18   Remove the hood striker (see Chapter 11) and front grille.

19   Remove the air intake cover fasteners and cover from the top of the engine.

20   Disconnect the hood struts then raise

and support the hood in an upright position or remove the hood (see Chapter 11).

21   Remove the battery (see Chapter 5).

22   Remove the air intake duct and filter housing (see Chapter 4).

23   Remove the front exhaust pipe (see Section 6).

24   Remove the engine mount-to-crossmember nuts.

25   Remove the intercooler (see Chapter 4).

26   Disconnect the electrical connectors around the front of the engine including the air conditioning compressor and alternator.

27   Remove the high-pressure fuel pump case shield bolts and shield.

28   Remove the upper roll mount through bolts and remove the roll mount.

29   On CVT models, disconnect the wiring harness retainer and move the harness out of the way.

30   Raise the vehicle and support it securely on jackstands.

31   Connect a chain engine lifting chain (see Chapter 2B) to the engine, use an engine hoist to lift the engine until the studs from the engine mounts clear the crossmember, then place blocks of wood between the mounts and the crossmember.

32   Move the oil cooler hoses out of the way.

All models

33   Disconnect the spark plug wires (see Chapter 1) or the ignition coils (see Chapter 5) from each cylinder.

34   Remove the bolts from the valve cover and separate the cover from the cylinder head. Depending on the tools you are using, it may be easier to remove the lower valve cover bolts from under the vehicle. If this is the case, raise the vehicle and support it securely on jackstands.

Installation

35   Install a new valve cover gasket and spark plug seals (see illustrations).

4.11 Remove the bolts from the valve cover (early 2.5L SOHC non-turbocharged model shown)

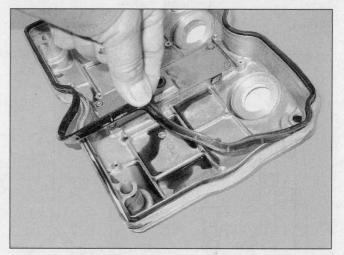

4.35a When replacing the valve cover gasket, make sure it seats in its groove properly

4.35b Replace the spark plug seals before installing the valve cover

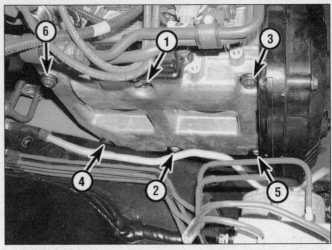

4.36 Valve cover bolt tightening sequence (2.5L SOHC non-turbocharged engines)

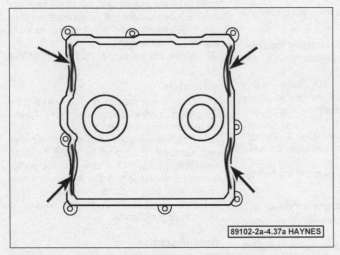

4.37a Apply THREE BOND sealant to the specified areas of the valve cover (2.5L DOHC non-turbocharged models and 2.0L turbocharged models)

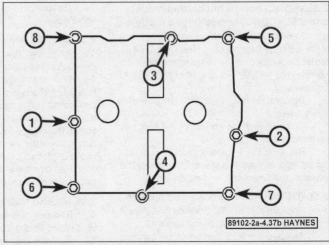

4.37b Valve cover bolt tightening sequence (2.5L DOHC non-turbocharged models and 2.0L turbocharged models)

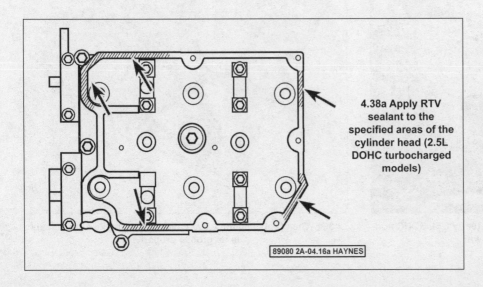

4.38a Apply RTV sealant to the specified areas of the cylinder head (2.5L DOHC turbocharged models)

36   On (SOHC) non-turbocharged models: Use the correct bolt tightening sequence (see illustration) and tighten the bolts to the torque listed in this Chapter's Specifications.

37   On 2.5L (DOHC) non-turbocharged models and 2.0L turbocharged models: Apply RTV sealant to the specified areas of the valve cover (see illustration). Install the valve cover and tighten the bolts, in sequence (see illustration), to the torque listed in this Chapter's Specifications.

38   On 2.5L (DOHC) turbocharged models: Apply RTV sealant to the specified areas of the cylinder head (see illustration). Install the valve cover and tighten the bolts, in sequence (see illustration), to the torque listed in this Chapter's Specifications.

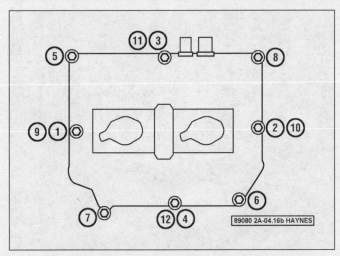

4.38b Valve cover bolt tightening sequence (2.5L DOHC turbocharged models)

5.6 Location of the coolant hoses on the throttle body

5 Intake manifold - removal and installation

Warning: *Wait until the engine is completely cool before beginning this procedure.*

Removal

1   On 2.5L (DOHC) turbocharged models, have the air conditioning system refrigerant recovered by a licensed air conditioning technician, then remove the air conditioning compressor (see Chapter 3).

2   Relieve the fuel pressure (see Chapter 4), then disconnect the cable from the negative terminal of the battery (see Chapter 5).

3   Remove the engine cover fasteners and lift the cover off the engine, if equipped.

4   Remove the air filter housing, the resonator and air intake ducts, as necessary, for access to the intake manifold (see Chapter 4). **Note:** *Depending on the year and model of the vehicle, the air filter housing and/or resonator may not need to be removed.*

5   On 2.5L (SOHC) models, detach the spark plug wires from the ignition coil. **Note:** *Mark the positions of the wires so they don't get mixed up.*

6   Clamp-off and disconnect the coolant hoses from the throttle body (see illustration). Place a rag under the connections to catch any coolant left in the hoses and throttle body.

7   Disconnect the electrical connectors from the fuel injectors, the CKP, CMP, ECT, knock sensors, oxygen sensors, oil switching valve, etc. (see Chapters 4 and 6). Label the connectors to insure correct reassembly.

8   Remove the drivebelt cover and drivebelts (see Chapter 1).

9   Remove the power steering pump (see

5.14 Typical location of the EGR pipe (A) and EGR valve (B) - early model shown, later model similar

Chapter 10). Position the power steering pump off to the side without disconnecting the power steering fluid lines.

10   Remove the alternator (see Chapter 5).

11   On non-turbocharged models, remove the air conditioning compressor and the mounting bracket (see Chapter 3). Position the compressor off to the side without disconnecting the refrigerant lines. **Warning:** *The air conditioning system is under high pressure. DO NOT loosen any fittings unless the system has been discharged. Air conditioning refrigerant should be properly discharged into an approved container at a dealer service department or an automotive air conditioning repair facility.* **Note:** *On some models the air conditioning compressor will not interfere with intake manifold removal.*

12   Disconnect the PCV hose (see Chapter 4) and all vacuum lines from the intake manifold. Label the vacuum hoses to insure

correct reassembly.

13   Disconnect the fuel delivery and return hoses from the fuel rail. Remove the fuel rails from each cylinder head and keep the injectors attached to the fuel rail (see Chapter 4).

2.5L (SOHC) non-turbocharged models

14   Remove the EGR pipe and the EGR valve (see illustration). **Note:** *Some models are not equipped with an EGR system. Refer to Chapter 6 for additional information.*

15   Disconnect the electrical connector to the throttle body (see Chapter 4).

16   Remove the air assist injector solenoid valve and bracket (see Chapter 6) from the intake manifold.

17   Disconnect the vacuum hose, the vent hose and the purge hose from the evaporation pipe. Label all the hoses for correct reassembly.

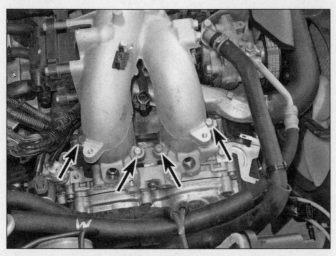

5.18 Location of the intake manifold mounting bolts on the right cylinder head - early SOHC model shown

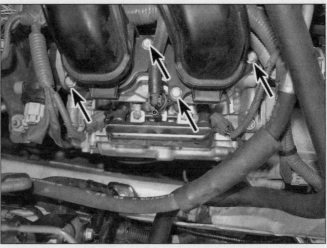

5.23 Location of the upper intake manifold mounting bolts on the right cylinder head - later (DOHC) non-turbocharged model shown

18   Remove the intake manifold mounting bolts (see illustration) and carefully lift the manifold off of the engine with the throttle body attached.

2.5L (DOHC) non-turbocharged models and all turbocharged models

Intake manifold (upper manifold)
19   Disconnect the electrical connector to the throttle body (see Chapter 4).
20   On turbocharged models, remove the intercooler (see Chapter 4).
21   Disconnect the oil flow control solenoid valve connector (see Chapter 6).
22   Disconnect the vacuum hoses from the purge control solenoid valve (see Chapter 6). Label the hoses for correct reassembly.
23   Remove the intake manifold mounting bolts (see illustration) and carefully lift the manifold off of the engine with the throttle body attached. As you lift the manifold, check for any hoses or wires that may still be connected.

Tumble generator valve assembly (lower manifold)
24   Disconnect the connectors from the tumble generator valve position sensor and the tumble generator valve actuator (see Chapter 6).
25   Remove the fuel injector rail (see Chapter 4) from the lower intake manifold. Remove the coolant reservoir brace if it's in the way of the left side lower manifold.
26   Remove the lower intake manifold mounting bolts and carefully separate the lower intake manifold from the cylinder heads.

Installation
27   Scrape away any traces of sealant or old gasket materials from the intake manifold mounting surfaces and clean the gasket surface with a rag and lacquer thinner.

Note: *When installing the manifold, always use new gaskets or O-rings, and do not use sealant on the gaskets. Clean the threads of the bolts with a wire brush before installation.*

2.5L (SOHC) non-turbocharged models
28   Carefully place the intake manifold onto the engine and install the mounting bolts, tightening them in several steps to the torque listed in this Chapter's Specifications.

2.5L (DOHC) non-turbocharged models and all turbocharged models
29   Carefully place the tumble generator valve assemblies (lower manifolds) onto the cylinder heads and install the mounting bolts, tightening them in several steps to the torque listed in this Chapter's Specifications.
30   Carefully place the intake manifold (upper) onto the tumble generator valve assemblies and install the mounting bolts, tightening them in several steps to the torque listed in this Chapter's Specifications.

All models
31   Install the fuel rail and injectors (see Chapter 4).
32   Attach the hose to the PCV valve (see Chapter 6).
33   Attach the EGR supply pipe to the manifold, if equipped.
34   Connect the wiring connectors and vacuum and fuel hoses.
Note: *Check all hoses for cracks and damage at this time (see Chapter 1). Replace them with new ones if necessary.*
35   Connect the coolant hoses to the throttle body.
36   Check the coolant level, adding as necessary (see Chapter 1). When starting the engine, check carefully for coolant, fuel or vacuum leaks.
37   On 2.5L (DOHC) turbocharged models,

have the A/C system evacuated, charged and leak tested by the shop that discharged it.

6   Exhaust manifold - removal and installation

Warning: *The engine must be completely cool before beginning this procedure.*

Removal
1   Disconnect the cable from the negative terminal of the battery (see Chapter 5).
2   Raise the vehicle and support it securely on jackstands.
3   Remove the engine splash shield(s) (see illustration).
4   Disconnect the front and rear oxygen sensor connectors (see Chapter 6).

Non-turbocharged models
5   Remove the heat shields from the exhaust pipes and the exhaust manifold (see illustration).
Note: *Spray penetrating lubricant on the bolts and studs to prevent thread stripping.*
6   Remove the bolts from the exhaust manifold connector at the center exhaust pipe.
7   Remove the nuts from the exhaust manifold on both cylinder heads (see illustrations).
8   Remove the exhaust manifold.

Turbocharged models
9   Remove the heat shields from the exhaust pipes and the exhaust manifold(s).
Note: *Spray penetrating lubricant on the bolts and studs to prevent thread stripping.*
10   Working on the center of the exhaust manifold, remove the bolts from the turbocharger joint pipe.
11   Remove the nuts from the exhaust manifold on both cylinder heads. Remove the center exhaust pipe and separate it from the left and right exhaust manifolds if the entire assembly is difficult to remove.

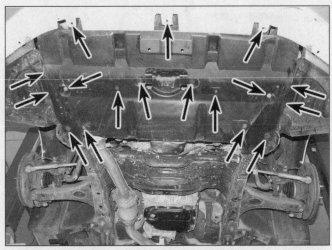

6.3 Location of the engine splash shield fasteners on Legacy models - Forester models have either a two piece splash shield or a one piece that is similar

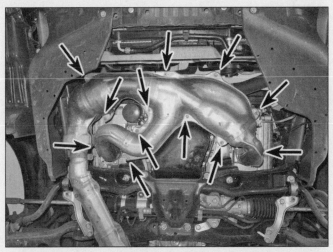

6.5 Typical 2.5L (SOHC) engine heat shield fastener locations

6.7a Location of the exhaust manifold nuts on the right-side cylinder head

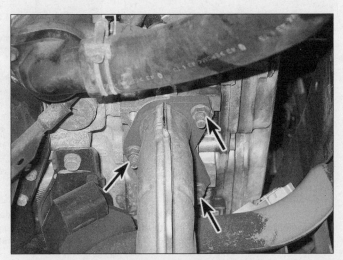

6.7b Location of the exhaust manifold nuts on the left-side cylinder head

Installation

12 Using a scraper, thoroughly clean the mating surfaces on the cylinder heads, manifold(s) and exhaust pipe. Remove all residue with brake system cleaner.

13 Check that the mating surfaces are perfectly flat and not damaged in any way. Warped or damaged manifolds will require replacement. Install the new gaskets to the cylinder head and place the manifold on the cylinder heads. Tighten the bolts evenly to the torque listed in this Chapter's Specifications.

14 Connect the center pipe (non-turbocharged models) or turbocharger joint pipe (turbocharged models) to the manifold and tighten the nuts evenly to the torque listed in the Chapter 4 Specifications.

15 The remainder of installation is the reverse of removal.

16 Reconnect the battery (see Chapter 5).

17 Run the engine and check for exhaust leaks.

7 Timing belt and sprockets - removal, inspection and installation

Warning: *Wait until the engine is completely cool before beginning this procedure.*

Note: *It's a good idea to replace the water pump (see Chapter 3) and the timing belt tensioners whenever the timing belt is replaced.*

Removal

1 Position the engine at TDC for cylinder number 1 (see Section 3).

2 Disconnect the cable from the negative terminal of the battery (see Chapter 5).

3 Remove the drivebelts (see Chapter 1).

4 On models equipped with a stopper rod mount, remove the mount bolts and rod assembly from the front of the engine.

Note: *On turbocharged models, the power steering pump and bracket will need to be removed with the stopper rod mount (see Chapter 10).*

5 Remove the engine cooling fan(s) and shroud (see Chapter 3).

6 Remove the crankshaft pulley (see Section 9).

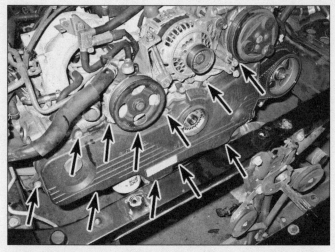

7.7a Location of the right-side timing belt cover mounting bolts

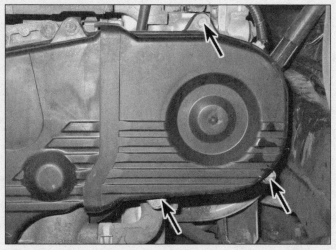

7.7b Location of the left-side timing belt cover mounting bolts

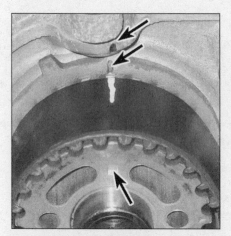

7.9a The two crankshaft sprocket alignment notches must align with the notch in the oil pump flange

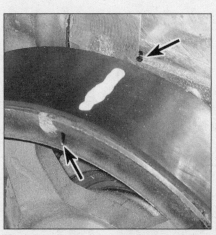

7.9b The right-side camshaft sprocket must align with the seam on the cylinder head/camshaft end cap

7.9c The left-side camshaft sprocket must align with the notch in the rear timing belt cover

Non-turbocharged engines

7   Remove the outer belt covers (see illustrations). There are two covers; one larger cover that extends over the right-side camshaft and the crankshaft sprocket and another smaller cover on the left side.

8   On manual transaxle models, remove the timing belt guide fasteners and guide.

9   Turn the crankshaft and align the marks on the crankshaft sprocket, the left camshaft sprocket and the right camshaft sprocket with the notches on the oil pump, the inner timing belt cover and the cylinder head seam (see illustrations).

Note: *The right camshaft sprocket alignment notch must align with the mark on the cylinder head seam. Only the left camshaft sprocket uses the rear timing belt cover for the alignment mark.*

10   Use white paint to clearly mark these alignment marks in relation to the engine block (center) and the inner belt cover (left) or the cylinder head (right) (see illustration 7.9a, 7.9b and 7.9c).

11   Use paint to mark the direction of belt rotation if the arrow has faded (see illustration). If the original timing belt marks have faded, paint new marks across the belt at the exact points of the alignment notches.

7.11 Paint an arrow on the belt to indicate timing belt rotation

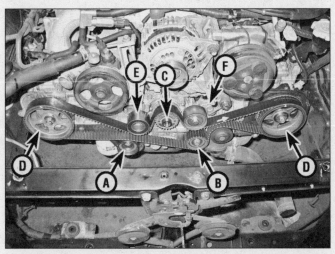

7.12 Timing belt details - (SOHC) non-turbocharged engines

A   Idler pulley number 1   D   Camshaft sprocket
B   Idler sprocket number 2   E   Idler pulley
C   Crankshaft sprocket   F   Tensioner

7.15 Remove the crankshaft sprocket from the crankshaft

7.20a Location of the timing marks on the crankshaft sprocket

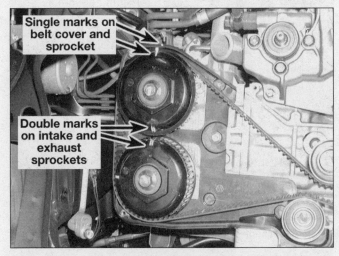

7.20b Location of the timing marks on the right-side intake and exhaust camshaft sprockets

12   Remove idler pulley number 1 to release the timing belt tension (see illustration). Remove idler sprocket number 2 to make clearance for the timing belt.

13   Remove the timing belt.

Caution: *Do not rotate the camshaft sprockets with the timing belt removed or the valve heads may contact the piston crowns, resulting in bent valves.*

14   If only the timing belt is to be replaced, proceed to the Inspection and Installation Steps. If the sprockets are to be replaced, continue with the following Steps.

15   Remove the crankshaft pulley sprocket from the crankshaft (see illustration). If it doesn't slip off, use two screwdrivers behind it to evenly pry it off.

16   Remove the timing belt tensioner (see illustration 7.12).

17   Keep the camshaft sprocket timing mark aligned with the mark on the inner cover, and remove the sprocket bolt while holding the sprocket with a pin wrench or similar tool. Remove both camshaft sprockets and mark them left and right. Do not interchange the left and right camshaft sprockets.

Turbocharged models

18   Disconnect the vacuum hoses and tube retainers from the belt covers then remove the outer belt cover fasteners and remove the covers. There are two side covers and one central cover.

19   Remove the timing belt guide fasteners and guides, if equipped.

20   Turn the crankshaft to align the marks on the crankshaft and left and right camshaft sprockets with the notches on the rear timing belt cover and the cylinder head (see illustrations).

21   Use white paint to clearly mark these alignment marks in relation to the engine block (center) and the inner belt covers (left and right).

22   Use paint to mark the direction of belt rotation if the arrow has faded (see illustration 7.11). If the original timing belt marks (yellow diagonal lines) have faded, paint new marks across the belt at the exact points of the alignment notches.

23   Install camshaft sprocket locking tools. One tool locks the right-side intake and exhaust camshaft sprockets together while the other tool locks the left-side intake and exhaust camshaft sprockets together. These tools are available at most auto parts stores.

Caution: *These tools are necessary to lock the camshaft sprockets in a stationary position to prevent any valve-to-piston contact*

7.20c Location of the timing marks on the left-side intake and exhaust camshaft sprockets

7.24 Remove idler pulley number 1 to release the timing belt tension

7.28 Location of the tensioner on a turbocharged engine

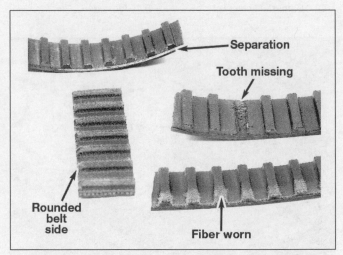

7.33 Check the timing belt for cracked and missing teeth

24   Remove idler pulley number 1 (lower) to release the timing belt tension (see illustration). Remove idler sprocket number 2 (upper) to make clearance for the timing belt.

25   Remove the timing belt.

Caution: *Do not rotate the camshaft sprockets with the timing belt removed or the valve heads may contact each other (or the piston[s]), resulting in bent valves.*

26   If only the timing belt is to be replaced, proceed to the Inspection and Installation Steps. If the sprockets are to be replaced, continue with the following Steps.

27   Remove the crankshaft sprocket from the crankshaft (see illustration 7.15). If it doesn't slip off, use two screwdrivers behind it to evenly pry it off.

28   Remove the bolt and remove the timing belt tensioner (see illustration).

Sprocket removal (if necessary)

29   On non-turbocharged models, hold the camshaft sprocket from turning using a a two-pin spanner then use a breaker bar and socket to remove the sprocket bolt an slide the sprocket off of the camshaft.

Note: *On turbocharged models, the intake and exhaust camshafts are equipped with actuator sprockets.*

30   On turbocharged models, remove the actuator cover fasteners then remove the cover. Keeping the camshaft sprocket timing mark aligned with the mark on the inner cover, hold the camshaft sprocket with special tool #ST 499977500, then use an Allen wrench on a socket adapter to remove the sprocket bolt. Remove the camshaft sprockets and mark them left and right.

Caution: *Do not try to disassemble the camshaft sprocket actuators.*

Inspection

Caution: *Do not bend, twist or turn the timing belt inside out. Do not allow it to come in contact with oil, coolant or fuel. Do not use timing belt tension to keep the camshaft or crank-* *shaft from turning when installing the sprocket bolt(s). Do not turn the crankshaft or camshaft more than a few degrees (necessary for tooth alignment) while the timing belt is removed.*

31   Rotate the tensioner pulley and idler pulley by hand and move it side-to-side to detect roughness and excessive play. Replace them if they don't turn smoothly or if play is noted.

32   If the timing belt was broken during engine operation, the belt may have been fouled by debris or may have been damaged by a defective component in the area of the timing belt; check for belt material in the teeth of the sprockets. Any defective parts or debris in the sprockets must be cleaned out of all the sprockets before installing the new belt or the belt will not mesh properly when installed.

Note: *If one of the sprockets is damaged or worn, replace the sprockets as a set.*

33   If the belt teeth are cracked or pulled off (see illustration), the oil pump or camshaft(s) may have seized.

34   If there is noticeable wear or cracks in

the belt, check to see if there are nicks or burrs on the sprockets.

35   If there is wear or damage on only one side of the belt (see illustration 7.33), check the belt guide and the alignment of all sprockets. Also check the oil seals at the front of the engine and replace them if they are leaking.

36   Replace the timing belt with a new one if obvious wear or damage is noted or if it is the least bit questionable. Correct any problems which contributed to belt failure prior to belt installation.

Note: *We recommend replacing the belt whenever it is removed, since belt failure will almost certainly lead to expensive engine damage.*

Installation

Caution: *Before starting the engine, carefully rotate the crankshaft by hand through at least two full revolutions (use a socket and breaker bar on the crankshaft pulley center bolt). If you feel any resistance, STOP! There is something wrong - most likely, the valves are contacting the pistons. You must find the problem before proceeding.*

Note: *If the inner timing belt covers were removed from the engine (only necessary if the cylinder heads had been removed or the engine was to be overhauled), continue as below. If the inner covers were not removed, proceed to Step 43.*

37   If removed as part of the camshaft sprocket and tensioner removal, install the tensioner bracket on the cylinder block.

38   Attach the seals and inner timing belt cover mounts to the left and right inner timing belt covers (see illustration), then install the assembly on the cylinder head and block.

39   Install the camshaft sprockets or actuators. On models equipped with camshaft sprocket actuators, install the actuator cover and fasteners. Tighten the sprocket/actuator fasteners to the torque listed in this Chapter's Specifications.

40   Install the crankshaft sprocket onto the crankshaft. Make sure the crankshaft and camshaft sprocket timing marks noted during removal are still aligned (see illustrations 7.9a, 7.9b and 7.9c [non-turbocharged engines] or 7.20a, 7.20b and 7.20c [turbocharged engines]). If necessary, rotate the sprockets slightly to align the timing marks.

41   Install idler sprocket number 2 and tighten the bolt to the torque listed in this Chapter's Specifications.

42   Place the tensioner assembly onto a vertical press and gradually press the plunger in until the holes align - press the plunger in very slowly, taking at least three minutes to complete the procedure.

43   Once the plunger is compressed, insert a stopper pin through the holes - DO NOT force the adjuster rod past this point or damage to the tensioner assembly will occur.

44   Reinstall the tensioner. Make sure the tensioner plunger is locked in place with a stopper pin. Install the assembly onto the

7.38 Typical right-side timing belt inner cover mounting bolts (turbocharged models shown)

engine. Tighten the bolt to the torque listed in this Chapter's Specifications.

Non-turbocharged models

45   Install the timing belt onto the sprockets and pulleys (see illustrations 7.9a, 7.9b and 7.9c) making sure that all the timing marks noted during removal align with the marks on the engine and the arrow indicates the correct direction of rotation. Be careful to allow for belt correction at the tensioner when the timing belt tensioner is released and the left camshaft sprocket rotates slightly.

46   Install the idler pulley number 1. Tighten the bolt to the torque listed in this Chapter's Specifications.

47   Apply tension to the timing belt then remove the stopper pin from the tensioner adjuster. Double-check all the timing marks for correct alignment.

48   Install the timing belt guide, if equipped, and tighten the mounting bolts to the torque listed in this Chapter's Specifications. Maintain the proper clearance between the guides and timing belt as listed in this Chapter's Specifications.

Turbocharged models

49   Install the timing belt onto the sprockets and pulleys (see illustrations 7.20a, 7.20b and 7.20c) making sure that all the timing marks noted during removal align with the marks on the engine and the arrow indicates the correct direction of rotation. Be careful to allow for belt correction at the tensioner when the timing belt tensioner is released and the left intake camshaft sprocket rotates slightly.

Note: *The exhaust camshaft sprockets on turbocharged models are also equipped with separate timing notches offset 90 degrees to the main timing marks. These secondary alignment timing notches should align with the notch in each of the inner timing belt covers.*

50   Install the idler pulley number 1. Tighten the bolt to the torque listed in this Chapter's Specifications.

51   Remove the stopper pin from the tensioner adjuster. Double-check all the tim-

ing marks for correct alignment.

52   Install the timing belt guide(s), if equipped, and tighten the mounting bolts to the torque listed in this Chapter's Specifications. Maintain the proper clearance between the guide(s) and timing belt (see this Chapter's Specifications).

53   Remove the special camshaft sprocket locking tools.

All models

54   Install the timing belt covers.

55   Install the crankshaft pulley (see Section 9).

56   The remainder of installation is the reverse of removal.

---

8   Timing chain cover, timing chains and sprockets - removal, inspection and installation

Warning: *Wait until the engine is completely cool before beginning this procedure.*

Removal

1   Disconnect the cable from the negative terminal of the battery (see Chapter 5).

2   Raise the vehicle and support it securely on jackstands.

3   Drain the engine oil and cooling system (see Chapter 1).

4   Remove the drivebelts (see Chapter 1).

5   Remove the radiator (see Chapter 3).

6   Remove the water pump pulley (see Chapter 3).

7   Remove the exhaust manifold (see Section 6).

8   On models with hydraulic power steering, remove the power steering pump (see Chapter 10).

9   Remove the alternator (see Chapter 5).

10   Remove the drivebelt tensioner and idler pulley (see Chapter 1).

11   Remove the crankshaft pulley (see Section 9).

12   Remove the engine harness bracket

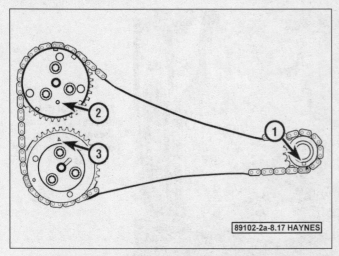

8.17 Right-side timing chain sprocket alignment details

1   *Crankshaft keyway and timing mark*
2   *Intake camshaft sprocket timing mark*
3   *Exhaust camshaft sprocket timing mark*

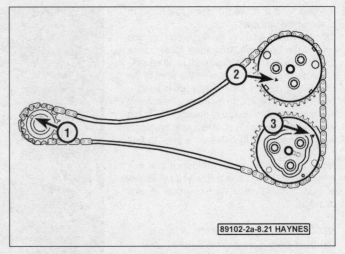

8.21 Left-side timing chain sprocket alignment details

1   *Crankshaft key way and timing mark*
2   *Intake camshaft sprocket timing mark*
3   *Exhaust camshaft sprocket timing mark*

bolts from the the front of the timing chain cover.

13   Disconnect the electrical connectors from the oil pressure switch, the oil control solenoids and the camshaft position sensors (see Chapter 6).

14   Remove the oil dipstick tube mounting bolt, then remove the tube from the cover and replace the O-ring.

15   Remove the timing cover mounting bolts, noting the their original locations. Locate the prying point along the case, then use a screwdriver or small prybar to carefully separate the cover from the engine at these points.

Caution: *The timing cover bolts are different sizes and must be installed in their original locations.*

16   Remove and replace the O-rings for the timing chain cover from the cylinder heads, case and upper oil pan.

17   Insert the crankshaft pulley bolt into the end of the crankshaft then use a ratchet and socket to rotate the engine until the key on the crankshaft is at the six o'clock position, the alignment marks on the right-side camshafts should be pointing at each other, with the intake camshaft mark at the six o'clock position and the exhaust camshaft mark at twelve o'clock position (see illustration).

18   Rotate the link plate on the outside of the right-side timing chain tensioner clockwise then push the tensioner plunger into the tensioner body and hold in this position. Insert a Allen wrench or paper clip through the link plate and into the hole in the tensioner body to lock the tensioner plunger in the compressed position.

19   Remove the right-hand tensioner mounting bolts and remove the tensioner then remove the lower right-side chain guide,

upper guide mounting bolt and guide.

20   Remove the right-side timing chain from the camshaft sprockets and crankshaft sprocket.

Note: *Note when the right-side timing chain is in this position (see illustration 8.17), the right-side intake and exhaust camshafts are kept at a zero-lift position, meaning the valves are closed. The right-side intake camshaft or exhaust camshaft can be independently rotated while the timing chain is removed.*

Caution: *The camshafts can't be rotated at the same time or the valve heads will contact each other and bend the valves. If the camshafts must be rotated at the same time, they may be turned slightly and only by hand.*

21   With the right-side chain removed, rotate the engine until the key on the crankshaft is at the ten o'clock position, with the intake camshaft mark at approximately the eight o'clock position and the exhaust camshaft mark at approximately the two o'clock position (see illustration).

22   Rotate the link plate on the outside of the left-side timing chain tensioner clockwise then push the tensioner plunger into the tensioner body and hold in this position. Insert a Allen wrench or paper clip through the link plate and into the hole in the tensioner body to hold the tensioner plunger in the compressed position.

23   Remove the left-hand tensioner mounting bolts and tensioner then slide the end of the upper left-side chain guide off of the pivot. Remove and discard the tensioner O-ring.

24   Remove the left-side timing chain from the sprockets and crankshaft sprocket, then remove the lower chain guide.

25   Rotate the crankshaft clockwise, approximately 200-degrees until the key on the crankshaft is at the ten o'clock position. In this

position the all the pistons are down and out of contact with the valves.

26   Using a two-pin spanner wrench, rotate the left-side intake camshaft only, approximately 180-degrees until the mark on the camshaft sprocket is at the eight o'clock position.

Note: *Note when the left-side timing chain is in this position (see illustration 8.17), only the left-side exhaust camshaft is in the zero-lift position, meaning the valves are closed. The left-side intake camshaft or exhaust camshaft can be independently rotated while the timing chain is removed.*

Caution: *The left-side camshafts can't be rotated at the same time or the valve heads will contact each other and bend the valves. If the camshafts must be rotated at the same time, they may be turned slightly and only by hand.*

Warning: *Once the left-side camshafts are in this position, do not turn either camshaft - valve damage will occur.*

Sprocket removal (if necessary)

27   On 2.5L (DOHC) non-turbocharged models, insert a three inch long 1/4 inch (6 mm) bolt or rod through the hole in the exhaust camshaft sprocket to prevent it from turning, then use a breaker bar and socket to remove the sprocket bolts and slide the sprocket off of the camshaft.

Note: *On turbocharged models the intake and exhaust camshafts are equipped with actuator sprockets.*

28   On 2.5L (DOHC) non-turbocharged intake sprockets and both sprockets on turbocharged models, hold the camshaft sprocket actuator from turning with special tool #ST 18334AA030 and 18355AA000 two-pin spanner wrench, then use a breaker bar and

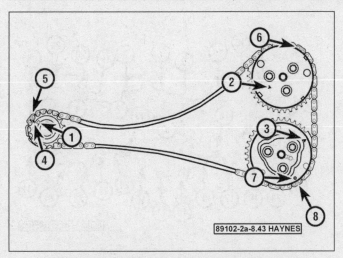

8.43 Left-side timing chain timing alignment details

1   Crankshaft sprocket mark location
2   Intake camshaft sprocket face mark location
3   Exhaust camshaft sprocket face mark location
4   Crankshaft sprocket timing mark location
5   Timing chain yellow link
6   Timing chain orange link
7   Exhaust camshaft sprocket (to chain) timing mark
8   Timing chain orange link

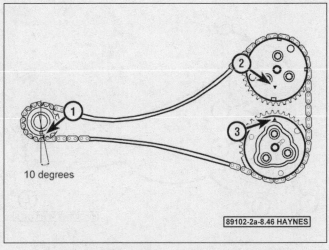

8.46 Left-side timing chain sprockets alignment details

1   Crankshaft sprocket mark location
2   Intake camshaft sprocket face mark location
3   Exhaust camshaft sprocket face mark location

socket to remove the sprocket actuator bolts and slide the sprocket off of the camshaft. Remove the camshaft sprockets and mark them Left and Right.

Caution: *Do not try to disassemble the camshaft sprocket actuators.*

Inspection

29   Clean all parts with solvent and dry with compressed air, if available.
30   Inspect the chain tensioners for excessive wear or other damage. Drain all the oil out of the chain tensioners if there to be reused.
31   Inspect the timing chain guides for deep grooves, excessive wear, or other damage.
32   Inspect the timing chains for excessive wear or damage.
33   Inspect the crankshaft and camshaft sprockets for chipped or broken teeth, excessive wear, or damage.
34   Replace any component that is in questionable condition.

Installation

Caution: *Before starting the engine, carefully rotate the crankshaft by hand through at least two full revolutions (use a socket and breaker bar on the crankshaft pulley center bolt). If you feel any resistance, STOP! There is something wrong - most likely, the valves are contacting the pistons. You must find the problem before proceeding.*

35   Using a gasket scraper, scrape off all traces of the old gasket from the cylinder heads, case and the oil pan. Be especially careful not to nick or gouge the gasket sealing surfaces of the crankcases (they are made of aluminum and are quite soft).
36   Install the camshaft sprockets or actuators and tighten the sprocket/actuator bolts to the torque listed in this Chapter's Specifications.
37   Clean the camshaft sprockets with a small amount of solvent and dry it thoroughly to locate the timing marks.
38   Check the keyway on the crankshaft sprocket, it should be at the ten o'clock position.
39   Verify the intake camshaft sprocket mark is at the eight o'clock position (see illustration 8.43).
40   If the intake camshaft sprocket must be aligned, rotate the crankshaft to the six o'clock position the align the intake camshaft. Once the intake camshaft is aligned, rotate the crankshaft counterclockwise, approximately 200 degrees until the key on the crankshaft is at the ten o'clock position.
41   Verify the left-side exhaust camshaft mark on the camshaft sprocket is at the two o'clock position (see illustration 8.43).
42   Install the left-side lower chain guide and tighten the bolt securely.
43   Place the left-side timing chain onto the chain guide, then match the yellow colored link of the chain with the mark on the crankshaft sprocket. Match the two orange colored links with timing marks on the intake camshaft sprocket and exhaust camshaft sprocket (see illustration).

Note: *The intake camshaft timing mark is a small line, located on the top of the camshaft sprocket, not the face of the sprocket.*

44   Install a new left-side tensioner O-ring on to the cylinder block.
45   Install the left-side chain guide on to the pivot and against the chain then install the tensioner and tighten the mounting bolts to the torque listed in this Chapter's Specifications.
46   Remove the retaining pin from the the left-side tensioner. Rotate the crankshaft clockwise making sure the crankshaft rotates smoothly and there is no binding. Continue rotating the crankshaft clockwise until the crankshaft key is at the six o'clock position, the mark on the face of the intake camshaft is at the six o'clock position and the mark on the exhaust sprocket is at the twelve o'clock position (see illustration). The left-side chain is now aligned for the installation of the right-side chain.
47   With the left-side chain installed and the sprockets aligned (see illustration 8.46) place the mark on the face of right-side intake camshaft sprocket at the 6 o'clock position and the mark on the exhaust camshaft sprocket at the 12 o'clock position (see illustration 8.17).
48   Install the right-side upper chain guide and tighten the bolt securely.
49   Place the right-side timing chain under the chain guide, then match the yellow colored link of the chain with the mark on the crankshaft sprocket. Match the two orange colored links with timing chain timing marks on the intake camshaft sprocket and exhaust

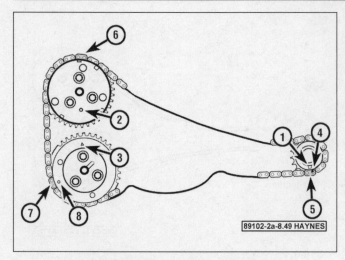

8.49 Right-side timing chain details

1 *Crankshaft key location*
2 *Intake camshaft sprocket face mark location*
3 *Exhaust camshaft sprocket face mark location*
4 *Crankshaft sprocket timing mark location*
5 *Timing chain yellow link*
6 *Timing chain orange link*
7 *Timing chain orange link*
8 *Exhaust sprocket timing chain alignment mark*

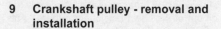

8.57 Timing chain cover bolt tightening sequence

camshaft sprocket (see illustration).
Note: *The intake camshaft sprocket timing chain alignment mark is a small line, located on the top of the camshaft sprocket not the face of the sprocket.*

50 Install the right-side lower chain guide onto the pivot and against the chain, then install the tensioner and tighten the mounting bolts to the torque listed in this Chapter's Specifications.

51 Remove the retaining pin from the the right-side tensioner. Rotate the crankshaft clockwise, making sure the crankshaft rotates smoothly and there is no binding. Continue rotating the crankshaft clockwise until the crankshaft key is at the six o'clock position,

the mark on the face of the intake camshaft is at the six o'clock position and the mark on the exhaust sprocket is at the twelve o'clock position (see illustration 8.17).

52 Clean the cylinder heads, case, oil pan and timing chain cover with solvent and dry it thoroughly. Wipe all the gasket surfaces clean with a rag soaked in brake system cleaner.

53 Install new O-rings to the cylinder heads, case and upper oil pan.

54 Apply liquid gasket (Three Bond or equivalent), at the gaps where the cylinder heads and cases meet.

55 Apply a 1/8-inch (5 mm) bead of liquid gasket (Three Bond or equivalent) to the perimeter sealing surface of the timing chain

cover and the five bolt hole areas on the cover.

56 Install the cover, then install the mounting bolts in their original bolt hole locations and tighten the bolts hand tight.

57 Tighten the timing chain cover bolts in sequence (see illustration) to the torque listed in this Chapter's Specifications.

58 The remainder of installation is the reverse of removal. After refilling with new coolant, fresh oil and installing a new oil filter, start the engine and check for oil leaks.

9 Crankshaft pulley - removal and installation

1 Disconnect the cable from the negative battery terminal (see Chapter 5).

2 Remove the drivebelts (see Chapter 1).

3 Raise the vehicle and support it securely on jackstands.

4 Remove the under-vehicle splash shield (see illustration 6.3).

5 On 2013 and later models, remove the secondary cooling fan and shroud (see Chapter 3).

6 If you're removing the crankshaft pulley as part of the timing chain or timing belt removal procedure, set the engine at TDC for cylinder no. 1 (see Section 3).

7 Prevent the pulley from turning by holding it with a two pin spanner that engages with the slots in the pulley hub (see illustrations), then use a large ratchet or breaker bar and socket to unscrew the crankshaft pulley center bolt.

9.7a Use a two-pin holding tool to prevent the crankshaft pulley from turning while removing the crankshaft bolt with a breaker bar and socket

9.7b If a chain wrench is used, wrap a piece of old drivebelt around the pulley to prevent damage to it

9.8 Remove the crankshaft pulley from the crankshaft (it should slide right off)

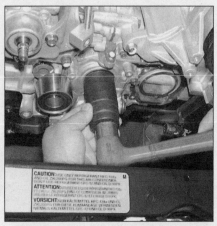

10.5 Drive the new seal in with a hammer and a deep socket

11.3 Measure from the end of the cylinder head (A) to the face of the seal (B) before removing the camshaft seals

8   Slide the pulley off the nose of the crankshaft (see illustration).
9   If you're replacing the crankshaft front oil seal, see Section 11.
10   Lubricate the hub of the pulley with clean engine oil, then slide it onto the crankshaft.
11   Install the crankshaft pulley bolt, then tighten the bolt to the torque listed in this Chapter's Specifications.
12   The remainder of installation is the reverse of removal.

10   Crankshaft front oil seal - replacement

1   Disconnect the cable from the negative terminal of the battery (see Chapter 5).
2   Remove the timing belt and crankshaft sprocket (see Section 7).
3   Carefully pry the seal out of the cover with a seal puller or a large screwdriver.
Caution: *Be careful not to scratch, gouge or distort the area that the seal fits into or an oil leak will develop.*
Note: *An alternative method is to drill two 1/8-inch holes in the seal, being careful not to hit the seal housing or crankshaft. Screw two self-tapping screws into the holes and pull on them, alternating side to side, with a slide-hammer or self-locking pliers on the screws.*
4   Clean the bore to remove any old seal material and corrosion. Position the new seal in the bore with the seal lip (usually the side with the spring) facing IN (toward the engine). A small amount of oil applied to the outer edge of the new seal will make installation easier - but don't overdo it!
5   Drive the seal into the bore with a large socket and hammer until it's completely seated (see illustration). Select a socket that's the same outside diameter as the seal and make sure the new seal is pressed into place until it bottoms against the cover flange, to the same depth as the original seal.
6   Install the sprocket and timing belt (see Section 7).

7   The remainder of installation is the reverse of removal.

11   Camshaft oil seals (timing belt engines only) - replacement

1   Remove the timing belt and camshaft sprocket(s) (see Section 7).
2   Unbolt and remove the inner timing belt covers to access the camshaft seals.
3   Measure the depth of the installed seal so that the new seal can be installed in the same location (see illustration).
4   Use a seal puller to pry the old camshaft seal from the cylinder head.
5   Install the new seal by gently tapping the seal into the cylinder head recess using a deep socket and hammer.
Note: *Drive the seal in squarely, to the same depth as the original seal was installed.*
6   The remainder of installation is the reverse of removal.

12   Camshafts and valve actuating components - removal, inspection and installation

Removal

2011 and 2012 Legacy turbo/all 2013 and later Legacy models and all 2012 and later Forester models

1   Remove the engine (see Chapter 2B). On timing chain models, remove the timing chain cover, timing chains and sprockets (see Section 8). On timing belt models, remove the timing belt, camshaft sprockets and inner timing belt covers (see Section 7).

2012 and earlier Legacy non-turbo/2010 Legacy turbo and all 2010 and earlier Forester models

2   Remove the timing belt, camshaft sprock-

ets and inner timing belt covers (see Section 7).

All models

3   Remove the valve covers (see Section 4).
4   Remove the Camshaft Position (CMP) sensors (see Chapter 6).
Note: *On 2.5L (DOHC) non-turbocharged models and 2.0L turbocharged models, the camshafts are meant to be removed as an assembly with the camshaft carrier.*

2.5L (SOHC) non-turbocharged engines

5   Working in the reverse of the tightening sequence (see illustration 12.32b), gradually loosen the rocker arm bolts.
6   Install special tool #18258AA000 onto the intake rocker arm assembly to lock it in position before lifting the assembly from the cylinder head.
Caution: *If the special service tool is not available, hold the rocker arm shaft from each end to prevent the rockers from popping off once the bolts are removed.*
7   Store all the components in an organized manner.
8   Remove the timing belt tensioner and the tensioner bracket (see Section 7).
9   Remove the oil dipstick tube.
10   Remove the camshaft end cap assembly. Follow the reverse of the tightening sequence (see illustration 11.32a). Carefully remove the camshaft from the cylinder head. Remove the camshaft oil seal and the end plug from the camshaft end cap assembly.
Caution: *When removing the camshaft, make sure the camshaft lobes do not nick the journal bores.*

2.5L (DOHC) turbocharged models

11   Check the valve clearances (see Section 14). Write down all of your measurements.
12   Disconnect the VVT oil flow control solenoid connectors from each cylinder head (see Chapter 6), if equipped.
13   Remove the timing belt tensioner and the tensioner bracket (see Section 7). Remove the oil dipstick tube.

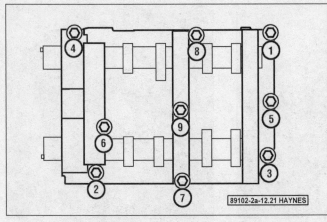

12.21 Camshaft carrier loosening sequence - left-side shown, right-side similar

12.26 Check the lifters for scuffing, cracks or chips

12.29a Measure the camshaft bearing journal diameter

12.29b Measure the camshaft lobe at its greatest dimension . . .

12.29c . . . and subtract the camshaft lobe diameter at its smallest dimension to obtain the lobe lift specification

14   Remove the oil pipe from the VVT oil flow control solenoid and the cylinder head (see Chapter 6), if equipped.

15   Working from the outer bolts to the center bolts, gradually loosen the intake camshaft cap bolts. Lift the intake camshaft cap assembly from the cylinder head.

16   Working from the outer bolts to the center bolts, gradually loosen the exhaust camshaft cap bolts. Lift the exhaust camshaft cap assembly from the cylinder head.

17   Store all the components in an organized manner so they won't get mixed up.

18   Remove the valve lifters if the valve clearance must be adjusted.

2.5L (DOHC) non-turbocharged models and 2.0L turbocharged models

19   Remove the fuel injectors and fuel rail (see Chapter 4).

20   On 2.0L models, remove the scavenge pump oil line banjo fittings and oil pump lines from the right-side cylinder head and the high-pressure fuel pump from the left-side cylinder head (see Chapter 4).

21   Remove the camshaft carrier bolts in sequence (see illustration), evenly at a 1/4-

turn at a time until the bolts are all removed then remove the camshaft carrier assembly.

22   Remove the two O-rings at the front of the cylinder head then remove the roller rocker arms from the cylinder head keeping them in order. The must be installed in their original locations.

23   Remove the valve shim and roller rocker arm pivot (lash adjuster) from the cylinder head.

24   Remove the camshaft carrier bolts and separate the camshafts from the carrier.

25   Store all the components in an organized manner so they won't get mixed up.

Inspection

26   On 2.5L (DOHC) turbocharged models, remove the lifters from the cylinder heads. Keep the lifters organized so they can be returned to their original locations. The lifters should come out by hand. Check each lifter for signs of wear (see illustration). Measure the lifter outer diameter and verify with this Chapter's Specifications. Measure the inside diameter of the lifter bore in the cylinder head. If the distance between the outer diameter and

the inner diameter (bore) exceeds the lifter-to-bore measurement listed in this Chapter's Specifications, replace the cylinder head.

Caution: *Do not use pliers to remove the lifters. If they are varnished and can't be removed easily, spray some carburetor cleaner around their bores and let it soak in.*

27   Check the pivot seat in each rocker arm and the pivot faces. Look for galling, stress cracks and unusual wear patterns. If the rocker arms are worn or damaged, replace them with new ones.

28   Visually examine the camshaft lobes, journals, bearing caps, pivot points and metal-to-metal contact areas. Check for score marks, pitting and evidence of overheating (blue, discolored areas). If wear is excessive or damage is evident, the component will have to be replaced. Also check the front of the camshaft for wear where the seal rides.

29   Using a micrometer, measure camshaft journal diameter and lobe height (see illustrations), and compare your measurements to this Chapter's Specifications. If the lobe height is less than the minimum allowable, the camshaft is worn and must be replaced.

30   On 2.5L (SOHC) non-turbocharged

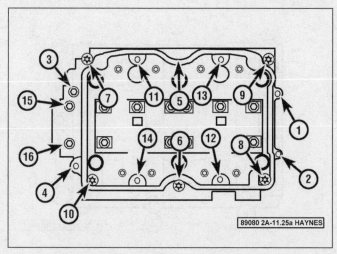

12.32a Camshaft end cap tightening sequence (2.5L SOHC non-turbocharged engines)

12.32b Rocker arm bolt tightening sequence (2.5L SOHC non-turbocharged engines)

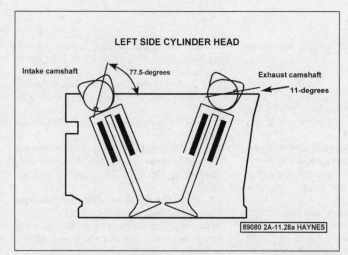

12.35a Install the camshaft at the correct angle to avoid damaging the valves during installation. The left-side intake camshaft will have to be rotated 80-degrees clockwise, and the left-side exhaust camshaft will have to be rotated 45-degrees counterclockwise after the camshafts have been installed

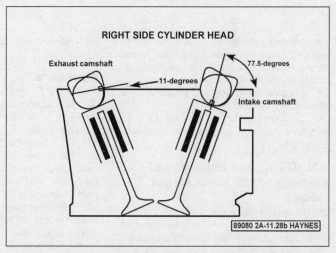

12.35b Right-side camshaft angle. The right-side cylinder head camshafts do not have to be rotated after installation to align the timing marks

engines, measure the inside diameter of each camshaft journal bore. If the oil clearance (bore diameter minus the camshaft journal diameter) is greater than the listed in this Chapter's Specifications, the cylinder head, camshaft and camshaft end cap must be replaced (the clearance can also be checked with Plastigage). On turbocharged engines, install the camshafts onto the cylinder head (with the lifters removed) and use Plastigage to determine the oil clearance.

Installation
31 Lubricate the camshaft journals and lobes with camshaft installation lubricant.

2.5L (SOHC) non-turbocharged engines
32 Prepare the camshaft end cap assembly for installation. Apply a bead of anaerobic

sealant approximately 0.12 inch (3 mm) wide onto the outer edge of the end cap assembly and allow the RTV sealant to set-up (follow the manufacturer's recommendations). Install the camshafts carefully onto the cylinder heads. Use camshaft installation lubricant applied to the camshaft lobes. Install the end cap assembly and tighten the bolts, in sequence (see illustration), to the torque listed in this Chapter's Specifications. Install the rocker arm assembly and tighten the bolts, in sequence (see illustration), to the torque listed in this Chapter's Specifications. Install a new camshaft oil seal (see Section 11) and the end plug.
Note: *The end plug must be installed with a special tool, and must be even with the outer edge of the cylinder head and the end cap assembly.*
33 Using a special spring installer tool,

rotate the spring stopper counterclockwise to lock the adjuster pin.
34 Adjust the valve clearances (see Section 14).

2.5L (DOHC) turbocharged engines
35 Lubricate the valve lifters with camshaft installation lubricant and install them in their original locations. If any valve clearance was out of specification, calculate the proper-thickness of lifter to install. Apply camshaft installation lubricant to the camshaft lobes. Install the camshafts with the base circle of the camshaft lobes nearest the valve lifters (see illustrations).
36 Apply a small amount of anaerobic sealant to each number one cap sealing surface. Lubricate the bearing surface of the camshaft caps with camshaft installation lubricant and install them in their original locations. Tighten

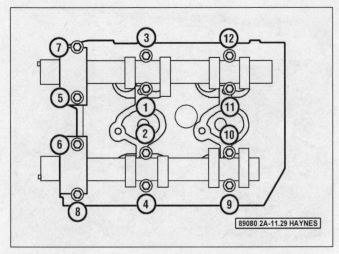

12.36 Camshaft bearing cap tightening sequence - 2.5L (DOHC) turbocharged engines

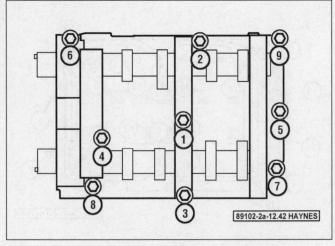

12.42 Camshaft carrier tightening sequence - left-side shown, right-side similar

the camshaft bearing cap bolts in the recommended sequence (see illustration) to the torque listed in this Chapter's Specifications. Install new camshaft oil seals (see Section 11).

37   Check and, if necessary, adjust the valve clearances (see Section 14).

38   Connect the VVT oil flow control solenoid connectors on each cylinder head (see Chapter 6).

2.5L (DOHC) non-turbocharged models and 2.0L turbocharged models

39   Lubricate the roller rocker arm pivots (lash adjusters) and shims with camshaft installation lubricant and install them in their original locations. If any valve clearance was out of specification, calculate the proper-thickness of shim to install. Apply camshaft installation lubricant to the camshaft lobes.

40   Install the roller rocker pivots, shims to the cylinder head then reinstall the roller rocker arms in their original locations.

41   Prepare the camshaft cap assembly for installation. Apply a bead of anaerobic sealant approximately 0.12 inch (3 mm) wide onto the outer edge of the end cap assembly and allow the RTV sealant to set-up (follow the manufacturer's recommendations). Install the camshafts carefully into the carrier. Use camshaft installation lubricant applied to the camshaft lobes. Install the camshaft cap assembly and tighten the bolts evenly to the torque listed this Chapter's Specifications. Rotate the camshaft carrier to the zero lift position (see Section 8).

42   Apply a bead of THREE BOND anaerobic sealant approximately 0.14 inch (5 mm) wide onto the sealing surface of the camshaft carrier outer edge and allow the RTV sealant to set-up (follow the manufacturer's recommendations). Install the camshaft carrier to the cylinder head and tighten the bolts in sequence (see illustration) evenly to

the torque listed this Chapter's Specifications.

All models

43   On 2.5L (SOHC) models and 2.5L (DOHC) turbocharged models, install the camshaft sprockets or actuators and timing belt (see Section 7).

44   On 2.5L (DOHC) non-turbocharged and 2.0L turbocharged models, install the timing chain cover, timing chains and sprockets (see Section 8) then install the engine assembly (see Chapter 2B).

45   Install the valve covers (see Section 4).

Note: *On 2.5L (DOHC) non-turbocharged and 2.0L turbocharged models, install the valve covers before installing the engine assembly.*

46   The remainder of the installation is the reverse of removal.

Note: *Use new gaskets on the valve covers.*

47   Start the engine, listen for unusual valve train noises and check for oil leaks at the valve cover gaskets.

13   Cylinder heads - removal and installation

Warning: *Wait until the engine is completely cool before beginning this procedure.*

Removal

1   Relieve the fuel pressure (see Chapter 4).

2   Disconnect the cable from the negative terminal of the battery (see Chapter 5).

3   Drain the cooling system and remove the spark plugs (see Chapter 1).

4   On 2011 and 2012 Legacy turbo/all 2013 and later Legacy models and all 2012 and later Forester models, remove the engine from the vehicle (see Chapter 2B) and place the engine on a stand.

5   On timing belt models, remove the timing belt, camshaft sprockets and inner timing belt covers (see Section 7).

6   On timing chain models, remove the timing chain cover and timing chains (see Section 8).

7   Remove the camshafts (see Section 12).

8   On 2.0L turbocharged models, remove the high-pressure fuel delivery lines (see Chapter 4) and the EGR cooler (see Chapter 6).

9   Disconnect the exhaust manifold from the cylinder heads (see Section 6).

Note: *Apply penetrating oil to the fasteners before beginning the procedure, and allow it to soak-in for awhile.*

10   Remove the intake manifold and the tumble generator valve (lower intake manifolds) assemblies, if equipped (see Section 5). Remove any hoses or brackets bolted to the cylinder heads.

11   When removing the right-side cylinder head remove the EGR tube, if equipped (see Chapter 6) from the rear of the cylinder head.

12   On 2013 and later models, when removing the left-side cylinder head remove the air conditioning compressor mounting bolts (see Chapter 3) and move the compressor out of the way with out disconnecting the lines.

13   Loosen the cylinder head bolts in the reverse of the tightening sequence (see illustration 13.18a or 13.18b).

14   Remove the cylinder heads and the old gaskets.

Note: *The block and cylinder heads are aluminum. Do not pry between the cylinder heads and the crankcase, as damage to the gasket sealing surfaces may result. Instead use a soft-faced hammer to tap the cylinder heads and break the gasket seal.*

15   Cylinder head disassembly and inspection procedures should be performed by a qualified automotive machine shop.

13.16 Be careful not to gouge the aluminum surfaces of the cylinder head or block when removing the old gasket material

13.17 Place the new head gasket over the dowels in the block - look for markings on the gaskets to indicate TOP or FRONT

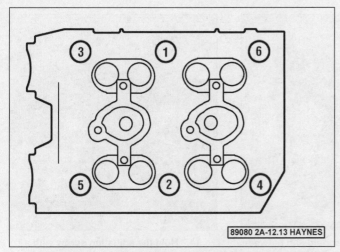

89080 2A-12.13 HAYNES

13.18a Cylinder head bolt tightening sequence - 2.5L (SOHC) engines and all 2.5L (DOHC) turbocharged engines

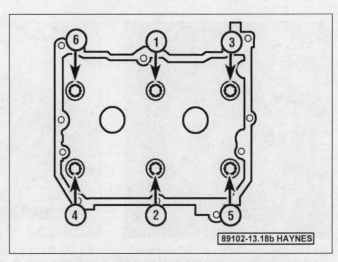

89102-13.18b HAYNES

13.18b Cylinder head bolt tightening sequence (Steps 1, 2, 4, 5 and 6) - 2.5L (DOHC) non-turbocharged models and all 2.0L turbocharged models

Installation

16   Clean the gasket mating surfaces of the cylinder heads and crankcase (see illustration) with brake system cleaner. They must be clean and oil-free.

17   Install the cylinder head gasket onto the cylinder head locating dowels on the engine block (see illustration).

18   Install the cylinder head(s). Lubricate the bolt threads and washers with engine oil, then install them hand-tight. Use a torque-angle meter (available at most automotive parts stores) or mark the bolt heads with white paint, and tighten the bolts, in sequence (see illustrations), to the torque and angle listed in this Chapter's Specifications.

19   The remainder of installation is the reverse of removal.

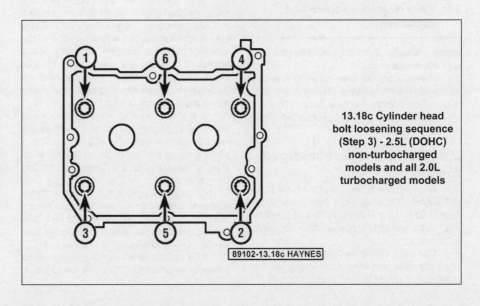

89102-13.18c HAYNES

13.18c Cylinder head bolt loosening sequence (Step 3) - 2.5L (DOHC) non-turbocharged models and all 2.0L turbocharged models

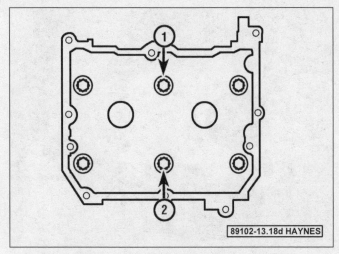

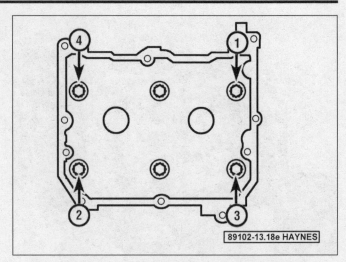

13.18d Cylinder head bolt tightening sequence (Step 7) - 2.5L (DOHC) non-turbocharged models and all 2.0L turbocharged models

13.18e Cylinder head bolt tightening sequence (Step 8) - 2.5L (DOHC) non-turbocharged models and all 2.0L turbocharged models

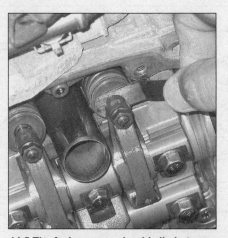

14.4 Align the arrow on the left camshaft sprocket with the notch in the inner timing belt cover

14.5 The feeler gauge should slip between the valve stem tip and rocker arm with a slight amount of drag

14.7 Hold the adjusting screw with a screwdriver and tighten the locknut

14   Valve clearance - check and adjustment

Note: *The valve clearances must be checked with the engine cold.*
1   Remove the air filter housing and the resonator (see Chapter 4). Remove the battery and the battery tray (see Chapter 5).
2   Remove the valve covers (see Section 4).

2.5L SOHC non-turbocharged models

3   Remove the timing belt cover from the left side (driver's) cylinder head (see Section 7). It is only necessary to see the timing marks on the left side sprocket for valve adjustment.
4   Use the timing mark (arrow) on the camshaft sprocket (see illustration) to position the number one piston at TDC (see Section 3).

5   With the number one piston at TDC, measure the clearance of the intake and exhaust valves on the number one cylinder (see illustration). Insert a feeler gauge of the specified thickness (see this Chapter's Specifications) between the valve stem tip and the rocker arm. The feeler gauge should slip between the valve stem tip and rocker arm with a slight amount of drag.
6   If the clearance is incorrect (too loose or too tight), loosen the locknut and turn the adjusting screw slowly until you can feel a slight drag on the feeler gauge as you withdraw it from between the valve stem tip and the rocker arm.
7   Once the clearance is adjusted, hold the adjusting screw with a screwdriver (to keep it from turning) and tighten the locknut (see illustration). Recheck the clearance to make sure it hasn't changed after tightening the locknut.
8   The valves in the remaining cylinders can now be checked. It is essential to adjust

cylinder 3 next, followed by 2 and finally 4 (follow the firing order sequence). Before checking clearances, bring each cylinder (in firing order) to TDC by turning the crankshaft 180 degrees in a clockwise direction (the camshaft sprocket will rotate 90-degrees for each 180-degree turn of the crankshaft). Verify TDC by checking the position of the arrow on the camshaft sprocket. With the number 1 cylinder at TDC, the arrow should be pointing straight UP. Be sure the valves are closed at each adjustment position.
9   If necessary, repeat the adjustment procedure described in Steps 5, 6 and 7 until all the valves are adjusted to specifications.
10   Install the valve covers (use new gaskets) (see Section 4).
11   Install the spark plug wires and the various hoses and vacuum lines (if removed).
12   Start the engine and check for oil leakage between the valve covers and the cylinder heads.

2.5L DOHC non-turbocharged and 2.0L turbocharged models

13   Remove the engine from the vehicle (see Chapter 2B).

14   Remove the left and right side valve cover (see Section 4).

15   Place the number one cylinder at TDC (see Section 3). Using feeler gauges, measure the number 1 intake valve, number 1 exhaust and the number 3 exhaust valve clearances between the camshaft lobe and the roller rocker. Write down your measurements.

16   Rotate the engine 360-degrees. Using feeler gauges, measure the number 3 intake valve clearances between the camshaft lobe and the roller rocker. Write down your measurement.

17   Place the number two cylinder at TDC. Using feeler gauges, measure the number 2 intake valve, number 2 exhaust and the number 4 exhaust valve clearances between the camshaft lobe and the roller rocker. Write down your measurements.

18   Rotate the engine 360-degrees. Using feeler gauges, measure the number 4 intake valve clearances between the camshaft lobe and the roller rocker. Write down your measurement.

19   After all the valve clearances are checked and recorded, replace the shim on any roller rocker arm pivot (lash adjuster) with a clearance that is out of specification. Remove the timing chains (see Section 8), camshaft(s) from the necessary cylinder head(s) (see Section 12).

20   Measure the thickness of the shim with a micrometer. To calculate the correct thickness of a replacement shim that will place the valve clearance within the specified value, use the following formula:

Engine type FB25#####A

Intake valve

   $S = (T + 1.54 \times (0.0051 \text{ inch } (0.13 \text{ mm})))$

Exhaust valve

   $S = (T + 1.69 \times (0.0087 \text{ inch } (0.22 \text{ mm})))$

S = Shim thickness needed
V = Measured camshaft clearance to roller
T = Old shim thickness

Engine type FB25#####F

Intake valve

   $S = (T + 1.69 \times (0.0051 \text{ inch } (0.13 \text{ mm})))$

Exhaust valve

   $S = (T + 1.87 \times (0.0087 \text{ inch } (0.22 \text{ mm})))$

S = Shim thickness needed
V = Measured camshaft clearance to roller
T = Old shim thickness

21   Select a shim with a thickness as close as possible to the thickness calculated. Shims are available in varying sizes. Consult with a dealer parts department or other qualified automotive parts department for availability and part numbers for each shim.

22   Repeat this procedure until all the valves which are out of clearance have been corrected.

23   Installation is the reverse of removal.

2.5L DOHC turbocharged models

24   Remove the timing belt cover from the right-side camshaft assembly to expose the timing belt sprocket (see Section 7).

25   Turn the crankshaft pulley clockwise until the arrow mark on the camshaft sprocket is set approximately at the 2:30 clock position. Using feeler gauges, measure the number 1 intake valve and the number 3 exhaust valve clearances. Write down your measurements.

26   Turn the crankshaft until the timing marks on the sprocket are at approximately the 4:30 clock position. Measure the number 2 exhaust valve and the number 3 intake valve clearances.

27   Turn the crankshaft until the timing marks on the sprocket are at approximately the 7:30 clock position. Measure the number 2 intake valve and the number 4 exhaust valve clearances.

28   Turn the crankshaft until the timing marks on the sprocket are at approximately the 10:30 clock position. Measure the number 1 exhaust valve and the number 4 intake valve clearances.

29   After all the valve clearances are checked and recorded, replace the lifter on any valve with a clearance that is out of specification. Remove the camshaft(s) from the necessary cylinder head(s) (see Section 12).

30   Measure the thickness of the lifter with a micrometer. To calculate the correct thickness of a replacement lifter that will place the valve clearance within the specified value, use the following formula:

Intake valve

   $S = (V + T) - 0.0075 \text{ inch } (0.19 \text{ mm})$

Exhaust valve

   $S = (V + T) - 0.0138 \text{ inch } (0.35 \text{ mm})$

15.13a Remove the oil pan bolts (not all bolts are visible in this view)

T = thickness of the old lifter
V = valve clearance measured
S = thickness of the new lifter

31   Select a lifter with a thickness as close as possible to the thickness calculated. Lifters are available in size increments of 0.0004 inch (0.01 mm). Consult with a dealer parts department or other qualified automotive parts department for availability and part numbers for each lifter.

32   Repeat this procedure until all the valves which are out of clearance have been corrected.

33   Installation of the spark plugs, valve cover, spark plug wires and boots, etc. is the reverse of removal.

15   Oil pan(s) - removal and installation

Note: *The 2.5L DOHC non-turbocharged and 2.0L turbocharged engines are equipped with an upper and lower oil pan. 2.5L SOHC engines and 2.5L DOHC turbocharged engines are equipped with only a lower oil pan.*

Removal

Lower oil pan

1   Disconnect the cable from the negative terminal of the battery (see Chapter 5).

2   Remove the air filter housing, intake ducts and the resonator (see Chapter 4). **Note:** *Depending on the year and model of the vehicle, the air filter housing may not need to be removed.*

3   On turbocharged models, remove the intercooler (see Chapter 4).

4   Remove the engine support brace (see Section 19).

5   Remove the radiator support brackets (see Chapter 3).

6   Raise the vehicle and support it securely on jackstands. Remove the front wheels and tires.

7   Remove the engine splash shield (see Section 6).

8   On non-turbocharged models, remove the exhaust manifold (see Section 6). **Note:** *It will be necessary to remove the exhaust manifold for added clearance when the engine is raised for oil pan bolt access.*

9   Drain the engine oil and remove the oil filter (see Chapter 1).

10   Remove the dipstick tube. Locate the dipstick tube mounting bolt on the cylinder head, remove the bolt and slide the dipstick tube out of the lower dipstick tube housing located on the oil pan. **Note:** *Depending on the year and model of the vehicle, the dipstick tube mounting bracket may be located slightly differently.*

11   Connect an engine hoist to the engine (see Chapter 2B).

12   Remove the nuts from the engine mounts at the frame (see Section 19), then raise the engine two inches with the engine hoist.

13   Remove the bolts securing the oil pan to the engine (see illustrations).

15.13b Remove the rear oil pan bolts through the access holes in the crossmember

15.15 Remove the oil pump pickup tube bolts and remove the pickup tube with the lower oil pan

Note: *There are two oil pan bolt access holes in thecenter crossmember (see illustration).*

14   Tap on the pan with a soft-faced hammer to break the gasket seal, then lower the oil pan from the engine. A thin putty knife can be inserted between the pan and the block to break the gasket seal, but the block is aluminum, so do not use a screwdriver or other sharp tool at the pan/block interface.

Caution: *Before using force on the oil pan, be sure all the bolts have been removed.*

15   If the oil pump pickup tube interferes with oil pan removal, remove the pickup tube bolts and remove the oil pan and pickup tube from the vehicle (see illustration).

Upper oil pan - 2.5L (DOHC) non-turbocharged and 2.0L turbocharged engines only

16   Remove the engine from the vehicle and attach the motor to an engine stand (see Chapter 2B).

17   Remove the water pump and thermostat cover (see Chapter 3).

18   Remove the lower oil pan (see Steps 13 through 15).

19   Remove the timing chain cover (see Section 8).

20   If not already removed, disconnect the oil pan level sensor and wiring harness.

21   Remove the upper oil pan mounting bolts and remove the upper oil pan.

Installation

22   Using a gasket scraper, scrape off all traces of the old gasket from the engine block and the oil pan. Be especially careful not to nick or gouge the gasket sealing surfaces of the crankcases (they are made of aluminum and are quite soft).

23   Clean the oil pan with solvent and dry it thoroughly. Check the gasket sealing surfaces for distortion. If the oil pan is distorted at the bolt hole areas, straighten the flange by supporting it from below on a wood block and tapping the bolt holes with the rounded end of a ball-peen hammer. Wipe the gasket surfaces clean with a rag soaked in lacquer thinner or acetone.

Upper oil pan - 2.5L DOHC non-turbocharged and 2.0L turbocharged engines only

24   With the upper oil pan sealing surface clean, apply a 1/8 inch (5 mm) bead of THREE

BOND sealant to the mounting surface of the upper pan.

25   Install the upper oil pan to the cylinder block then install the mounting bolts hand tight.

26   Tighten the upper oil pan mounting bolts in sequence (see illustration) to the torque listed in this Chapter's Specifications.

27   Install the lower oil pan (see Steps 29 through 31).

28   Install the engine (see Chapter 2B), remainder of installation is the reverse of removal. After refilling with fresh oil and installing a new filter, start the engine and check for oil leaks.

Lower oil pan

29   Install a new O-ring on the pickup tube and place it in the oil pan.

30   Apply a thin coat of gasket sealant to the new oil pan gasket in place it carefully on the oil pan.

31   Raise the oil pan in position and install the pickup tube. Tighten the mounting bolts to the torque listed in this Chapter's Specifications. Be careful not to disturb the gasket. Install the oil pan to the engine block and tighten the bolts hand-tight. Working from the center of the pan out to the ends, tighten the bolts to the torque listed in this Chapter's Specifications. Do not overtighten the bolts or oil leaks may occur.

32   The remainder of installation is the reverse of removal. After refilling with fresh oil and installing a new filter, start the engine and check for oil leaks.

16   Oil pump - removal, inspection and installation

Warning: *Wait until the engine is completely cool before beginning this procedure.*

Note: *On 2.0L turbocharged engines and 2.5L DOHC non-turbocharged engines, the oil pump is not serviceable separately from the timing chain cover.*

Removal

1   Raise the front of the vehicle and support it securely on jackstands.

2   Drain the engine oil and remove the oil filter (see Chapter 1).

3   Remove the timing belt, the tensioner and crankshaft sprocket (see Section 7).

4   Remove the upper timing belt idler pulley, idler pulley number 1, then idler sprocket number 2 (see Section 7).

5   Drain the coolant (see Chapter 1).

6   Remove the radiator (see Chapter 3).

7   Remove the coolant pipes from the oil cooler at the front of the engine.

8   Remove the water pump (see Chapter 3).

9   Remove the radiator (see Chapter 3).

10   Remove the Crankshaft Position (CKP) sensor (see Chapter 6).

15.26 Upper oil pan tightening sequence

89102-2a-15.26 HAYNES

16.11 Remove the oil pump mounting bolts

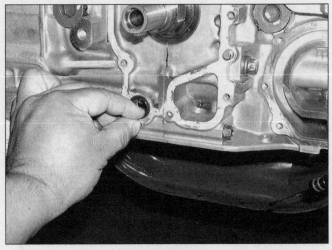

**16.22 Install a new O-ring into the oil pump housing or
engine block**

11   Remove the mounting bolts and the oil pump (see illustration). Place a drain pan under the oil pump to catch the oil that will be spilled as the pump is removed.

Inspection

12   Remove the pump cover screws from the back of the oil pump assembly and remove the cover.
13   Apply alignment marks to the inner and outer rotors so they can be installed in their original relationship to each other. Withdraw the rotors from the pump housing. Remove the relief valve plug, washer, spring and relief valve from the pump housing.
14   Clean the components with solvent, dry them thoroughly and inspect for any obvious damage.
15   Carefully check the interior surface of the pump housing and the exterior surfaces of the rotors for score marks and damage.
16   Check the relief valve and spring for damage.
17   Check the pump housing for clogged oil passages, case cracks and damage.
18   If there is damage to any of the components, replace the oil pump assembly.
19   Install the rotors in the pump housing, then use a feeler gauge to measure the rotor tip clearance between the rotor tips; the outer rotor-to-oil pump housing clearance between the outer rotor and the pump body; and the rotor-to-cover clearance, using a depth micrometer or a precision straightedge and feeler gauge to measure the rotor-to-cover clearance (endplay). If any clearance exceeds the limit listed in this Chapter's Specifications, replace the oil pump assembly. If it checks good, reinstall the pump cover and tighten the mounting screws to the torque listed in this Chapter's Specifications.

Installation

20   Lubricate the relief valve with clean engine oil and install the relief valve, spring, washer and plug.
21   Lubricate the rotors with clean engine oil and install the rotors into the pump housing, aligning the matchmarks made previously. Install the rotor cover.
22   Replace the oil pump housing-to-engine block O-ring and install a new crankshaft oil seal (see illustration).
23   Apply a bead of anaerobic sealant to the oil pump housing sealing surface. Install the oil pump onto the engine block and tighten the oil pump housing bolts to the torque listed in this Chapter's Specifications.
24   The remainder of installation is the reverse of removal. Refill the engine with fresh oil and install a new filter (see Chapter 1). On turbo models, refill the cooling system (see Chapter 1). Start the engine and check for proper oil pressure and oil leaks.

---

17   Flywheel/driveplate - removal and installation

Removal

1   Remove the transaxle (see Chapter 7A or 7B). If equipped with a manual transaxle, remove the clutch disc and pressure plate (see Chapter 8).
2   Remove the attaching bolts and separate the flywheel/driveplate from the crankshaft.

Installation

3   Apply thread locking compound to the bolt threads. On automatic transaxle models, align the small hole in the driveplate with

the mark on the backplate. Hold the flywheel/driveplate in position and install the bolts.
Note: *The flywheel/driveplate can only be installed in one position, since the bolt holes are not equally spaced. If the bolt holes do not align, rotate the flywheel/driveplate relative to the crankshaft until they all are in exact alignment.*
4   Hold the flywheel/driveplate with an appropriate tool so that it doesn't turn, and tighten the bolts, in a crisscross pattern, to the torque listed in this Chapter's Specifications.
5   Install the clutch disc and clutch cover assembly (see Chapter 8), if equipped.
6   Install the transaxle (see Chapter 7A or 7B).

---

18   Rear main oil seal - replacement

1   Remove the transaxle (see Chapter 7A or 7B) and, on manual transaxle models, the clutch assembly (see Chapter 8).
2   Remove the flywheel/driveplate (see Section 17).
3   Note the installation depth of the seal and then pry the rear main oil seal from the back of the block with a seal removal tool. Be very careful not to nick the crankshaft seal surface with the tool.
4   Clean the seal bore and make sure the seal mounting surface is free of burrs.
5   Lubricate the new seal's inner lip with multi-purpose grease, and the outer diameter with clean engine oil.
6   Drive the new seal in place squarely with a seal driver. Drive the seal to the original depth as noted during removal.
7   Install the flywheel/driveplate, clutch assembly (if equipped) and transaxle.

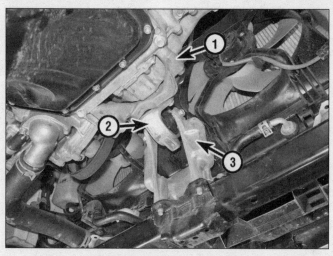

19.10 Front engine mount details

1   Mount-to-engine bracket   3   Mount-to-body bracket
2   Front mount

19.19 Location of the upper engine mount bolts

19   Engine mounts - check and replacement

Check

1   Engine mounts seldom require attention, but broken or deteriorated mounts should be replaced immediately or the added strain placed on the driveline components may cause damage.

2   During the check, the engine must be raised slightly to remove the weight from the mounts. Disconnect the cable from the negative terminal of the battery (see Chapter 5).

3   Raise the vehicle and support it securely on jackstands, then position the jack under the engine oil pan. Place a wood block between the jack head and the oil pan, then carefully raise the engine just enough to take the weight off the mounts.

4   Check the mounts to see if the rubber is cracked, hardened or separated from the metal plates. Sometimes the rubber will split right down the center. Rubber preservative may be applied to the mounts to slow deterioration.

5   Check for relative movement between the mount plates and the engine or frame (use a large screwdriver or pry bar to attempt to move the mounts). If movement is noted, lower the engine and tighten the mounting fasteners to the torque listed in this Chapter's Specifications.

Replacement

6   Disconnect the cable from the negative terminal of the battery (see Chapter 5).

Front engine mount

7   Raise the vehicle and support it securely on jackstands.

8   Connect an engine hoist to the engine (see Chapter 2B).

9   Remove the engine splash shield (see illustration 6.3).

10   Remove the engine mount bracket-to-body bolts (see illustration).

11   Using a an engine hoist, raise the front of the engine high enough to take the weight off of the front mount, but do not force the engine up too high. If anything interferes before the mounts are free, remove the component for clearance. Block the engine in this position with wood blocks.

12   Remove the mount through bolt then remove the mount-to-body bracket.

13   Remove the mount-to-engine bracket bolts and separate the mount form the bracket.

14   If necessary remove the mount bracket-to-engine bolts and remove the bracket.

15   Install a new engine mount on to the bracket. Install the bolts and tighten them to the torque listed in this Chapter's Specifications.

16   Install the engine mount bracket-to-body bolts, then raise the engine and remove the wood blocks and lower the engine to its original height and install the through bolt and nut then tighten the fasteners to the torque listed in this Chapter's Specifications.

Upper engine mount

17   Remove the air filter housing (see Chapter 4).

18   On turbocharged models, remove the intercooler (see Chapter 4).

19   Remove the upper engine mount brace mounting bolts (see illustration) and remove the mount from the engine compartment.

20   Installation is the reverse of removal.

Lower engine mounts

Note: *It will be necessary to remove components that will interfere with the engine when it is raised.*

21   Raise the vehicle and support it securely on jackstands.

22   Connect an engine hoist to the engine (see Chapter 2B).

23   Remove the engine splash shield (see Section 6).

24   Remove the exhaust manifolds from the cylinder heads (see Section 6).

25   Remove the engine mount locknut from the stud projecting through the crossmember (see illustrations).

26   Raise the front of the engine high enough for the mount stud to clear the crossmember, but do not force the engine up too high. If anything interferes before the mounts are free, remove the component for clearance. Block the engine in this position with wood blocks.

27   Remove the two bolts securing the mount to the engine block and remove the mount.

28   Slip the new engine mount between the crossmember and the engine. Install the bolts into the engine block and tighten them to the torque listed in this Chapter's Specifications.

29   Lower the engine slowly, making sure that both lower studs go through their respective holes in the crossmember. Remove the wood blocks and lower the engine to its original height and tighten the fasteners to the torque listed in this Chapter's Specifications.

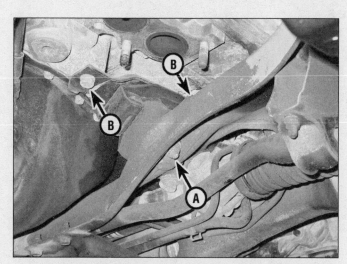

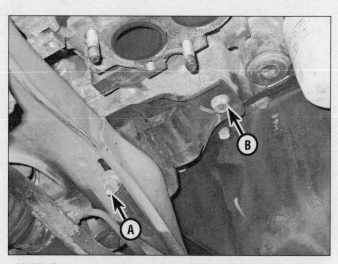

19.25a Remove the lock nut (A) and the engine mount bolts (B - one bolt hidden from view) - right side mount

19.25b Remove the lock nut (A) and the engine mount bolts (B - one bolt hidden from view) - left side mount

Notes

Chapter 2 Part B
General engine overhaul procedures

Contents

Specifications

General

Bore and stroke		
2.0L turbocharged (DOHC) engines	3.39 x 3.39 inches	86.0 x 86.0 mm
2.5L engines		
Legacy models		
2012 and earlier models	3.92 x 3.11 inches	99.5 x 79.0 mm
2013 and later models	3.70 x 3.54 inches	94.0 x 9.0 mm
Forester models		
Non-turbocharged (DOHC) engines	3.70 x 3.54 inches	94.0 x 9.0 mm
Turbocharged (DOHC) engines	3.92 x 3.11 inches	99.5 x 79.0 mm
Displacement		
2.0L turbocharged (DOHC) engines	121.92 cubic inches	1,998 cc
2.5L engines		
Legacy models		
2012 and earlier engines	149.94 cubic inches	2,457 cc
2013 and later engines	152.43 cubic inches	2,498 cc
Forester models		
Non-turbocharged (DOHC) engines	152.43 cubic inches	2,498 cc
Turbocharged (DOHC) engines	149.93 cubic inches	2.457 cc
Cylinder compression pressure (at 200 to 300 rpm)		
2.0L turbocharged (DOHC) engines	196 to 254 psi	1,350 to 1,750 kPa
2.5L engines		
Non-turbocharged (SOHC) engines	148 to 185 psi	1,020 to 1,275 kPa
Non-turbocharged (DOHC) engines		
Legacy models	142 to 171 psi	981 to 1,177 kPa
Forester models	152 to 203 psi	1,050 to 1,400 kPa

General (continued)

Compression ratio
  2.0L turbocharged (DOHC) engines 10.6:1
  2.5L engines
    Non-turbocharged (SOHC) engines 10.0:1
    Non-turbocharged (DOHC) engines
      Legacy models
        2014 and earlier models.. 10.0:1
        2015 and later models.. 10.3:1
      Forester models 10.0:1
    Turbocharged (DOHC) engines
      Legacy models
        2011 and earlier models.. 8.4:1
        2012 models.. 9.5:1
      Forester models 8.4:1

Oil pressure

2.0L engines		
@ 600 rpm	5.1 psi	35 kPa
@ 6,000 rpm	46.6 psi	321 kPa
2.5L engines		
Legacy models		
SOHC engines		
@ 600 rpm	14 psi	98 kPa
@ 5000 rpm	43 psi	294 kPa
DOHC engines		
2012 and earlier models		
@ 600 rpm	14 psi	98 kPa
@ 6,000 rpm	56.8 psi	392 kPa
2013 models		
@ 600 rpm	4.3 psi	30 kPa
@ 6,000 rpm	37.7 psi	260 kPa
2014 and later models		
@ 600 rpm	5.8 psi	40 kPa
@ 6,000 rpm	46.8 psi	323 kPa
Forester models		
Non-turbocharged DOHC engines		
2012 models		
@ 600 rpm	5.8 psi	40 kPa
@ 6,000 rpm	46.8 psi	323 kPa
2013 and 2014 models		
@ 600 rpm	4.3 psi	30 kPa
@ 6,000 rpm	37.7 psi	260 kPa
2015 and later models		
@ 600 rpm	5.8 psi	40 kPa
@ 6,000 rpm	46.8 psi	323 kPa
Turbocharged DOHC engines		
@ 600 rpm	14 psi	98 kPa
@ 5,000 rpm	43 psi	294 kPa

Valves

Valve clearance .... See Chapter 2A

Crankcase

Mating surface warpage limit...	0.001 inch	0.025 mm
Surface grinding limit...	0.004 inch	0.100 mm

Torque specifications

	Ft-lbs (unless otherwise indicated)	Nm

Note: *One foot-pound (ft-lb) of torque is equivalent to 12 inch-pounds (in-lbs) of torque. Torque values below approximately 15 ft-lbs are expressed in inch-pounds, because most foot-pound torque wrenches are not accurate at these smaller values.*

	Ft-lbs (unless otherwise indicated)	Nm
Engine-to-transaxle bolts	37	50
Connecting rod cap bolts/nuts		
Non-turbocharged models		
SOHC engine models	33	45
DOHC engine models		
Step 1	89 in-lbs	10
Step 2	16.2	22
Turbocharged models*	38.4	52
Crankcase halves mounting bolts		
2012 and earlier non-turbocharged models and all 2.5L turbocharged models (see illustrations 16.5a, 16.5b and 16.5c)		
Step 1, Bolts A through D (long bolts)	88 in-lbs	10
Step 2, Bolts E through J (long bolts)	88 in-lbs	10
Step 3, Bolts A through D (long bolts)	159 in-lbs	18
Step 4, Bolts E through J (long bolts)	159 in-lbs	18
Step 5		
Bolts A and C (long bolts)	Tighten bolts an additional 90-degrees	
Bolts B and D (long bolts)	29.5	40
Step 6, Bolts E through J (long bolts)	Tighten bolts an additional 90-degrees	
Step 7, Bolts A through G (perimeter bolts)	18.5	25
Step 8, Bolt H	53 in-lbs	6
2013 and later 2.5L non-turbocharged models and 2.0L turbocharged models (see illustrations 16.5d through 16.5j)		
Step 1, see illustration 16.5d	25.8	35
Step 2, see illustration 16.5e	Loosen the bolts 180-degrees	
Step 3, see illustration 16.5d	25.8	35
Step 4, see illustration 16.5f	Loosen the bolts 180-degrees	
Step 5, see illustration 16.5g	12.5	17
Step 6, see illustration 16.5g	Tighten bolts an additional 60-degrees	
Step 7, see illustration 16.5h	Loosen the bolts 180-degrees	
Step 8, see illustration 16.5i	2.5	17
Step 9, see illustration 16.5i	Tighten bolts an additional 60-degrees	
Step 10, see illustration 16.5j (perimeter bolts)	18.4	25
Crankcase service hole plugs - 2012 and earlier non-turbocharged models and all 2.5L turbocharged models		
Plugs	51.5	70
Cover screws (left rear)	53 in-lbs	6
Torque converter bolts	See Chapter 7B	

* Use new connecting rod cap bolts

1.10a An engine block being bored. An engine rebuilder will use special machinery to recondition the cylinder bores

1.10b If the cylinders are bored, the machine shop will normally hone the engine on a machine like this

1   General information - engine overhaul

1   Included in this portion of Chapter 2 are general information and diagnostic testing procedures for determining the overall mechanical condition of your engine.

2   The information ranges from advice concerning preparation for an overhaul and the purchase of replacement parts and/or components to detailed, step-by-step procedures covering removal and installation.

3   The following Sections have been written to help you determine whether your engine needs to be overhauled and how to remove and install it once you've determined it needs to be rebuilt. For information concerning in-vehicle engine repair, see Chapter 2A.

4   This Chapter's Specifications are general in nature and include only those necessary for testing the oil pressure and checking the engine compression. Refer to Chapter 2A for additional engine Specifications.

5   It's not always easy to determine when, or if, an engine should be completely overhauled, because a number of factors must be considered.

6   High mileage is not necessarily an indication that an overhaul is needed, while low mileage doesn't preclude the need for an overhaul. Frequency of servicing is probably the most important consideration. An engine that's had regular and frequent oil and filter changes, as well as other required maintenance, will most likely give many thousands of miles of reliable service. Conversely, a neglected engine may require an overhaul very early in its service life.

7   Excessive oil consumption is an indication that piston rings, valve seals and/or valve guides are in need of attention. Make sure that oil leaks aren't responsible before deciding that the rings and/or guides are bad. Perform a cylinder compression check to determine the extent of the work required (see Section 3). Also check the vacuum readings under various conditions (see Section 4).

8   Check the oil pressure with a gauge installed in place of the oil pressure sending unit and compare it to this Chapter's Specifications (see Section 2). If it's extremely low, the bearings and/or oil pump are probably worn out.

9   Loss of power, rough running, knocking or metallic engine noises, excessive valve train noise and high fuel consumption rates may also point to the need for an overhaul, especially if they're all present at the same time. If a complete tune-up doesn't remedy the situation, major mechanical work is the only solution.

10   An engine overhaul involves restoring the internal parts to the specifications of a new engine. During overhaul, the piston rings are replaced and the cylinder walls are reconditioned (rebored and/or honed) (see illustrations). If a rebore is done by an automotive repair shop, new oversize pistons will also be installed. The main bearings and connecting rod bearings are generally replaced with new ones and, if necessary, the crankshaft may be reground to restore the journals (see illustra-tion). Generally, the valves are serviced as well, since they're usually in less-than-perfect condition at this point. While the engine is being overhauled, other components, such as the starter and alternator, can be rebuilt as well. The end result should be similar to a new engine that will give many hours of trouble free miles.

Note: *Critical cooling system components such as hoses, drivebelts, thermostat and water pump should be replaced with new parts when an engine is overhauled. The radiator should be checked carefully to ensure that it isn't clogged or leaking (see Chapter 3). If you purchase a rebuilt engine or short block, some rebuilders will not warranty their engines unless the radiator has been professionally flushed. Also, we don't recommend overhauling the oil pump - always install a new one when the engine is rebuilt.*

11   Overhauling the internal components on today's engines is a difficult and time-consuming task which requires a significant amount of specialty tools and is best left to a professional engine rebuilder (see illustrations). A competent engine rebuilder will handle the inspection

1.10c A crankshaft having a main bearing journal ground

1.11a A machinist checks for a bent connecting rod, using specialized equipment

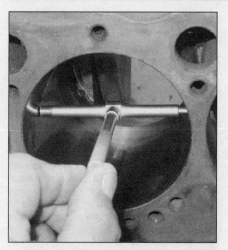

1.11b A bore gauge being used to check a cylinder bore

1.11c Uneven piston wear like this indicates a bent connecting rod

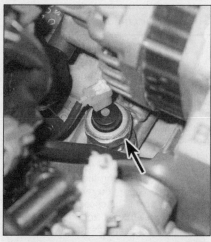

2.2a On models with a timing belt, the oil pressure sending unit is located below the alternator

of your old parts and offer advice concerning the reconditioning or replacement of the original engine. Never purchase parts or have machine work done on other components until the block has been thoroughly inspected by a professional machine shop. As a general rule, time is the primary cost of an overhaul, especially since the vehicle may be tied up for a minimum of two weeks or more. Be aware that some engine builders only have the capability to rebuild the engine you bring them while other rebuilders have a large inventory of rebuilt exchange engines in stock. Also be aware that many machine shops could take as much as two weeks time to completely rebuild your engine depending on shop workload. Sometimes it makes more sense to simply exchange your engine for another engine that's already rebuilt to save time.

2 Oil pressure check

1 Low engine oil pressure can be a sign of an engine in need of rebuilding. A low oil pressure indicator (often called an idiot light) is not a test of the oiling system. Such indicators only come on when the oil pressure is dangerously low. Even a factory oil pressure gauge in the instrument panel is only a relative indication, although much better for driver information than a warning light. A better test is with a mechanical (not electrical) oil pressure gauge.
2 Locate the oil pressure indicator sending unit (see illustrations).
3 Unscrew and remove the oil pressure sending unit and then screw in the hose for your oil pressure gauge (see illustration). If

necessary, install an adapter fitting. Use Teflon tape or thread sealant on the threads of the adapter and/or the fitting on the end of your gauge's hose.
Caution: *If it's necessary to remove the alternator for the check, completely remove the drivebelt, and also cover the B+ connector to the alternator with electrical tape.*
4 Connect an accurate tachometer to the engine, according to the tachometer manufacturer's instructions.
5 Check the oil pressure with the engine running (normal operating temperature) at the specified engine speed, and compare it to this Chapter's Specifications. If it's extremely low, the bearings and/or oil pump are probably worn out.

2.2b On models with a timing chain, the oil pressure sending unit is located on the front of the engine, below the oil filter

2.3 Remove the oil pressure sending unit and attach an oil pressure gauge - be sure the fittings you use have the same thread as the sending unit

3   Cylinder compression check

1   A cylinder compression check will tell you what mechanical condition the upper end of your engine (pistons, rings, valves, head gaskets) is in. Specifically, it can tell you if the compression is down due to leakage caused by worn piston rings, defective valves and seats or a blown head gasket.
Note: *The engine must be at normal operating temperature and the battery must be fully charged for this check.*
2   Begin by cleaning the area around the spark plugs before you remove them (compressed air should be used, if available). The idea is to prevent dirt from getting into the cylinders as the compression check is being done.
3   Remove all of the spark plugs from the engine (see Chapter 1).
4   On 2009 SOHC Legacy/2009 and 2010 SOHC Forester models (models with a coil pack), disable the ignition system by unplugging the wiring harness from the ignition coil pack (see Chapter 5) (on all other models, the ignition coils will already have been removed for spark plug removal). Disable the fuel system by removing the fuel pump fuse (see Chapter 4).
Note: *Follow the* Fuel pressure relief *procedure in Chapter 4 for disabling the fuel system.*
5   Install a compression gauge in the spark plug hole (see illustration).
6   Have an assistant depress the accelerator pedal and crank the engine over at least seven compression strokes while you watch the gauge. The compression should build up quickly in a healthy engine. Low compression on the first stroke, followed by gradually increasing pressure on succes-

sive strokes, indicates worn piston rings. A low compression reading on the first stroke, which doesn't build up during successive strokes, indicates leaking valves or a blown head gasket (a cracked head could also be the cause). Deposits on the undersides of the valve heads can also cause low compression. Record the highest gauge reading obtained.
7   Repeat the procedure for the remaining cylinders and compare the results to this Chapter's Specifications.
8   Add some engine oil (about three squirts from a plunger-type oil can) to each cylinder, through the spark plug hole, and repeat the test.
9   If the compression increases after the oil is added, the piston rings are definitely worn. If the compression doesn't increase significantly, the leakage is occurring at the valves or head gasket. Leakage past the valves may be caused by burned valve seats and/or faces or warped, cracked or bent valves.
10   If two adjacent cylinders have equally low compression, there's a strong possibility that the head gasket between them is blown. The appearance of coolant in the combustion chambers or the crankcase would verify this condition.
11   If one cylinder is slightly lower than the others, and the engine has a slightly rough idle, a worn lobe on the camshaft could be the cause.
12   If the compression is unusually high, the combustion chambers are probably coated with carbon deposits. If that's the case, the cylinder head(s) should be removed and decarbonized.
13   If compression is way down or varies greatly between cylinders, it would be a good idea to have a leak-down test performed by an automotive repair shop. This test will pin-

point exactly where the leakage is occurring and how severe it is.

4   Vacuum gauge diagnostic checks

1   A vacuum gauge provides inexpensive but valuable information about what is going on in the engine. You can check for worn rings or cylinder walls, leaking head or intake manifold gaskets, restricted exhaust, stuck or burned valves, weak valve springs, improper ignition or valve timing and ignition problems.
2   Unfortunately, vacuum gauge readings are easy to misinterpret, so they should be used in conjunction with other tests to confirm the diagnosis.
3   Both the absolute readings and the rate of needle movement are important for accurate interpretation. Most gauges measure vacuum in inches of mercury (in-Hg). The following references to vacuum assume the diagnosis is being performed at sea level. As elevation increases (or atmospheric pressure decreases), the reading will decrease. For every 1,000 foot increase in elevation above approximately 2,000 feet, the gauge readings will decrease about one inch of mercury.
4   Connect the vacuum gauge directly to the intake manifold vacuum, not to ported (throttle body) vacuum (see illustration). Be sure no hoses are left disconnected during the test or false readings will result.
5   Before you begin the test, allow the engine to warm up completely. Block the wheels and set the parking brake. With the transaxle in Park, start the engine and allow it to run at normal idle speed.
Warning: *Keep your hands and the vacuum gauge clear of the fans, drivebelt and rotating components.*

3.5 A compression gauge with a threaded fitting for the spark plug hole is preferred over the type that requires hand pressure to maintain the seal

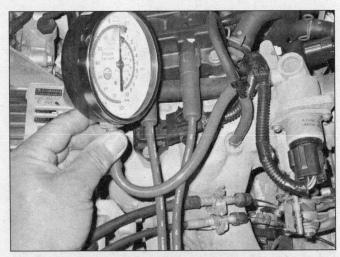

4.4 An inexpensive vacuum gauge can tell a lot about the tune and general condition of an engine - test engine vacuum before beginning an overhaul

6   Read the vacuum gauge; an average, healthy engine should normally produce about 17 to 22 in-Hg with a fairly steady needle (see illustration). Refer to the following vacuum gauge readings and what they indicate about the engine's condition:

7   A low, steady reading usually indicates a leaking gasket between the intake manifold and cylinder head(s) or throttle body, a leaky vacuum hose, late ignition timing or incorrect camshaft timing. Check ignition timing with a timing light and eliminate all other possible causes, utilizing the tests provided in this Chapter before you remove the timing belt cover to check the timing marks.

8   If the reading is three to eight inches below normal and it fluctuates at that low reading, suspect an intake manifold gasket leak at an intake port or a faulty fuel injector.

9   If the needle has regular drops of about two-to-four inches at a steady rate, the valves are probably leaking. Perform a compression check or leak-down test to confirm this.

10   An irregular drop or down-flick of the needle can be caused by a sticking valve or an ignition misfire. Perform a compression check or leak-down test and read the spark plugs.

11   A rapid vibration of about four in-Hg vibration at idle combined with exhaust smoke indicates worn valve guides. Perform a leak-down test to confirm this. If the rapid vibration occurs with an increase in engine speed, check for a leaking intake manifold gasket or head gasket, weak valve springs, burned valves or ignition misfire.

12   A slight fluctuation, say one inch up and down, may mean ignition problems. Check all the usual tune-up items and, if necessary, run the engine on an ignition analyzer.

13   If there is a large fluctuation, perform a compression or leak-down test to look for a weak or dead cylinder or a blown head gasket.

14   If the needle moves slowly through a wide range, check for a clogged PCV system, incorrect idle fuel mixture, throttle body or intake manifold gasket leaks.

15   Check for a slow return after revving the engine by quickly snapping the throttle open until the engine reaches about 2,500 rpm and let it shut. Normally the reading should drop to near zero, rise above normal idle reading (about 5 in-Hg over) and then return to the previous idle reading. If the vacuum returns slowly and doesn't peak when the throttle is snapped shut, the rings may be worn. If there is a long delay, look for a restricted exhaust system (often the muffler or catalytic converter). An easy way to check this is to temporarily disconnect the exhaust ahead of the suspected part and redo the test.

5   Engine rebuilding alternatives

1   The do-it-yourselfer is faced with a number of options when purchasing a rebuilt engine. The major considerations are cost, warranty, parts availability and the time required for the rebuilder to complete the project. The decision to replace the engine block, piston/connecting rod assemblies and crankshaft depends on the final inspection results of your engine. Only then can you make a cost effective decision whether to have your engine overhauled or simply purchase an exchange engine for your vehicle.

2   Some of the rebuilding alternatives include:

3   **Individual parts** - If the inspection procedures reveal that the engine block and most engine components are in reusable condition, purchasing individual parts and having a rebuilder rebuild your engine may be the most economical alternative. The block, crankshaft and piston/connecting rod assemblies should all be inspected carefully by a machine shop first.

4   **Long block** - A long block consists of an engine block plus an oil pump, oil pan, cylinder heads, valve cover, camshaft and valve train components, timing sprockets and chain or gears and timing cover. All components are installed with new bearings, seals and gaskets incorporated throughout. The installation of manifolds and external parts is all that's necessary.

5   **Low mileage used engines** - Some companies now offer low mileage used engines which is a very cost effective way to get your vehicle up and running again. These engines often come from vehicles which have been totaled in accidents or come from other countries which have a higher vehicle turn over rate. A low mileage used engine also usually has a similar warranty like the newly remanufactured engines.

6   Give careful thought to which alternative is best for you and discuss the situation with local automotive machine shops, auto parts dealers and experienced rebuilders before ordering or purchasing replacement parts.

6   Engine removal - methods and precautions

1   If you've decided that an engine must be removed for overhaul or major repair work, several preliminary steps should be taken. Read all removal and installation procedures carefully prior to committing to this job.

2   Locating a suitable place to work is extremely important. Adequate work space, along with storage space for the vehicle, will

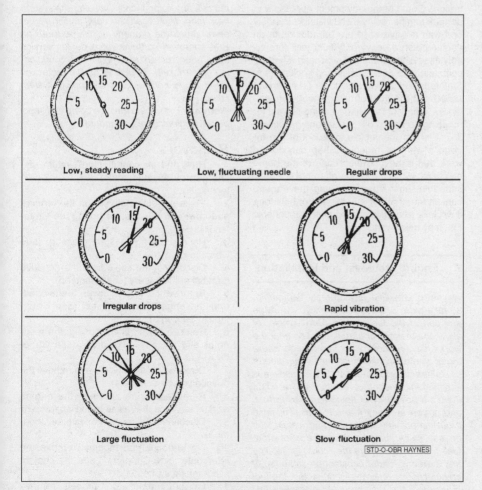

Low, steady reading   Low, fluctuating needle   Regular drops

Irregular drops   Rapid vibration

Large fluctuation   Slow fluctuation

STD-O-OBR HAYNES

4.6 Typical vacuum gauge readings

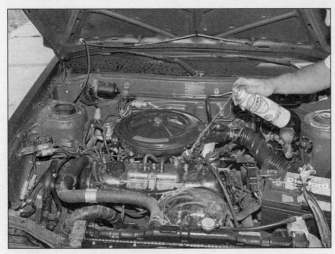

6.3a After tightly wrapping water-vulnerable components, use a spray cleaner on everything, with particular concentration on the greasiest areas, usually around the valve cover and lower edges of the block. If one section dries out, apply more cleaner

6.3b Depending on how dirty the engine is, let the cleaner soak in according to the directions and then hose off the grime and cleaner. Get the rinse water down into every area you can get at; then dry important components with a hair dryer or paper towels

be needed. If a shop or garage isn't available, at the very least a flat, level, clean work surface made of concrete or asphalt is required.

3   Cleaning the engine compartment and engine before beginning the removal procedure will help keep tools clean and organized (see illustrations).

4   An engine hoist will also be necessary. Make sure the hoist is rated in excess of the weight of the engine. Safety is of primary importance, considering the potential hazards involved in removing the engine from the vehicle.

5   If you're a novice at engine removal, get at least one helper. One person cannot easily do all the things you need to do to remove an engine from the engine compartment. Also helpful is to seek advice and assistance from someone who's experienced in engine removal.

6   Plan the operation ahead of time. Arrange for or obtain all of the tools and equipment you'll need prior to beginning the job (see illustration). Some of the equipment necessary to perform engine removal and installation safely and with relative ease are (in addition to an engine hoist) a heavy duty floor jack (preferably fitted with a transaxle jack head adapter), complete sets of wrenches and sockets (see *Maintenance techniques, tools and working facilities* at the front of this manual), wooden blocks, plenty of rags and cleaning solvent for mopping up spilled oil, coolant and gasoline.

7   Plan for the vehicle to be out of use for quite a while. A machine shop can do the work that is beyond the scope of the home mechanic. Machine shops often have a busy schedule, so before removing the engine, consult the shop for an estimate of how long it will take to rebuild or repair the components that may need work.

7   Engine - removal and installation

Warning: *Gasoline is extremely flammable, so take extra precautions when you work on any part of the fuel system. Don't smoke or allow open flames or bare light bulbs near the work area, and don't work in a garage where a gas-type appliance (such as a water heater or clothes dryer) is present. Since gasoline is carcinogenic, wear fuel-resistant gloves when there's a possibility of being exposed to fuel, and, if you spill any fuel on your skin, rinse it off immediately with soap and water. Mop up any spills immediately and do not store fuel-soaked rags where they could ignite. The fuel system is under constant pressure, so, if any fuel lines are to be disconnected, the fuel pressure in the system must be relieved first (see Chapter 4). When you perform any kind of work on the fuel system, wear safety glass-*

es and have a Class B type fire extinguisher on hand.
Warning: *The air conditioning system is under high pressure. DO NOT loosen any fittings or remove any components until after the system has been discharged. Air conditioning refrigerant should be properly discharged into an EPA-approved container at a dealer service department or an automotive air conditioning repair facility. Always wear eye protection when disconnecting air conditioning system fittings.*
Warning: *The engine must be completely cool before beginning this procedure.*

Removal

1   Have the air conditioning system discharged by an automotive air conditioning technician.

2   Place protective covers on the fenders and cowl and remove the hood (see Chapter 11).

3   Relieve the fuel system pressure (see Chapter 4).

4   Disconnect the cable from the negative terminal of the battery (see Chapter 5).

5   Remove the engine cover, if equipped, and the engine splash shield (see Chapter 2A, Section 6).

6   Remove the air filter housing, the resonator and the air intake ducts (see Chapter 4).

7   Drain the cooling system and remove the drivebelts (see Chapter 1).

8   Remove the fan shrouds, the engine cooling fans and the radiator (see Chapter 3).

9   Disconnect the heater hoses (see Chapter 3).

10   On turbocharged models, remove the intercooler (see Chapter 4) and the coolant filler tank (see Chapter 3).

11   On 2.0L turbocharged models, remove the Secondary Air Injection pump (see Chapter 6).

6.6 Get an engine stand sturdy enough to firmly support the engine while you're working on it. Stay away from three-wheeled models; they have a tendency to tip over more easily, so get a four-wheeled unit.

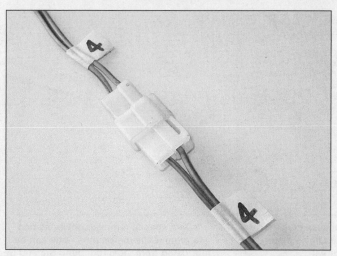

7.12 Label each wire before unplugging the connector

7.28a Attach the chain to the engine lift bracket located on the rear of the engine . . .

12   Clearly label and disconnect all vacuum lines, emissions hoses, wiring harness connectors, ground straps and fuel lines. Masking tape and/or a touch up paint applicator work well for marking items (see illustration). Take instant photos or sketch the locations of components and brackets.

13   Remove the battery and the battery tray (see Chapter 5).

14   Remove the hood (see Chapter 11).

15   Detach the ground cable from the engine ground terminal in the engine compartment.

16   Disconnect the air conditioning lines from the air conditioning compressor (see Chapter 3).

17   On models with hydraulic power steering, remove the power steering pump and brackets without disconnecting the power steering fluid hoses, and tie the assembly out of the way (see Chapter 10).

18   Disconnect the wires from the starter solenoid and remove the starter (see Chapter 5).

19   On automatic transaxle models, remove the rubber service plug and remove the torque converter-to-driveplate bolts.

20   Remove the upper engine brace (see Chapter 2A). Remove the air filter housing upper and side mounting brackets from the engine compartment.

21   Remove the starter (see Chapter 5).

22   Disconnect the fuel lines from the fuel rail (see Chapter 4) and plug the lines.

23   Raise the front of the vehicle and support it securely on jackstands. Block the rear wheels to keep the vehicle from rolling.

24   Remove the exhaust manifold (see Chapter 2A).

25   Remove the engine-to-transaxle lower mounting nuts and bolts.

26   Drain the engine oil (see Chapter 1).

27   Remove the engine oil cooler lines and brackets, if equipped.

28   Support the engine from above with a hoist. Attach the hoist chain to the engine lifting brackets (see illustrations). If no brackets

are present, you will have to fasten the chains to a substantial part of the engine - one that is strong enough to take the weight, but in a location that will provide good balance. If you're attaching a chain to the stud on the engine, or are using a bolt passing through the chain and into a threaded hole, place a washer between the nut or bolt head and the chain and tighten the nut or bolt securely.

29   Support the transaxle with a floor jack.

30   Remove the transaxle-to-engine bolts (see Chapter 7A or 7B).

31   Use the hoist to take the weight off the engine mounts, then remove the engine mount stud nuts (see Chapter 2A).

32   Check to make sure everything is disconnected, then slowly lift the engine out of the vehicle. The engine will probably need to be tilted and/or maneuvered as it's lifted out, so have an assistant handy.

Warning: *Do not place any part of your body under the engine when it is supported only by a hoist or other lifting device.*

33   Remove the flywheel/driveplate and mount the engine on an engine stand or set the engine on the floor and support it so it doesn't tip over. Then disconnect the engine hoist.

Installation

34   Check the engine mounts. If they're worn or damaged, replace them (see Chapter 2A).

35   On automatic transaxle models, inspect the converter seal and bushing.

36   Attach the hoist to the engine, remove the engine from the engine stand and install the flywheel/driveplate (see Chapter 2A).

37   Carefully guide the engine into place, lowering it slowly and moving it back into the engine compartment until the engine mounts can be secured.

38   With the engine still supported by the hoist, use the floor jack under the transaxle, if necessary, to adjust of the angle of the transaxle to bring it into alignment with the engine.

7.28b . . . and to a solid mounting point on the front of the engine (if no lifting bracket is present)

39   Install and tighten all the transaxle-to-engine bolts and the nuts on the engine mounts to the torque listed in this Chapter's Specifications, then remove the hoist and jack.

40   Reinstall the remaining components in the reverse order of removal.

41   Add coolant, oil, power steering and transaxle fluid as needed (see Chapter 1).

42   Run the engine and check for proper operation and leaks. Shut off the engine and recheck the fluid levels.

43   Have the air conditioning system evacuated, charged and leak tested by the shop that discharged it.

8   Engine overhaul - disassembly sequence

1   It's much easier to remove the external components if it's mounted on a portable engine stand. A stand can often be rented quite cheaply from an equipment rental yard.

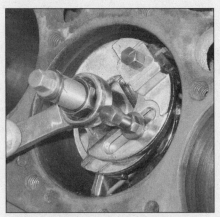

9.1 Before you try to remove the pistons, use a ridge reamer to remove the raised material (ridge) from the top of the cylinders

9.2 Remove the four access plugs (arrow indicates one) that allows piston pin removal

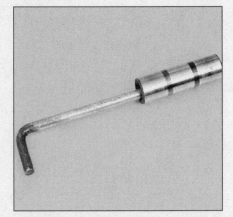

9.4a A special removal tool is needed to remove the piston pins - one can be fabricated from steel rod; bend the end to grab the rear edge and extract the pin

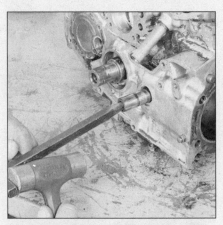

9.4b If the pins are varnished from high mileage, you may have to use a slide hammer or hit the bent end of your homemade tool to force the pin out

9.10 Checking the connecting rod endplay (side clearance)

Before the engine is mounted on a stand, the flywheel/driveplate should be removed from the engine.

2   If a stand isn't available, it's possible to remove the external engine components with it blocked up on the floor. Be extra careful not to tip or drop the engine when working without a stand.

3   If you're going to obtain a rebuilt engine (long block), all external components must come off first, to be transferred to the replacement engine. These components include:

   Flywheel/driveplate
   Ignition system components
   Emissions-related components
   Engine mounts and mount brackets
   Intake manifold
   Fuel injection components
   Oil filter/oil cooler
   Spark plug wires and spark plugs
   Thermostat and housing assembly
   Coolant crossover pipe
   Water pump
   Oil separator cover

Note: *When removing the external components from the engine, pay close attention to*

details that may be helpful or important during installation. Note the installed position of gaskets, seals, spacers, pins, brackets, washers, bolts and other small items.

4   If you're going to rebuild the engine, disassemble the engine in the following order. See Section 5 for additional information regarding the different possibilities to be considered.

   Remove the external components listed above
   Remove the cylinder heads
   Remove the pistons
   Separate the crankcase halves
   Remove the crankshaft and connecting rods

---

9   Pistons - removal

Note: *On 2013 and later non-turbocharged models and 2.0L turbocharged models the piston and connecting rods are removed as a unit prior to separating the case halves.*

1   Temporarily install the crankshaft pulley bolt in the crankshaft front end so you can turn the crankshaft. Check for the presence

of a wear ridge at the top of each cylinder. If a ridge has formed, it must be machined out before the pistons are removed (see illustration).

2012 and earlier non-turbocharged models and 2.5L turbocharged models

2   Using an Allen wrench, remove the plugs from the four service holes for access to the piston pin circlips (see illustration).

Note: *These plugs may be difficult to remove. Soak them first with penetrating oil. If you have to hit the Allen wrench with a hammer, make sure the wrench is inserted fully into the plug to avoid rounding off the hexagonal opening.*

3   To remove the piston pin circlips from a piston, position that piston at bottom dead center by turning the crankshaft, then insert needle-nose pliers through the service holes and remove the circlips.

Note: *Use a small flashlight to see that the circlip is positioned directly at the access hole. You may have to make small movements of the crankshaft to align the piston just right.*

4   Use a special removal tool to pull the piston pins out through the service hole (see illustrations).

5   Keep the pistons and pins together and mark them so they can be reinstalled in their original locations.

6   The pistons can remain in the cylinder bores until the crankcase is separated, then driven out with a wooden or plastic hammer handle, or they can be removed first.

7   If desired, remove the pistons before separating the crankcase as follows:

a)   Turn the crankshaft very slowly until the connecting rods push the pistons out slightly.

b)   Insert the piston pins (clean and oil them first for easy installation) into the connecting rods (through the service holes), then turn the crankshaft until the pin pushes the piston from the bore.

c)   Pull out the pistons.

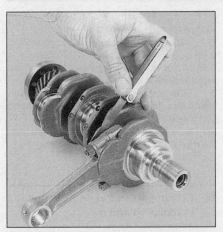

12.1 Checking the connecting rod endplay (side clearance)

2013 and later 2.5L non-turbocharged models and 2.0L turbocharged models

8   Remove the cylinder heads and upper oil pan (see Chapter 2A).

9   After the cylinder ridges have been removed, turn the engine so the crankshaft is facing up.

10   Before the main bearing cap assembly and connecting rods are removed, check the connecting rod endplay with feeler gauges. Slide them between the first connecting rod and the crankshaft throw until the play is removed (see illustration). Repeat this procedure for each connecting rod. The endplay is equal to the thickness of the feeler gauge(s). Check with an automotive machine shop for the endplay service limit (a typical endplay should measure between 0.005 to 0.015 inch [0.127 to 0.381 mm]). If the play exceeds the service limit, new connecting rods will be required. If new rods (or a new crankshaft) are installed, the endplay may fall under the minimum allowable. If it does, the rods will have to be machined to restore it. If necessary, consult an automotive machine shop for advice.

11   Check the connecting rods and caps for identification marks. If they aren't plainly marked, use paint or marker (see illustration 12.2) to clearly identify each rod and cap (1, 2, 3, etc., depending on the cylinder they're associated with). Do not interchange the rod caps. Install the exact same rod cap onto the same connecting rod.

Caution: *Do not use a punch and hammer to mark the connecting rods or they may be damaged.*

12   Loosen each of the connecting rod cap bolts 1/2-turn at a time until they can be removed by hand.

13   Remove the number one connecting rod cap and bearing insert. Don't drop the bearing insert out of the cap.

14   Remove the bearing insert and push the connecting rod/piston assembly out through the top of the engine. Use a wooden or plastic

hammer handle to push on the upper bearing surface in the connecting rod. If resistance is felt, double-check to make sure that all of the ridge was removed from the cylinder.

15   Repeat the procedure for the remaining cylinders.

16   After removal, reassemble the connecting rod caps and bearing inserts in their respective connecting rods and install the cap bolts finger tight. Leaving the old bearing inserts in place until reassembly will help prevent the connecting rod bearing surfaces from being accidentally nicked or gouged.

17   The pistons and connecting rods are now ready for inspection and overhaul at an automotive machine shop.

10   Crankcase - separation

1   On 2013 and later non-turbocharged models and 2.0L turbocharged models, remove the pistons and connecting rods (see Section 9).

2   In order to separate the crankcase halves, remove the bolts from the left side and loosen the right side bolts 1 to 2 turns.

3   Place the crankcase on a workbench with the right side (cylinder numbers 1 and 3) facing UP.

4   Remove the bolts from the right side of the crankcase (see illustration 16.5b or 16.5d).

5   Pull straight up on the right crankcase half to separate the two sections. You may have to tap the right crankcase section with a soft-faced hammer to break the gasket seal.

6   On 2012 and earlier models and 2.5L turbocharged models, be careful when separating the halves; do not allow the connecting rods to fall and damage the crankcase. The crankshaft and connecting rod assembly will remain in the left half.

7   On 2013 and later 2.5L non-turbocharged models and 2.0L turbocharged models, be careful when separating the halves; the crankshaft bearings are attached to the case and can fall out - the bearings must be kept in order.

11   Crankshaft and connecting rods (2012 and earlier non-turbocharged models and 2.5L turbocharged models) - removal

1   Separate the crankcase (see Section 10) and remove the crankshaft rear oil seal.

2   Before lifting out the crankshaft/connecting rod assembly, check the crankshaft endplay. Gently pry or push the crankshaft all the way to the rear of the engine. Slip feeler gauges between the crankshaft and the thrust face of the center main bearing to determine the clearance (which is equivalent to crankshaft endplay). A typical crankshaft endplay will fall between 0.003 to 0.010 inch (0.076 to 0.254 mm). If it is greater than that, check

12.2 If the connecting rods or caps are not marked, use permanent ink or paint to mark the caps to the rods by cylinder number (for example, this would be number 4 cylinder connecting rod)

the crankshaft thrust surfaces for wear after it's removed. If no wear is evident, new main bearings should correct the endplay.

Note: *The thrust bearing is located at the #5 (rear) bearing.*

3   Carefully lift out the crankshaft and store it where it will not fall or get damaged.

4   Remove the main bearings from the case halves. If they will be reused, store them in a clearly marked container so they can be reinstalled in their original locations.

12   Connecting rods and bearings (2012 and earlier non-turbocharged models and all 2.5L turbocharged models) - removal

1   Before removing the connecting rods from the crankshaft, check the endplay (side clearance) with a feeler gauge (see illustration). Slide the feeler gauge between the first connecting rod and the crankshaft throw until the play is removed. Repeat this procedure for each connecting rod. The endplay is equal to the thickness of the feeler gauge(s). Check with an automotive machine shop for the endplay service limit (a typical endplay limit should measure between 0.005 to 0.015 inch [0.127 to 0.381 mm]). If the play exceeds the service limit, new connecting rods will be required. If new rods (or a new crankshaft) are installed, the endplay may fall under the minimum allowable. If it does, the rods will have to be machined to restore it. If necessary, consult an automotive machine shop for advice.

2   If the rods and caps are not numbered, carefully mark the connecting rods and caps so they can be reinstalled in the same position on the same crankshaft journal (see illustration). Mark the connecting rod and cap at the front of the crankshaft with one dot, the second connecting rod and cap with two dots

14.4 Place Plastigage on each connecting rod bearing journal parallel to the crankshaft centerline

14.5 Use the scale on the Plastigage package to determine the bearing oil clearance - measure the widest part of the Plastigage and use the correct scale; it comes with both standard and metric scales

and so on (both the rods and caps must be marked since they are going to be separated). Loosen the cap nuts or bolts on one connecting rod in three steps, carefully lift off the cap and bearing insert, then carefully remove the connecting rod and remaining bearing insert from the crankshaft journal. Temporarily reassemble the connecting rod, the bearing and the cap to prevent mixing up parts.

3   Repeat the procedure for the remaining connecting rods. Be very careful not to nick or scratch the crankshaft journals with the connecting rod bolts.

4   Without mixing them up, clean the parts with solvent and dry them thoroughly. Make sure the oil holes are clear.

13   Engine overhaul - reassembly sequence

1   To assemble the engine, install the following items in the order given:

Crankshaft and connecting rods
Join the crankcase halves
Pistons
Cylinder heads
Camshafts
Rocker arm assembly (non-turbo models)
Oil pump
Timing belt and sprockets
Valve covers
Oil strainer/pick-up tube
Oil pan
Flywheel/driveplate and housing
Engine external components

14   Connecting rods and bearings - installation and oil clearance check

1   Once the crankshaft and connecting rods have been cleaned and inspected and the decision has been made concerning bearing replacement, the connecting rods can be

reinstalled on the crankshaft.
Note: *If new bearings are being used, check the oil clearances before final installation of the connecting rods. If the clearances are within the specified limits, proceed with the installation. Never assume that the clearances are correct even though new bearings are involved.*

2   Make sure the bearing faces and backs are perfectly clean, then fit them to the connecting rod and cap. The tab on each bearing must be engaged in the recess in the cap or connecting rod.

3   Clean the number one connecting rod journal on the crankshaft, then slip the number one connecting rod into place. Make sure the mark on the side of the connecting rod is facing the front of the crankshaft.

4   Apply a length of Plastigage to the crankshaft journal, just off center (see illustration). Gently install the connecting rod cap in place, without turning the connecting rod on the journal. Make sure the mating mark on the cap is on the same side as the mark on the connecting rod. Lubricate the threads of the connecting rod nuts or bolts and tighten them to the torque listed in this Chapter's Specifications.

5   Remove the connecting rod nuts or bolts without allowing the connecting rod to turn on the journal, then remove the cap. Examine the Plastigage and compare its width to the scale on the Plastigage package (see illustration). The connecting rod oil clearance is usually about 0.001 to 0.002 inch (0.025 to 0.05 mm). Consult an automotive machine shop for the clearance specified for the rod bearings on your engine. If the clearance is within Specifications, proceed with checking the other three connecting rods.

6   If the connecting rod clearances are all within Specifications, lubricate both halves of the bearings of connecting rod number 1 with moly-based assembly lube, and install the connecting rod nuts or bolts and tighten them

to the torque listed in this Chapter's Specifications, working up to it in three steps.

7   Repeat the procedure for the remaining connecting rods: do not mix up the connecting rods and caps and do not install the connecting rods backwards.

8   After each connecting rod has been installed, rotate the the crankshaft by hand and check for any obvious binding.

9   As a final step, the connecting rod side clearance must be rechecked (see Section 12).

15   Crankshaft and main bearings - installation and oil clearance check

1   Before installation of the crankshaft, the main bearing oil clearance must be checked.

2   Position the left crankcase section on a workbench with the bearing saddles facing up. Wipe the main bearing surfaces of the crankcase with a clean lint-free cloth. They must be kept spotlessly clean.

3   Clean the back sides of the main bearing inserts and lay one bearing half in each main bearing saddle in the crankcase on the workbench and the other bearing half from each set in the corresponding location in the remaining crankcase section. Make sure the tab on the bearing insert fits into the recess in the crankcase. Do not hammer the bearings into place and do not nick or gouge the bearing faces. No lubrication should be used at this time.

4   Clean the faces of the bearings in the crankcase and the crankshaft main bearing journals with a clean, lint-free cloth. Once you are certain that the crankshaft is clean, carefully lay it in position in the (left) crankcase section on the workbench.

5   Trim three pieces of Plastigage so that they are slightly shorter than the width of the main bearings and place one piece on each crankshaft main bearing journal, parallel with the journal axis (see illustration 14.4).

6   Clean the faces of the bearings in the right crankcase, then carefully lay it in position. Do not disturb the Plastigage.

7   Install the crankcase bolts and tighten them (see Section 14). Do not rotate the crankshaft at any time during this operation.

8   Remove the bolts and carefully lift off the right crankcase section. Do not disturb the Plastigage or rotate the crankshaft.

9   Compare the width of the crushed Plastigage on each journal to the scale printed on the Plastigage container to obtain the main bearing oil clearances (see illustration 14.5). A typical main bearing oil clearance should fall between 0.0015 to 0.0023 inch (0.038 to 0.058 mm). Check with an automotive machine shop for the crankshaft main bearing oil clearance limits for your engine.

10   If the clearance is not correct, double-check to make sure that you have the right size bearing inserts. Also, recheck the crankshaft main bearing journal diameters and

15.12 Apply engine assembly lubricant to the main bearing inserts before final assembly

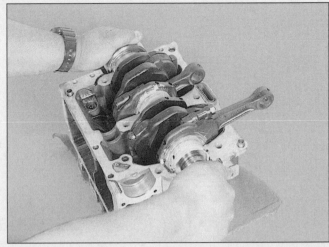

15.13 Install the crankshaft in the left crankcase - 2012 and earlier non-turbocharged models and all turbocharged models shown

make sure that no dirt or oil was between the bearing inserts and the main bearing caps or the block when the clearance was measured.

11   Remove all traces of the Plastigage from the bearing faces and/or journals. To prevent damage to the bearing surfaces, use a wood or plastic tool.

12   Carefully lift the crankshaft out of the crankcase. Clean the bearing faces, then apply a thin layer of engine assembly lube to each of the bearing faces in both crankcase halves (see illustration). Coat the thrust bearing faces as well.

13   Carefully lay the crankshaft in the left crankcase section. On 2012 and earlier non-turbocharged models and all turbocharged models, make sure the connecting rods are directed into the cylinder bores (see illustration).

14   Reassemble the crankcase halves (see Section 16).

16 Crankcase - reassembly

1   Clean the block mating surfaces with lacquer thinner or acetone (they must be clean and oil-free).

2   Install the crankshaft and connecting rods (timing belt models), or crankshaft (timing chain models) to the left crankcase.

3   Install new O-rings in the left crankcase section. Apply a thin layer of anaerobic sealant to the crankcase mating surfaces (see illustrations).

Caution: *DO NOT allow the sealant to flow into the O-ring grooves, oil passages or bearing grooves when the case is joined together!*

4   Carefully lower the right crankcase section into position on the left crankcase and install the right-side bolts, tightening them lightly. Reposition the engine block horizontally

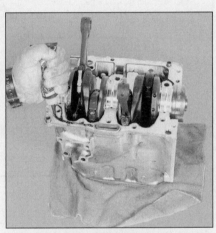

16.3a Apply a bead of anaerobic sealant to the face of the left crankcase (timing belt models)

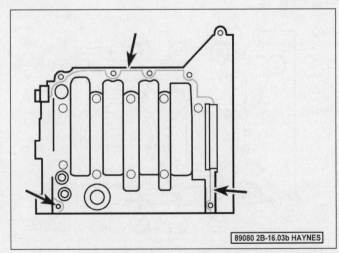

16.3b Apply a bead of anaerobic sealant to the face of the left crankcase (timing chain models)

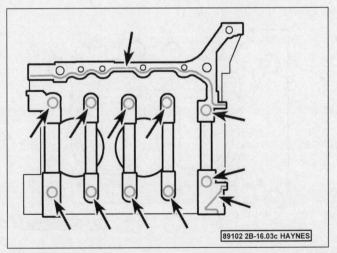

16.3c Run the bead to the inside of the bolt holes to ensure proper sealing of the crankcase (timing chain models)

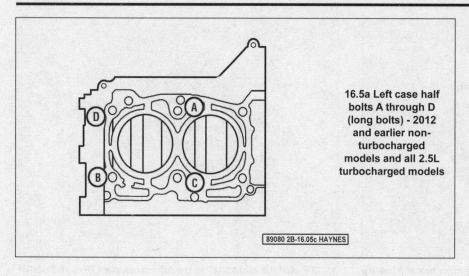

16.5a Left case half bolts A through D (long bolts) - 2012 and earlier non-turbocharged models and all 2.5L turbocharged models

89080 2B-16.05c HAYNES

and install the left-side bolts. On 2013 and later 2.5L non-turbocharged models and all 2.0L turbocharged models, install one of the upper rear cylinder head bolts hand tight to help align the cases.

5   Tighten the bolts, in alphabetical order (see illustrations), to the torque steps listed in this Chapter's Specifications. Follow the tightening sequence carefully to allow the crankcase halves to mate evenly and uniformly.

6   Install a new rear main oil seal into the crankcase (see Chapter 2A). Apply a thin bead of RTV sealant to the perimeter of the oil separator cover and install the cover.

7   Install the pistons (Section 18).

8   Install a new front oil seal in the oil pump housing (see Chapter 2A).

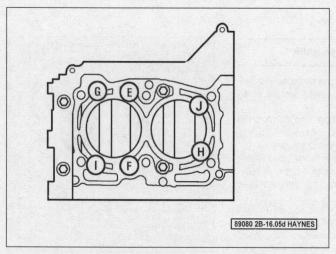

89080 2B-16.05d HAYNES

16.5b Right case half bolts E through J (long bolts) - 2012 and earlier non-turbocharged models and all 2.5L turbocharged models

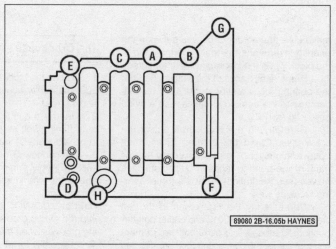

89080 2B-16.05b HAYNES

16.5c Location of Bolts A through G (perimeter bolts) and Bolt H on 2012 and earlier non-turbocharged models and all 2.5L turbocharged models (tighten them in alphabetical order)

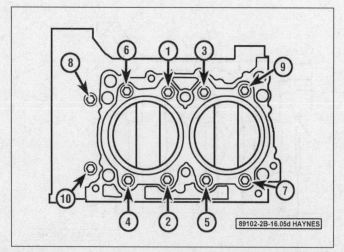

89102-2B-16.05d HAYNES

16.5d Case bolts tightening sequence - 2012 and later (DOHC) 2.5L non-turbocharged models and all 2.0L turbocharged models

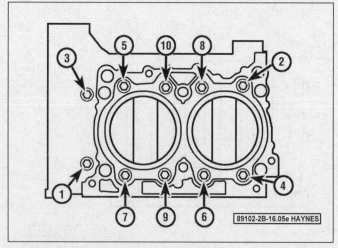

89102-2B-16.05e HAYNES

16.5e Case bolt loosening sequence - 2012 and later 2.5L (DOHC) non-turbocharged models and all 2.0L turbocharged models

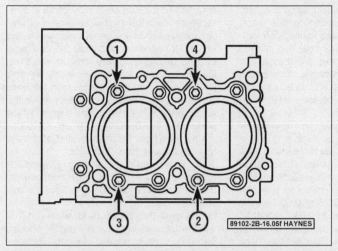

16.5f Case bolt loosening sequence - 2012 and later (DOHC) 2.5L non-turbocharged models and all 2.0L turbocharged models

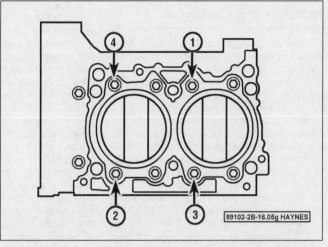

16.5g Case bolts tightening sequence - 2012 and later (DOHC) 2.5L non-turbocharged models and all 2.0L turbocharged models

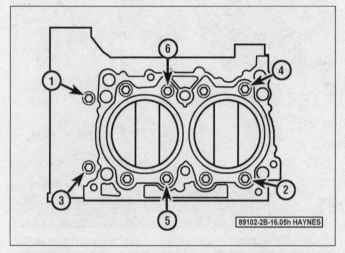

16.5h Case bolt loosening sequence - 2012 and later (DOHC) 2.5L non-turbocharged models and all 2.0L turbocharged models

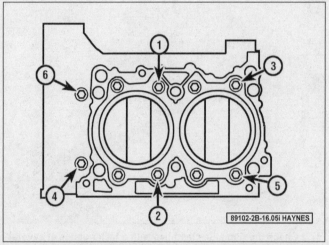

16.5i Case bolt tightening sequence - 2012 and later (DOHC) 2.5L non-turbocharged models and all 2.0L turbocharged models

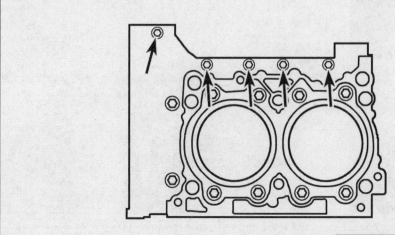

16.5j Remaining bolt locations - 2012 and later (DOHC) 2.5L non-turbocharged models and all 2.0L turbocharged models

17   Piston rings - installation

1   Lay out the pistons and the new ring sets so the ring sets will be matched with the same piston and cylinder during the side clearance check, end gap measurement and engine assembly.

2   Before installing the rings on the pistons, the piston ring side clearance must be checked by laying a new ring in each groove and slipping a feeler gauge in beside it (see illustration). Check the clearance at three or four locations around each groove. Use the correct ring for each groove - they are different. A typical ring groove clearance for compression rings would be around 0.0015 to 0.004-inch (0.038 mm to 0.101 mm). Check with an automotive machine shop for the clearance for your particular engine. If the side clearance is excessive new pistons will have to be used.

3   The ring end gaps must also be checked. It's assumed that the piston ring side clearance has been checked and verified correct.

4   Insert the top (number one) ring into the first cylinder and square it up with the cylinder walls by pushing it in with the top of the piston (see illustration). The ring should be near the bottom of the cylinder, at the lower limit of ring travel.

5   To measure the end gap, slip feeler gauges between the ends of the ring until a gauge equal to the gap width is found (see illustration). The feeler gauge should slide between the ring ends with a slight amount of drag. A typical ring gap should fall between 0.010 and 0.020 inch (0.25 to 0.50 mm) for compression rings and up to 0.030 inch (0.76 mm) for the oil ring steel rails. If the gap is larger or smaller than specified, double-check to make sure you have the correct rings before proceeding.

6   If the gap is too small, it must be enlarged or the ring ends may come in contact with each other during engine operation, which can cause serious damage to the engine. If necessary, increase the end gaps by filing the ring ends very carefully with a fine file. Mount the file in a vise equipped with soft jaws, slip the ring over the file with the ends contacting the file face and slowly move the ring to remove material from the ends. When performing this operation, file only by pushing the ring from the outside end of the file towards the vise (see illustration).

7   Excess end gap isn't critical unless it's greater than 0.040 inch (1.01 mm). Again, double-check to make sure you have the correct ring type.

8   Repeat the procedure for each ring that will be installed in the first cylinder and for each ring in the remaining cylinders. Remember to keep rings, pistons and cylinders matched up.

9   Once the ring end gaps have been

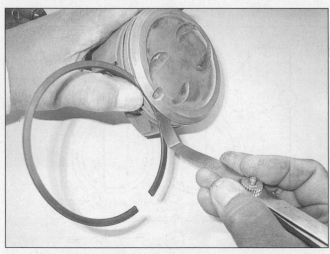

17.2 Check the ring side clearance with a feeler gauge at several points around the piston

17.4 Install the piston ring into the cylinder then push it down into position using a piston so the ring will be square in the cylinder

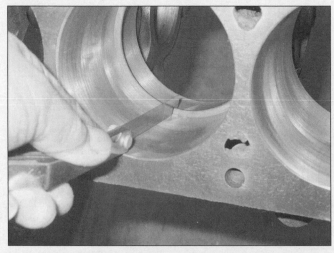

17.5 With the ring square in the cylinder, measure the ring end gap with a feeler gauge

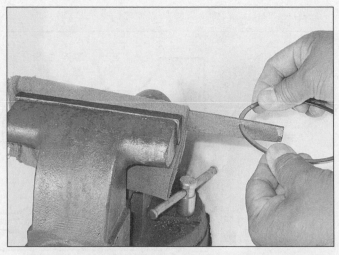

17.6 If the ring end gap is too small, clamp a file in a vise as shown and file the piston ring ends - remove all raised material

checked/corrected, the rings can be installed on the pistons.

10   The oil control ring (lowest one on the piston) is usually installed first. It's composed of three separate components. Slip the spacer/expander into the groove (see illustration). Next, install the upper side rail in the same manner (see illustration). Don't use a piston ring installation tool on the oil ring side rails, as they may be damaged. Instead, place one end of the side rail into the groove between the spacer/expander and the ring land, hold it firmly in place and slide a finger around the piston while pushing the rail into the groove. Finally, install the lower side rail. Make sure the upper rail spin stopper is aligned with the side-hole in the piston.

11   After the three oil ring components have been installed, check to make sure that both the upper and lower side rails can be rotated smoothly inside the ring grooves.

12   The number two (middle) ring is installed next. It's usually stamped with a mark which must face up, toward the top of the piston. Do not mix up the top and middle rings, as they have different cross-sections.

Note: *Always follow the instructions printed on the ring package or box - different manufacturers may require different approaches.*

13   Use a piston ring installation tool and make sure the identification mark is facing the top of the piston, then slip the ring into the middle groove on the piston (see illustration). Don't expand the ring any more than necessary to slide it over the piston.

14   Install the number one (top) ring in the same manner. Make sure the mark is facing up. Be careful not to confuse the number one and number two rings.

15   Repeat the procedure for the remaining pistons and rings.

---

18   Pistons - installation

1   Position the piston ring end gaps at the correct intervals around the piston (see illustration). On the upper oil ring make sure the tab end of the ring or "stopper" is located in the side hole on the piston ring channel.

2012 and earlier non-turbocharged models and 2.5L turbocharged models

2   Install new piston pin circlips in the inner piston pin bore groove of each piston. Make sure the piston is positioned correctly and the circlip is installed in the groove opposite the crankcase service hole when the piston is installed.

3   Lubricate the skirt and rings with clean engine oil. Install a piston ring compressor on the number one piston. Leave the skirt protruding about 1-inch to guide the piston into the cylinder. The rings must be compressed as far as possible.

4   Carefully rotate the crankshaft until the number one and two connecting rods are at bottom dead center. Align the connecting rods with the center of the cylinder.

17.10a Installing the spacer/expander in the oil ring groove

17.10b DO NOT use a piston ring installation tool when installing the oil control side rails and make sure the upper rail spin stopper is aligned with the side hole in the piston ring grove

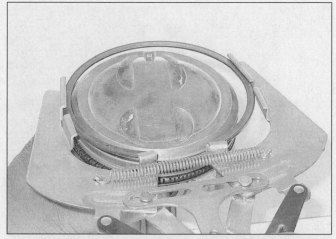

17.13 Use a piston ring installation tool to install the number 2 and the number 1 (top) rings - be sure the directional mark on the piston ring(s) is facing toward the top of the piston

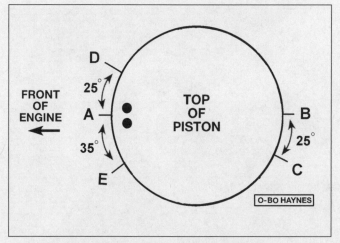

18.1 Position of the piston ring end gaps

A	Top compression ring gap	C	Upper oil ring gap
B	Second compression ring gap	D	Expander ring gap
		E	Lower oil ring gap

5   Gently guide the number one piston into the cylinder. Make sure the mark on the piston crown faces the front (timing belt end) of the engine. Tap the exposed edge of the ring compressor so that it is contacting the crankcase around its entire circumference.

6   Carefully tap on the top of the piston with a wood or plastic hammer handle (see illustration). The piston rings may try to pop out of the ring compressor just before entering the cylinder bore, so keep some pressure on the ring compressor. Work slowly, and if any resistance is felt as the piston rings enter the cylinder, stop immediately. Find out what is hanging up and fix it before proceeding. Do not, for any reason, force the piston into the cylinder, as you will break a ring and/or the piston.

7   Push the piston in until the piston pin bore and the small end of the connecting rod are aligned in the service hole.

Caution: *Fabricate an alignment tool to insert into the service hole and align the connecting rod with the piston pin bore.*

8   Lubricate the piston pin with clean engine oil, then slip it through the service hole into the piston and connecting rod. If resistance is felt, do not force the pin. Instead, check to make sure the pin bore and connecting rod are aligned.

9   Install the new outer circlip in the piston pin bore groove.

Caution: *Make sure the circlip is seated properly in the groove or serious engine damage may result.*

10   Repeat the procedure for the number two piston. Apply RTV sealant to the service hole plug gaskets and install the gaskets and plugs. Tighten the plugs to the torque listed in this Chapter's Specifications.

11   Turn the engine over (crankshaft snout facing down) and rotate the crankshaft until the number three and four connecting rods are at bottom dead center. Align the connecting rods with the center of the cylinder.

12   Repeat the piston and pin installation procedure for pistons three and four.

13   Apply RTV sealant to the service hole plug and cover gaskets and install the plug and cover. Tighten the plug and cover screws to the torque listed in this Chapter's Specifications.

2013 and later 2.5L non-turbocharged models and 2.0L turbocharged models

14   Before installing the piston/connecting rod assemblies, the cylinder walls must be perfectly clean, the top edge of each cylinder bore must be chamfered, and the crankshaft must be in place.

15   Remove the cap from the end of the number one connecting rod (refer to the marks made during removal). Remove the original bearing inserts and wipe the bearing surfaces of the connecting rod and cap with a clean, lint-free cloth. They must be kept spotlessly clean.

Connecting rod bearing oil clearance check

16   Clean the back side of the new upper bearing insert, then lay it in place in the connecting rod.

17   Make sure the tab on the bearing fits into the recess in the rod. Don't hammer the bearing insert into place and be very careful not to nick or gouge the bearing face. Don't lubricate the bearing at this time.

18   Clean the back side of the other bearing insert and install it in the rod cap. Again, make sure the tab on the bearing fits into the recess in the cap, and don't apply any lubricant. It's critically important that the mating surfaces of the bearing and connecting rod are perfectly clean and oil free when they're assembled.

19   Position the piston ring gaps at the intervals around the piston as shown (see illustration 18.1).

20   Lubricate the piston and rings with clean engine oil and attach a piston ring compressor to the piston. Leave the skirt protruding about 1/4-inch to guide the piston into the cylinder. The rings must be compressed until they're flush with the piston.

21   Rotate the crankshaft until the number one connecting rod journal is at BDC (bottom dead center) and apply a liberal coat of engine oil to the cylinder walls.

22   With the "front" arrow mark on the piston facing towards the front (timing chain end) of the engine, gently insert the piston/connecting rod assembly into the number one cylinder bore and rest the bottom edge of the ring compressor on the engine block.

23   Tap the top edge of the ring compressor to make sure it's contacting the block around its entire circumference.

24   Gently tap on the top of the piston with the end of a wooden or plastic hammer handle (see illustration 18.6) while guiding the end of the connecting rod into place on the crankshaft journal. The piston rings may try to pop out of the ring compressor just before entering the cylinder bore, so keep some downward pressure on the ring compressor. Work slowly, and if any resistance is felt as the piston enters the cylinder, stop immediately. Find out what's hanging up and fix it before proceeding. Do not, for any reason, force the piston into the cylinder - you might break a ring and/or the piston.

25   Once the piston/connecting rod assembly is installed, the connecting rod bearing oil clearance must be checked before the rod cap is permanently installed.

26   Cut a piece of the appropriate size Plastigage slightly shorter than the width of the connecting rod bearing and lay it in place on the number one connecting rod journal, parallel with the journal axis (see illustration).

27   Clean the connecting rod cap bearing face and install the rod cap. Make sure the mating mark on the cap is on the same side

18.6 Use a plastic or wooden hammer handle to push the piston into the cylinder

18.26 Place Plastigage on each connecting rod bearing journal parallel to the crankshaft centerline

as the mark on the connecting rod (see illustration 12.2).

28   Install the old rod bolts and tighten them to the torque listed in this Chapter's Specifications. DO NOT rotate the crankshaft at any time during this operation.

Note: *Use a thin-wall socket to avoid erroneous torque readings that can result if the socket is wedged between the rod cap and the bolt. If the socket tends to wedge itself between the fastener and the cap, lift up on it slightly until it no longer contacts the cap.*

29   Remove the fasteners and detach the rod cap, being careful not to disturb the Plastigage. If the connecting rod fasteners have any type of wear or distortion they cannot be reused.

30   Compare the width of the crushed Plastigage to the scale printed on the Plastigage envelope to obtain the oil clearance (see illustration). The connecting rod bearing oil clearance is usually about 0.001 to 0.002 inch. Consult an automotive machine shop for the clearance specified for the rod bearings on your engine.

31   If the clearance is not as specified, the bearing inserts may be the wrong size (which means different ones will be required). Before deciding that different inserts are needed, make sure that no dirt or oil was between the bearing inserts and the connecting rod or cap when the clearance was measured. Also, recheck the journal diameter. If the Plastigage was wider at one end than the other, the journal may be tapered. If the clearance still exceeds the limit specified, the bearing will have to be replaced with an undersize bearing.

Caution: *When installing a new crankshaft, always use a standard size bearing.*

Final installation

32   Carefully scrape all traces of the Plastigage material off the rod journal and/or bearing face. Be very careful not to scratch the bearing - use your fingernail or the edge of a plastic card.

33   Make sure the bearing faces are perfectly clean, then apply a uniform layer of clean moly-base grease or engine assembly lube to both of them. You'll have to push the piston into the cylinder to expose the face of the bearing insert in the connecting rod.

34   Slide the connecting rod back into place on the journal, install the rod cap, install the

18.30 Use the scale on the Plastigage package to determine the bearing oil clearance - be sure to measure the widest part of the Plastigage and use the correct scale; it comes with both standard and metric scales

new bolts and tighten them to the torque listed in this Chapter's Specifications.

35   Repeat the entire procedure for the remaining pistons/connecting rods.

36   The important points to remember are:

(a) Keep the back sides of the bearing inserts and the insides of the connecting rods and caps perfecltly clean when assembling them.

b) Make sure you have the correct piston/rod assembly for each cyinder.

c) The mark on the piston must face the front (timing chain end) of he engine.

d) Lubricate the cylinder walls liberally with clean oil.

e) Lubricate the bearing faces when installing the old rod caps after the oil clearance has been checked.

19   Initial start-up and break-in after overhaul

Warning: *Have a fire extinguisher handy when starting the engine for the first time.*

1   Once the engine has been installed in the vehicle, double-check the engine oil and coolant levels (Chapter 1).

2   With the spark plugs out of the engine and the ignition system and fuel pump disabled, crank the engine until oil pressure registers on the gauge or the light goes out.

3   Install the spark plugs, hook up the plug wires (non-turbo models) or install the ignition

coils (turbo models) and restore the ignition system and fuel pump functions.

4   Start the engine. It may take a few moments for the fuel system to build up pressure, but the engine should start without a great deal of effort.

5   After the engine starts, it should be allowed to warm up to normal operating temperature. While the engine is warming up, make a thorough check for fuel, oil and coolant leaks.

6   Shut the engine off and recheck the engine oil and coolant levels.

7   Drive the vehicle to an area with minimum traffic, accelerate from 30 to 50 mph, then allow the vehicle to slow to 30 mph with the throttle closed. Repeat the procedure 10 or 12 times. This will load the piston rings and cause them to seat properly against the cylinder walls. Check again for oil and coolant leaks.

8   Drive the vehicle gently for the first 500 miles (no sustained high speeds) and keep a constant check on the oil level. It is not unusual for an engine to use oil during the break-in period.

9   At approximately 500 to 600 miles, change the oil and filter (Chapter 1).

10   For the next few hundred miles, drive the vehicle normally. Do not pamper it or abuse it.

11   After 2000 miles, change the oil and filter again and consider the engine broken in.

ENGINE BEARING ANALYSIS

Debris

Babbitt bearing embedded with debris from machinings

Microscopic detail of debris

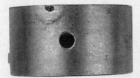

Microscopic detail of gouges

Overplated copper alloy bearing gouged by cast iron debris

Aluminum bearing embedded with glass beads

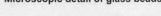

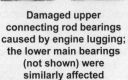

Damaged lining caused by dirt left on the bearing back

Microscopic detail of glass beads

Misassembly

Result of a lower half assembled as an upper - blocking the oil flow

Excessive oil clearance is indicated by a short contact arc

Polished and oil-stained backs are a result of a poor fit in the housing bore

Result of a wrong, reversed, or shifted cap

Overloading

Damage from excessive idling which resulted in an oil film unable to support the load imposed

Damaged upper connecting rod bearings caused by engine lugging; the lower main bearings (not shown) were similarly affected

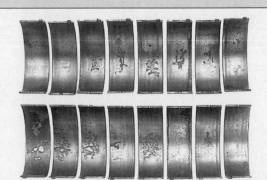
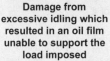

The damage shown in these upper and lower connecting rod bearings was caused by engine operation at a higher-than-rated speed under load

Misalignment

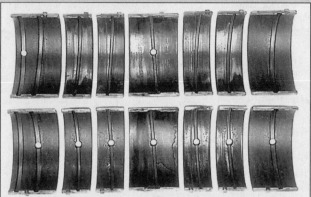

A warped crankshaft caused this pattern of severe wear in the center, diminishing toward the ends

A poorly finished crankshaft caused the equally spaced scoring shown

A tapered housing bore caused the damage along one edge of this pair

A bent connecting rod led to the damage in the "V" pattern

Lubrication

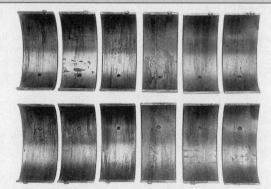

Result of dry start: The bearings on the left, farthest from the oil pump, show more damage

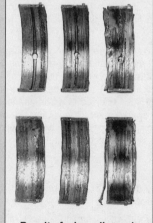

Result of a low oil supply or oil starvation

Severe wear as a result of inadequate oil clearance

Corrosion

Microscopic detail of corrosion

Corrosion is an acid attack on the bearing lining generally caused by inadequate maintenance, extremely hot or cold operation, or inferior oils or fuels

Microscopic detail of cavitation

Example of cavitation - a surface erosion caused by pressure changes in the oil film

Damage from excessive thrust or insufficient axial clearance

Bearing affected by oil dilution caused by excessive blow-by or a rich mixture

COMMON ENGINE OVERHAUL TERMS

B

Backlash - The amount of play between two parts. Usually refers to how much one gear can be moved back and forth without moving the gear with which it's meshed.

Bearing Caps - The caps held in place by nuts or bolts which, in turn, hold the bearing surface. This space is for lubricating oil to enter.

Bearing clearance - The amount of space left between shaft and bearing surface. This space is for lubricating oil to enter.

Bearing crush - The additional height which is purposely manufactured into each bearing half to ensure complete contact of the bearing back with the housing bore when the engine is assembled.

Bearing knock - The noise created by movement of a part in a loose or worn bearing.

Blueprinting - Dismantling an engine and reassembling it to EXACT specifications.

Bore - An engine cylinder, or any cylindrical hole; also used to describe the process of enlarging or accurately refinishing a hole with a cutting tool, as to bore an engine cylinder. The bore size is the diameter of the hole.

Boring - Renewing the cylinders by cutting them out to a specified size. A boring bar is used to make the cut.

Bottom end - A term which refers collectively to the engine block, crankshaft, main bearings and the big ends of the connecting rods.

Break-in - The period of operation between installation of new or rebuilt parts and time in which parts are worn to the correct fit. Driving at reduced and varying speed for a specified mileage to permit parts to wear to the correct fit.

Bushing - A one-piece sleeve placed in a bore to serve as a bearing surface for shaft, piston pin, etc. Usually replaceable.

C

Camshaft - The shaft in the engine, on which a series of lobes are located for operating the valve mechanisms. The camshaft is driven by gears or sprockets and a timing chain. Usually referred to simply as the cam.

Carbon - Hard, or soft, black deposits found in combustion chamber, on plugs, under rings, on and under valve heads.

Cast iron - An alloy of iron and more than two percent carbon, used for engine blocks and heads because it's relatively inexpensive and easy to mold into complex shapes.

Chamfer - To bevel across (or a bevel on) the sharp edge of an object.

Chase - To repair threads with a tap or die.

Combustion chamber - The space between the piston and the cylinder head, with the piston at top dead center, in which air-fuel mixture is burned.

Compression ratio - The relationship between cylinder volume (clearance volume) when the piston is at top dead center and cylinder volume when the piston is at bottom dead center.

Connecting rod - The rod that connects the crank on the crankshaft with the piston. Sometimes called a con rod.

Connecting rod cap - The part of the connecting rod assembly that attaches the rod to the crankpin.

Core plug - Soft metal plug used to plug the casting holes for the coolant passages in the block.

Crankcase - The lower part of the engine in which the crankshaft rotates; includes the lower section of the cylinder block and the oil pan.

Crank kit - A reground or reconditioned crankshaft and new main and connecting rod bearings.

Crankpin - The part of a crankshaft to which a connecting rod is attached.

Crankshaft - The main rotating member, or shaft, running the length of the crankcase, with offset throws to which the connecting rods are attached; changes the reciprocating motion of the pistons into rotating motion.

Cylinder sleeve - A replaceable sleeve, or liner, pressed into the cylinder block to form the cylinder bore.

D

Deburring - Removing the burrs (rough edges or areas) from a bearing.

Deglazer - A tool, rotated by an electric motor, used to remove glaze from cylinder walls so a new set of rings will seat.

E

Endplay - The amount of lengthwise movement between two parts. As applied to a crankshaft, the distance that the crankshaft can move forward and back in the cylinder block.

F

Face - A machinist's term that refers to removing metal from the end of a shaft or the face of a larger part, such as a flywheel.

Fatigue - A breakdown of material through a large number of loading and unloading cycles. The first signs are cracks followed shortly by breaks.

Feeler gauge - A thin strip of hardened steel, ground to an exact thickness, used to check clearances between parts.

Free height - The unloaded length or height of a spring.

Freeplay - The looseness in a linkage, or an assembly of parts, between the initial application of force and actual movement. Usually perceived as slop or slight delay.

Freeze plug - See Core plug.

G

Gallery - A large passage in the block that forms a reservoir for engine oil pressure.

Glaze - The very smooth, glassy finish that develops on cylinder walls while an engine is in service.

H

Heli-Coil - A rethreading device used when threads are worn or damaged. The device is installed in a retapped hole to reduce the thread size to the original size.

I

Installed height - The spring's measured length or height, as installed on the cylinder head. Installed height is measured from the spring seat to the underside of the spring retainer.

J

Journal - The surface of a rotating shaft which turns in a bearing.

K

Keeper - The split lock that holds the valve spring retainer in position on the valve stem.

Key - A small piece of metal inserted into matching grooves machined into two parts fitted together - such as a gear pressed onto a shaft - which prevents slippage between the two parts.

Knock - The heavy metallic engine sound, produced in the combustion chamber as a result of abnormal combustion - usually detonation. Knock is usually caused by a loose or worn bearing. Also referred to as detonation, pinging and spark knock. Connecting rod or main bearing knocks are created by too much oil clearance or insufficient lubrication.

L

Lands - The portions of metal between the piston ring grooves.

Lapping the valves - Grinding a valve face and its seat together with lapping compound.

Lash - The amount of free motion in a gear train, between gears, or in a mechanical assembly, that occurs before movement can begin. Usually refers to the lash in a valve train.

Lifter - The part that rides against the cam to transfer motion to the rest of the valve train.

M

Machining - The process of using a machine to remove metal from a metal part.

Main bearings - The plain, or babbit, bearings that support the crankshaft.

Main bearing caps - The cast iron caps, bolted to the bottom of the block, that support the main bearings.

O

O.D. - Outside diameter.

Oil gallery - A pipe or drilled passageway in the engine used to carry engine oil from one area to another.

Oil ring - The lower ring, or rings, of a piston; designed to prevent excessive amounts of oil from working up the cylinder walls and into the combustion chamber. Also called an oil-control ring.

Oil seal - A seal which keeps oil from leaking out of a compartment. Usually refers to a dynamic seal around a rotating shaft or other moving part.

O-ring - A type of sealing ring made of a special rubberlike material; in use, the O-ring is compressed into a groove to provide the sealing action.

Overhaul - To completely disassemble a unit, clean and inspect all parts, reassemble it with the original or new parts and make all adjustments necessary for proper operation.

P

Pilot bearing - A small bearing installed in the center of the flywheel (or the rear end of the crankshaft) to support the front end of the input shaft of the transmission.

Pip mark - A little dot or indentation which indicates the top side of a compression ring.

Piston - The cylindrical part, attached to the connecting rod, that moves up and down in the cylinder as the crankshaft rotates. When the fuel charge is fired, the piston transfers the force of the explosion to the connecting rod, then to the crankshaft.

Piston pin (or wrist pin) - The cylindrical and usually hollow steel pin that passes through the piston. The piston pin fastens the piston to the upper end of the connecting rod.

Piston ring - The split ring fitted to the groove in a piston. The ring contacts the sides of the ring groove and also rubs against the cylinder wall, thus sealing space between piston and wall. There are two types of rings: Compression rings seal the compression pressure in the combustion chamber; oil rings scrape excessive oil off the cylinder wall.

Piston ring groove - The slots or grooves cut in piston heads to hold piston rings in position.

Piston skirt - The portion of the piston below the rings and the piston pin hole.

Plastigage - A thin strip of plastic thread, available in different sizes, used for measuring clearances. For example, a strip of plastigage is laid across a bearing journal and mashed as parts are assembled. Then parts are disassembled and the width of the strip is measured to determine clearance between journal and bearing. Commonly used to measure crankshaft main-bearing and connecting rod bearing clearances.

Press-fit - A tight fit between two parts that requires pressure to force the parts together. Also referred to as drive, or force, fit.

Prussian blue - A blue pigment; in solution, useful in determining the area of contact between two surfaces. Prussian blue is commonly used to determine the width and location of the contact area between the valve face and the valve seat.

R

Race (bearing) - The inner or outer ring that provides a contact surface for balls or rollers in bearing.

Ream - To size, enlarge or smooth a hole by using a round cutting tool with fluted edges.

Ring job - The process of reconditioning the cylinders and installing new rings.

Runout - Wobble. The amount a shaft rotates out-of-true.

S

Saddle - The upper main bearing seat.

Scored - Scratched or grooved, as a cylinder wall may be scored by abrasive particles moved up and down by the piston rings.

Scuffing - A type of wear in which there's a transfer of material between parts moving against each other; shows up as pits or grooves in the mating surfaces.

Seat - The surface upon which another part rests or seats. For example, the valve seat is the matched surface upon which the valve face rests. Also used to refer to wearing into a good fit; for example, piston rings seat after a few miles of driving.

Short block - An engine block complete with crankshaft and piston and, usually, camshaft assemblies.

Static balance - The balance of an object while it's stationary.

Step - The wear on the lower portion of a ring land caused by excessive side and back-clearance. The height of the step indicates the ring's extra side clearance and the length of the step projecting from the back wall of the groove represents the ring's back clearance.

Stroke - The distance the piston moves when traveling from top dead center to bottom dead center, or from bottom dead center to top dead center.

Stud - A metal rod with threads on both ends.

T

Tang - A lip on the end of a plain bearing used to align the bearing during assembly.

Tap - To cut threads in a hole. Also refers to the fluted tool used to cut threads.

Taper - A gradual reduction in the width of a shaft or hole; in an engine cylinder, taper usually takes the form of uneven wear, more pronounced at the top than at the bottom.

Throws - The offset portions of the crankshaft to which the connecting rods are affixed.

Thrust bearing - The main bearing that has thrust faces to prevent excessive endplay, or forward and backward movement of the crankshaft.

Thrust washer - A bronze or hardened steel washer placed between two moving parts. The washer prevents longitudinal movement and provides a bearing surface for thrust surfaces of parts.

Tolerance - The amount of variation permitted from an exact size of measurement. Actual amount from smallest acceptable dimension to largest acceptable dimension.

U

Umbrella - An oil deflector placed near the valve tip to throw oil from the valve stem area.

Undercut - A machined groove below the normal surface.

Undersize bearings - Smaller diameter bearings used with re-ground crankshaft journals.

V

Valve grinding - Refacing a valve in a valve-refacing machine.

Valve train - The valve-operating mechanism of an engine; includes all components from the camshaft to the valve.

Vibration damper - A cylindrical weight attached to the front of the crankshaft to minimize torsional vibration (the twist-untwist actions of the crankshaft caused by the cylinder firing impulses). Also called a harmonic balancer.

W

Water jacket - The spaces around the cylinders, between the inner and outer shells of the cylinder block or head, through which coolant circulates.

Web - A supporting structure across a cavity.

Woodruff key - A key with a radiused backside (viewed from the side).

Notes

Chapter 3
Cooling, heating and air conditioning systems

Contents

Specifications

General

Coolant type and capacity	See Chapter 1	
Thermostat rating		
Opening temperature range		
2012 and earlier Legacy models		
Non-turbocharged engines...	187 to 194 degrees F	86 to 90 degrees C
Turbocharged engines		
2013 and 2014 Legacy models	189 to 196 degrees F	87 to 91 degrees C
2015 and later Legacy models	194 to 201 degrees F	90 to 94 degrees C
2013 and earlier Forester models		
Non-turbocharged engines...	176 to 183 degrees F	80 to 84 degrees C
Turbocharged engines	169 to 176 degrees F	76 to 80 degrees C
2014 and later Forester models..	187 to 194 degrees F	86 to 90 degrees C
Fully open temperature		
2012 and earlier Legacy models		
Non-turbocharged engines...	203 degrees F	95 degrees C
Turbocharged engines	196 degrees F	91 degrees C
2013 and 2014 Legacy models...	208 degrees F	98 degrees C
2015 and later Legacy models...	212 degrees F	100 degrees C
2013 and earlier Forester models		
Non-turbocharged engines...	203 degrees F	95 degrees C
Turbocharged engines	196 degrees F	91 degrees C
2014 and later Forester models..	203 degrees F	95 degrees C
Radiator cap pressure	14 to 18 psi	96 to 124 kPa
Refrigerant capacity		
R134a systems	Refer to HVAC specification tag	

Torque specifications

	Ft-lbs (unless otherwise indicated)	**Nm**

Note: *One foot-pound (ft-lb) of torque is equivalent to 12 inch-pounds (in-lbs) of torque. Torque values below approximately 15 ft-lbs are expressed in inch-pounds, because most foot-pound torque wrenches are not accurate at these smaller values.*

	Ft-lbs	Nm
Air conditioning lines-to-compressor	88.8 in-lbs	10
Air conditioning lines-to-condenser	44.4 in-lbs	5
Air conditioning lines-to-evaporator	66 in-lbs	7.5
Compressor bracket-to-engine mounting bolts	26	36
Compressor-to-bracket mounting bolts	19.5	26.5
Condenser mounting bolts	62 in-lbs	7
Engine coolant passage	53 in-lbs	6
Radiator bracket mounting bolts	106.8 in-lbs	12
Thermostat housing bolts		
Turbocharged engines		
2012 and earlier models	79.2 in-lbs	9
Non-turbocharged engines		
2012 and earlier models	106.8 in-lbs	12
2013 and later models	56.4 in-lbs	6.4
Water pump bolts		
Legacy models		
2012 and earlier non-turbocharged models		
Step 1	106.8 in-lbs	12
Step 2	106.8 in-lbs	12
2013 and later non-turbocharged models	56.4 in-lbs	6.4
Forester models		
Non-turbocharged models	56.4 in-lbs	6.4
Turbocharged models		
2.5L engines		
Step 1	106.8 in-lbs	12
Step 2	106.8	12
2.0L engines	56.4 in-lbs	6.4
Water pump pulley bolts (2011 and later 2.5L (DOHC) engines and 2.0L engines)	123.6 in-lbs	14

1 General information

Warning: *Do not allow antifreeze to come in contact with your skin or painted surfaces of the vehicle. Rinse off spills immediately with plenty of water. Antifreeze is highly toxic if ingested. Never leave antifreeze lying around in an open container or in puddles on the floor; children and pets are attracted by its sweet smell and may drink it. Check with local authorities about disposing of used antifreeze. Many communities have collection centers which will see that antifreeze is disposed of safely. Never dump used antifreeze on the ground or pour it into drains.*

Engine cooling system

1 All modern vehicles employ a pressurized engine cooling system with thermostatically controlled coolant circulation. The cooling system consists of a radiator, a coolant reservoir, a pressure cap (located on the radiator), a thermostat, two cooling fans, and a water pump.

2 The water pump circulates coolant through the engine. The coolant flows around each cylinder and around the intake and exhaust ports, near the spark plug areas and in close proximity to the exhaust valve guides.

3 A thermostat controls engine coolant temperature. During warm up, the closed thermostat prevents coolant from circulating through the radiator. As the engine nears normal operating temperature, the thermostat opens and allows hot coolant to travel through the radiator, where it's cooled before returning to the engine.

Heating system

4 The heating system consists of a blower fan and heater core located in a housing under the dash, the hoses connecting the heater core to the engine cooling system and the heater/air conditioning control head on the dashboard. Hot engine coolant is circulated through the heater core. When the heater mode is activated, a flap door in the housing opens to expose the heater core to the passenger compartment through air ducts. A fan switch on the control head activates the blower motor, which forces air through the core, heating the air.

Air conditioning system

5 The air conditioning system consists of a condenser mounted in front of the radiator, an evaporator mounted adjacent to the heater core, a compressor mounted on the engine, a receiver-drier or accumulator and the plumbing connecting all of the above components.

6 A blower fan forces the warmer air of the passenger compartment through the evaporator core (sort of a radiator-in-reverse), transferring the heat from the air to the refrigerant. The liquid refrigerant boils off into low pressure vapor, taking the heat with it when it leaves the evaporator.

2 Troubleshooting

Coolant leaks

1 A coolant leak can develop anywhere in the cooling system, but the most common causes are:

a) A loose or weak hose clamp
b) A defective hose
c) A faulty pressure cap
d) A damaged radiator
e) A bad heater core
f) A faulty water pump
g) A leaking gasket at any joint that carries coolant

2 Coolant leaks aren't always easy to find. Sometimes they can only be detected when the cooling system is under pressure. Here's where a cooling system pressure tester comes in handy. After the engine has cooled completely, the tester is attached in place of the pressure cap, then pumped up to the pressure value equal to that of the pressure cap rating (see illustration). Now, leaks that only exist when the engine is fully warmed up will become apparent. The tester can be left connected to locate a nagging slow leak.

Coolant level drops, but no external leaks

3 If you find it necessary to keep adding coolant, but there are no external leaks, the probable causes include:

a) A blown head gasket
b) A leaking intake manifold gasket (only on engines that have coolant passages in the manifold)
c) A cracked cylinder head or cylinder block

4 Any of the above problems will also usually result in contamination of the engine oil, which will cause it to take on a milkshake-like appearance. A bad head gasket or cracked head or block can also result in engine oil contaminating the cooling system.

5 Combustion leak detectors (also known as block testers) are available at most auto parts stores. These work by detecting exhaust gases in the cooling system, which indicates a compression leak from a cylinder into the coolant. The tester consists of a large bulb-type syringe and bottle of test fluid (see illustration). A measured amount of the fluid is added to the syringe. The syringe is placed over the cooling system filler neck and, with the engine running, the bulb is squeezed and a sample of the gases present in the cooling system are drawn up through the test fluid (see illustration). If any combustion gases are present in the sample taken, the test fluid will change color.

6 If the test indicates combustion gas is present in the cooling system, you can be sure that the engine has a blown head gasket or a crack in the cylinder head or block, and will require disassembly to repair.

2.2 The cooling system pressure tester is connected in place of the pressure cap, then pumped up to pressurize the system

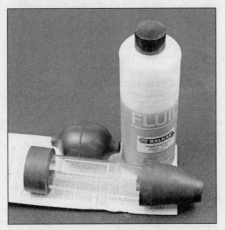
2.5a The combustion leak detector consists of a bulb, syringe and test fluid

2.5b Place the tester over the cooling system filler neck and use the bulb to draw a sample into the tester

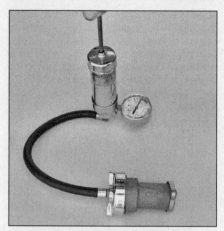

2.8 Checking the cooling system pressure cap with a cooling system pressure tester

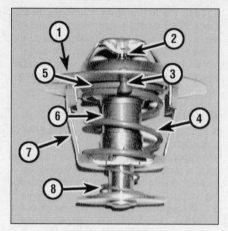

2.10 Typical thermostat:

1   *Flange*
2   *Piston*
3   *Jiggle valve*
4   *Main coil spring*
5   *Valve seat*
6   *Valve*
7   *Frame*
8   *Secondary coil spring*

2.28 The water pump weep hole is generally located on the underside of the pump

Pressure cap

Warning: *Wait until the engine is completely cool before beginning this check.*

7   The cooling system is sealed by a spring-loaded cap, which raises the boiling point of the coolant. If the cap's seal or spring are worn out, the coolant can boil and escape past the cap. With the engine completely cool, remove the cap and check the seal; if it's cracked, hardened or deteriorated in any way, replace it with a new one.

8   Even if the seal is good, the spring might not be; this can be checked with a cooling system pressure tester (see illustration). If the cap can't hold a pressure within approximately 1-1/2 lbs of its rated pressure (which is marked on the cap), replace it with a new one.

9   The cap is also equipped with a vacuum relief spring. When the engine cools off, a vacuum is created in the cooling system. The vacuum relief spring allows air back into the system, which will equalize the pressure and prevent damage to the radiator (the radiator tanks could collapse if the vacuum is great enough). If, after turning the engine off and allowing it to cool down you notice any of the cooling system hoses collapsing, replace the pressure cap with a new one.

Thermostat

10   Before assuming the thermostat (see illustration) is responsible for a cooling system problem, check the coolant level (see Chapter 1), drivebelt tension (see Chapter 1) and temperature gauge (or light) operation.

11   If the engine takes a long time to warm up (as indicated by the temperature gauge or heater operation), the thermostat is probably stuck open. Replace the thermostat with a new one.

12   If the engine runs hot or overheats, a thorough test of the thermostat should be performed.

13   Definitive testing of the thermostat can only be made when it is removed from the vehicle. If the thermostat is stuck in the open

position at room temperature, it is faulty and must be replaced.

Caution: *Do not drive the vehicle without a thermostat. The computer may stay in open loop and emissions and fuel economy will suffer.*

14   To test a thermostat, suspend the (closed) thermostat on a length of string or wire in a pot of cold water.

15   Heat the water on a stove while observing thermostat. The thermostat should fully open before the water boils.

16   If the thermostat doesn't open and close as specified, or sticks in any position, replace it.

Electric cooling fan

17   If the engine is overheating and the cooling fan is not coming on when the engine temperature rises to an excessive level, unplug the fan motor electrical connector(s) and connect the motor directly to the battery with fused jumper wires. If the fan motor doesn't come on, replace the motor.

18   If the radiator fan motor is okay, but it isn't coming on when the engine gets hot, the fan relay might be defective. A relay is used to control a circuit by turning it on and off in response to a control decision by the Powertrain Control Module (PCM). These control circuits are fairly complex, and checking them should be left to a qualified automotive technician. Sometimes, the control system can be fixed by simply identifying and replacing a bad relay.

19   Locate the fan relays in the engine compartment fuse/relay box.

20   Test the relay (see Chapter 12).

21   If the relay is okay, check all wiring and connections to the fan motor. Refer to the wiring diagrams at the end of the manual. If

no obvious problems are found, the problem could be the Engine Coolant Temperature (ECT) sensor or the Powertrain Control Module (PCM). Have the cooling fan system and circuit diagnosed by a dealer service department or repair shop with the proper diagnostic equipment.

Belt-driven cooling fan

22   Disconnect the cable from the negative terminal of the battery (Chapter 5) and rock the fan back and forth by hand to check for excessive bearing play.

23   With the engine cold (and not running), turn the fan blades by hand. The fan should turn freely.

24   Visually inspect for substantial fluid leakage from the clutch assembly. If problems are noted, replace the clutch assembly.

25   With the engine completely warmed up, turn off the ignition switch and disconnect the negative battery cable from the battery. Turn the fan by hand. Some drag should be evident. If the fan turns easily, replace the fan clutch.

Water pump

26   A failure in the water pump can cause serious engine damage due to overheating.

Drivebelt-driven water pump

27   There are two ways to check the operation of the water pump while it's installed on the engine. If the pump is found to be defective, it should be replaced with a new or rebuilt unit.

28   Water pumps are equipped with weep (or vent) holes (see illustration). If a failure occurs in the pump seal, coolant will leak from the hole.

29   If the water pump shaft bearings fail, there may be a howling sound at the pump while it's running. Shaft wear can be felt with the drivebelt removed if the water pump pulley is rocked up and down (with the engine off).

Note: *Don't mistake drivebelt slippage, which causes a squealing sound, for water pump bearing failure.*

Timing chain or timing belt-driven water pump

30 Water pumps driven by the timing chain or timing belt are located underneath the timing chain or timing belt cover.

31 Checking the water pump is limited because of where it is located. However, some basic checks can be made before deciding to remove the water pump. If the pump is found to be defective, it should be replaced with a new or rebuilt unit.

32 One sign that the water pump may be failing is that the heater (climate control) may not work well. Warm the engine to normal operating temperature, confirm that the coolant level is correct (see Chapter 1), then run the heater and check for hot air coming from the ducts.

33 Check for noises coming from the water pump area. If the water pump impeller shaft or bearings are failing, there may be a howling sound at the pump while the engine is running.

Note: *Be careful not to mistake drivebelt noise (squealing) for water pump bearing or shaft failure.*

34 It you suspect water pump failure due to noise, wear can be confirmed by feeling for play at the pump shaft. This can be done by rocking the drive sprocket on the pump shaft up and down. To do this you will need to remove the tension on the timing chain or belt as well as access the water pump.

All water pumps

35 In rare cases or on high-mileage vehicles, another sign of water pump failure may be the presence of coolant in the engine oil. This condition will adversely affect the engine in varying degrees.

Note: *Finding coolant in the engine oil could indicate other serious issues besides a failed water pump, such as a blown head gasket or a cracked cylinder head or block.*

36 Even a pump that exhibits no outward signs of a problem, such as noise or leakage, can still be due for replacement. Removal for close examination is the only sure way to tell. Sometimes the fins on the back of the impeller can corrode to the point that cooling efficiency is diminished significantly.

Heater system

37 Little can go wrong with a heater. If the fan motor will run at all speeds, the electrical part of the system is okay. The three basic heater problems fall into the following general categories:

a) *Not enough heat*
b) *Heat all the time*
c) *No heat*

38 If there's not enough heat, the control valve or door is stuck in a partially open position, the coolant coming from the engine isn't hot enough, or the heater core is restricted. If the coolant isn't hot enough, the thermostat in the engine cooling system is stuck open, allowing coolant to pass through the engine so rapidly that it doesn't heat up quickly enough.

If the vehicle is equipped with a temperature gauge instead of a warning light, watch to see if the engine temperature rises to the normal operating range after driving for a reasonable distance.

39 If there's heat all the time, the control valve or the door is stuck wide open.

40 If there's no heat, coolant is probably not reaching the heater core, or the heater core is plugged. The likely cause is a collapsed or plugged hose, core, or a frozen heater control valve. If the heater is the type that flows coolant all the time, the cause is a stuck door or a broken or kinked control cable.

Air conditioning system

41 If the cool air output is inadequate:

a) *Inspect the condenser coils and fins to make sure they're clear*
b) *Check the compressor clutch for slippage.*
c) *Check the blower motor for proper operation.*
d) *Inspect the blower discharge passage for obstructions.*
e) *Check the system air intake filter for clogging.*

42 If the system provides intermittent cooling air:

a) *Check the circuit breaker, blower switch and blower motor for a malfunction.*
b) *Make sure the compressor clutch isn't slipping.*
c) *Inspect the plenum door to make sure it's operating properly.*
d) *Inspect the evaporator to make sure it isn't clogged.*
e) *If the unit is icing up, it may be caused by excessive moisture in the system, incorrect super heat switch adjustment or low thermostat adjustment.*

43 If the system provides no cooling air:

a) *Inspect the compressor drivebelt. Make sure it's not loose or broken.*
b) *Make sure the compressor clutch engages. If it doesn't, check for a blown fuse.*
c) *Inspect the wire harness for broken or disconnected wires.*
d) *If the compressor clutch doesn't engage, bridge the terminals of the A/C pressure switch(es) with a jumper wire; if the clutch now engages, and the system is properly charged, the pressure switch is bad.*
e) *Make sure the blower motor is not disconnected or burned out.*
f) *Make sure the compressor isn't partially or completely seized.*
g) *Inspect the refrigerant lines for leaks.*
h) *Check the components for leaks.*
i) *Inspect the receiver-drier/accumulator or expansion valve/tube for clogged screens.*

44 If the system is noisy:

a) *Look for loose panels in the passenger compartment.*

b) *Inspect the compressor drivebelt. It may be loose or worn.*
c) *Check the compressor mounting bolts. They should be tight.*
d) *Listen carefully to the compressor. It may be worn out.*
e) *Listen to the idler pulley and bearing and the clutch. Either may be defective.*
f) *The winding in the compressor clutch coil or solenoid may be defective.*
g) *The compressor oil level may be low.*
h) *The blower motor fan bushing or the motor itself may be worn out.*
i) *If there is an excessive charge in the system, you'll hear a rumbling noise in the high pressure line, a thumping noise in the compressor, or see bubbles or cloudiness in the sight glass.*
j) *If there's a low charge in the system, you might hear hissing in the evaporator case at the expansion valve, or see bubbles or cloudiness in the sight glass.*

---

3 Air conditioning and heating system - check and maintenance

Air conditioning system

Warning: *The air conditioning system is under high pressure. Do not loosen any hose fittings or remove any components until after the system has been discharged. Air conditioning refrigerant should be properly discharged into an EPA-approved recovery/recycling unit at a dealer service department or an automotive air conditioning repair facility. Always wear eye protection when disconnecting air conditioning system fittings.*

Caution: *All models covered by this manual use environmentally friendly R-134a. This refrigerant (and its appropriate refrigerant oils) are not compatible with R-12 refrigerant system components and must never be mixed or the components will be damaged.*

Caution: *When replacing entire components, additional refrigerant oil should be added equal to the amount that is removed with the component being replaced. Be sure to read the can before adding any oil to the system, to make sure it is compatible with the R-134a system.*

1 The following maintenance checks should be performed on a regular basis to ensure that the air conditioning continues to operate at peak efficiency.

a) *Inspect the condition of the compressor drivebelt. If it is worn or deteriorated, replace it (Chapter 1).*
b) *Check the drivebelt tension (see Chapter 1).*
c) *Inspect the system hoses. Look for cracks, bubbles, hardening and deterioration. Inspect the hoses and all fittings for oil bubbles or seepage. If there is any evidence of wear, damage or leakage, replace the hose(s).*

3.1 The evaporator drain hose is located on the passenger's side of the firewall

3.9 Insert a thermometer in the center vent, turn on the air conditioning system and wait for it to cool down; depending on the humidity, the output air should be 35 to 40 degrees cooler than the ambient air temperature

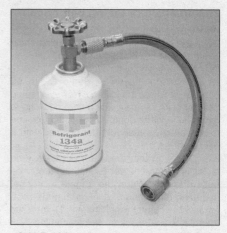

3.11 R-134a automotive air conditioning charging kit

d) *Inspect the condenser fins for leaves, bugs and any other foreign material that may have embedded itself in the fins. Use a fin comb or compressed air to remove debris from the condenser.*

e) *Make sure the system has the correct refrigerant charge.*

f) *If you hear water sloshing around in the dash area or have water dripping on the carpet, check the evaporator housing drain tube (see illustration) and insert a piece of wire into the opening to check for blockage.*

2   It's a good idea to operate the system for about ten minutes at least once a month. This is particularly important during the winter months because long term non-use can cause hardening, and subsequent failure, of the seals. Note that using the Defrost function operates the compressor.

3   If the air conditioning system is not work-ing properly, proceed to Step 6 and perform the general checks outlined below.

4   Because of the complexity of the air con-ditioning system and the special equipment necessary to service it, in-depth troubleshoot-ing and repairs beyond checking the refriger-ant charge and the compressor clutch opera-tion are not included in this manual. However, simple checks and component replacement procedures are provided in this Chapter. For more complete information on the air condi-tioning system, refer to the *Haynes Automo-tive Heating and Air Conditioning Manual.*

5   The most common cause of poor cool-ing is simply a low system refrigerant charge. If a noticeable drop in system cooling ability occurs, one of the following quick checks will help you determine if the refrigerant level is low.

Checking the refrigerant charge

6   Warm the engine up to normal operating temperature.

7   Place the air conditioning temperature selector at the coldest setting and put the blower at the highest setting.

8   After the system reaches operating tem-perature, feel the larger pipe exiting the evap-orator at the firewall. The outlet pipe should be cold (the tubing that leads back to the compressor). If the evaporator outlet pipe is warm, the system probably needs a charge.

9   Insert a thermometer in the center air distribution duct (see illustration) while oper-ating the air conditioning system at its maxi-mum setting - the temperature of the output air should be 35 to 40 degrees F below the ambient air temperature (down to approxi-mately 40 degrees F). If the ambient (outside) air temperature is very high, say 110 degrees F, the duct air temperature may be as high

as 60 degrees F, but generally the air condi-tioning is 35 to 40 degrees F cooler than the ambient air.

10   Further inspection or testing of the sys-tem requires special tools and techniques and is beyond the scope of the home mechanic.

Adding refrigerant

Caution: *Make sure any refrigerant, refrig-erant oil or replacement component you purchase is designated as compatible with R-134a systems.*

Caution: *Never add more than one can of re-frigerant to the system. If more refrigerant than that is required, the system should be evacu-ated and leak tested.*

11   Purchase an R-134a automotive charg-ing kit at an auto parts store (see illustration). A charging kit includes a can of refrigerant, a tap valve and a short section of hose that can be attached between the tap valve and the system low side service valve.

Warning: *Wear protective eyewear when dealing with pressurized refrigerant cans.*

12   Back off the valve handle on the charg-ing kit and screw the kit onto the refrigerant can, making sure first that the O-ring or rub-ber seal inside the threaded portion of the kit is in place.

13   Remove the dust cap from the low-side charging port and attach the hose's quick-connect fitting to the port (see illustration).

Warning: *DO NOT hook the charging kit hose to the system high side! The fittings on the charging kit are designed to fit only on the low side of the system.*

14   Warm up the engine and turn On the air conditioning. Keep the charging kit hose away from the fan and other moving parts.

Note: *The charging process requires the compressor to be running. If the clutch cycles off, you can put the air conditioning switch on*

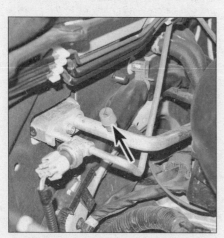

3.13 Location of the low-side charging port

High and leave the car doors open to keep the clutch on and compressor working. The compressor can be kept on during the charging by removing the connector from the pressure switch and bridging it with a paper clip or jumper wire during the procedure.

15   Turn the valve handle on the kit until the stem pierces the can, then back the handle out to release the refrigerant. You should be able to hear the rush of gas. Keep the can upright at all times, but shake it occasionally. Allow stabilization time between each addition.

Note: *The charging process will go faster if you wrap the can with a hot-water-soaked rag to keep the can from freezing up.*

16   If you have an accurate thermometer, you can place it in the center air conditioning duct inside the vehicle and keep track of the output air temperature. A charged system that is working properly should cool down to approximately 40 degrees F. If the ambient (outside) air temperature is very high, say 110 degrees F, the duct air temperature may be as high as 60 degrees F, but generally the air conditioning is 35 to 40 degrees F cooler than the ambient air.

17   When the can is empty, turn the valve handle to the closed position and release the connection from the low-side port. Reinstall the dust cap.

18   Remove the charging kit from the can and store the kit for future use with the piercing valve in the UP position, to prevent inadvertently piercing the can on the next use.

Heating systems

19   If the carpet under the heater core is damp, or if antifreeze vapor or steam is coming through the vents, the heater core is leaking. Remove it (see Section 11) and install a new unit (most radiator shops will not repair a leaking heater core).

20   If the air coming out of the heater vents isn't hot, the problem could stem from any of the following causes:

a) The thermostat is stuck open, preventing the engine coolant from warming up enough to carry heat to the heater core. Replace the thermostat (see Section 4).

b) There is a blockage in the system, preventing the flow of coolant through the heater core. Feel both heater hoses at the firewall. They should be hot. If one of them is cold, there is an obstruction in one of the hoses or in the heater core, or the heater control valve is shut. Detach the hoses and back flush the heater core with a water hose. If the heater core is clear but circulation is impeded, remove the two hoses and flush them out with a water hose.

c) If flushing fails to remove the blockage from the heater core, the heater core must be replaced (see Section 11).

Eliminating air conditioning odors

21   Unpleasant odors that often develop in air conditioning systems are caused by the growth of a fungus, usually on the surface of the evaporator core. The warm, humid environment there is a perfect breeding ground for mildew to develop.

22   The evaporator core on most vehicles is difficult to access, and factory dealerships have a lengthy, expensive process for eliminating the fungus by opening up the evaporator case and using a powerful disinfectant and rinse on the core until the fungus is gone. You can service your own system at home, but it takes something much stronger than basic household germ-killers or deodorizers.

23   Aerosol disinfectants for automotive air conditioning systems are available in most auto parts stores, but remember when shopping for them that the most effective treatments are also the most expensive. The basic procedure for using these sprays is to start by running the system in the RECIRC mode for ten minutes with the blower on its highest speed. Use the highest heat mode to dry out

the system and keep the compressor from engaging by disconnecting the wiring connector at the compressor.

24   The disinfectant can usually comes with a long spray hose. Insert the nozzle into an intake port inside the cabin, and spray according to the manufacturer's recommendations (see illustration). Try to cover the whole surface of the evaporator core, by aiming the spray up, down and sideways. Follow the manufacturer's recommendations for the length of spray and waiting time between applications.

25   Once the evaporator has been cleaned, the best way to prevent the mildew from coming back again is to make sure your evaporator housing drain tube is clear (see illustration 3.1).

Automatic heating and air conditioning systems

26   Some vehicles are equipped with an optional automatic climate control system. This system has its own computer that receives inputs from various sensors in the heating and air conditioning system. This computer, like the PCM, has self-diagnostic capabilities to help pinpoint problems or faults within the system. Vehicles equipped with automatic heating and air conditioning systems are very complex and considered beyond the scope of the home mechanic. Vehicles equipped with automatic heating and air conditioning systems should be taken to dealer service department or other qualified facility for repair.

---

4   Thermostat - replacement

1   The thermostat is located at the front of the engine, bolted to the front of the water pump on 2012 and earlier Legacy models and Forester 2.5L turbocharged models; to the bottom of the water pump housing on 2013 and later Legacy models and all non-turbocharged Forester models. On 2.0L turbocharged models, the thermostat is located on the left side of the water pump housing. The thermostat allows for quicker warm-ups and governs the normal operating temperature of the engine.

Warning: *Wait until the engine is completely cool before starting this procedure.*

2   Raise the front of the vehicle and support it securely on jackstands.

3   Drain the cooling system (see Chapter 1).

4   Remove the front exhaust pipe-to-cylinder head nuts, then remove the catalytic converter-to-exhaust pipe nuts/bolts and remove the front exhaust pipe assembly.

5   Place the drain pan under the thermostat housing.

Note: *If the lower radiator hose is old, you may want to remove it from the thermostat housing cover and replace it. Otherwise, the cover can be removed with the radiator hose still attached.*

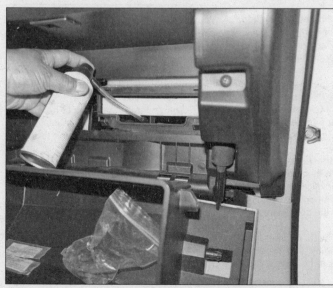

3.24 Insert the nozzle of the disinfectant can into the return-air intake behind the glove box

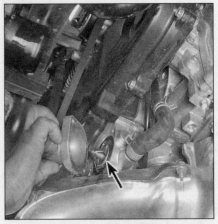

4.6a Remove the thermostat housing cover bolts (2012 and earlier Legacy models/Forester 2.5L turbocharged models)

4.6b Thermostat housing cover bolts (2013 and later Legacy models/non-turbo Forester models)

4.7a Note the installed direction of the thermostat and remove it from the housing (2012 and earlier Legacy models/ Forester 2.5L turbocharged models)

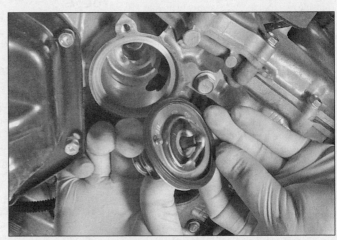

4.7b Thermostat removal - 2013 and later Legacy models/ non-turbo Forester models

4.9 Install a new seal around the thermostat flange

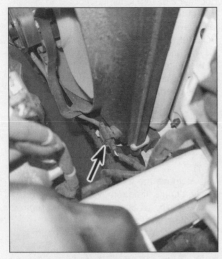

5.5 Disconnect the fan motor electrical connector - secondary fan connector shown

6   Remove the bolts and lift off the housing cover (see illustrations). You may have to tap the cover with a soft-faced hammer to break the gasket seal.

7   Note how the thermostat is installed, then remove it (see illustrations).

8   Clean the mating surfaces of the thermostat housing and cover. Do not nick or gouge the sealing surfaces.

9   Install a new seal on the thermostat (see illustration), then place the thermostat into the housing spring side first. Make sure that the thermostat flange is properly seated in the recessed area of the housing as noted during removal.

10   Carefully position the housing cover, install the bolts and tighten them to the torque listed in this Chapter's Specifications.

11   Place the radiator hose onto the housing cover (if removed), install the hose clamp and tighten it securely.

12   Refill the radiator with coolant (see Chapter 1). Start the engine and check for leaks around the thermostat housing and the lower radiator hose.

5   Cooling fan - removal and installation

Warning: *Wait until the engine is completely cool before beginning this procedure.*

1   Raise the vehicle and support it securely on jackstands.

2   Remove the engine splash shield from the bottom of the engine compartment (see Chapter 2A, Section 6).

3   Remove the air intake duct from above the radiator, if applicable (see Chapter 4).

4   Remove the coolant reservoir (see Section 6).

Note: *This step may not be necessary for removing individual fan assemblies on the passenger's side.*

5   Disconnect the fan motor electrical (see illustration) connector(s).

Note: *It may be necessary to move or detach the upper radiator hose from the radiator.*

6   Remove the shroud mounting bolts and remove the shroud(s) from the radiator (see illustrations).

5.6a Main cooling fan and shroud mounting fastener locations

5.6b Secondary cooling fan and shroud mounting fastener locations

7   Remove the fan motor mounting bolts and harness clips from the shroud (see illustration), then remove the fan motor and fan.

8   If the fan motor is being replaced, remove the fan from the old motor and attach it to the new motor (see illustration).

9   Installation is the reverse of removal. Refill the cooling system (see Chapter 1). Start the engine and allow it to reach normal operating temperature, then verify proper fan operation.

6   Radiator and coolant reservoir - removal and installation

Warning: *Do not allow antifreeze to come in contact with your skin or painted surfaces of the vehicle. Flush contaminated areas immediately with plenty of water. Don't store new coolant or leave old coolant lying around where it's accessible to children or pets - they're at-* *tracted by its sweet smell. Ingestion of even a small amount of coolant can be fatal! Wipe up garage floor and drip pan spills immediately. Keep antifreeze containers covered and repair cooling system leaks as soon as they're noticed.*

Warning: *Wait until the engine is completely cool before starting this procedure.*

Radiator

1   Set the parking brake and block the rear wheels. Raise the front of the vehicle and support it securely on jackstands. Remove the splash shield beneath the radiator (see Chapter 2A, Section 6).

2   Drain the cooling system (see Chapter 1). If the coolant is relatively new or in good condition, save it and reuse it.

3   Remove the radiator support cover fasteners (see illustration) and remove the cover. On 2015 and later Legacy models, remove the front bumper cover (see Chapter 11).

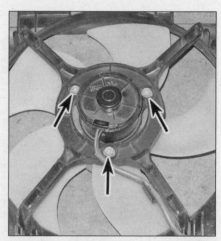

5.7 Remove the fasteners securing the fan motor

5.8 Fan blade fastener - early model shown

6.3 Radiator support cover fastener locations - Legacy models shown, Forester models similar

6.6a Upper radiator hose and clamps

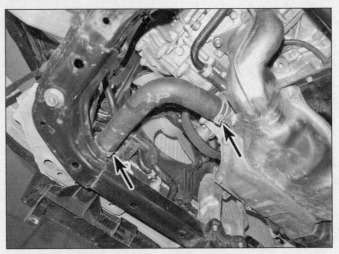

6.6b Lower radiator hose and clamps

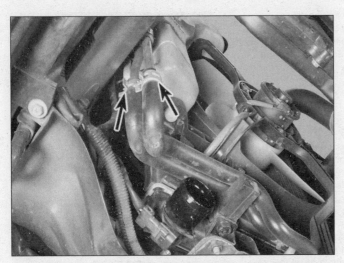

6.7a 5-speed automatic transaxle fluid cooler line connections

6.7b CVT transaxle fluid cooler line connections

4   Remove the air intake duct from above the radiator, if applicable (see Chapter 4).

5   Remove the coolant reservoir (see Steps 21 through 23).

6   Disconnect the upper and lower radiator hoses from the radiator by loosening the hose clamps (see illustrations).

7   On automatic transaxle and CVT transaxle models, disconnect the fluid cooler lines from the radiator (see illustrations).

Note: *Plug the ends of the transaxle cooling lines to minimize fluid loss and contamination.*

8   Disconnect the fan electrical connectors then remove the cooling fans (see Section 5).

9   On 2015 and later models Legacy models, remove the condenser lower bracket-to-radiator mounting bolts then remove the bracket-to-condenser bolts and remove the lower brackets. Secure the condenser to the radiator support.

10   On 2015 and later models Forester models, remove the upper and lower condenser-

to-radiator mounting bolts and secure the condenser to the radiator support.

11   Remove the radiator mounting brackets (see illustration). Remove any clips, brackets, harnesses or hoses that may be attached to the radiator or fan shroud.

12   Carefully lift the radiator up and out (see illustration). Don't spill coolant on the vehicle or scratch the paint.

13   Inspect the radiator for leaks and damage. If it needs repair, have a radiator shop or dealer service department perform the work as special techniques are required.

14   Bugs and dirt can be removed from the radiator by spraying it with a garden hose nozzle from the back side. The radiator should be flushed out with a garden hose before reinstallation.

15   Check the radiator rubber mounts for deterioration and replace them if necessary (see illustration).

16   Installation is the reverse of removal.

Guide the radiator into the mounts (see illustration) until it seats completely.

17   Tighten the radiator bracket bolts to the torque listed in this Chapter's Specifications.

18   Fill the cooling system with the proper coolant (see Chapter 1).

19   Start the engine and allow it to reach normal operating temperature while checking for leaks. Recheck the coolant level and add more if required.

20   Check and add transaxle fluid as needed (see Chapter 1).

Coolant reservoir

21   Pull the radiator overflow hose out from the tank.

22   On 2014 and earlier Legacy models and all Forester models, depress the locking tab, then rotate the tank counterclockwise and remove it (see illustrations).

23   On 2015 and later Legacy models, remove the two mounting bolts and remove the reservoir.

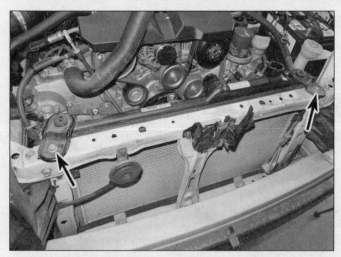

6.11 Radiator mounting brackets and fasteners

6.12 Slowly lift the radiator upwards making sure there is nothing connected and you are not damaging the cooler fins

6.15 Radiator lower rubber mounts

6.16 Make sure the mounting posts on the radiator are centered into the lower mounts

6.22a Depress the reservoir locking tab . . .

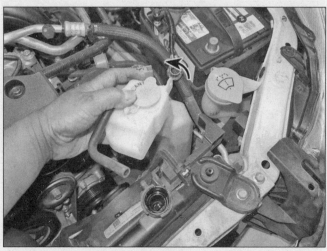

6.22b . . . then rotate the reservoir out of the bracket

24   Prior to installation make sure the reservoir is clean and free of debris which could be drawn into the radiator (wash inside it with soapy water and a long brush if necessary). It will be easier to read the coolant level if the tank is cleaned.

25   Installation is the reverse of removal. Fill the cooling system with the proper coolant (see Chapter 1).

7   Water pump - replacement

Warning: *Wait until the engine is completely cool before starting this procedure.*

1   Drain the cooling system (see Chapter 1).
2   Remove the drivebelt(s) (see Chapter 1).
3   Remove the cooling fans (see Section 5).

2012 and earlier 2.5L (SOHC) engines and 2013 and earlier 2.5L turbocharged engines

4   Disconnect the radiator hose and the bypass hose(s) from the water pump (see illustration).
5   Remove both cooling fans from the radiator (see Section 5).
6   Remove the drivebelt cover and drivebelts (see Chapter 1).
7   Remove the timing belt (see Chapter 2A).
8   Remove the crankshaft pulley (see Chapter 2A).
9   Remove the timing belt tensioner and the idler pulley(s) located below (and on turbo models, above) the water pump (see Chapter 2A).
10   On turbocharged engines, remove the Camshaft Position (CMP) sensor (see Chapter 6).
11   Remove the sprocket(s) from the left side camshafts (see Chapter 2A).
12   Remove the left side rear timing belt

7.4 Remove the lower radiator hose, bypass hose clamps and hose from the water pump (non-turbo models shown, turbo models are similar)

cover (see Chapter 2A).
13   Remove the mounting bracket for the belt tensioner (see Chapter 2A).
14   Loosen the water pump mounting bolts (see illustrations), then separate the water pump and gasket from the engine. You may have to tap the pump gently with a soft-faced hammer to break the gasket seal.

2011 and later 2.5L (DOHC) non-turbocharged engines and 2.0L engines

15   Raise the vehicle up and support it securely on jackstands.
16   Remove the engine lower splash shield fasteners and splash shield from under the vehicle.
17   Remove the front exhaust assembly (see Chapter 6, Section 17).
18   Hold the water pump from turning using a two-pin spanner wrench placed into the holes (see illustrations) on the pump pulley then loosen and remove the bolts.

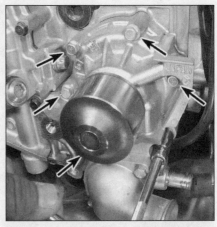

7.14a Remove the water pump mounting bolts

7.14b Remove the pump and gasket

7.18a Insert the pins of the spanner into the holes on the pulley . . .

7.18b . . . then loosen the bolts while keeping the pulley from turning

7.20a Loosen all the bolts then remove four of the five bolts

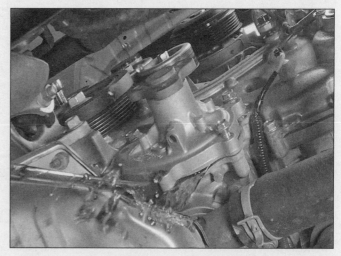

7.20b Use a screwdriver to release the pump from the upper oil pan - be prepared for coolant spillage

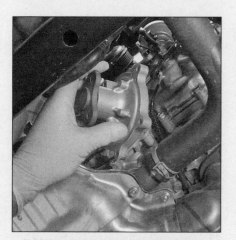

7.21 Remove the water pump from the upper oil pan

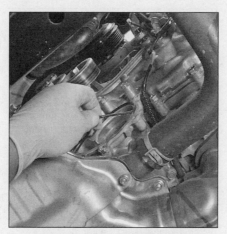

7.22 Remove the gasket from the sealing surface

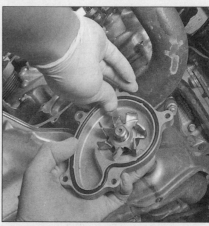

7.27 Install a new gasket into the groove on the pump body making sure it is completely seated in the groove

19   Place a drain pan under the pump.
20   Remove the water pump-to-upper oil pan bolts then pry the pump loose from the upper oil pan (see illustrations).
21   Remove the remaining water pump bolt and the water pump (see illustration).
22   Remove the old O-ring gasket from the upper oil pan mounting surface (see illustration) and clean the mating surfaces thoroughly. Do not nick or gouge the gasket sealing surfaces.

All models

23   Remove all traces of the old gasket material from the engine mounting surface and clean it thoroughly. Do not nick or gouge the gasket sealing surfaces.
24   Make sure the bolt threads and the threaded holes in the engine are clear of corrosion.
25   Compare the new pump to the old one to make sure they're identical.

26   On 2012 and earlier 2.5L (SOHC) engines and 2013 and earlier 2.5L turbo-charged engines, coat both sides of a new gasket with gasket sealant and then install the gasket onto the pump.
27   On 2011 and later 2.5L (DOHC) engines and 2.0L engines, install a new gasket into the groove on the water pump housing (see illustration).
28   Apply a small amount of RTV sealant to the threads of each mounting bolt.
29   Carefully move the water pump into position while keeping the gasket in place. Install the mounting bolts finger tight making certain that the water pump and gasket are aligned correctly on the engine.
30   Tighten the bolts, in 1/4-turn increments, to the torque listed in this Chapter's Specifications. Don't over-tighten the bolts or the pump may become distorted and leak.
Note: *Start with the center-most bolt on the right side of the pump and work in a clockwise*

direction. Tighten them once again after the torque specification has been achieved.
31   The remainder of installation is the reverse of removal. On 2011 and later 2.5L (DOHC) engines and 2.0L engines, install the water pump pulley and tighten the bolts to the torque listed in this Chapter's Specifications.
32   Attach the hoses to the pump and tighten the hose clamps securely.
33   Refill the cooling system and check the drivebelt tension (see Chapter 1).

8   Coolant temperature indicator - check

Warning: *Wait until the engine is completely cool before beginning this procedure.*
1   The coolant temperature indicator system consists of a temperature gauge on the dash and a sensor mounted on the engine. On all models, an Engine Coolant Tempera-

9.4 Disconnect the electrical connector from the power transistor - blower motor resistor similar

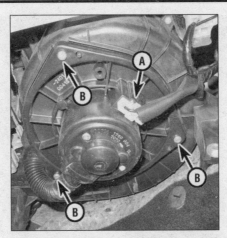

9.10 Blower motor electrical connector (A) and mounting screws (B)

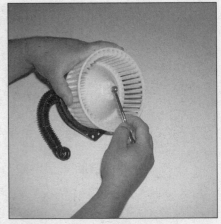

9.11 Remove the fastener that retains the blower fan to the motor

ture (ECT) sensor (see Chapter 6), which is an information sensor for the Powertrain Control Module (PCM), provides a signal to the PCM which controls and actuates the temperature gauge.

2   If an overheating indication has occurred, first check the coolant level in the system (see Chapter 1) and that the coolant mixture is correct (see your Owner's Manual). Also, refer to the *Troubleshooting* section at the front of this manual before assuming that the temperature indicator is faulty.

3   Start the engine and warm it up for 10 minutes. If the temperature gauge has not moved from the C position, check the wiring harness connections going to the instrument cluster.

4   If there is a problem with the ECT sensor, it is very likely that the CHECK ENGINE light will be illuminated and the sensor or circuit will need repair (see Chapter 6).

10.3 Typical early style control cable

9   Blower motor resistor/transistor and blower motor - replacement

Warning: *The models covered by this manual are equipped with a Supplemental Restraint System (SRS), more commonly known as airbags. Always disable the airbag system before working in the vicinity of any airbag system component to avoid the possibility of accidental deployment of the airbag, which could cause personal injury (see Chapter 12).*
Note: *Models that have the automatic climate control feature are equipped with a power transistor and models with manual climate control have a blower motor resistor.*

1   Disconnect the cable from the negative battery terminal (see Chapter 5).

2   On 2014 and earlier models, use a trim tool to pull out the cover fasteners under the passenger's side lower instrument panel cover under the glove box, then remove the panel. On 2015 and later models, the fasteners (hooked shaped) are molded into the panel; use a small screwdriver to release the three hook-shaped fasteners and remove the panel.

Blower motor resistor/ transistor

3   On 2014 and later Forester models, remove the glove box (see Chapter 11) then remove the floor duct fasteners and duct.

4   Disconnect the electrical connector from the blower motor resistor or power transistor (see illustration).
Note: *On 2014 and later non-turbocharged Forester models, the PCM must be removed (see Chapter 6) to access the blower motor resistor.*

5   On Legacy models and 2013 and earlier Forester models, remove the blower motor resistor/transistor mounting screws and remove it from the heater/air conditioning case.

6   On 2014 and later Forester models, depress the two locking claws on the sides of the transistor while sliding the transistor downwards and out of the bracket.

7   Installation is the reverse of removal.

Blower motor

8   Locate the cover under the glove box then use a trim tool to pull the cover fasteners out and remove the cover.

9   Disconnect the electrical connector from the blower motor (see illustration 9.10).

10   Remove the blower motor mounting screws and remove the blower motor assembly (see illustration).

11   Remove the fan from the motor (see illustration).

12   Installation is the reverse of removal.

10   Heater/air conditioning control assembly - removal and installation

Warning: *The models covered by this manual are equipped with a Supplemental Restraint System (SRS), more commonly known as airbags. Always disarm the airbag system before working in the vicinity of any airbag system component to avoid the possibility of accidental deployment of the airbag, which could cause personal injury (see Chapter 12). Do not use a memory saving device to preserve the PCM's memory when working on or near the airbag system components.*

1   Disconnect the cable from the negative battery terminal (see Chapter 5).

Forester models

2   On manual control A/C models, remove the knee bolster (see Chapter 11).

3   Disconnect the two control cables, one on the driver's side (see illustration) and one on the passenger's side.

10.10 Control unit mounting screw locations

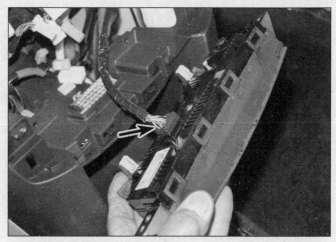

10.12 Disconnect the electrical connector to the control unit - manual control models have two electrical connectors

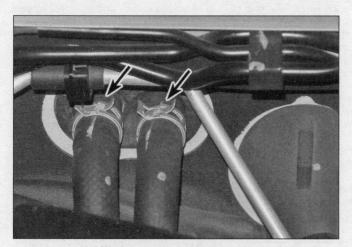

11.4 Disconnect the heater hose clamps

11.5 Remove the refrigerant line-to-expansion valve mounting bolt

4   On all models, remove the center trim panel (or bezel) assembly by carefully prying the panel out from the instrument panel (see Chapter 11).
5   Disconnect the electrical connector(s) from the back side of the control assembly.
6   Remove the control assembly mounting fasteners, then disengage the two retaining clips at the top of the control assembly and separate the assembly from the panel.
7   Installation is the reverse of removal.

Legacy models

8   Remove the instrument panel center trim panel (see Chapter 11).
Note: *The center trim panel is very long. It starts at the instrument cluster and ends at the register vent on the passenger's side.*
9   Remove the radio and, if equipped, the navigation unit (see Chapter 12).
10   On 2014 and earlier models, remove the control unit mounting screws (see illustration), then disconnect the plastic retaining claws and remove the control unit from the center

trim panel.
11   On 2015 and later models, disengage the seven retaining clips, then carefully remove he control unit from the instrument panel.
12   Disconnect the electrical connector(s) from the control unit (see illustration).
13   Installation is the reverse of removal.

11 Heater core - removal and installation

Warning: *The models covered by this manual are equipped with a Supplemental Restraint System (SRS), more commonly known as airbags. Always disable the airbag system before working in the vicinity of any airbag system component to avoid the possibility of accidental deployment of the airbag, which could cause personal injury (see Chapter 12).*
Warning: *The air conditioning system is under high pressure. DO NOT loosen any fittings or remove any components until after the system has been discharged. Air conditioning refriger-*

ant must be properly discharged into an EPA-approved container at a dealer service department or an automotive air conditioning repair facility. Always wear eye protection when disconnecting air conditioning system fittings.
Warning: *Wait until the engine is completely cool before beginning this procedure.*

Removal

1   Before having the refrigerant discharged the oil in the system must be allowed to return to the compressor (see Section 12, Step 1) then have the refrigerant discharged and recovered by an air conditioning technician.
2   Disconnect the cable from the negative battery terminal (see Chapter 5).
3   Drain the cooling system (see Chapter 1).
4   Disconnect the heater hoses from the firewall (see illustration).
5   Disconnect the refrigerant line fittings from the air conditioning evaporator (see illustration).
6   Disconnect the temperature control

11.11a Left side heater and evaporator housing fastener . . .

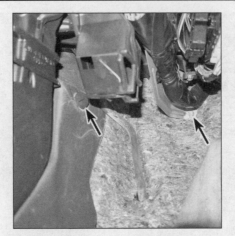

11.11b . . . center fastener . . .

11.11c . . . and the right side fastener

cables from the heater unit (see illustration 10.3), if equipped.
Note: *Models equipped with the automatic temperature control feature do not have a temperature control cable.*
7   On 2.0L turbocharged engines, remove the intercooler (see Chapter 4).
8   On later models, remove the Powertrain Control Module (PCM) (see Chapter 6).
9   Remove the center console, the instrument panel and the support beam from behind the instrument panel (see Chapter 11).
10   Remove the blower motor housing fasteners.
11   Remove the fasteners for the heater housing and then lift it from the vehicle (see illustrations).
Note: *Put some shop towels on the vehicle's floor to protect the carpeting from spilled coolant. If the coolant spills on any painted surfaces, wash it off immediately with cold water.*
12   Remove the screws for the cover on the heater core tubes from the heater housing, then remove the tubes support.
13   Remove the heater core tubes locking clips by prying the clips off then separate the tubes from the heater core. Remove and discard the O-rings.
14   Remove the heater core cover screws from the heater housing and remove the cover. Pull the heater core straight out of the housing.

Installation

15   Slide the new heater core into the housing, making sure that the sealing foam is in place, and secure the heater core cover (if applicable). Reassemble the heater core housing (if applicable).
16   On 2008 and later models, install new O-rings onto the tubes. Lubricate the tubes and insert them into the core until the locking clips can be installed. Install the tube support and cover.
17   Install the heater housing in the vehicle.

18   Install any heater ducts which may have been removed or separated.
19   Install the support beam, the instrument panel and the center console. Install the air-bag control module (if removed).
20   Install the temperature control cable, if equipped.
21   Connect the heater hoses and the refrigerant lines at the firewall. If the hoses are hardened or split at the end, replace them with new ones.
22   Fill the radiator with coolant (see Chapter 1) and reconnect the battery (see Chapter 5).
23   Start the vehicle and operate the heater controls. Check for any leakage around the hose connections.

12   Air conditioning compressor - removal and installation

Warning: *The air conditioning system is under high pressure. Do not loosen any hose fittings or remove any components until after the system has been discharged. Air conditioning refrigerant must be properly discharged into an EPA-approved recovery/recycling unit at a dealer service department or an automotive air conditioning repair facility. Always wear eye protection when disconnecting air conditioning system fittings.*
Caution: *When replacing entire components, additional refrigerant oil should be added equal to the amount that is removed with the component being replaced. Read the label on the container before adding any oil to the system to confirm that it is compatible with the R-134a system.*

Removal

1   Before having the refrigerant discharged, the oil in the system must be allowed to return to the compressor as follows:

a)   *Start the engine and bring the engine speed up to 1,500 rpm and hold.*
b)   *Turn the air conditioning switch to the ON position and place the temperature dial to the MAX cool position. Place the fresh/recirculate switch to the recirculate position and the fan to the MAX position.*
c)   *Allow the engine to run with the air conditioning system set in these positions for 10 minutes, then stop the engine.*

2   Have the refrigerant discharged and recovered by an air conditioning technician.
Caution: *Don't operate the air conditioning system on the way to get the system discharged. Make sure it is turned Off.*
3   Disconnect the cable from the negative battery terminal (see Chapter 5).
4   Remove the drivebelt cover bolt and cover (see illustration).
5   Remove the drivebelts (see Chapter 1).
6   Remove the alternator (see Chapter 5)
7   On 2.0L engine models, remove the secondary air injection pump (see Chapter 6).

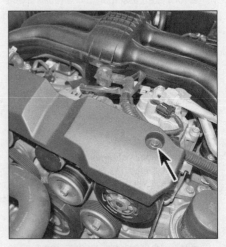

12.4 Remove the drivebelt cover bolt - non-turbo Legacy model shown

12.8 Disconnect the electrical connector to the air compressor (1) then disconnect the harness retainers (2) and move the harness out of the way

12.10 Air compressor mounting details - 2.5L non-turbocharged model shown

1   Refrigerant line mounting bolts
2   Compressor mounting bolts

8   Disconnect the alternator harness retainers and the air conditioning compressor clutch electrical connector (see illustration).

9   Disconnect the refrigerant lines from the compressor (see illustration 12.10). Plug the open fittings immediately to prevent entry of dirt and moisture.

10   On all models except 2.0L models, remove the compressor-to-bracket mounting bolts and remove the compressor (see illustration).

11   On 2.0L models, remove the compressor bracket-to-engine mounting bolts then remove the compressor and brackets as an assembly then remove the compressor-to-bracket bolts and separate the brackets from the compressor.

Installation

12   If a new compressor is being installed, follow the new compressor's accompanying directions on draining the excess oil from it prior to installation.

13   The clutch may have to be transferred from the old compressor to the new unit.

14   Installation is the reverse of removal. Use new O-rings (lightly coated with fresh refrigerant oil) at the line fittings. Tighten the compressor mounting bolts and line fittings to the torque listed in this Chapter's Specifications.

Note: Only use O-rings that are designed specifically for R-134a A/C system applications.

15   Reconnect the battery (see Chapter 5).

16   Have the system evacuated, recharged and leak tested by the shop that discharged it.

13   Air conditioning condenser - removal and installation

Warning: The air conditioning system is under high pressure. Do not loosen any hose fittings or remove any components until after the

system has been discharged. Air conditioning refrigerant must be properly discharged into an EPA-approved recovery/recycling unit at a dealer service department or an automotive air conditioning repair facility. Always wear eye protection when disconnecting air conditioning system fittings.

Caution: When replacing entire components, additional refrigerant oil should be added equal to the amount that is removed with the component being replaced. Read the label on the container before adding any oil to the system to confirm that it is compatible with the R-134a system.

Note: The receiver-drier is integrated with the condenser and is not serviceable separately.

Removal

1   Before having the refrigerant discharged, the oil in the system must be allowed to return to the compressor (see Section 12 Step 1),

then have the refrigerant discharged and recovered by an air conditioning technician.

2   Disconnect the cable from the negative battery terminal (see Chapter 5).

3   Remove the air intake duct from above the radiator, if necessary (see Chapter 4).

4   Remove the radiator support cover fasteners (see illustration 6.3) and remove the cover. On 2015 and later Legacy models, remove the front bumper cover (see Chapter 11).

5   Remove the radiator brackets (see Section 6) and lean the radiator back to access the refrigerant lines.

6   Disconnect the refrigerant lines from the condenser and plug or cap all openings immediately to prevent dirt or moisture from enter the system (see illustrations).

Note: Depending on what model and year you're working on, the line fittings can be found on either one or both sides of the condenser.

13.6a Remove the condenser line fitting from the back side . . .   13.6b . . . and the front side

7   Remove the condenser mounting bolts (see illustration). Lean the radiator back and use the gap to carefully lift the condenser from its lower mounts to remove it.

Installation

8   When installing a new condenser, drain the oil from the old condenser into a measured container. Install that amount of fresh refrigerant oil into the new condenser.
9   Carefully lower the condenser in place between the radiator and the radiator support. Make sure the lower guides on the condenser are properly seated in the mounts.
10   Installation is the reverse of removal. Use new O-rings (lightly coated with fresh refrigerant oil) at the line fittings. Tighten the compressor mounting bolts and line fittings to the torque listed in this Chapter's Specifications.
Note: *Only use O-rings that are designed specifically for R-134a A/C system applications.*
11   Reconnect the battery (see Chapter 5).
12   Have the system evacuated, recharged and leak tested by the shop that discharged it.

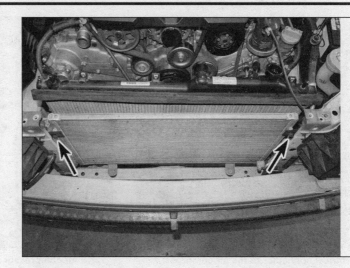

13.7 Condenser mounting bolts (radiator support removed for clarity)

Chapter 4 Part
Fuel and exhaust systems

Contents

Specifications

Fuel pressure (at idle)

Forester
  2013 and earlier models
Non-turbo models	49 to 58 psi	340 to 400 kPa
Turbo models		
With fuel pressure regulator vacuum hose disconnected	41 to 46 psi	284 to 314 kPa
With fuel pressure regulator vacuum hose connected	33 to 38 psi	230 to 260 kPa
2014 and later models	49 to 58 psi	340 to 400 kPa

Legacy
  2010 and earlier models
Non-turbo models	49 to 50 psi	338 to 348 kPa
Turbo models		
With fuel pressure regulator vacuum hose disconnected	41 to 46 psi	284 to 314 kPa
With fuel pressure regulator vacuum hose connected	33 to 38 psi	230 to 260 kPa

  2011 and later models
Non-turbo models	49 to 58 psi	340 to 400 kPa
Turbo models		
With fuel pressure regulator vacuum hose disconnected	48 to 52 psi	328 to 358 kPa
With fuel pressure regulator vacuum hose connected	40 to 44 psi	274 to 304 kPa

Torque specifications

Note: *One foot-pound (ft-lb) of torque is equivalent to 12 inch-pounds (in-lbs) of torque. Torque values below approximately 15 ft-lbs are expressed in inch-pounds, because most foot-pound torque wrenches are not accurate at these smaller values.*

	Ft-lbs (unless otherwise indicated)	**Nm**
Fuel tank strap bolts	24	33
Fuel pump module/sub module nuts	36 in-lbs	4.4
Fuel rail mounting bolts		
Turbo	168 in-lbs	19
Non-turbo		
Forester		
2010 and earlier models	168 in-lbs	19
2011 and later models	56 in-lbs	6.4
Legacy		
2012 and earlier models	168 in-lbs	19
2013 and later models	56 in-lbs	6.4
Throttle body mounting bolts	71 in-lbs	8
Turbocharger assembly		
Turbocharger-to-bracket bolts	24	33
Exhaust pipe-to-cylinder head nuts	31	42.5
Exhaust pipe front center to rear center bolts	31	42.5
Joint pipe-to-turbocharger nuts	31	42.5
Oil inlet pipe banjo bolts		
Upper	142 in-lbs	16
Lower	15	20
Coolant pipe banjo bolts		
2007 and earlier models	24	33
2008 and later models	17	23
Intercooler-to-turbocharger and left-side mounting bolt		
(2013 and earlier Forester)	142 in-lbs	16
High pressure fuel pump (2014 and later Forester turbo models)		
Torx Plus bolts	15	21
High pressure fuel delivery pipe	18	25

1   General information

Fuel system warnings

1   Gasoline is extremely flammable and repairing fuel system components can be dangerous. Consider your automotive repair knowledge and experience before attempting repairs which may be better suited for a professional mechanic.

a)   *Don't smoke or allow open flames or bare light bulbs near the work area*

b)   *Don't work in a garage with a gas-type appliance (water heater, clothes dryer)*

c)   *Use fuel-resistant gloves. If any fuel spills on your skin, wash it off immediately with soap and water*

d)   *Clean up spills immediately*

e)   *Do not store fuel-soaked rags where they could ignite*

f)   *Prior to disconnecting any fuel line, you must relieve the fuel pressure (see Section 3)*

g)   *Wear safety glasses*

h)   *Have a proper fire extinguisher on hand*

2   The fuel system in 2014 and later Forester turbo models is made up of a low-pressure system and a high-pressure system.

Before any work on the high-pressure system can be performed, the pressure on the low-pressure side must be relieved, then wait at least two hours before loosening any fittings in the high-pressure side.

Fuel system

3   The fuel system consists of the fuel tank, electric fuel pump/fuel level sending unit (located in the fuel tank), fuel rail and fuel injectors. The fuel injection system is a multi-port system; multi-port fuel injection uses timed impulses to inject the fuel directly into the intake port of each cylinder. The Powertrain Control Module (PCM) controls the injectors. The PCM monitors various engine parameters and delivers the exact amount of fuel required into the intake ports.

4   Fuel is circulated from the fuel pump to the fuel rail through fuel lines running along the underside of the vehicle. Various sections of the fuel line are either rigid metal or nylon, or flexible fuel hose. The various sections of the fuel hose are connected either by quick-connect fittings or threaded metal fittings.

5   2014 and later Forester models with turbocharged engines are equipped with a direct injection, high-pressure fuel system. This includes a low-pressure fuel system as described above, and a high-pressure fuel system that includes a high-pressure fuel pump and high-pressure fuel lines.The high-pressure fuel lines feed direct injection fuel injectors that spray fuel directly into the combustion chamber under extremely high pressure.

Exhaust system

6   The exhaust system consists of the exhaust manifold(s), catalytic converter(s), muffler(s), tailpipe and all connecting pipes, flanges and clamps. The catalytic converters are an emission control device added to the exhaust system to reduce pollutants.

2   Troubleshooting

Fuel pump

1   The fuel pump is located inside the fuel tank. Sit inside the vehicle with the windows closed, turn the ignition key to ON (not START) and listen for the sound of the fuel pump as it's briefly activated. You will only hear the sound for a second or two, but that sound tells you that the pump is working. Alternatively, have an assistant listen at the fuel filler cap.

2   If the pump does not come on, check the fuel pump relay fuses and relay (see illustrations). If the fuses and relay are okay, check the wiring back to the fuel pump. If the fuses, relay and wiring are okay, the fuel pump is probably defective. If the pump runs continuously with the ignition key in the ON position, the Powertrain Control Module (PCM) is probably defective. Have the PCM checked by a professional mechanic.

Fuel injection system

Note: *The following procedure is based on the assumption that the fuel pump is working and the fuel pressure is adequate (see Section 4).*

3   Check all electrical connectors that are related to the system. Check the ground wire connections for tightness.

4   Verify that the battery is fully charged (see Chapter 5).

5   Inspect the air filter element (see Chapter 1).

6   Check all fuses related to the fuel system (see Chapter 12).

7   Check the air induction system between the throttle body and the intake manifold for air leaks. Also inspect the condition of all vacuum hoses connected to the intake manifold and to the throttle body.

8   Remove the air intake duct from the throttle body and look for dirt, carbon, varnish, or other residue in the throttle body, particularly around the throttle plate. If it's dirty, clean it with carb cleaner, a toothbrush and a clean shop towel.

9   With the engine running, place an automotive stethoscope against each injector, one at a time, and listen for a clicking sound that indicates operation (see illustration).

Warning: *Stay clear of the drivebelt and any rotating or hot components.*

10   If you can hear the injectors operating, but the engine is misfiring, the electrical circuits are functioning correctly, but the injectors might be dirty or clogged. Try a commercial injector cleaning product (available at auto

parts stores). If cleaning the injectors doesn't help, replace the injectors.

11   If an injector is not operating (it makes no sound), disconnect the injector electrical connector and measure the resistance across the injector terminals with an ohmmeter. Compare this measurement to the other injectors. If the resistance of the non-operational injector is quite different from the other injectors, replace it.

12   If the injector is not operating, but the resistance reading is within the range of resistance of the other injectors, the PCM or the circuit between the PCM and the injector might be faulty.

---

3   Fuel pressure relief procedure

Warning: *Gasoline is extremely flammable. See* Fuel system warnings *in Section 1.*

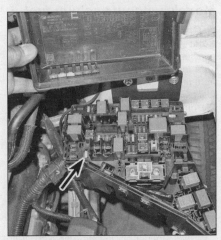

2.2a Fuel pump fuse location in the engine compartment fuse box (Legacy models)

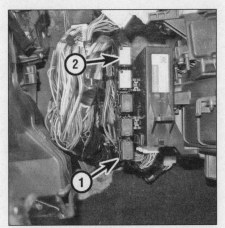

2.2c Fuel pump relay location (behind the glove box) - 2013 and earlier Forester models

2.2d Fuel pump relay location (behind the glove box) - all Legacy models and 2014 and later Forester models

1   *Legacy models*
2   *2014 and later Forester models*

Warning: *The fuel system in 2014 and later Forester models is made up of a low-pressure system and a high-pressure system. Once the pressure on the low-pressure side has been relieved, wait at least two hours before loosening any high-pressure side fittings or lines.*

1   Remove the fuel filler cap to relieve any pressure built-up in the fuel tank.

2   Remove the fuel pump fuse from the underhood fuse/relay box (see Section 2).

3   Attempt to start the engine; it should immediately stall. Crank the engine several more times to ensure the fuel system has been completely relieved. Disconnect the cable from the negative terminal of the battery (see Chapter 5) before working on the fuel system.

4   It's a good idea to cover any fuel connection to be disassembled with rags to absorb the residual fuel that may leak out. Properly dispose of the rags.

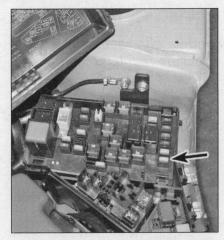

2.2b Fuel pump fuse location in the engine compartment fuse box (Forester models)

2.9 An automotive stethoscope is used to listen to the fuel injectors in operation

4   Fuel pressure - check

Warning: *Gasoline is extremely flammable. See* Fuel system warnings *in Section 1.*
Warning: *The fuel system in 2014 and later Forester models is made up of a low-pressure system and a high-pressure system. Once the pressure on the low-pressure side has been relieved, wait at least two hours before loosening any high-pressure side fittings or lines.*
Note: *The following procedure assumes that the fuel pump is receiving voltage and runs (see Section 2).*

1   Relieve the fuel system pressure (see Section 3).
2   Disconnect the fuel supply line at the fuel rail (see illustration), then use an adapter to connect the fuel pressure gauge between the fuel line and the fuel rail (see illustration).
Note: *The pressure gauge can also be tee'd into the fuel feed line at the fuel pulsation damper at the left side of the engine compartment, on models so equipped (see Section 12).*
3   Reinstall the fuel pump relay fuse.

Models with vacuum fuel pressure regulator

4   Start the engine and allow it to idle. Compare the pressure reading with the engine running value listed in this Chapter's Specifications. Disconnect and plug the vacuum hose from the fuel pressure regulator (see Section 12) - the pressure should increase immediately (see the values listed in this Chapter's Specifications). If the pressure readings are correct, the system is operating properly.
5   If the fuel pressure is not within specifications, check the following:

a) *If the pressure is higher than specified, check for vacuum at the hose to the fuel pressure regulator. Vacuum must fluctuate with the increase or decrease in the engine rpm. If vacuum is present, check for a pinched or clogged fuel return hose or pipe. If the return line is not obstructed, replace the fuel pressure regulator.*
b) *If the pressure is lower than specified, check for a restriction in the fuel filter or fuel line. If the fuel filter and lines are OK, start the engine (if possible) and slowly pinch the return hose shut. If the pressure rises to normal or above, replace the fuel pressure regulator (see Section 12). If the pressure is still low, replace the fuel pump (see Section 7).*

Warning: *Don't allow the fuel pressure to exceed 50 psi.*
Note: *A leaking fuel injector could also cause lower-than-normal fuel pressure, but would most likely set a diagnostic trouble code.*
6   Turn off the engine. Fuel pressure should not fall more than 8 psi over five minutes. If it does, the problem could be a leaky fuel injector, fuel line leak, or faulty fuel pump module.
7   Relieve the fuel system pressure (see Section 3) and remove the fuel pressure gauge. Reconnect the fuel line and wipe up any spilled gasoline.

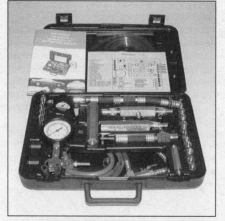

4.2a This fuel pressure testing kit contains all the necessary fittings and adapters, along with the fuel pressure gauge, to test most automotive systems

Models without vacuum fuel pressure regulator

Note: *On 2014 and later Forester models equipped with direct injection, the fuel pressure test is only testing the supply pressure from the fuel tank pump to the high-pressure fuel pump.*
Warning: *Never attempt to measure fuel pressure on the high-pressure side of the system.*
8   Start the engine and allow it to idle. Note the gauge reading as soon as the pressure stabilizes, and compare it with the pressure listed in this Chapter's Specifications.
9   If the fuel pressure is not within specifications, check the following:

a) *Check for a restriction in the fuel system (kinked fuel line, plugged fuel pump inlet strainer or clogged fuel filter). If no restrictions are found, replace the fuel pump module (see Section 7).*
b) *If the fuel pressure is higher than specified, replace the fuel pump module (see Section 7).*

10   Turn off the engine. Fuel pressure should not fall more than 8 psi over five minutes. If it does, the problem could be a leaky fuel injector, fuel line leak, or faulty fuel pump module.
11   Disconnect the fuel pressure gauge. Wipe up any spilled gasoline.

5   Fuel lines and fittings - general information and disconnection

Warning: *Gasoline is extremely flammable. See* Fuel system warnings *in Section 1.*
1   Relieve the fuel pressure before servicing fuel lines or fittings (see Section 3), then disconnect the cable from the negative battery terminal (see Chapter 5) before proceeding.
2   The fuel supply line connects the fuel pump in the fuel tank to the fuel rail on the engine. The Evaporative Emission (EVAP) system lines connect the fuel tank to the EVAP canister and connect the canister to the

4.2b Location of the fuel feed line connection at the fuel rail (2013 Legacy shown)

intake manifold.
3   Whenever you're working under the vehicle, inspect all fuel and evaporative emission lines for leaks, kinks, dents and other damage. Always replace a damaged fuel or EVAP line immediately.
4   If you find signs of dirt in the lines during disassembly, disconnect all lines and blow them out with compressed air. Inspect the fuel strainer on the fuel pump pick-up unit for damage and deterioration.

Steel tubing

5   It is critical that the fuel lines be replaced with lines of equivalent type and specification.
6   Some steel fuel lines have threaded fittings. When loosening these fittings, hold the stationary fitting with a wrench while turning the tube nut.

Plastic tubing

Warning: *When removing or installing plastic fuel line tubing, be careful not to bend or twist it too much, which can damage it. Also, plastic fuel tubing is NOT heat resistant, so keep it away from excessive heat.*
7   When replacing fuel system plastic tubing, use only original equipment replacement plastic tubing.

Flexible hoses

8   When replacing fuel system flexible hoses, use only original equipment replacements.
9   Don't route fuel hoses (or metal lines) within four inches of the exhaust system or within ten inches of the catalytic converter. Make sure that no rubber hoses are installed directly against the vehicle, particularly in places where there is any vibration. If allowed to touch some vibrating part of the vehicle, a hose can easily become chafed and it might start leaking. A good rule of thumb is to maintain a minimum of 1/4-inch clearance around a hose (or metal line) to prevent contact with the vehicle underbody.

Disconnecting Fuel Line Fittings

Two-tab type fitting; depress both tabs with your fingers, then pull the fuel line and the fitting apart

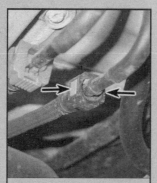

On this type of fitting, depress the two buttons on opposite sides of the fitting, then pull it off the fuel line

Threaded fuel line fitting; hold the stationary portion of the line or component (A) while loosening the tube nut (B) with a flare-nut wrench

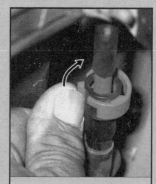

Plastic collar-type fitting; rotate the outer part of the fitting

Metal collar quick-connect fitting; pull the end of the retainer off the fuel line and disengage the other end from the female side of the fitting . . .

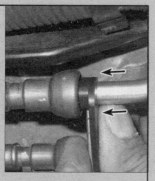

. . . insert a fuel line separator tool into the female side of the fitting, push it into the fitting and pull the fuel line off the pipe

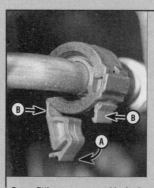

Some fittings are secured by lock tabs. Release the lock tab (A) and rotate it to the fully-opened position, squeeze the two smaller lock tabs (B) . . .

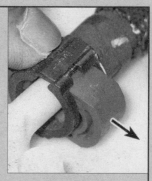

. . . then push the retainer out and pull the fuel line off the pipe

Spring-lock coupling; remove the safety cover, install a coupling release tool and close the tool around the coupling . . .

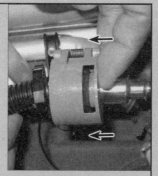

. . . push the tool into the fitting, then pull the two lines apart

Hairpin clip type fitting: push the legs of the retainer clip together, then push the clip down all the way until it stops and pull the fuel line off the pipe

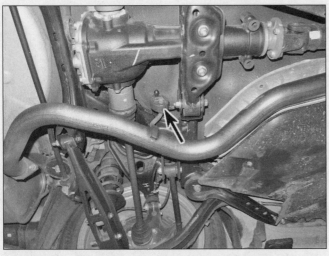

6.1 A typical exhaust system hanger. Inspect regularly and replace at the first sign of damage or deterioration

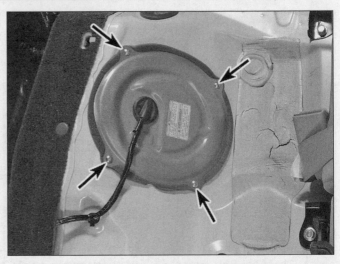

7.3 Fuel pump module access cover screws

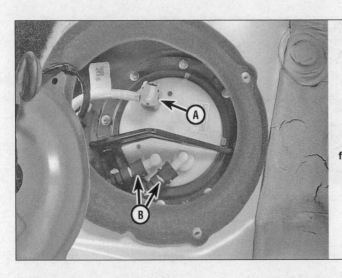

7.4 Fuel pump module electrical connector (A) and fuel supply line quick-connect fitting (B)

d) *Apply anti-seize compound to the threads of all exhaust system fasteners during reassembly.*

e) *Allow sufficient clearance between newly installed parts and all points on the underbody to avoid overheating the floor pan and possibly damaging the interior carpet and insulation. Pay particularly close attention to the catalytic converter and heat shield.*

7   Fuel pump/Fuel Pump Control Module (FPCM) - removal and installation

Fuel pump module

Warning: *Gasoline is extremely flammable. See* Fuel system warnings *in Section 1.*
Note: *The fuel pump module includes the fuel pump, the fuel level sending unit, a fuel filter and, on mechanical returnless pumps, a fuel pressure regulator. On electronic returnless pumps there is no regulator; fuel pressure is regulated by a Fuel Pump Control Module (FPCM). None of these components is separately serviceable*

1   Disconnect the cable from the negative battery terminal (see Chapter 5). Relieve the fuel system pressure (see Section 3).
2   Remove the rear seat cushion (see Chapter 11). Fold back the floor mat as necessary to allow access.
3   Remove the fuel pump access cover screws (see illustration).
Caution: *The fuel pump module access cover is on the right (passenger's) side.*
4   Disconnect the electrical connector and the fuel supply line quick-connect fitting from the fuel pump module (see illustration).

6   Exhaust system servicing - general information

Warning: *Allow exhaust system components to cool before inspection or repair. Also, when working under the vehicle, make sure it is securely supported on jackstands.*
1   The exhaust system consists of the exhaust manifolds, catalytic converter, muffler, tailpipe and all connecting pipes, flanges and clamps. The exhaust system is isolated from the vehicle body and from chassis components by a series of rubber hangers (see illustration). Periodically inspect these hangers for cracks or other signs of deterioration, replacing them as necessary.
2   Conduct regular inspections of the exhaust system to keep it safe and quiet. Look for any damaged or bent parts, open seams, holes, loose connections, excessive corrosion or other defects which could allow exhaust

fumes to enter the vehicle. Do not repair deteriorated exhaust system components; replace them with new parts.
3   If the exhaust system components are extremely corroded, or rusted together, a cutting torch is the most convenient tool for removal. Consult a properly-equipped repair shop. If a cutting torch is not available, you can use a hacksaw, or if you have compressed air, there are special pneumatic cutting chisels that can also be used. Wear safety goggles to protect your eyes from metal chips and wear work gloves to protect your hands.
4   Here are some simple guidelines to follow when repairing the exhaust system:

a) *Work from the back to the front when removing exhaust system components.*
b) *Apply penetrating oil to the exhaust system component fasteners to make them easier to remove.*
c) *Use new gaskets, hangers and clamps.*

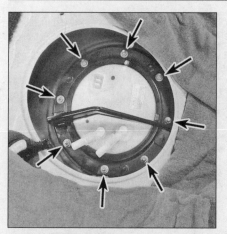

7.5a Remove the pump cover mounting fasteners . . .

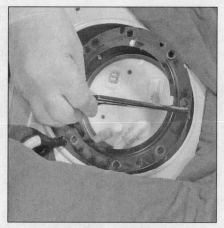

7.5b . . . then remove the cover

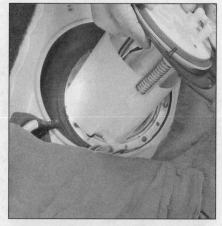

7.6a Remove the fuel pump module at an angle to prevent damage to the float arm

5   Remove the fuel pump cover assembly mounting nuts and the cover (see illustrations).
6   Carefully pull the fuel pump module out of the tank, angling it as necessary to protect the fuel level sensor float arm, then remove the seal (see illustration).
7   Inspect the seal ring and replace it if it shows any sign of deterioration.
8   Installation is the reverse of removal.

Fuel level sending unit

9   Disconnect the electrical connector and harness for the sending unit from the fuel pump module.
10   Depress the retainer tab(s) while sliding the fuel level sending unit off the fuel pump module.
11   Installation is reverse of removal.

Fuel Pump Control Module (FPCM)

Note: *Only Legacy and 2013 and earlier Forester turbocharged models are equipped with an FPCM.*
12   On Legacy models, remove the carpet trim from the right rear part of the trunk. On Forester models, remove the right-rear side quarter trim panel.
13   Disconnect the electrical connector from the FPCM.
14   Remove the fastener and remove the FPCM.
15   Installation is the reverse of removal.

High-pressure fuel pump

Note: *2014 and later Forester turbocharged models are equipped with a direct injection, high-pressure fuel system.*
16   Release the fuel pressure (see Section 3).
Warning: *After releasing the fuel pressure, wait at least two hours before proceeding.*
17   Disconnect the battery negative cable (see Chapter 5).
18   Remove the fuel filler cap.

7.6b Remove and inspect the seal

19   Remove the intake manifold (see Chapter 2A, Section 5).
20   Remove the insulators for the high-pressure fuel pump, fuel pipe 1 and fuel pipe 2.
21   Remove the high-pressure fuel delivery pipe from the high-pressure fuel pump and fuel rail. Disconnect the fuel feed hose quick-disconnect fitting from the low-pressure fuel system at the high-pressure fuel pump.
22   Disconnect the high-pressure fuel pump electrical connector.
23   Remove the two Torx Plus bolts and remove the high-pressure fuel pump from the engine.
24   Remove the fuel pump lifter from the bore. Clean it, then lubricate the bottom of the lifter and the bore of the fuel pump case with engine oil.
25   Installation is reverse of removal. Coat the opening in the engine for the high-pressure fuel pump with clean engine oil prior to installation.
26   Tighten all fasteners to the torque values listed in this Chapter's Specifications.
27   Start the engine and check for leaks.

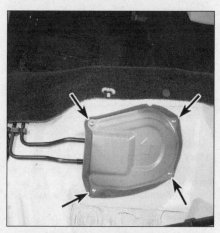

8.4 Sub-compartment fuel level sending unit access plate screws

8   Sub-compartment fuel level sending unit - removal and installation

Warning: *Gasoline is extremely flammable, so take extra precautions when you work on any part of the fuel system. See Fuel system warnings in Section 1.*
Note: *The fuel pump/fuel level sending unit assembly consists of the fuel level sending unit, an integral filter and the holder to which everything is attached. You cannot replace the components separately.*
1   Relieve the fuel system pressure (see Section 3).
2   Disconnect the cable from the negative battery terminal (see Chapter 5).
3   Remove the rear seat (see Chapter 11). Remove the rear floor mat if necessary to gain access.
4   There are two access plates; remove the left (driver's side) plate screws (see illustration), and remove the plate from the body floor pan.

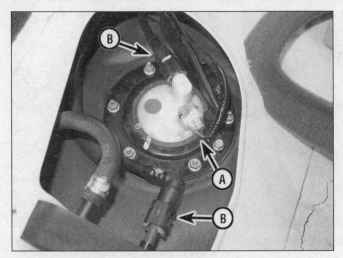

8.5 Sub-compartment fuel level sending unit electrical connector (A) and fuel supply line quick-connect fitting (B)

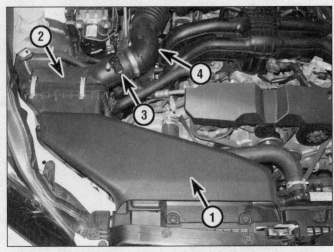

10.1 Air filter housing details (Legacy shown)

1   *Fresh air intake duct*   3   *MAF/IAT sensor*
2   *Air filter case halves*   4   *Air intake duct*

5   Disconnect the electrical connector from the sending unit, then disconnect the fuel supply and return hose quick-connect fittings (see illustration). If you're unfamiliar with quick-connect fittings, refer to Section 5.
6   Remove the sub-compartment fuel level sending unit mounting nuts. Lift the unit out of the fuel tank. angling the sending unit as necessary to protect the float arm from damage.
7   After removing the sending unit, remove the old gasket and inspect it for cracks, tears and deterioration. If the gasket is cracked, torn or deteriorated, replace it.
8   Installation is the reverse of removal.

---

9   Fuel tank - removal and installation

Warning: *Gasoline is extremely flammable, so take extra precautions when you work on any part of the fuel system. See* Fuel system warnings *in Section 1.*
Note: *The following procedure is much easier to perform if the fuel tank is empty.*
1   Remove the fuel tank filler cap to relieve fuel tank pressure.
2   Relieve the fuel system pressure (see Section 3).
3   Disconnect the cable from the negative battery terminal (see Chapter 5).
4   Remove the rear seat and floor mat (see Chapter 11).
5   Disconnect the electrical connector from the fuel pump/fuel level sending unit harness (see illustration 7.4).
6   Remove the sub-compartment fuel level sending unit access plate (see illustration 8.4), and disconnect the fuel supply and return hose quick-connect fittings (see illustration 8.5). If you're unfamiliar with quick-connect fittings, refer to Section 5.
7   Loosen the rear wheel lug nuts. Raise the vehicle and support it securely on jackstands.

Remove the rear wheels.
8   Remove the left and right covers from the front of the fuel tank (if equipped).
9   To drain the left (driver's) side of the fuel tank, remove the sub-compartment fuel level sending unit (see Section 8) and siphon the fuel into an approved fuel container. To drain the right side of the tank, remove the fuel pump module (see Section 7).
Warning: *Don't start the siphoning action by mouth; use a siphoning kit (available at most auto parts stores).*
10   Remove the rear exhaust pipe and muffler and heat shield from under the vehicle (if equipped).
11   On 2014 and later Forester models, remove the rear differential (see Chapter 8 Section 16). On 2013 and earlier Forester models and all Legacy models, remove the rear subframe/suspension assembly (see Chapter 10 Section 11).
12   Remove the rear fuel tank covers.
13   Disconnect the fuel filler neck hose and the fuel tank pressure sensor hose.
14   Disconnect the air vent hose from the EVAP pipe assembly and disconnect the EVAP hose from the pressure control solenoid valve.
15   Support the fuel tank.
16   Remove the fuel tank strap bolts, then carefully lower the fuel tank, making sure nothing is still connected.
17   Installation is the reverse of removal. Tighten the fuel tank strap bolts to the torque listed in this Chapter's Specifications

---

10   Air filter housing - removal and installation

Non-turbocharged models

1   On these models, the air filter housing, which is located at the right front corner of

the engine compartment, is connected to the throttle body by the rear air intake duct. A resonator, which is connected to and located below the front air intake duct, connects the front air intake duct to the air filter housing. If you need to remove some or all of the induction assembly on one of these models, disassemble it in the sequence indicated in the caption for the accompanying illustration.

Turbocharged models

2   On these models, the air filter housing is located at the right front corner of the engine compartment and is almost identical to non-turbocharged models. If you need to remove some or all of the induction assembly on one of these models, disassemble it in the sequence indicated in illustration 10.1, 1 through 4.

---

11   Throttle body - removal and installation

Warning: *Gasoline is extremely flammable, so take extra precautions when you work on any part of the fuel system. See* Fuel system warnings *in Section 1.*
Warning: *Wait until the engine is completely cool before beginning this procedure.*
1   Disconnect the cable from the negative battery terminal (see Chapter 5).
2   Remove the engine cover (if equipped).
3   On non-turbocharged models, remove the air filter housing (see Section 10) and air inlet tube.
4   On turbocharged models, remove the intercooler (see Section 16) and intake air duct. On some models, it may be necessary to remove the air bypass pipe and/or the PCV pipe assembly prior to removing the intake air duct.

11.5 Disconnect the electrical connector from the throttle body

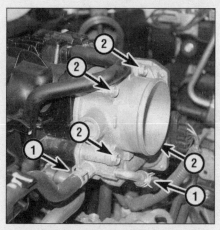

11.7 Coolant lines (1) and throttle body mounting bolts (2)

11.8 Remove the throttle body gasket

5   On all models, disconnect the electrical connector from the throttle body (see illustration).

6   Carefully mark and disconnect the coolant hoses from the throttle body. Clamp-off or plug the coolant hoses to prevent leakage.

7   Remove the four throttle body mounting bolts and remove the throttle body from the intake manifold (see illustration).

8   Remove and discard the old throttle body gasket (see illustration). This may be a gasket or O-ring depending on model. Thoroughly clean the gasket mating surfaces. If scraping is necessary, be careful not to damage the gasket surfaces or allow material to drop into the manifold.

9   While the throttle body is removed, inspect the bore for carbon deposits and/or a build-up of residue. If it's dirty, clean it out with aerosol carburetor cleaner. Make sure that the can of cleaner states specifically that it's safe for use with oxygen sensors and catalytic converters.

10   Installation is the reverse of removal. Be sure to use a new gasket, and tighten the throttle body mounting bolts to the torque listed in this Chapter's Specifications.

11   If a significant amount of coolant was lost when the hoses were disconnected, check the coolant level and top it off as necessary (see Chapter 1).

12 Fuel pressure pulsation damper and pressure regulator - removal and installation

Warning: *Gasoline is extremely flammable, so take extra precautions when you work on any part of the fuel system. See* Fuel system warnings *in Section 1.*

1   Relieve the fuel system pressure (see Section 3).

2   Disconnect the cable from the negative terminal of the battery (see Chapter 5).

Fuel pressure pulsation damper (2014 and later Forester models)

Note: *The pulsation damper(s) is located between the fuel lines on the driver's side of the engine compartment, near the brake master cylinder. Some models have two fuel dampers; one in the supply line and one in the return line. The two dampers are not interchangeable, so be careful not to mix them up if you are removing them both at the same time.*

3   Loosen the clamps, then disconnect and plug the fuel damper hoses.

4   Place new clamps on the hoses, install the damper and tighten the clamps securely.

Fuel pressure regulator and damper (2013 and earlier Forester turbo models and 2012 and earlier Legacy turbo models)

Note: *On these models, the assembly is located in a junction between the fuel supply and return lines, on the driver's side of the engine compartment, near the brake master cylinder.*

5   Disconnect the vacuum hose from the fuel pressure regulator.

6   Disconnect the fuel hoses from the fuel pressure regulator and damper.

7   Remove the regulator cover, then remove the two fuel pressure regulator mounting screws.

8   Remove and discard the old O-ring from the fuel pressure regulator.

9   Install a new O-ring on the fuel pressure regulator. Apply a light coat of clean engine oil to the new O-ring.

10   Installation is the reverse of removal. Tighten the pressure regulator mounting screws and all hose clamps securely.

11   Start the engine and check for leaks.

13 Fuel rail and injectors - removal and installation

Warning: *Gasoline is extremely flammable. See* Fuel system warnings *in Section 1.*

Note: *Even if you only removed the fuel rail assembly to replace a single injector or a leaking O-ring, it's a good idea to remove all of the injectors from the fuel rail and replace all of the O-rings at the same time.*

1   Relieve the fuel system pressure (see Section 3).

2   Disconnect the cable from the negative battery terminal (see Chapter 5).

Non-turbocharged models
2012 and earlier Legacy models

Note: *The fuel rails and injectors are removed with the intake manifold.*

3   Remove the intake manifold (see Chapter 2A, Section 5).

4   Remove the bolts securing the fuel rail to the intake manifold.

5   Remove the fuel rail mounting bolts, lift up the rail and pull out the injectors.

Note: *To remove the fuel rail and the injectors from the intake manifold, grasp the rail firmly and pull. If either injector is difficult to dislodge from its mounting hole in the intake manifold, wiggle the injector(s) from side-to-side while simultaneously pulling on the fuel rail.*

6   Remove and discard the old injector O-ring.

7   Install a new O-ring on the injector. Apply a light coat of engine oil to the O-ring to protect it during installation of the injector.

8   The remainder of installation is the reverse of removal. Tighten all fasteners to the torque listed in this Chapter's Specifications.

13.10 Remove fuel rail shield to expose the injectors and rail

13.11 Disconnect the fuel line at the rail

13.12 Remove bolts and remove fuel rail and injectors

13.13 Remove and replace the injector O-rings

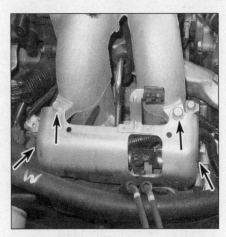

13.18 To detach the protector for the right or left side, remove the four bolts securing the cover

13.19 To disconnect the electrical connectors (A) from the fuel injectors, depress the release tabs and pull off the connectors. (B) are the fuel rail mounting bolts

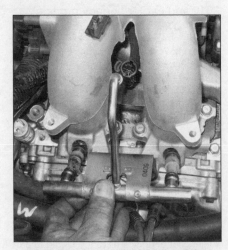

13.21 To remove the fuel rail and the injectors from the intake manifold, grasp the rail firmly and pull. If either injector is difficult to dislodge from its mounting hole in the intake manifold, wiggle the injector(s) from side-to-side while simultaneously pulling on the fuel rail (right fuel rail)

2013 and later Legacy models and 2011 and later Forester models

9   For the passenger side fuel rail and injectors, remove the air intake duct, the resonator and the air filter housing (see Section 10).
10   For either side, remove the bolts and intake manifold shields to expose the fuel rail and injectors (see illustration).
11   On models with quick-disconnect fittings at the fuel rails, disconnect the fuel lines from the fuel rails before removing the bolts (see illustration).
12   Remove the fuel rail mounting bolts, lift up the rail and pull out the injectors (see illustration). Some models are equipped with clips securing the injectors to the fuel rails.
13   Remove and discard the old injector O-rings (see illustration).
14   Install a new O-ring on the injector. Apply a light coat of engine oil to the O-ring to protect it during installation of the injector.
15   The remainder of installation is the reverse of removal. Tighten all fasteners to

the torque listed in this Chapter's Specifications.

2010 and earlier Forester models

Right-side fuel rail and injectors removal

16   Remove the air intake duct, the resonator and the air filter housing (see Section 10).
17   Disconnect the spark plug wires from the spark plugs for the No. 1 and No. 3 cylinders (see Chapter 1).
18   Remove the fuel rail protector (see illustration).
19   Disconnect the electrical connectors from the fuel injectors (see illustration).
20   Remove the fuel rail mounting bolts.
21   Remove the fuel rail and injectors from the intake manifold as a single assembly (see illustration).
22   Use clean shop towels to plug the injector holes in the intake manifold to prevent debris from entering the combustion chambers.

13.28 The one-piece protectors are secured by five bolts

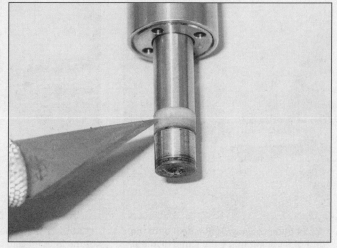

13.49 To remove the Teflon sealing ring, cut it off with a hobby knife (be careful not to scratch the injector groove)

23   Place the fuel rail/injector assembly on a clean workbench.

24   Carefully pull the injectors out of the fuel rail(s).

25   Remove and discard the old O-rings from each injector.

Left fuel rail and injectors removal

26   Disconnect the spark plug wires from the spark plugs for the No. 2 and No. 4 cylinders (see Chapter 1).

27   Disconnect the PCV hose from the pipe on the left valve cover (see Chapter 6).

28   Remove the fuel rail protector(s) (see illustration).

29   Disconnect the electrical connectors from the fuel injectors.

30   Disconnect the quick-connect fittings from the fuel rail.

31   Remove the fuel rail mounting bolts (see illustration 13.19).

Note: *In addition to the fuel rail mounting bolts, similar to the the right-side fuel rail bolts shown in illustration 13.19, there's another bolt securing the line leading to the rail, higher up on the manifold.*

32   Remove the fuel rail and injectors from the intake manifold as a single assembly. The rear fuel rail pipe snakes around the backside of the intake manifold and emerges between the two intake runners, so be careful when removing the fuel rail.

33   Remove and discard the old O-rings from each injector.

Installation

34   Install new O-rings on each injector. Apply a light coat of engine oil to each new O-ring to protect it when installing the injector into the fuel rail and the intake manifold.

35   Carefully install the injectors into the fuel rail.

36   Install the fuel rail and injectors as a single assembly. Carefully work each injector

into its mounting hole in the intake manifold until it's fully seated. Be careful not to damage the injector O-rings.

37   Install the fuel rail mounting bolts and tighten them to the torque listed in this Chapter's Specifications.

38   The remainder of installation is the reverse of removal.

Turbocharged models

39   Remove the intake manifold (see Chapter 2A).

Note: *On Legacy models and 2013 and earlier Forester models, the fuel rails and injectors are removed with the intake manifold.*

40   On Legacy models and 2013 and earlier Forester models, remove the fuel rail cover fasteners and remove the cover(s).

41   On 2014 and later Forester models, remove the three insulators to access the fuel rails. Remove the fuel delivery pipe from between the left and right fuel rails.

42   On all models, disconnect the fuel injector electrical connectors.

2.5L engine

43   Remove the fuel rail mounting bolts, lift up the rail and pull out the injectors.

44   Remove and discard the old injector O-ring.

45   Install a new O-ring on the injector. Apply a light coat of engine oil to the O-ring to protect it during installation of the injector.

46   The remainder of installation is the reverse of removal. Tighten all fasteners to the torque listed in this Chapter's Specifications.

2.0L engine

47   Remove the bolts and detach the fuel rail from the injectors.

48   Using an injector extractor tool, pull the injectors from the cylinder head.

49   Remove the old combustion chamber

Teflon sealing ring and the upper O-ring and support ring from each injector (see illustration).

Caution: *Be extremely careful not to damage the groove for the seal or the rib in the floor of the groove. If you damage the groove or the rib, you must replace the injector.*

50   Before installing the new Teflon seal on each injector, thoroughly clean the groove for the seal and the injector shaft. Remove all combustion residue and varnish with a clean shop rag.

Teflon seal installation using the special tools

51   The manufacturer recommends that you use the tools included in the special injector tool set described above to install the Teflon lower seals on the injectors: Install the special seal assembly cone on the injector, install the special sleeve on the injector and use the sleeve to push on the assembly cone, which pushes the Teflon seal into place on its groove. Do NOT use any lubricants to do so.

52   Pushing the Teflon seal into place in its groove expands it slightly. There is a two-sided sizing sleeve in the special tool set with two different inside diameters. Using a clockwise rotating motion of about 180 degrees, install the slightly larger sleeve onto the injector and over the Teflon seal until the sleeve hits its stop, then carefully turn the sleeve counterclockwise as you pull it off the injector. Use the slightly smaller sizing sleeve the same way. The seal is now sized. Repeat this step for each injector.

Teflon seal installation without special tools

53   If you don't have the special injector tool set, the Teflon seal can be installed using this method: First, find a socket that is equal or very close in diameter to the diameter of the end of the fuel injector.

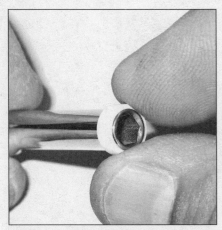

13.54 Slide the new Teflon seal onto the end of a socket that's the same diameter as the end of the fuel injector . . .

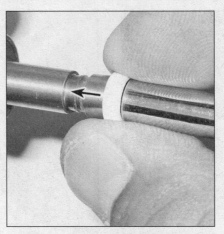

13.55 . . . align the socket with the end of the injector and slide the seal onto the injector and into its mounting groove

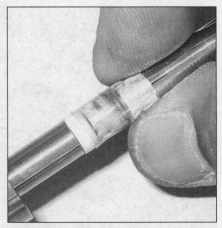

13.56a Use the socket to push a short section of plastic tubing onto the end of the injector and over the new seal . . .

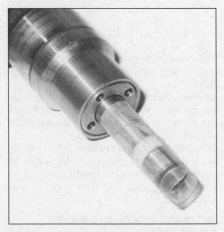

13.56b . . . then leave the plastic tubing in place for several hours to compress the new seal

13.57 Note that the upper O-ring (1) is installed above the support ring (2)

54   Work the new Teflon seal onto the end of the socket (see illustration).

55   Place the socket against the end of the injector (see illustration) and slide the seal from the socket onto the injector. Do NOT use any lubricants to do so. Continue pushing the seal onto the injector until it seats into its mounting groove.

56   Because the inside diameter of the seal has to be stretched open to fit over the bore of the socket and the injector, its outside diameter is now slightly too large - it is no longer flush with the surface of the injector. It must be shrunk it back to its original size. To do so, push a piece of plastic tubing with an interference fit onto the end of the socket; a plastic straw that fits tightly on the injector will work. After pushing the plastic tubing onto the socket about an inch, snip off the rest of the tubing, then use the socket to push the tubing onto the end of the injector (see illustration) and slide it onto the injector until it completely covers the new seal (see illustration). Leave the tubing on for a few hours, then remove it. The seal should now be shrunk back to its

original outside diameter, or close to it.

Injector and fuel rail installation

57   Install the new support ring at the upper end of the injector. Lubricate the new upper O-ring with clean engine oil and install it on the injector. Do NOT oil the new Teflon seal. Note that the seal is installed above the spacer (see illustration).

58   Thoroughly clean the injector bores with a small nylon brush.

59   Install the new injector holder to the bottom of each injector.

60   Install the fuel injectors in the fuel rail and secure them with new retainers, then install the fuel rail and injectors. The bores in the cylinder head are slightly tapered, so you will encounter some resistance as the Teflon seal nears the bottom of the bore.

61   Install the fuel rail bolts, tightening them alternately until they are seated, then tighten them to the torque listed in this Chapter's Specifications.

62   The remainder of installation is the reverse of removal. Clean the high-pressure

fuel line fittings on the fuel rails, then apply a little clean engine oil to the threads. Install the new high-pressure fuel line, tightening the fittings to the torque listed in this Chapter's Specifications.

14   Turbocharger - description and inspection

Description

1   A turbocharger system increases engine horsepower by means of an exhaust gas-driven turbine that turns an impeller, or compressor, which in turn pressurizes the air entering the intake manifold. The faster the engine speed, the higher the speed of the exhaust gases and the speed of the exhaust gas-driven turbine. And the faster the exhaust gases, the faster the compressor spins, which pumps even more air into the intake manifold. As the amount of air being pumped into the intake manifold increases, so does the pressure of the air entering the manifold. This pressurized air is known as boost. The amount of boost (or intake manifold pressure) is controlled by the wastegate, a pop-off valve that's controlled by the Powertrain Control Module (PCM).

2   The turbocharger system consists of the turbocharger assembly, the PCM and an array of information sensors, the wastegate controller solenoid valve, the wastegate controller, the wastegate valve, the air bypass valve and the intercooler. The rest of the system - the throttle body and the intake manifold - isn't that much different from the components used on a normally-aspirated engine.

Turbocharger assembly

3   The turbocharger assembly is actually composed of two separate castings. The housing for the turbine is cast iron; the housing for the compressor is aluminum. A common shaft riding on full-floating bearings connects the turbine and the compressor. The

turbocharger assembly is water-cooled. Coolant is pumped by the water pump through a line from the right cylinder head, then through cooling passages near the turbine shaft bearings, then out of the turbocharger housing and into the coolant reservoir. The turbocharger is lubricated by engine oil pumped through the turbocharger housing by the engine oil pump. The lubrication system also helps to cool the bearings for the turbine shaft by carrying away some of the heat generated by the exhaust gases moving through the turbine housing.

14.4 A typical wastegate valve (A) and wastegate controller (B) (early style, other models similar)

Wastegate valve

4   The wastegate valve (see illustration) is designed to restrict the maximum boost level by allowing some of the exhaust gases to bypass the turbine when boost pressure gets too high. As long as the boost is below the predetermined threshold, the wastegate is closed, and all exhaust gases are directed through to the turbine housing. But when the boost pressure exceeds the specified level, some of the exhaust gases are diverted to the exhaust pipe by way of the wastegate valve. The wastegate valve is controlled by the wastegate controller.

Wastegate controller

5   The wastegate controller housing has two chambers inside it. One chamber contains atmospheric pressure (14.7 psi). The other chamber is connected to the output side of the compressor by a hose, and the pressure inside this chamber can be anywhere between atmospheric and the predetermined boost threshold. The two chambers are divided by a spring-loaded diaphragm, which is connected to the wastegate valve. As long as the boost pressure on the output side of the compressor is below the predetermined threshold, the wastegate controller is inactive. But when the boost pressure hits or exceeds the threshold, the controller opens the wastegate valve.

Wastegate controller solenoid valve

6   As the vehicle is driven into higher altitudes, the air thins and the atmospheric pressure goes down, which means that turbocharging pressure is also diminished. The wastegate controller solenoid valve, which is controlled by the PCM, keeps the wastegate controller closed to optimize the pressure on the outlet side of the compressor.

Intercooler

7   Have you ever noticed how your vehicle's engine seems to make more power under a load (accelerating, passing, going uphill, etc.) on a cool morning than it does later in the day when the ambient air temperature is higher? That's because the cooler morning air is denser (has more oxygen in it), which means that it can produce more power when mixed with fuel and burned. The intake air that's compressed by a turbocharger is very hot. And because hot air expands, it results in lower effective supercharging efficiency because hot air is not as dense as cold air, which means that it has less oxygen in

it, which means that it will make less power when mixed with fuel and burned in the combustion chambers. But as this hot intake air passes through the air-cooled intercooler, it cools down significantly, which makes it denser again and therefore able to provide more oxygen for the combustion process.

Air bypass valve

8   When the throttle plate is snapped shut during deceleration, a sudden rise in air pressure inside the passage between the turbocharger outlet and the throttle body occurs. If not for the air bypass valve (also known as a blow-off valve), this would cause a braking effect on the turbocharger. The air bypass valve reduces this effect by routing the excess air back to the turbocharger inlet duct. Here's how it works: The air bypass valve is mounted on the intercooler. A diaphragm housing on the bypass valve is connected to the intake manifold by a vacuum hose. When you lift your foot off the accelerator pedal, the throttle plate closes, intake manifold vacuum goes up and pulls the diaphragm up into its housing. The diaphragm is connected to a valve that opens and allows air from the intercooler to be directed through a passage back to the turbocharger inlet duct. When you accelerate again, intake manifold vacuum goes down, the spring-loaded diaphragm closes the valve and all air is once again directed from the intercooler through throttle body and into the intake manifold.

PCM and information sensors

9   For explanations of what the PCM and the various sensors do, refer to Chapter 6.

Inspection

10   Though it's a relatively simple device, the turbocharger is a precision component. Special tools are needed to disassemble and overhaul a turbocharger, so servicing should be left to a dealer service department. However, you can inspect some things yourself, such as a cracked turbo mounting flange, a blocked or restricted oil supply line, a worn out or overheated turbine/compressor shaft bearing or a defective wastegate actuator.

11   A turbocharger has its own distinctive

sound, so a change in the quality or the quantity of noise can be a sign of potential problems. But before assuming that a funny sound is caused by a defective turbocharger, inspect the exhaust manifold for cracks and loose connections. For example, a high-pitched or whistling sound might indicate an intake air or exhaust gas leak. Inspect the turbocharger mounting flange at the exhaust manifold and make sure that the hose clamp that attaches the air intake duct to the turbocharger is tight.

12   If an unusual sound is coming from the turbocharger, turn the engine off and allow it to cool completely, then remove the intake duct between the air cleaner housing and the turbocharger. Reach inside the housing and turn the compressor wheel to make sure it spins freely. If it doesn't, it's possible the turbo lubricating oil has sludged or coked up from overheating. Push in on the turbine wheel and check for binding. The turbine should rotate freely with no binding or rubbing on the housing. If it does the turbine or compressor shaft bearing is worn out.

Warning: *Inspect the turbocharger with the engine off and cool to the touch. Touching or reaching inside a hot and/or operating turbocharger can cause serious injury.*

13   The turbocharger is lubricated by engine oil. Oil is delivered to the turbocharger by a supply line that's tapped into the right cylinder head. Oil travels to the turbocharger, where it lubricates the shaft and bearings. A return pipe routes the heated oil back to the crankcase. Because the turbine and compressor wheels spin at speeds up to 140,000 rpm, severe damage can result from the interruption or contamination of the oil supply to the turbocharger bearings. Look for leaks in the oil supply line. If a fitting is leaking, tighten it and note whether the leak stops. If the supply line itself is leaking, replace it. Remove the oil return line (on the bottom) and inspect it for obstructions. A blocked return line can cause a loss of oil through the turbocharger seals. Burned oil on the turbine housing is a sign of a blocked return line.

Caution: *Whenever a major engine bearing such as a main, connecting rod or camshaft bearing is replaced, flush the turbocharger oil passages with clean oil.*

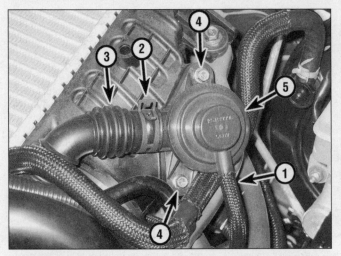 

15.2 Air bypass valve assembly (2013 and earlier models):

1	Vacuum hose	4	Mounting bolts
2	Spring-type hose clamp	5	Air bypass valve
3	Air bypass hose		

16.4 Intake duct-to-intercooler clamp

16.5 Intercooler-to-turbocharger bolts (A) and left side mounting bolt (B)

15 Air bypass valve - removal and installation

1   Remove the engine cover, if equipped (see Chapter 2A).

Forester

2013 and earlier models

2   Disconnect the vacuum hose and air bypass hose from the air bypass valve (see illustration).
3   Remove the air bypass valve mounting bolts.
4   Remove the air bypass valve.
5   Installation is the reverse of removal.

2014 and later models

6   Disconnect the vacuum hose and air bypass hose from the air bypass valve.
7   Remove the air intake duct containing the air bypass valve.
8   Loosen the clamp and remove the air bypass valve.
9   Installation is the reverse of removal.

Legacy

10   Remove the collector cover.
11   Disconnect the vacuum line from the PCV pipe.
12   Loosen the air bypass valve clamp at the intake duct.
13   Raise and support the vehicle on jackstands and remove the engine under cover.
14   Remove the air bypass valve from the bypass tube and intake air duct.
15   Installation is the reverse of removal.

16 Intercooler - removal and installation

Forester

2013 and earlier models

1   Disconnect the cable from the negative terminal of the battery (see Chapter 5).
2   Remove the engine cover, if equipped.
3   Loosen the hose clamp that secures the air bypass duct to the air bypass valve, then

disconnect the bypass duct from the bypass valve (see illustration 16.5).
4   Loosen the clamp that secures the air intake duct to the intercooler (see illustration).
5   Remove the intercooler-to-turbocharger bolts (see illustration).
6   Remove the intercooler left-side mounting bolt and remove the intercooler.
7   If you're simply removing the intercooler to access some other component, no disassembly is required.
8   If you're removing the intercooler to replaceit, remove the air bypass valve and install it on the new intercooler.
9   Installation is the reverse of removal. Be sure to use a new gasket between the intercooler and turbocharger, and tighten the intercooler-to-turbocharger bolts and the left-side mounting bolt to the torque listed in this Chapter's Specifications.

2014 and later models

10   Disconnect the cable from the negative terminal of the battery.
11   Remove the engine cover.
12   Disconnect the PCM connectors.
13   Loosen the intercooler duct hose clamps.
14   Remove the bolts attaching the intercooler to the intercooler mounts.
15   Detach the intercooler duct hoses and remove the intercooler from the vehicle.
16   Installation is the reverse of removal.

Legacy

17   Remove the collector cover.
18   Loosen the intercooler duct hose clamps.
19   Remove the bolts attaching the intercooler to the intercooler mounts.
20   Detach the intercooler duct hoses and remove the intercooler from the vehicle.
21   Installation is the reverse of removal.

17.3 Intercooler bracket mounting fasteners (2013 and earlier models shown)

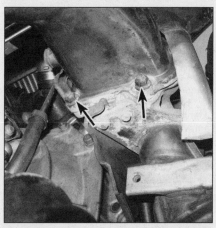

17.5a From under the vehicle, remove the center exhaust pipe lower nut/bolts . . .

17.5b . . . then remove the remaining nuts/bolts from above

17.6 To disconnect the joint pipe from the turbocharger, remove the fasteners (two of three shown)

17.10 Oil inlet line mounting bracket (1) and upper banjo bolt (2) (lower banjo bolt not shown)

17 Turbocharger - removal and installation

Warning: *Wait until the engine is completely cool before beginning this procedure.*
Caution: *The turbocharger is a precision component that has been assembled and balanced to very fine tolerances. Do not disassemble it or try to repair it. Turbochargers should only be overhauled or repaired by authorized turbocharged repair facilities. An incorrectly assembled turbocharger could result in damage to the turbocharger and/or the engine.*

Removal
2013 and earlier Forester models

1 Disconnect the cable from the negative battery terminal (see Chapter 5).
2 Remove the engine cover, if equipped (see Chapter 2A).
3 Remove the intercooler (see Section 16)

and the mounting bracket (see illustration).
4 Drain the engine coolant and oil (see Chapter 1).
5 Raise the vehicle and support it securely on jackstands, then remove the center exhaust pipe (see illustrations).
6 Disconnect the turbocharger joint pipe from the turbocharger (see illustration).
7 Loosen the spring type hose clamp and disconnect the coolant return hose from the metal coolant line.
8 Loosen the big hose clamp that secures the turbocharger to the intake duct.
9 Remove the bolt that secures the oil inlet line mounting bracket to the turbocharger.
10 Remove the banjo bolts at both ends of the oil inlet line (see illustration) and remove the oil inlet line from the turbocharger.
Note: *Not all models have a banjo bolt on each end, some models have a compression fitting that is unscrewed instead.*
11 Loosen the hose clamps on both ends

of the coolant hose and remove the coolant hose.
12 Remove the right turbocharger mounting bracket.
13 Loosen the spring type hose clamp that secures the oil outlet hose to the underside of the turbocharger, then disconnect the oil outlet hose from the turbocharger.
14 Remove the turbocharger.
15 If you're only removing the turbocharger to access some other component(s), no further disassembly is necessary.
16 If you're replacing the turbocharger, strip off all the remaining parts and install them on the new turbocharger unit.

2014 and later Forester models and all Legacy models

17 Remove the engine cover and disconnect the negative battery cable.
18 Remove the intake air duct (see Section 10).

19   Raise and support the vehicle and remove the vehicle engine under cover and the engine under cover.

20   Drain the engine coolant (see Chapter 1, Section 21).

21   Disconnect the oxygen sensor connectors an harness clips (see Chapter 6, Section 12).

22   Disconnect the coolant hose between the tank and water pump.

23   Remove the electric cooling fan motor assembly (see Chapter 3, Section 5).

24   Disconnect the intake air duct from the turbocharger.

25   Working under the vehicle, disconnect the oil supply lines and the bracket. Secure the lines using a wrench when attempting to loosen to prevent the assembly from rotating.

26   Disconnect the vacuum line and bolts securing the intake air duct to the turbocharger.

27   Remove the bolts and disconnect the front center exhaust pipe from the rear center exhaust pipe.

28   Disconnect the rear center exhaust pipe from the bracket and remove the rear center exhaust pipe from the vehicle.

29   Remove the oil catch tank from the turbocharger.

30   Remove the two fasteners securing the turbocharger to the bracket.

31   Support the front exhaust pipe (bolted to the cylinder heads and includes the turbocharger) using a floor jack.

32   Remove the six nuts attaching the front exhaust pipes to the cylinder heads and remove the front exhaust pipe and turbocharger.

33   Remove the shield and turbocharger nuts. The brackets will also be removed with the turbocharger.

34   If you're only removing the turbocharger to access some other component(s), no further disassembly is necessary.

35   If you're replacing the turbocharger, strip off all the remaining parts and install them on the new turbocharger unit.

Installation

36   When installing the turbocharger:

a) *Use new sealing washers for the oil inlet pipe banjo fittings and, if removed, for the coolant pipe banjo fittings.*

b) *Tighten the oil inlet pipe banjo bolts and, if removed, the coolant pipe banjo bolts to the torque listed in this Chapter's Specifications.*

c) *Use a new gasket and nuts when reconnecting the joint pipe to the turbocharger. If you're reconnecting the joint pipe to the old turbo unit, it's a good idea to clean the threads on the mounting studs with a thread chaser.*

d) *Apply anti-seize compound to the mounting studs and tighten the joint pipe nuts to the torque listed in this Chapter's Specifications.*

37   Installation is otherwise the reverse of removal. Be sure to use new gaskets and tighten the fasteners to the torque values listed in this Chapter's Specifications.

38   Refill the engine coolant and oil (see Chapter 1, Section 6).

39   Start the engine and check for coolant, oil and exhaust leaks.

Notes

Notes

Chapter 5
Engine electrical systems

Contents

Specifications

Firing order	1-3-2-4
Charging voltage	13.5 to 15 volts

Ignition coil
2009 SOHC Legacy/2009 and 2010 SOHC Forester models
Secondary resistance only	11.2 k-ohms +/- 15 percent
All other models	Not available

Torque specifications

Note: *One foot-pound (ft-lb) of torque is equivalent to 12 inch-pounds (in-lbs) of torque. Torque values below approximately 15 foot-pounds are expressed in inch-pounds, because most foot-pound torque wrenches are not accurate at these smaller values.*

	Ft-lbs (unless otherwise indicated)	Nm
Alternator bolts		
Forester		
2013 and earlier		
Non-turbo		
Upper bolt	18	25
Lower bolt	27	36
Turbo		
Pivot bolt	16	22
Adjuster bolt	18	25
2014 and later	18	25
Legacy	18	25
Starter bolt/nuts	37	50

1   General information and precautions

General information

Ignition system

1   The electronic ignition system consists of the Crankshaft Position (CKP) sensor, the Camshaft Position (CMP) sensor, the Knock Sensor (KS), the Powertrain Control Module (PCM), the ignition switch, the battery, the individual ignition coils or a coil pack, and the spark plugs. For more information on the CKP, CMP and KS sensors, as well as the PCM, refer to Chapter 6.

Charging system

2   The charging system includes the alternator (with an integral voltage regulator), the Powertrain Control Module (PCM), the Body Control Module (BCM), a charge indicator light on the dash, the battery, a fuse or fusible link and the wiring connecting all of these components. The charging system supplies electrical power for the ignition system, the lights, the radio, etc. The alternator is driven by a drivebelt.

Starting system

3   The starting system consists of the battery, the ignition switch, the starter relay, the Powertrain Control Module (PCM), the Body Control Module (BCM), the Transmission Range (TR) switch, the starter motor and solenoid assembly, and the wiring connecting all of the components.

Precautions

4   Always observe the following precautions when working on the electrical system: Be extremely careful when servicing engine electrical components. They are easily damaged if checked, connected or handled improperly.

   a) *Never leave the ignition switched on for long periods of time when the engine is not running.*

   b) *Never disconnect the battery cables while the engine is running.*

   c) *Maintain correct polarity when connecting battery cables from another vehicle during jump starting (see* Booster battery (jump) starting *at the front of this manual).*

   d) *Always disconnect the cable from the negative battery terminal before working on the electrical system, but read the battery disconnection procedure first (see Section 3).*

5   It's also a good idea to review the safety-related information regarding the engine electrical systems located in the *Safety first!* section at the front of this manual before beginning any operation included in this Chapter.

2   Troubleshooting

Ignition system

1   If a malfunction occurs in the ignition system, do not immediately assume that any particular part is causing the problem. First, check the following items:

   a) *Make sure that the cable clamps at the battery terminals are clean and tight (see Chapter 1, Section 7).*

   b) *Test the condition of the battery (see Steps 21 through 24). If it doesn't pass all the tests, replace it.*

   c) *Check the ignition coil or coil pack connections.*

   d) *Check any relevant fuses in the engine compartment fuse and relay box (see Chapter 12). If they're burned, determine the cause and repair the circuit.*

Check

Warning: *Because of the high voltage generated by the ignition system, use extreme care when performing a procedure involving ignition components.*

Note: *Most problems with the ignition system will result in a Diagnostic Trouble Code (DTC) being stored in the Powertrain Control; Module (PCM). See Chapter 6 for information on*

how to extract trouble codes from the PCM.
Note: *You'll need a spark tester for the following test. Spark testers are available at most auto supply stores.*

2   If the engine turns over but won't start, verify that there is sufficient ignition voltage to fire the spark plugs as follows.

3   On models with a coil-over-plug type ignition system, remove a coil and install the tester between the boot at the lower end of the coil and the spark plug (see illustration). On models with spark plug wires, disconnect a spark plug wire from a spark plug and install the tester between the spark plug wire boot and the spark plug.

Caution: *Do NOT crank the engine or allow it to run for more than five seconds; running the engine for more than five seconds may set a Diagnostic Trouble Code (DTC) for a cylinder misfire.*

4   Crank the engine and note whether or not the tester flashes.

Models with a coil-over-plug type ignition system

5   If the tester flashes during cranking, the coil is delivering sufficient voltage to the spark plug to fire it. Repeat this test for each cylinder to verify that the other coils are OK.

6   If the tester doesn't flash, remove a coil from another cylinder and swap it for the one being tested. If the tester now flashes, you know that the original coil is bad. If the tester still doesn't flash, the PCM or wiring harness is probably defective. Have the PCM checked out by a dealer service department or other qualified repair shop (testing the PCM is beyond the scope of the do-it-yourselfer because it requires expensive special tools).

7   If the tester flashes during cranking but a misfire code (related to the cylinder being tested) has been stored, the spark plug could be fouled or defective, or the coil could be be malfunctioning under load.

Models with spark plug wires

8   If the tester flashes during cranking, sufficient voltage is reaching the spark plug to fire it.

9   Repeat this test on the remaining cylinders.

10   Proceed on this basis until you have verified that there's a good spark from each spark plug wire. If there is, then you have verified that the coils in the coil pack are functioning correctly and that the spark plug wires are OK.

11   If there is no spark from a spark plug wire, then either the coil is bad, the plug wire is bad or a connection at one end of the plug wire is loose. Assuming that you're using new plug wires or known good wires, then the coil is probably defective. Also inspect the coil pack electrical connector. Make sure that it's clean, tight and in good condition.

12   If all the coils are firing correctly, but the engine misfires, then one or more of the plugs might be fouled. Remove and check the spark plugs or install new ones (see Chapter 1).

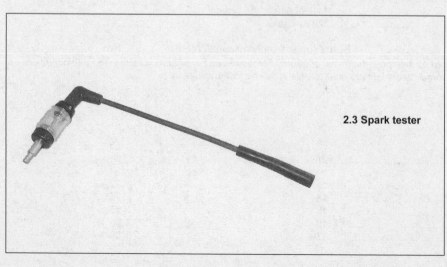

2.3 Spark tester

13   No further testing of the ignition system is possible without special tools. If the problem persists, have the ignition system tested by a dealer service department or other qualified repair shop.

Charging system

14   If a malfunction occurs in the charging system, do not automatically assume the alternator is causing the problem. First check the following items:

a) *Check the drivebelt tension and condition (see Chapter 1). Replace it if it's worn or deteriorated.*

b) *Make sure the alternator mounting bolts are tight.*

c) *Inspect the alternator wiring harness and the connectors at the alternator and voltage regulator. They must be in good condition, tight and have no corrosion.*

d) *Check the fusible link (if equipped) or main fuse in the underhood fuse/relay box. If it is burned, determine the cause, repair the circuit and replace the link or fuse (the vehicle will not start and/or the accessories will not work if the fusible link or main fuse is blown).*

e) *Start the engine and check the alternator for abnormal noises (a shrieking or squealing sound indicates a bad bearing).*

f) *Check the battery. Make sure it's fully charged and in good condition (one bad cell in a battery can cause overcharging by the alternator).*

g) *Disconnect the battery cables (negative first, then positive). Inspect the battery posts and the cable clamps for corrosion. Clean them thoroughly if necessary (see Chapter 1). Reconnect the cables (positive first, negative last).*

Alternator - check

15   Use a voltmeter to check the battery voltage with the engine off. It should be at least 12.6 volts (see illustration 2.21).

16   Start the engine and check the battery voltage again. It should now be approximately 13.5 to 15 volts.

17   If the voltage reading is more or less than the specified charging voltage, the voltage regulator is probably defective, which will require replacement of the alternator (the voltage regulator is not replaceable separately). Remove the alternator (see Section 7) and have it bench tested (most auto parts stores will do this for you).

18   The charging system (battery) light on the instrument cluster lights up when the ignition key is turned to ON, but it should go out when the engine starts.

19   If the charging system light stays on after the engine has been started, there is a problem with the charging system. Before replacing the alternator, check the battery condition, alternator belt tension (see Chapter 1) and electrical cable connections.

20   If replacing the alternator doesn't restore voltage to the specified range, have the charging system tested by a dealer service department or other qualified repair shop.

Battery - check

21   Check the battery state of charge. Visually inspect the indicator eye on the top of the battery (if equipped with one); if the indicator eye is black in color, charge the battery (see Chapter 1). Next perform an open circuit voltage test using a digital voltmeter. With the engine and all accessories Off, touch the negative probe of the voltmeter to the negative terminal of the battery and the positive probe to the positive terminal of the battery (see illustration). The battery voltage should be 12.6 volts or slightly above. If the battery is less than the specified voltage, charge the battery before proceeding to the next test. Do not proceed with the battery load test unless the battery charge is correct.

Note: *The battery's surface charge must be removed before accurate voltage measurements can be made. Turn on the high beams for ten seconds, then turn them off and let the vehicle stand for two minutes.*

22   Disconnect the negative battery cable, then the positive cable from the battery.

23   Perform a battery load test. An accurate check of the battery condition can only be performed with a load tester (see illustration). This test evaluates the ability of the battery to operate the starter and other accessories during periods of high current draw. Connect the load tester to the battery terminals. Load test the battery according to the tool manufacturer's instructions. This tool increases the load demand (current draw) on the battery.

24   Maintain the load on the battery for 15 seconds and observe that the battery voltage does not drop below 9.6 volts. If the battery condition is weak or defective, the tool will indicate this condition immediately.

Note: *Cold temperatures will cause the minimum voltage reading to drop slightly. Follow the chart given in the manufacturer's instructions to compensate for cold climates. Minimum load voltage for freezing temperatures (32 degrees F) should be approximately 9.1 volts.*

Starting system

The starter rotates, but the engine doesn't

25   Remove the starter (see Section 8). Check the overrunning clutch and bench test the starter to make sure the drive mechanism extends fully for proper engagement with the flywheel ring gear. If it doesn't, replace the starter.

26   Check the flywheel ring gear for missing teeth and other damage. With the ignition turned off, rotate the flywheel so you can check the entire ring gear.

The starter is noisy

27   If the solenoid is making a chattering noise, first check the battery (see Steps 21

2.21 To test the open circuit voltage of the battery, touch the black probe of the voltmeter to the negative terminal and the red probe to the positive terminal of the battery; a fully charged battery should be at least 12.6 volts

2.23 Connect a battery load tester to the battery and check the battery condition under load following the tool manufacturer's instructions

through 24). If the battery is okay, check the cables and connections.

28   If you hear a grinding, crashing metallic sound when you turn the key to Start, check for loose starter mounting bolts. If they're tight, remove the starter and inspect the teeth on the starter pinion gear and flywheel ring gear. Look for missing or damaged teeth.

29   If the starter sounds fine when you first turn the key to Start, but then stops rotating the engine and emits a zinging sound, the problem is probably a defective starter drive that's not staying engaged with the ring gear. Replace the starter.

The starter rotates slowly

30   Check the battery (see Steps 21 through 24).

31   If the battery is okay, verify all connections (at the battery, the starter solenoid and motor) are clean, corrosion-free and tight. Make sure the cables aren't frayed or damaged.

32   Check that the starter mounting bolts are tight so it grounds properly. Also check the pinion gear and flywheel ring gear for evidence of a mechanical bind (galling, deformed gear teeth or other damage).

The starter does not rotate at all

33   Check the battery (see Steps 21 through 24).

34   If the battery is okay, verify all connections (at the battery, the starter solenoid and motor) are clean, corrosion-free and tight. Make sure the cables aren't frayed or damaged.

35   Check all of the fuses in the underhood fuse/relay box.

36   Check that the starter mounting bolts are tight so it grounds properly.

37   Check for voltage at the starter solenoid "S" terminal when the ignition key is turned to the start position. If voltage is present, replace the starter/solenoid assembly. If no voltage is present, the problem could be the starter relay, the Transmission Range (TR) switch (see Chapter 6) or clutch start switch (see Chapter 8), or with an electrical connector somewhere in the circuit (see the wiring diagrams).

Also, on many modern vehicles, the Powertrain Control Module (PCM) and the Body Control Module (BCM) control the voltage signal to the starter solenoid; on such vehicles a special scan tool is required for diagnosis.

3   Battery - disconnection

Caution: *Always disconnect the cable from the negative battery terminal FIRST and hook it up LAST or the battery may be shorted by the tool being used to loosen the cable clamps.*

1   Some systems on the vehicle require battery power to be available at all times, either to maintain continuous operation (alarm system, power door locks, etc.), or to maintain control unit memory (radio station presets, Powertrain Control Module and other control units). When the battery is disconnected, the power that maintains these systems is cut. So, before you disconnect the battery, please note that on a vehicle with power door locks, it's a wise precaution to remove the key from the ignition and to keep it with you, so that it does not get locked inside if the power door locks should engage accidentally when the battery is reconnected!

Warning: *Some memory savers deliver a considerable amount of current in order to keep vehicle systems operational after the main battery is disconnected. If you're using a memory saver, make sure that the circuit concerned is actually open before servicing it.*

Warning: *If you're going to work near any of the airbag system components, the battery MUST be disconnected and a memory saver must NOT be used. If a memory saver is used, power will be supplied to the airbag, which means that it could accidentally deploy and cause serious personal injury.*

2   Devices known as "memory-savers" can be used to avoid some of these problems. Precise details vary according to the device used. The typical memory saver is plugged into the cigarette lighter and is connected to a spare battery. Then the vehicle battery can be disconnected from the electrical system. The memory saver will provide sufficient current

to maintain audio unit security codes, PCM memory, etc. and will provide power to always hot circuits such as the clock and radio memory circuits.

3   To disconnect the battery for service procedures requiring power to be cut from the vehicle, loosen the cable end bolt and disconnect the cable from the negative battery terminal (see Section 4). Isolate the cable end to prevent it from coming into accidental contact with the battery terminal.

4   Battery - removal and installation

1   Disconnect the cable from the negative battery terminal first, then disconnect the cable from the positive battery terminal (see illustration).

2   Remove the battery hold-down clamp.

3   Lift out the battery. Be careful - it's heavy.

Note: *Battery straps and handlers are available at most auto parts stores for reasonable prices. They make it easier to remove and carry the battery.*

4   While the battery is out, inspect the battery tray. The battery tray itself is plastic, so it won't corrode. But if any corrosion from the battery terminals has fallen onto the tray, remove it and rinse it off with water. Also inspect the area below the battery tray for for any deposits of corrosion. If there's any sign of corrosion, clean the deposits with a mixture of baking soda and water to prevent further corrosion. Flush the area with plenty of clean water and dry thoroughly.

5   If you are replacing the battery, make sure you get one that's identical, with the same dimensions, amperage rating, cold cranking rating, etc. Also, remove the heat shield from the old battery and install it on the new battery.

6   Installation is the reverse of removal.

5   Battery cables - replacement

1   When removing the cables, always disconnect the cable from the negative battery terminal first and hook it up last, or you might accidentally short out the battery with the tool you're using to loosen the cable clamps. Even if you're only replacing the cable for the positive terminal, disconnect the negative cable from the battery first.

2   Disconnect the old cables from the battery, then trace each of them to their opposite ends and disconnect them. Note the routing of each cable before disconnecting it to ensure correct installation.

3   If you are replacing any of the old cables, take them with you when buying new cables. It is vitally important that you replace the cables with identical parts.

4   Clean the threads of the solenoid or ground connection with a wire brush to remove rust and corrosion. Apply a light coat of battery terminal corrosion inhibitor or petro-

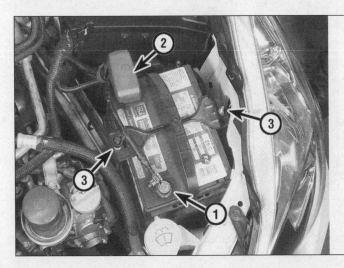

4.1 Battery details

1   *Negative cable*
2   *Positive cable (under cover)*
3   *Hold-down J-bolt/nuts*

6.3 Depress this release tab and pull off the connector

6.4 Ignition coil mounting bolts

6.10 Ignition coil locations (left cylinder bank)

leum jelly to the threads to prevent future corrosion.

5   Attach the cable to the solenoid or ground connection and tighten the mounting nut/bolt securely.

6   Before connecting a new cable to the battery, make sure that it reaches the battery post without having to be stretched.

7   Connect the cable to the positive battery terminal first, then connect the ground cable to the negative battery terminal.

6   Ignition coil(s) - removal and installation

2009 SOHC Legacy/2009 and 2010 SOHC Forester models (coil pack)

Note: *The ignition coil assembly is located on the top of the intake manifold on 2003 and earlier models. 2004 and later models use a similar coil unit, but it's mounted vertically and is located on the left front intake runner instead of the top of the manifold. However, it's removed and installed exactly the same way as the earlier unit.*

1   Disconnect the cable from the negative battery terminal (see Section 3).

2   Disconnect the spark plug wires from the ignition coil (see Chapter 1).

3   Disconnect the electrical connector from the ignition coil (see illustration).

4   Remove the ignition coil mounting bolts (see illustration) and remove the coil assembly.

5   Installation is the reverse of removal.

All other models (coil-on-plug)

Note: *These ignition coils are mounted directly on top of each spark plug. There are no spark plug wires. Once you have removed the components that are in the way, replacing one*

of these coils is simply a matter of disconnecting the electrical connector and removing a mounting bolt.

Left-side coils

6   Disconnect the cable from the negative battery terminal (see Section 3).

7   Remove the battery (see Section 4).

8   If necessary, remove the secondary air pump or air pump hose (see Chapter 6).

9   Disconnect the electrical connector from the ignition coil.

10   Remove the ignition coil retaining bolt, then detach the coil unit from the spark plug by pulling it straight out to the side (see illustration).

Note: *On some models, turn the No. 4 cylinder ignition coil 180 degrees to remove.*

11   Installation is the reverse of removal.

Right-side coils

12   Disconnect the cable from the negative battery terminal (see Section 3).

13   Remove the air filter housing (see Chapter 4).

14   Disconnect the electrical connector from the ignition coil unit.

15   Remove the ignition coil retaining bolt, then detach the coil unit from the spark plug by pulling it straight out to the side.

16   Installation is the reverse of removal.

7   Alternator - removal and installation

1   Disconnect the cable from the negative battery terminal (see Section 3).

2   Remove the engine cover and engine cover bracket if necessary.

3   Remove the drivebelt cover and bracket and remove the alternator drivebelt (see Chapter 1).

4   Disconnect the battery cable and the electrical connector from the alternator (see illustration).

5   On models with manual alternator belt adjustment, remove the adjustment bolt and adjuster.

7.4 Lift the cover (1) and remove the nut to disconnect the battery cable from the B+ terminal, then depress this release tab (2) and disconnect the electrical connector from the alternator. Remove the bracket (3) if equipped

7.6 Remove the idler pulley if necessary to gain access to the lower alternator bolt

7.7 Alternator mounting details

1   Drivebelt cover bracket bolts
2   Alternator upper mounting bolts

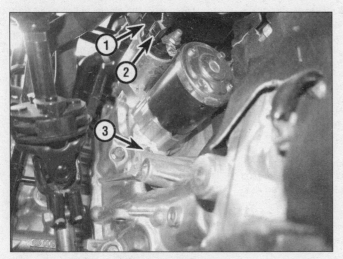

8.4 Starter details

1   Battery cable (under cover)
2   Electrical connector
3   Starter lower mounting bolt

8.6 Starter upper mounting bolt

6   On models with an automatic belt tensioner, remove the idler pulley to remove the alternator lower bolts (see illustration).
7   Remove the alternator bolts and alternator from the vehicle (see illustration).
8   Installation is the reverse of removal.
9   On 2013 and earlier turbocharged Forester models, adjust the drivebelt tension (see Chapter 1).

8   Starter motor - removal and installation

1   Disconnect the cable from the negative battery terminal (see Section 3).
2   On non-turbo models, remove the air intake duct (see Chapter 4). On turbo models, remove the intercooler (see Chapter 4).
3   Raise the vehicle and support it securely on jackstands.

4   Disconnect the wire and the large cable from the terminals on the starter solenoid (see illustration).
5   Remove the starter lower mounting bolt.
6   Remove the upper starter motor mounting bolt (see illustration).
7   Remove the lower starter motor mounting bolt or nut and detach the starter from the engine (see illustration 8.4).
8   Installation is the reverse of removal.

Chapter 6
Emissions and engine control systems

Contents

Specifications

Torque specifications

Note: *One foot-pound (ft-lb) of torque is equivalent to 12 inch-pounds (in-lbs) of torque. Torque values below approximately 15 foot-pounds are expressed in inch-pounds, because most foot-pound torque wrenches are not accurate at these smaller values.*

	Ft-lbs (unless otherwise indicated)	Nm
Exhaust Gas Recirculation (EGR) valve mounting bolts	168 in-lbs	19
Knock sensor retaining bolt	18	24
Oxygen sensors		
Non-turbo	16	21
Turbo		
Front	22	30
Rear	16	21
Exhaust		
Front exhaust manifold-to-cylinder head nuts	22	30
Exhaust pipe mounting flange nuts and bolts		
Rear center-to-rear exhaust flange nuts	13	18
Front center-to-rear center flange bolts	31	42
Exhaust pipe-to-turbocharger mounting nuts	31	42
Secondary air injection pump mounting bolts	168 in-lbs	19
Tumble generator valve-to-cylinder head bolts	18	24

1   General information

1   To prevent pollution of the atmosphere from incompletely burned and evaporating gases, and to maintain good driveability and fuel economy, a number of emission control systems are incorporated. They include the:

Catalytic converter

2   A catalytic converter is an emission control device in the exhaust system that reduces certain pollutants in the exhaust gas stream. There are two types of converters: oxidation converters and reduction converters.

3   Oxidation converters contain a monolithic substrate (a ceramic honeycomb) coated with the semi-precious metals platinum and palladium. An oxidation catalyst reduces unburned hydrocarbons (HC) and carbon monoxide (CO) by adding oxygen to the exhaust stream as it passes through the substrate, which, in the presence of high temperature and the catalyst materials, converts the HC and CO to water vapor (H_2O) and carbon dioxide (CO_2).

4   Reduction converters contain a monolithic substrate coated with platinum and rhodium. A reduction catalyst reduces oxides of nitrogen (NOx) by removing oxygen, which in the presence of high temperature and the catalyst material produces nitrogen (N) and carbon dioxide (CO_2).

5   Catalytic converters that combine both types of catalysts in one assembly are known as "three-way catalysts" or TWCs. A TWC can reduce all three pollutants.

Evaporative Emissions Control (EVAP) system

6   The Evaporative Emissions Control (EVAP) system prevents fuel system vapors (which contain unburned hydrocarbons) from escaping into the atmosphere. On warm days, vapors trapped inside the fuel tank expand until the pressure reaches a certain threshold. Then the fuel vapors are routed from the fuel tank through the fuel vapor vent valve and the fuel vapor control valve to the EVAP canister, where they're stored temporarily until the next time the vehicle is operated. When the conditions are right (engine warmed up, vehicle up to speed, moderate or heavy load on the engine, etc.) the PCM opens the canister purge valve, which allows fuel vapors to be drawn from the canister into the intake manifold. Once in the intake manifold, the fuel vapors mix with incoming air before being drawn through the intake ports into the combustion chambers where they're burned up with the rest of the air/fuel mixture. The EVAP system is complex and virtually impossible to troubleshoot without the right tools and training.

Exhaust Gas Recirculation (EGR) system

7   The EGR system reduces oxides of nitrogen by recirculating exhaust gases from the exhaust manifold, through the EGR valve and intake manifold, then back to the combustion chambers, where it mixes with the incoming air/fuel mixture before being consumed. These recirculated exhaust gases dilute the incoming air/fuel mixture, which cools the combustion chambers, thereby reducing NOx emissions.

8   The EGR system consists of the Powertrain Control Module (PCM), the EGR valve, the EGR valve position sensor and various other information sensors that the PCM uses to determine when to open the EGR valve. The degree to which the EGR valve is opened is referred to as "EGR valve lift." The PCM is programmed to produce the ideal EGR valve lift for varying operating conditions. The EGR valve position sensor, which is an integral part of the EGR valve, detects the amount of EGR valve lift and sends this information to the PCM. The PCM then compares it with the appropriate EGR valve lift for the operating conditions. The PCM increases current flow to the EGR valve to increase valve lift and reduces the current to reduce the amount of lift. If EGR flow is inappropriate to the operating conditions (idle, cold engine, etc.) the PCM simply cuts the current to the EGR valve and the valve closes.

Secondary Air Injection (AIR) system

9   Some models are equipped with a secondary air injection (AIR) system. The secondary air injection system is used to reduce tailpipe emissions on initial engine start-up. The system uses an electric motor/pump assembly, relay, air shut-off valve, check valves and tubing to inject fresh air directly into the exhaust manifolds. The fresh air (oxygen) reacts with the exhaust gas in the catalytic converter to reduce HC and CO levels. The air pump and solenoid are controlled by the PCM through the AIR relay. During initial start-up, the PCM energizes the AIR relay, the relay supplies battery voltage to the air pump which opens and allows air to flow through the tubing into the exhaust manifolds. The PCM will operate the air pump until closed loop operation is reached (approximately four minutes). During normal operation, the check valves prevent exhaust backflow into the system.

Powertrain Control Module (PCM)

10   The Powertrain Control Module (PCM) is the brain of the engine management system. It also controls a wide variety of other vehicle systems. In order to program the new PCM, the dealer needs the vehicle as well as the new PCM. If you're planning to replace the PCM with a new one, there is no point in trying to do so at home because you won't be able to program it yourself.

Positive Crankcase Ventilation (PCV) system

11   The Positive Crankcase Ventilation (PCV) system reduces hydrocarbon emissions by scavenging crankcase vapors, which are rich in unburned hydrocarbons. A PCV valve or orifice regulates the flow of gases into the intake manifold in proportion to the amount of intake vacuum available.

12   The PCV system generally consists of the fresh air inlet hose, the PCV valve or orifice and the crankcase ventilation hose (or PCV hose). The fresh air inlet hose connects the air intake duct to a pipe on the valve cover. The crankcase ventilation hose (or PCV hose) connects the PCV valve or orifice in the valve cover to the intake manifold.

Information Sensors

Accelerator Pedal Position (APP) sensor - as you press the accelerator pedal, the APP sensor alters its voltage signal to the PCM in proportion to the angle of the pedal, and the PCM commands a motor inside the throttle body to open or close the throttle plate accordingly

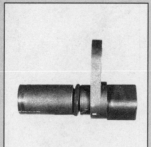

Camshaft Position (CMP) sensor - produces a signal that the PCM uses to identify the number 1 cylinder and to time the firing sequence of the fuel injectors

Crankshaft Position (CKP) sensor - produces a signal that the PCM uses to calculate engine speed and crankshaft position, which enables it to synchronize ignition timing with fuel injector timing, and to detect misfires

Engine Coolant Temperature (ECT) sensor - a thermistor (temperature-sensitive variable resistor) that sends a voltage signal to the PCM, which uses this data to determine the temperature of the engine coolant

Fuel tank pressure sensor - measures the fuel tank pressure and controls fuel tank pressure by signaling the EVAP system to purge the fuel tank vapors when the pressure becomes excessive

Intake Air Temperature (IAT) sensor - monitors the temperature of the air entering the engine and sends a signal to the PCM to determine injector pulse-width (the duration of each injector's on-time) and to adjust spark timing (to prevent spark knock)

Knock sensor - a piezoelectric crystal that oscillates in proportion to engine vibration which produces a voltage output that is monitored by the PCM. This retards the ignition timing when the oscillation exceeds a certain threshold

Manifold Absolute Pressure (MAP) sensor - monitors the pressure or vacuum inside the intake manifold. The PCM uses this data to determine engine load so that it can alter the ignition advance and fuel enrichment

Mass Air Flow (MAF) sensor - measures the amount of intake air drawn into the engine. It uses a hot-wire sensing element to measure the amount of air entering the engine

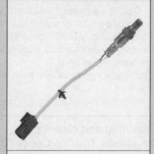

Oxygen sensors - generates a small variable voltage signal in proportion to the difference between the oxygen content in the exhaust stream and the oxygen content in the ambient air. The PCM uses this information to maintain the proper air/fuel ratio. A second oxygen sensor monitors the efficiency of the catalytic converter

Throttle Position (TP) sensor - a potentiometer that generates a voltage signal that varies in relation to the opening angle of the throttle plate inside the throttle body. Works with the PCM and other sensors to calculate injector pulse width (the duration of each injector's on-time)

Photos courtesy of Wells Manufacturing, except APP and MAF sensors.

2.4a Simple code readers are an economical way to extract DTCs when the CHECK ENGINE light comes on

2.4b Hand-held scan tools like these can extract DTCs and also perform diagnostics

2   On Board Diagnosis (OBD) system

General description

1   All models are equipped with the second generation OBD-II system. This system consists of an on-board computer known as the Powertrain Control Module (PCM), and information sensors, which monitor various functions of the engine and send data to the PCM. This system incorporates a series of diagnostic monitors that detect and identify fuel injection and emissions control system faults and store the information in the computer memory. This system also tests sensors and output actuators, diagnoses drive cycles, freezes data and clears codes.

2   The PCM is the brain of the electronically controlled fuel and emissions system. It receives data from a number of sensors and other electronic components (switches, relays, etc.). Based on the information it receives, the PCM generates output signals to control various relays, solenoids (fuel injectors) and other actuators. The PCM is specifically calibrated to optimize the emissions, fuel economy and driveability of the vehicle.

3   It isn't a good idea to attempt diagnosis or replacement of the PCM or emission control components at home while the vehicle is under warranty. Because of a federally-mandated warranty which covers the emissions system components and because any owner-induced damage to the PCM, the sensors and/or the control devices may void this warranty, take the vehicle to a dealer service department if the PCM or a system component malfunctions.

Scan tool information

4   Because extracting the Diagnostic Trouble Codes (DTCs) from an engine management system is now the first step in troubleshooting many computer-controlled systems and components, a code reader, at the very least, will be required (see illustration). More powerful scan tools can also perform many of the diagnostics once associated with expensive factory scan tools (see illustration). If you're planning to obtain a generic scan tool for your vehicle, make sure that it's compatible with OBD-II systems. If you don't plan to purchase a code reader or scan tool and don't have access to one, you can have the codes extracted by a dealer service department or an independent repair shop.

Note: *Some auto parts stores even provide this service.*

3   Obtaining and clearing Diagnostic Trouble Codes (DTCs)

1   All models covered by this manual are equipped with on-board diagnostics. When the PCM recognizes a malfunction in a monitored emission or engine control system, component or circuit, it turns on the Malfunction Indicator Light (MIL) on the dash. The PCM will continue to display the MIL until the problem is fixed and the Diagnostic Trouble Code (DTC) is cleared from the PCM's memory. You'll need a scan tool to access any DTCs

stored in the PCM.

2   Before outputting any DTCs stored in the PCM, thoroughly inspect ALL electrical connectors and hoses. Make sure that all electrical connections are tight, clean and free of corrosion. And make sure that all hoses are correctly connected, fit tightly and are in good condition (no cracks or tears).

Accessing the DTCs

3   The Diagnostic Trouble Codes (DTCs) can only be accessed with a code reader or scan tool. Professional scan tools are expensive, but relatively inexpensive generic code readers or scan tools (see illustrations 2.4a and 2.4b) are available at most auto parts stores. Simply plug the connector of the scan tool into the Data Link Connector (see illustration). Then follow the instructions included with the scan tool to extract the DTCs.

4   Once you have outputted all of the stored DTCs, look them up on the accompanying DTC chart.

5   After troubleshooting the source of each DTC, make any necessary repairs or replace the defective component(s).

Clearing the DTCs

6   Clear the DTCs with the code reader or scan tool in accordance with the instructions provided by the tool's manufacturer.

Diagnostic Trouble Codes

7   The accompanying tables are a list of the Diagnostic Trouble Codes (DTCs) that can be accessed by a do-it-yourselfer working at home (there are many, many more DTCs available to professional mechanics with proprietary scan tools and software, but those codes cannot be accessed by a generic scan tool). If, after you have checked and repaired the connectors, wire harness and vacuum hoses (if applicable) for an emission-related system, component or circuit, the problem persists, have the vehicle checked by a dealer service department or other qualified repair shop.

3.3 The Data Link Connector (DLC) is located at the lower edge of the dash, below the steering column

OBD-II trouble codes

Note: *Not all trouble codes apply to all models.*

Code	Probable cause
P0010	Intake camshaft position actuator, open circuit (Bank 1)
P0011	Intake camshaft position timing over-advanced (Bank 1)
P0012	Intake camshaft position timing, over-retarded (Bank 1)
P013A	Oxygen sensor slow response, rich to lean (Bank 1, Sensor 2)
P013C	Oxygen sensor slow response, rich to lean (Bank 2, Sensor 2)
P013E	Oxygen sensor delayed response, rich to lean (Bank 1, Sensor 2)
P014A	Oxygen sensor delayed response, rich to lean (Bank 2, Sensor 2)
P0014	Exhaust AVCS system, 1 performance
P0016	Crankshaft position-to-camshaft position correlation (Bank 1)
P0017	Crankshaft and camshaft(s) timing circuit B - system failure (Bank 1)
P0018	Crankshaft position-to-camshaft position correlation (Bank 2)
P0019	Crankshaft and camshaft(s) timing circuit B - system failure (Bank 2)
P0020	Intake camshaft position actuator, open circuit (Bank 2)
P0021	Intake camshaft position timing over-advanced (Bank 2)
P0022	Intake camshaft position timing over-retarded (Bank 2)
P0024	Exhaust AVCS system, 2 performance
P0030	Oxygen sensor heater control circuit (Bank 1, Sensor 1)
P0031	Oxygen sensor control circuit low (Bank 1, Sensor 1)
P0032	Oxygen sensor control circuit high (Bank 1, Sensor 1)
P0037	Oxygen sensor control circuit low (Bank 1, Sensor 2)
P0038	Oxygen sensor control circuit high (Bank 1, Sensor 2)
P0040	Oxygen sensor signals swapped (Bank 1, Sensor 1/Bank 2, Sensor 1)
P0041	Oxygen sensor signals swapped (Bank 1, Sensor 2/Bank 2, Sensor 2)
P0050	Oxygen sensor heater control circuit (Bank 2, Sensor 1)
P0053	Oxygen sensor heater resistance (Bank 1, Sensor 1)
P0054	Oxygen sensor heater resistance (Bank 1, Sensor 2)
P0055	Oxygen sensor heater resistance (Bank 1, Sensor 3)
P0059	Oxygen sensor heater resistance (Bank 2, Sensor 1)

OBD-II trouble codes (continued)
Note: *Not all trouble codes apply to all models.*

Code	Probable cause
P0060	Oxygen sensor heater resistance (Bank 2, Sensor 2)
P0068	Manifold Absolute Pressure (MAP) sensor/Mass Air Flow (MAF) sensor-to-throttle position correlation
P0097	Intake Air Temperature (IAT) sensor 2 circuit, low voltage
P0098	Intake Air Temperature (IAT) sensor 2 circuit, high voltage
P0101	Mass or volume air flow circuit range or performance problem
P0102	Mass or volume air flow A circuit, low voltage
P0103	Mass or volume air flow circuit, high input voltage
P0104	Mass Air Flow (MAF) sensor A circuit, intermittent or erratic signal
P0106	Manifold Absolute Pressure (MAP) sensor circuit, range or performance problem
P0107	Manifold Absolute Pressure (MAP) sensor circuit, low voltage
P0108	Manifold Absolute Pressure (MAP) sensor circuit, high voltage
P0109	Manifold Absolute Pressure (MAP) sensor circuit, intermittent signal
P0111	Intake Air Temperature (IAT) sensor circuit, range or performance problem
P0112	Intake Air Temperature (IAT) sensor circuit, low voltage
P0113	Intake Air Temperature (IAT) sensor circuit, high voltage
P0114	Intake Air Temperature (IAT) sensor circuit, intermittent or erratic signal
P0116	Engine Coolant Temperature (ECT) sensor circuit, range or performance problem
P0117	Engine Coolant Temperature (ECT) sensor circuit, low voltage
P0118	Engine Coolant Temperature (ECT) sensor circuit, high voltage
P0119	Engine Coolant Temperature (ECT) sensor circuit, intermittent or erratic signal
P0121	Throttle Position (TP) sensor A circuit, range or performance problem
P0122	Throttle Position (TP) sensor A circuit, low voltage
P0123	Throttle Position (TP) sensor A circuit, high voltage
P0125	Insufficient coolant temperature for closed loop fuel control
P0128	Coolant temperature below coolant thermostat's regulating temperature
P0130	Oxygen sensor circuit malfunction (Bank 1, Sensor 1)
P0131	Oxygen sensor circuit, low voltage (Bank 1, Sensor 1)
P0132	Oxygen sensor circuit, high voltage (Bank 1, Sensor 1)

Code	Probable cause
P0133	Oxygen sensor circuit, slow response (Bank 1, Sensor 1)
P0134	Oxygen sensor circuit, no activity detected (Bank 1, Sensor 1)
P0135	Oxygen sensor heater circuit malfunction (Bank 1, Sensor 1)
P0137	Oxygen sensor circuit low (Bank 1, Sensor 2)
P0138	Oxygen sensor circuit, high voltage (Bank 1, Sensor 2)
P0139	Oxygen sensor circuit, slow response (Bank 1, Sensor 2)
P013A	Oxygen sensor slow response, rich to lean (Bank 1, Sensor 2)
P013B	Oxygen sensor slow response, lean to rich (Bank 1, Sensor 2)
P013E	Oxygen sensor delayed response, rich to lean (Bank 1, Sensor 2)
P013F	Oxygen sensor delayed response, lean to rich (Bank 1, Sensor 2)
P0140	Oxygen sensor circuit, no activity detected (Bank 1, Sensor 2)
P0141	Oxygen sensor heater circuit problem (Bank 1, Sensor 2)
P0144	Oxygen sensor circuit, high voltage (Bank 1, Sensor 3)
P0147	Oxygen sensor heater circuit malfunction (Bank 1, Sensor 3)
P0148	Fuel delivery error
P014C	Oxygen sensor slow response, rich to lean (Bank 1, Sensor 1)
P014D	Oxygen sensor slow response, lean to rich (Bank 1, Sensor 1)
P015A	Oxygen sensor delayed response, rich to lean (Bank 1, Sensor 1)
P015B	Oxygen sensor delayed response, lean to rich (Bank 1, Sensor 1
P0150	Oxygen sensor circuit malfunction (Bank 2, Sensor 1)
P0152	Oxygen sensor circuit, high voltage (Bank 2, Sensor 1)
P0153	Oxygen sensor circuit, slow response (Bank 2, Sensor 1)
P0154	Oxygen sensor circuit, no activity detected (Bank 2, Sensor 1)
P0155	Oxygen sensor heater circuit malfunction (Bank 2, Sensor 1)
P0158	Oxygen sensor circuit, high voltage (Bank 2, Sensor 2)
P0159	Oxygen sensor circuit, slow response (Bank 2, Sensor 2)
P0161	Oxygen sensor heater circuit malfunction (Bank 2, Sensor 2)
P0171	System too lean (Bank 1)
P0172	System too rich (Bank 1)
P0174	System too lean (Bank 2)

OBD-II trouble codes (continued)

Note: *Not all trouble codes apply to all models.*

Code	Probable cause
P0175	System too rich (Bank 2)
P0180	Fuel temperature sensor circuit malfunction
P0181	Fuel temperature sensor circuit, range or performance problem
P0182	Fuel temperature sensor circuit, low voltage
P0183	Fuel temperature sensor circuit, high voltage
P0191	Fuel rail pressure sensor circuit, range or performance problem
P0192	Fuel rail pressure sensor circuit, low voltage
P0193	Fuel rail pressure sensor circuit, high voltage
P0196	Engine Oil Temperature (EOT) sensor circuit, range or performance problem
P0197	Engine Oil Temperature (EOT) sensor circuit, low voltage
P0198	Engine Oil Temperature (EOT) sensor circuit, high voltage
P0201	Cylinder 1 injector problem
P0202	Cylinder 2 injector problem
P0203	Cylinder 3 injector problem
P0204	Cylinder 4 injector problem
P0205	Injector open circuit, cylinder 5
P0206	Injector open circuit, cylinder 6
P0217	Engine coolant over-temperature condition
P0218	Transaxle fluid temperature over-temperature condition
P0219	Engine over-speed condition
P0221	Throttle Position (TP) sensor circuit, range or performance problem
P0222	Throttle Position (TP) sensor circuit, low voltage
P0223	Throttle Position (TP) sensor circuit, high voltage
P0230	Fuel pump primary circuit malfunction
P0231	Fuel pump secondary circuit, low voltage
P0232	Fuel pump secondary circuit, high voltage
P0244	Turbocharger wastegate solenoid "A", range or performance problem
P0245	Turbocharger wastegate solenoid "A", low voltage

Code	Probable cause
P0246	Turbocharger wastegate solenoid "A", high voltage
P025A	Fuel pump module control circuit open
P025B	Fuel pump module control circuit range or performance problem
P0298	Engine oil over-temperature condition
P0300	Random misfire detected
P0301	Cylinder 1 misfire
P0302	Cylinder 2 misfire
P0303	Cylinder 3 misfire
P0304	Cylinder 4 misfire
P0315	Crankshaft position system variation not learned
P0316	Misfire detected on start-up (first 1000 revolutions)
P0320	Ignition/distributor engine speed input circuit
P0325	Knock sensor 1 circuit malfunction (Bank 1)
P0326	Knock sensor 1 circuit, range or performance problem (Bank 1)
P0327	Knock sensor 1 circuit, low (Bank 1 or single sensor)
P0328	Knock sensor 1 circuit, high (Bank 1 or single sensor)
P0330	Knock sensor 2 circuit malfunction (Bank 2)
P0331	Knock sensor 2 circuit, range or performance problem (Bank 2)
P0335	Crankshaft position sensor "A" circuit, problem
P0336	Crankshaft position sensor "A" circuit, range or performance problem
P0340	Camshaft Position (CMP) sensor circuit malfunction (Bank 1 or single sensor)
P0341	Camshaft Position (CMP) sensor circuit, range or performance problem (Bank 1 or single sensor)
P0344	Camshaft Position (CMP) sensor circuit, intermittent signal (Bank 1 or single sensor)
P0345	Camshaft Position (CMP) sensor circuit malfunction (Bank 2)
P0346	Camshaft Position (CMP) sensor circuit, range or performance problem (Bank 2)
P0349	Camshaft Position (CMP) sensor circuit, intermittent signal (Bank 2)
P0350	Ignition coil primary/secondary circuit malfunction
P0351	Ignition coil A primary/secondary circuit malfunction
P0352	Ignition coil B primary/secondary circuit malfunction
P0353	Ignition coil C primary/secondary circuit malfunction

OBD-II trouble codes (continued)

Note: *Not all trouble codes apply to all models.*

Code	Probable cause
P0354	Ignition coil D primary/secondary circuit malfunction
P0355	Ignition coil E primary/secondary circuit malfunction
P0356	Ignition coil F primary/secondary circuit malfunction
P0365	Camshaft position sensor "B" circuit, problem (Bank 1)
P0366	Camshaft position sensor "B" circuit, range or performance problem (Bank 1)
P0390	Camshaft position sensor "B" circuit, problem (Bank 2)
P0391	Camshaft position sensor "B" circuit, range or performance problem (Bank 2)
P0400	Exhaust Gas Recirculation (EGR) system flow
P0401	Exhaust Gas Recirculation (EGR) system, insufficient flow detected
P0402	Exhaust Gas Recirculation (EGR) system, excessive flow detected
P0403	Exhaust Gas Recirculation (EGR) system control circuit malfunction
P0405	Exhaust Gas Recirculation (EGR) system, differential pressure feedback sensor circuit, low voltage
P0406	Exhaust Gas Recirculation (EGR) system, differential pressure feedback sensor circuit, high voltage
P0410	Secondary Air Injection (AIR) system
P0411	Secondary Air Injection (AIR) system, incorrect flow detected
P0412	Secondary Air Injection (AIR) system, switching valve circuit malfunction
P0413	Secondary Air Injection (AIR) system switching valve "A" circuit, open
P0414	Secondary Air Injection (AIR) system switching valve "A" circuit, shorted
P0416	Secondary Air Injection (AIR) system switching valve "B" circuit, open
P0417	Secondary Air Injection (AIR) system switching valve "B" circuit, shorted
P0420	Catalyst system efficiency below threshold (Bank 1)
P0430	Catalyst system efficiency below threshold (Bank 2)
P0441	Evaporative Emission (EVAP) system, incorrect purge flow
P0442	Evaporative Emission (EVAP) system, small leak detected
P0443	Evaporative Emission (EVAP) system, purge control valve circuit malfunction
P0446	Evaporative Emission (EVAP) system, vent control circuit malfunction
P0451	Evaporative Emission (EVAP) system, pressure sensor range or performance problem
P0452	Evaporative Emission (EVAP) system, pressure sensor, low voltage

Code	Probable cause
P0453	Evaporative Emission (EVAP) system, pressure sensor, high voltage
P0454	Evaporative Emission (EVAP) system, pressure sensor, intermittent signal
P0455	Evaporative Emission (EVAP) system, gross leak detected/no flow
P0456	Evaporative Emission (EVAP) system, very small leak detected
P0457	Evaporative Emission (EVAP) system, leak detected (fuel cap loose or off)
P0458	Evaporative Emission (EVAP) system, purge control valve circuit low voltage
P0459	Evaporative Emission (EVAP) system, purge control valve circuit high voltage
P0460	Fuel level sensor circuit malfunction
P0461	Fuel level sensor circuit, range or performance problem
P0462	Fuel level sensor circuit, low voltage
P0463	Fuel level sensor circuit, high voltage
P04AC	Evaporative Emission (EVAP) system, purge control valve "B" circuit, low voltage
P04AD	Evaporative Emission (EVAP) system, purge control valve "B" circuit, high voltage
P04DB	Crankcase ventilation system, disconnected
P0480	Fan 1 control circuit malfunction
P0481	Fan 2 control circuit malfunction
P0483	Fan performance
P0491	Secondary Air Injection (AIR) system, insufficient flow (Bank 1)
P0500	Vehicle Speed Sensor (VSS)
P0503	Vehicle Speed Sensor (VSS), intermittent, erratic or high signal
P0505	Idle Air Control (IAC) system
P0506	Idle Air Control (IAC) system, rpm lower than expected
P0507	Idle Air Control (IAC) system, rpm higher than expected
P050A	Idle Air Control (IAC) system performance problem
P050B	Cold start ignition timing performance problem
P050E	Cold start engine exhaust temperature out of range
P0511	Idle Air Control (IAC) system circuit malfunction
P0512	Starter request circuit malfunction
P0513	Incorrect immobilizer key used
P052A	Cold start camshaft position timing over-advanced (Bank 1)

OBD-II trouble codes (continued)

Note: *Not all trouble codes apply to all models.*

Code	Probable cause
P052B	Cold start camshaft position timing over-retarded (Bank 1)
P052C	Cold start camshaft position timing over-advanced (Bank 2)
P052D	Cold start camshaft position timing over-retarded (Bank 2)
P0528	Fan speed sensor circuit, no signal
P0532	Air conditioning refrigerant pressure sensor circuit, low voltage
P0533	Air conditioning refrigerant pressure sensor circuit, high voltage
P0534	Air conditioning refrigerant charge loss
P0537	Air conditioning evaporator temperature sensor circuit, low voltage
P0538	A/C evaporator temperature sensor circuit, high voltage
P053A	Positive Crankcase Ventilation (PCV) heater control circuit open
P0552	Power Steering Pressure (PSP) sensor circuit, low voltage
P0553	Power Steering Pressure (PSP) sensor circuit, high voltage
P0560	System voltage, range or performance problem
P0562	System voltage low
P0563	System voltage high
P0571	Brake switch circuit malfunction
P0572	Brake switch circuit, low voltage
P0573	Brake switch circuit, high voltage
P0579	Cruise control multifunction input circuit, range or performance problem
P0581	Cruise control multifunction input circuit, high voltage
P0600	Serial communication link
P0601	Powertrain Control Module (PCM), memory checksum error
P0602	Powertrain Control Module (PCM) programming error
P0603	Powertrain Control Module (PCM), Keep Alive Memory (KAM) error
P0604	Powertrain Control Module (PCM), Random Access Memory (RAM) error
P0605	Powertrain Control Module (PCM), Read Only Memory (ROM) error
P0606	Powertrain Control Module (PCM) processor
P0607	Powertrain Control Module (PCM) performance

Code	Probable cause
P060A	InternalControl Module monitoring processor, performance problem
P060B	Internal Control Module A and/or D circuit processing, performance problem
P060C	Internal control module main processor performance
P060D	Internal control module accelerator pedal position performance
P0610	Powertrain Control Module (PCM) options error
P0616	Starter relay circuit, low voltage
P0617	Starter relay circuit, high voltage
P061B	Internal control module torque calculation performance
P061C	Internal control module engine rpm performance
P061D	Internal control module engine air mass performance
P061F	Internal control module throttle actuator controller performance
P062C	Internal control module vehicle speed performance
P062F	InternalControl Module EEPROM, error
P0620	Alternator control circuit malfunction
P0622	Alternator field terminal, circuit malfunction
P0625	Alternator field terminal, low circuit voltage
P0626	Alternator field terminal, high circuit voltage
P0627	Fuel pump, open control circuit
P062F	Internal control module EEPROM error
P0642	Sensor reference voltage (VREF) circuit below VREF minimum voltage
P0643	Sensor reference voltage (VREF) circuit, high voltage
P0645	Air conditioning clutch relay control circuit malfunction
P064D	Internal control module oxygen sensor processor performance (Bank 1)
P064E	Internal control module oxygen sensor processor performance (Bank 2)
P0657	Actuator supply voltage, open circuit
P065B	Alternator control circuit range or performance problem
P0660	Intake Manifold Tuning Valve (IMTV) control circuit, open circuit (Bank 1)
P0663	Intake Manifold Tuning Valve (IMTV) control circuit, open circuit (Bank 2)
P0685	Powertrain Control Module (PCM) power relay control circuit open
P0689	Powertrain Control Module (PCM) power relay sense circuit, low voltage

OBD-II trouble codes (continued)

Note: *Not all trouble codes apply to all models.*

Code	Probable cause
P0690	Powertrain Control Module (PCM) power relay sense circuit, high voltage
P0703	Brake switch input circuit malfunction
P0704	Clutch switch input circuit malfunction
P0705	Transmission Range (TR) sensor circuit (PRNDL) input problem
P0706	Transmission Range (TR) sensor circuit, range or performance problem
P0707	Transmission Range (TR) sensor circuit, low voltage
P0708	Transmission range sensor circuit, high voltage
P0711	Transmission fluid temperature sensor circuit, range or performance problem
P0712	Transmission fluid temperature sensor circuit, low input
P0713	Transmission fluid temperature sensor circuit, high input
P0715	Input/turbine speed sensor circuit malfunction
P0716	Input/turbine speed sensor circuit, range or performance problem
P0717	Input/turbine speed sensor circuit, no signal
P0720	Output Shaft Speed (OSS) sensor circuit malfunction
P0721	Output Shaft Speed (OSS) sensor circuit, range or performance problem
P0722	No signal from Output Shaft Speed (OSS) sensor
P0723	Output Shaft Speed (OSS) sensor circuit, intermittent signal
P06B8	Internal control module Non-volatile random access memory (NVRAM) error
P0729	Gear 6 incorrect ratio
P0730	Incorrect gear ratio
P0731	Incorrect gear ratio, first gear
P0732	Incorrect gear ratio, second gear
P0733	Incorrect gear ratio, third gear
P0734	Incorrect gear ratio, fourth gear
P0735	Incorrect gear ratio, fifth gear
P0736	Incorrect gear ratio, reverse gear
P0741	Torque converter clutch, circuit performance problem or stuck in Off position
P0742	Torque converter clutch circuit, stuck in On position

Code	Probable cause
P0744	Torque converter clutch circuit, intermittent
P0745	Pressure control solenoid malfunction
P0751	Shift solenoid A, performance problem or stuck in Off position
P0752	Shift solenoid A, stuck in On position
P0753	Shift solenoid A, electrical problem
P0756	Shift solenoid B, performance problem or stuck in Off position
P0757	Shift solenoid B, stuck in On position
P0758	Shift solenoid B, electrical problem
P0761	Shift solenoid C, performance problem or stuck in Off position
P0762	Shift solenoid C, stuck in On position
P0763	Shift solenoid C, electrical problem
P0766	Shift solenoid D, performance problem or stuck in Off position
P0767	Shift solenoid D, stuck in On position
P0768	Shift solenoid D, electrical problem
P0771	Shift solenoid E, performance problem or stuck in Off position
P0772	Shift solenoid E, stuck in On position
P0773	Shift solenoid E, electrical problem
P0777	Pressure control solenoid "B" stuck On
P0778	Pressure control solenoid "B" electrical
P0780	Shift malfunction
P0791	Intermediate shaft speed sensor circuit malfunction
P0812	Reverse input circuit malfunction
P0815	Upshift switch circuit malfunction
P0817	Starter disable circuit malfunction
P0830	Clutch pedal switch circuit malfunction
P0840	Transmission fluid pressure sensor circuit malfunction
P0841	Transmission fluid pressure sensor/switch "A" circuit range/performance problem
P0882	Transmission control module (TCM) power input signal low
P0894	Transmission component slipping
P0961	Pressure control (PC) solenoid A - control circuit range/performance problem

OBD-II trouble codes (continued)

Note: *Not all trouble codes apply to all models.*

Code	Probable cause
P0962	Pressure control (PC) solenoid A - control circuit low
P0963	Pressure control (PC) solenoid A - control circuit high
P0973	Shift solenoid (SS) A - control circuit low
P0974	Shift solenoid (SS) A - control circuit high
P0976	Shift solenoid (SS) B - control circuit low
P0977	Shift solenoid (SS) B - control circuit high
P0978	Shift solenoid (SS) C - control circuit range/performance problem
P0979	Shift solenoid (SS) C - control circuit low
P0980	Shift solenoid (SS) C - control circuit high
P0981	Shift solenoid (SS) D - control circuit range/performance problem
P0982	Shift solenoid (SS) D - control circuit low
P0983	Shift solenoid (SS) D - control circuit high
P0984	Shift solenoid (SS) E - control circuit range/performance problem
P0985	Shift solenoid (SS) E - control circuit low
P0986	Shift solenoid (SS) E - control circuit high
P0997	Shift solenoid (SS) F - control circuit range/performance problem
P0998	Shift solenoid (SS) F - control circuit low
P0999	Shift solenoid (SS) F - control circuit high

4.3 APP sensor details

1   *Electrical connector*
2   *Mounting nuts*

4   Accelerator Pedal Position (APP) sensor - replacement

Note: *The APP sensor is at the upper end of the accelerator pedal assembly. If you need to replace the APP sensor you must replace the APP sensor and the accelerator pedal as a single assembly. The APP sensor is not removable.*

1   Disconnect the cable from the negative battery terminal (see Chapter 5).

2   Remove the driver's side knee bolster (see Chapter 11).

3   Using a flashlight if necessary, disconnect the electrical connector from the APP sensor (see illustration).

4   Remove the accelerator pedal assembly mounting nuts and remove the pedal assembly.

5   Installation is the reverse of removal.

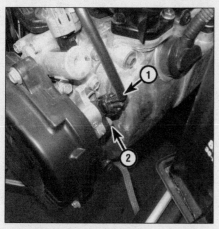

5.2 CMP sensor electrical connector (1) and mounting bolt (2)

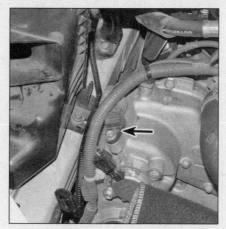

5.8a Right bank CMP sensor

5.8b Left bank CMP sensor

5   Camshaft Position (CMP) sensor - replacement

Non-turbocharged models
2011 and earlier Forester and 2012 and earlier Legacy

Note: *These models are equipped with a single CMP sensor. The CMP sensor is mounted on a support that is bolted to the left cylinder head, between the backside of the timing belt cover and the front end of the valve cover.*

1   Disconnect the cable from the negative battery terminal (see Chapter 5).

2   Disconnect the electrical connector from the CMP sensor (see illustration).

3   Remove the CMP sensor support mounting bolts, then remove the support and sensor as an assembly.

Note: *You can't remove the CMP sensor from the support without first removing the support because there isn't enough clearance to remove sensor mounting bolt.*

4   Detach the CMP sensor from the sensor support.

5   Installation is the reverse of removal.

2012 and later Forester and 2013 and later Legacy models

Note: *These models are equipped with 2 CMP sensors.*

6   Disconnect the cable from the negative battery terminal.

7   For access to the passenger side sensor, remove the intake air duct before the air filter housing.

8   Disconnect the electrical connector from the CMP sensor (see illustrations).

9   Remove the bolt attaching the CMP sensor to the cylinder head.

10   If the sensor is to be reused, replace the O-ring.

11   Installation is the reverse of removal.

Turbocharged models

Note: *There and four CMP sensors on turbocharged models. The CMP sensors are located on the back end of the cylinder heads, at the outer rear corner of each head.*

12   Remove the engine cover, if equipped (see Chapter 2A).

13   Disconnect the cable from the negative battery terminal (see Chapter 5).

14   If removing the left intake CMP on Legacy or 2013 and earlier Forester models, remove the intake manifold (see Chapter 2A).

15   On all other models, you should be able to access the intake CMP sensors after pushing aside the electrical wiring and hoses in the area.

16   If you're replacing an exhaust CMP sensor, raise the vehicle and support it securely on jackstands. Remove the lower engine splash shield. You should be able to access the CMP sensor after removing the harness cover.

17   Disconnect the electrical connector from the CMP sensor.

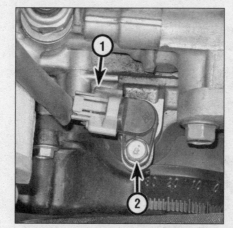

7.4 CKP sensor electrical connector (1), and mounting bolt (2)

18   Remove the CMP sensor mounting bolt and remove the sensor.

19   Installation is the reverse of removal.

6   Clutch Pedal Position (CPP) switch - replacement

Note: *The CPP switch is also known as the clutch start switch.*

1   If you need to replace the CPP switch, refer to Chapter 8.

7   Crankshaft Position (CKP) sensor - replacement

2012 and earlier Legacy models, 2010 and earlier Forester non-turbocharged models and 2013 and earlier Forester tuborcharged models

Note: *The CKP sensor is located on the top front of the engine block, just below the alternator and above the timing belt cover.*

1   Disconnect the cable from the negative battery terminal (see Chapter 5).

2   Remove the engine cover, if equipped (see Chapter 2A).

3   Remove the accessory drivebelt (see Chapter 1).

Note: *On some models it may also be necessary to remove the alternator for full access to the CKP sensor (see Chapter 5).*

4   Depress the release tab and disconnect the electrical connector from the CKP sensor (see illustration).

5   Remove the sensor mounting bolt (see illustration 8.4) and remove the sensor.

6   Installation is the reverse of removal.

7.10 Locating CKP sensor at rear of block

8.5 Disconnect the electrical connector (1)
from the ECT sensor (2)

8.10 Locating the ECT sensor on
later models

2013 and later Legacy models, 2011 and later Forester non-turbocharged models and 2014 and later Forester turbocharged models

Note: *The CKP sensor is located on the top rear of the engine block where it bolts to the transaxle, near the two engine grounds.*

7   Disconnect the cable from the negative battery terminal.
8   Remove the engine cover.
9   Remove the intake air duct between the throttle body and the air filter housing.
10   Locate the CKP sensor and disconnect the electrical connector (see illustration).
11   Remove the bolt and remove the CKP sensor.
12   Installation is reverse of removal.

---

8   Engine Coolant Temperature (ECT) sensor - replacement

Warning: *Wait until the engine is completely cool before beginning this procedure.*

9.5 Disconnect
the knock sensor
electrical connector,
then remove the
mounting bolt

1   Disconnect the cable from the negative terminal of the battery (see Chapter 5).
2   Partially drain the engine coolant so it's below the level of the sensor (see Chapter 1).

2012 and earlier Legacy models, 2010 and earlier Forester non-turbocharged models and 2013 and earlier Forester tuborcharged models

Note: *The ECT sensor is located on top of the engine block, under the right side of the alternator.*

3   Remove the engine cover, if equipped (see Chapter 2A).
4   Remove the alternator (see Chapter 5).
5   Disconnect the electrical connector from the ECT sensor (see illustration).
6   Unscrew and remove the sensor.
7   Wrap the threads of the ECT sensor with Teflon tape.
8   Installation is the reverse of removal. Refill the cooling system (see Chapter 1).

2013 and later Legacy models, 2011 and later Forester non-turbocharged models and 2014 and later Forester turbocharged models

9   Remove the engine cover, if equipped.
10   Locate the ECT and disconnect the electrical connector (see illustration).
11   Unscrew and remove the sensor.
12   Wrap the threads of the ECT sensor with Teflon tape.
13   Installation is the reverse of removal. Refill the cooling system.

---

9   Knock sensor - replacement

Note: *The knock sensor is located on the back left of the engine block, under the intake manifold, near the EGR pipe.*

1   Remove the engine cover, if equipped (see Chapter 2A).
2   Disconnect the cable from the negative battery terminal (see Chapter 5).
3   On turbocharged models, remove the intercooler (see Chapter 4).
4   On non-turbocharged models, remove the air intake duct between the throttle body and the air filter housing (see Chapter 4).
5   Disconnect the knock sensor electrical connector (see illustration).
6   Remove the knock sensor mounting bolt and remove the sensor.
Note: *On models with a connector on the sensor itself, the knock sensor should be installed so that the connector is positioned at a 90-degree angle relative to the front of engine. On models with a harness attached to the sensor, the knock sensor should be installed so that the connector is positioned at a 60-degree angle relative to the front of engine.*
7   Installation is the reverse of removal. Install the sensor in its original position, and tighten the knock sensor retaining bolt to the torque listed in this Chapter's Specifications.

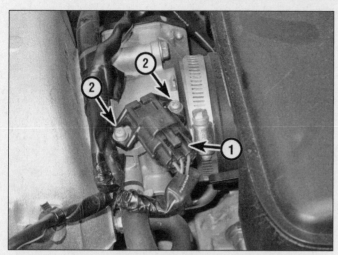

10.2a MAP sensor electrical connector (1) and mounting screws (2) (throttle body mounted version shown)

10.2b Identifying MAP sensor (intake manifold mounted version shown)

10   Manifold Absolute Pressure (MAP) sensor - replacement

Note: *On 2012 and earlier Legacy models, 2010 and earlier Forester non-turbocharged models and 2013 and earlier Forester tuborcharged models, the MAP sensor is located on the throttle body. On 2013 and later Legacy models, 2011 and later Forester non-turbocharged models and 2014 and later Forester turbocharged models, the MAP sensor is located on the intake manifold, near the throttle body.*

1   Disconnect the cable from the negative battery terminal (see Chapter 5).

2   Depress the release tab and disconnect the electrical connector from the MAP sensor (see illustrations).

3   Remove the MAP sensor mounting screws and remove the MAP sensor.

4   Remove and discard the old MAP sensor O-ring (see illustration 12.5).

5   Installation is the reverse of removal. Install a new O-ring.

11   Mass Air Flow/Intake Air Temperature (MAF/IAT) sensor - replacement

Note: *The sensor is located on top of the air filter housing.*

1   Disconnect the cable from the negative battery terminal (see Chapter 5).

2   Disconnect the electrical connector from the MAF/IAT sensor (see illustration).

3   Remove the MAF/IAT sensor mounting screws and remove the sensor.

4   Installation is the reverse of removal.

12   Oxygen sensors - general information and replacement

General information

1   Use special care when servicing an oxygen sensor:

a) *Oxygen sensors have a permanently attached pigtail and electrical connector that can't be removed from the sensor. Damage to or removal of the pigtail or the electrical connector will ruin the sensor.*

b) *Keep grease, dirt and other contaminants away from the electrical connector and the oxygen sensor.*

c) *Do not use cleaning solvents of any kind on an oxygen sensor.*

d) *Do not drop or roughly handle an oxygen sensor.*

Replacement

Note: *Because it is installed in the exhaust manifold or catalytic converter, both of which contract when cool, an oxygen sensor might be very difficult to loosen when the engine is cold. Rather than risk damage to the sensor, start and run the engine for a minute or two, then shut it off. Be careful not to burn yourself during the following procedure.*

Non-turbocharged models

2   Disconnect the cable from the negative terminal of the battery (see Chapter 5).

3   Raise the vehicle and support it securely on jackstands.

Upstream oxygen sensor

Note: *The upstream oxygen sensor is located just behind the flange between the two exhaust manifolds and the front end of the catalytic converter.*

4   On 2011 and later Forester models, remove the radiator fan assembly (see Chapter 3, Section 5).

5   Remove the intake air duct before the air filter housing to gain access to the sensor connectors (see Chapter 4, Section 10).

6   Locate the upstream oxygen sensor. Disconnect the electrical connector, then go

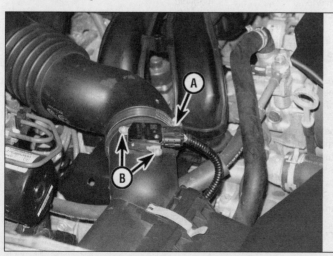

11.2 MAF/IAT sensor electrical connector (A) and mounting screws (B)

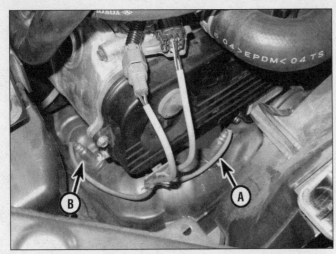

12.6a Location of the upstream (A) and downstream (B) oxygen sensors (2010 and earlier Forester and 2012 and earlier Legacy models shown)

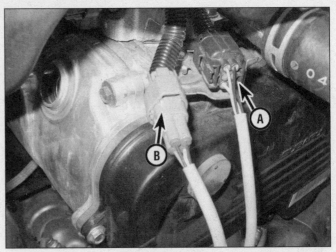

12.6b Location of the upstream (A) and downstream (B) oxygen sensor electrical connectors (2010 and earlier Forester and 2012 and earlier Legacy models shown)

12.12 A typical downstream oxygen sensor on a non-turbocharged model

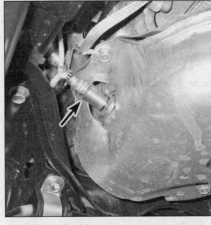

12.23 A typical upstream oxygen sensor location on a turbocharged model. Use an oxygen sensor socket, if possible

back under the vehicle and unscrew the sensor (see illustrations). We recommend using an oxygen sensor socket where possible, because it protects the sensor from damage during removal and installation. However, on many of these models you will have to use a large wrench because there isn't enough room to put an oxygen sensor socket on the sensor.

7   Clean the threads of the sensor bore in the exhaust manifold.

8   If you're going to install the old sensor, apply anti-seize compound to the threads of the sensor to facilitate future removal. If you're going to install a new oxygen sensor, it's not necessary to apply anti-seize compound to the threads. The threads on new sensors already have anti-seize compound on them.

9   Installation is otherwise the reverse of removal. Tighten the sensor to the torque listed in this Chapter's Specifications.

Downstream oxygen sensor

Note: *The downstream oxygen sensor is located on the catalytic converter.*

10   Remove the vehicle under cover if equipped.

11   Trace the electrical lead from the downstream oxygen sensor to the electrical connector and disconnect it.

12   Unscrew and remove the sensor with an oxygen sensor socket (see illustration).

13   Clean the threads of the sensor bore in the catalytic converter.

14   If you're going to install the old sensor, apply anti-seize compound to the threads of the sensor to facilitate future removal.

15   If you're going to install a new oxygen sensor, it's not necessary to apply anti-seize compound to the threads. The threads on new sensors already have anti-seize compound on them.

16   Installation is otherwise the reverse of

removal. Tighten the sensor to the torque listed in this Chapter's Specifications.

Turbocharged models

17   Disconnect the cable from the negative terminal of the battery (see Chapter 5).

Upstream oxygen sensor

Note: *The upstream oxygen sensor is located on the right exhaust manifold.*

18   On Legacy and 2014 and later Forester models, remove the radiator fan assembly (see Chapter 3, Section 5).

19   Disconnect the upstream oxygen sensor electrical connector.

20   Detach the clips for the upstream oxygen sensor harness.

21   If necessary, loosen the right front wheel lug nuts. Raise the front of the vehicle and support it securely on jackstands. Remove the right front wheel.

22   To access the upstream oxygen sensor, remove the engine under cover.

23   Unscrew the oxygen sensor (see illustration) and remove it from the right exhaust manifold.

Note: *If the sensor is difficult to loosen, spray the base of the sensor with some penetrating oil and give it some time to soak into the threads, then try again.*

24   If you're going to install the old oxygen sensor, apply anti-seize compound to the threads of the sensor to facilitate future removal.

25   If you're installing a new oxygen sensor, it's not necessary to apply anti-seize compound to the threads; the threads on new sensors already have anti-seize compound on them.

26   Installation is otherwise the reverse of removal. Tighten the sensor to the torque listed in this Chapter's Specifications. Tighten the wheel lug nuts to the torque listed in the Chapter 1 Specifications.

12.28 A typical downstream oxygen sensor on a turbocharged model

13.2 Depress the release tab and disconnect the PSP switch electrical connector

Downstream oxygen sensor

Note: *The downstream oxygen sensor is located on the downstream catalytic converter.*

27   Raise the vehicle and support it securely on jackstands.

28   Locate the oxygen sensor (see illustration), trace the sensor electrical harness to its connector and disconnect the connector.

29   On some models it may be necessary to detach the sensor harness clips from the upper side of the crossmember.

30   Unscrew the oxygen sensor and remove it from the downstream catalytic converter.

Note: *If the sensor is difficult to loosen, spray the base of the sensor with some penetrating oil and give it some time to soak into the threads, then try again.*

31   If you're going to install the old oxygen sensor, apply anti-seize compound to the threads of the sensor to facilitate future removal.

32   If you're installing a new oxygen sensor, it's not necessary to apply anti-seize compound to the threads; the threads on new sensors already have anti-seize compound on them.

33   Installation is otherwise the reverse of removal. Tighten the downstream oxygen sensor to the torque listed in this Chapter's Specifications.

---

13 Power Steering Pressure (PSP) switch - replacement

Note: *The PSP switch is located on the power steering pump on most models.*

1   Disconnect the cable from the negative terminal of the battery (see Chapter 5).

2   Disconnect the PSP switch electrical connector (see illustration).

3   Unscrew and remove the PSP switch.

4   Installation is the reverse of removal. Tighten the PSP switch securely.

5   Check the power steering fluid level, adding as necessary (see Chapter 1).

14.5 Push the locking tab straight in and unplug the electrical connector from the TR sensor

---

14 Transmission Range (TR) sensor - replacement

Note: *The TR sensor is located on the right side of the transaxle. The TR switch is also called the inhibitor switch.*

1   Disconnect the cable from the negative terminal of the battery (see Chapter 5).

2   Put the shift lever in Neutral.

3   Raise the vehicle and support it securely on jackstands.

4   Remove the center exhaust pipe section (see Chapter 4). On later models you might also have to remove the front part of the exhaust system (see Chapter 4).

5   Disconnect the electrical connector from the TR sensor (see illustration).

6   Disconnect the shift cable from the manual lever and from the transaxle (see illustration) and set it aside.

7   Carefully drive out the roll pin from the end of the shift shaft (see illustration), then slide the shift arm off of the shaft.

Caution: *Do not use excessive force to drive out the roll pin or damage to the shaft will occur.*

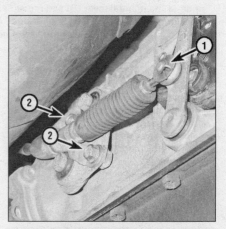

14.6 Remove the cotter pin (1) (and washer) securing the cable to the manual lever, remove the two cable bracket mounting bolts (2), then slide the end of the cable off the pin on the manual lever

14.7 Use a pin punch to carefully drive out the roll pin

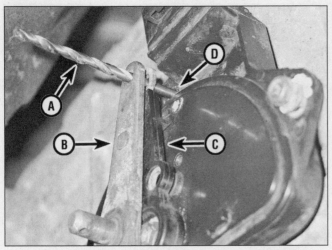

14.10 Insert a 5/32-inch drill bit (A) through the holes in the ends of the manual lever (B) and the sensor lever (C), and into the alignment hole (D) in the sensor body (typical earlier model shown, later models similar)

15.46 Identifying the secondary speed sensor

8   Remove the TR sensor mounting bolts.
9   Slide the sensor off of the shaft.
10   To adjust the TR sensor, place the sensor in position and loosely install the TR sensor bolts. Insert a 5/32-inch drill bit through the alignment holes in the ends of the manual and sensor levers, and into the alignment hole in the sensor body (see illustration). Tighten the sensor bolts securely.
11   Installation is otherwise the reverse of removal.

15   Vehicle Speed Sensor (VSS) - replacement

1   Disconnect the cable from the negative terminal of the battery (see Chapter 5).
Note: *Three speed sensors are used on the automatic transaxle: the front VSS, the torque converter turbine speed sensor, and the rear VSS. The front VSS and the torque converter turbine speed sensor are wired into the same harness and must be replaced together. The front VSS is located at the upper left rear part of the main transaxle case. The torque converter turbine speed sensor is located at the left front of the main transaxle case. The rear VSS is located on the left side of the transaxle extension housing.*

Front VSS and torque converter turbine speed sensor - automatic transaxle

2   On non-turbo models, remove the air intake duct/resonator from the throttle body.
3   On turbocharged models, remove the intercooler (see Chapter 4).
4   Remove the upper engine mount (pitching stopper) (see Chapter 2A).
5   Disconnect the transaxle harness electrical connector and detach it from the bracket.
6   Raise the vehicle and support it securely

on jackstands.
7   Drain the transaxle fluid (see Chapter 1), then reinstall the drain plug, tightening it to the torque listed in the Chapter 1 Specifications.
8   If you're working on a non-turbo model, remove the entire exhaust system; if you're working on a turbo model, remove the rear and center portion of the exhaust system (see Chapter 4).
9   Remove the heat shield and the driveshaft (see Chapter 8).
10   Support the transaxle with a floor jack (preferably one with a transmission jack head adapter).
11   Unbolt the crossmember from the floor pan and lower the transaxle.
12   Disconnect the fluid lines from the transaxle.
Caution: *Don't lose the ball and spring when removing the retaining screw from the outlet line.*
13   Remove the retaining bolts and remove the front VSS and the torque converter turbine speed sensor from the transaxle case.
14   Remove the transaxle fluid pan.
15   Disconnect the electrical connector from the rear VSS.
16   Follow the VSS wiring harness into the transaxle and disconnect the electrical connectors. Also remove the screw and detach the ground wire. Push the harness through the transaxle case.
17   Installation is the reverse of removal, noting the following points:
   a) *Make sure the harness grommet seats properly in the transaxle case.*
   b) *Clean the mating surfaces of the fluid pan and transaxle, then apply a bead of RTV sealant to the flange of the pan. Install the pan and tighten the bolts to the torque listed in this Chapter's Specifications.*
   c) *Tighten the sensor mounting bolts to the torque listed in this Chapter's Specifications.*

Primary speed sensor - CVT transaxle, non-turbocharged models

18   If you're working on a 2012 or earlier model, remove the air intake duct between the throttle body and air filter housing (see Chapter 4).
19   If you're working on a 2013 or later model, remove the CVT transaxle from the vehicle (see Chapter 7B).
20   Disconnect the electrical connector from the sensor.
21   Remove the bolt and the speed sensor.
22   If the sensor is to be reinstalled, use a new O-ring.
23   Installation is reverse of removal.

Primary speed sensor - CVT transaxle, turbocharged models

24   The sensor is located on the top of the transmission.
25   Disconnect the negative battery cable.
26   Remove the intercooler (see Chapter 4 Section 16).
27   Clean the area around the speed sensor.
28   Disconnect the speed sensor electrical connector.
29   Remove the bolt and the speed sensor.
30   If the sensor is to be reinstalled, use a new O-ring.
31   Installation is reverse of removal.

Front wheel speed sensor - CVT transaxle, turbocharged models (TR690)

Note: *This is a transaxle-mounted speed sensor, not to be confused with the ABS wheel speed sensor.*
32   Disconnect the negative battery cable.

33   Raise and support the vehicle on jackstands.
34   Clean the area around the speed sensor.
35   Disconnect the speed sensor electrical connector.
36   Remove the bolt and the speed sensor.
Note: *Be prepared to catch any fluid that may spill out of the speed sensor opening.*
37   If the sensor is to be reinstalled, use a new O-ring.
38   Installation is reverse of removal.

Rear VSS - automatic transaxles

39   Raise and support the vehicle on jackstands.
40   Disconnect the electrical connector from the rear VSS, then remove the retaininig bolt and remove the sensor from the transaxle extension housing.
Note: *Be prepared to catch any fluid that may spill out of the speed sensor opening.*
41   If the sensor is to be reinstalled, use a new O-ring.
42   Installation is the reverse of removal.

Secondary speed sensor - CVT transaxles

43   On Forester models, remove the CVT transaxle from the vehicle (see Chapter 7B).
44   Remove the transaxle cover over the speed sensor.
45   On Legacy models, raise and support the vehicle.
46   Disconnect the speed sensor electrical connector (see illustration).
47   Remove the bolt and the speed sensor.
Note: *On Legacy models, be prepared to catch any fluid that may spill out of the speed sensor opening.*
48   If the sensor is to be reinstalled, use a new O-ring.
49   Installation is reverse of removal.

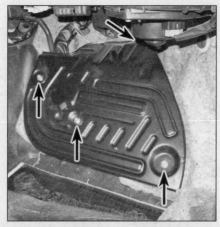

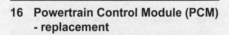
16.2 PCM protective cover retaining bolts (the exact shape of these covers varies somewhat among different models but they're all quite similar) (2013 and earlier Forester shown)

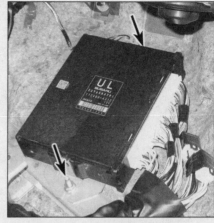
16.3 Remove the PCM mounting nuts (2013 and earlier Forester shown)

16   Powertrain Control Module (PCM) - replacement

Caution: *To avoid electrostatic discharge damage to the PCM, handle it only by its case. Do not tough the electrical terminals during removal and installation. If available, ground yourself to the vehicle with an anti-static ground strap, available at computer supply stores.*
1   Disconnect the cable from the negative battery terminal (see Chapter 5).

2013 and earlier Forester models

Note: *The PCM is located inside the vehicle, on the lower part of the right (passenger's) side firewall, under the carpet and a protective cover.*

2   Fold back the passengers side carpet and remove the protective cover retaining bolts (see illustration) and remove the cover.
3   Remove the PCM mounting nuts (see illustration).
4   Disconnect the electrical connectors from the PCM (see illustration). Do not pull on the wires. Only pull on the plastic connectors.
5   Remove the PCM.
6   Installation is the reverse of removal.

All Legacy models and 2014 and later Forester models

7   Remove the glove box (see Chapter 11).
8   Disconnect the electrical connectors from the PCM (see illustration).
9   Remove the mounting nuts and detach the PCM from its bracket.
10   Installation is the reverse of removal.

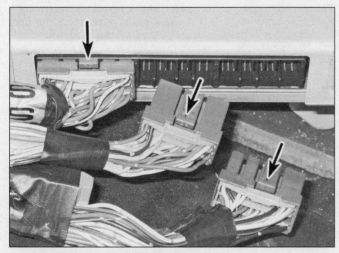
16.4 Depress the release tab on each electrical connector and carefully pull it out of the PCM (2013 and earlier Forester shown)

16.8 PCM electrical connectors

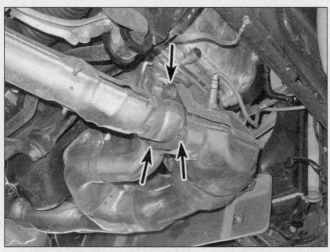

17.7 Front catalyst flange bolts and nuts (non-turbocharged models)

17.8 Rear catalyst flange bolts and nuts (non-turbocharged models)

17 Catalytic converters - description and component replacement

General description

1   The catalytic converter is an emission control device installed in the exhaust system that reduces pollutants from the exhaust gas stream. There are two types of converters: The oxidation catalyst reduces the levels of hydrocarbon (HC) and carbon monoxide (CO) by adding oxygen to the exhaust stream to produce water vapor (H_2O) and carbon dioxide (CO_2). The reduction catalyst lowers the levels of oxides of nitrogen (NOx) by removing oxygen from the exhaust gases to produce nitrogen (N) and oxygen. These two types of catalysts are combined into a three-way catalyst that reduces all three pollutants.
2   The amount of oxygen entering the catalyst is critical to its operation because without oxygen it cannot convert harmful pollutants into harmless compounds. The catalyst is most efficient at capturing and storing oxygen when it converts the exhaust gases of an intake charge that's mixed at the ideal (stoi-

chiometric) air/fuel ratio of 14.7:1. If the air/fuel ratio is leaner than stoichiometric for an extended period of time, the catalyst will store even more oxygen. But if the air/fuel ratio is richer than stoichiometric for any length of time, the oxygen content in the catalyst can become totally depleted. If this condition occurs, the catalyst will not convert anything!
3   Because the catalyst's ability to store oxygen is such an important factor in its operation, it can also be considered a factor in the catalyst's eventual inability to do its job. The PCM monitors the oxygen content going into and coming out of the catalyst by comparing the voltage signals from the upstream and downstream oxygen sensors. When the catalyst is functioning correctly, there is very little oxygen to monitor at the outlet end of the catalyst because it's capturing, storing and releasing oxygen as needed to convert HC, CO and NOx into more benign substances. But as the catalyst ages, it slowly loses its ability to store oxygen, and the downstream oxygen sensor tells the PCM that the oxygen content in the catalyzed exhaust gases is going up. When the amount of oxygen exiting the catalyst reaches a specified threshold, the

PCM stores a Diagnostic Trouble Code (DTC) and turns on the Malfunction Indicator Light (MIL).

Component replacement

4   Disconnect the cable from the negative battery terminal (see Chapter 5).

Non-turbocharged models

Note: *On these models, the upstream and downstream catalysts, and the exhaust pipe that connects them, are part of each exhaust pipe assembly. So if you have to replace either catalyst, you must replace each exhaust pipe assembly.*
5   Raise the vehicle and support it securely on jackstands.
6   Remove the upstream and downstream oxygen sensors (see Section 12).
7   Remove the front mounting flange bolts and nuts (see illustration).
8   Remove the rear mounting flange bolts and nuts (see illustration) and remove the front center exhaust pipe/catalyst assembly.
9   Remove the nuts attaching the front exhaust pipe to the cylinder heads and remove the front exhaust pipe/catalyst assembly (see illustration).
10   Installation is the reverse of removal.

Turbocharged models

Note: *The upstream and downstream catalysts are both part of the center exhaust pipe. To replace either of these catalysts, you must first remove the center exhaust pipe, then unbolt the catalyst that you want to replace.*
11   Remove the engine cover, if equipped (see Chapter 2A).
12   On 2013 and earlier Forester models, remove the intercooler (see Chapter 4) and the intercooler mounting bracket (see Chapter 4, Section 16).
13   Raise the vehicle and support it securely on jackstands.
14   Remove the engine under cover (see Chapter 2A).

17.9 Identifying front (A) and center front (B) exhaust pipes (2014 Forester shown)

15   Working under the vehicle, remove the bolts that secure the lower edge of the turbo-charger cover, if equippped.

16   Remove the turbocharger upper cover.

17   Unbolt the center exhaust pipe from the turbocharger.

18   Working under the vehicle, disconnect the electrical connector from the rear oxygen sensor (see Section 12).

19   Unbolt the center exhaust pipe from the rear exhaust pipe.

20   Disconnect the brackets for the exhaust pipe.

21   Remove the center exhaust pipe.

22   Unbolt the front exhaust pipe/catalytic converter from the rear exhaust pipe/catalytic converter.

23   When bolting the two catalytic converters back together, use a new gasket at the flange.

24   Installation is otherwise the reverse of removal.

18.11 Location of the purge control solenoid valve (2014 Legacy shown)

18 Evaporative Emissions Control (EVAP) system - description and component replacement

Description

1   The Evaporative Emissions Control (EVAP) system absorbs fuel vapors (unburned hydrocarbons) and, during engine operation, releases them into the intake manifold from which they're drawn into the intake ports where they mix with the incoming air-fuel mixture.

2   The EVAP system consists of the fuel tank filler neck cap, the fuel cut valve, the EVAP canister, the drain filter, the drain valve, the fuel tank pressure sensor, the pressure control solenoid valve, the shut-off valve, the vent valve and the purge control solenoid valve. Everything except the purge control solenoid valve is located underneath the vehicle, tucked between the right rear wheelwell and the right inside corner of the rear bumper cover. The EVAP canister purge valve is located in the engine compartment.

3   Modern EVAP systems are quite complex. But basically, here's how it works: The gasoline inside the fuel tank evaporates constantly and produces fuel vapors. The pressure control solenoid valve monitors the pressure inside the tank and keeps the Powertrain Control Module (PCM) informed. When the PCM senses that the pressure has exceeded the specified threshold, it energizes the pressure control solenoid valve, which opens, allowing the vapors to migrate to the EVAP canister. The canister stores these vapors until the PCM energizes the purge control solenoid valve, which opens and purges the EVAP canister, allowing intake manifold vacuum to pull the vapors from the canisters into the intake manifold.

4   When the EVAP system is being purged and stored vapors inside the canister are being pulled out of the canister by intake manifold vacuum, a vacuum condition would quickly result inside the canister if it were not vented to atmospheric pressure. So during purging, atmospheric air is drawn into the EVAP canister through the drain filter, where any impurities are removed. From the drain filter, air is drawn through the drain valve, then into the canister.

5   The EVAP system diagnostic monitor is an OBD-II test that the PCM runs to check the EVAP system and the fuel tank for leaks. When the PCM runs the OBD-II EVAP system monitor, it energizes the atmospheric pressure switching solenoid, which closes off the passage between the fuel filler neck pipe (atmospheric pressure) and the fuel tank. The PCM also closes the drain valve during OBD-II system monitoring.

6   During refueling, three different valves play a role in protecting the EVAP system from being contaminated by raw gasoline. The shut-off valve, which is located at the top of the fuel filler neck pipe, closes the EVAP line to prevent the fuel nozzle from accidentally pumping fuel into the EVAP system. Down at the fuel tank, the fuel cut valve, which is an integral component of the fuel tank - it's built into the top of the tank - prevents fuel from entering the EVAP system during refueling. As the fuel level in the tank rises, a float in the fuel cut valve moves up and closes the hole in the bottom of the fuel cut valve so that no fuel can enter the EVAP system. As the level of fuel inside the fuel tank rises during refueling, fuel vapors are produced in the space between the rising fuel level and the roof of the tank. The vent valve, which is also located on the fuel tank, allows these vapors to migrate to the EVAP canister. When the pressure inside the fuel tank exceeds atmospheric pressure, a spring-loaded diaphragm opens and allows the excessive pressure to push the vapors into the canister. The EVAP system's ability to vent vapors to the canister during refueling is the principal feature of the vehicle's On-Board Refueling Vapor Recovery (ORVR) system. The vent valve also has a float inside it that blocks the vapor passage through the valve once the tank is full.

7   In the event that an EVAP line becomes kinked or pinched, the fuel tank filler neck cap has a relief valve that prevents the formation of a vacuum inside the tank. When the EVAP system is functioning normally, the fuel tank filler neck cap is sealed by a sealing ring that's compressed when you screw on the cap. If a vacuum develops inside the fuel tank, atmospheric pressure forces a spring inside the filler cap to open a valve in the bottom of the cap, which open the fuel tank to the atmosphere. Air at atmospheric pressure is drawn into the relative vacuum of the fuel tank, keeping the air inside the tank (above the fuel) equalized with the outside atmospheric pressure.

Component replacement

Purge control solenoid valve

Note: *The purge control solenoid valve is located on the left rear of the intake manifold on non-turbocharged models, and on the right front of the intake manifold on turbocharged models. 2014 and later turbocharged models use two purge control solenoid valves.*

8   Remove the engine cover, if equipped.

9   Disconnect the cable from the negative battery terminal (see Chapter 5).

10   If necessary, remove the intercooler to access the purge solenoid (see Chapter 4, Section 16).

11   Disconnect the electrical connector from the purge control solenoid valve (see illustration).

12   On models with a bracket, remove the purge control solenoid valve mounting bracket mounting bolts, and remove the bracket and solenoids as a single assembly from the intake manifold.

13   On models without a bracket, remove the bolt and the purge solenoid from the intake manifold.

14   Clearly label, then disconnect the two EVAP hoses from the purge control solenoid valve.

15   Remove the purge control solenoid valve mounting bolt and remove the valve from the bracket if equipped.

16   Installation is the reverse of removal. Reconnect the EVAP hoses to their correct ports on the purge control solenoid valve.

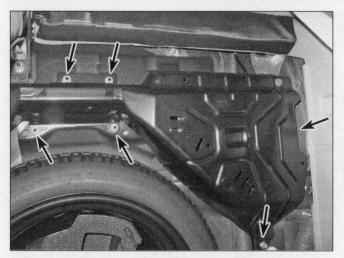

18.21 Remove the floor cover fasteners

18.22 Canister connection details

1	Purge hose	4	Drain valve
2	Vent hose		electrical connector
3	Drain hose	5	PCV drain hose

EVAP canister and leak check valve

Note: *On 2013 and earlier Forester models and all Legacy models, the leak check valve is part of the canister and removed with the canister.*

2013 and earlier Forester models

Note: *The canister is located in the rear of the vehicle. The leak check valve is attached to the canister.*

17 Disconnect the cable from the negative battery terminal (see Chapter 5).
18 Raise the rear of the vehicle and support it securely on jackstands.
19 Open the liftgate, then remove the mat.
20 Fold the right rear seat back all the way down.
21 Remove the clips from the back of the seat. Remove the floor cover fasteners and remove the covers (see illustration).
Note: *There are either two or three covers in the floorboard area, depending on the year*

and model.
22 On the front end of the EVAP canister, disconnect the electrical connector from the drain valve. Clearly label, then disconnect the EVAP hoses from the EVAP canister assembly (see illustration).
23 Disconnect the quick-connect fitting from the rear end of the EVAP canister. If you're unfamiliar with quick-connect fittings, refer to Chapter 4.
24 Disconnect the vent hose.
25 Remove the three EVAP canister mounting bolts/nuts (see illustration) and remove the canister assembly.
26 Installation is the reverse of removal. Reconnect the hoses to their correct ports on the EVAP canister.

2014 and later Forester models

Note: *The canister and leak check valve are located above the rear differential.*

27 Disconnect the negative battery cable.

28 Raise and support the rear of the vehicle.
29 Remove the rear exhaust pipe.
30 Remove the rear driveshaft (see Chapter 8, Section 12).
31 Support the rear differential using a floor jack.
32 Remove the upper differential-to-subframe nuts (see Chapter 8).
33 Remove the lower differential mount-to-subframe bolts.
34 Disengage the upper studs from the crossmember. Lower the differential until the upper studs are about even with the lower mount bolt holes in the subframe.
35 Disconnect the EVAP hoses and electrical connector from the leak check valve (see illustration).
36 Remove the clip and the leak check valve from the vehicle.
37 Disconnect the canister hoses and connector from the canister (see illustration).

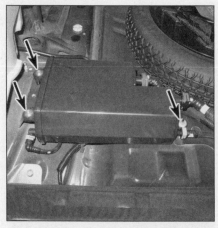

18.25 EVAP canister mounting fasteners

18.35 Identifying leak check valve
(2014 and later Forester)

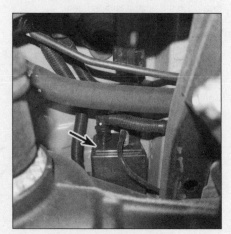

18.37 EVAP canister location
(2014 and later Forester)

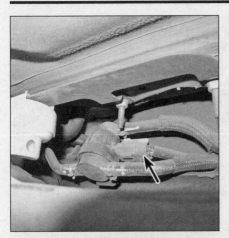

18.55 Disconnect the pressure control solenoid valve electrical connector

18.61 Remove the fuel filler ring retaining screws

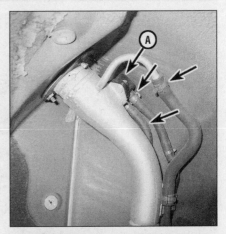

18.64 Disconnect any EVAP hoses connected to the fuel filler neck pipe and the shut valve (A)

38   Unbolt the canister and remove from the vehicle.
39   Installation is reverse of removal.

Legacy models

Note: *The canister is located above the left rear wheel, protected by the inner fender liner. The leak check valve is attached to the canister.*

40   Disconnect the negative battery cable.
41   Raise and support the rear of the vehicle on jackstands and remove the left rear wheel.
42   Remove the inner fender liner to access the canister.
43   Disconnect the canister hoses and connector behind the strut assembly. Remove the harness clip attaching the hoses and harness to the vehicle.
44   Unbolt the canister and remove from the vehicle.
45   Disconnect the hoses from the canister.
46   Installation is reverse of removal.

Fuel tank pressure sensor

Note: *Fuel tank pressure sensors are installed on 2012 and earlier Forester turbocharged models and all 2012 and earlier Legacy models.*

47   Disconnect the cable from the negative battery terminal (see Chapter 5).
48   Remove the fuel filler cap to equalize the pressure inside the fuel tank.
49   Raise the rear of the vehicle and support it securely on jackstands.
50   Disconnect the electrical connectors from the fuel tank pressure sensor.
51   Disconnect the fuel tank pressure hose from the fuel tank pressure sensor.
52   Remove the fuel tank pressure sensor mounting bracket nut and remove the sensor.
53   Installation is reverse of removal.

Pressure control solenoid valve

Note: *2013 and earlier Forester turbocharged and 2012 and earlier Legacy turbocharged*

models are equipped with a pressure control solenoid. The pressure control solenoid valve is located below the EVAP canister.

54   Raise the rear of the vehicle and support it securely on jackstands. Remove the pressure control solenoid valve mounting bracket bolt.
55   Disconnect the electrical connector from the pressure control solenoid valve (see illustration).
56   Separate the pressure control solenoid valve from its mounting bracket.
57   Clearly label, then disconnect, the two EVAP hoses from the pressure control solenoid valve.
58   Disconnect the vacuum hose from the pressure control solenoid valve.
59   Installation is the reverse of removal. Reconnect the hoses to the correct ports on the pressure control solenoid valve.

Shut valve

Note: *2013 and earlier Forester turbocharged and 2012 and earlier Legacy turbocharged models are equipped with a shut valve. The shut valve is located near the top of the fuel filler neck pipe. To replace the shut valve, the fuel filler neck pipe must be removed.*

60   Disconnect the cable from the negative battery terminal (see Chapter 5).
61   Open the fuel filler cap door, unscrew the cap. On Forester models, remove the filler ring retaining screws and the fuel filler ring (see illustration). On Legacy models, rotate the filler ring clockwise to unscrew and remove.
62   Loosen the right rear wheel lug nuts. Raise the vehicle and support it securely on jackstands. Remove the right rear wheel.
63   Remove the splash shield from the right rear wheelwell (see Chapter 11).
64   Carefully label each EVAP hose, then disconnect them from the fuel filler neck pipe (see illustration).

65   Remove the fasteners securing the fuel filler neck pipe to the vehicle body (see illustration).
66   Trace the fuel filler neck pipe to its lower end, loosen the hose clamp securing the filler hose to the filler neck pipe, and disconnect the hose from the pipe.

Note: *If you're unable to remove the hose from the filler neck pipe, wait until after you have unbolted the lower end of the pipe in the next step, then pull the pipe out of the hose.*

67   Remove the fuel filler neck pipe lower mounting bolt and remove the filler neck assembly.
68   Remove the two shut valve mounting nuts and remove the shut valve from the fuel filler neck pipe.
69   Installation is the reverse of removal. Tighten the wheel lug nuts to the torque listed in the Chapter 1 Specifications.

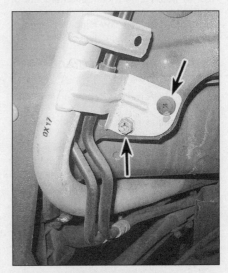

18.65 Fuel filler neck pipe mounting fasteners

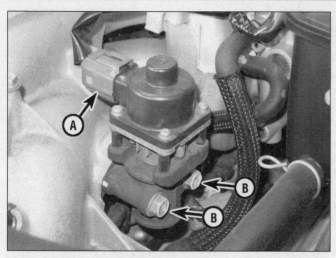

19.5a EGR valve electrical connector (A) and mounting bolts (B) (2010 Forester shown)

19.5b EGR valve location - intake manifold removed (2013 Legacy shown)

19 Exhaust Gas Recirculation (EGR) system - description and component replacement

Note: *Only non-turbocharged models are equipped with an Exhaust Gas Recirculation (EGR) system.*

Description

1   When your vehicle is under load, the temperature inside the combustion chambers heats up. When the temperature inside the combustion chambers reaches 2500 degrees F, the engine begins to produce oxides of nitrogen (NOx), which is an odorless, colorless and toxic gas. The EGR system reduces NOx by introducing a controlled amount of spent exhaust gases into the intake manifold, which lowers combustion chamber temperatures and reduces the creation of NOx.

Component replacement
EGR valve
Note: *The EGR valve is located on the intake manifold.*
2   Disconnect the cable from the negative battery terminal (see Chapter 5).
3   On Forester models, if necessary, remove the intake air duct between the air filter housing and throttle body (see Chapter 4).
4   Disconnect the electrical connector from the EGR valve.
5   Remove the EGR mounting bolts (see illustrations) and remove the EGR valve from the intake manifold or water passage, as applicable.
6   Remove and discard the old EGR valve gasket.
7   Remove all exhaust deposits from the EGR valve mating surfaces. Look for exhaust deposits in the valve outlet. Remove deposit build-up with a scraper or screwdriver.

Caution: *Don't wash the EGR valve in solvents or degreaser, either of which will permanently damage the diaphragm inside the valve.*
8   If the EGR passage contains an excessive build-up of deposits, clean it out with a wire wheel. Make sure that all loose particles are completely removed to prevent them from clogging the EGR valve or from being ingested into the engine.
9   Installation is the reverse of removal. Install a new gasket and tighten the EGR valve mounting bolts to the torque listed in this Chapter's Specifications.

20 Positive Crankcase Ventilation (PCV) system - description and component replacement

Description

1   The Positive Crankcase Ventilation (PCV) system reduces hydrocarbon emissions by directing blow-by gases and crankcase vapors into the intake manifold, where they're mixed with intake air before being drawn into the combustion chambers where they're consumed along with the air/fuel mixture. The PCV system does this by circulating fresh air from the air filter housing through a series of hoses into the crankcase, where the fresh air mixes with blow-by gases before being drawn from the crankcase by intake vacuum, through the PCV valve and then into the intake manifold.
2   During idle and part-throttle conditions, intake manifold vacuum is high. Blow-by gases and crankcase vapors flow from the crankcase into the intake manifold through the PCV valve and the crankcase ventilation hose (also known as the PCV hose) into the intake manifold. The strong intake manifold vacuum also pulls fresh air from the air intake

duct or the air filter housing through the fresh air inlet hoses into the crankcase.
3   During wide-open throttle conditions, intake manifold vacuum is not high enough to pull fresh air into the crankcase or to pull blow-by gases or crankcase vapors out of the crankcase. Instead, other hoses allow some of the blow-by gases and crankcase vapors to flow out of the crankcase and into the air intake duct or air filter housing, from which they're pulled into the intake manifold along with intake air.
4   There is no scheduled maintenance interval for the PCV valve or the PCV system hoses. But over time the PCV system might become less efficient as an oily residue of sludge builds up inside the PCV valve and the hoses. One symptom of a clogged PCV system is leaking seals. When crankcase vapors can't escape, pressure builds inside the bottom end and eventually causes crankshaft seals to leak. So anytime that you're changing the oil filter, air filter, fuel filter, spark plugs, etc., it's a good idea to pull off the PCV hoses and inspect them. If the hoses are clogged, remove them and clean them out. If they're cracked, torn or deteriorated, replace them.

Component replacement
PCV valve
5   Remove the air intake duct assembly (see Chapter 4).
6   On turbo models, it may be necessary to remove the intercooler to access the PCV valve and hose (see Chapter 4, Section 16).
7   The crankcase ventilation hose, or PCV hose (see illustrations) connects the PCV valve to the intake manifold.
8   Remove the PCV hose and inspect the hose for cracks, tears and deterioration. If the hose is damaged or worn, replace it.
9   Remove the PCV valve from the engine.
10   Installation is the reverse of removal.

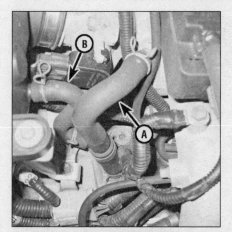

20.7a Typical crankcase ventilation (or PCV) hose (A) and PCV hose-to-air filter housing hose (B)

20.7b Identifying PCV valve and hose - intake manifold removed (2013 Legacy non-turbo shown)

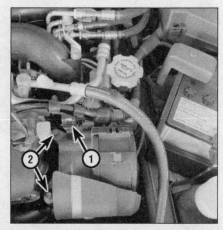

21.3 Secondary air pump details - top view

1   *Harness retaining clip*
2   *Pump mounting bolts*

21 Secondary air injection system - description and component replacement

Description

1   The secondary air injection system, which is only used on 2013 and earlier Forester turbocharged models, is a PCM-controlled system that pumps extra air into the exhaust system during open-loop operation (cold starts), to help oxidize unburned hydrocarbons until the oxygen sensors and the catalytic converters are warmed up. The system consists of a PCM-controlled electric air pump and two secondary air combination valves, one for each exhaust manifold. When the PCM energizes the relays for the secondary air combination valves, they open the left and right secondary air combination valves and the secondary air pump, and air is pumped into the exhaust manifolds. The left secondary air combination valve is located on the front of the right cylinder head, and the right valve is located on top of the right part of the engine block.

Component replacement

Secondary air injection pump

Note: *The secondary air injection pump is located at the left front corner of the engine compartment, to the left of the air conditioning compressor.*

2   Disconnect the cable from the negative battery terminal (see Chapter 5).
3   Detach the wiring harness clip from the top of the secondary air injection pump (see illustration).
4   Remove the pump mounting bolts
5   Disconnect the pump's electrical connector (see illustration).
6   Lift the pump up and disconnect the air hose, then remove the pump.
7   Installation is the reverse of removal. Tighten the pump mounting bolts to the torque listed in this Chapter's Specifications.

Secondary air injection combination valves

8   Disconnect the cable from the negative battery terminal (see Chapter 5).
9   Remove the intercooler (see Chapter 4, Section 16).

Left valve

10   Disconnect the electrical connector from the left secondary air combination valve.
11   Disconnect and remove the air duct.
12   Unbolt the outlet pipe from the secondary air combination valve. Remove and discard the old gasket between the valve and the outlet pipe.
13   Unbolt and remove the left secondary air combination valve.
14   Installation is the reverse of removal. Use a new gasket when reconnecting the outlet pipe to the secondary air combination valve.

Right valve

15   Remove the left secondary air combination valve.
16   Remove the intake manifold (see Chapter 2A).
17   Disconnect the electrical connector from the right secondary air combination valve.
18   Unbolt the outlet pipe from the right secondary air combination valve outlet pipe. Remove and discard the old gasket between the valve and the outlet pipe.
19   Unbolt and remove the right secondary air combination valve.
20   Installation is the reverse of removal. Install a new gasket when reconnecting the outlet pipe to the secondary air combination valve.

21.5 Secondary air pump details - left-side view

1   *Electrical connector*
2   *Hose clamp*

22 Tumble generator - description and component replacement

Description

1   The tumble generator system is used on all turbocharged models. The tumble generator valves reduce emissions during start-ups. A tumble generator valve swirls the air entering the combustion chamber, which improves the dispersion (mixing) of the air/fuel mixture.
2   The tumble generator valves (butterfly valves) are housed in the lower intake manifolds (Subaru refers to the lower intake manifolds as tumble generator housings). There is one valve for each intake runner, and each pair of valves is fitted to a common shaft. There are two actuators. The actuator for the left cylinder head is located at the rear end of

22.11 Tumble generator valve actuator details

1   *Electrical connector*
2   *Mounting screw (other screw not visible)*

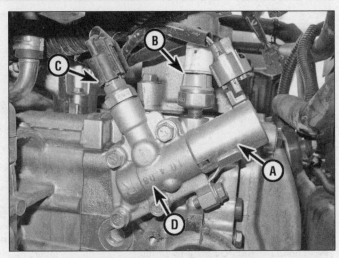

23.5 Oil switching solenoid valve (OSV) and holder assembly (right side shown, left OSV similar):

A   *OSV valve*
B   *Variable valve lift diagnosis oil pressure switch*
C   *Oil temperature sensor*
D   *OSV holder*

the lower intake manifold, and the actuator for the right cylinder head is located at the front end of the lower intake manifold.
3   When you start a cold engine, the PCM determines that the engine coolant is cold, turns on a timer and energizes the tumble generator valve actuator, which (almost, but not quite) closes the butterfly valves. When the valves are closed, air entering the combustion chambers is forced to go through a very small cross-sectional area, which means that it moves through this bottleneck at very high speed, which creates a tumbling motion (swirl), which enables the mixture to be burned more completely. The timer turns off the tumble generator valve actuator once the engine is warmed up. The system only operates during cold start-ups.

Tumble generator valve actuator assembly replacement

4   On turbocharged models, relieve the fuel system pressure (see Chapter 4).
5   Disconnect the cable from the negative battery terminal (see Chapter 5).

Turbocharged models

Note: *On turbocharged models, the actuator cannot be separated from the tumble generator valve.*

6   Remove the intake manifold (see Chapter 2A, Section 5).
7   Remove the fuel injectors (see Chapter 4, Section 13).
8   Remove the mounting six bolts and the tumble generator valve assembly from the intake manifold.
9   On 2014 and later Forester models, remove the three mounting bolts and the intake adapter and cylinder head plates from the engine.

10   Installation is the reverse of removal. Tighten the valve actuator mounting bolts securely.

Non-turbocharged models

11   Disconnect the electrical connector from the actuator valve (see illustration).
12   Remove the screws and detach the valve from the tumble generator.
13   Installation is the reverse of removal. Be sure to use a new gasket, and tighten the screws securely.

---

23   Variable Valve Lift (VVL) system (2012 and earlier models) - component replacement

Oil switching solenoid valves (OSV) and OSV holders

Note: *There are two oil switching solenoid valves; they are located on the cylinder heads.*

Right valve and holder, and oil temperature sensor

1   Disconnect the cable from the negative battery terminal (see Chapter 5).
2   Remove the air intake duct between the throttle body and air filter housing (see Chapter 4).
3   Detach the engine harness electrical connector from its bracket.
4   Disconnect the electrical connector from the OSV.
5   Remove the OSV retaining bolt and remove the OSV (see illustration).
6   Remove the oil temperature sensor.
7   Remove the variable valve lift diagnosis oil pressure switch.
8   Remove the OSV holder mounting bolts and remove the holder.

9   Remove and discard the old switching valve holder gasket.
10   Installation is the reverse of removal. Install a new switching valve holder gasket and tighten all bolts securely.

Left valve and holder

11   Disconnect the cable from the negative battery cable (see Chapter 5).
12   Remove the accessory drivebelts (see Chapter 1).
13   Remove the crankshaft pulley (see Chapter 2A).
14   Remove the timing belt cover and the timing belt (see Chapter 2A).
15   Remove the left camshaft sprocket (see Chapter 2A).
16   Remove the rear timing belt cover (see Chapter 2A).
17   Disconnect the electrical connector from the OSV (see illustration 23.5).
18   Remove the OSV retaining bolt and remove the OSV.
19   Remove the variable valve lift diagnosis oil pressure switch.
20   Remove the OSV holder mounting bolts and remove the holder.
21   Remove and discard the old switching valve holder gasket.
22   Installation is the reverse of removal. Install a new switching valve holder gasket and tighten all bolts securely.

Variable valve lift diagnosis oil pressure switch

Note: *There are two variable valve lift diagnosis pressure switches, one for each cylinder head. The left switch is located on the upper front end of the left cylinder head, behind the left OSV. The right switch is located on the upper rear end of the of the right cylinder head, just ahead of the right OSV.*

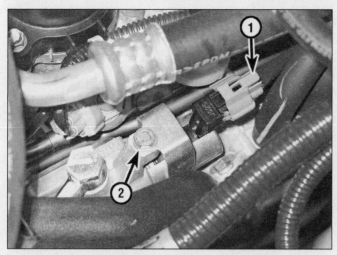

24.6a Left variable valve timing solenoid valve/oil flow control solenoid valve electrical connector (1) and retaining bolt (2)

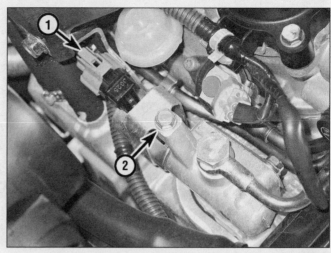

24.6b Right variable valve timing solenoid valve/oil flow control solenoid valve electrical connector (1) and retaining bolt (2)

23   Detach the engine harness electrical connector from its bracket.

24   Unscrew and remove the variable valve lift diagnosis oil pressure switch (see illustration 23.5).

25   Installation is the reverse of removal. Tighten the variable valve lift diagnosis oil pressure switch securely.

24   Variable Valve Timing (VVT) system - description and component replacement

Description

1   The variable valve timing system, adjusts the opening and closing timing of the intake valves (non-turbocharged models) and exhaust valves (turbocharged models) by altering the phase angle of the camshaft sprockets relative to the camshafts. The Powertrain Control Module (PCM) continuously monitors the angle (position) of the crankshaft, engine speed, vehicle speed, throttle opening and other inputs, then determines the optimal phase angle of the camshaft sprockets.

2   Inside each intake camshaft sprocket are hydraulic chambers that can either advance or retard the cam sprocket in relation to the position of the camshaft. The flow of engine oil into and out of these two chambers is controlled by the oil flow control solenoid valves (there are two of them, one for each intake camshaft sprocket). The PCM continuously commands the oil flow control solenoid valve to move a spool inside the oil flow control solenoid valves, which directs engine oil in or out of chambers inside the intake camshaft sprockets. One of these chambers, when filled with oil, advances the sprocket. The other chamber, when filled with oil, retards the sprocket. The oil flow control solenoid valves

are located on top of and at the front end of the valve covers.

Component replacement
Oil control solenoid valves

Forester (2010 and earlier non-turbocharged and 2013 and earlier turbocharged models)/Legacy (2012 and earlier non-turbocharged and all turbocharged models)

3   Remove the engine cover, if equipped (see Chapter 2A).

4   Disconnect the cable from the negative battery terminal (see Chapter 5).

5   If you're going to remove the right variable valve timing solenoid(s) valve/oil flow control solenoid valve, remove the air intake duct (see Chapter 4).

6   Depress the release tab and disconnect the electrical connector from the variable valve timing solenoid valve/oil flow control solenoid valve (see illustrations).

7   Remove the variable valve timing

solenoid(s) valve/oil flow control solenoid valve retaining bolt and remove the solenoid valve.

8   Installation is the reverse of removal. Tighten the retaining bolt securely.

Forester (2011 and later non-turbocharged and 2014 and later turbocharged models), Legacy (2013 and later non-turbocharged models)

9   Disconnect the negative battery cable (see Chapter 5).

10   To access the passenger side solenoid(s), remove the intake air duct (see Chapter 4).

11   To access the passenger side solenoid(s) it may help to remove the coolant reservoir.

12   Disconnect the electrical connector and remove the bolts to remove the intake or exhaust oil control solenoid (see illustration).

13   If the solenoid is to be reused, install a new O-ring. Apply clean engine oil to the O-ring prior to installation.

14   Installation is reverse of removal.

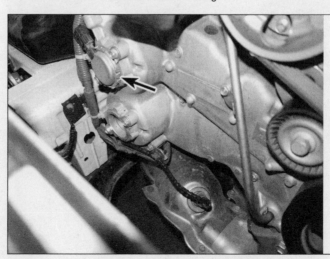

24.12 Oil control solenoid, intake, right bank (2013 Legacy non-turbo shown)

25 Oil temperature sensor/oil pressure switch - replacement

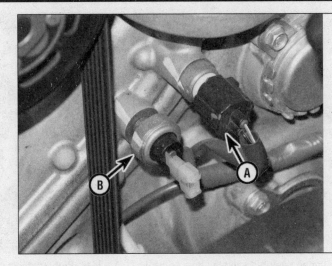

Forester (2010 and earlier non-turbocharged and 2013 and earlier turbocharged models), 2012 and earlier Legacy models

Note: *These models are only equipped with a oil pressure switch.*

1   Disconnect the negative battery cable (see Chapter 5).
2   Remove the alternator (see Chapter 5, Section 7).
3   Disconnect the electrical connector and remove the oil pressure switch.
4   Use a thread sealant on the threads prior to installation.
5   Installation is reverse of removal.

Forester (2011 and later non-turbocharged and 2014 and later turbocharged models), 2013 and later Legacy models

6   Disconnect the negative battery cable (see Chapter 5).
7   Disconnect the electrical connector for the oil pressure switch or oil temperature sensor (see illustration).
8   Remove the switch or sensor.
9   On the oil pressure switch, use a thread sealant on the threads prior to installation. On the oil temperature sensor, install new gasket prior to installation.
10   Installation is reverse of removal.

25.7 Identifying the oil temperature sensor (A) and oil pressure switch (B)

Notes

Notes

Chapter 7 Part A
Manual transaxle

Contents

Specifications

Torque specifications

Note: *One foot-pound (ft-lb) of torque is equivalent to 12 inch-pounds (in-lbs) of torque. Torque values below approximately 15 foot-pounds are expressed in inch-pounds, because most foot-pound torque wrenches are not accurate at these smaller values.*

	Ft-lbs	Nm
Back-up light switch/neutral switch..	24	32
Front engine mount (Legacy)		
Mount-to-engine bolts	18	25
Through bolt/nut	33	45
Transaxle-to-engine fasteners..	37	50
Transaxle mount bolts/nuts...	26	35
Transaxle main mounting bracket (Legacy)		
Bolts 55	75	
Nuts 33	45	
Pitching stopper bolts (Forester)		
Body end	43	58
Engine end	37	50

1　General information

1　There are two manual transaxles used on these models: the five-speed (5MT) on 2013 and earlier Forester models, and the six-speed (6MT) on 2014 and later Forester models, and all Legacy models. Both transaxles are fully-synchronized. The transaxle is actually several components bolted together into a single assembly: the clutch housing; the main case, which houses the differential and transmission; and the rear case. The transaxle is removed and installed as a single assembly; do not try to separate any of these components from the transaxle. If the transaxle must be replaced, obtain a complete new, rebuilt or used assembly.

2.5 Remove the extension housing oil seal with a seal removal tool or a large screwdriver; make sure you don't damage the splines on the output shaft

2　Oil seal replacement

1　Oil leaks frequently occur as a result of a worn extension housing oil seal or driveaxle oil seal, a vehicle speed sensor (VSS) seal or back-up light switch seal. Replacement of these seals is relatively easy, since the repairs can be performed without removing the transaxle from the vehicle. If you see puddles of lubricant under the transaxle, raise the vehicle and place it securely on jackstands, and try to determine the source of the leak.

Extension housing oil seal

2　The extension housing oil seal is located at the extreme rear end of the transaxle, where the driveshaft is attached. If the extension housing seal is leaking, there will be a buildup of lubricant on the front end of the driveshaft, and lubricant may even be dripping from the rear of the transaxle.

3　Remove the driveshaft from the transaxle (see Chapter 8).

4　Remove the heat shield.

5　Using a seal removal tool or screwdriver (see illustration), carefully pry the oil seal out of the rear of the transaxle. Do not damage the splines on the output shaft.

6　If the oil seal cannot be removed with a screwdriver or prybar, a special oil seal removal tool (available at auto parts stores) will be required.

7　Using a seal driver or a large deep socket as a drift, install the new oil seal (see illustration). Drive it into the bore squarely and make sure it's completely seated.

8　Lubricate the splines of the output shaft and the outside of the driveshaft sleeve yoke with lightweight grease, then install the driveshaft. Be careful not to damage the lip of

the new seal.

9　Installation is the reverse of the removal.

Driveaxle oil seals

Note: *This procedure applies to manual and automatic transaxles.*

10　Remove the exhaust manifold (see Chapter 2A) and the center exhaust pipe (see Chapter 4).

11　Place a drain pan under the transaxle.

12　Remove the driveaxle(s) from the transaxle (see Chapter 8).

13　Use a special seal removal tool to pry the driveaxle oil seal from the transaxle. If necessary, remove the oil seal using a blunt screwdriver (see illustration). Be careful not to damage the transaxle while removing the oil seal.

14　Using a large section of pipe or a large deep socket as a drift, install the new oil seal into the transaxle (see illustration). Drive it into the bore squarely and make sure it's completely seated.

15　Lightly oil the driveaxle seal then install the driveaxles (see Chapter 8).

16　Installation is the reverse of removal.

17　Check the transaxle lubricant level (manual transaxle) or differential lubricant level (automatic transaxle), adding as necessary to bring it to the appropriate level (see Chapter 1).

3　Shift lever - removal and installation

2013 and earlier Forester models

1　Disconnect the cable from the negative terminal of the battery (see Chapter 5).

2　Unscrew and remove the shift lever knob

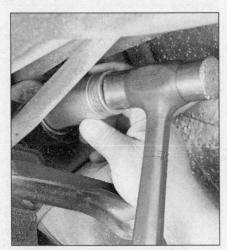

2.7 Make sure the seal is square to the bore, then use a hammer and seal driver or large socket to tap the new extension housing seal into place; make sure the outside diameter of the socket is slightly smaller than the outside diameter of the new seal

2.13 Remove the driveaxle oil seal using a seal removal tool

2.14 Using a large section of pipe or a large deep socket to install the new oil seal

3.4 Shift lever details

1   Shift rod-to-lever through-bolt
2   Shift lever through-bolt nut
3   Insulator mounting bolts

3.10 Remove the stay (A) from the transaxle bracket (B)

from the shift lever.
3   Remove the center console and the shift lever boot (see Chapter 11).
4   Remove the shift rod-to-shift lever through-bolt, then the insulator assembly bolts (see illustration).
5   Remove the boot and insulator assembly from the plate assembly.
6   Separate the plate assembly from the center console.
7   Raise the vehicle and support it securely on jackstands.
8   Remove the rear exhaust pipe and the muffler (see Chapter 4).
9   Remove the heat shield.
10   On non-STI models, remove the transaxle stay fasteners and remove the stay

from the end of the transaxle (see illustration).
11   Remove the rod from the joint (see illustration).
12   Remove the rubber cushion from the stay (see illustration).
13   Remove the pin and separate the joint from the assembly (see illustration).
14   Lower the vehicle and remove the shift lever from inside the vehicle.
15   Installation is the reverse of removal. Make sure that all fasteners are tight.

2014 and later Forester models and all Legacy models

16   Disconnect the cable from the negative

terminal of the battery (see Chapter 5).
17   Raise the vehicle and support it securely on jackstands.
18   Remove the center rear exhaust pipe.
19   Remove the heat shield.
20   Remove the shift cable cover plate.
21   Disconnect the shift cables from the shift lever assembly.
22   Remove the four nuts and the cable cover assembly from below the shift lever.
23   Working inside of the vehicle, unscrew the gear shift knob.
24   Remove the center console (see Chapter 11, Section 24).
25   Remove the four bolts and remove the shift lever assembly from the vehicle.
26   Installation is the reverse of removal.

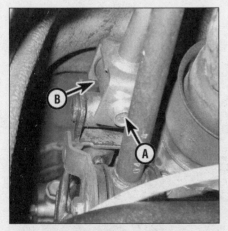

3.11 Use a socket and wrench to remove the rod through bolt (A) from the joint (B) on the stay bracket

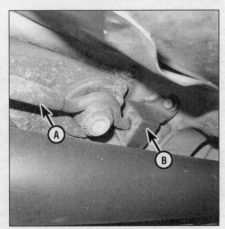

3.12 Remove the rod (A) from the rubber mount (B)

3.13 Using a pin-punch and hammer, drive the roll pin (A) out of the joint assembly (B)

4.2 The back-up light switch (A) and neutral switch (B) are located on the left side of the transaxle

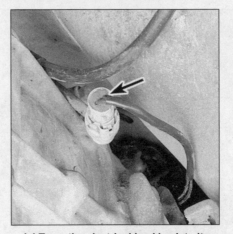

4.4 Trace the electrical lead back to its connector, unplug the connector and hook up an ohmmeter to the connector terminals

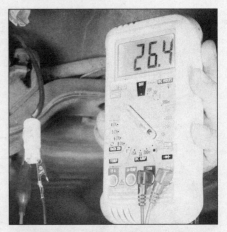

4.5 The back-up light switch should have continuity only in Reverse; the neutral switch should have continuity only in Neutral

4   Back-up light and neutral switches - check and replacement

Check

1   Raise the vehicle and support it securely on jackstands.

2   The back-up light switch and neutral switches (see illustration) are located on the left side of the transaxle. The back-up light switch is located on the left side of the rear case; the neutral switch is located just behind the back-up light switch.

3   On turbo models, remove the intercooler (see Chapter 4).

4   To check either switch, trace the electrical lead back to its connector and hook up an ohmmeter (see illustration).

5   To check the back-up light switch, put the transaxle into reverse and verify that there's continuity (zero or low resistance) (see illustration). Then put the transaxle in any other gear and verify that there's no continuity (high or infinite resistance).

6   To check the neutral switch, put the transaxle in Neutral and verify that there's continuity (zero or low resistance) (see illustration 4.5). Then put the transaxle in any other gear and verify that there's no continuity (high or infinite resistance).

Note: *The neutral switch on 5-speed models has four wires and on 6-speed models there are six wires. Place the switch connector with the locking tab on top (looking into the open end of the connector), then check the wires on the right (5-speed models) or left (6-speed models) column of wires.*

7   If either switch fails to operate as described, replace it.

Replacement

8   Unscrew and remove the old switch. Install the new switch (make sure the washer is installed) and tighten it to the torque listed in this Chapter's Specifications.

9   Verify that the new switch works properly (see above), then plug in the electrical connector.

5   Transaxle mount - check and replacement

Mount

1   Raise the vehicle and support it securely on jackstands.

2   Insert a large screwdriver or prybar into the space between the transaxle and the crossmember and try to pry the transaxle up slightly (see illustration). The transaxle should move very little. If it moves a lot, inspect the rubber portions of the two mounts. If either mount is damaged, replace the transaxle mount assembly.

3   To replace a mount, remove the bolts attaching the mount to the crossmember and to the transaxle (see illustration).

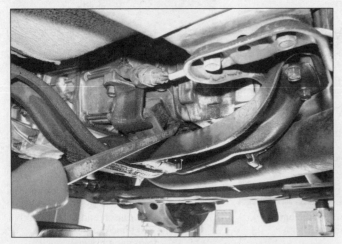

5.2 To check the transaxle mount, insert a large prybar between the rubber portion of the mount and the crossmember, then try to lever the transaxle up slightly; if it moves easily and excessively, replace the mount

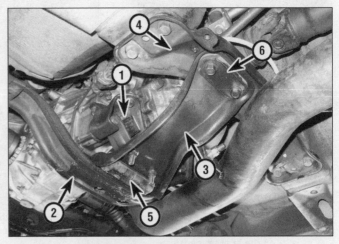

5.3 Typical transaxle mount details

1 Transaxle mount	4 Rear crossmember
2 Front crossmember	5 Damper (if equipped)
3 Center crossmember	6 Cushion and plate

4   Raise the transaxle slightly with a jack and remove the mount.

5   Installation is the reverse of removal. Tighten the bolts securely.

Pitching stopper (dog bone) - Forester

6   Disconnect the cable from the negative terminal of the battery (see Chapter 5).

7   On turbocharged models, remove the intercooler (see Chapter 4, Section 16).

8   On non-turbocharged models, remove the intake air duct between the air filter housing and the throttle body (see Chapter 4).

9   Locate and remove the pitching stopper bolts and the pitching stopper.

10   Installation is reverse of removal. Tighten the fasteners to the torque listed in this Chapter's Specifications.

6   Manual transaxle - removal and installation

Removal

1   Open the hood and prop it open with the hood stay.

2   Disconnect the cable from the negative terminal of the battery (see Chapter 5).

3   Remove the air intake duct, the resonator and the air filter housing (see Chapter 4).

4   On turbocharged models, remove the intercooler (see Chapter 4).

5   Remove the air filter housing support brackets.

6   Clearly label, then unplug, all electrical connectors accessible from above that would interfere with transaxle removal.

7   Unbolt the battery ground cable at the transaxle.

8   Remove the starter (see Chapter 5).

9   Remove the clutch release cylinder (see Chapter 8) and secure to the vehicle body using wire or similar.

Forester models

10   Remove the throttle body (see Chapter 4, Section 11).

11   Support the rear of the engine with an engine hoist or support fixture (see Chapter 2B). Remove the pitching stopper (see Section 5).

12   Remove the upper transaxle-to-engine bolts opposite the starter.

13   Raise the vehicle and support it securely on jackstands.

14   Remove the engine splash shield (see Chapter 2A).

15   Remove the exhaust manifold (see Chapter 2A), the center exhaust pipe, the rear exhaust pipe (turbocharged models) and the muffler (see Chapter 4).

16   Remove the driveshaft (see Chapter 8).

17   Remove the heat shield.

18   Remove the hanger bracket from the right side of the transaxle.

19   On 2013 and earlier models, remove the gear shift rod and the stay from the transaxle.

20   On 2014 and later models, disconnect the shift cables from the shift lever assembly (see Section 3).

21   Remove the stay from the transaxle.

22   If equipped, remove the front suspension height sensor.

23   Detach the stabilizer bar links from the lower control arms (see Chapter 10).

24   Separate the lower balljoints from the steering knuckles (see Chapter 10).

25   Remove the front driveaxles (see Chapter 8).

26   Remove the lower transaxle-to-engine nuts/bolts.

27   Place a transaxle jack or a floor jack equipped with a transmission adapter head under the transaxle. As a safety measure, secure the transaxle to the jack head with a tie-down, or a piece of chain or rope.

28   Remove the transmission crossmember.

29   Move the transaxle jack to the rear slightly to disengage the input shaft from the splines on the clutch disc, then slowly lower the transaxle assembly. Keep a hand on the transaxle while lowering the assembly.

Legacy models

30   Disconnect the throttle body and MAP sensor connectors.

31   Raise the vehicle and support it securely on jackstands.

32   Remove the engine splash shield.

33   Remove the center exhaust pipe and remove the exhaust heat shield from under the vehicle.

34   Remove the exhaust hanger bracket.

35   Remove the steering shaft universal joint (see Chapter 10, Section 17).

36   Disconnect the shift cables from the shift lever assembly (see Section 3).

37   Detach the stabilizer bar links from the lower control arms (see Chapter 10, Section 4).

38   Separate the lower balljoints from the steering knuckles (see Chapter 10).

39   Remove the front driveaxles (see Chapter 8, Section 14).

40   Working in the engine compartment, remove the nuts securing the engine mount and main transaxle mounting bracket together.

41   Remove the drivebelt cover.

42   Support the engine with an engine hoist or support fixture.

43   Slightly raise the engine and remove the front engine mount under the crank pulley.

44   Remove the bolts and let the battery cable bracket hang free.

45   Remove the bolts and the left and right main transaxle mounting brackets from the vehicle.

46   Remove the upper transaxle-to-engine bolts opposite the starter.

47   Place a transaxle jack or a floor jack equipped with a transmission adapter head under the transaxle. As a safety measure, secure the transaxle to the jack head with a tie-down, or a piece of chain or rope.

48   Remove the lower transaxle-to-engine bolts opposite the starter.

49   Remove the transmission crossmember.

50   Move the transaxle jack to the rear slightly to disengage the input shaft from the splines on the clutch disc, then slowly lower the transaxle assembly. Keep a hand on the transaxle while lowering the assembly.

Installation

51   Installation is reverse of removal, noting the following items:

a)   *Apply a little multi-purpose grease to the input shaft splines.*

b)   *Slowly and carefully slide the transaxle forward and insert the input shaft into the clutch hub. If the input shaft hangs up, rotate the crankshaft or the transaxle output shaft until the input shaft splines are aligned with the clutch hub splines.*

c)   *Tighten all fasteners to the specifications listed in this Chapter's Specifications.*

d)   *Bleed the air from the clutch hydraulic lines if necessary (see Chapter 8, Section 5).*

e)   *Refill the transaxle lubricant.*

f)   *Start the engine and check the exhaust system for any leaks or noise.*

g)   *Check the shift linkage for smooth operation.*

7   Manual transaxle overhaul - general information

1   Overhauling a manual transaxle is a difficult job for the do-it-yourselfer. It involves the disassembly and reassembly of many small parts. Numerous clearances must be precisely measured and, if necessary, changed with select fit spacers and snap-rings. If transaxle problems arise, you can remove and install the transaxle yourself, but overhaul should be left to a transaxle repair shop. Rebuilt transaxles may be available - check with your dealer parts department and auto parts stores. At any rate, the time and money involved in an overhaul are almost sure to exceed the cost of a rebuilt unit.

2   Nevertheless, it's not impossible for an inexperienced mechanic to rebuild a transaxle if the special tools are available and the job is done in a deliberate step-by-step manner so nothing is overlooked.

3   The tools necessary for an overhaul include internal and external snap-ring pliers, a bearing puller, a slide hammer, a set of pin punches, a dial indicator and possibly a hydraulic press. In addition, a large, sturdy workbench and a vise or transaxle stand will be required.

4   During disassembly of the transaxle, make careful notes of how each piece comes off, where it fits in relation to other pieces and what holds it in place. Note how the parts are installed as you remove them; this will

make it much easier to get the transaxle back together.

5   Before taking the transaxle apart for repair, it will help if you have some idea what area of the transaxle is malfunctioning. Certain problems can be closely tied to specific areas in the transaxle, which can make component examination and replacement easier.

Refer to the *Troubleshooting* section at the front of this manual for information regarding possible sources of trouble.

Chapter 7 Part B
Automatic transaxle

Contents

Specifications

Torque specifications

Note: *One foot-pound (ft-lb) of torque is equivalent to 12 inch-pounds (in-lbs) of torque. Torque values below approximately 15 foot-pounds are expressed in inch-pounds, because most foot-pound torque wrenches are not accurate at these smaller values.*

	Ft-lbs (unless otherwise indicated)	Nm
Shift cable plate bolts (transaxle end)	18.5	25
Shift cable adjusting nut A	71 in-lbs	8
Torque converter bolts	18.5	25
Transaxle-to-engine nuts/bolts	37	50

1 General information

1 Vehicles covered in this chapter are equipped with either a four-speed (4AT) automatic transaxle, five-speed (5AT) automatic transaxle, or one of two Continuously Variable Transaxles (CVT) TR580 or TR690. All information on the automatic and CVT transaxle is included in this Part of Chapter 7. Information for the manual transaxles can be found in Chapter 7A.

2 There are two types of shift levers; standard shift type and sport model type. The sport model can be operated in standard mode and sport mode. Sport mode is selected by moving the shift lever laterally from DRIVE (move to the left) where sport shifting can be selected by moving the shift lever forward for upshifts or back for downshifts.

3 Because of the complexity of automatic and CVT transaxles and the specialized tools and equipment necessary to perform most service operations, this Chapter contains only those procedures related to to routine maintenance, general diagnosis and transaxle removal and installation.

4 If the transaxle requires major repair work, it should be left to a dealer service department or other qualified repair shop. Once properly diagnosed, however, you can remove and install the transaxle yourself to save the expense, and have the repair work done by a transmission shop.

2 Diagnosis - general

Automatic transaxle malfunctions may be caused by five general conditions:

a) *Poor engine performance*
b) *Improper adjustments*
c) *Hydraulic malfunctions*
d) *Mechanical malfunctions*
e) *Malfunctions in the Powertrain Control Module (PCM) or its signal network*

1 Diagnosis of these problems should always begin with a check of the easily repaired items: fluid level and condition (see Chapter 1), and shift cable adjustment (see Section 3). Next, perform a road test to deter-

mine if the problem has been corrected or if more diagnosis is necessary. Because the transaxle relies on many sensors in the engine control system, and since the transmission shift points are controlled by the Powertrain Control Module, you'll also want to check to see if any trouble codes have been stored in the PCM (see Chapter 6 for a list of trouble codes and how to extract them). If the problem persists after the preliminary tests and corrections are completed, additional diagnosis should be done by a dealer service department or transmission repair shop. Refer to the *Troubleshooting* section at the front of this manual for transaxle problem diagnosis.

Preliminary checks

2   Drive the vehicle to warm the transaxle to normal operating temperature.
3   Check the fluid level (see Chapter 1):
   a) *If the fluid level is unusually low, add enough fluid to bring the level within the designated area of the dipstick, then check for external leaks.*
   b) *If the fluid level is abnormally high, drain off the excess, then check the drained fluid for contamination by coolant. The presence of engine coolant in the automatic transaxle fluid indicates that a failure has occurred in the internal radiator walls that separate the coolant from the transaxle fluid (see Chapter 1).*
   c) *If the fluid is foaming, drain it and refill the transaxle, then check for coolant in the fluid or a high fluid level.*
4   Check the engine idle speed.
Note: *If the engine is malfunctioning, do not proceed with the preliminary checks until it has been repaired and runs normally.*
5   Inspect the shift cable (see Section 3). Make sure that it's properly adjusted and that it operates smoothly.
6   Check the Transmission Range (TR) sensor adjustment (see Chapter 6).

Fluid leak diagnosis

7   Most fluid leaks are easy to locate visually. Repair usually consists of replacing a seal or gasket. If a leak is difficult to find, the following procedure may help.
8   Identify the fluid. Make sure it's transmission fluid and not engine oil or brake fluid (automatic transmission fluid is a deep red color, and CVT fluid is a transparent light green color).
9   Try to pinpoint the source of the leak. Drive the vehicle several miles, then park it over a large sheet of cardboard. After a minute or two, you should be able to locate the leak by determining the source of the fluid dripping onto the cardboard.
10   Make a careful visual inspection of the suspected component and the area immediately around it. Pay particular attention to gasket mating surfaces. A mirror is often helpful for finding leaks in areas that are hard to see.
11   If the leak still cannot be found, clean the suspected area thoroughly with a degreaser or solvent, then dry it.

12   Drive the vehicle for several miles at normal operating temperature and varying speeds. After driving the vehicle, visually inspect the suspected component again.
13   Once the leak has been located, the cause must be determined before it can be properly repaired. If a gasket is replaced but the sealing flange is bent, the new gasket will not stop the leak. The bent flange must be straightened.
14   Before attempting to repair a leak, check to make sure that the following conditions are corrected or they may cause another leak.
Note: *Some of the following conditions cannot be fixed without highly specialized tools and expertise. Such problems must be referred to a transmission shop or a dealer service department.*

Gasket leaks

15   Check the pan periodically. Make sure the bolts are tight, no bolts are missing, the gasket is in good condition and the pan is flat (dents in the pan may indicate damage to the valve body inside).
16   If the pan gasket is leaking, the fluid level or the fluid pressure may be too high, the vent may be plugged, the pan bolts may be too tight, the pan sealing flange may be warped, the sealing surface of the transaxle housing may be damaged, the gasket may be damaged or the transaxle casting may be cracked or porous. If sealant instead of gasket material has been used to form a seal between the pan and the transaxle housing, it may be the wrong sealant.

Seal leaks

17   If a transaxle seal is leaking, the fluid level or pressure may be too high, the vent may be plugged, the seal bore may be damaged, the seal itself may be damaged or improperly installed, the surface of the shaft protruding through the seal may be damaged or a loose bearing may be causing excessive shaft movement.

3.8 Remove the locking clip (A) from the shift lever on the transaxle and detach the cable, then remove the shift cable bracket bolts (B)

18   Make sure the dipstick tube seal is in good condition and the tube is properly seated. Periodically check the area around the speedometer gear or vehicle speed sensor for leakage. If transaxle fluid is evident, check the O-ring for damage. Also inspect the driveshaft oil seal for leakage.

Case leaks

19   If the case itself appears to be leaking, the casting is porous and will have to be repaired or replaced.
20   Make sure the oil cooler hose fittings are tight and in good condition. The transaxle oil cooler lines on these models are equipped with quick connect fittings - always inspect the O-rings if a leak is suspected.

Fluid comes out vent pipe or fill tube

21   If this condition occurs, the transaxle is overfilled, there is coolant in the fluid, the case is porous, the dipstick is incorrect, the vent is plugged or the drain back holes are plugged.

---

3   Shift cable - check, replacement and adjustment

Warning: *The models covered by this manual are equipped with a Supplemental Restraint System (SRS), more commonly known as airbags. Always disable the airbag system before working in the vicinity of any airbag system component to avoid the possibility of accidental deployment of the airbag(s), which could cause personal injury (see Chapter 12). Do not use a memory saving device to preserve the PCM or radio memory when working on or near airbag system components*

Check

1   Firmly apply the parking brake and try to momentarily operate the starter in each shift lever position. The starter should only operate when the shift lever is in the Park or Neutral positions. If the starter operates in any position other than Park or Neutral, adjust the shift cable (see below). If, after adjustment, the starter still operates in positions other than Park or Neutral, the TR sensor is defective (see Chapter 6).

Replacement

2   Disconnect the cable from the negative terminal of the battery (see Chapter 5).
3   Make sure the shift lever is in the Neutral position.
4   Raise the vehicle and support it securely on jackstands.
5   Remove the engine splash shield (see Chapter 2A).
6   Remove the exhaust manifold (see Chapter 2A), the exhaust pipe and the muffler (see Chapter 4).
7   Remove the heat shield fasteners and heat shield from under the vehicle.
8   Remove the locking clip from the shift lever on the transaxle (see illustration).

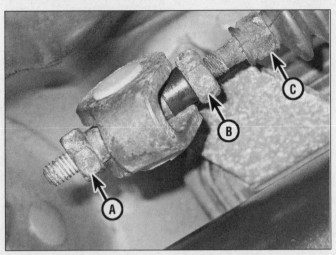

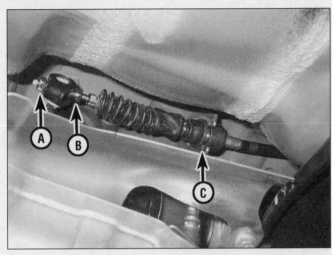

3.10 Use a back-up wrench to hold the shift cable when removing adjusting nut A from the cable end

A   *Adjusting nut A*
B   *Adjusting nut B*
C   *Hold here with a wrench to prevent turning*

3.19 Details of the shift cable adjustment

A   *Adjusting nut A*
B   *Adjusting nut B*
C   *Late model cable bracket clamp*

9   Remove the two bolts and shift cable bracket from the shift cable plate assembly.
10   Working under the vehicle on the shift lever linkage, remove the shift cable end (see illustration).
11   Separate the shift cable from the mounting bracket.
Note: *The clamp must be expanded to remove the shift cable from the mounting bracket (see illustration 3.19).*
12   Remove the shift cable from the vehicle.
13   Installation is the reverse of removal. Tighten the shift cable plate assembly bolts to the torque listed in this Chapter's Specifications. Adjust the cable (see below).

Adjustment
14   Make sure the shift lever is in the Neutral position.
15   Raise the vehicle and support it securely on jackstands.
16   Remove the engine splash shield (see Chapter 2A).
17   Remove the center exhaust pipe and the muffler (see Chapter 4).
18   Remove the heat shield fasteners and remove the heat shield.
19   Working under the vehicle below the console linkage, loosen adjusting nuts A and B on both sides of the cable end (see illustration).
20   Turn adjusting nut B until it contacts the linkage arm.
21   Install a back-up wrench onto adjusting nut B to keep it from rotating and tighten adjusting nut A to the torque listed in this Chapter's Specifications.
22   Remove the jackstands and lower the vehicle.
23   Move the shift lever through all gear positions and verify that the indicated positions correspond with the actual gear positions at the shift lever console. Also verify that the engine will start only in Park and Neutral,

and that the back-up lights come on when the shift lever is placed in Reverse. If necessary, readjust the cable until these conditions are met. It may also be necessary to adjust the TR sensor (see Chapter 6).

---

4   Shift lever - replacement

Knob
1   On 2013 and earlier Forester models, unscrew the shift knob to remove.
2   On 2014 and later Forester and all Legacy models, perform one of the following:
   a) *On models with a shift boot, pull the boot down from the bottom of the shift knob to expose the retaining clip.*
   b) *On models without a shift boot, pull the lower trim ring down from the bottom of the shift knob to expose the retaining clip.*
   c) *Remove the retainer clip and remove the shift knob.*
3   Installation is reverse of removal.

Shift lever assembly
4   Disconnect the cable from the negative terminal of the battery (see Chapter 5).
5   Make sure the shift lever is in the Neutral position.
6   Raise the vehicle and support it securely on jackstands.
7   Disconnect the shift cable from the shift lever on the transaxle (see Section 3).
8   Lower the vehicle and remove the center console (see Chapter 11).
9   Remove the shift lever knob.
Note: *On some models, it is not necessary to remove the shift lever grip for to access the various components of the shift lever system.*
10   Depress the tabs on each side of the shift lever indicator base and lift the base up and over the shift lever.
11   Unplug the electrical connector.
12   Remove the shift lever base mounting bolts (see illustration) and remove the shift lever assembly.
13   Installation is the reverse of removal. Adjust the shift cable (see Section 3).

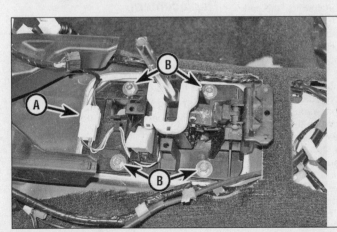

4.12 Disconnect the electrical connectors (A) then remove the mounting bolts (B) from the base of the shift lever assembly

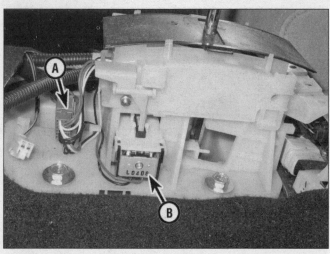

5.12 Disconnect the electrical connector (A) to the shift lock solenoid (B)

6.3 Location of the TCM on a non-turbocharged model - turbocharged models slightly different

5   Brake Transmission Shift Interlock (BTSI) system - description, check and replacement

Warning: *The models covered by this manual are equipped with a Supplemental Restraint System (SRS), more commonly known as airbags. Always disable the airbag system before working in the vicinity of any airbag system component to avoid the possibility of accidental deployment of the airbag(s), which could cause personal injury (see Chapter 12). Do not use a memory saving device to preserve the PCM or radio memory when working on or near airbag system components.*

Description

1   The Brake Transmission Shift Interlock (BTSI) system incorporates two solenoid-operated devices; one mounted next to the ignition key lock cylinder and the other mounted onto the shift lever assembly under the center console. The BTSI system is also equipped with an Integrated Module that receives information from the brake pedal switch, the park position switch and the Transmission Range (TR) sensor for proper activation of the key lock solenoid (ignition lock cylinder) and the shift lock solenoid (console shift lever). The shift lock solenoid locks the shift lever into the Park position when the ignition key is in the LOCK or ACC position. When the ignition key is in the RUN position, a magnetic holding device is energized. When the system is functioning correctly, the only way to unlock the shift lever and move it out of Park is to depress the brake pedal. The BTSI system also prevents the ignition key from being turned to the LOCK or ACC position unless the shift lever is fully locked into the Park position.

Check

2   Verify that the ignition key can be removed only in the Park position.
3   When the shift lever is in the Park position, you should be able to rotate the ignition key from OFF to LOCK. But when the shift lever is in any gear position other than Park (including Neutral), you should not be able to rotate the ignition key to the LOCK position.
4   You should not be able to move the shift lever out of the Park position when the ignition key is turned to the OFF position.
5   You should not be able to move the shift lever out of the Park position when the ignition key is turned to the RUN or START position until you depress the brake pedal.
6   You should not be able to move the shift lever out of the Park position when the ignition key is turned to the ACC or LOCK position.
7   Once in gear, with the ignition key in the RUN position, you should be able to move the shift lever between gears, or put it into Neutral or Park, without depressing the brake pedal.
8   If the BTSI system doesn't operate as described, replace it.

Replacement
Key lock solenoid
9   The key lock solenoid must be replaced as a single unit along with the ignition lock cylinder (see Chapter 12).

Shift lock solenoid - 2013 and earlier Legacy models
10   Disconnect the cable from the negative terminal of the battery (see Chapter 5).
11   Remove the center console (see Chapter 11).
12   Disconnect the electrical connector from the shift lock solenoid (see illustration).
13   Depress the tabs on the sides of the console indicator panel and lift the panel up and

over the shift lever.
14   Press the shift lock release button, then slide the shift lever into neutral "N" position.
15   Remove the through-bolt from the front of the shifter, then lift up the plate guide.
16   Using a small blade screwdriver, disconnect the electrical connector from the plate and remove the guide.
17   Lift the detent spring up at the rear of the shifter, then push the shift lever backwards. Holding the shift lever in this position, remove the shift lock solenoid from the side of the shift lever assembly.
18   With the solenoid off of the shift lever assembly, lift the electrical connector retaining claws up from the sides to expose the wire terminals. The wires must be released from the connector to remove the solenoid. Mark the wires to the electrical connector, then use a small pin punch or screwdriver to push the top four wires out of the top row of the connector (the bottom row has six wires).
19   Installation is the reverse of removal.

Shift lock solenoid - 2014 and later Forester models and all Legacy models
20   Remove the shift lever assembly (see Section 4).
21   Remove the spacer and the gasket from the underside of the shift lever assembly.
22   Disconnect the connector from the shift lever assembly base.
23   On the underside of the shift lever assembly, use a small flat-bladed screwdriver to release the lock tab and use a second small, flat-bladed screwdriver to slide the shift lock solenoid from the shift lever base.
24   Use a terminal tool to remove the shift lock solenoid terminal from the connector.
25   Installation is reverse of removal.

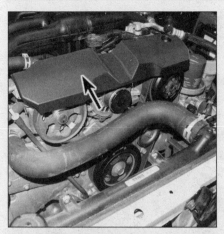

7.9 Remove the drivebelt cover (Legacy shown)

7.12 Pitching stopper-to-transaxle bolt

7.15a Pull out the rubber plug that covers the torque converter bolt access hole

6 Transmission Control Module (TCM) - removal and installation

Warning: *The models covered by this manual are equipped with a Supplemental Restraint System (SRS), more commonly known as airbags. Always disable the airbag system before working in the vicinity of any airbag system component to avoid the possibility of accidental deployment of the airbag(s), which could cause personal injury (see Chapter 12). Do not use a memory saving device to preserve the PCM or radio memory when working on or near airbag system components.*

All Forester models and 2014 and earlier Legacy models

1   Disconnect the cable from the negative terminal of the battery (see Chapter 5).
2   Remove the knee bolster from the left side of the lower instrument panel (see Chapter 11).
3   Disconnect the Transmission Control Module (TCM) connector (see illustration).
4   Unscrew the mounting nuts from the TCM bracket and remove the TCM.
Note: *On some models, it may be easier to remove the bracket and the TCM together, then remove the bracket from the TCM.*
5   Installation is the reverse of removal.
6   A new TCM must learn the operating parameters before the vehicle can be driven. Have the TCM programmed by a dealer service department or other qualified automotive repair facility.

2015 and later Legacy models

7   Disconnect the cable from the negative battery terminal (see Chapter 5).
8   Remove the intake air duct between the air cleaner assembly and the throttle body.
9   At the rear of the engine compartment, locate the transaxle case cover.
10   Disconnect the two transaxle connectors and remove the ground bolt and ground connection.

11   Remove the transaxle case cover to expose the TCM.
12   Unlock the TCM connector and disconnect from the TCM.
13   Remove the bolts and remove the TCM from the transaxle.
14   Installation is the reverse of removal.
15   A new TCM must learn the operating parameters before the vehicle can be driven. Have the TCM programmed by a dealer service department or other qualified automotive repair facility.

7 Automatic transaxle - removal and installation

Removal

1   Open the hood and prop it open with the hood stay.
2   Disconnect the cable from the negative terminal of the battery (see Chapter 5).
3   On non-turbo models, remove the air intake duct, the resonator and the air filter housing (see Chapter 4).
4   On turbocharged models, remove the intercooler (see Chapter 4).
5   Remove the air filter housing support brackets.
6   Disconnect the transaxle harness connectors.
7   Clearly label and unplug any other electrical connectors that would interfere with removal.
8   Remove the bolt(s) and detach the battery ground cable(s) from the transaxle.
9   Remove the drivebelt cover (see illustration).
10   Remove the starter (see Chapter 5).
11   On CVT models, unbolt the CVT cooler and secure it to the vehicle body using wire or similar. Disconnect the cooler hoses at the transaxle. Disconnect any additional CVT hoses required for transaxle removal.

7.15b Remove the torque converter bolts through the access hole

Forester models

12   Support the rear of the engine with an engine hoist or support fixture (see Chapter 2B). Unbolt the pitching stopper from the bracket on the transaxle (see illustration).
13   On non-turbo models, remove the throttle body (see Chapter 4, Section 11).
14   Install a wrench onto the crankshaft pulley for the purpose of rotating the engine for access to the torque converter bolts. Remove the drivebelt cover plate, if necessary for access (see Chapter 1).
15   Remove the rubber service plug (see illustration). Mark the relationship of the torque converter to the driveplate and remove the four torque converter-to-driveplate bolts (see illustration).
16   Remove the upper transaxle-to-engine bolts.
17   Raise the vehicle and support it securely on jackstands.
18   Remove the automatic transaxle fluid dipstick tube.
19   Remove the engine splash shield (see Chapter 2A).

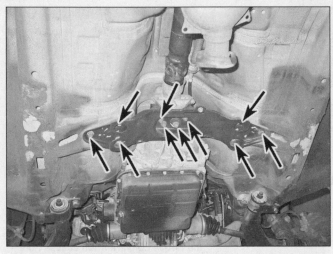

7.31 Location of the transaxle crossmember mounting bolts

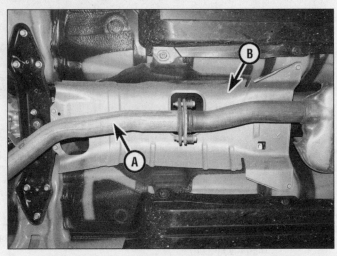

7.38 Remove the center rear exhaust pipe (A) and the exhaust shield (B)

20   Remove the exhaust manifold (see Chapter 2A), the center exhaust pipe (and the rear exhaust pipe on turbocharged models), and the muffler (see Chapter 4).

21   Remove the driveshaft (see Chapter 8).

22   Drain the fluid from the transaxle (see Chapter 1).

23   Disconnect the transaxle fluid cooler hoses from the metal lines.

24   Remove the heat shield fasteners and shield.

25   Disconnect the shift cable from the lever on the transaxle and detach the cable bracket and shift cable from the transaxle (see Section 3).

26   Detach the stabilizer bar links from the lower control arms (see Chapter 10).

27   Separate the lower balljoints from the steering knuckles (see Chapter 10).

28   Remove the front driveaxles (see Chapter 8).

29   Place a transaxle jack or a floor jack equipped with a transmission adapter head under the transaxle. As a safety measure,

secure the transaxle to the jack head with a tie-down, or a piece of chain or rope.

30   Remove the lower transaxle-to-engine nuts/bolts.

31   Remove the rear crossmember (see illustration).

32   Move the jack to the rear slightly to disengage the torque converter from the engine, then slowly lower the transaxle and torque converter assembly. Keep a hand on the torque converter, which can fall out once the transaxle is detached from the engine.

Legacy models

33   On 2013 and earlier models, remove the clips and the grille bracket (see Chapter 11).

34   On 2015 and later models, remove the TCM (see Section 6).

35   Loosen the front wheel lug nuts, then raise and support the vehicle on jackstands and remove the front wheels.

36   Remove the engine under cover.

37   Drain the transaxle (see Chapter 1).

38   Remove the center rear exhaust pipe

and the exhaust shield on the vehicle body (see illustration).

39   Remove the driveshaft (see Chapter 8, Section 12).

40   Disconnect the shift cable from the lever on the transaxle and detach the cable bracket and shift cable from the transaxle (see Section 3).

41   Disconnect the steering shaft universal joint from the steering gear (see Chapter 10).

42   Disconnect the tie-rod ends from the steering knuckles (see Chapter 10).

43   Detach the stabilizer bar links from the stabilizer bar (see Chapter 10).

44   Separate the lower balljoints from the steering knuckles (see Chapter 10).

45   Remove the driveaxles (see Chapter 8, Section 14).

46   Loosen the bolt at the bottom of the transaxle bracket.

47   Remove the bolts and let the battery cable bracket hang free.

48   Remove the rubber service plug (see illustration 7.15a). Mark the relationship of the torque converter to the driveplate and remove the four torque converter-to-driveplate bolts (see illustration 7.15b).

49   Remove the nuts from the transaxle mounting brackets.

50   Support the engine with an engine hoist or support fixture.

51   Slightly raise the engine and remove the front engine mount through-bolt (see illustration).

52   Remove the bolts and the left and right main transaxle mounting brackets from the vehicle.

53   Remove the upper transaxle-to-engine bolts.

54   Place a transaxle jack or a floor jack equipped with a transmission adapter head under the transaxle. As a safety measure, secure the transaxle to the jack head with a tie-down, or a piece of chain or rope.

7.51 Front engine mount through-bolt

7.55a Remove the exhaust hanger bracket . . .

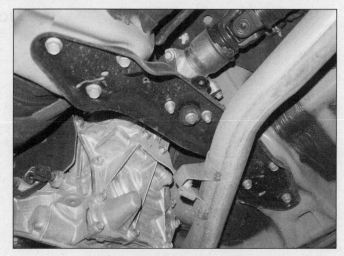

7.55b . . . and the rear crossmember

55   Remove the hanger bracket and rear crossmember (see illustrations).
56   Lower the rear of the transaxle.
57   Remove the lower transaxle-to-engine nuts/bolts.
58   Move the jack to the rear slightly to disengage the torque converter from the engine, then slowly lower the transaxle and torque converter assembly. Keep a hand on the torque converter, which can fall out once the transaxle is detached from the engine.

Installation

59   Installation is reverse of removal, noting the following points:

a) *Replace the driveaxle oil seals, if necessary (see Chapter 7A, Section 2).*
b) *Support the transaxle on the jack and raise it into alignment with the engine. Slowly and carefully slide the transaxle forward until the engine and transaxle*

are fully engaged.
c) *Line up the marks you made on the torque converter and driveplate, install the torque converter-to-driveplate bolts and tighten them to the torque listed in this Chapter's Specifications.*
d) *Fill the transaxle with the recommended automatic transmission fluid (see Chapter 1).*
e) *Start the engine and check the exhaust system for any leaks or noise.*
f) *Check the shift cable for smooth operation.*

8   Automatic transaxle overhaul - general information

1   In the event of a problem occurring, it will be necessary to establish whether the fault is electrical, mechanical or hydraulic in nature, before repair work can be contemplated. Diagnosis requires detailed knowledge of the transaxle's operation and construction, as well as access to specialized test equipment, and so is deemed to be beyond the scope of this manual. It is therefore essential that problems with the automatic transaxle are referred to a dealer service department or other qualified repair facility for assessment.
2   Note that a faulty transaxle should not be removed before the vehicle has been diagnosed by a knowledgeable technician equipped with the proper tools, as troubleshooting must be performed with the transaxle installed in the vehicle.

Note

Chapter 8
Clutch and driveline

Contents

Specifications

General

Clutch switch adjustment
   Switch-to-pedal plate gap .... 0.04 to 0.08 inch   1.1 to 2.1 mm

Torque specifications

Note: *One foot-pound (ft-lb) of torque is equivalent to 12 inch-pounds (in-lbs) of torque. Torque values below approximately 15 foot-pounds are expressed in inch-pounds, because most foot-pound torque wrenches are not accurate at these smaller values.*

	Ft-lbs (unless otherwise indicated)	**Nm**
Center bearing retaining bolts	38	52
Clutch pressure plate-to-flywheel bolts	142 in-lbs	16
Clutch master cylinder nuts	159 in-lbs	18
Clutch release cylinder bolts	27	37
Clutch release lever access plug (6-speed models)	34	46
Rear differential mounting bolts/nuts		
Rear differential-to-cross member nuts	52	70
Differential mount-to-vehicle bolts/nuts	81	110
Differential mount-to-differential nuts	37	50
Driveshaft-to-pinion flange nuts/bolts	23	31
Front driveaxle nut	162	220
Rear driveaxle nut	140	190
Rear differential pinion flange nut		
Forester		
2010 and earlier models	134	182
2011 to 2013 models	123 to 145	167 to 196
2014 and later models		
T-type	123 to 145	167 to 196
VA1-type	119 to 162	162 to 220
Legacy		
T-type		
2011 and earlier models	134	182
2012 and later models	123 to 145	167 to 196
VA-type		
2011 and earlier models	141	191
2012 and later models	120 to 162	162 to 220

1   General information

1   The Sections in this Chapter deal with the components from the rear of the engine to the rear wheels (except for the transaxle, which is covered in Chapters 7A and 7B) and to the front wheels. In this Chapter, the components are grouped into three categories: clutch, driveshaft and driveaxles. Separate Sections in this Chapter cover checks and repair procedures for components in each group.

2   Since nearly all these procedures involve working under the vehicle, make sure it's safely supported on sturdy jackstands or a hoist where the vehicle can be safely raised and lowered (see *Jacking and towing* at the front of this manual).

2   Clutch - description and check

1   All vehicles with a manual transaxle have a single dry plate, diaphragm spring-type clutch. The clutch disc has a splined hub which allows it to slide along the splines of the transaxle input shaft. The clutch and pressure plate are held in contact by spring pressure exerted by the diaphragm in the pressure plate.

2   The clutch release system is operated by hydraulic pressure. The hydraulic release system consists of the clutch pedal, a master cylinder and reservoir, a release (or slave) cylinder and the hydraulic line connecting the two components.

3   When the clutch pedal is depressed, a pushrod pushes against brake fluid inside the master cylinder, applying hydraulic pres-

sure to the release cylinder, which pushes the release bearing against the diaphragm fingers of the clutch pressure plate.

4   Terminology can be a problem when discussing the clutch components because common names are in some cases different from those used by the manufacturer. For example, the driven plate is also called the clutch plate or disc, the clutch release bearing is sometimes called a throwout bearing, the release cylinder is sometimes called the slave cylinder.

5   Unless you're replacing components with obvious damage, perform these preliminary checks to diagnose clutch problems:

a) *The first check should be of the fluid level in the master cylinder. If the fluid level is low, add fluid as necessary (see Chapter 1) and inspect the hydraulic system for leaks. If the master cylinder reservoir is dry, bleed the system (see Section 5) and recheck the clutch operation.*

b) *To check clutch spin-down time, run the engine at normal idle speed with the transaxle in Neutral (clutch pedal up - engaged). Disengage the clutch (pedal down), wait several seconds and shift the transaxle into Reverse. No grinding noise should be heard. A grinding noise would most likely indicate a bad pressure plate or clutch disc.*

c) *To check for complete clutch release, run the engine (with the parking brake applied to prevent vehicle movement) and hold the clutch pedal approximately 1/2-inch from the floor. Shift the transaxle between 1st gear and Reverse several times. If the shift is rough, component failure is indicated.*

d) *Visually inspect the pivot bushing at the top of the clutch pedal to make sure there's no binding or excessive play.*

3   Clutch master cylinder - removal and installation

1   Remove the knee bolster panel (see Chapter 11).

Caution: *Do not allow brake fluid to come in to contact with the paint as it will damage the finish.*

2   Working under the dashboard, remove the clevis pin retaining clip (see illustration), depress the tangs on the tip of the clevis pin, then push out the pin to disconnect the clutch master cylinder pushrod from the clutch pedal.

Removal

Forester models

3   On 2014 and later Forester models, remove the intake air duct from between the air cleaner assembly and the throttle body.

4   Using a flare-nut wrench, disconnect the hydraulic line from the master cylinder and drain the fluid into a suitable container (see illustration).

5   Remove the master cylinder mounting nuts and remove the unit from the engine compartment.

Legacy models

6   Working under the dashboard, disconnect the clutch travel sensor electrical connector.

7   Disconnect the brake pipes from the clutch master cylinder.

3.2 Remove the clevis pin retaining clip

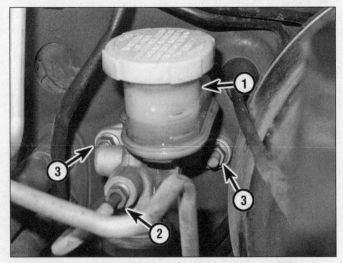

3.4 Clutch master cylinder details (2013 and earlier Forester models shown)

1	Clutch master cylinder reservoir	2	Hydraulic line
		3	Mounting nuts

8   Remove the fasteners and remove the clutch master cylinder from the pedal bracket.

Installation

9   Installation is the reverse of removal, noting the following:

a) *Bleed the hydraulic system (see Section 5).*

b) *Tighten the mounting nuts to the torque listed in this Chapter's Specifications.*

---

4   Clutch release cylinder - removal and installation

Removal

1   Remove the air intake duct and filter housing (see Chapter 4). On turbo models, remove the intercooler (see Chapter 4).
2   Remove the banjo bolt and disconnect the hydraulic line at the release cylinder (see illustration). Discard the sealing washers; new ones should be used upon installation. Have a small can and rags handy, as some fluid will be spilled as the line is removed.
3   Remove the release cylinder mounting bolts.
4   Remove the release cylinder.

Installation

5   Install the release cylinder on the clutch housing. Tighten the mounting bolts to the torque listed in this Chapter's Specifications. Make sure the pushrod is seated in the release lever pocket.
6   Connect the hydraulic line to the release cylinder, using new sealing washers. Tighten the connection securely.
7   Fill the clutch master cylinder with the brake fluid listed in the Chapter 1 Specifications.
8   Bleed the system (see Section 5).
9   The remainder of installation is the reverse of removal. Tighten the mounting bolts to the torque listed in this Chapter's Specifications.

---

5   Clutch hydraulic system - bleeding

1   Bleed the hydraulic system whenever any part of the system has been removed or the fluid level has fallen so low that air has been drawn into the master cylinder. The bleeding procedure is very similar to bleeding a brake system.
2   Fill the clutch master cylinder reservoir with new brake fluid conforming to DOT 3 specifications.
Caution: *Do not re-use any of the fluid coming from the system during the bleeding operation or use fluid which has been inside an open container for an extended period of time.*
3   Have an assistant depress the clutch pedal and hold it. Open the bleeder valve on the release cylinder, allowing fluid and any

air to escape. Close the bleeder valve when the flow of fluid (and bubbles) ceases. Once closed, have your assistant release the pedal.
4   Continue this process until all air is evacuated from the system, indicated by a solid stream of fluid being ejected from the bleeder valve each time with no air bubbles. Keep a close watch on the fluid level inside the brake master cylinder reservoir - if the level drops too far, air will get into the system and you'll have to start all over again.
Note: *Wash the area with water to remove any excess brake fluid.*
5   Check the fluid level again, and add some, if necessary, to bring it to the appropriate level (see Chapter 1). Check carefully for proper operation before placing the vehicle into normal service.

---

6   Clutch components - removal, inspection and installation

Warning: *Dust produced by clutch wear is hazardous to your health. DO NOT blow it out with compressed air and DO NOT inhale it. DO NOT use gasoline or petroleum-based solvents to remove the dust. Brake system cleaner should be used to flush the dust into a drain pan. After the clutch components are wiped clean with a rag, dispose of the contaminated rags and cleaner in a covered, marked container.*

Removal

1   Access to the clutch components is normally accomplished by removing the transaxle, leaving the engine in the vehicle. If the engine is being removed for major overhaul, check the clutch for wear and replace worn components as necessary. However, the relatively low cost of the clutch components compared to the time and trouble spent gaining access to them warrants their replacement anytime the engine or transaxle is removed, unless they are new or in near-perfect condition. The following procedures are based on the assumption the engine will stay in place.
2   Remove the transaxle from the vehicle

(see Chapter 7A). Support the engine while the transaxle is out. Preferably, an engine support fixture or a hoist should be used to support it from above (see Chapter 2B).
3   The clutch fork and release bearing can remain attached to the transaxle housing for the time being.
4   To support the clutch disc during removal, install a clutch alignment tool through the clutch disc hub.
5   Carefully inspect the flywheel and pressure plate for indexing marks. The marks are usually an X, an O or a white letter. If they cannot be found, scribe or paint marks yourself so the pressure plate and the flywheel will be in the same alignment during installation (see illustration).
6   Turning each bolt a little at a time, loosen the pressure plate-to-flywheel bolts. Work in a criss-cross pattern until all spring pressure is relieved. Then hold the pressure plate securely and completely remove the bolts, followed by the pressure plate and clutch disc.

Inspection

7   Ordinarily, when a problem occurs in the clutch, it can be attributed to wear of the clutch driven plate assembly (clutch disc).

4.2 Release cylinder banjo bolt (Forester shown)

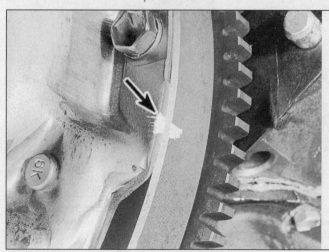

6.5 Mark the relationship of the pressure plate to the flywheel (if you're planning to re-use the old pressure plate)

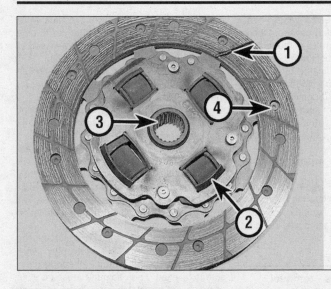

6.9 The clutch disc

1　**Lining** - *this will wear down in use*
2　**Springs or dampers** - *check for cracking and deformation*
3　**Splined hub** - *the splines must not be worn and should slide smoothly on the transmission input shaft splines*
4　**Rivets** - *these secure the lining and will damage the flywheel or pressure plate if allowed to contact the surfaces*

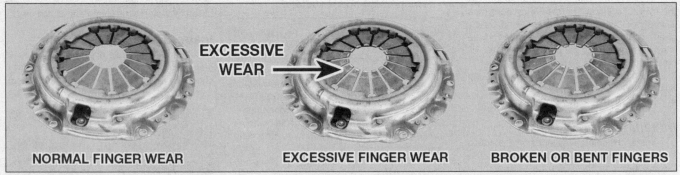

NORMAL FINGER WEAR　　EXCESSIVE WEAR　EXCESSIVE FINGER WEAR　　BROKEN OR BENT FINGERS

6.11a Replace the pressure plate if excessive wear or damage are noted

However, all components should be inspected at this time.
8　Inspect the flywheel for cracks, heat checking, grooves and other obvious defects. If the imperfections are slight, a machine shop can machine the surface flat and smooth, which is highly recommended regardless of the surface appearance. Refer to Chapter 2A for the flywheel removal and installation procedure.

9　Inspect the lining on the clutch disc. There should be at least 1/16-inch of lining above the rivet heads. Check for loose rivets, distortion, cracks, broken springs and other obvious damage (see illustration). As mentioned above, ordinarily the clutch disc is routinely replaced, so if in doubt about the condition, replace it with a new one.
10　The release bearing should also be replaced along with the clutch disc (see Section 7).

11　Check the machined surfaces and the diaphragm spring fingers of the pressure plate (see illustrations). If the surface is grooved or otherwise damaged, replace the pressure plate. Also check for obvious damage, distortion, cracking, etc. Light glazing can be removed with emery cloth or sandpaper. If a new pressure plate is required, new and re-manufactured units are available.
12　Check the pilot bearing in the end of the crankshaft for excessive wear, scoring, dryness, roughness and any other obvious damage. If any of these conditions are noted, replace the bearing (see Section 8).

Installation

13　Before installation, clean the flywheel and pressure plate machined surfaces with brake cleaner, lacquer thinner or acetone. It's important that no oil or grease is on these surfaces or the lining of the clutch disc. Handle the parts only with clean hands.
14　Position the clutch disc and pressure plate against the flywheel with the clutch held in place with an alignment tool (see illustration). Make sure the disc is installed properly (most replacement clutch discs will be marked "flywheel side" or something similar - if not marked, install the clutch disc with

6.11b Inspect the pressure plate surface for excessive score marks, cracks and signs of overheating

6.14 Center the clutch disc in the pressure plate with the clutch alignment tool

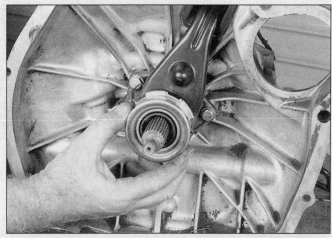

7.2a Disengage the retaining clips from the release bearing . . .

7.2b . . . and slide the release bearing off the input shaft; note which end of the bearing faces toward the clutch pressure plate diaphragm fingers - this is the bearing surface, and the bearing must be installed this way

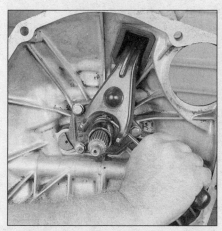

7.3a The release lever is secured to the ballstud by a wire retainer spring on the backside of the lever; to disengage the lever from the ballstud, insert a screwdriver behind the lever and carefully but firmly pry it off . . .

7.3b . . . then pull the release lever and the old rubber dust boot out through the hole in the bellhousing

7.4 To check the release bearing, turn it while pushing on it at the same time; the bearing should rotate smoothly and quietly; if it's rough or noisy, replace it

the damper springs toward the transaxle). If installing existing parts, install them with the indexing marks made during installation properly aligned.

15   Tighten the pressure plate-to-flywheel bolts only finger tight, working around the pressure plate.

16   Center the clutch disc by ensuring the alignment tool extends through the splined hub and into the pilot bearing in the crankshaft. Wiggle the tool up, down or side-to-side as needed to center the disc. Tighten the pressure plate-to-flywheel bolts a little at a time, working in a criss-cross pattern to prevent distorting the cover. After all of the bolts are snug, tighten them to the torque listed in this Chapter's Specifications. Remove the alignment tool.

17   Using high-temperature grease, lubricate the inner groove of the release bearing

(see Section 7). Also place a small amount of grease on the release lever contact areas and the transaxle input shaft bearing retainer.

18   Install the clutch release bearing (see Section 7).

19   Install the transaxle and all components removed previously.

---

7   Clutch release bearing - removal, inspection and installation

Removal

1   Remove the transaxle (see Chapter 7A).

2   Remove the release bearing retaining clips (or springs) from the bearing and remove the bearing from the input shaft (see illustrations).

3   If the release lever pivots on a ballstud (5-speed models), pry the release lever from the ballstud and remove the lever and the rubber sealing boot from the transaxle (see illustrations). If it is necessary to remove the lever of the type that pivots on a cross shaft (6-speed models), remove the plug and knock out the release lever shaft.

Inspection

4   Hold the bearing and rotate the outer portion while applying pressure (see illustration). If the bearing doesn't turn smoothly or if it's noisy, replace it. Wipe the bearing with a clean shop rag and inspect it for cracks, wear and other damage. Do NOT immerse the bearing in solvent; it's a sealed unit, so putting it into solvent will ruin it.

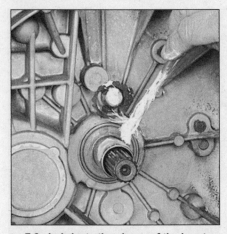

7.6a Lubricate the sleeve of the input shaft bearing retainer and the end of the ballstud with high-temperature grease

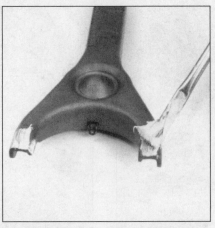

7.6b Lubricate the lever-to-bearing contact points on the two release lever fingers . . .

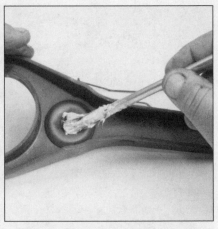

7.6c . . . then turn over the lever and lubricate the pocket for the ballstud and the retainer spring

8.5 A slide hammer with an internal puller attachment is handy for removing a pilot bearing

8.6 Tap the bearing into place with a bearing driver or a socket that is slightly smaller than the outside diameter of the bearing

Installation

5   Replace the release bearing retaining clips, or the release bearing/ballstud retainer spring, if they're deformed or weak.

6   Apply a light coat of grease to the sleeve of the input shaft bearing retainer and the input shaft splines (see illustration), and to the contact surfaces of the release lever (see illustrations).

7   Installation is essentially the reverse of removal. Make sure the release lever is properly positioned on the ballstud, then push it firmly until the ballstud pops into place between the two sides of the retainer spring.

8   Install the release bearing and secure it with the retaining clips.

9   On some 6-speed models, slide the release bearing onto the input shaft bearing retainer, then insert the fork from the top until the bearing and lever tabs are locked in place. Slide the release lever cross shaft into the case and through the release lever, aligning

the slot in the end of the cross shaft with the roll pin in the case. Install the cross shaft plug and tighten the plug to the torque listed in this Chapter's Specifications

10   Install the transaxle (see Chapter 7A).

8   Pilot bearing - inspection and replacement

1   The clutch pilot bearing is a needle roller type bearing which is pressed into the rear of the crankshaft. It's greased at the factory and does not require additional lubrication. Its primary purpose is to support the front of the transaxle input shaft. The pilot bearing should be inspected whenever the clutch components are removed from the engine, and replaced if you have any doubt about its condition.
Note: *If the engine has been removed from the vehicle, disregard the following steps*

which don't apply.

2   Remove the transaxle (see Chapter 7A).

3   Remove the clutch components (see Section 6).

4   Using a flashlight, inspect the bearing for excessive wear, scoring, dryness, roughness and any other obvious damage. If any of these conditions are noted, replace the bearing.

5   Removal can be accomplished with a special puller available at most auto parts stores, or with a slide hammer and an internal puller attachment (see illustration).

6   To install the new bearing, lightly lubricate the outside surface with grease, then drive it into the recess with a bearing driver or socket (see illustration). Some bearings have an O-ring seal, which must face out.

7   Install the clutch components, transaxle and all other components removed previously. Tighten all fasteners to the recommended torque specifications.

9 Clutch Pedal Position (CPP) switch - check and replacement

Note: *The CPP switch is also referred to as the clutch start switch.*

Check

1   Verify that the engine will not start when the clutch pedal is released.
2   Verify that the engine will start when the clutch pedal is depressed all the way.
3   If the engine won't start with the pedal depressed, or starts with the pedal released, unplug the electrical connector to the switch. The clutch start switch is located near the top of the clutch pedal. Check continuity between the connector terminals with the clutch pedal depressed.
4   If there's continuity between the terminals with the pedal depressed, the switch is okay; if there's no continuity between the terminals with the pedal depressed, replace the switch. If there's continuity between the terminals when the clutch pedal is released, replace the switch.

Replacement

5   Remove the knee bolster panel (see Chapter 11).
6   Unplug the switch electrical connector.
7   Loosen the locknut and unscrew the switch from the clutch pedal bracket.
8   Installation is the reverse of removal. To adjust the switch, loosen the locknut and turn the switch in or out, until there is a 0.04 to 0.08 inch (1.1 to 2.1 mm) gap between the clutch switch and the stop plate.

10 Driveshafts, universal joints and driveaxles - general information

Driveshafts and universal joints

1   The driveshaft transmits power between the transaxle and the rear differential. Universal joints are located at either end of the driveshaft; a third U-joint is installed behind the center bearing.
2   The driveshaft employs a splined sleeve yoke at the front end, which slips into the extension housing. This arrangement allows the driveshaft to slide back-and-forth within the extension housing during vehicle operation. An oil seal prevents fluid from leaking out of the extension housing and keeps dirt from entering the transaxle. If leakage is evident at the front of the driveshaft, replace the oil seal (see Chapter 7A).
3   The rear end of the driveshaft is bolted to the differential pinion flange.
4   A center bearing supports the connection between the front and rear tubes of the driveshaft. The center bearing is a ball-type bearing mounted in a rubber cushion attached to the vehicle floorpan. The bearing is pre-

12.5 Remove the four yoke-to-flange nuts and bolts

lubricated and sealed at the factory.
5   The driveshaft assembly requires very little service. The universal joints are lubricated for life, and cannot be rebuilt; if a U-joint on one of these models is worn or damaged, replace the driveshaft (see Section 12).
6   Since the driveshaft is a balanced unit, it's important that no undercoating, mud, etc. be allowed to stay on it. When the vehicle is raised for service it's a good idea to clean the driveshaft and inspect it for any obvious damage. Also, make sure the small weights used to originally balance the driveshaft are in place and securely attached. Whenever the driveshaft is removed it must be reinstalled in the same relative position to preserve the balance.
7   Problems with the driveshaft are usually indicated by a noise or vibration while driving the vehicle. A road test should verify if the problem is the driveshaft or another vehicle component. Refer to the *Troubleshooting* section at the front of this manual. If you suspect trouble, inspect the driveline (see Section 11).

Driveaxles

8   All models are equipped with a pair of front driveaxles and two rear driveaxles. The front and rear driveaxle assemblies are identical in design. Some driveaxles consist of an inner and outer ball-and-cage type CV joint connected by an axleshaft; others have a tri-pot inner joint and a ball-and-cage outer joint. The inner CV joint can be disassembled; the axleshaft and outer CV joint are a single assembly and cannot be disassembled.

11 Driveline inspection

1   Raise the rear of the vehicle and support it securely on jackstands. Block the front wheels to keep the vehicle from rolling off the stands.
2   Visually inspect the driveshaft. Look for any dents or cracks in the tubing. If any are found, the driveshaft must be replaced.
3   Check for oil leakage at the front and rear of the driveshaft. Leakage where the driveshaft enters the transaxle indicates a defective transaxle/transfer case seal (see Chapter 7A). Leakage where the driveshaft joins the differential indicates a defective pin-

ion seal (see Section 13).
4   While under the vehicle, have an assistant rotate a rear wheel so the driveshaft will rotate. As it does, make sure the universal joints are operating properly without binding, noise or looseness. Listen for any noise from the center bearing (if equipped), indicating it's worn or damaged. Also check the rubber portion of the center bearing for cracking or separation, which will necessitate replacement.
5   The universal joint can also be checked by gripping your hands on either side of the joint and attempting to twist the joint. Any movement at all in the joint is a sign of considerable wear. Lifting up on the shaft will also indicate movement in the universal joints.
6   Check all driveshaft U-joint mounting bolts; make sure they're tight.
7   Check for looseness in the CV joints of the front and rear driveaxles. Also check for grease or oil leakage from around the driveaxles by inspecting the rubber boots and both ends of each axle. Leakage at the wheel end of a driveaxle indicates a torn or damaged rubber boot. If the tear is serious, the surface of the wheel housing will be splattered with grease. Oil leakage at the differential end of a driveaxle could also indicate a damaged boot (again, look for signs of oil being thrown onto the surrounding components), or it could indicate a defective side gear oil seal.

12 Driveshaft - removal and installation

Removal

1   Disconnect the cable from the negative battery terminal (see Chapter 5). Raise the vehicle and support it securely on jackstands. Place the transaxle in Neutral with the parking brake off.
2   Remove the heat shield cover.
3   On some models, it may be necessary to remove the center and rear exhaust pipes to access the heat shield cover. For exhaust removal, refer to Chapter 4.
4   Place match marks on the rear U-joint yoke and the differential pinion flange.
5   Remove the yoke-to-pinion flange bolts and nuts (see illustration).

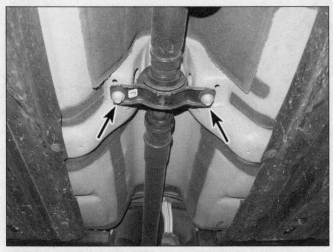

12.6 Remove the center bearing retaining bolts

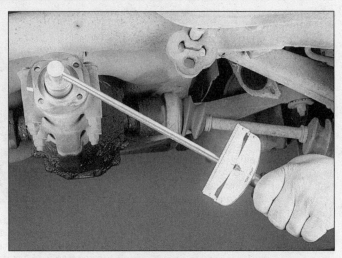

13.3 Using an inch-pound torque wrench, measure the turning torque of the pinion flange; jot down this number and save it for reassembly

13.4 Holding the flange with a suitable tool (such as this pin spanner braced by an exhaust hanger bracket), remove the retaining nut (if you don't have a pin spanner, try a pair of large water pump pliers or a plumber's wrench)

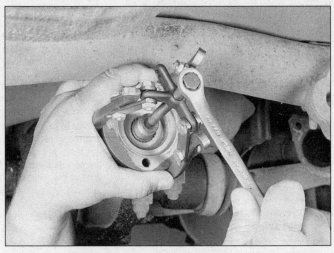

13.5 Sometimes you can remove the pinion flange by simply pulling it off; if not, use a small puller

6   Remove the center bearing retaining bolts (see illustration).

7   Pull the sleeve yoke out of the extension housing and remove the driveshaft. Plug the extension housing to prevent transaxle lubricant from leaking out.

8   The center bearing is not serviceable and the entire driveshaft must be replaced if the bearing is bad.

Installation

9   Lubricate the sleeve yoke splines, then remove the extension housing plug and carefully insert the sleeve yoke into the extension housing. Make sure you don't damage the extension housing seal or the splines of the transaxle output shaft.

10   Raise the center bearing into place,

install the center bearing retaining bolts and tighten them to the torque listed in this Chapter's Specifications.

11   Align the match marks on the rear U-joint yoke and the pinion flange, connect the yoke to the flange with the nuts and bolts and tighten them to the torque listed in this Chapter's Specifications.

12   The remainder of installation is the reverse of removal.

13   Rear differential pinion seal - replacement

1   Raise the vehicle and support it securely on jackstands. Place the transaxle in Neutral with the parking brake off.

2   Remove the driveshaft (see Section 12).

3   Using an inch-pound torque wrench, measure the turning torque of the pinion flange (see illustration). Jot down this figure and save it for reassembly.

4   Holding the flange with a suitable tool, remove the retaining nut (see illustration).

5   Remove the pinion flange; use a puller if necessary (see illustration).

6   Remove the old seal (see illustration).

7   Install a new seal (see illustration).

8   Installation is the reverse of removal. Gradually tighten the pinion flange retaining nut to the minimum torque listed in this Chapter's Specifications; as you're tightening the nut, use the figure you recorded prior to disassembly to periodically check the pinion flange turning torque. By the time the retaining nut's minimum specified torque is reached, the turn-

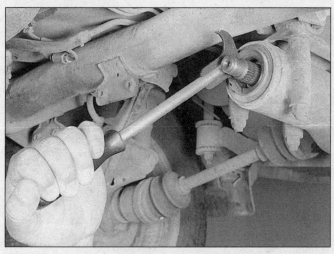

13.6 Remove the old seal with a seal removal tool (shown) or with a large screwdriver

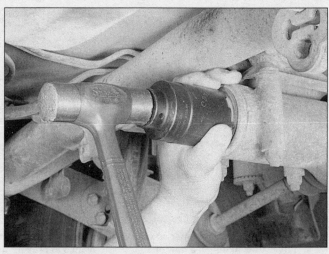

13.7 Install the new seal with a large socket; make sure the seal is square to the bore, then carefully tap it into place until it's fully seated

14.1a Before you can remove the driveaxle nut, unstake it: Using a small punch, restore the inner edge of the nut where it's been peened over to lock the nut onto the driveaxle

14.1b With the vehicle on the ground, have an assistant put the transaxle in gear and apply the brakes while you break the driveaxle nut loose with a breaker bar

14.6 Disengage the driveaxle from the steering knuckle

ing torque of the pinion flange should be the same as it was before disassembly. When this figure is attained, tighten the nut to increase the turning torque by five inch-pounds.

9   Install the driveshaft (see Section 12).

10   Lower the vehicle.

14   Driveaxles - removal and installation

Front driveaxle

1   Remove the wheel cover. Unstake, then loosen, the driveaxle nut (see illustrations). **Caution:** *Just break the nut loose at this time. If it is loosened very much or removed with the wheel on the ground (supporting the weight of the vehicle), the front hub bearings can be damaged.*

2   Loosen the wheel lug nuts, raise the vehicle and support it securely on jackstands.

3   Remove the wheel.

4   On models equipped with automatic headlight leveling, remove the height sensor.

5   Disconnect the control arm balljoint from the steering knuckle (see Chapter 10).

6   Remove the driveaxle nut, then pull the driveaxle assembly out of the steering knuckle (see illustration). Make sure you don't damage the lip of the inner steering knuckle seal. If the outer CV joint splines are stuck in the hub, knock the driveaxle loose with a hammer and punch. If that doesn't break the splines loose, remove the brake disc (see Chapter 9) and push the driveaxle from the hub using a two-jaw puller.

7   Pry the inner CV joint out of the differential (see illustration).

8   This is a good time to check the hub and

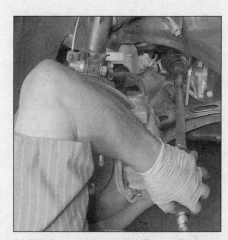

14.7 Using a prybar, carefully pry the inner end of the driveaxle from the transaxle

14.9 Pry the circlip off the inner end of the driveaxle and install a new one

14.10a Insert a punch into the disc cooling vanes to prevent the hub from turning . . .

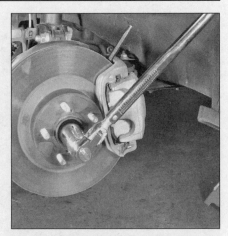

14.10b . . . tighten the nut to the specified torque . . .

14.10c . . . then stake the collar of the nut into the slot in the end of the driveaxle

14.16 Pry the driveaxle stub shaft out of the differential (use one of the bearing retainer plate bolts as a fulcrum - do NOT use the bearing retainer or you might crack it)

bearing unit in the knuckle, replacing it if necessary (see Chapter 10).

9   Replace the circlip on the inner end of the driveaxle with a new one (see illustration).

10   Installation is the reverse of removal. Insert a punch into the brake disc cooling vanes and allow it to rest on the caliper; install a NEW driveaxle/hub nut and tighten it to the torque listed in this Chapter's Specifications. Stake the collar of the nut into the slot in the driveaxle (see illustrations).

11   Lower the vehicle and tighten the wheel lug nuts to the torque listed in the Chapter 1 Specifications.

12   Check the transaxle lubricant level (manual transaxle) or differential lubricant level (automatic transaxle), adding as necessary (see Chapter 1).

Rear driveaxle

13   Unstake, then loosen, the driveaxle nut (see illustrations 14.1a and 14.1b).

Caution: *Just break the nut loose at this time. If it is loosened very much or removed with the wheel on the ground (supporting the weight of the vehicle) the hub bearings can be damaged.*

14   Loosen the rear wheel lug nuts, raise the vehicle and support it securely on jackstands. Remove the rear wheels.

15   Unbolt the trailing link and the rear lateral link from the rear knuckle (see Chapter 10).

16   Pry the rear driveaxle out of the differential (see illustration).

17   Remove the driveaxle nut, pull the rear knuckle outward, then pull the driveaxle assembly out of the rear knuckle.

18   This is a good time to inspect the rear hub and bearing assembly; if necessary, replace it (see Chapter 10).

19   Replace the circlip on the inner end of the driveaxle with a new one (see illustration 14.9).

20   Installation is the reverse of removal. Tighten the suspension fasteners to the

torque values listed in the Chapter 10 Specifications. Brace a long prybar across two of the wheel studs and let it rest on the ground, then tighten the NEW driveaxle/hub nut to the torque listed in this Chapter's Specifications. Stake the collar of the nut into the slit in the driveaxle (see illustration 14.10c).

21   Check the differential lubricant level, adding as necessary (see Chapter 1).

22   Install the wheel and lug nuts. Lower the vehicle and tighten the lug nuts to the torque listed in the Chapter 1 Specifications.

15   Rear differential side gear seals - replacement

1   The rear differential side gear seals can become worn and leak gear lubricant onto the differential housing and inner CV joint. If your differential is covered with gear lube, replace the seals.

2   Loosen the rear wheel lug nuts, block the front wheels, raise the rear of the vehicle and support it securely on jackstands. Remove the rear wheel(s).

3   Drain the gear lubricant from the differential (see Chapter 1).

4   Remove the rear driveaxle(s) (see Section 14).

5   Carefully pry out the driveaxle oil seal with a seal removal tool or a large screwdriver. Be careful not to damage or scratch the seal bore.

6   Using a seal installer or a large deep socket as a drift, install the new oil seal. Drive it into the bore squarely and make sure it's completely seated.

7   Installation is the reverse of removal. Lubricate the lip of the new seal with multi-purpose grease before installing the driveaxles. Be careful not to damage the lip of the new seal.

8   Fill the rear differential with the type and quantity of lubricant listed in the Chapter 1 Specifications.

9   Install the wheel and lug nuts, then lower the vehicle. Tighten the lug nuts to the torque listed in the Chapter 1 Specifications.

10   Drive the vehicle, then inspect for leaks around the seal and retainer.

16   Rear differential - removal and installation

Removal

1   Loosen the rear wheel lug nuts, block the front wheels and raise the rear of the vehicle. Support it securely on jackstands. Remove the rear wheels.

2   Drain the lubricant from the differential (see Chapter 1), then disconnect the oil temperature switch electrical connector, if equipped.

16.7 Differential-to-rear subframe mounting fasteners

3   Disconnect the driveshaft from the rear differential (see Section 12). Remove the rear exhaust pipe and muffler (see Chapter 4).

4   Unbolt the trailing link and the rear lateral link from the rear knuckle (see Chapter 10).

5   Pry the inner CV joints out of the differential just far enough to release the circlips (see Section 14).

6   Support the differential with a floor jack.

7   Remove the differential-to-rear subframe mounting fasteners (see illustration).

8   Lower the differential enough to separate the driveaxles from the differential. If the driveaxles are difficult to remove from the differential, use a prybar to remove them.

9   Support the driveaxles out of the way by securing them to the subframe with a piece of wire.

10   Carefully lower the differential and remove it from under the vehicle.

11   With the differential removed from the vehicle, now would be a good time to check or replace the rubber mounts for the differential mounting brackets and/or the rear crossmember.

Installation

12   Place the differential on the jack head and position it directly underneath the mounting bracket and crossmember.

13   Raise the differential enough to install the driveaxles into the differential.

14   Raise the differential into position and loosely install the rear mounting nuts, then the front mounting nuts. Tighten all mounting fasteners securely.

15   Install the driveshaft (see Section 12).

16   Fill the differential with the type and amount of lubricant listed in the Chapter 1 Specifications.

17   Install the wheels, remove the jack and lower the vehicle to the ground. Tighten the wheel lug nuts to the torque listed in the Chapter 1 Specifications.

Notes

Chapter 9
Brakes

Contents

Specifications

General

Brake fluid type	See Chapter 1	
Brake pedal freeplay		
Legacy		
2010 to 2012	0.079 to 0.197 inch	2 to 5 mm
2013 to 2014	0.008 to.020 inch	0.2 to 0.5 mm
2015 and later models	0.020 to 0.11 inch	0.5 to 2.7 mm
Forester		
2015 and earlier models	0.020 to 0.079 inch	0.5 to 2.0 mm
2016 models	0.020 to 0.11 inch	0.5 to 2.7 mm
Brake pedal height		
Legacy		
2015 and earlier models	5.51 to 5.91 inches	140 to 150 mm
2016 models	4.92 to 5.31 inches	125 to 135 mm
Forester		
2013 and earlier models	5.91 to 6.29 inches	150 to 160 mm
2014 and later models	5.51 to 5.91 inches	140 to 150 mm
Power brake booster pushrod length	5.37 inches	136.3 mm
Parking brake travel	7 to 8 clicks	

Disc brakes (front and rear)

Minimum brake pad thickness	See Chapter 1	
Disc minimum thickness	Refer to the dimension marked on the disc	
Disc runout limit	0.0020 inch	0.050 mm

Torque specifications

	Ft-lbs (unless otherwise indicated)	Nm

Note: *One foot-pound (ft-lb) of torque is equivalent to 12 inch-pounds (in-lbs) of torque. Torque values below approximately 15 foot-pounds are expressed in inch-pounds, because most foot-pound torque wrenches are not accurate at these smaller values.*

	Ft-lbs (unless otherwise indicated)	Nm
Brake hose-to-caliper banjo bolt	156 in-lbs	18
Brake hose bracket to strut	24	33
Caliper support bracket bolt		
Legacy		
Front	89	120
Rear	49	66
Forester		
Front	59	80
Rear	49	66
Caliper mounting bolts-to-caliper support bracket		
All models except 2016 Legacy	20	27
2016 Legacy	37	50
Master cylinder mounting nut	120 in-lbs	13
Brake booster mounting nuts	156 in-lbs	18
Brake line flair nut	132 to 168 in-lbs	15 to 19
Wheel speed sensor	24	33
Wheel lug nuts	See the Chapter 1 Specifications	

1   General information

1   The vehicles covered by this manual are equipped with hydraulically operated front and rear brake systems. The front brakes are disc type and the rear brakes are either disc or drum type. Both the front and rear brakes are self adjusting. The disc brakes automatically compensate for pad wear, while the drum brakes incorporate an adjustment mechanism which is activated as the parking brake is applied.

Hill start assist

2   Some models may feature a hill start assist system. The system engages when the vehicle is on an incline (of three degrees or greater) and is in gear (not park or neutral). The system utilizes the wheel speed sensors, yaw and a lateral sensor (G sensors) to determine the inclination of the vehicle and if it is moving on the incline. When these conditions occur, the hill start assist system actuates the parking brake to hold the vehicle. When the brake pedal is released the vehicle will stay at that position until the gas pedal is depressed.

Hydraulic system

3   The hydraulic system consists of two separate circuits. The master cylinder has separate reservoir chambers for the two circuits, and, in the event of a leak or failure in one hydraulic circuit, the other circuit will remain operative.

Power brake booster

4   The power brake booster - which utilizes engine manifold vacuum and atmospheric pressure to provide assistance to the hydraulically operated brakes - is mounted on the firewall in the engine compartment.

Parking brake

5   The parking brake operates the rear brakes only. There are two types of parking brake systems utilized on these vehicles: a mechanical system and a fully electronic system. Servicing the two different systems are similar in some aspects but for the electronic parking brake system a scanner is required to perform a lot of the service work.

Service

6   After completing any operation involving disassembly of any part of the brake system, always test drive the vehicle to check for proper braking performance before resuming normal driving. When testing the brakes, perform the tests on a clean, dry, flat surface. Conditions other than these can lead to inaccurate test results.

7   Test the brakes at various speeds with both light and heavy pedal pressure. The vehicle should stop evenly without pulling to one side or the other. Avoid locking the brakes, because this slides the tires and diminishes braking efficiency and control of the vehicle.

8   Tires, vehicle load and wheel alignment are factors which also affect braking performance.

Precautions

9   There are some general cautions and warnings involving the brake system on this vehicle:

a) *Use only brake fluid conforming to specifications listed in the Chapter 1 Specifications.*

b) *The brake pads and linings contain fibers which are hazardous to your health if inhaled. Whenever you work on brake system components, clean all parts with brake system cleaner. Do not allow the fine dust to become airborne. Also, wear an approved filtering mask.*

c) *Safety should be paramount whenever any servicing of the brake components is performed. Do not use parts or fasteners which are not in perfect condition, and be sure that all clearances and torque specifications are adhered to. If you are at all unsure about a certain procedure, seek professional advice. Upon completion of any brake system work, test the brakes carefully in a controlled area before putting the vehicle into normal service. If a problem is suspected in the brake system, don't drive the vehicle until it's fixed.*

2   Troubleshooting

PROBABLE CAUSE	CORRECTIVE ACTION

No brakes - pedal travels to floor

PROBABLE CAUSE	CORRECTIVE ACTION
1 Low fluid level 2 Air in system	1 and 2 Low fluid level and air in the system are symptoms of another problem a leak somewhere in the hydraulic system. Locate and repair the leak
3 Defective seals in master cylinder	3 Replace master cylinder
4 Fluid overheated and vaporized due to heavy braking	4 Bleed hydraulic system (temporary fix). Replace brake fluid (proper fix)

Brake pedal slowly travels to floor under braking or at a stop

PROBABLE CAUSE	CORRECTIVE ACTION
1 Defective seals in master cylinder	1 Replace master cylinder
2 Leak in a hose, line, caliper or wheel cylinder	2 Locate and repair leak
3 Air in hydraulic system	3 Bleed the system, inspect system for a leak

Brake pedal feels spongy when depressed

PROBABLE CAUSE	CORRECTIVE ACTION
1 Air in hydraulic system	1 Bleed the system, inspect system for a leak
2 Master cylinder or power booster loose	2 Tighten fasteners
3 Brake fluid overheated (beginning to boil)	3 Bleed the system (temporary fix). Replace the brake fluid (proper fix)
4 Deteriorated brake hoses (ballooning under pressure)	4 Inspect hoses, replace as necessary (it's a good idea to replace all of them if one hose shows signs of deterioration)

Troubleshooting (continued)

PROBABLE CAUSE	CORRECTIVE ACTION

Brake pedal feels hard when depressed and/or excessive effort required to stop vehicle

PROBABLE CAUSE	CORRECTIVE ACTION
1 Power booster faulty	1 Replace booster
2 Engine not producing sufficient vacuum, or hose to booster clogged, collapsed or cracked	2 Check vacuum to booster with a vacuum gauge. Replace hose if cracked or clogged, repair engine if vacuum is extremely low
3 Brake linings contaminated by grease or brake fluid	3 Locate and repair source of contamination, replace brake pads or shoes
4 Brake linings glazed	4 Replace brake pads or shoes, check discs and drums for glazing, service as necessary
5 Caliper piston(s) or wheel cylinder(s) binding or frozen	5 Replace calipers or wheel cylinders
6 Brakes wet	6 Apply pedal to boil-off water (this should only be a momentary problem)
7 Kinked, clogged or internally split brake hose or line	7 Inspect lines and hoses, replace as necessary

Excessive brake pedal travel (but will pump up)

PROBABLE CAUSE	CORRECTIVE ACTION
1 Drum brakes out of adjustment	1 Adjust brakes
2 Air in hydraulic system	2 Bleed system, inspect system for a leak

Excessive brake pedal travel (but will not pump up)

PROBABLE CAUSE	CORRECTIVE ACTION
1 Master cylinder pushrod misadjusted	1 Adjust pushrod
2 Master cylinder seals defective	2 Replace master cylinder
3 Brake linings worn out	3 Inspect brakes, replace pads and/or shoes
4 Hydraulic system leak	4 Locate and repair leak

Brake pedal doesn't return

PROBABLE CAUSE	CORRECTIVE ACTION
1 Brake pedal binding	1 Inspect pivot bushing and pushrod, repair or lubricate
2 Defective master cylinder	2 Replace master cylinder

Brake pedal pulsates during brake application

PROBABLE CAUSE	CORRECTIVE ACTION
1 Brake drums out-of-round	1 Have drums machined by an automotive machine shop
2 Excessive brake disc runout or disc surfaces out-of-parallel	2 Have discs machined by an automotive machine shop
3 Loose or worn wheel bearings	3 Adjust or replace wheel bearings
4 Loose lug nuts	4 Tighten lug nuts

Brakes slow to release

PROBABLE CAUSE	CORRECTIVE ACTION
1 Malfunctioning power booster	1 Replace booster
2 Pedal linkage binding	2 Inspect pedal pivot bushing and pushrod, repair/lubricate
3 Malfunctioning proportioning valve	3 Replace proportioning valve
4 Sticking caliper or wheel cylinder	4 Repair or replace calipers or wheel cylinders
5 Kinked or internally split brake hose	5 Locate and replace faulty brake hose

Brakes grab (one or more wheels)

PROBABLE CAUSE	CORRECTIVE ACTION
1 Grease or brake fluid on brake lining	1 Locate and repair cause of contamination, replace lining
2 Brake lining glazed	2 Replace lining, deglaze disc or drum

PROBABLE CAUSE

CORRECTIVE ACTION

Vehicle pulls to one side during braking

PROBABLE CAUSE	CORRECTIVE ACTION
1 Grease or brake fluid on brake lining	1 Locate and repair cause of contamination, replace lining
2 Brake lining glazed	2 Deglaze or replace lining, deglaze disc or drum
3 Restricted brake line or hose	3 Repair line or replace hose
4 Tire pressures incorrect	4 Adjust tire pressures
5 Caliper or wheel cylinder sticking	5 Repair or replace calipers or wheel cylinders
6 Wheels out of alignment	6 Have wheels aligned
7 Weak suspension spring	7 Replace springs
8 Weak or broken shock absorber	8 Replace shock absorbers

Brakes drag (indicated by sluggish engine performance or wheels being very hot after driving)

PROBABLE CAUSE	CORRECTIVE ACTION
1 Brake pedal pushrod incorrectly adjusted	1 Adjust pushrod
2 Master cylinder pushrod (between booster and master cylinder)	2 Adjust pushrod incorrectly adjusted
3 Obstructed compensating port in master cylinder	3 Replace master cylinder
4 Master cylinder piston seized in bore	4 Replace master cylinder
5 Contaminated fluid causing swollen seals throughout system	5 Flush system, replace all hydraulic components
6 Clogged brake lines or internally split brake hose(s)	6 Flush hydraulic system, replace defective hose(s)
7 Sticking caliper(s) or wheel cylinder(s)	7 Replace calipers or wheel cylinders
8 Parking brake not releasing	8 Inspect parking brake linkage and parking brake mechanism, repair as required
9 Improper shoe-to-drum clearance	9 Adjust brake shoes
10 Faulty proportioning valve	10 Replace proportioning valve

Brakes fade (due to excessive heat)

PROBABLE CAUSE	CORRECTIVE ACTION
1 Brake linings excessively worn or glazed	1 Deglaze or replace brake pads and/or shoes
2 Excessive use of brakes	2 Downshift into a lower gear, maintain a constant slower speed (going down hills)
3 Vehicle overloaded	3 Reduce load
4 Brake drums or discs worn too thin	4 Measure drum diameter and disc thickness, replace drums or discs as required
5 Contaminated brake fluid	5 Flush system, replace fluid
6 Brakes drag	6 Repair cause of dragging brakes
7 Driver resting left foot on brake pedal	7 Don't ride the brakes

Brakes noisy (high-pitched squeal)

PROBABLE CAUSE	CORRECTIVE ACTION
1 Glazed lining	1 Deglaze or replace lining
2 Contaminated lining (brake fluid, grease, etc.)	2 Repair source of contamination, replace linings
3 Weak or broken brake shoe hold-down or return spring	3 Replace springs
4 Rivets securing lining to shoe or backing plate loose	4 Replace shoes or pads
5 Excessive dust buildup on brake linings	5 Wash brakes off with brake system cleaner
6 Brake drums worn too thin	6 Measure diameter of drums, replace if necessary
7 Wear indicator on disc brake pads contacting disc	7 Replace brake pads
8 Anti-squeal shims missing or installed improperly	8 Install shims correctly

Troubleshooting (continued)

PROBABLE CAUSE	CORRECTIVE ACTION

Brakes noisy (scraping sound)

1 Brake pads or shoes worn out; rivets, backing plate or brake	1 Replace linings, have discs and/or drums machined (or replace) shoe metal contacting disc or drum

Brakes chatter

1 Worn brake lining	1 Inspect brakes, replace shoes or pads as necessary
2 Glazed or scored discs or drums	2 Deglaze discs or drums with sandpaper (if glazing is severe, machining will be required)
3 Drums or discs heat checked	3 Check discs and/or drums for hard spots, heat checking, etc. Have discs/drums machined or replace them
4 Disc runout or drum out-of-round excessive	4 Measure disc runout and/or drum out-of-round, have discs or drums machined or replace them
5 Loose or worn wheel bearings	5 Adjust or replace wheel bearings
6 Loose or bent brake backing plate (drum brakes)	6 Tighten or replace backing plate
7 Grooves worn in discs or drums	7 Have discs or drums machined, if within limits (if not, replace them)
8 Brake linings contaminated (brake fluid, grease, etc.)	8 Locate and repair source of contamination, replace pads or shoes
9 Excessive dust buildup on linings	9 Wash brakes with brake system cleaner
10 Surface finish on discs or drums too rough after machining	10 Have discs or drums properly machined (especially on vehicles with sliding calipers)
11 Brake pads or shoes glazed	11 Deglaze or replace brake pads or shoes

Brake pads or shoes click

1 Shoe support pads on brake backing plate grooved or	1 Replace brake backing plate excessively worn
2 Brake pads loose in caliper	2 Loose pad retainers or anti-rattle clips
3 Also see items listed under Brakes chatter	

Brakes make groaning noise at end of stop

1 Brake pads and/or shoes worn out	1 Replace pads and/or shoes
2 Brake linings contaminated (brake fluid, grease, etc.)	2 Locate and repair cause of contamination, replace brake pads or shoes
3 Brake linings glazed	3 Deglaze or replace brake pads or shoes
4 Excessive dust buildup on linings	4 Wash brakes with brake system cleaner
5 Scored or heat-checked discs or drums	5 Inspect discs/drums, have machined if within limits (if not, replace discs or drums)
6 Broken or missing brake shoe attaching hardware	6 Inspect drum brakes, replace missing hardware

Rear brakes lock up under light brake application

1 Tire pressures too high	1 Adjust tire pressures
2 Tires excessively worn	2 Replace tires
3 Defective proportioning valve	3 Replace proportioning valve

Brake warning light on instrument panel comes on (or stays on)

1 Low fluid level in master cylinder reservoir (reservoirs with fluid level sensor)	1 Add fluid, inspect system for leak, check the thickness of the brake pads and shoes
2 Failure in one half of the hydraulic system	2 Inspect hydraulic system for a leak
3 Piston in pressure differential warning valve not centered	3 Center piston by bleeding one circuit or the other (close bleeder valve as soon as the light goes out)

PROBABLE CAUSE   CORRECTIVE ACTION

Brake warning light on instrument panel comes on (or stays on) (continued)

4 Defective pressure differential valve or warning switch	4 Replace valve or switch
5 Air in the hydraulic system	5 Bleed the system, check for leaks
6 Brake pads worn out (vehicles with electric wear sensors - small	6 Replace brake pads (and sensors) probes that fit into the brake pads and ground out on the disc when the pads get thin)

Brakes do not self adjust

Disc brakes

1 Defective caliper piston seals	1 Replace calipers. Also, possible contaminated fluid causing soft or swollen seals (flush system and fill with new fluid if in doubt)
2 Corroded caliper piston(s)	2 Same as above

Drum brakes

1 Adjuster screw frozen	1 Remove adjuster, disassemble, clean and lubricate with high-temperature grease
2 Adjuster lever does not contact star wheel or is binding	2 Inspect drum brakes, assemble correctly or clean or replace parts as required
3 Adjusters mixed up (installed on wrong wheels after brake job)	3 Reassemble correctly
4 Adjuster cable broken or installed incorrectly (cable-type adjusters)	4 Install new cable or assemble correctly

Rapid brake lining wear

1 Driver resting left foot on brake pedal	1 Don't ride the brakes
2 Surface finish on discs or drums too rough	2 Have discs or drums properly machined
3 Also see Brakes drag	

3   Anti-lock Brake System (ABS) - general information

General information

1   The anti-lock brake system is designed to maintain vehicle steerability, directional stability and optimum deceleration under severe braking conditions on most road surfaces. It does so by monitoring the rotational speed of each wheel and controlling the brake line pressure to each wheel during braking. This prevents the wheels from locking up.

2   The ABS system has three main components - the wheel speed sensors, the ECU and the hydraulic unit (see illustration). Four wheel speed sensors - one at each wheel - send a variable voltage signal to the control unit, which monitors these signals, compares them to its program and determines whether a wheel is about to lock up. When a wheel is about to lock up, the control unit signals the hydraulic unit to reduce hydraulic pressure (or not increase it further) at that wheel's brake caliper. Pressure modulation is handled by electrically-operated solenoid valves. In addition, some vehicles will also include a YAW sensor (G sensor) to determine the inclination and general angle of the vehicle during a turn or on a hill.

3   If a problem develops within the system, an ABS warning light will glow on the dashboard. Sometimes, a visual inspection of the ABS system can help you locate the problem. Carefully inspect the ABS wiring harness. Pay particularly close attention to the harness and connections near each wheel. Look for signs of chafing and other damage caused by incorrectly routed wires. If a wheel sensor harness is damaged, the sensor must be replaced.

Warning: *Do NOT try to repair an ABS wiring harness. The ABS system is sensitive to even the smallest changes in resistance. Repairing the harness could alter resistance values and cause the system to malfunction. If the ABS wiring harness is damaged in any way, it must be replaced.*

Caution: *Make sure the ignition is turned off before unplugging or reattaching any electrical connections.*

3.2 The ABS control module and hydraulic control unit is located at the right side of the engine compartment, forward of the strut tower

3.9a ABS front wheel speed sensor

3.9b ABS rear wheel speed sensor

Diagnosis and repair

4   If a dashboard warning light comes on and stays on while the vehicle is in operation, the ABS system requires attention. Although special electronic ABS diagnostic testing tools are necessary to properly diagnose the system, you can perform a few preliminary checks before taking the vehicle to a dealer service department.

a) Check the brake fluid level in the reservoir.
b) Verify that the computer electrical connectors are securely connected.
c) Check the electrical connectors at the hydraulic control unit.
d) Check the fuses.
e) Follow the wiring harness to each wheel and verify that all connections are secure and that the wiring is undamaged.

5   If the above preliminary checks do not rectify the problem, the vehicle should be diagnosed by a dealer service department or other qualified repair shop. Due to the complex nature of this system, all actual repair

4.4 Wash the brake assembly with brake system cleaner; do NOT use compressed air to blow off the brake dust

work must be done by a qualified automotive technician.

Wheel speed sensor - removal and installation

6   Loosen the wheel lug nuts, raise the vehicle and support it securely on jackstands. Remove the wheel.

7   Make sure the ignition key is turned to the Off position.

8   Trace the wiring back from the sensor, detaching all brackets and clips while noting its correct routing, then disconnect the electrical connector.

9   Remove the mounting bolt and carefully pull the sensor out from the knuckle (see illustrations).

10   Installation is the reverse of removal. Tighten the mounting bolt to the torque listed in this Chapter's Specifications.

11   Install the wheel and lug nuts. Lower the vehicle and tighten the lug nuts to the torque listed in the Chapter 1 Specifications.

4   Disc brake pads - replacement

Warning: *Disc brake pads must be replaced on both front or both rear wheels at the same time; never replace the pads on only one side. Also, the dust created by the brake system is harmful to your health. Never blow it out with compressed air and don't inhale any of it. An approved filtering mask should be worn when working on the brakes. Do not, under any circumstances, use petroleum-based solvents to clean brake parts. Use brake system cleaner only!*
Caution: *Brake fluid will damage paint. Wash off any spills immediately with water to avoid paint damage.*
Note: *This procedure applies to front and rear brakes.*

1   Loosen the wheel lug nuts, raise the front or rear of the vehicle and support it securely on jackstands.

2   Remove the wheels. Release the parking brake if you're working on the rear brakes.

3   Remove about two-thirds of the fluid from the master cylinder reservoir. Position a drain pan under the brake assembly.

4   Before beginning, wash down the entire brake assembly with brake system cleaner (see illustration).

5   To replace the brake pads, follow the accompanying illustrations, beginning with illustration 4.5a. Stay in order and read the caption under each illustration. Work on one brake assembly at a time so that you'll have something to refer to if you get in trouble. To replace the rear brake pads, follow the same photos (the rear brake pad and caliper are slightly smaller than the front setup but are otherwise virtually identical).

6   While the pads are removed, inspect the caliper for brake fluid leaks and ruptures in the piston boot. Replace the caliper if necessary (see Section 5). Also inspect the brake disc carefully (see Section 6). If machining is necessary, follow the information in that Section to remove the disc. If you're replacing the rear pads, this would be a good time to remove the caliper and disc and inspect the parking brake shoes (see Section 12).

7   Before installing the caliper guide pins, make sure you clean them and inspect them for corrosion, scoring and other damage. If they're damaged or worn, replace them. Tighten the caliper bolts to the torque listed in this Chapter's Specifications.

8   Install the brake pads on the opposite wheel, then install the wheels and lower the vehicle. Tighten the wheel lug nuts to the torque listed in the Chapter 1 Specifications.

9   Add brake fluid to the reservoir until it's full (see Chapter 1). Pump the brakes several times to seat the pads against the discs, then check the fluid level again.

10   Check the operation of the brakes before driving the vehicle in traffic. Try to avoid heavy brake applications until the brakes have been applied lightly several times to seat the pads.

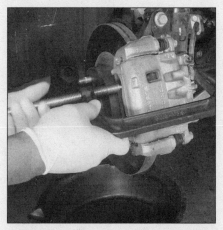

4.5a Depress the piston(s) into the caliper with a C-clamp to make room for the new brake pads

4.5b Remove the lower caliper bolt (on the lower pin), then swing the caliper up for access to the brake pads. To detach the caliper completely, remove both caliper bolts but do not let the caliper hang by the brake hose

4.5c Remove the outer brake pad and shims, then remove the shim(s) from the pad (if a shim is damaged, replace it)

4.5d Remove the inner brake pad and shims, then remove the shims from the pad

4.5e Remove the lower anti-rattle clip, clean and inspect it, then set it aside for re-use; if it is damaged, replace it

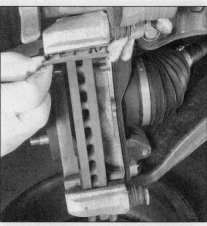

4.5f Remove the upper anti-rattle clip, clean and inspect it, then set it aside for re-use; if it is damaged, replace it

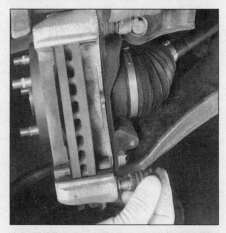

4.5g If the caliper doesn't slide well on the guide pins, remove the caliper from the caliper support, then clean and inspect both pins; if either pin is damaged or worn, replace it

4.5h Inspect the pin dust boots; if they're torn or cracked, replace them. Lubricate the pins with high-temperature grease

4.5i The brake pads may have either one or two shims; apply anti-squeal compound to the backing plates of the new pads . . .

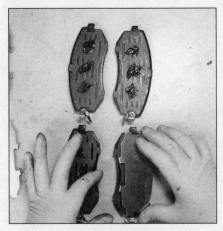

4.5j . . . then install the shim(s) on the pads

4.5k Install the lower anti-rattle clip on the caliper support bracket . . .

4.5l . . . and the upper anti-rattle clip

4.5m Install the inner and outer brake pads and shims; make sure the pads are correctly seated in the caliper support

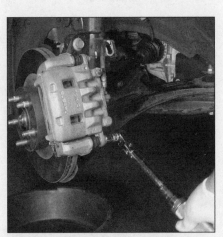

4.5n Slide the caliper back onto the guide pin, if removed, then pivot it down over the new pads, install the caliper bolt and tighten it to the torque listed in this Chapter's Specifications

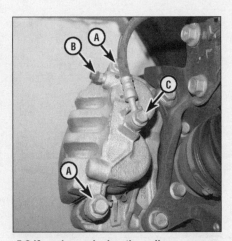

5.2 If you're replacing the caliper, remove the brake hose-to-caliper banjo bolt; discard the old sealing washers and use new ones on installation (non-Brembo models shown, Brembo models similar)

A   Caliper mounting bolts
B   Caliper bleeder screw
C   Banjo fitting bolt

5   Brake caliper - removal and installation

Warning: *The dust created by the brake system is harmful to your health. Never blow it out with compressed air and don't inhale any of it. An approved filtering mask should be worn when working on the brakes. Do not, under any circumstances, use petroleum-based solvents to clean brake parts. Use brake system cleaner only!*

Note: *Always replace the calipers in pairs (front/front, rear/rear) - never replace just one of them.*

Removal

1   Loosen the wheel lug nuts, raise the front or rear of the vehicle and support it securely on jackstands. Release the parking brake lever if you're working on the rear brakes. Remove the disc brake pads (see Section 4).
2   Place a container under the caliper and have some rags handy to catch any spilled brake fluid. Remove the brake hose-to-caliper banjo bolt (see illustration). Plug the hose to prevent contaminants from entering the brake hydraulic system and to prevent fluid from leaking out the hose.

Note: *If you're only removing the caliper for access to other components, don't disconnect the hose from the caliper.*

3   Unbolt and remove the caliper from the caliper support bracket.

Installation

4   Install the brake pads (see Section 4).
5   Clean the caliper guide pins, then lubricate the pins with high-temperature (see illustrations 4.5g and 4.5h).
6   Install the caliper assembly and, if necessary, reconnect the brake line to the caliper. Use new sealing washers and tighten the banjo bolt and the caliper bolts to the torque listed in this Chapter's Specifications.
7   Install the wheel and lug nuts. Lower the vehicle and tighten the lug nuts to the torque listed in the Chapter 1 Specifications.
8   Bleed the brake system (see Section 9).

6.3 The brake pads on this vehicle were obviously neglected, as they wore down completely and cut deep grooves into the disc - wear this severe means the disc must be replaced

6.4 Check brake disc runout with a dial indicator; check both sides of the disc

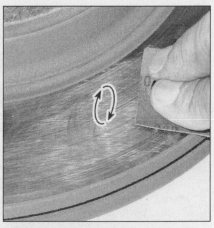

6.5 Using a swirling motion, remove the glaze from the disc with sandpaper or emery cloth

6.6a The minimum thickness of this disc is cast into the hub area (typical), look for the minimum thickness for your disc in this area

6.6b Measure the thickness of the disc with a micrometer and compare it to the specified minimum thickness

6   Brake disc - inspection, removal and installation

Warning: *The dust created by the brake system is harmful to your health. Never blow it out with compressed air and don't inhale any of it. An approved filtering mask should be worn when working on the brakes. Do not, under any circumstances, use petroleum-based solvents to clean brake parts. Use brake system cleaner only!*

Inspection

1   Loosen the wheel lug nuts, raise the vehicle and support it securely on jackstands. Remove the wheel and install the lug nuts to hold the disc in place against the hub flange.
Note: *If the lug nuts don't contact the disc when screwed on all the way, install washers*

under them. If you're checking the rear disc, release the parking brake.

2   Remove the brake caliper as outlined in Section 5. It isn't necessary to disconnect the brake hose. After removing the caliper bolts, suspend the caliper out of the way with a piece of wire. Don't let the caliper hang by the hose and don't stretch or twist the hose.

3   Visually inspect the disc surface for score marks and other damage. Light scratches and shallow grooves are normal after use and may not always be detrimental to brake operation, but deep scoring requires disc removal and refinishing by an automotive machine shop. Check both sides of the disc (see illustration). If pulsating has been noticed during application of the brakes, suspect disc runout.

4   To check disc runout, place a dial indicator at a point about 1/2-inch from the outer edge of the disc (see illustration). Set the indi-

cator to zero and turn the disc. The indicator reading should not exceed the specified allowable runout limit. If it does, the disc should be refinished by an automotive machine shop.

5   The discs should be resurfaced regardless of the dial indicator reading, as this will impart a smooth finish and ensure a perfectly flat surface, eliminating any brake pedal pulsation or other undesirable symptoms related to questionable discs. At the very least, if you elect not to have the discs resurfaced, remove the glaze from the surface with emery cloth or sandpaper, using a swirling motion (see illustration).

6   It's absolutely critical that the disc not be machined to a thickness under the specified minimum thickness. The minimum (or discard) thickness is cast or stamped into the disc. The disc thickness can be checked with a micrometer (see illustrations).

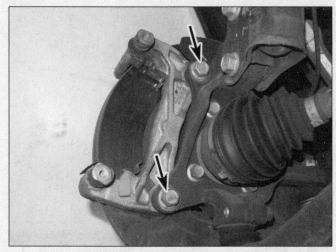

6.7a Front caliper support bracket mounting bolts

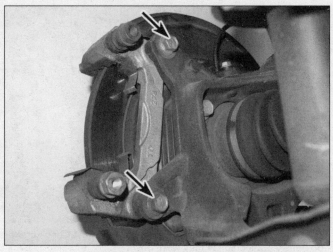

6.7b The rear caliper support bracket mounting bolts

6.8 If the disc is stuck, thread two 8 mm bolt(s) into the threaded holes in the disc and tighten them to force the disc off the hub

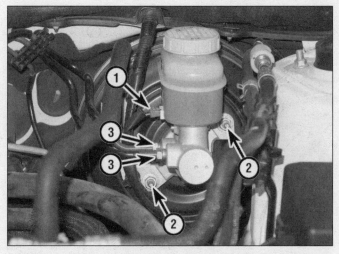

7.2 Master cylinder electrical connector (1), mounting nuts (2) and brake line fittings (3)

Removal

7   Remove the caliper support bracket bolts (see illustrations) and remove the support bracket.

8   Slide the disc off the hub. If the disc is stuck to the hub and won't come off, thread two bolts into the holes provided and tighten them (see illustration).

9   If you're removing a rear disc and it won't come off (but isn't stuck to the hub flange), back-off the parking brake adjuster (see Section 12).

10   If you're removing a rear disc, inspect the parking brake shoes (see Section 12).

Installation

11   Thoroughly clean all parts. Install the disc.

12   Install the caliper support bracket and tighten the bracket bolts to the torque listed in this Chapter's Specifications.

13   Install the brake pads and caliper (see Sections 4 and 5) and tighten the caliper bolts to the torque listed in this Chapter's Specifications.

14   Install the wheel and lug nuts, then lower the vehicle to the ground. Tighten the lug nuts to the torque listed in the Chapter 1 Specifications. Depress the brake pedal a few times to bring the brake pads into contact with the disc. Bleeding won't be necessary unless the brake hose was disconnected from the caliper. Check the operation of the brakes carefully before driving the vehicle.

---

7   Master cylinder - removal and installation

Removal

1   Place some shop rags underneath the master cylinder to catch any spilled brake fluid,

then remove the brake fluid from the reservoir.
Caution: *Brake fluid will damage paint. Cover all body parts and be careful not to spill fluid during this procedure.Clean any spilled fluid immediately and wash the area thoroughly with water.*

Note: *A large syringe or poultry baster works well for removing the brake fluid from the reservoir but cannot be used for anything else afterwards.*

2   Unplug the electrical connector from the brake fluid level indicator (see illustration).

3   Place some rags or newspapers under the brake line fittings. Using a flare-nut wrench, unscrew the brake line tube nuts and allow any residual fluid to drain onto the rags.

4   Remove the master cylinder-to-power brake booster mounting nuts.

5   Remove the master cylinder from the engine compartment, being careful not to spill any fluid.

7.8 The best way to bleed air from the master cylinder before installing it on the vehicle is with a pair of bleeder tubes that direct brake fluid back into the reservoir during bleeding

8.3 Remove the brake hose from these three points

Installation

6   If a new master cylinder is being installed, the power brake booster pushrod length must be checked and adjusted. Refer to Section 11 for check and adjustment procedures.

7   Bench bleed the new master cylinder before installing it. Mount the master cylinder in a vise, with the jaws of the vise clamping on the mounting flange.

8   Attach a pair of master cylinder bleeder tubes to the outlet ports of the master cylinder (see illustration).

9   Fill the reservoir with brake fluid of the recommended type (see Chapter 1).

10   Slowly push the pistons into the master cylinder (a large Phillips screwdriver can be used for this) - air will be expelled from the pressure chambers and into the reservoir. Because the tubes are submerged in fluid, air can't be drawn back into the master cylinder when you release the pistons.

11   Repeat the procedure until no more air bubbles are present.

12   Remove the bleed tubes, one at a time, and install plugs in the open ports to prevent fluid leakage and air from entering. Install the reservoir cap.

13   Replace the O-ring seal on the master cylinder (if equipped) and then place it over the studs on the booster and tighten the attaching nuts only finger tight at this time.

Caution: *If your vehicle is equipped with an O-ring between the master cylinder and booster it is not there to prevent brake fluid leaks but to insure a good vacuum seal from the master cylinder to the booster. Failure to replace the O-ring can result in a hard pedal and no power assist.*

14   Thread the brake line fittings into the master cylinder. Since the master cylinder is still a bit loose, it can be moved slightly in order for the fittings to thread in easily. Be careful not to cross-thread or strip the fittings as they are installed.

15   Fully tighten the mounting nuts, then the brake line fittings. Tighten the master cylinder mounting nuts to the torque listed in this Chapter's Specifications.

16   Fill the master cylinder reservoir with fluid, then bleed the master cylinder and the brake system (see Section 9). To bleed the cylinder on the vehicle, have an assistant depress the brake pedal and hold the pedal to the floor. Loosen the fitting just enough to allow air and fluid to escape then tighten it lightly. Repeat this procedure on both fittings until the fluid is clear of air bubbles and then tighten the fittings securely.

Caution: *Have plenty of rags on hand to catch the fluid - brake fluid will ruin painted surfaces. After the bleeding procedure is completed, rinse the area under the master cylinder with clean water.*

17   The remainder of installation is the reverse of removal. Test the operation of the brake system carefully before placing the vehicle into normal service.

Warning: *Do not operate the vehicle if you are in doubt about the effectiveness of the brake system. On models equipped with ABS, it is possible for air to become trapped in the anti-lock brake system hydraulic control unit, so, if the pedal continues to feel spongy after repeated bleedings or the BRAKE or ANTI-LOCK light stays on, have the vehicle towed to a dealer service department or other qualified shop to be bled with the aid of a scan tool.*

8   Brake hoses and lines - check and replacement

1   About every six months, with the vehicle raised and placed securely on jackstands, the flexible hoses which connect the steel brake lines with the front and rear brake assemblies should be inspected for cracks, chafing of the outer cover, leaks, blisters and other damage. These are important and vulnerable parts of the brake system and inspection should be complete. A light and mirror will be needed for a thorough check. If a hose exhibits any of the above defects, replace it with a new one.

Note: *In some cases, a problem of a stuck caliper that won't release may not be the caliper at all but, the rubber brake line has internally failed. A bulge in the rubber hose is a good indicator the hose has internally failed.*

Flexible hoses

2   Clean all dirt away from the ends of the hose.

3   Unscrew the metal tube nut with a flare nut wrench, pull the retaining clip straight out from the hose fitting at the frame bracket and remove the hose from the bracket. On front hoses, remove the hose mounting bolt from the bracket on the strut (see illustration).

4   Disconnect the hose from the caliper and discard the sealing washers.

5   Attach the new brake hose to the caliper using new sealing washers. Tighten the brake hose banjo bolt to the torque listed in this Chapter's Specifications.

6   Installation is the reverse of removal. Make sure that the hose is routed correctly and not twisted.

7   Bleed the brake system (see Section 9).

Metal brake lines

Note: *Metal brake line failure is usually due to salt corrosion or abrasive movement or both. If you believe that a metal line has failed follow the line from the ABS controller or the master cylinder and look for a leak along the length of the brake line.*

8   When replacing brake lines, use the correct parts. Don't use copper tubing for any brake system components. Purchase steel brake lines from a dealer parts department or auto parts store.

9   Prefabricated brake line, with the tube ends already flared and fittings installed, is available at auto parts stores and dealer parts departments. These lines can be bent to the

9.1 Have an assistant depress the brake pedal and hold it down. Briefly loosen the line fitting to allow air and fluid to escape. Repeat this procedure on both line fittings until the fluid is clear of air bubbles

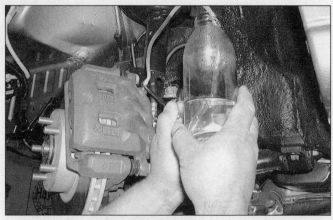

9.8 When bleeding the brakes, a hose is connected to the bleeder screw at the caliper or wheel cylinder and submerged in brake fluid - air will be seen as bubbles in the tube and container (all air must be expelled before moving to the next wheel)

proper shapes using a tubing bender.

10   When installing a new line, make sure it's supported in the original brackets and has plenty of clearance between moving or hot components.

11   After installation, check the master cylinder fluid level and add fluid as necessary. Bleed the brake system as outlined in Section 9 and test the brakes carefully before placing the vehicle into normal operation.

9   Brake hydraulic system - bleeding

Warning: *If air has found its way into the hydraulic control unit on models with ABS, the system must be bled with the use of a scan tool. If the brake pedal feels spongy even after bleeding the brakes, or the ABS light on the instrument panel does not go off, or if you have any doubts whatsoever about the effectiveness of the brake system, have the vehicle towed to a dealer service department or other repair shop equipped with the necessary tools for bleeding the system.*

Warning: *Wear eye protection when bleeding the brake system. If the fluid comes in contact with your eyes, immediately rinse them with water and seek medical attention.*

Note: *Bleeding the brake system is necessary to remove any air that's trapped in the system when it's opened during removal and installation of a hose, line, caliper, wheel cylinder or master cylinder.*

1   It will probably be necessary to bleed the system at all four brakes if air has entered the system due to low fluid level, or if the brake lines have been disconnected at the master cylinder. If the master cylinder has run dry (due to a leak in the system) or the master cylinder has been replaced, begin by bleeding the master cylinder (see illustration).

2   If a brake line was disconnected only at a wheel, then only that caliper or wheel cylin-

der must be bled.

3   If a brake line is disconnected at a fitting located between the master cylinder and any of the brakes, that part of the system served by the disconnected line must be bled.

4   Remove any residual vacuum (or hydraulic pressure) from the brake power booster by applying the brake several times with the engine off.

5   Remove the master cylinder reservoir cap and fill the reservoir with brake fluid. Reinstall the cap.

Note: *Check the fluid level often during the bleeding operation and add fluid as necessary to prevent the fluid level from falling low enough to allow air bubbles into the master cylinder.*

6   Have an assistant on hand, as well as a supply of new brake fluid, an empty clear plastic container, a length of plastic, rubber or vinyl tubing to fit over the bleeder valve and a wrench to open and close the bleeder valve.

7   Beginning at the right rear wheel, loosen the bleeder screw slightly, then tighten it to a point where it's snug but can still be loosened quickly and easily.

8   Place one end of the tubing over the bleeder screw fitting and submerge the other end in brake fluid in a container (see illustration).

9   Have the assistant slowly depress the brake pedal and hold it in the depressed position.

10   While the pedal is held depressed, open the bleeder screw just enough to allow a flow of fluid to leave the valve. Watch for air bubbles to exit the submerged end of the tube. When the fluid flow slows after a couple of seconds, tighten the screw and have your assistant release the pedal.

11   Repeat Steps 9 and 10 until no more air is seen leaving the tube, then tighten the bleeder screw and proceed to the left rear wheel, the right front wheel and the left front wheel, in that order, and perform the same

procedure. Check the fluid in the master cylinder reservoir frequently.

Note: *Always use fresh brake fluid when bleeding the brake system. Only use an unopened container of brake fluid and only purchase enough brake fluid to accomplish the task you're doing. Brake fluid is "hydroscopic," meaning it will draw moisture to itself. Opened or old brake fluid will contain moisture which can boil under heavy braking conditions and disable the brake system. There are test strips you can purchase at most parts stores to check your brake fluid for moisture contamination.*

12   Refill the master cylinder with fluid at the end of the operation.

13   Check the operation of the brakes. The pedal should feel solid when depressed, with no sponginess. If necessary, repeat the entire process.

Warning: *Do not operate the vehicle if you are in doubt about the effectiveness of the brake system. On models equipped with ABS, it's possible for air to become trapped in the anti-lock brake system hydraulic control unit, so, if the pedal continues to feel spongy after repeated bleedings or the BRAKE or ANTI-LOCK light stays on, have the vehicle towed to a dealer service department or other qualified shop to be bled with the aid of a scan tool.*

10   Parking brake - cable adjustment, removal and installation

Mechanical parking brake
Cable adjustment

1   Before adjusting the parking brake, make sure that the brake hydraulic system is free of all air (see Section 9) and the parking brake shoes have been adjusted properly.

2   Fully engage and release the parking brake lever five times.

3   Count how many clicks the brake lever travels before it becomes fully engaged. The

10.18 Electronic parking brake controller and cable location

A   *Electronic parking brake controller*
B   *Electronic parking brake cable routing*

11.9 Push the retaining clip tabs inwards and pull out the clevis pin

correct number is seven to eight clicks. If the parking brake lever needs more than this number of clicks before it's fully applied, the cable is stretched. If it applies the brakes in less than this number, the cable is too tight. Adjust the parking brake as follows.

4   Remove the center console cover (see Chapter 11).

5   Back off the locknut, then turn the adjuster nut clockwise to tighten the cable or counterclockwise to loosen it.

6   Pull up on the parking brake lever again and count how many clicks it takes to fully apply the parking brake. Repeat the adjustment procedure if necessary.

7   After the adjustment is made, tighten the locknut against the adjuster nut.

Note: *If the correct adjustment cannot be achieved, it's possible (but rare) the cables may be stretched beyond the point of adjustment, and are in need of replacement.*

8   Install the center console cover (see Chapter 11).

Removal and installation

9   Remove the center console (see Chapter 11).

10   Remove the rear seat cushion (see Chapter 11).

11   Loosen the cable locknut and adjuster nut and remove the right and left cables from the equalizer fastener.

12   Loosen the rear wheel lug nuts, raise the rear of the vehicle and support it securely on jackstands. Remove the rear wheels.

13   Trace the routing of the rear cables and remove all clamps and/or clips attaching the cables to the vehicle body or suspension.

14   Disengage the cable from the rear brake assembly (see Section 12).

15   Detach the cable from the brake backing plate.

16   Installation is the reverse of removal. Make sure that the cables are routed so that they're not kinked and so that nothing interferes with them.

17   Adjust the cables.

Electronic parking brake

18   The electronic parking brake system requires the use of a special factory scanner in order to perform any service on the system. Take your vehicle to the appropriate repair facility that is equipped with the proper equipment. Do not attempt any repairs without the scanner. For location of the electronic parking brake controller and cable routing (see illustration).

19   The system does have an emergency bypass feature that can be performed in the event a failure has occurred.

Emergency release of the electronic parking brake

20   Park the vehicle on a flat and level surface.

21   Place the shift lever in Park on the automatic transmission vehicles, First or reverse for the manual transmission models.

22   Block the wheels to avoid the vehicle moving.

23   Remove the emergency brake release tool from the vehicles tool service bag.

24   Locate the white emergency release cap on the passenger side of the car just in front of the rear tire area. It is underneath the car near the center of the vehicle. Align the tool with the mechanical release port. Remove the white colored cap by turning the tool counter clockwise. Then puncture the protective plastic film covering the release lug. The lug is made onto the end of the armature of the EPB motor (Electronic Parking Brake).

25   Slide the tool into the slot and engage the adjuster.

26   Turn the adjuster clockwise approximately 200 to 250 turns.

27   Replace the parking brake actuator cap.

11   Power brake booster - check, removal and installation

1   The power brake booster unit requires no special maintenance apart from periodic inspection of the vacuum hose and the case.

Warning: *Do not, under any circumstances, try to repair or disassemble the brake booster. There is a very large spring under a great deal of pressure inside the booster. Personal injury can result from attempting to disassemble a brake booster.*

Operating check

2   Depress the brake pedal several times with the engine off and make sure there is no change in the pedal reserve distance (the minimum distance to the floor).

3   Hold the pedal depressed and start the engine. If the pedal should go down further. Then, release the pedal. If the pedal returns to its original position (where it was before you pumped the pedal) the booster is operating normally.

Airtightness check

4   Start the engine and turn it off after one or two minutes. Depress the pedal several times slowly. If the pedal goes down farther the first time but gradually rises after the second or third depression, the booster is airtight.

5   Depress the brake pedal while the engine is running, then stop the engine with the brake pedal depressed. If there is no change in the pedal reserve travel after holding the pedal for 30 seconds, the booster is airtight.

Removal

6   If the booster is defective, replace it with a new or rebuilt unit. The booster cannot be overhauled.

7   Disconnect the vacuum hose from the booster unit.

8   Remove the master cylinder (see Section 7).

9   Working from inside of the vehicle, remove the cotter pin and the pushrod clevis pin, and disconnect the booster pushrod clevis from the brake pedal (see illustration).

11.10 Power brake booster mounting nuts (one hidden in this photo)

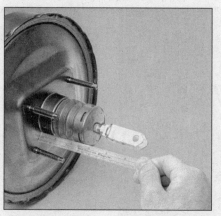

11.11 Measure the distance between the booster and the hole in the clevis

12.3a If a rear disc proves difficult or impossible to remove, pull out the adjuster hole access plug

12.3b Back the adjuster off with a brake adjuster tool or flat tip screwdriver enough to remove the disc

12.4 Wash the parking brake assembly with brake system cleaner before disassembling anything

12.5 The maximum allowable diameter is stamped on the inside of the disc

10   Remove the four booster-to-firewall nuts (see illustration), then remove the booster from the vehicle.

Installation

11   If you're installing a new power brake booster, adjust the pushrod. Measure the length of the booster pushrod from the base of the brake booster to the center of the clevis pin hole (see illustration); compare your measurement to the length listed in this Chapter's Specifications. If the pushrod is out of specification, loosen the locknut and screw the pushrod in or out.

12   Installation is the reverse of removal. Tighten the booster-to-firewall nuts to the torque listed in this Chapter's Specifications.

13   Bleed the brake system (see Section 9).

12   Parking brake shoes - inspection and replacement

Warning: *Parking brake shoes must be replaced on both wheels at the same time - never replace the shoes on only one wheel.*

Also, the dust created by the brake system is harmful to your health. Never blow it out with compressed air and don't inhale any of it. An approved filtering mask should be worn when working on the brakes. Do not, under any circumstances, use petroleum-based solvents to clean brake parts. Use brake system cleaner only!

1   Loosen the rear wheel lug nuts, raise the rear of the vehicle and support it securely on jackstands. Block the front wheels to keep the vehicle from rolling off the stands.

2   Remove the rear wheels. Release the parking brake. On the electronic parking brake models the parking brake must be turned to the service position by way of a scanner.

3   Remove the brake discs (see Section 6). It's not necessary to disconnect the brake hoses from the brake calipers. Support the calipers with wire. It may be difficult or impossible to remove the discs if the parking brake shoes have worn them excessively. On the mechanical parking brake models, if you can't pull off the discs, remove the access hole plug for the parking brake shoe adjuster, then using a brake adjuster tool or a narrow screwdriver, back off the brake shoes by turn-

ing the star wheel on the adjuster (see illustrations). On electronic parking brake models, use the appropriate scanner to set the vehicle in "Parking Brake Removal" mode before removing the discs or use the parking release procedure described in Section 10.

4   Wash the parking brake assemblies with brake system cleaner before beginning work (see illustration). Do not use compressed air to blow off the brake assembly.

5   Wash the brake discs and check the parking brake drums for score marks, deep grooves, hard spots (which will appear as small discolored areas) and cracks. If the parking brake drums are worn, scored or out-of-round, they can be resurfaced. Resurfacing will eliminate the possibility of out-of-round drums. If the drums are worn so much that they can't be resurfaced without exceeding the maximum allowable diameter stamped into the drum portion of the disc (see illustration) install new ones. At the very least, if you elect not to have them resurfaced, remove the glazing from the surface with sandpaper or emery cloth using a swirling motion. This is also a good time to inspect the discs themselves for wear (see Section 6).

12.6a Unhook the leading shoe return spring from the anchor pin plate

12.6b Unhook the trailing shoe return spring from the anchor pin plate

12.6c Unhook and remove the lower return spring from the shoes

12.6d Remove the adjuster, noting which direction it is installed

12.6e Unhook the strut spring . . .

12.6f . . . and remove the strut

12.6g Push in on the hold-down spring and twist the pin 90-degrees to release it (repeat on the other shoe). Remove the shoes from the backing plate

12.6h Remove the C-clip and washer and unhook the parking brake lever from the trailing shoe

12.6i Clean off the backing plate, then lubricate the brake shoe contact areas with high-temperature grease

6   To replace the parking brake shoes, follow the accompanying photos, beginning with illustration 12.6a. Stay in order and read the caption under each illustration. Work on only one parking brake assembly at a time. Do not begin disassembling the second parking brake assembly until you have reassembled the first. That way, you will have one assembled parking brake to use as a reference, if necessary.

7   Repeat this procedure for the other parking brake assembly.
8   Install the brake discs (see Section 6). To adjust the parking brake shoes, turn the adjuster until the shoes rub on the drum, then back off the adjuster slightly just until the shoes no longer contact the drum. On electronic emergency brake models follow the procedures and steps provided with the scanner.

9   Install the caliper support brackets, the brake pads and the calipers (see Sections 4 and 5).
10   Install the rear wheels and lug nuts, lower the vehicle and tighten the lug nuts to the torque listed in the Chapter 1 Specifications. Adjust the parking brake (see Section 10). Test the brakes for proper operation before driving the vehicle in traffic.

12.6j Connect the parking brake lever to the new shoe and install the washer . . .

12.6k . . . and C-clip. Squeeze the ends of the clip together to secure it to the pin

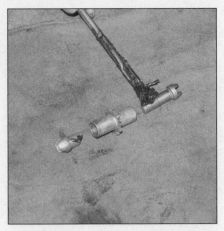

12.6l Clean the adjuster and lubricate the threads and moving components with high-temperature brake grease

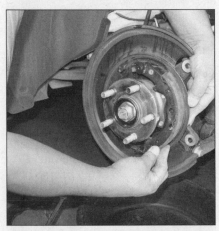

12.6m Install the trailing shoe on the backing plate and secure it with the pin and hold-down spring

12.6n Install the adjuster (with the threaded part facing the rear) and connect the lower return spring to the bottom of each shoe . . .

12.6o . . . then install the leading shoe to the backing plate and secure it with the pin and hold-down spring

12.6p Install the strut between the shoes

12.6q Connect the strut spring to the trailing shoe and strut . . .

12.6r . . . then install the upper return springs to the shoes and anchor pin plate

13.3 Brake light switch

A   Electrical connection   B   Brake light switch lock nut

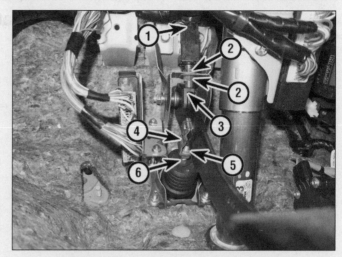

14.2 Brake pedal adjustment details (typical shown):

1   Brake light switch and connector
2   Brake light switch mounting/adjusting nuts
3   Brake pedal stop
4   Clevis
5   Clevis locknut
6   Power brake booster pushrod

13   Brake light switch - replacement

1   Disconnect the cable from the negative battery terminal (see Chapter 5).
2   Remove the driver's side knee bolster trim panel (see Chapter 11).
3   Disconnect the electrical connector from the brake light switch (see illustration), located near the top of the brake pedal.
4   Remove the nut closest to the brake pedal stop, then remove the switch.
5   To install the new switch, rotate it until the plunger on the switch is completely compressed, and the threaded end of the switch is just against the brake pedal stop.
6   Check and adjust the brake pedal height and freeplay (see Section 14).

7   Tighten the switch mounting nuts securely.
8   Connect the brake light switch electrical connector, reconnect the battery, then check the rear brake lights for proper operation.

14   Brake pedal height and freeplay - adjustment

1   Pedal free play is the distance the brake pedal travels from a fully up position to the point that it starts to push on the brake booster. To check the free play lift up on the brake pedal and measure the distance when applying a downward pressure of no more than 2 ft. lbs. of force.
2   Disconnect the electrical connector from

the brake light switch. Loosen the switch mounting nuts and turn the brake light switch until the pedal height listed in this Chapter's Specifications is obtained (see illustration).
3   Tighten the mounting nuts securely, connect the electrical connector and check the brake lights for proper operation. They should come on when the brake pedal is depressed, and go out when it is released.
4   To adjust pedal freeplay (the distance the pedal travels before it begins to move the power brake pushrod), loosen the locknut on the power brake pushrod (at the clevis that attaches the pushrod to the brake pedal) and turn the pushrod (pliers may be necessary) until the proper amount of freeplay is obtained. Tighten the locknut securely.

Notes

Chapter 10
Suspension and steering systems

Contents

Specifications

Torque specifications

Note: *One foot-pound (ft-lb) of torque is equivalent to 12 inch-pounds (in-lbs) of torque. Torque values below approximately 15 foot-pounds are expressed in inch-pounds, because most foot-pound torque wrenches are not accurate at these smaller values.*

Front suspension

	Ft-lbs	Nm
Balljoint		
Balljoint-to-control arm nut	37	50
Steering knuckle-to-balljoint pinch bolt	29	39
Front hub and bearing assembly-to-knuckle bolts	48	65
Driveaxle/hub nut	See Chapter 8	
Control arm		
Legacy		
Front bushing bolt/nut*	70	95
Rear bushing stud nut	103	140
Forester		
Front bushing bolt/nut*	70	95
Rear bushing bolt/nut	81	110
Rear bushing support plate bolts*	44	60
Stabilizer bar		
Bracket bolts	18	25
Link nuts	44	60
Strut/coil spring assembly		
Upper mounting nuts	15	20
Strut-to-knuckle bolts/nuts*	114	155
Damper rod-to-mount nut*	41	55
Brake hose bracket to strut	24	33
Front crossmember	44	60

The manufacturer states that these self-locking nuts must be replaced whenever removed.

Rear suspension

Rear hub and bearing assembly-to-knuckle bolts	48	65
Driveaxle hub nut*	See Chapter 8	
Shock absorber/coil spring		
Upper mounting nuts*	22	30
Lower mounting bolt/nut*		
Legacy	88	120
Forester		
2011 and earlier models	88	120
2012 through 2014 models	59	80
2015 and later models	63	85
Damper rod-to-mount nut*	18	25
Rear suspension links		
Legacy		
Front lateral link		
Link to subframe	88	120
Link to knuckle	44	60
Rear lateral link (both ends)	59	80
Trailing arm		
Arm to subframe	88	120
Arm to knuckle	59	80
Stabilizer bar		
Link nuts	24	33
Bracket bolts	28	38
Upper control arm		
Arm to subframe	59	80
Arm to knuckle	59	80
Forester		
Front lateral link		
Link to subframe	74	100
Link to knuckle	44	60
Rear lateral link (both ends)	59	80
Trailing arm		
Arm subframe	66	90
Arm to knuckle	66	90
Stabilizer bar		
Bracket bolts	22	30
Link nuts	28	38
Upper control arm		
Arm to subframe	66	90
Arm to knuckle	59	80

Steering

Power steering pump		
Banjo fitting at the pump	30	40
Pump-to-bracket mounting bolts	12	16
Bracket-to-engine mounting bolts		
Step 1	12	16
Step 2	26	36
Tie-rod end-to-steering knuckle nut (castle nuts)	20	27
Tie-rod locking nut	63	85
Steering gear mounting bolts	44	60
Front crossmember support plate	44	60
Steering wheel nut	28	39

The manufacturer states that these self-locking nuts must be replaced whenever removed.

1.1 Front suspension and steering components

1	Strut/coil spring assembly	4	Balljoint	7	Stabilizer bar
2	Tie-rod end	5	Control arm	8	Stabilizer bar bracket
3	Steering knuckle	6	Stabilizer bar link		

1.2 Rear suspension components

1	Stabilizer bar	4	Rear knuckle	7	Upper control arm
2	Rear lateral link	5	Trailing link	8	Subframe
3	Shock absorber/coil spring assembly	6	Front lateral link		

1   General information

Suspension

1   The front suspension is fully independent (see illustrations). It consists of strut/coil spring assemblies, control arms, steering knuckles and a stabilizer bar. The upper end of each strut is attached to the body and the lower end is bolted to the steering knuckle. The lower end of the knuckle is attached to the control arm by a balljoint. The inner end of the control arm is bolted to a crossmember. The stabilizer bar is attached to the crossmember by a pair of clamps and is connected to the control arms by links.

2   The rear suspension is also fully independent (see illustration). It consists of shock absorber/coil spring assemblies, trailing arms, lateral suspension links (control arms), knuckles and a stabilizer bar. The upper end of each shock absorber is attached to the body and the lower end is bolted to the rear lateral link. The knuckle is positioned by the links and the trailing arm. The inner ends of the links are bolted to the subframe; the outer ends of the links are bolted to the knuckle. The front ends of the trailing arms are bolted to the unibody structure; the rear ends of the trailing arms are bolted to the knuckles. The stabilizer bar is attached to the subframe by a pair of clamps and is connected to the control arms by links.

Steering

3   All models use a power-assisted rack-and-pinion type steering gear. The steering gear is connected to the steering knuckles by a pair of tie-rods. 2014 and earlier Legacy models/2013 and earlier Forester models use hydraulic power steering, while 2015 and later Legacy models/2014 and later Forester models use electric power steering.

Precautions

4   Frequently, when working on the suspension or steering system components, you may come across fasteners which seem impossible to loosen. These fasteners on the underside of the vehicle are continually subjected to water, road grime, mud, etc., and can become rusted or frozen, making them extremely difficult to remove. In order to unscrew these stubborn fasteners without damaging them (or other components), be sure to use lots of penetrating oil and allow it to soak in for a while. Using a wire brush to clean exposed threads will also ease removal of the nut or bolt and prevent damage to the threads. Sometimes a sharp blow with a hammer and punch will break the bond between a nut and bolt threads, but care must be taken to prevent the punch from slipping off the fastener and ruining the threads. Heating the stuck fastener and surrounding area with a torch sometimes helps too, but isn't recommended because of the obvious dangers associated with fire. Long breaker bars and extension, or cheater, pipes will increase leverage, but never use an extension pipe on a ratchet - the ratcheting mechanism could be damaged. Sometimes tightening the nut or bolt first will help to break it loose. Fasteners that require drastic measures to remove should always be replaced with new ones.

5   Since most of the procedures dealt with in this Chapter involve jacking up the vehicle and working underneath it, a good pair of jackstands will be needed. A hydraulic floor jack is the preferred type of jack to lift the vehicle, and it can also be used to support certain components during various operations.

Caution: *Never, under any circumstances, rely on a jack to support the vehicle while working on it. Whenever any of the suspension or steering fasteners are loosened or removed they must be inspected and, if necessary, replaced with new ones of the same part number or of original equipment quality and design. Torque specifications must be followed for proper reassembly and component retention. Never attempt to heat or straighten any suspension or steering components. Instead, replace any bent or damaged part with a new one.*

2   Strut/coil spring assembly (front) - removal and installation

Warning: *Struts and/or coil springs must be replaced in pairs - never replace just one of them.*

Removal

1   Loosen the front wheel lug nuts, block the rear wheels, raise the front of the vehicle and support it securely on jackstands. Remove the front wheels.

2   Detach the brake hose from its bracket on the strut (see illustration).

3   Remove ABS sensor from the steering knuckle, if equipped (see illustration).

4   Mark the relationship of the strut bolts to the strut flange, and the strut to the knuckle, then remove the strut-to-knuckle nuts and bolts (see illustrations).

Note: *If a new strut is being installed, it is still important to mark the bolt position; there is an indexing mark on the strut flange, and the proper alignment mark on the bolt must line up with it when installed to preserve the camber setting.*

2.2 These bolts can rust in place and can be stubborn to remove. A little penetrating oil can help

2.3 Squeeze the protruding hooks together then push them through the bracket

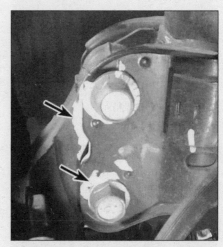

2.4 Mark the relationship of the strut-to-knuckle bolts

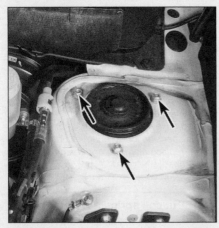

2.5 Strut upper mounting nuts; mark one stud and the strut tower to aid installation

3.3 Install the spring compressor in accordance with the tool manufacturer's instructions and compress the spring until all pressure is relieved from the upper spring seat

3.4 Remove the damper shaft nut

3.5 Remove the upper mount from the damper shaft

3.6 Remove the upper spring seat from the damper shaft

5   In the engine compartment, remove the strut-to-strut tower mounting nuts (see illustration). Support the strut with one hand (or have an assistant hold it) while doing this.

6   Remove the strut assembly. If you're planning to replace either the strut or the coil spring, refer to Section 3.

Installation

Note: *The manufacturer recommends using new self-locking strut upper mounting nuts when installing the strut assembly to the strut tower.*

7   Place the strut assembly in position and install, but don't tighten, the upper mounting nuts.

8   Insert the steering knuckle into the strut flange. Install the strut-to-steering knuckle bolts, aligning the marks on the upper bolt with the mark on the strut flange. Tighten the bolts and nuts to the torque listed in this Chapter's Specifications.

9   Connect the ABS sensor harness to the strut.

10   Reattach the brake hose bracket to the strut.

11   Install the wheels and lug nuts.

12   Lower the vehicle and tighten the lug nuts to the torque listed in the Chapter 1 Specifications. Tighten the strut upper mounting nuts to the torque listed in this Chapter's Specifications.

13   Have the front end alignment checked and, if necessary, adjusted.

---

3   Strut/coil spring - replacement

Warning: *Struts and/or coil springs must be replaced in pairs - never replace just one of them.*

Note: *You'll need a spring compressor for this procedure. Spring compressors are available on a daily rental basis at most auto parts stores or equipment yards.*

1   If the struts or coil springs exhibit the telltale signs of wear (leaking fluid, loss of damping capability, chipped, sagging or cracked coil springs), explore all options before beginning any work. The strut/shock absorber assemblies are not serviceable and must be replaced if a problem develops. However, strut assemblies complete with springs may be available on an exchange basis, which eliminates much time and work. Whichever route you choose to take, check on the cost and availability of parts before disassembling your vehicle.

Warning: *Disassembling a strut is potentially dangerous and utmost attention must be directed to the job, or serious injury may result. Use only a high quality spring compressor and carefully follow the manufacturer's instructions furnished with the tool. After removing the coil spring from the strut assembly, set it aside in a safe, isolated area.*

Disassembly

2   Remove the strut and spring assembly (see Section 2).

3   Mount the strut assembly in a vise. Line the vise jaws with wood or rags to prevent damage to the unit and don't tighten the vise excessively. Following the tool manufacturer's instructions, install the spring compressor (which can be obtained at most auto parts stores or equipment yards on a daily rental basis) on the spring and compress it sufficiently to relieve all pressure from the upper spring seat (see illustration). This can be verified by wiggling the spring.

4   Loosen the damper shaft nut with a socket wrench (see illustration).

5   Remove the nut and lift off the upper strut mount (see illustration). Remove the spacer. Inspect the bearing in the strut mount for smooth operation. If it doesn't turn smoothly, replace the strut mount. Check the rubber portion of the strut mount for cracking and general deterioration. If there is any separation of the rubber, replace it.

6   Remove the upper spring seat (see illustration), the rubber seat and the dust cover. Inspect the upper seat, the rubber seat and the dust cover for cracking and hardness. Replace all damaged parts.

7   Carefully lift the compressed spring from the assembly (see illustration) and set it in a safe place.
Warning: *Never place your head near the end of the spring!*
8   Slide the rubber bumper off the damper shaft. Inspect it for cracking and hardness. If it's worn or damaged, replace it.

Reassembly

Note: *The manufacturer recommends using a new self-locking nut when assembling the strut.*
9   Fully compress and retract the damper rod at least four times to purge air that may be in the strut.
10   Extend the damper rod to its full length and install the rubber bumper.
11   Carefully place the coil spring onto the lower insulator, with the end of the spring resting in the lowest part of the insulator (see illustration).
12   Install the dust cover, the rubber seat and the upper spring seat.
13   Install the spacer and the upper strut mount. Install a new self-locking nut and tighten it to the torque listed in this Chapter's Specifications.
14   Remove the spring compressor.
15   Install the strut/coil spring assembly (see Section 2).

4   Stabilizer bar, bushings and links (front) - removal and installation

Note: *The manufacturer recommends using new self-locking mounting nuts when installing the stabilizer bar links.*
1   Loosen the wheel lug nuts. Block the rear wheels, raise the front of the vehicle and place it securely on jackstands. Remove the front wheels.
2   Remove the under-vehicle splash shield,

then remove the stabilizer bar link nuts (see illustration).
Note: *Insert an Allen wrench in the end of the link's ballstud to hold it while removing the link nut.*
3   Remove the stabilizer bar bushing clamps.
4   Disconnect the tie-rod end from the right-side steering knuckle (see Section 15).
5   Rotate the ends of the stabilizer bar towards the front of the vehicle and maneuver it out from the right side of the vehicle.
6   Remove the bushings from the stabilizer and inspect them for cracks or deterioration. Inspect the stabilizer bar for cracks in the curved portions and deformation. Replace any parts, as necessary.
7   Installation is the reverse of removal. Tighten the fasteners to the torque listed in this Chapter's Specifications.
8   Install the wheels and lug nuts and lower the vehicle.
9   Tighten the lug nuts to the torque listed in the Chapter 1 Specifications.

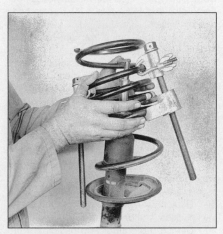

3.7 Remove the compressed spring assembly; keep the ends of the spring pointed away from your body

5   Control arm and subframe (front) - removal and installation

Note: *The manufacturer recommends using new self-locking mounting nuts when installing the control arm.*
1   Loosen the front wheel lug nuts, block the rear wheels, raise the front of the vehicle and support it securely on jackstands. Remove the front wheel.
2   Remove the under-vehicle splash shield.

Control arm

3   Disconnect the stabilizer bar from the control arm (see Section 4).
4   Detach the balljoint from the steering knuckle (see Section 6).
5   Remove the front and rear bushing bolts (see illustration). If needed, pry the bushing end of the control arm off to remove.
6   Inspect the control arm bushings for cracks or deterioration. Inspect the control arm itself for cracks and deformations.

3.11 When installing the spring, make sure the end fits into the recessed portion of the lower seat

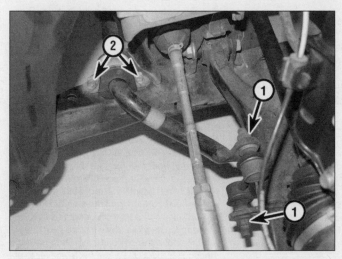

4.2 Stabilizer bar details

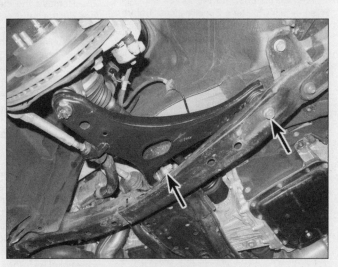

5.5 Control arm bushing fasteners

1   Link nuts   2   Bushing bracket bolts

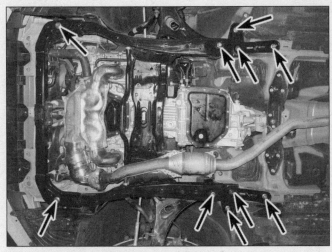

5.22 Subframe mounting bolt locations

6.8 Separate the balljoint from the control arm with a puller or balljoint separator

6.9 Use a screwdriver (1) to pry open the slot in the steering knuckle to facilitate removal of the balljoint from the knuckle

Replace any damaged parts.

7   Installation is the reverse of removal. Tighten all fasteners to the torque settings listed in this Chapter's Specifications. Before tightening the control arm pivot bolt and bushing bolt, raise the outer end of the control arm with a floor jack to simulate normal ride height, then tighten the fasteners to the torque listed in this Chapter's Specifications.

8   Install the wheel and lug nuts, then lower the vehicle.

9   Tighten the wheel lug nuts to the torque listed in the Chapter 1 Specifications.

Subframe

Note: *The manufacturer recommends using new bolts when installing the subframe.*

10   Disconnect the cable from the negative terminal of the battery (see Chapter 5).

11   Remove the radiator cover (see Chapter 3).

12   On models with hydraulic power steering, remove the banjo bolt and detach the power steering hose from the power steering pump.

13   Remove the air intake duct and the throt-

tle body (see Chapter 4).

Note: *Don't disconnect the coolant hoses from the throttle body; just detach the throttle body and set it aside.*

14   Support the engine from above with an engine support fixture.

15   Remove the under-vehicle splash shield.

16   Detach the steering intermediate shaft U-joint from the steering gear (see Section 17).

Warning: *Don't allow the steering wheel to turn after the shaft has been disconnected - the airbag clockspring could become damaged.*

17   Remove the front and center exhaust pipes and the heat shields.

18   Remove the through-bolt from the front engine mount (see Chapter 2A). Unbolt the transaxle mounts from the subframe.

19   Detach the tie-rod ends from the steering knuckles (see Section 15).

20   Detach the control arm balljoints from the steering knuckles (see Section 6).

21   Support the subframe with two floor jacks (one on each side).

22   Remove the subframe mounting bolts (see illustration).

23   Lower the subframe from the chassis.

24   Installation if the reverse of removal. Tighten the mounting bolts, from front to rear, to the torque listed in this Chapter's Specifications.

6   Balljoints - check and replacement

Check

1   Inspect the control arm balljoints for looseness anytime either of them is separated from the control arm. See if you can turn the ballstud in its socket with your fingers. If the balljoint is loose, or if the ballstud can be turned, replace the balljoint. You can also check the balljoints with the suspension assembled as follows.

2   Raise the front of the vehicle and support it securely on jackstands.

3   Wipe each balljoint clean and inspect the seal for cuts and tears. If the seal is damaged it can be replaced, but it's a good idea to go ahead and replace the balljoint.

4   Place a large prybar under the balljoint and resting on the wheel, then try to pry the balljoint up while feeling for movement between the balljoint and steering knuckle. Now, pry between the control arm and the steering knuckle and try to pry down while feeling for movement between the balljoint and steering knuckle. If any movement is evident in either check, the balljoint is worn and should be replaced.

5   Have an assistant grasp the tire at the top and bottom and move the top of the tire in-and-out. Check for looseness in the balljoint stud castellated nut. If any looseness is felt, suspect a worn balljoint stud or a widened hole in the control arm. If the latter problem exists, the control arm should be replaced as well as the balljoint.

Replacement

6   Loosen the front wheel lug nuts. Block the rear wheels, raise the front of the vehicle and support it securely on jackstands. Remove the front wheel.

7   Detach the stabilizer bar link from the control arm (see Section 9). Remove the cotter pin and loosen, but don't remove, the castle nut on the ballstud.

8   Separate the control arm from the balljoint with a two-jaw puller, balljoint separator or picklefork tool (see illustration).

Note: *The use of a picklefork tool will most likely damage the balljoint boot, but if the balljoint is being replaced, it doesn't matter. For all other operations requiring the control arm to be separated from the steering knuckle, the balljoint can easily be detached from the steering knuckle (as shown in the next Step).*

9   Remove the balljoint pinch bolt from the steering knuckle. Use a large screwdriver to pry open the slot in the steering knuckle, then pull the balljoint out of the knuckle (see illustration).

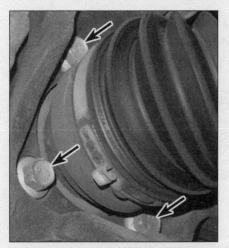

7.4 Hub and bearing assembly-to-steering knuckle bolts (three of four shown)

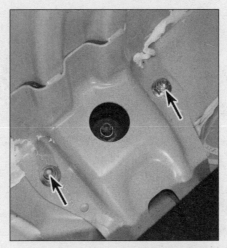

8.1 The rear upper shock mounting fasteners are located in the trunk/luggage compartment (Legacy model shown)

8.5 Shock-to-rear lateral link mounting fasteners

10 Install the balljoint into the knuckle and tighten the pinch bolt to the torque listed in this Chapter's Specifications.

11 Reattach the control arm to the balljoint (steering knuckle) and tighten the castle nut to the torque listed in this Chapter's Specifications. Install a new cotter pin. Install the wheels and lower the vehicle. Tighten the wheel lug nuts to the torque listed in the Chapter 1 Specifications.

Note: *If necessary, tighten the castle nut an additional amount (up to 60 degrees) to allow insertion of the cotter pin. Never loosen the nut to allow cotter pin insertion.*

7 Steering knuckle/hub assembly - removal, bearing replacement and installation

Warning: *Dust created by the brake system is harmful to your health. Never blow it out with compressed air and don't inhale any of it. Do not, under any circumstances, use petroleum-based solvents to clean brake parts. Use brake system cleaner only.*

Note: *The manufacturer recommends using new self-locking mounting nuts when installing the strut assembly to the steering knuckle.*

Note: *The hub and bearing unit can be replaced without removing the steering knuckle.*

1 Loosen the front wheel lug nuts, block the rear wheels, raise the front of the vehicle and support it securely on jackstands. Remove the front wheel.

2 Unstake and loosen the driveaxle/hub nut (see Chapter 8).

3 Remove the brake caliper, the caliper support bracket and the brake disc. On models with ABS, remove the front wheel speed sensor and carefully secure it aside (see Chapter 9).

Hub and bearing unit

4 Remove the four bolts from the back side of the steering knuckle and detach the hub and bearing unit from the knuckle (see illustration). If the driveaxle splines stick in the hub, tap it out with a soft-faced hammer or use a puller to push it out of the hub.

Caution: *Be careful not to overextend the inner CV joint.*

5 Installation is the reverse of the removal procedure. Tighten the hub-to-knuckle bolts to the torque listed in this Chapter's Specifications.

6 Tighten the driveaxle/hub nut to the torque listed in the Chapter 8 Specifications.

Steering knuckle/hub assembly

7 Disconnect the tie-rod end from the steering knuckle (see Section 15).

8 Loosen, but do not remove, the strut-to-steering knuckle nuts (see Section 2).

Note: *Mark the relationship of the upper bolt to the strut flange to preserve the camber angle on reassembly.*

9 Separate the control arm from the steering knuckle (see Section 5).

10 Remove the strut-to-knuckle nuts and bolts.

11 Remove the driveaxle/hub nut and pull the steering knuckle off the outer CV joint. If the hub sticks to the CV joint splines, push the shaft out of the hub with a two-jaw puller (see Chapter 8).

Caution: *Be careful not to overextend the inner CV joint.*

12 Unbolt the hub assembly from the steering knuckle (see illustration 7.4).

13 While the suspension is disassembled, inspect and, if necessary, replace any component that is not serviceable.

14 Installation is the reverse of removal. Align the mark on the upper strut-to-knuckle

bolt with the mark on the strut flange, and tighten all fasteners to the torque listed in this Chapter's Specifications.

15 Tighten the driveaxle/hub nut to the torque listed in the Chapter 8 Specifications.

16 Install the wheel and lug nuts, then lower the vehicle.

17 Tighten the lug nuts to the torque listed in the Chapter 1 Specifications.

18 Have the front end alignment checked and, if necessary, adjusted.

8 Shock absorber/coil spring assembly (rear) - removal and installation

Note: *The manufacturer recommends using new self-locking mounting nuts when installing the shock assembly.*

1 On Legacy models, move the carpet in the trunk to access the shock upper mounting nuts (see illustration). On Forester models, remove the luggage compartment floor mat, cover, cargo bin and access cover to access the shock upper mounting nuts.

2 Loosen the rear wheel lug nuts, block the front wheels, raise the rear of the vehicle and support it securely on jackstands. Remove the rear wheels.

3 Place a floor jack under the rear knuckle and raise it till it just contacts the knuckle.

4 Disconnect the rear stabilizer link from the lower arm (see Section 9).

5 Remove the shock-to-rear lateral link fasteners (see illustration). If the bolt is difficult to remove, raise the knuckle slightly with the jack until the bolt comes out easily.

6 Remove the rear lateral link-to-knuckle through-bolt and nut, then separate the link from the strut.

7 Have an assistant support the shock, then remove the shock upper mounting nuts.

9.2 Rear stabilizer bar link nuts (A) and bracket bolts (B)

10.2 Trailing arm fasteners

11.2 Scribe or paint alignment marks on the adjuster bolt cam and subframe

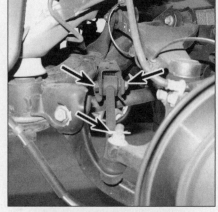

11.4 Front lateral link fasteners

8   If you need to disassemble the shock/coil spring assembly to replace either the shock or the coil spring, refer to Section 3.

9   Installation is the reverse of removal. Use the jack to raise the rear suspension to simulate normal ride height, then tighten all fasteners to the torque listed in this Chapter's Specifications.

10   If you need to disassemble the shock/coil spring assembly to replace either the shock or the coil spring, refer to Section 3.

11   Install the wheels and lug nuts, then lower the vehicle.

12   Tighten the wheel lug nuts to the torque listed in the Chapter 1 Specifications.

9   Stabilizer bar, bushings and links (rear) - removal and installation

Note: *The manufacturer recommends using new self-locking nuts when installing the stabilizer bar links.*

1   Raise the rear of the vehicle and support it securely on jackstands. Block the front wheels to prevent the vehicle from rolling.

2   Detach the stabilizer bar links from the bar (see illustration).
Note: *If the ballstud turns while loosening the nut, hold it with an Allen wrench.*

3   Unbolt the bushing brackets from each side of the stabilizer bar, then remove the bar.

4   Pull the bushings off the bar and inspect them for cracks or other damage. If the bushings are damaged, replace them. Check the stabilizer bar links for loose balljoints and replace them as necessary.

5   Installation is the reverse of removal. Tighten all fasteners to the torque listed in this Chapter's Specifications.

10   Trailing arm - removal and installation

Note: *The manufacturer recommends using new self-locking mounting nuts when installing the trailing arm.*

1   Loosen the rear wheel lug nuts, block the front wheels, raise the rear of the vehicle and support it securely on jackstands. Remove the rear wheel.

2   Remove the nut and pivot bolt that attach the forward end of the trailing arm to the trailing arm bracket (see illustration).

3   Remove the nut and bolt that attach the trailing arm to the rear knuckle.

4   Remove the trailing arm.

5   Inspect the trailing arm bushings. If they're cracked, hardened or otherwise worn, have them pressed out and new ones pressed in at an automotive machine shop or replaced entirely.

6   Installation is the reverse of removal. After the bolts and nuts have been installed, raise the rear knuckle with a floor jack to simulate normal ride height, then tighten the trailing arm bolts to the torque listed in this Chapter's Specifications.

11   Suspension links and subframe (rear) - removal and installation

1   Loosen the rear wheel lug nuts, block the front wheels, raise the rear of the vehicle and support it securely on jackstands. Remove the rear wheel.

Suspension links
Removal
Front lateral link

2   To ensure that the correct toe-in is maintained, scribe or paint alignment marks on the adjuster bolt washer and subframe before removing the bolt (see illustration).

3   Remove the trailing arm (see Section 10).

4   Remove the cotter pin from the ballstud on the outer end of the link, then remove the fasteners that attach the link to the rear knuckle and the subframe (see illustration). Use a balljoint separator to detach the outer end of the link from the knuckle.

5   Inspect the link bushings. If they're cracked, dried out, or otherwise worn, have them pressed out and new ones pressed in at an automotive machine shop.

11.6 Rear lateral link fasteners

11.28 Locations of the subframe mounting fasteners

Rear lateral link

6   Remove the fasteners that attach the shock absorber and stabilizer bar link to the rear lateral link, then remove the fasteners that connect the link to the rear knuckle and the subframe (see illustration).

7   Inspect the rear lateral link bushings. If they're cracked, dried out, or otherwise worn, have them pressed out and new ones pressed in at an automotive machine shop or replace the lateral link entirely.

Upper control arm

8   Remove the rear subframe.

9   Remove the pinch bolt nut and bolt, then separate the upper arm from the rear knuckle.

10   Remove the fasteners that attach the upper arm to the subframe.

11   Inspect the link bushings. If they're cracked, dried out, or otherwise worn, have them pressed out and new ones pressed in at an automotive machine shop.

Installation

12   Installation is the reverse of removal. If the front lateral link was removed, align the matchmarks on the inner link fastener and the crossmember, and be sure to use a new nut on the outer ballstud. After all fasteners have been installed, raise the rear knuckle with a floor jack to simulate normal ride height, then tighten the link fasteners to the torque listed in this Chapter's Specifications. Install the rear wheel and lower the vehicle. Tighten the wheel lug nuts to the torque listed in the Chapter 1 Specifications.

13   Have the rear wheel alignment checked and, if necessary, adjusted.

Subframe

14   Disconnect the negative battery terminal (see Chapter 1).

15   Loosen the rear wheel lug nuts, raise the rear of the vehicle and support it securely on jackstands. Remove the wheels.

16   Remove the driveshaft (see Chapter 8).

17   Support the front and rear exhaust pipe, then unbolt the rear exhaust pipe and muffler.

18   Remove rear brake calipers (see Chapter 9). Don't disconnect the brake hoses, but support the calipers with lengths of wire - don't let them hang by the hoses.

19   Remove the wheel speed sensors from the rear knuckles (see Chapter 9).

20   Remove the brake hose bracket fasteners and separate the hoses from the rear knuckles.

21   Detach the parking brake cables from the parking brake shoe levers, and also unbolt the cable brackets and detach the cables from the backing plates.

22   Disconnect the electrical connectors from the wheel speed sensors (see Chapter 9).

23   Remove the shock absorber lower mounting bolts.

24   Detach any wiring harnesses from the subframe.

25   If equipped, detach the headlight leveling sensor from the rear lateral link.

26   Remove the fuel tank protectors.

27   Remove the subframe-to-unibody stays.

28   Support the subframe with two floor jacks, then remove the subframe mounting bolts (see illustration).

29   Carefully lower the subframe.

Caution: *It's a good idea to work with an assistant for this step.*

30   Installation if the reverse of removal. Tighten the mounting bolts to the torque listed in this Chapter's Specifications.

12   Hub and bearing assembly (rear) - replacement

1   Loosen the rear wheel lug nuts, block the front wheels, raise the rear of the vehicle and support it securely on jackstands. Remove the rear wheels.

2   Remove the rear driveaxle/hub nut (see Chapter 8).

3   Remove the brake disc (see Chapter 9).

4   Remove the hub mounting bolts from the back of the knuckle (see illustration). Suspend the backing plate safely aside.

5   Push the driveaxle through the hub splines as the hub and bearing assembly is removed. If the driveaxle sticks in the hub, you'll have to push it out with a puller (see Chapter 8).

Caution: *Be careful not to overextend the inner CV joint. Once the hub has been removed, support the outer end of the driveaxle with a length of wire or rope.*

6   Installation is the reverse of removal, noting the following:

a) *Tighten the hub mounting bolts to the torque listed in this Chapter's Specifications.*

b) *Tighten the brake caliper mounting bracket bolts, caliper mounting bolts and the wheel speed sensor bolt to the torque listed in the Chapter 9 Specifications.*

c) *Tighten the driveaxle/hub nut to the torque listed in the Chapter 8 Specifications.*

d) *Tighten the wheel lug nuts to the torque listed in the Chapter 1 Specifications.*

12.4 Rear hub and bearing assembly mounting bolts

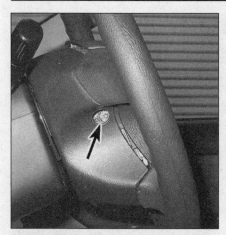

14.2 On 2011 and earlier Legacy models and 2013 and earlier Forester models, the airbag module is retained by two Torx screws

14.3a Pry the airbag retaining springs away from the pins on the back of the airbag module to release them (2012 and later Legacy models and 2014 and later Forester models)

e) *Tighten the wheel lug nuts to the torque listed in the Chapter 1 Specifications.*

14   Steering wheel, driver's airbag module and clockspring - removal and installation

Warning: *These vehicles are equipped with a Supplemental Restraint System (SRS), more commonly known as airbags. Always disable the airbag system before working in the vicinity of any airbag system component to avoid the possibility of accidental deployment of the airbag(s), which could cause personal injury (see Chapter 12).*
Warning: *Do not use a memory saving device to preserve the PCM or radio memory when working on or near airbag system components.*

Removal

1   Park the vehicle with the wheels pointing straight ahead. Disconnect the cable from the negative terminal of the battery (see Chapter 5). Disable the airbag system (see Chapter 12).
2   On 2011 and earlier Legacy models and 2013 and earlier Forester models, use a T30 Torx bit to remove the airbag retaining screws from the sides of the steering wheel (see illustration).
3   On 2012 and later Legacy models and 2014 and later Forester models, use a screwdriver or Allen wrench inserted into the holes in the steering wheel to pry the airbag retaining springs away from the airbag retaining pins (see illustrations).
4   Carefully lift the airbag module away from the steering wheel and disconnect the electrical connectors (see illustration).
Note: *The small yellow safety clips must be UP when installing the airbag. Push the safety clips DOWN after the connector has seated into place.*

13   Knuckle/hub assembly (rear) - removal and installation

1   Loosen the rear driveaxle/hub nut (see Chapter 8).
2   Loosen the rear wheel lug nuts, block the front wheels, raise the rear of the vehicle and support it securely on jackstands. Remove the rear wheel.
3   Remove the brake disc and the parking brake assembly (see Chapter 9).
4   Remove the rear wheel speed sensor (see Chapter 9).
5   Remove the hub and wheel bearing assembly (see Section 12).
6   Support the rear knuckle with a floor jack, then disconnect the trailing arm (see Section 10) and suspension links from the knuckle (see Section 11).
7   Remove the knuckle and inspect the

bushing for wear. If bushing replacement is necessary, have a qualified automotive shop perform the work.

All models
8   Installation is the reverse of removal, noting the following:
a) *Raise the rear knuckle with a floor jack to simulate normal ride height, then tighten the various link, support and trailing arm fasteners to the torque listed in this Chapter's Specifications.*
b) *Tighten the brake component fasteners to the torque listed in the Chapter 9 Specifications.*
c) *Tighten the driveaxle/hub nut to the torque listed in the Chapter 8 Specifications.*
d) *On vehicles equipped with drum brakes, bleed the brake system (see Chapter 9).*

14.3b Here's what one of the airbag module retaining springs looks like. There is one on each spoke of the steering wheel

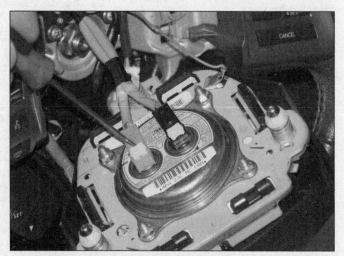

14.4 Pry up the lock tabs and disconnect the airbag module electrical connectors

5   Remove the airbag module and store it in a safe location.

Warning: *Carry the airbag module with the trim side facing away from you, and set the airbag module down with the trim side facing up. Don't place anything on top of the airbag module.*

6   Loosen the steering wheel retaining nut until it meets the end of the steering shaft; don't remove the nut.

7   Release the steering wheel from the steering shaft using a steering wheel puller (see illustrations). The puller screw must be in contact with the steering shaft. Once the steering wheel is released, remove the puller and the retaining nut, then mark the relationship of the steering wheel hub to the steering shaft. The index mark will help ensure that the steering wheel is installed in its original position on the steering shaft.

Caution: *Don't thread the bolts of the puller into the steering wheel more than five turns, as they could contact the airbag clockspring and damage it.*

8   Disconnect any remaining electrical connectors and lift the steering wheel off the shaft, feeding the wiring harness through the hole in the wheel.

Caution: *Do not turn the clockspring, steering shaft or front wheels while the steering wheel is removed. The airbag clockspring could be damaged if the steering wheel is reinstalled with these components misaligned. If one of the components is turned, perform the alignment procedures found later in this section.*

9   If it is necessary to remove the clockspring, remove the steering column covers (see Chapter 11), then unplug its electrical connectors (see illustration).

Installation

10   With the wheels pointing straight ahead, make absolutely sure that the airbag clockspring is centered. This shouldn't be a problem as long as you have not turned the steering shaft while the wheel was removed. If for

14.7a Use a steering wheel puller to release the steering wheel from the steering shaft

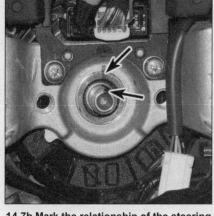

14.7b Mark the relationship of the steering wheel hub to the steering shaft

some reason the shaft was turned, center the clockspring as follows:

a) *Legacy models and 2014 and later Forester models: Rotate the clockspring counterclockwise until it stops (don't apply too much force, though).*
b) *2013 and earlier Forester models: Rotate the clockspring clockwise until it stops (don't apply too much force, though).*
c) *2012 and earlier Legacy models: Rotate the clockspring clockwise about 3 turns until the small arrows on the clockspring are aligned at the bottom.*
d) *2013 and earlier Forester models: Rotate the clockspring counterclockwise about 3-1/4 turns until the small arrows on the clockspring are aligned at the bottom.*
e) *2013 and later Legacy models and 2014 and later Forester models: Rotate the clockspring clockwise about 2-1/2 turns until the orange roller appears in the window and the small arrows on the clock-*

spring align at the bottom (see illustration).

11   Installation is the reverse of removal, noting the following:

a) *Make sure the airbag clockspring is centered before installing the steering wheel.*
b) *When installing the steering wheel, align the marks on the steering shaft and the steering wheel hub.*
c) *Tighten the steering wheel nut to the torque listed in this Chapter's Specifications.*
d) *Carefully install the airbag module to the steering wheel, making sure all electrical connectors are properly connected. On 2012 and later Legacy models and 2014 and later Forester models, push down to make sure the retaining springs engage their pins.*
e) *Enable the airbag system (see Chapter 12).*

14.9 Clockspring electrical connector (A) and lower retaining hooks (B)

14.10 Clockspring centering details (2013 and later Legacy models and 2014 and later Forester models)

1   *Orange roller appears in window (2013 and later Legacy/2014 and later Forester)*
2   *Alignment arrows*

15.2a Loosen and back off the jam nut from the tie-rod end . . .

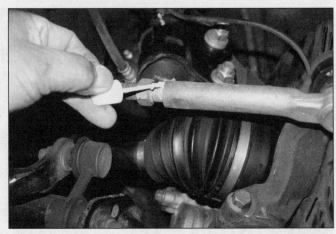

15.2b . . . and mark the position of the tie-rod end on the tie-rod

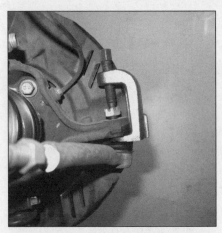

15.4 Install a suitable small puller or tie-rod removal tool such as the one shown to force the tie-rod end ballstud out of the steering knuckle

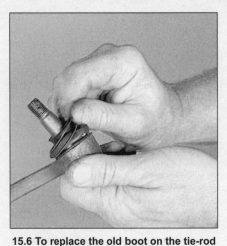

15.6 To replace the old boot on the tie-rod end, remove the boot retaining ring

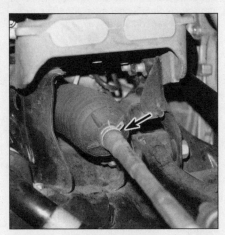

16.3 Remove the small spring clamp and large wire clamp (not shown) to remove the steering gear boot

15   Tie-rod ends - removal and installation

1   Loosen the front wheel lug nuts. Block the rear wheels. Raise the front of the vehicle and support it securely on jackstands. Remove the front wheel.
2   Loosen the jam nut enough to mark the position of the tie-rod end in relation to the threads (see illustrations).
3   Remove the cotter pin and loosen - but don't remove - the nut on the tie-rod end stud.
4   Disconnect the tie-rod end from the steering knuckle with a puller (see illustration). Remove the nut and separate the tie-rod end from the steering knuckle.
5   Unscrew the tie-rod end from the tie-rod.
6   If you're planning to install the old tie-rod end, you should inspect the tie-rod end boot for cracks or tears. If it's damaged, remove the boot retaining ring (see illustration), slide off the old boot, and wipe off the balljoint with a clean rag. Lubricate the new boot with chassis grease, slide it on, and install the boot ring.

7   Thread the tie-rod end on to the marked position and insert the tie-rod end stud into the steering knuckle. Tighten the jam nut securely.
8   Install the nut on the stud and tighten it to the torque listed in this Chapter's Specifications. Install a new cotter pin.
9   Install the wheel and lug nuts. Lower the vehicle and tighten the wheel lug nuts to the torque listed in the Chapter 1 Specifications.
10   Have the alignment checked and, if necessary, adjusted.

16   Steering gear boots - replacement

1   Loosen the front wheel lug nuts, raise the vehicle and support it securely on jackstands. Remove the wheel.
2   Remove the tie-rod end (see Section 15).
3   Remove the steering gear boot clamps and slide off the boot (see illustration).
4   To prevent damage to the new boot, wrap the threads on the end of the tie-rod with

tape before installation.
5   Slide the new boot into position until it seats in the groove on the steering gear, then install new clamps.
6   Remove the tape from the tie-rod and install the tie-rod end (see Section 15).
7   Install the wheel and lug nuts. Lower the vehicle and tighten the lug nuts to the torque listed in the Chapter 1 Specifications.
8   Have the alignment checked and, if necessary, adjusted.

17   Steering gear - removal and installation

Warning: *Make sure the steering shaft is not turned while the steering gear is removed or you could damage the airbag clockspring. To prevent the shaft from turning, place the ignition key in he lock position or thread the seatbelt through the steering wheel and clip it into place.*

1   Disconnect the cable from the negative terminal of the battery (see Chapter 5).
2   Loosen the front wheel lug nuts. Block

17.5 Legacy power steering lines shown

17.7 Turn the steering shaft to position it in a good spot to remove the pinch bolt. Do not turn the steering shaft after it is separated

18.3 Remove the drivebelt cover to access the power steering pump

18.7 Disconnect the fluid lines

the rear wheels, raise the front of the vehicle and support it securely on jackstands. Remove the front wheels.

3   Disconnect the tie-rod ends from the steering knuckles (see Section 15).

4   Remove the stabilizer bar (see Section 4).

5   Models with hydraulic power steering: On Forester models, remove the center power steering hose coupling to drain the fluid. On Legacy models disconnect the lines at the steering gear (see illustration). Turn the steering wheel left and to the right to push out any fluid still in the steering gear.

6   Mark the relationship of the U-joint connecting the steering shaft to the steering gear input shaft.

7   Remove the steering shaft U-joint pinch bolt (see illustration).

8   On Legacy models, remove the subframe (see Section 5).

9   On Forester models, remove the lower engine cover and front exhaust pipe.

10   On Forester models, remove the front crossmember support bracket and jack plate.

11   Remove the steering gear mounting bolts and remove the steering gear.

12   Installation is the reverse of removal, noting the following:

a) *Align the mark on the U-joint with the mark on the shaft, tighten the steering gear mounting bolts, the U-joint pinch bolt and the tie-rod end-to-steering knuckle nuts to the torque listed in this Chapter's Specifications.*

b) *Tighten the jacking plate and crossmember support plate, if equipped, to the torque listed in this Chapter's Specifications.*

c) *Tighten the exhaust pipe fasteners to the torque listed in the Chapter 4 Specifications.*

d) *Install the wheels and lug nuts. Lower the vehicle and tighten the lug nuts to the torque listed in the Chapter 1 Specifications.*

e) *Fill the steering system with the recommended fluid, then check for leaks (see Chapter 1).*

f) *Bleed the system (see Section 20).*

g) *Have the wheel alignment checked and, if necessary, adjusted.*

18   Power steering pump - removal and installation

Removal

1   Disconnect the cable from the negative terminal of the battery (see Chapter 5).

2   Using a syringe, remove the power steering fluid from the power steering pump reservoir.

3   Remove the drivebelt pulley cover (see illustration).

4   Remove the drivebelt (see Chapter 1).

5   On turbocharged models, remove the air intake duct (see Chapter 4).

6   Disconnect the power steering pump electrical connector.

7   Disconnect the fluid lines from the power steering pump (see illustration).

18.8 Rotate the pulley to gain access to each of the pump bolts

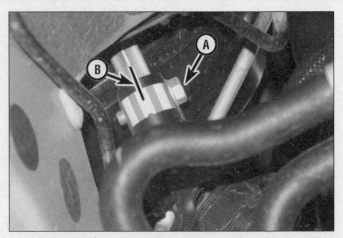

19.3 Mark the universal joint and steering shaft before removing the pinch bolt

A   Pinch bolt   B   Match mark

19.5 Remove the various connectors, harnesses and components from the steering column

19.6 Steering column mounting bolts

8   Remove the pump bracket mounting bolts (see illustration).
9   Remove the single rear pump-to-bracket mounting bolt. Pry the pump from the bottom of the bracket and remove the pump.

Installation

10   Installation is the reverse of removal. Tighten the pump mounting fasteners to the torque listed in this Chapter's Specifications. Tighten all other fasteners securely. Refer to Chapter 1 for drivebelt installation.
11   Add new power steering fluid and check for any leaks in the system (see Chapter 1). Bleed the power steering system (see Section 20).

19   Steering column - removal and installation

Warning: *These vehicles are equipped with a Supplemental Restraint System (SRS), more commonly known as airbags. Always disable the airbag system before working in the vicin-*ity of any airbag system component to avoid the possibility of accidental deployment of the airbag(s), which could cause personal injury (see Chapter 12).*
Warning: *Do not use a memory saving device to preserve the PCM or radio memory when working on or near airbag system components.*
1   Remove the steering wheel (see Section 14).
2   Remove the driver's side knee bolster (see Chapter 11).
3   Mark the relationship of the universal joint to the steering shaft, then remove the steering shaft-to-U-joint pinch bolt (see illustration).
4   Remove the steering column covers and the lower instrument trim panel (see Chapter 11).
5   Disconnect all electrical connectors, and remove any harnesses and electrical components attached to the steering column that would interfere with removal (see illustration).
6   Remove the steering column mounting bolts, then carefully guide the steering column out from the instrument panel (see illustra-tion).
Caution: *Secure the steering shaft to keep it from turning. If it is turned, the clockspring can be damaged.*
7   Installation is the reverse of removal, noting the following points:
 a) *Align the mark on the U-joint with the mark on the steering shaft and tighten the steering column mounting bolts and the U-joint pinch bolt to the torque listed in this Chapter's Specifications.*
 b) *If the steering shaft was turned while the steering column was removed, re-center the clockspring (see Section 14).*

20   Power steering system - bleeding

1   The power steering system must be bled whenever a line is disconnected. Bubbles can be seen in power steering fluid that has air in it and the fluid will often have a tan or milky appearance. Low fluid level can cause air to mix with the fluid, resulting in a noisy pump as well as foaming of the fluid.

2   Open the hood and check the fluid level. in the reservoir, adding the specified fluid necessary to bring it up to the proper level (see Chapter 1).

3   Start the engine and slowly turn the steering wheel several times from left-to-right and back again. Do not turn the wheel completely from lock-to-lock. Check the fluid level, topping it up as necessary until it remains steady and no more bubbles are visible.

21 Wheels and tires - general information

1   All models covered by this manual are equipped with metric-sized radial tires (see illustration). Use of other size or type of tires may affect the ride and handling of the vehicle. Don't mix different types of tires, such as radials and bias belted, on the same vehicle as handling may be seriously affected. It's recommended that tires be replaced in pairs on the same axle, but if only one tire is being replaced, be sure it's the same size, structure and tread design as the other.

2   Because tire pressure has a substantial effect on handling and wear, the pressure on all tires should be checked at least once a month or before any extended trips (see Chapter 1).

3   Wheels must be replaced if they are bent, dented, leak air, have elongated bolt holes, are heavily rusted, out of vertical symmetry or if the lug nuts won't stay tight. Wheel repairs that use welding or peening are not recommended.

4   Tire and wheel balance is important to the overall handling, braking and performance of the vehicle. Unbalanced wheels can adversely affect handling and ride characteristics as well as tire life. Whenever a tire is installed on a wheel, the tire and wheel should be balanced by a shop with the proper equipment.

22 Wheel alignment - general information

1   A wheel alignment refers to the adjustments made to the wheels so they are in proper angular relationship to the suspension and the ground. Wheels that are out of proper alignment not only affect vehicle control, but also increase tire wear. The alignment angles normally measured are camber, caster and toe-in (see illustration). Toe-in and camber on the front, and toe-in on the rear are the only adjustable angles on these vehicles. The other angles should be measured to check for bent or worn suspension parts.

2   Wheel alignment is a very exacting process, one in which complicated and expensive machines are necessary to perform the job properly. You should have a technician with the proper equipment perform these tasks. We will, however, use this space to give you

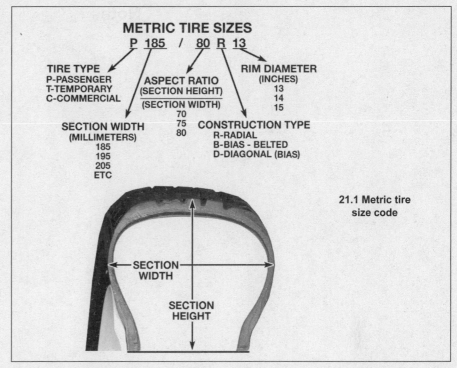

21.1 Metric tire size code

a basic idea of what is involved with a wheel alignment so you can better understand the process and deal intelligently with the shop that does the work.

3   Toe-in is the turning in of the wheels. The purpose of a toe specification is to ensure parallel rolling of the wheels. In a vehicle with zero toe-in, the distance between the front edges of the wheels will be the same as the distance between the rear edges of the wheels. The actual amount of toe-in is normally only a fraction of an inch. On the front end, toe-in is controlled by the tie-rod end position on the tie-rod. On the rear end, it's controlled by a cam bolt on the inner end of the rearmost control arm or link. Incorrect toe-in will cause the tires to wear improperly by making them scrub against the road surface.

4   Camber is the tilting of the wheels from vertical when viewed from one end of the vehicle. When the wheels tilt out at the top, the camber is said to be positive (+). When the wheels tilt in at the top the camber is negative (-). The amount of tilt is measured in degrees from vertical and this measurement is called the camber angle. This angle affects the amount of tire tread which contacts the road and compensates for changes in the suspension geometry when the vehicle is cornering or traveling over an undulating surface. On the front end, camber is adjusted by a cam bolt (the upper strut-to-knuckle bolt). Rear camber is not adjustable.

5   Caster is the tilting of the front steering axis from the vertical. A tilt toward the rear is positive caster and a tilt toward the front is negative caster.

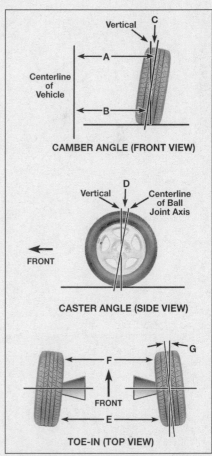

22.1 Camber, caster and toe-in angles

A minus B = C (degrees camber)
D = caster (expressed in degrees)
E minus F = toe-in (measured in inches)
G = toe-in (expressed in degrees)

Notes

Chapter 11
Body

Contents

1   General information

Warning: *The models covered by this manual are equipped with a Supplemental Restraint System (SRS), more commonly known as airbags. Always disable the airbag system before working in the vicinity of any airbag system components to avoid the possibility of accidental deployment of the airbags, which could cause personal injury (see Chapter 12).*

1   Certain body components are particularly vulnerable to accident damage and can be unbolted and repaired or replaced. Among these parts are the hood, doors, trunk lid, liftgate, bumpers and front fenders.

2   Only general body maintenance practices and body panel repair procedures within the scope of the do-it-yourselfer are included in this Chapter.

Make sure the damaged area is perfectly clean and rust free. If the touch-up kit has a wire brush, use it to clean the scratch or chip. Or use fine steel wool wrapped around the end of a pencil. Clean the scratched or chipped surface only, not the good paint surrounding it. Rinse the area with water and allow it to dry thoroughly

Thoroughly mix the paint, then apply a small amount with the touch-up kit brush or a very fine artist's brush. Brush in one direction as you fill the scratch area. Do not build up the paint higher than the surrounding paint

2   Repairing minor paint scratches

1   No matter how hard you try to keep your vehicle looking like new, it will inevitably be scratched, chipped or dented at some point. If the metal is actually dented, seek the advice of a professional. But you can fix minor scratches and chips yourself. Buy a touch-up paint kit from a dealer service department or an auto parts store. To ensure that you get the right color, you'll need to have the specific make, model and year of your vehicle and, ideally, the paint code, which is located on a special metal plate under the hood or in the door jamb.

3   Body repair - minor damage

Plastic body panels

1   The following repair procedures are for minor scratches and gouges. Repair of more serious damage should be left to a dealer service department or qualified auto body shop. Below is a list of the equipment and materials necessary to perform the following repair procedures on plastic body panels.

Wax, grease and silicone removing
*   *solvent*
Cloth-backed body tape
Sanding discs
Drill motor with three-inch disc holder
Hand sanding block
Rubber squeegees
Sandpaper
Non-porous mixing palette
Wood paddle or putty knife
Curved-tooth body file
Flexible parts repair material

Flexible panels (bumper trim)

2   Remove the damaged panel, if necessary or desirable. In most cases, repairs can be carried out with the panel installed.

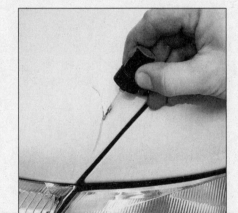

If the vehicle has a two-coat finish, apply the clear coat after the color coat has dried

3   Clean the area(s) to be repaired with a wax, grease and silicone removing solvent applied with a water-dampened cloth.
4   If the damage is structural, that is, if it extends through the panel, clean the backside of the panel area to be repaired as well. Wipe dry.
5   Sand the rear surface about 1-1/2 inches beyond the break.
6   Cut two pieces of fiberglass cloth large enough to overlap the break by about 1-1/2 inches. Cut only to the required length.
7   Mix the adhesive from the repair kit according to the instructions included with the kit, and apply a layer of the mixture approximately 1/8-inch thick on the backside of the panel. Overlap the break by at least 1-1/2 inches.
8   Apply one piece of fiberglass cloth to the adhesive and cover the cloth with additional adhesive. Apply a second piece of fiberglass cloth to the adhesive and immediately cover the cloth with additional adhesive in sufficient quantity to fill the weave.
9   Allow the repair to cure for 20 to 30 minutes at 60-degrees to 80-degrees F.

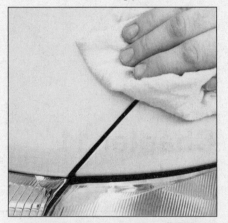

Wait a few days for the paint to dry thoroughly, then rub out the repainted area with a polishing compound to blend the new paint with the surrounding area. When you're happy with your work, wash and polish the area

10   If necessary, trim the excess repair material at the edge.
11   Remove all of the paint film over and around the area(s) to be repaired. The repair material should not overlap the painted surface.
12   With a drill motor and a sanding disc (or a rotary file), cut a "V" along the break line approximately 1/2-inch wide. Remove all dust and loose particles from the repair area.
13   Mix and apply the repair material. Apply a light coat first over the damaged area; then continue applying material until it reaches a level slightly higher than the surrounding finish.
14   Cure the mixture for 20 to 30 minutes at 60-degrees to 80-degrees F.
15   Roughly establish the contour of the area being repaired with a body file. If low areas or pits remain, mix and apply additional adhesive.
16   Block sand the damaged area with sandpaper to establish the actual contour of the surrounding surface.

17   If desired, the repaired area can be temporarily protected with several light coats of primer. Because of the special paints and techniques required for flexible body panels, it is recommended that the vehicle be taken to a paint shop for completion of the body repair.

Steel body panels

Repair of dents

Note: *These photos illustrate a method of repairing simple dents. They are intended to supplement* Body repair - minor damage *in this Chapter and should not be used as the sole instructions for body repair on these vehicles.*

18   When repairing dents, the first job is to pull the dent out until the affected area is as close as possible to its original shape. There is no point in trying to restore the original shape completely as the metal in the damaged area will have stretched on impact and cannot be restored to its original contours. It is better to bring the level of the dent up to a point that is about 1/8-inch below the level of the surrounding metal. In cases where the dent is very shallow, it is not worth trying to pull it out at all.

19   If the backside of the dent is accessible, it can be hammered out gently from behind using a soft-face hammer. While doing this, hold a block of wood firmly against the opposite side of the metal to absorb the hammer blows and prevent the metal from being stretched.

20   If the dent is in a section of the body which has double layers, or some other factor makes it inaccessible from behind, a different technique is required. Drill several small holes through the metal inside the damaged area, particularly in the deeper sections. Screw long, self-tapping screws into the holes just enough for them to get a good grip in the metal. Now pulling on the protruding heads of the screws with locking pliers can pull out the dent.

21   The next stage of repair is the removal of paint from the damaged area and from an inch or so of the surrounding metal. This is easily done with a wire brush or sanding disk in a drill motor, although it can be done just as effectively by hand with sandpaper. To complete the preparation for filling, score the surface of the bare metal with a screwdriver or the tang of a file or drill small holes in the affected area. This will provide a good grip for the filler material. To complete the repair, see the Section on filling and painting.

Repair of rust holes or gashes

22   Remove all paint from the affected area and from an inch or so of the surrounding metal using a sanding disk or wire brush mounted in a drill motor. If these are not available, a few sheets of sandpaper will do the job just as effectively.

23   With the paint removed, you will be able to determine the severity of the corrosion and decide whether to replace the whole panel, if possible, or repair the affected area. New body panels are not as expensive as most

people think and it is often quicker to install a new panel than to repair large areas of rust.

24   Remove all trim pieces from the affected area except those which will act as a guide to the original shape of the damaged body, such as headlight shells, etc. Using metal snips or a hacksaw blade, remove all loose metal and any other metal that is badly affected by rust. Hammer the edges of the hole in to create a slight depression for the filler material.

25   Wire-brush the affected area to remove the powdery rust from the surface of the metal. If the back of the rusted area is accessible, treat it with rust inhibiting paint.

26   Before filling is done, block the hole in some way. This can be done with sheet metal riveted or screwed into place, or by stuffing the hole with wire mesh.

27   Once the hole is blocked off, the affected area can be filled and painted. See the following subsection on filling and painting.

Filling and painting

28   Many types of body fillers are available, but generally speaking, body repair kits which contain filler paste and a tube of resin hardener are best for this type of repair work. A wide, flexible plastic or nylon applicator will be necessary for imparting a smooth and contoured finish to the surface of the filler material. Mix up a small amount of filler on a clean piece of wood or cardboard (use the hardener sparingly). Follow the manufacturer's instructions on the package, otherwise the filler will set incorrectly.

29   Using the applicator, apply the filler paste to the prepared area. Draw the applicator across the surface of the filler to achieve the desired contour and to level the filler surface. As soon as a contour that approximates the original one is achieved, stop working the paste. If you continue, the paste will begin to stick to the applicator. Continue to add thin layers of paste at 20-minute intervals until the level of the filler is just above the surrounding metal.

30   Once the filler has hardened, the excess can be removed with a body file. From then on, progressively finer grades of sandpaper should be used, starting with a 180-grit paper and finishing with 600-grit wet-or-dry paper. Always wrap the sandpaper around a flat rubber or wooden block, otherwise the surface of the filler will not be completely flat. During the sanding of the filler surface, the wet-or-dry paper should be periodically rinsed in water. This will ensure that a very smooth finish is produced in the final stage.

31   At this point, the repair area should be surrounded by a ring of bare metal, which in turn should be encircled by the finely feathered edge of good paint. Rinse the repair area with clean water until all of the dust produced by the sanding operation is gone.

32   Spray the entire area with a light coat of primer. This will reveal any imperfections in the surface of the filler. Repair the imperfections with fresh filler paste or glaze filler and once more smooth the surface with sandpa-

per. Repeat this spray-and-repair procedure until you are satisfied that the surface of the filler and the feathered edge of the paint are perfect. Rinse the area with clean water and allow it to dry completely.

33   The repair area is now ready for painting. Spray painting must be carried out in a warm, dry, windless and dust free atmosphere. These conditions can be created if you have access to a large indoor work area, but if you are forced to work in the open, you will have to pick the day very carefully. If you are working indoors, dousing the floor in the work area with water will help settle the dust that would otherwise be in the air. If the repair area is confined to one body panel, mask off the surrounding panels. This will help minimize the effects of a slight mismatch in paint color. Trim pieces such as chrome strips, door handles, etc., will also need to be masked off or removed. Use masking tape and several thickness of newspaper for the masking operations.

34   Before spraying, shake the paint can thoroughly, then spray a test area until the spray painting technique is mastered. Cover the repair area with a thick coat of primer. The thickness should be built up using several thin layers of primer rather than one thick one. Using 600-grit wet-or-dry sandpaper, rub down the surface of the primer until it is very smooth. While doing this, the work area should be thoroughly rinsed with water and the wet-or-dry sandpaper periodically rinsed as well. Allow the primer to dry before spraying additional coats.

35   Spray on the top coat, again building up the thickness by using several thin layers of paint. Begin spraying in the center of the repair area and then, using a circular motion, work out until the whole repair area and about two inches of the surrounding original paint is covered. Remove all masking material 10 to 15 minutes after spraying on the final coat of paint. Allow the new paint at least two weeks to harden, then use a very fine rubbing compound to blend the edges of the new paint into the existing paint. Finally, apply a coat of wax

4   Body repair - major damage

1   Major damage must be repaired by an auto body shop specifically equipped to perform body and frame repairs. These shops have the specialized equipment required to do the job properly.

2   If the damage is extensive, the frame must be checked for proper alignment or the vehicle's handling characteristics may be adversely affected and other components may wear at an accelerated rate.

3   Due to the fact that all of the major body components (hood, fenders, etc.) are separate and replaceable units, any seriously damaged components should be replaced rather than repaired. Sometimes the components can be found in a wrecking yard that specializes in used vehicle components, often at considerable savings over the cost of new parts.

These photos illustrate a method of repairing simple dents. They are intended to supplement *Body repair - minor damage* in this Chapter and should not be used as the sole instructions for body repair on these vehicles.

1 If you can't access the backside of the body panel to hammer out the dent, pull it out with a slide-hammer-type dent puller. Tap with a hammer near the edge of the dent to help 'pop' the metal back to its original shape, about 1/8-inch below the surface of the surrounding metal

2 Using coarse-grit sandpaper, remove the paint down to the bare metal. Clean the repair area with wax/silicone remover.

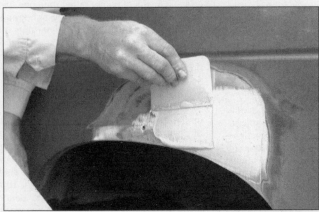

3 Following label instructions, mix up a batch of plastic filler and hardener, then quickly press it into the metal with a plastic applicator. Work the filler until it matches the original contour and is slightly above the surrounding metal

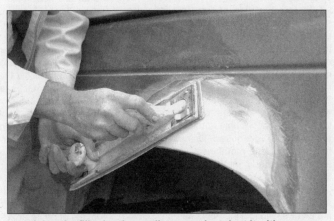

4 Let the filler harden until you can just dent it with your fingernail. File, then sand the filler down until it's smooth and even. Work down to finer grits of sandpaper - always using a board or block - ending up with 360 or 400 grit

5 When the area is smooth to the touch, clean the area and mask around it. Apply several layers of primer to the area. A professional-type spray gun is being used here, but aerosol spray primer works fine

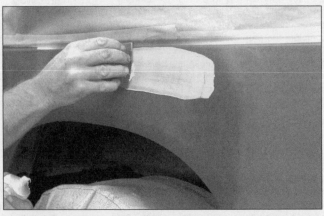

6 Fill imperfections or scratches with glazing compound. Sand with 360 or 400-grit and re-spray. Finish sand the primer with 600 grit, clean thoroughly, then apply the finish coat. Don't attempt to rub out or wax the repair area until the paint has dried completely (at least two weeks)

5   Upholstery, carpets and vinyl trim - maintenance

Upholstery and carpets

1   Every three months remove the floormats and clean the interior of the vehicle (more frequently if necessary). Use a stiff whiskbroom to brush the carpeting and loosen dirt and dust, then vacuum the upholstery and carpets thoroughly, especially along seams and crevices.

2   Dirt and stains can be removed from carpeting with basic household or automotive carpet shampoos available in spray cans. Follow the directions and vacuum again, then use a stiff brush to bring back the nap of the carpet.

3   Most interiors have cloth or vinyl upholstery, either of which can be cleaned and maintained with a number of material-specific cleaners or shampoos available in auto supply stores. Follow the directions on the product for usage, and always spot-test any upholstery cleaner on an inconspicuous area (bottom edge of a backseat cushion) to ensure that it doesn't cause a color shift in the material.

4   After cleaning, vinyl upholstery should be treated with a protectant.

Note: *Make sure the protectant container indicates the product can be used on seats - some products may make a seat too slippery.*

Caution: *Do not use protectant on vinyl-covered steering wheels.*

5   Leather upholstery requires special care. It should be cleaned regularly with saddle-soap or leather cleaner. Never use alcohol, gasoline, nail polish remover or thinner to clean leather upholstery.

6   After cleaning, regularly treat leather upholstery with a leather conditioner, rubbed in with a soft cotton cloth. Never use car wax on leather upholstery.

7   In areas where the interior of the vehicle is subject to bright sunlight, cover leather seating areas of the seats with a sheet if the vehicle is to be left out for any length of time.

Vinyl trim

8   Don't clean vinyl trim with detergents, caustic soap or petroleum-based cleaners. Plain soap and water works just fine, with a soft brush to clean dirt that may be ingrained. Wash the vinyl as frequently as the rest of the vehicle.

9   After cleaning, application of a high-quality rubber and vinyl protectant will help prevent oxidation and cracks. The protectant can also be applied to weather-stripping, vacuum lines and rubber hoses, which often fail as a result of chemical degradation, and to the tires.

6   Fastener and trim removal

1   There is a variety of plastic fasteners used to hold trim panels, splash shields and other parts in place in addition to typical screws, nuts and bolts. Once you are familiar with them, they can usually be removed without too much difficulty.

2   The proper tools and approach can pre-

Fasteners

This tool is designed to remove special fasteners. A small pry tool used for removing nails will also work well in place of this tool

A Phillips head screwdriver can be used to release the center portion, but light pressure must be used because the plastic is easily damaged. Once the center is up, the fastener can easily be pried from its hole

Here is a view with the center portion fully released. Install the fastener as shown, then press the center in to set it

This fastener is used for exterior panels and shields. The center portion must be pried up to release the fastener. Install the fastener with the center up, then press the center in to set it

This type of fastener is used commonly for interior panels. Use a small blunt tool to press the small pin at the center in to release it . . .

. . . the pin will stay with the fastener in the released position

Reset the fastener for installation by moving the pin out. Install the fastener, then press the pin flush with the fastener to set it

This fastener is used for exterior and interior panels. It has no moving parts. Simply pry the fastener from its hole like the claw of a hammer removes a nail. Without a tool that can get under the top of the fastener, it can be very difficult to remove

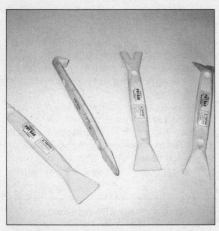

6.4 These small plastic pry tools are ideal for prying off trim panels

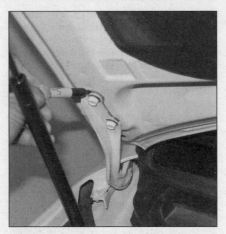

7.2 Before removing the hood, draw a line around the hinge plate

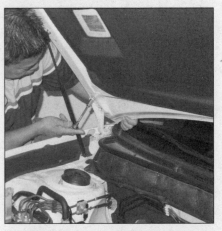

7.6 With an assistant holding the opposite side of the hood, use your shoulder to support the hood while removing the hood hinge bolts

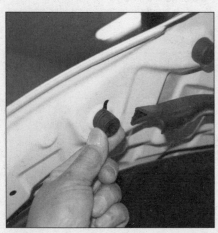

7.13 Screw the hood bumpers in or out to adjust the hood flush with the fenders

8.1 Remove these three hood latch retaining bolts

vent added time and expense to a project by minimizing the number of broken fasteners and/or parts.

3   The illustrations below show various types of fasteners that are typically used on most vehicles and how to remove and install them (see illustrations 6.5a through 6.5h). Replacement fasteners are commonly found at most auto parts stores, if necessary.

4   Trim panels are typically made of plastic and their flexibility can help during removal. The key to their removal is to use a tool to pry the panel near its retainers to release it without damaging surrounding areas or breaking-off any retainers. The retainers will usually snap out of their designated slot or hole after force is applied to them. Stiff plastic tools designed for prying on trim panels are available at most auto parts stores (see illustration). Tools that are tapered and wrapped in protective tape, such as a screwdriver or small pry tool, are also very effective when used with care.

7   Hood - removal, installation and adjustment

Note: *The hood is heavy and somewhat awkward to remove and install - at least two people should perform this procedure.*

Removal and installation

1   Use blankets or pads to cover the cowl area of the body and fenders. This will protect the body and paint as the hood is lifted off.
2   Make marks or scribe a line around the hood hinge to ensure proper alignment during installation (see illustration).
3   Disconnect the hood support struts.
4   Remove the plastic clip securing the insulator pad to the hood.
5   Disconnect any wires that will interfere with removal.
6   With an assistant still helping you sup-

port the hood, remove the hinge-to-hood bolts (see illustration).
7   Lift off the hood.
8   Installation is the reverse of removal.

Adjustment

9   Fore-and-aft and side-to-side adjustment of the hood is done by moving the hinge plate slot after loosening the bolts or nuts.
10   Scribe a line around the entire hinge plate so you can determine the amount of movement (see illustration 7.2).
11   Loosen the bolts or nuts and move the hood into correct alignment. Move it only a little at a time. Tighten the hinge bolts and carefully lower the hood to check the position.
12   After installing the hood, adjust the hood release latch (see Section 8), if necessary. The latch can be adjusted fore-and-aft so that the hood closes securely and flush with the fenders. To make the adjustment, scribe a line or mark around the latch mounting flange to provide a reference point, then loosen the latch bolts and reposition the latch as necessary. Tighten the latch mounting bolts securely.
13   Also, if necessary, adjust the hood bumpers (see illustration) so that the hood is flush with the fenders when it's closed.
14   The hood latch assembly, as well as the hinges, should be periodically lubricated with lithium-base grease to prevent binding and wear.

8   Hood latch and release cable - removal and installation

Latch

1   Scribe a line around the latch to aid alignment when installing, detach the latch retaining bolts from the radiator support (see illustration), and remove the latch.

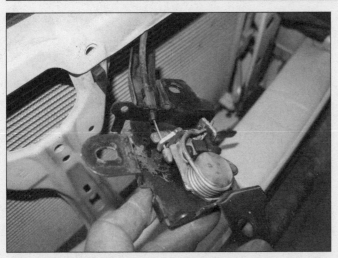

8.2 Flip the hood latch over to disengage the hood release cable from the latch mechanism

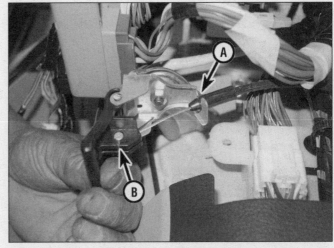

8.7 Pry the cable casing out of the bracket (A), then pass the cable through the slot in the lever (B)

2   Note the routing of the hood release cable, then disengage the cable from the latch assembly (see illustration).

3   Installation is the reverse of removal.

Cable

4   Disconnect the hood release cable from the latch assembly as described above.

5   Attach a piece of stiff wire to the end of the cable, trace the cable back to the firewall and detach all cable retaining clips.

6   Remove the driver's side knee bolster (see Section 25).

7   Detach the cable from the release lever bracket (see illustration).

8   Disengage the cable from the hood release lever.

9   Pull the old cable into the passenger compartment until you can see the stiff wire that you attached to the cable. A grommet insulates the cable hole in the firewall from the elements. The new cable should have a new grommet, so you can remove and discard the old cable grommet. Make sure the new grommet is already on the new cable (if not, slip the old grommet onto the new cable), then detach the old cable from the wire and attach the new cable to the wire.

10   Working from the engine compartment side of the firewall, pull the wire through the cable hole in the firewall.

11   Installation is otherwise the reverse of the removal. Working in the passenger compartment, push the grommet into place with your fingers. Make sure it's fully seated in the hole in the firewall.

9   Radiator grille - removal and installation

Legacy

1   Remove the front bumper cover.

2   Remove the screws from the back side of the bumper that secure the grille to the bumper fascia.

3   Release the hooks and remove the grille.

4   Installation is the reverse of removal, making sure the hooks are completely locked into the bumper cover.

Forester

Upper grille

5   Remove the upper fasteners (see illustration).

6   Remove the lower fasteners.

7   Remove the two outside edge nuts securing the grille to the bumper fascia. Then lift the grille off.

8   Installation is the reverse of removal.

Forester

Lower grille

9   Remove the front bumper cover (see Section 10).

10   Remove the screws from the back side of the bumper that secure the grille to the bumper fascia.

11   Release the hooks and remove the grille.

12   Installation is the reverse of removal, making sure the hooks are completely locked into the bumper cover.

9.5 Upper fasteners are plastic clips

10.2a Remove the fasteners securing the front part of the left and right splash shields

10.2b Remove the fasteners from the bottom of the cover. Legacy model shown

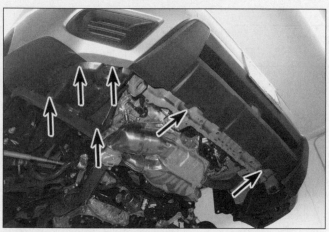

10.2c Forester bottom cover fasteners

10.4 Remove the upper fasteners (other models similar)

10 Bumper covers - removal and installation

Front bumper cover

Note: *The front bumper cover should be re-moved with the help of an assistant to prevent damage during removal.*

1   Raise the vehicle and support it securely on jackstands.

2   Detach the front part of the fender splash shields from the bumper cover, then remove the bumper cover screws and clips along the bottom edge of the cover (see illustrations).

Note: *The number of screws and fasteners used will vary by year and model.*

3   Apply protective tape to the edges of the front bumper cover where it contacts the headlights.

4   Remove the cover fasteners along the top edge of the grille (see illustration).

5   Remove the screws and clips secur-ing the front bumper at the wheel well edge (see illustration). These fasteners are located at the top of the bumper and inside the inner wheel wells.

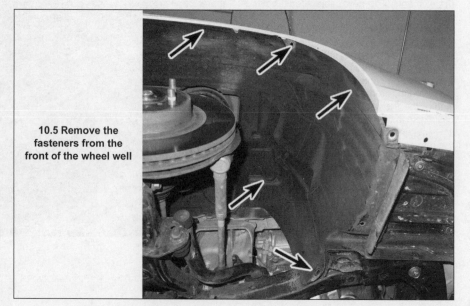

10.5 Remove the fasteners from the front of the wheel well

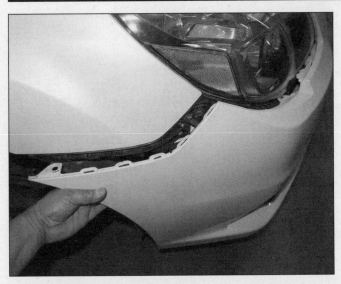

10.7 Release the bumper cover clips from the fender

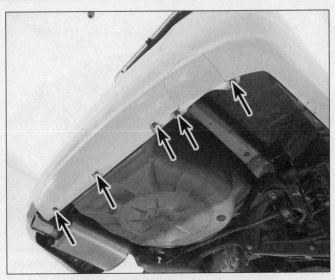

10.10a Remove the fasteners from the lower edge
(Legacy model shown)

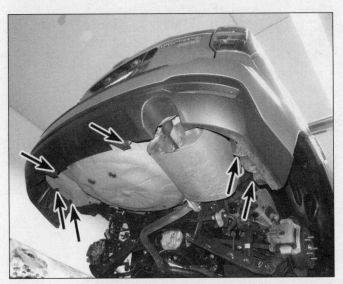

10.10b Forester models are similar

10.11 Remove the fasteners from the wheel opening

6   Disconnect the front fog light connectors (if equipped).
7   Release both sides of the bumper cover from the clips at the upper edge where the bumper meets up with the fender (see illustration), and remove the front bumper cover.
8   Installation is the reverse of removal.

Rear bumper cover

9   Raise the vehicle and support it securely on jackstands.
10   Working under the vehicle, detach the plastic clips and screws securing the lower edge of the bumper cover (see illustrations).
11   Remove the bumper cover screws from the rear wheel openings (see illustration).

12   Remove the rear tail lamp assemblies.
13   Open the trunk or rear liftgate and remove the screws and clips securing the upper edge of the bumper cover. Pull the bumper cover out and away from the vehicle.
14   Installation is the reverse of removal.

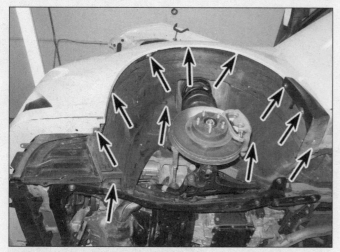

11.2a Legacy model wheel well splash shield fastener locations

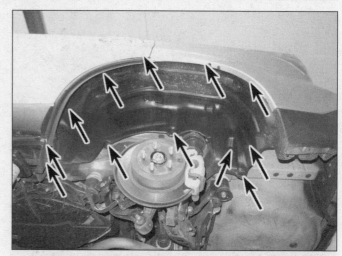

11.2b Forester model wheel well splash shield fastener locations

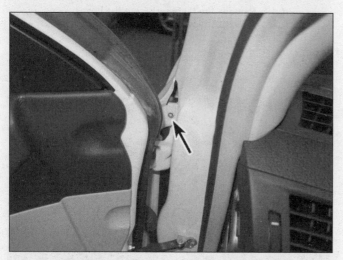

11.5 Fender upper corner fastener location

11.8 Remove the lower mounting bolts

11 Front fender - removal and installation

1   Loosen the front wheel lug nuts, raise the vehicle and support it securely on jackstands. Remove the wheel.

2   Remove the inner fender splash shield from the wheel wells (see illustrations).

3   Remove the cowl trim panel (see Section 27).

4   Remove the front bumper cover (see Section 10).

5   Open the front door and remove the fender corner fasteners (see illustration).

6   Remove the side sill spoiler fasteners along the perimeter of the sill and lower the sill.

7   Remove the headlight housings (see Chapter 12).

8   Remove the lower fender fasteners (see illustrations).

9   Remove the fender mounting bolts (see illustration).

Note: *Some models have a fender trim panel that must be carefully pried off and removed to access the mounting bolts.*

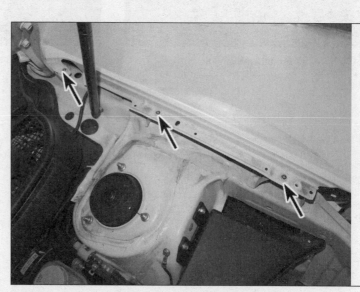

11.9 Remove the bolts from the top of the fender

12.1 Carefully pry off the sail panel

12.2 Remove the inside release handle trim screw

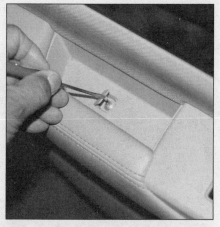

12.3a On Legacy models, carefully pry the screw cover off in the door pull to expose the screw

10   Detach the fender. It's a good idea to have an assistant support the fender while it's being moved away from the vehicle to prevent damage to the surrounding body panels.
11   Installation is the reverse of removal.

12   Door and liftgate trim panels - removal and installation

Door trim panel

1   Pry off the sail panel from the corner of the door panel (see illustration), and disconnect the speaker electrical connector, if equipped.
2   Use a small screwdriver to pry back the screw cover and remove the screw from the inside door release handle (see illustration).
3   Use a small screwdriver to pry back the screw cover from the door pull pocket (see illustrations). Remove the screw.
4   On the bottom edge of the door panel there is a slot in the middle section. Use a flat trim tool in this slot to unhook the door fasteners. Work you way around the door to insure all the fasteners have come loose (see illustration).
5   With door panel off of the door now disconnect the cables for the inside latch and door lock.
6   Disconnect the electrical connections for the door locks and power windows (if equipped).
7   For access to the handle, latch, lock and window regulator mechanisms, carefully peel back the plastic watershield (see illustration).

12.3b On Forester models, pull the pull handle trim off with a flat trim tool to expose the grab handle screws. The same screw cover is used on the inside door release handle as the Legacy models

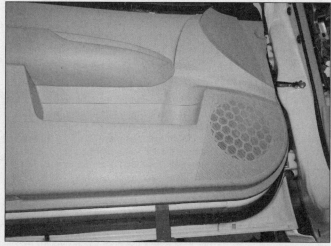

12.4 Use a flat bladed trim tool to pry the door panel off of the door

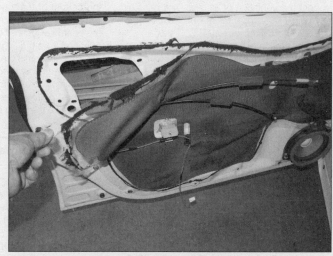

12.7 Carefully peel the watershield from the door so that it can be reinstalled

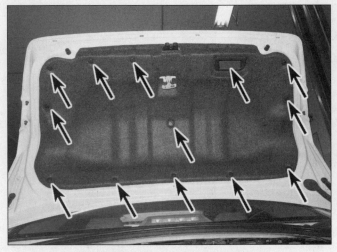

12.11 Trunk lid trim panel clip locations

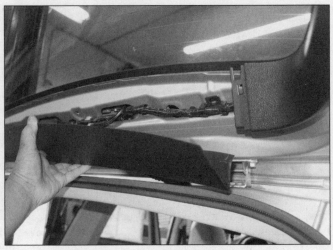

12.12a Start by removing the upper trim panel . . .

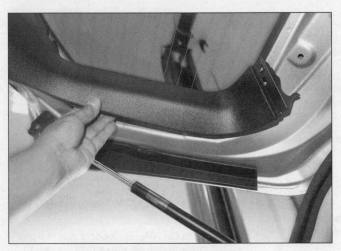

12.12b . . . then the side trim

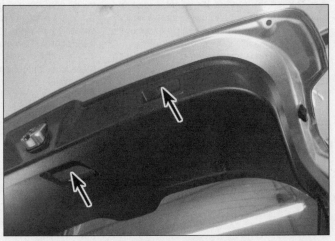

12.13 Two screws secure the lower section in place. The rest of the fasteners are pressure clips

8   Before installing the door trim panel, inspect the condition of all clips, and reinstall any which may have fallen out. Reinstall the plastic watershield.

9   Installation is the reverse of removal.

Note: *When installing door trim panel retaining clips, make sure the clips are lined up with their mating holes first, then gently press the clips in with the palm of your hand.*

Trunk lid trim panel

10   Open the trunk and release the trim clips by prying the center section of the clip out (partially not all the way off), then pry the clip off.

11   Once all the clips have been removed the trim panel can be removed (see illustration).

Liftgate trim panel

12   Open the liftgate and use a trim panel tool to pry the trim panels from around the liftgate glass area (see illustrations).

13   For the larger bottom panel, start from the bottom of the trim panel and remove the two screws (see illustration) then work around the perimeter until all the fasteners have been released from the liftgate.

14   Installation is the reverse of removal.

Note: *When installing liftgate trim panel retaining clips, make sure the clips are lined up with their mating holes first, then gently tap the clips in with the palm of your hand.*

13   Door - removal, installation and adjustment

Note: *The door is heavy and somewhat awkward to remove and install - at least two people should perform this procedure.*

Removal and installation

1   Open the door all the way and support it on jacks or blocks covered with rags to prevent damaging the paint.

2   Remove the threshold panel, then the kick panel (see illustrations) and disconnect the door electrical connector from the body harness.

3   Detach the rubber conduit between the body and the door and pull the wiring harness through the conduit.

4   Unbolt the door stop strut from the door jamb (see illustration).

5   Mark around the door hinges with a pen or a scribe to facilitate realignment during reassembly.

6   With an assistant holding the door, remove the hinge-to-door bolts and lift off the door (see illustrations).

7   Installation is the reverse of removal.

Adjustment

8   Having proper door to body alignment is a critical part of a well functioning door assembly. First check the door hinge pins for excessive play. Fully open the door and lift up and down on the door without lifting the body. If

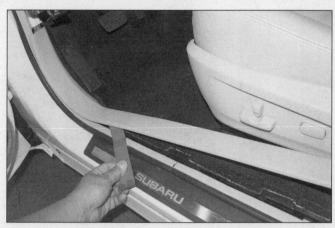

13.2a Carefully pry off the threshold panel

13.2b Remove the fastener(s) securing the kick panel, then carefully pry it off

13.4 Remove the door stop strut retaining bolt (and nuts if you're replacing the strut)

13.6a Remove the lower door-to-hinge bolts . . .

a door has 1/16-inch or more excessive play, the hinges should be replaced.

9   Door-to-body alignment adjustments are made by loosening the hinge-to-body bolts or hinge-to-door bolts and moving the door. Proper body alignment is achieved when the top of the doors are parallel with the roof section, the front door is flush with the fender, the rear door is flush with the rear quarter panel and the bottom of the doors are aligned with the lower rocker panel. If these goals can't be reached by adjusting the hinge-to-body or hinge-to-door bolts, body alignment shims may have to be purchased and inserted behind the hinges to achieve correct alignment.

10   To adjust the door closed position, scribe a line or mark around the striker plate to provide a reference point, then verify that the door latch is contacting the center of the latch striker. If it isn't, adjust the vertical position of the striker (see illustration).

11   If necessary, adjust the horizontal position of the striker, so that the door panel is flush with the center pillar or rear quarter panel, and provides positive engagement with the latch mechanism.

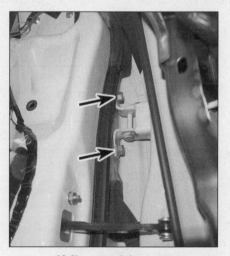

13.6b . . . and the upper door-to-hinge bolts

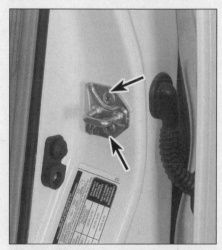

13.10 Adjust the door lock striker by loosening the mounting screws and gently tapping the striker in the desired direction

14.2 Remove the inside door handle screws

14.6a Remove the trim cap from the end of the door

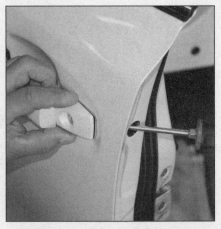

14.6b Use a Torx bit driver tool to remove the screw

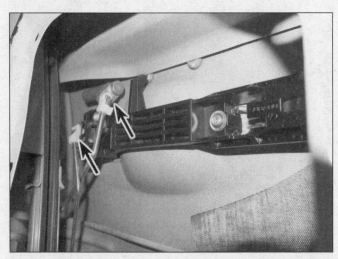

14.7a Remove the linkage arms from the outside door handle

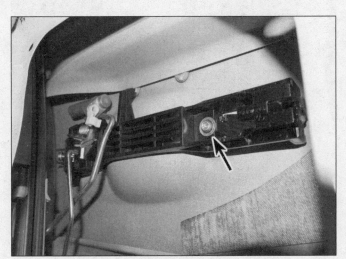

14.7b Remove the Torx screw from inside the door

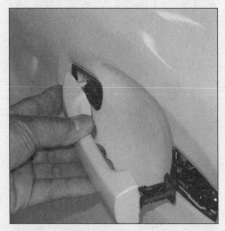

14.8 Pull back slightly and pull outwards to remove the handle

14   Door handles, key lock cylinder and latch - removal and installation

1   Raise the window, then remove the door trim panel and watershield (see Section 12).

Inside handle

2   On some models, the inside handle is mounted on the back side of the door panel. Remove the door handle retaining screws and remove the handle from the door panel (see illustration). On all others the inside handle is mounted on the door itself.

3   Installation is the reverse of removal.

Outside handle

4   Remove the door panel (see Section 12).

5   Remove the actuating rod from the outside handle.

6   Remove the screw cover from the end of the door, then loosen Torx bit through the hole (see illustrations).

7   Remove the linkage arms and inner Torx screw (see illustrations).

8   Pull back on the outside handle to release the front and pull outwards (see illustration). Remove the outer side spacer from the outside of the door.

9   On models with keyless entry, disconnect the electrical connectors to the outside lock/handle.

10   Installation is the reverse of removal.

Key lock cylinder

11   Remove the door trim panel (see Section 12).

12   Remove the screw cover from the end

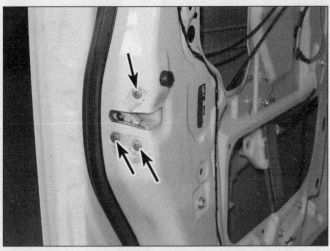

14.18 Remove the latch screws from the end of the door

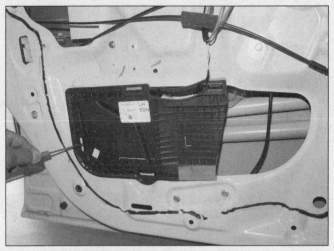

15.2 Pry the splash guard off

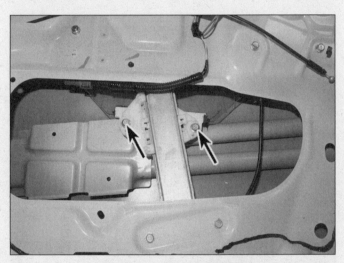

15.3 Window glass retainer bolts

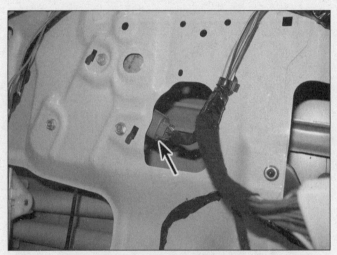

16.3 Window regulator electrical connection

of the door, then loosen Torx bit through the hole.

13   Detach the lock rod clamp from the key cylinder arm and remove the rod.

14   Remove the key lock cylinder from the handle.

15   Installation is the reverse of removal.

Door latch

16   Disengage the inside handle-to-latch actuating rods from the latch.

17   Working through the access hole on the inside of the door, disengage the outside handle-to-latch rods and the lock cylinder-to-latch rod from the latch assembly.

18   Remove the three latch retaining screws (see illustration), then remove the latch assembly from the door.

19   Installation is the reverse of removal.

15   Door window glass - removal and installation

1   Remove the door trim panel and the plastic watershield (see Section 12).

2   Remove the lower splash guard from the door (see illustration).

3   Temporally reattach the window switch or window crank handle and lower the window glass to a position to gain access to the mounting bolts that attach the glass to the track assembly (see illustration).

4   Tilt the front of the glass downwards, remove the rubber weather stripping, then remove the glass.

5   Installation is the reverse of removal. If it is necessary to adjust the glass, loosen the adjustment bolts then carefully raise the window and position the glass in the window opening so it is level and contacting the weatherstrip evenly all the way around. Have an assistant

press in slightly on the window to give it a bit of preload on the weatherstrip, then tighten the adjustment bolts. To fine-tune the adjustment, loosen the necessary adjustment bolts and move the up-stops, sashes or stabilizers as required, then tighten them securely. Verify that the window goes up and down smoothly, and that the door opens and closes easily. If the door pops when you open it or is hard to close, there is too much preload on the glass.

16   Door window glass regulator and motor - removal and installation

1   Remove the door trim panel and the plastic watershield (see Section 12).

2   Remove the door window glass (see Section 15).

3   Unplug the electrical connector from the window regulator motor (see illustration).

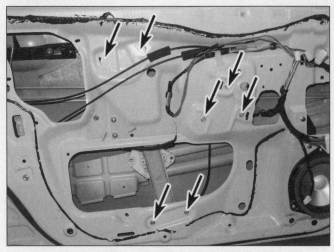

16.4 Window glass regulator assembly mounting bolts

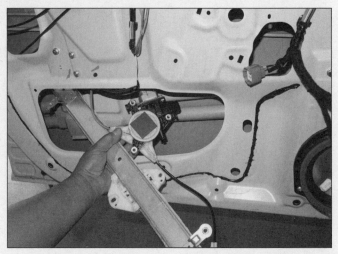

16.5 Lower the regulator assembly through the service hole

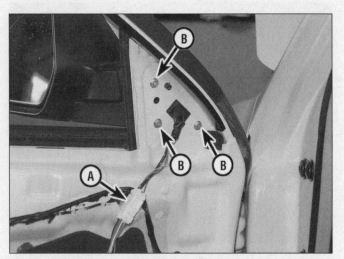

17.3 Mirror electrical connector (A) and mounting fasteners (B)

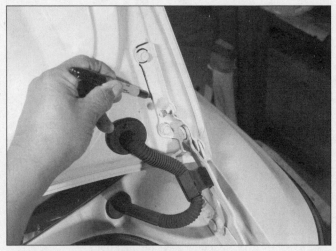

18.3 Draw around the hinge with a marking pen before loosening the bolts to ensure proper alignment of the trunk lid when it's reinstalled

4   Remove the regulator mounting bolts (see illustration).

5   Pull the regulator assembly through the service hole and remove it from the door (see illustration).

6   Remove the three motor-to-regulator fasteners and separate the motor from the regulator assembly.

7   Installation is the reverse of removal.

17   Outside mirrors - removal and installation

1   Remove the door trim panel (see Section 12).

2   Disconnect the mirror electrical connector.

3   Remove the mirror retaining screws (see

illustration) and remove the mirror from the vehicle.

4   Installation is the reverse of removal.

18   Trunk lid - removal and installation

Note: *The trunk lid is heavy and somewhat awkward to remove and install - at least two people should perform this procedure.*

1   Open the trunk lid and cover the edges of the trunk compartment with pads or cloths to protect the painted surfaces when the lid is removed.

2   Disconnect any cables or wire harness connectors attached to the trunk lid that would interfere with removal.

3   Make alignment marks around the hinge

mounting bolts to help with alignment during installation (see illustration).

4   While an assistant supports the trunk lid, disconnect the trunk lid support struts. Then, remove the lid-to-hinge bolts on both sides and lift the trunk lid from the vehicle.

5   Installation is the reverse of removal.

Note: *When reinstalling the trunk lid, align the lid-to-hinge bolts with the marks made during removal.*

19   Trunk lid latch and lock cylinder - removal and installation

Latch

1   Open the trunk and remove any trunk lid trim panels surrounding the latch (see Section 12).

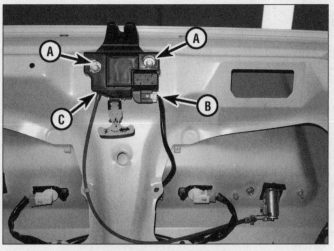

19.2 Trunk lid latch assembly

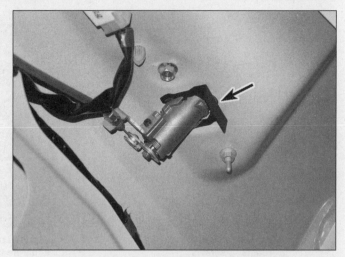

19.5 Slide the clip off to remove the lock cylinder

A   Latch fasteners   C   Latch cable
B   Electrical connector

20.2a Remove the circular clamp from the upper end of the support arm . . .

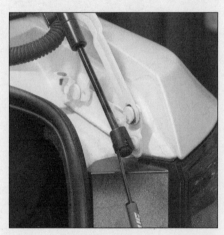

20.2b . . . then detach the lower end of the strut from the body in the same manner

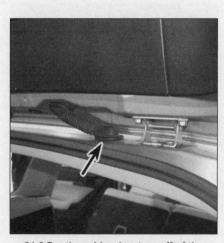

21.2 Pry the rubber boot up off of the wire harness retainer, then press in on the edges of the hard plastic retainer to remove it. The wire harness connector is just under the upper edge of the headliner. To reinstall, put the rubber boot back onto the plastic retainer first, then push the retainer into place

2   The trunk lid latch is retained by two fasteners. Detach these bolts, then disconnect the electrical connector and cable from the back of the latch (see illustration). Remove the latch.
3   Installation is the reverse of removal. Align the latch with the marks you made prior to removal.

Trunk lock cylinder

4   Open the trunk and remove any trunk trim panels surrounding the latch assembly.
5   Remove the clip to the trunk lock cylinder (see illustration). Then, remove the cable that is attached to the lock cylinder.
6   Slide the lock cylinder out of the trunk.
7   Installation is the reverse of removal.

20   Trunk/liftgate support struts - removal and installation

Note: *The liftgate is heavy and somewhat awkward to support - at least two people should perform this procedure.*
1   Open the trunk or liftgate and support it securely.
2   Slide the circular clamp off of the ends of the struts, then remove the "U" clips that secure the ends of the strut to the ballstuds (see illustrations).
Note: *Some replacement struts will come with new ballstuds. Remove the original ballstuds and replace them with the ones provided.*
3   Installation is the reverse of removal.

21   Liftgate - removal, installation and adjustment

Note: *The liftgate is heavy and somewhat awkward to remove and install - at least two people should perform this procedure.*

Removal and installation

1   Open the liftgate and support it securely.
2   Remove the liftgate trim panels and disconnect the rear washer hose and all wiring harness connectors leading to the liftgate (see illustration).
3   While an assistant supports the liftgate, detach the support struts from the liftgate (see Section 20).

23.3 Steering column cover retaining screws

23.4 Disengage the rear locking hooks to separate the covers

24.3 A trim tool works best to pry up the center trim

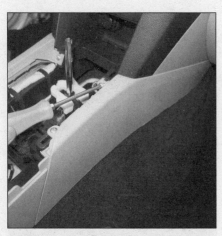

24.4a Remove the screw for the side panel

24.4b Pry the side panel off after the screw has been removed

24.4c On the Forester models, remove these two screws

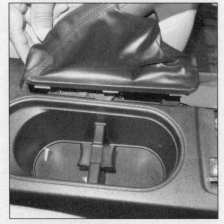

24.4d Forester models, pry the parking brake boot off of the center console

4   Draw a line around the liftgate hinges for a reference point to aid the installation procedure. Remove the hinge-to-liftgate bolts and remove the liftgate from the vehicle.

5   Installation is the reverse of removal.

Adjustment

6   Adjustments are made by loosening the hinge-to-liftgate bolts and moving the liftgate. Proper alignment is achieved when the edges of the liftgate are parallel with the rear quarter panel and the top of the tailgate.

7   To provide positive engagement with the latch mechanism, the latch striker may need to be adjusted. To access the striker, remove the trim piece between the bumper cover and the carpeting. Mark the relationship of the striker

to the body, loosen the striker bolts and move the striker fore-and-aft and/or side-to-side as necessary to achieve positive engagement.

22   Liftgate latch and outside handle - removal and installation

1   Open the liftgate and support it securely.

Latch

2   Remove the bolts from the latch assembly, then disconnect the electrical connector and the outer handle cable.

3   Remove the latch.

4   Installation is the reverse of removal.

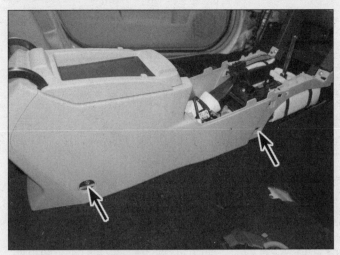

24.6a Console side screw locations, Legacy model shown

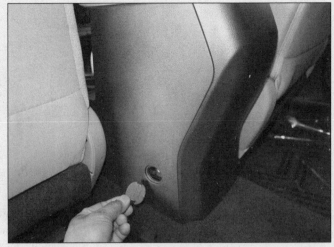

24.6b Forester model's rear console fasteners are similar to the Legacy

Liftgate opener button

5   Disconnect the cable from the negative battery terminal (see Chapter 5).
6   Remove the liftgate trim panel (see Section 12).
7   Disconnect the electrical connector from the liftgate opener button.
8   Hold down the locking hook and remove the button from the outside of the liftgate.
9   Installation is the reverse of removal.

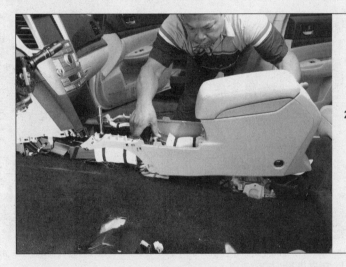

24.7 Lift the console out of the car

23   Steering column covers - removal and installation

Warning: *Models covered by this manual are equipped with a Supplemental Restraint System (SRS), more commonly known as airbags. Always disable the airbag system before working in the vicinity of any airbag system component to avoid the possibility of accidental deployment of the airbag, which could cause personal injury (see Chapter 12).*
1   Disconnect the cable from the negative terminal of the battery (see Chapter 5).
2   Remove the steering wheel (see Chapter 10).
3   Remove the steering column cover screws (see illustration).
4   Separate the cover halves (see illustration) and remove them from the steering column.
Note: *On keyless models, remove the ignition key cap on the lower steering column cover.*
5   Installation is the reverse of removal.

24   Center console - removal and installation

Warning: *Models covered by this manual are equipped with a Supplemental Restraint System (SRS), more commonly known as airbags. Always disable the airbag system be-*

fore working in the vicinity of any airbag system component to avoid the possibility of accidental deployment of the airbag, which could cause personal injury (see Chapter 12).
1   Disconnect the cable from the negative battery terminal (see Chapter 5).
2   On manual and automatic transmission models, remove the shift lever knob (see Chapter 7A).
Note: *It is not absolutely necessary, but it may be helpful to remove one or both front seats (see Section 28) to gain complete access to the center console.*
3   Using a flat bladed trim tool pry up the center trim panel and remove it (see illustration).
4   Remove the console side trim panels. One screw and four clips hold them in place (see illustrations).
5   If you did not remove the seats previously, now move the seats forward to gain access to the rear screws.
Caution: *If your vehicle has electric seats. Move seats forward then, disconnect battery again. Wait 60 seconds before proceeding*

with the rest of the procedures.
6   Remove the screws from each side (see illustrations).
7   Lift up on the front of the console to free it from the clips then, pull back a bit to clear the other components (see illustration).
8   Installation is the reverse of removal.

25   Dashboard trim panels - removal and installation

Warning: *The models covered by this manual are equipped with a Supplemental Restraint System (SRS), more commonly known as airbags. Always disarm the airbag system before working in the vicinity of any airbag system component to avoid the possibility of accidental deployment of the airbag, which could cause personal injury (see Chapter 12). Do not use a memory saving device to preserve the PCM's memory when working on or near airbag system components.*
1   Disconnect the cable from the negative terminal of the battery (see Chapter 5).

25.2 Carefully pry off the end trim panel

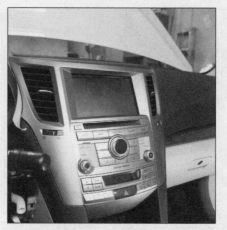

25.4a On Legacy models, pull out along the edge of the top vents to disengage the mounting clips

25.4b Forester models are slightly different, but basically are removed in the same manner

25.5 Pull out along the outer edges to release the trim panel. Legacy model shown

25.8 Remove the screws securing the trim to the dash panel

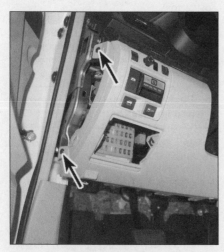

25.11 Knee bolster fasteners

Left and right dashboard end trim panels

2 Use a trim tool to carefully pry off the end trim panel (see illustration).

3 Installation is the reverse of removal.

Radio trim panel (Center trim panel)

Note: *Place protective tape along the outside edge of the center trim panel to avoid damaging the instrument cluster trim.*

4 Grasp along the top edge of the air inlet vent on each side of the radio and pull outward to release the pressure clips (see illustrations).

5 Grasp the expose edge of the trim panel and work your way around pulling outward as you go to release the remainder of the pressure clips (see illustration).

6 Installation is the reverse of removal.

Instrument cluster trim panel

7 Remove the steering column covers (see Section 23).

8 Remove the two screws securing the trim to the dash (see illustration).

9 Remove the panel.

10 Installation is the reverse of removal.

Knee bolster trim panel

11 Remove the driver's side end trim panel and remove the two knee bolster mounting fasteners hidden behind the side end panel (see illustration).

12 Remove the lower close out panel by removing the pressure clips.

13 Carefully pry around the edges of the panel to release it.

14 The remainder of the knee bolster is held on with pressure clips. Grasp the edge of the knee bolster and pull out firmly. Work your way around the inside edge of the knee bolster pulling out as you reach each corner.

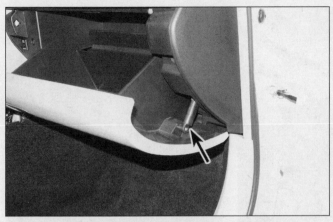

25.17 Disconnect the damper from the pin

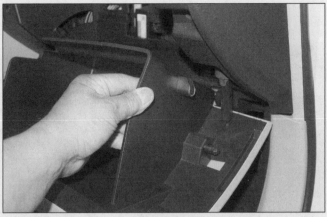

25.18 Push the corners inwards until the stops are clear of the instrument panel

26.6a Pull the top section free

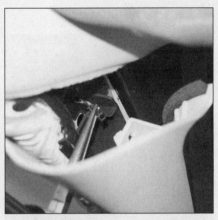

26.6b Grasp the retainer clip with long needle-pliers and pull it out of the A pillar

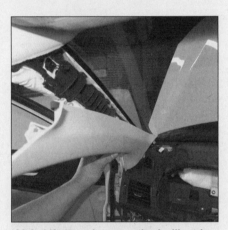

26.6c Lift up and remove the A pillar trim. Connect the retainer clip on the A pillar trim before reinstalling

15   Disconnect the electrical connectors, then remove the panel.
16   Installation is the reverse of removal.

Glove box

17   Open the glove box door and disconnect the damper from the right side of the glove box (see illustration).
18   Firmly grasp the corners of the glove box and push them inwards until the stops clear the sides, and remove the glove box (see illustration).
19   Remove the passenger side dash end trim plate. The plate is held on with pressure clips. Pry the plate off with a flat trim tool.
20   The glove box inner panel is held on with pressure clips. Pull the clips out and remove the inner panel and trim.
21   The glove box shelf is held in place with seven screws, three pressure clips, and one screw on the edge of the dash on the passenger side (under the end trim plate). Remove the screws and pry the glove box shelf out with a flat trim tool to release the pressure clips.
22   Installation is the reverse of removal.

26   Instrument panel - removal and installation

Warning: *Models covered by this manual are equipped with a Supplemental Restraint System (SRS), more commonly known as airbags. Always disable the airbag system before working in the vicinity of any airbag system component to avoid the possibility of accidental deployment of the airbag, which could cause personal injury (see Chapter 12).*
Note: *This is a difficult procedure for the home mechanic. There are many hidden fasteners, difficult angles to work in and many electrical connectors to tag and disconnect/connect. We recommend that this procedure be performed only by an experienced do-it-yourselfer.*
Note: *During removal of the instrument panel, make careful notes of how each piece comes off, where it fits in relation to other pieces and what holds it in place. If you note how each part is installed before removing it, getting the instrument panel back together again will be much easier.*
Note: *It is not necessary, but it is suggested to remove both front seats to allow additional*

working space and lessen the chance of damage to the seats during this procedure (see Section 28).
Note: *Keep in mind, the entire instrument panel assembly is installed at the factory as one complete unit. Only certain components needed to be removed, which are generally the components that will vary from one model to the next. (instrument cluster, HVAC housing, and entertainment systems). When removing the instrument panel assembly use care and don't pull on anything that feels like it is still attached. Check for any hidden fasteners in that area. Some models may have fasteners in various areas that are not noted in the procedures.*
1   Disconnect the cable from the negative battery terminal (see Chapter 5).
2   Remove the steering wheel (see Chapter 10).
3   Remove the center console (see Section 24).
4   Remove all of the dashboard trim panels (see Section 25).
5   Remove the instrument cluster (see Chapter 12).
6   Remove the front pillar trim (see illustrations).

26.12a Remove the speaker covers

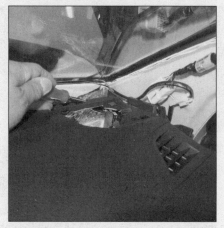

26.12b Remove the retaining bolts below the speaker

26.12c Remove the center support bolts from the passenger side . . .

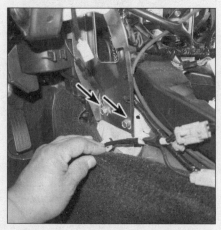

26.12d . . . then remove the center support bolts from the driver's side

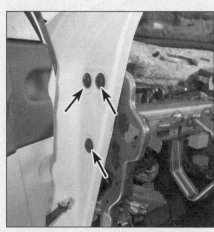

26.12e Remove the driver's side support bar bolts

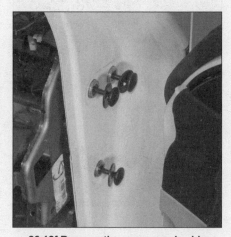

26.12f Remove the passenger's side support bar bolts

26.12g All the support bar bolts have a large collar that is part of the bolt

26.12h To remove just the dash trim panel these screws will need to be removed as well as the remaining silver-headed screws that secure the trim panel to the dash support bracket

7   Disconnect the steering column inter-mediate shaft (mark the shaft before remov-ing it). Now remove the fasteners securing the steering column to the dash support and lower the steering column out of the way. You can remove the steering column if needed. Remove all the electrical fasteners and shift cables to do so (see Chapter 10).

8   Remove the sill trim and kick panels from each side.

9   Remove the radio (see Chapter 12) and the heater control assembly (see Chapter 3).

10   Remove the glove box (see Section 25).

11   Disconnect the instrument panel electri-cal connectors.

Note: *A number of electrical connectors must be disconnected in order to remove the instru-ment panel. Most are designed so that they will only fit on the matching connector (male or female), but if there is any doubt, mark the connectors with masking tape and a marking pen before disconnecting them.*

12   Remove the fasteners securing the instrument panel (see illustrations). Fastener locations vary by model.

26.15 Carefully lift up on the dash trim to remove it from the vehicle

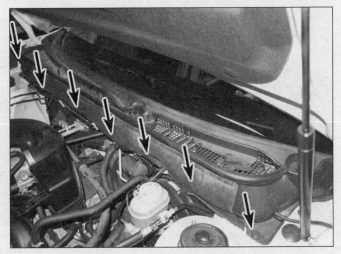

27.3 Cowl cover retaining clips

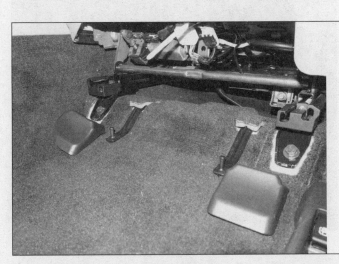

28.2a Front mounting bolts

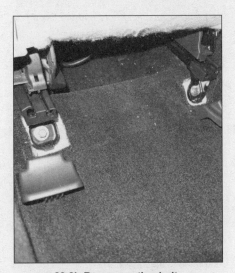

28.2b Rear mounting bolts

13   Remove the two support screws behind the radio area and the two support bolts behind the steering column just below the instrument cluster. There is also two screws on either side of the center portion were hidden by the center console side trim panels.

14   Pull the instrument panel away from the firewall and detach any electrical connectors interfering with removal.

15   Once all the electrical connectors are detached, lift the instrument panel slightly and then pull it away from the windshield. Remove it through the door opening (see illustration).

16   To double check yourself that all the mounting bolts have been removed here is a review of the locations of the various mounting bolts.

a) Two mounting bolts from the right end of the instrument panel
b) Six mounting bolts in the center and lower panel area
c) Three mounting bolts on the left end of the instrument panel
d) Four mounting bolts on the upper portion of the instrument panel.

Note: *Have an assistant help maneuver the dash assembly out of the vehicle.*

17   Installation is the reverse of removal.

27   Cowl cover - removal and installation

1   Remove the windshield wiper arms (see Chapter 12).
2   Remove the side panels from each end of the cowl.
3   Carefully pry up the plastic clips securing the cowl (see illustration). Then lift the cowling up far enough to disconnect the windshield washer hose. Now remove the cowling.
4   Installation is the reverse of removal.

28   Seats - removal and installation

Warning: *The front seat belts on some models are equipped with pre-tensioners, which are pyrotechnic (explosive) devices designed to retract the seat belts in the event of a collision. On models equipped with pre-tensioners, do not remove the front seat belt retractor assemblies, and do not disconnect the electrical connectors leading to the assemblies. Problems with the pre-tensioners will turn on the SRS (airbag) warning light on the dash. If any pre-tensioner problems are suspected, take the vehicle to a dealer service department.*

Warning: *On models with side-impact airbags, be sure to disarm the airbag system before beginning this procedure (see Chapter 12).*

Front seats

1   Position the seat all the way forward or all the way to the rear to access the retaining bolts.
2   Remove the bolt trim covers (if equipped) and remove the retaining bolts (see illustrations).

28.3 Typical seat electrical connectors

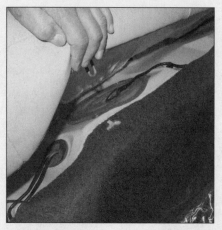

28.5 Pull up on the seat to detach the front clips

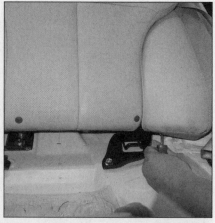

28.7a Reach up from the bottom to gain access to the retaining screw

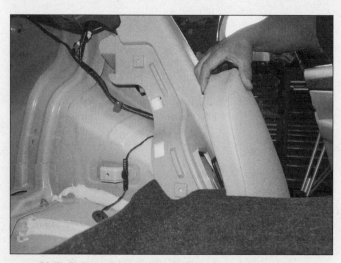

28.7b Pull out from the top to remove the side cushion

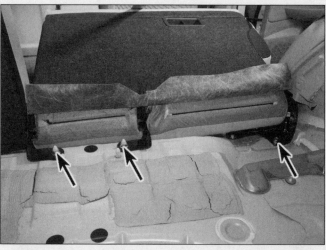

28.9 Remove the left side seat back-to-hinge mounting bolts

3   Tilt the seat front section upward and disconnect any electrical connectors (see illustration). Lift the seat from the vehicle.
4   Installation is the reverse of removal.

Rear seat

Lower cushion

5   Pull up sharply on each side of the lower cushion (in front of the seating areas) (see illustration), then lift the front of the seat up while pushing toward the rear to release the hook at the rear.
6   Installation is the reverse of removal.

Seat back cushion

7   Remove the lower cushion. On some of the Legacy models the side trim cushion on the back cushion is a separate piece and needs to be removed before the back cushion can be removed (see illustrations).
8   Remove the lower bolts retaining the seat back cushion. Then, fold the rear back rest down and remove the luggage compartment floor mat.

9   Separate the seat cover at the center of the seat back and remove the seat back-to-hinge mounting bolts (see illustration).
10   Lift (left side first) the inside corner of the seatback off the hinge, slide the seatback out of the outer hinge and remove the seat.
Note: *The hinge on the outside edge of the seatback has a pin and cannot be removed unless the seatback is in the down position.*
11   Installation is the reverse of removal.

---

29   Spoiler - removal and installation

Legacy

1   Open the trunk lid.
2   Disconnect the electrical connector from the high-mount brake light.
3   Remove the spoiler-to-trunk lid mounting nuts, making sure not to drop them into the trunk lid.
Note: *These models are equipped with either a small or large rear spoiler; the small spoil-*

er has four mounting nuts and the large has twelve.
4   Lift the spoiler off of the trunk lid.
5   Clean the trunk lid surface and mounting surface of the spoiler before installing the spoiler on the trunk.
6   Installation is the reverse of removal.

Forester

7   Remove the liftgate trim panel (see Section 12).
8   Disconnect the electrical connector from the high-mount brake light.
9   Disconnect the washer hose from the rear washer.
10   From inside the liftgate, remove the spoiler mounting fasteners.
11   Carefully pry up the spoiler up from the outside, disengaging the three plastic clips and remove the spoiler.
12   Installation is the reverse of removal.
Caution: *Make sure the harness grommet is seated between the spoiler and the liftgate to prevent water leaks.*

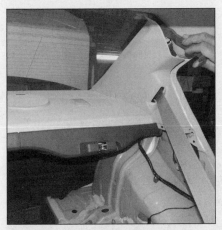

30.3a Pry the upper edge free first

30.3b On Forester models, pry around the edges to free the pressure clips, then pull straight up (direction of the arrows) to release the clips along the metal lip edge

30.4a Keep applying pressure with the trim tool to free the quarter panel from the retaining clips as you work your way to the bottom edge

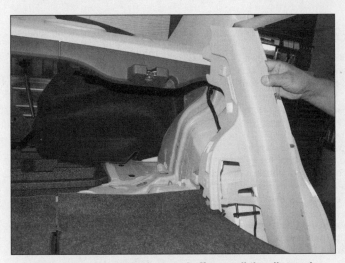

30.4b Lift the quarter trim panel off once all the clips and fasteners are removed

30.7 Screw and bolt locations

A   Screws   *B   Luggage bracket bolt*

30 Quarter trim panel - removal and installation

1   Remove the rear seat (see Section 28).
2   Remove the rear seat belt anchor bolts.
3   Pry the upper edge of the quarter panel free with a trim tool (see illustrations).
4   Work your way down the edge with the trim tool (see illustrations).
5   Installation is the reverse of removal.

Forester lower quarter panel trim

6   Remove the upper quarter panel trim
7   Remove the screws and the bolt out of the luggage rack bracket (see illustration), then pry around the edges with a flat trim tool to release the panel.

8   Remove the panel. Replace any pressure clips that didn't come off with the panel back onto the panel before reinstalling.
9   Installation is reverse of removal.

31 Parcel shelf trim panel - removal and installation

1   Remove the rear seat (see Section 28).
2   Remove the upper and lower quarter panel trim (see Section 30).
3   Remove the rear seat belt anchor bolts.
4   Remove the front trunk side trim panels.
5   Pry the upper trim cover off of the front of the parcel shelf (see illustration).
6   Remove the clips at the front of the panel, then lift the panel up and remove it.
7   Installation is the reverse of removal.

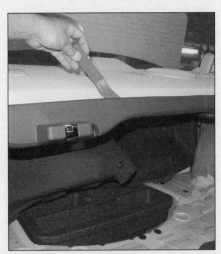

31.5 Pry the trim panel off to remove the parcel shelf

32.6 After the screws have been removed, pry the overhead console free

32.7 Overhead assist handles (Forester)

32   Headliner, sun visor, and sun roof removal and installation

Warning: *Models covered by this manual are equipped with a Supplemental Restraint System (SRS), more commonly known as airbags. Always disable the airbag system before working in the vicinity of any airbag system component to avoid the possibility of accidental deployment of the airbag, which could cause personal injury (see Chapter 12).*

1   Disconnect the negative battery terminal from the battery and wait at least 60 seconds before proceeding.

2   Remove the trim panels that are touching the headliner. For detail removal procedures see Section 25, Section 30, and Section 26.

3   Remove the center section trim panels (if applicable) as well as the seat belt shoulder bolt bracket.

4   Remove the sun visors retaining screws, then pull them down enough to disconnect the electrical connector. Now remove the sun visor.

5   Remove the sun visor hooks by pressing in on each side tabs with a flat screwdriver while pulling them downward.

6   Open the overhead console and remove the screws securing the console/light fixture, then pry the overhead console free (see illustration). Pry the side interior lamp fixtures out (if applicable) and disconnect the electrical leads.

7   Remove the overhead assist handles by prying out the screw caps and removing the screws securing the handle to the roof (see illustration).

8   Remove the headrests from the seats for added room.

9   Gently pull down on the edges of the headliner while observing any electrical or antenna cables that may be stuck to the liner.

10   Once all electrical leads are free lower the headliner down and guide it out of the vehicle.

11   Disconnect the sunroof motor electrical connector.

12   Remove the drain tubes from the four corners of the sun roof assembly.

13   Remove the sunroof cover bolts.

14   Remove the bolts securing the sunroof assembly to the roof line.

15   Carefully lower the sunroof assembly as you loosen the last bolt.

16   Installation is the reverse of removal.

Notes

Notes

Chapter 12
Chassis electrical system

Contents

1 General information

1 The electrical system is a 12-volt, negative ground type. Power for the lights and all electrical accessories is supplied by a lead/acid-type battery, which is charged by the alternator.

2 This Chapter covers repair and service procedures for the various electrical components not associated with the engine. Information on the battery, alternator and starter motor can be found in Chapter 5.

3 It should be noted that when portions of the electrical system are serviced, the cable should be disconnected from the negative terminal of the battery to prevent electrical shorts and/or fires.

2 Electrical troubleshooting - general information

1 A typical electrical circuit consists of an electrical component, any switches, relays, motors, fuses, fusible links or circuit breakers related to that component and the wiring and connectors that link the component to both the battery and the chassis. To help you pinpoint an electrical circuit problem, wiring diagrams are in Chapter 13.

2 Before tackling any troublesome electrical circuit, it would be wise to understand the basics of electrical theory and how a circuit in an automobile is connected. Knowing how any system works before attempting repairs will greatly reduce the possibility of replacing unneeded components. A good place to start is to study the appropriate wiring diagrams to get a complete understanding of what makes up that individual circuit. Trouble spots, for instance, can often be narrowed down by noting if other components related to the circuit are operating properly. Taking it step by step and following the guidelines provided will reduce your time in diagnosing electrical issues.

3 Electrical problems usually stem from simple causes, such as loose or corroded connections, worn or chafed wiring, a blown fuse, a melted fusible link, or faulty components. Visually inspect the condition of all fuses, wires and connections in a problem circuit before troubleshooting the circuit. Check not only the positive signals but the negative signals as well. Faulty grounds, or weak ground connections are a leading factor in system failures.

4 If test equipment and instruments are going to be utilized, be sure you understand how to use the equipment properly before attempting a repair. A bad diagnostic routine can start with bad equipment or the lack of proper use of the equipment. Use the wiring diagrams to plan ahead of time where you will make the necessary connections in order to accurately pinpoint your test connections as well as were the possible trouble could be.

5 The basic tools needed for electrical troubleshooting include a multi-meter that is capable of reading DC and AC voltage, Ohms (resistance), and Amps, a test light, jumper wires with alligator clips at each end, a jumper wire preferably with a circuit breaker incorporated, and a few sharp pins (straight pins

work well) which can be used to bypass electrical components (see illustrations). Before attempting to locate a problem with test instruments, use the wiring diagram(s) to decide where to make the connections.

Voltage checks

Note: *Keep in mind that some circuits receive voltage only when the ignition key is in the Accessory or Run position.*

6   Voltage checks should be performed if a circuit is not functioning properly. Connect one lead of a circuit tester to either the negative battery terminal or a known good ground. Always check your test light before checking the actual circuit you're working on to be sure it is making good contact with the negative and the positive leads. Connect the other lead to a connector in the circuit being tested, preferably nearest to the battery or fuse (see illustration). If the bulb of the tester lights, voltage is present, which means that the part of the circuit between the connector and the battery is problem free. Continue checking the rest of the circuit in the same fashion. When you reach a point at which no voltage is present, the problem lies between that point and the last test point with voltage. Most of the time the problem can be traced to a loose connection.

Finding a short

7   A short occurs when the path of electricity takes a route to ground that it was not designed for. This is usually associated with a blown fuse or melted fusible link. One method of finding shorts in a circuit is to remove the fuse and connect a test light or voltmeter in place of the fuse terminals. A fuse terminal has two connections. One is the supplied voltage to the fuse while the other is the send lead to that circuit. There should be no readable voltage at those two connectors because they should be of the same potential. Moving the wiring harness from side-to-side while watching the test light may also allow you to

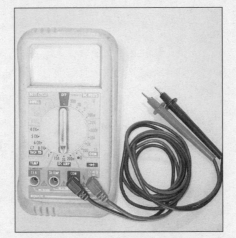

2.5a The most useful tool for electrical troubleshooting is a digital multimeter that can check volts, amps, and test continuity

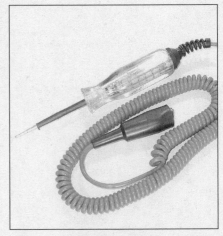

2.5b A test light is a very handy tool for checking voltage

find any chaffed wiring that might have blown the fuse originally. If the bulb is on, there is a negative and a positive potential at the fuse connection. When the light is on, there is a short to ground somewhere in that area, probably where the insulation has rubbed through. The same test can be performed on each component in the circuit, or on a switch.

Ground check

8   Perform a ground test to check whether a component is properly grounded. Disconnect the battery and connect one lead of a continuity tester or multimeter (set to the ohms scale), to a known good ground. Connect the other lead to the wire or ground connection being tested. If the resistance is low (less than 5 ohms), the ground is good. If the bulb on a self-powered test light does not go on, the ground is bad. A more accurate method is the voltage drop test. Place the positive side of your multimeter on the positive post

of the battery, then place the negative side on the chassis. Note the reading, then move the negative lead to the suspected bad ground area, such as the engine (which should have the same grounded leads to it). Take another reading. The two readings should be exactly the same.

Continuity check

9   A continuity check is done to determine if there are any breaks in a circuit - if it is passing electricity properly. With the circuit off (no power in the circuit), a self-powered continuity tester or multimeter can be used to check the circuit. Connect the test leads to both ends of the circuit (or to the power end and a good ground), and if the test light comes on the circuit is passing current properly (see illustration). If the resistance is low (less than 5 ohms), there is continuity; if the reading is 10,000 ohms or higher, there is a break somewhere in the circuit. The same procedure can

2.6 In use, a basic test light's lead is clipped to a known good ground, then the pointed probe can test connectors, wires or electrical sockets - if the bulb lights, the part being tested has battery voltage

2.9 With a multimeter set to the ohms scale, resistance can be checked across two terminals - when checking for continuity, a low reading indicates continuity, a high reading indicates lack of continuity

3.1a The engine compartment fuse box is located on the left side of the engine compartment. It includes a fuse and relay guide on the underside of the fuse box cover

3.1b The passenger compartment fuse box is located at the left end of the instrument panel

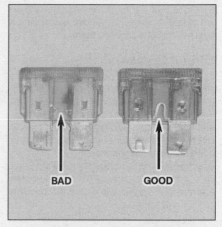

3.3 When a fuse blows, the element between the terminals melts

be used to test a switch, by connecting the continuity tester to the switch terminals. With the switch turned On, the test light should come on (or low resistance should be indicated on a meter).

Caution: *Always check your multimeter before hooking it up to any circuit so that you know you are on the right scale. If there is voltage present on a lead, and you are trying to measure resistance, you can do permanent damage to your meter if it is set on the wrong scale.*

Finding an open circuit

10   When diagnosing for possible open circuits, it is often difficult to locate them by sight because the connectors hide oxidation or terminal misalignment. Merely wiggling a connector on a sensor or in the wiring harness may correct the open circuit condition. Remember this when an open circuit is indicated when troubleshooting a circuit. Intermittent problems may also be caused by oxidized or loose connections.

11   Electrical troubleshooting is simple if you keep in mind that all electrical circuits are basically electricity running from the battery, through the wires, switches, relays, fuses and fusible links to each electrical component (light bulb, motor, etc.) and to ground, from which it is passed back to the battery. Any electrical problem is an interruption in the flow of electricity to and from the battery.

Finding a battery drain

Note: *Before attempting to find a drain, test the battery to be sure the battery itself is not the cause (see Chapter 5).*

12   Battery drain is any electrical load that is present when it shouldn't be, which will cause the battery to have insufficient amperage/voltage to restart the vehicle. Today's vehicles have what is referred to as parasitic battery drain. This is a normal process that occurs with all newer vehicles. Each of the different

computer based systems in the vehicle have a certain amount of constant current required to maintain enough electricity to restart. The required voltage is very small - so small, a standard test light or volt meter will not pick up the signal correctly. An amperage meter in line with the battery negative post and negative clamp is recommended to read the amount of current being passed to the vehicle. A reading of less than 0.02 to 0.04 amps indicates a lack of battery drain. Anything above that would indicate something has been left on, or one of the computer based systems is still activated.

13   Modules all have a sleep mode; this varies with each module or system. Some will carry out their functions shortly after the last door is closed or when the key is turned off. Delay systems such as dome light entry and exit are a good example of a module cycling through the sleep mode. When the light comes on, it's awake, and when it goes out a few seconds later, it's asleep.

14   Finding a battery drain can be quite challenging. If you are hesitant in trying to locate the drain, take your vehicle to your local dealer or qualified independent shop that specializes in electrical repairs.

---

3   Fuses, fusible links and circuit breakers - general information

Fuses

1   The electrical circuits of the vehicle are protected by a combination of fuses, circuit breakers and fusible links. There are two fuse boxes: the engine compartment fuse box and the passenger compartment fuse box. The engine compartment fuse box (see illustration) is located on the left side of the engine compartment on all models. The passenger compartment fuse box is located at the left end of the instrument panel (see illustration).

2   Each of the fuses is designed to protect

a specific circuit, as identified on the fuse cover. Spare fuses and a special removal tool are included in the fuse box cover.

3   Miniaturized fuses are employed in the fuse blocks. These compact fuses, with blade terminal design, allow fingertip removal and replacement. If an electrical component fails, always check the fuse first. The best way to check the fuses is with a test light. Check for power at the exposed terminal tips of each fuse. If power is present at one side of the fuse but not the other, the fuse is blown. A blown fuse can also be identified by visually inspecting it (see illustration).

4   To replace a fuse, simply pull out the bad fuse and push in a new fuse. Always replace a blown fuse with a replacement unit of the same type and amperage rating. Fuses of different amperage ratings are physically interchangeable, but don't replace a blown fuse with one rating with a replacement fuse with a different rating. Always replace bad fuses with new units with the exact same amperage rating. Replacing a fuse with one of a higher or lower value than specified is not recommended. Each electrical circuit needs a specific amount of protection. The amperage rating of every fuse is molded into the fuse body.

5   If the replacement fuse immediately fails, don't replace it again until the cause of the problem is isolated and corrected. In most cases, this will be a short circuit in the wiring caused by a broken or deteriorated wire.

Fusible links

6   Some circuits, such as the starter circuit that connects the starter motor and the alternator, are protected by fusible links. Fusible links are used in circuits that carry high current or are not ordinarily fused. Cartridge type fusible links (also referred to as maxi-fuses) are located in the engine compartment fuse and relay box and are similar to a large fuse. After disconnecting the negative terminal of the battery cable, simply unplug and replace a fusible link with a new unit of the same amper-

age. Some of the higher voltage maxi-fuses are bolted in place. To remove these, simply remove the bolts securing them.

Circuit breakers

7   Circuit breakers protect certain circuits, such as the power windows or heated seats. Depending on the vehicle's accessories, there might be one or two circuit breakers, and they're usually located inside the vehicle, where they're scattered throughout the area under the instrument panel.

8   Because circuit breakers reset automatically, an electrical overload in a circuit-breaker-protected system will cause the circuit to fail momentarily, then come back on. If the circuit does not come back on, check it immediately.

9   For a basic check, pull the circuit breaker up out of its socket on the fuse panel, but just far enough to probe with a voltmeter. The breaker should still contact the sockets.

10   With the voltmeter negative lead on a good chassis ground, touch each end prong of the circuit breaker with the positive meter probe. There should be battery voltage at each end. If there is battery voltage only at one end, the circuit breaker must be replaced.

11   Some circuit breakers must be reset manually.

4   Electrical connectors - general information

1   Most electrical connections on these vehicles are made with multiwire plastic connectors. The mating halves of many connectors are secured with locking clips molded into the plastic connector shells. The mating halves of some large connectors, such as some of those under the instrument panel, are held together by a bolt through the center of the connector.

2   To separate a connector with locking clips, use a small screwdriver to pry the clips

Electrical connectors

Most electrical connectors have a single release tab that you depress to release the connector

Some electrical connectors have a retaining tab which must be pried up to free the connector

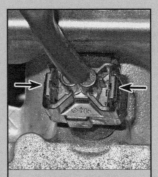

Some connectors have two release tabs that you must squeeze to release the connector

Some connectors use wire retainers that you squeeze to release the connector

Critical connectors often employ a sliding lock (1) that you must pull out before you can depress the release tab (2)

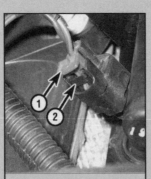

Here's another sliding-lock style connector, with the lock (1) and the release tab (2) on the side of the connector

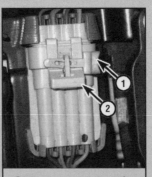

On some connectors the lock (1) must be pulled out to the side and removed before you can lift the release tab (2)

Some critical connectors, like the multi-pin connectors at the Powertrain Control Module employ pivoting locks that must be flipped open

apart carefully, then separate the connector halves. Pull only on the shell, never pull on the wiring harness, as you may damage the individual wires and terminals inside the connectors. Look at the connector closely before trying to separate the halves. Often the locking clips are engaged in a way that is not immediately clear. Additionally, many connectors have more than one set of clips.

3 Each pair of connector terminals has a male half and a female half. When you look at the end view of a connector in a diagram, be sure to understand whether the view shows the harness side or the component side of the connector. Connector halves are mirror images of each other, and a terminal shown on the right side end-view of one half will be on the left side end-view of the other half.

4 It is often necessary to take circuit voltage measurements with a connector connected. Whenever possible, carefully insert a small straight pin (not your meter probe) into the rear of the connector shell to contact the terminal inside, then clip your meter lead to the pin. This kind of connection is called back-probing. When inserting a test probe into a terminal, be careful not to distort the terminal opening. Doing so can lead to a poor connection and corrosion at that terminal later. Using the small straight pin instead of a meter probe results in less chance of deforming the terminal connector.

5   Relays - general information and testing

General information

1 Several electrical accessories in the vehicle, such as the fuel injection system, horns, starter, and fog lamps use relays to transmit the electrical signal to the component. Relays use a low-current circuit (the control circuit) to open and close a high-current circuit (the power circuit). If the relay is defective, that component will not operate properly. Most relays are mounted in the engine compartment fuse and relay box. There are also some

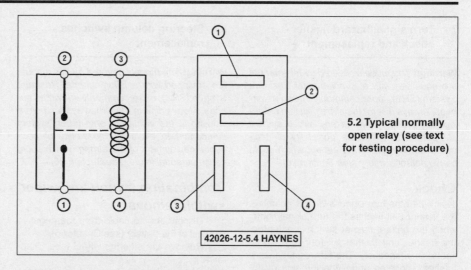

5.2 Typical normally open relay (see text for testing procedure)

42026-12-5.4 HAYNES

relays mounted on or near the passenger compartment fuse box, but they're not visible until you remove the knee bolster. If you suspect a faulty relay, simply remove it and test it using the procedure below. Or have it tested by a dealer service department. Defective relays cannot be repaired; they must be replaced with a new unit.

Testing

2 Most of the relays used in these vehicles are normally open relays (see illustration).

3 Refer to the wiring diagram for the circuit to determine the proper connections for the relay you're testing. If you can't determine the correct connection from the wiring diagrams, however, you may be able to determine the test connections from the information that follows.

4 Two of the terminals are the relay control circuit and connect to the relay coil. The other relay terminals are the power circuit. When the relay is energized, the coil creates a magnetic field that closes the larger contacts of the power circuit to provide power to the circuit loads.

5 To test a normally-open relay, use an ohmmeter to verify that there is no continuity between terminal No. 1 and No. 2 when the

power is disconnected. Then verify that there is continuity between terminal No. 1 and No. 2 when the No. 3 and No. 4 terminals are connected to power and ground.

6 If the relay fails the above test, replace it.

6   Remote keyless entry fob - battery replacement

1 Unscrew the two halves of the fob (see illustration).

2 Separate the two halves and remove the fob electrical unit (see illustration).

Caution: *Do not touch the circuit board or battery terminal contacts inside the key fob.*

3 Install the new battery, making sure the positive (+) terminal faces the bottom of the case (see illustration), then reassemble the two halves of the electrical unit and install it into the fob housing.

Caution: *Handle the battery by its edges only; holding it like a coin (touching both sides) can reduce the battery's life by partially discharging it.*

4 Snap the housing halves together and install the screw.

6.1 Use a small jeweler's-type screwdriver to remove the screw

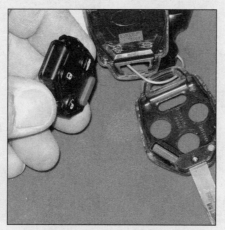

6.2 Carefully remove the electrical unit from the key fob housing

6.3 Be sure to have the battery polarity installed correctly

7   Turn signal/hazard flasher - check and replacement

Warning: *The models covered by this manual are equipped with a Supplemental Restraint System (SRS), more commonly known as airbags. Always disarm the airbag system before working in the vicinity of any airbag system component to avoid the possibility of accidental deployment of the airbag, which could cause personal injury (see Section 26).*

Check

1   When the turn signal switch is actuated, the flasher unit flashes the turn signal lights; when the hazard flasher switch is actuated, the flasher unit flashes all four turn signal lights simultaneously. The turn signal/hazard flasher is located under the left side of the dash on the driver's side.

2   When the flasher unit is functioning properly, an audible click can be heard during its operation. If the turn signals fail on one side or the other and the flasher unit does not make its characteristic clicking sound, or if it flashes much more rapidly than normal, a faulty turn signal bulb is indicated.

3   If both turn signals fail to blink, the problem may be due to a blown fuse, a faulty flasher unit, a broken switch or a loose or open connection. If a quick check of the fuse box indicates that the turn signal fuse has blown, check the wiring for a short before installing a new fuse.

Replacement

4   To remove the flasher, remove the knee bolster and the reinforcement panel behind it (see Chapter 11).

5   Unplug the electrical connector from the flasher unit, remove the mounting bolt and remove the unit.

6   Installation is the reverse of removal.

8   Steering column switches - replacement

Warning: *The models covered by this manual are equipped with a Supplemental Restraint System (SRS), more commonly known as airbags. Always disarm the airbag system before working in the vicinity of any airbag system component to avoid the possibility of accidental deployment of the airbag, which could cause personal injury (see Section 26).*

Combination switch and wiper switch removal

1   Disconnect the cable from the negative terminal of the battery (see Chapter 5).

2   Remove the steering wheel (see Chapter 10).

3   Remove the steering column covers (see Chapter 11).

4   Remove the airbag clockspring (see Chapter 10).

5   Disconnect the electrical connection to the wiper switch, then lift the clip hooks securing the switch to the column. Slide the wiper switch off (see illustration).

6   Disconnect the electrical connection to the combination switch then, remove the screws secure the switch to the column.

7   Slide the switch off of the column.

8   Installation is the reverse of removal.

9   Ignition switch and key lock cylinder - check and replacement

Warning: *The models covered by this manual are equipped with a Supplemental Restraint System (SRS), more commonly known as airbags. Always disarm the airbag system before working in the vicinity of any airbag system component to avoid the possibility of accidental deployment of the airbag, which could cause personal injury (see Section 26).*

1   Disconnect the cable from the negative terminal of the battery (see Chapter 5).

Note: *The manufacturer recommends removing the entire steering column to replace the lock cylinder. But, it can be done with it still in the vehicle. Use your own judgement as to which way you would prefer to accomplish the task. The following procedures are the same whether the column is in the car or out. The difference is the positions of the components. Out of the car you can maneuver the steering column. For steering column removal (see Chapter 10).*

2   Remove the instrument panel lower cover, the upper and lower steering column covers and the instrument cluster trim panel (see Chapter 11).

3   Depress the release tab on the ignition switch electrical connector to remove it (see illustration).

4   If equipped, remove the plate underneath the steering column assembly (see illustration).

5   On models with a tilt steering column, move the tilt lever down far enough to clear the ignition switch.

6   If you're just replacing the ignition switch (electrical part), remove the switch retaining screw and remove the switch. Otherwise leave it in place to be removed as an assembly with the key lock cylinder.

7   If you're replacing the key lock cylinder, use a hammer and punch to unscrew the two breakaway bolts (see illustration).

Note: *If the bolts can't be unscrewed using this method, you'll have to drill a hole down the center of each bolt and unscrew them with a screw extractor, or use a larger drill bit and drill out the entire bolt head.*

8   Remove the ignition switch and key lock cylinder as an assembly.

9   If you're replacing the key lock cylinder, remove the ignition switch from the key lock cylinder assembly (see illustration 9.4).

10   Installation is the reverse of removal. When installing the lock cylinder bolts, tighten them until their heads twist off.

8.5 Combination switch electrical connectors. Each switch can be removed separately

9.3 Disconnect the ignition switch electrical connector

9.4 Fastener locations

A   *Ignition switch fastener*
B   *Plate fasteners*

9.7 Using a hammer and punch, knock these breakaway bolts in a counterclockwise direction to unscrew them, remove the upper clamp and detach the key lock cylinder/ignition switch assembly from the steering column assembly by pulling it straight down

10.2a For Legacy models, follow the removal procedure in Chapter 11, then grasp the end while using a trim tool across the top edge and pull it free

10.2b On the Forester just push the panel (B) off by reaching in from the end trim panel (A) area

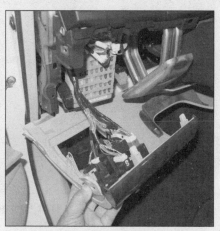

10.3a Tilt the panel down to expose the electrical connections

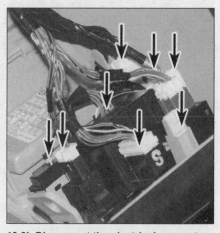

10.3b Disconnect the electrical connectors to remove the panel or the switches

10   Instrument panel switches - replacement

Warning: *The models covered by this manual are equipped with a Supplemental Restraint System (SRS), more commonly known as air-bags. Always disarm the airbag system before working in the vicinity of any airbag system component to avoid the possibility of accidental deployment of the airbag, which could cause personal injury (see Section 26).*
Note: *The procedure for removing and installing the heater and air conditioning control assembly is in Chapter 3.*

Illumination brightness control switch, remote control mirror switch and/or windshield wiper de-icer switch

1   All of these switches are located at the left end of the instrument panel, in the instrument panel lower cover.
2   Remove the dashboard end panel (see Chapter 11 for removal procedure). On the Forester model remove the dash end trim and push the switch panel outwards (see illustrations).
3   Tilt the panel down and disconnect the electrical connectors. Remove the screws securing the switches from the back side (see illustrations).

10.3c Remove the switch mounting screws to the switches you are replacing

10.5 Depress the tabs from the back side and push the switch outwards from the control panel

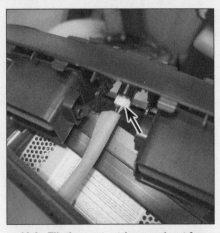

10.9a Tilt the center trim panel out far enough to get to the tabs for the switch

10.9b Leave the wire connector exposed through the opening so you can snap the switch back into place. That way the connector won't fall back through the dash

11.5a Legacy instrument cluster fastener locations

11.5b Forester instrument cluster fastener locations

11.6 Disconnect the instrument cluster electrical connectors (not all release tabs are the same type or in the same location on all instrument clusters)

Legacy hazard flasher switch

4   Remove the center trim panel and the HVAC control head (see Chapter 3).
5   Depress the tabs on the switch housing and push the switch out from the back side of the control unit (see illustration).
6   Installation is the reverse of removal.

Forester hazard flasher switch

7   Remove center trim panel and HVAC control head (see Chapter 11).
8   Press in on the side tabs of the switch and push it out through the front.
9   With switch pulled out of the center trim, now disconnect the electrical connector (see illustrations).
10   Installation is the reverse of removal.

---

11   Instrument cluster - removal and installation

Warning: *The models covered by this manual are equipped with a Supplemental Restraint System (SRS), more commonly known as air-bags. Always disarm the airbag system before working in the vicinity of any airbag system component to avoid the possibility of accidental deployment of the airbag, which could cause personal injury (see Section 26).*

1   Disconnect the cable from the negative terminal of the battery (see Chapter 5).
2   If the vehicle is equipped with a tilt steering column, lower the column to its lowest position.
3   Remove the center trim panel (see Chapter 11).
4   Remove the instrument cluster visor screws. Then, tilt the top out and pull upwards to release the bottom hooked clips.
5   Remove the four screws securing the cluster to the dash (see illustrations). Then tilt the cluster downward to gain access to the electrical connections.
6   Depress the release tabs and disconnect the electrical connectors from the backside of the instrument cluster (see illustration), then carefully remove the cluster.
7   Installation is the reverse of removal.

12.3a Legacy model radio mounting screws

12.3b Forester model radio mounting screws

12.4a Pull out the radio assembly and disconnect the electrical connectors and the antenna cable, Legacy model shown

12.4b Forester models are similiar

12.10 Door speaker mounting screws (front door shown, rear door similar)

12   Radio and speakers - removal and installation

Warning: *The models covered by this manual are equipped with a Supplemental Restraint System (SRS), more commonly known as airbags. Always disarm the airbag system before working in the vicinity of any airbag system component to avoid the possibility of accidental deployment of the airbag, which could cause personal injury (see Section 26).*

Radio

1   Disconnect the cable from the negative terminal of the battery (see Chapter 5).
2   Remove center panel (see Chapter 11).
3   Remove the radio mounting screws (see illustrations).

4   Pull out the radio and mounting bracket assembly far enough to disconnect the antenna lead and electrical connectors from the backside of the radio (see illustrations), and remove the radio.
5   Installation is the reverse of removal.

Satellite radio unit and navigation unit

6   Remove the radio (see Steps 1 through 4).
7   Remove the mounting screws and pull the satellite radio unit out from the instrument panel far enough to disconnect the electrical connectors from the back side, then remove the satellite radio.
8   Installation is the reverse of removal.

Speakers

Door speakers
Note: *This procedure applies to front and rear door speakers.*
9   Remove the door trim panel (see Chapter 11).
10   Remove the door speaker mounting screws (see illustration).
11   Pull out the speaker, disconnect the electrical connector and remove the speaker.
12   Installation is the reverse of removal.

Tweeter speakers
13   Remove the mirror sail panel (see Chapter 11).
14   Disconnect the electrical connector from the speaker.
15   Remove the speaker mounting screws and remove the speaker from the panel.
16   Installation is the reverse of removal.

12.18 Screw locations

12.19 The electrical connection can be reached from inside the trunk once the trim has been removed or disconnected when the speaker has been removed

14.2 Carefully pry off the protective cap from each windshield wiper arm

14.4 Mark the relationship of the arm to its shaft to ensure correct alignment when it's reinstalled

14.8 Windshield wiper motor linkage assembly mounting bolts (A) and electrical connector (B). Connector has already been disconnected

Sub woofer speaker

17   Remove the parcel shelf (see Chapter 11).
18   Remove the screws securing the speaker to the shelf (see illustration).
19   Disconnect the electrical connector and remove the speaker (see illustration).
20   Installation is the reverse of removal.

---

13   Antenna - removal and installation

Warning: *The models covered by this manual are equipped with a Supplemental Restraint System (SRS), more commonly known as airbags. Always disarm the airbag system before working in the vicinity of any airbag system component to avoid the possibility of accidental deployment of the airbag, which could cause personal injury (see Section 26).*
Note: *Our research has shown that there are several different types of antennas installed throughout the various years covered in this manual. Listed below are the various types of antennas that could fit your vehicle and the replacement procedures.*

Antenna mast and cable type (fender mounted)

1   Remove the antenna base mounting screws.
2   Remove the driver's side carpeting and the center console left side panel (see Chapter 11).
3   Trace the antenna cable down from the A-pillar, down through the kick panel area, across the floorpan and up the left side of the center console area, where it's connected to the cable that goes to the back of the radio. Disconnect the cable.
4   Attach a wire to the old antenna cable, then pull the cable up through the A-pillar. Attach the wire to the new antenna cable and run it back through the A-pillar. Once the cable has been correctly routed back to the radio cable, reconnect the two cables.
5   Installation is otherwise the reverse of removal.

Rear roof antenna

6   Remove the rear trim panel fasteners and remove the trim panels (see Chapter 11).
7   Carefully pull the headliner down enough to access the antenna mounting nut and

remove the nut.
8   Disconnect the electrical connectors and pull the antenna from the top of the roof.
9   Installation is the reverse of removal.

---

14   Wiper motors - replacement

Front wiper motor and linkage

1   Disconnect the cable from the negative terminal of the battery (see Chapter 5).
2   Remove the protective cap from each windshield wiper arm (see illustration).
3   Remove the nut securing each wiper arm to its shaft.
4   Before removing the wiper arm, mark the relationship of each wiper arm to its shaft (see illustration).
5   Remove the wiper arms.
6   Remove the cowl cover (see Chapter 11).
7   Disconnect the electrical connector from the wiper motor.
8   Remove the wiper motor and linkage assembly retaining bolts and nut (see illustration), and remove the assembly from the cowl.

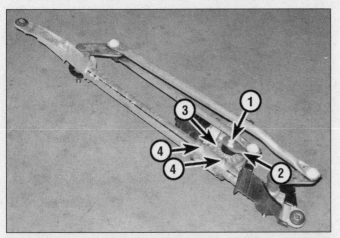

14.9 Remove the crank arm nut (1), mark the relationship of crank arm (2) to the mounting bracket (3), remove the crank arm, then remove the motor mounting bolts (4) (Not all the motor mounting bolts are shown in this view)

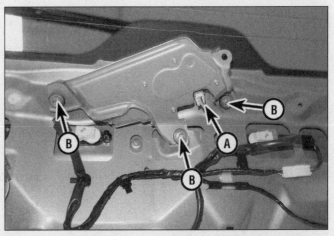

14.17 Forester rear wiper motor shown.

A   Electrical connector   B   Mounting bolts

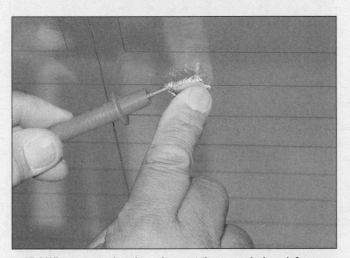

15.4 When measuring the voltage at the rear window defogger grid, wrap a piece of aluminum foil around the positive probe of the voltmeter and press the foil against the wire with your finger

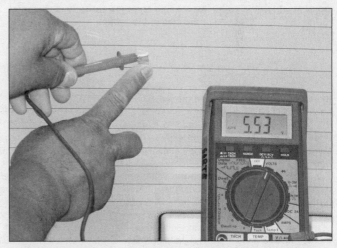

15.5 To determine if a heating element has broken, check the voltage at the center of each element; if the voltage is 5 or 6-volts, the element is unbroken, but if the voltage is 10 or 12-volts, the element is broken between the center and the ground side. If there is no voltage, the element is broken between the center and the positive side

9   Separate the wiper motor from the linkage assembly (see illustration).
10   Installation is the reverse of removal.

Rear wiper motor

11   Disconnect the cable from the negative terminal of the battery (see Chapter 5).
12   Flip up the wiper arm cover.
13   Remove the nut securing the wiper arm to the motor shaft and remove the arm.
14   Mark the relationship of the wiper arm to its shaft and remove the nut.
Note: *Note the installation sequence of the spacers and cushion used. These parts must be installed in the correct sequence when installing the rear wiper arm.*
15   Remove the liftgate trim panel (see Chapter 11).
16   Disconnect the electrical connector from the wiper motor.

17   Remove the wiper motor mounting bolts and remove the motor from the liftgate (see illustration).
18   Installation is the reverse of removal.

---

15   Rear window defogger - check and repair

1   The rear window defogger consists of a number of horizontal elements baked onto the glass surface.
2   Small breaks in the element can be repaired without removing the rear window.

Check

3   Turn the ignition switch and defogger system switches to the ON position. Using a voltmeter, place the positive probe against the

defogger grid positive terminal and the negative probe against the ground terminal. If battery voltage is not indicated, check the fuse, defogger switch and related wiring. If voltage is indicated, but all or part of the defogger doesn't heat, proceed with the following tests.
4   When measuring voltage during these tests, wrap a piece of aluminum foil around the tip of the voltmeter positive probe and press the foil against the heating element with your finger (see illustration). Place the negative probe on the defogger grid ground terminal.
5   Check the voltage at the center of each heating element (see illustration). If the voltage is 5 or 6-volts, the element is okay (there is no break). If there is not voltage, the element is broken between the center of the element and the positive end. If the voltage is 10 to 12 volts the element is broken between

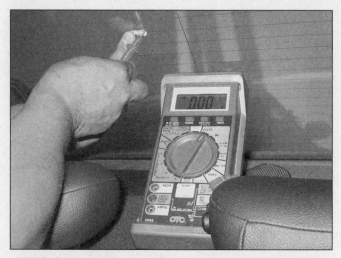

15.7 To find the break, place the voltmeter negative lead against the defogger ground terminal, place the voltmeter positive lead with the foil strip against the heating element at the positive terminal end and slide it toward the negative terminal end. The point at which the voltmeter reading changes abruptly is the point at which the element is broken

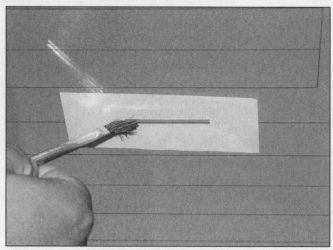

15.13 To use a defogger repair kit, apply masking tape to the inside of the window at the damaged area, then brush on the special conductive coating

the center of the element and ground. Check each heating element.

6 Connect the negative lead to a good body ground. The reading should stay the same. If it doesn't, the ground connection is bad.

7 To find the break, place the voltmeter negative probe against the defogger ground terminal. Place the voltmeter positive probe with the foil strip against the heating element at the positive terminal end and slide it toward the negative terminal end. The point at which the voltmeter deflects from several volts to zero is the point at which the heating element is broken (see illustration).

Repair

8 Repair the break in the element using a repair kit specifically recommended for this purpose, available at most auto parts stores. Included in this kit is plastic conductive epoxy.

9 Prior to repairing a break, turn off the system and allow it to cool off for a few minutes.

10 Lightly buff the element area with fine steel wool, then clean it thoroughly with rubbing alcohol.

11 Use masking tape to mask off the area being repaired.

12 Thoroughly mix the epoxy, following the instructions provided with the repair kit.

13 Apply the epoxy material to the slit in the masking tape, overlapping the undamaged area about 3/4-inch on either end (see illustration).

14 Allow the repair to cure for 24 hours before removing the tape and using the system.

16 Headlight bulbs - replacement

Warning: *Halogen gas-filled bulbs are under pressure and may shatter if the surface is scratched or the bulb is dropped. Wear eye protection and handle the bulbs carefully, grasping only the base whenever possible. Do not touch the surface of the bulb with your fingers because the oil from your skin could cause it to overheat and fail prematurely. If you do touch the bulb surface, clean it with rubbing alcohol.*

Warning: *Some models use high-intensity-discharge (HID) bulbs for the low beam bulbs. HID bulbs use an extremely high voltage. To avoid the risk of an electric shock and serious injury, do not attempt to replace these bulbs at home. Do not try to replace the high-beam bulbs either. And don't try to remove and install the headlight housing on these models. Instead, if the headlight housing, high-beam bulb or low-beam bulb needs service, have it done by a Subaru dealer or other qualified repair shop.*

1 Disconnect the cable from the negative terminal of the battery (see Chapter 5).

Legacy models

Low beam bulbs

2 For the right hand side bulb, remove the intake duct.

3 Turn the front wheels in the opposite direction as to the bulb you want to change.

4 Remove front mounting fasteners and pull back the inner fender splash shield (see Chapter 11).

5 Twist the headlight weather cap counterclockwise (see illustration). and remove the

cap. Then, disconnect the electrical connector to the bulb. (The following photos are with the headlight housing in place. More detail removal procedures are provided below with the headlight housing removed.)

6 Find the curled end of the wire fastener that holds the headlight in place. Push down and inward on the curled end of the wire to disengage the fastener. Rotate the fastener out of the way. Then, remove the bulb (see illustrations).

Note: *Illustrations shown with headlight housing removed for clarity.*

7 Installation is the reverse of removal

High-beam bulbs

8 Disconnect the electrical connector from the bulb.

9 For the right-side bulb, remove the intake duct.

10 Disconnect the electrical connector from the bulb, then remove the bulb from the headlight housing by turning it counterclockwise a quarter turn (see illustrations).

11 Installation is the reverse of removal.

Forester

Low beam bulbs

12 Disconnect the cable from the negative terminal of the battery (see Chapter 1).

13 For the right-side headlight, remove the intake air duct.

14 Reaching in from the engine side, disconnect the electrical connections to the headlight bulbs.

15 Rotate the bulb counterclockwise to remove it.

16 Installation is the reverse of removal.

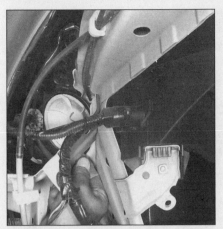

16.5a With the inner fender splash shield out of the way, reach up and rotate the weather cap counterclockwise to get to the headlight bulb

16.5b We used long-reach needle-nose pliers to get to the hold down wire

16.5c Once the wire has been unclipped, the bulb can be removed

16.6a Low beam bulb cover

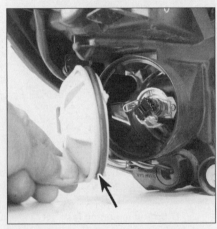

16.6b Rotate the cover counterclockwise to remove it

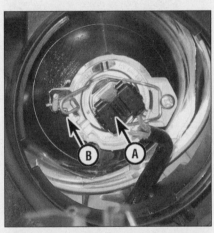

16.6c Disconnect the electrical connector (A) then, unlatch the curled end of the wire holder (B) and rotate it out of the way

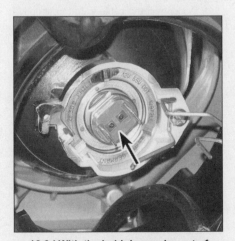

16.6d With the hold down wire out of the way pull the bulb straight out of the headlamp housing

16.10a Disconnect the electrical connector

16.10b To remove the high-beam bulb from the headlight housing, turn it counterclockwise a quarter turn

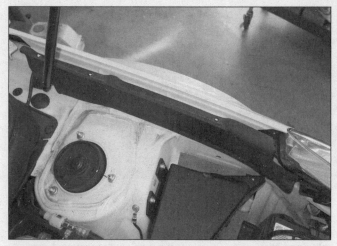

17.4 Fender inner cover trim needs to be removed to expose the headlamp housing retainers. Use a flat trim tool to release the clips along the top edge of the trim cover

17.6a Front headlight housing mounting bolts

17.6b (1) Pressure clip - (2) mounting bolts

17.6c Top mounting fastener

17.6d Top rear mounting fasteners

High beam bulbs

17   For the right-side headlight, remove the intake duct.

18   Reaching in from the engine side, disconnect the electrical connections to the

17.6e Pull the headlamp housing straight out to remove it

headlight bulbs.

19   Rotate the bulb counterclockwise to remove it.

20   Installation is the reverse of removal.

17   Headlight housings - removal and installation

Warning: *Some models use high-intensity-discharge (HID) bulbs for the low beam bulbs. HID bulbs use an extremely high voltage. To avoid the risk of an electric shock and serious injury, do not attempt to replace these bulbs at home. Do not try to replace the high-beam bulbs either. And don't try to remove and install the headlight housing on these models. Instead, if the headlight housing, high-beam bulb or low-beam bulb needs service, have it done by a Subaru dealer.*

Warning: *Many of these vehicles are equipped with halogen gas-filled headlight bulbs, which are under pressure and may shatter if the surface is damaged or the bulb is dropped. Wear eye protection and handle the bulbs carefully, grasping only the base whenever possible.*

Do not touch the surface of the bulb with your fingers because the oil from your skin could cause it to overheat and fail prematurely. If you do touch the bulb surface, clean it with rubbing alcohol.

1   Disconnect the cable from the negative terminal of the battery (see Chapter 5).

2   If you're removing the right headlight housing, remove the air intake duct (see Chapter 4).

3   Remove the radiator grille(s) and the front bumper cover (see Chapter 11).

4   Remove the fender inner cover trim (see illustration).

5   Disconnect the electrical connector(s) from the headlight bulb(s) (see Section 16) and from the parking, turn signal and side-marker light bulbs. Remove the upper fender apron.

6   Remove the headlight housing bolts (see illustrations) and disengage the pressure clips.

7   Pull out the headlight housing and disconnect any other electrical connectors from the housing.

8   Installation is the reverse of removal. Check the headlight adjustment (see Section 18).

18.1a Headlight adjustment screw location

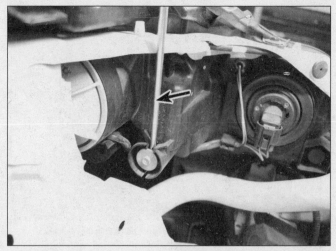

18.1b The headlight adjustment screw is located at the base of the headlight housing next to the bulb access cover. Use a Phillips screwdriver to make the adjustments

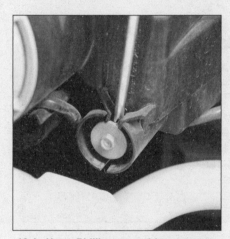

18.1c Use a Phillips screwdriver to rotate the adjuster wheel

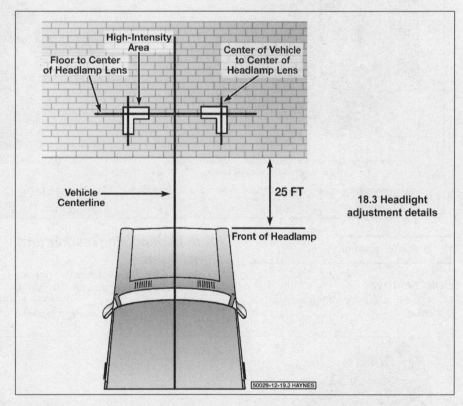

18.3 Headlight adjustment details

18 Headlights - adjustment

Note: *The headlights must be aimed correctly. If adjusted incorrectly they could blind the driver of an oncoming vehicle and cause a serious accident or seriously reduce your ability to see the road. The headlights should be checked for proper aim every 12 months and any time a new headlight is installed or front end bodywork is performed. It should be emphasized that the following procedure is only an interim step that will provide temporary adjustment until a properly equipped shop can adjust the headlights. Always have someone sitting in the driver's position to adjust the headlights.*

1   Each headlight has a single adjusting screw for adjusting up-and-down movement (see illustrations).

2   There are several methods for adjusting the headlights. The simplest method requires a blank wall 25 feet in front of the vehicle and a level floor.

3   Position masking tape vertically on the wall in reference to the vehicle centerline and the centerlines of both headlights (see illustration).

4   Position a horizontal tape line in reference to the centerline of all the headlights.

Note: *It might be easier to position the tape on the wall with the vehicle parked only a few inches away.*

5   Adjustment should be made with the vehicle sitting level, the gas tank half-full and no unusually heavy load in the vehicle.

6   Starting with the low beam adjustment, position the high intensity zone so it is two inches below the horizontal line and two inches to the right of the headlight vertical line. Adjustment is made by turning the adjusting screw to raise or lower the beam.

7   With the high beams on, the high intensity zone should be vertically centered with the exact center just below the horizontal line.

Note: *It might not be possible to position the headlight aim exactly for both high and low beams. If a compromise must be made, keep in mind that the low beams are the most used and have the greatest effect on driver safety.*

8   Have the headlights adjusted by a dealer service department or service station at the earliest opportunity.

Bulb removal

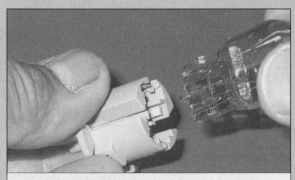

To remove many modern exterior bulbs from their holders, simply pull them out

On bulbs with a cylindrical base ("bayonet" bulbs), the socket is spring-loaded; a pair of small posts on the side of the base hold the bulb in place against spring pressure. To remove this type of bulb, push it into the holder, rotate it 1/4-turn counterclockwise, then pull it out

If a bayonet bulb has dual filaments, the posts are staggered, so the bulb can only be installed one way

To remove most overhead interior light bulbs, simply unclip them

19   Bulb replacement

Bulb removal

1   Typical bulb removal procedures (see illustration).

Front parking/side marker/turn signal lights

2   Remove the air intake duct for right side and inner fender cover trim for left side (if applicable).
3   Turn the bulb holder counterclockwise to remove it from the housing, then turn the bulb counterclockwise and remove it from the socket (see illustrations).
Note: *Illustrations shown with headlight housing removed*
4   Installation is the reverse of removal.

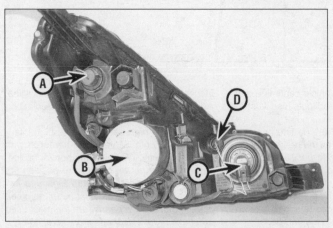

19.3a Bulb locations

A   *Turn/park lamp bulb*   C   *High beam headlamp*
B   *Low beam headlamp*   D   *Marker light*

19.3b Rotate a quarter turn counterclockwise to remove the bulb socket

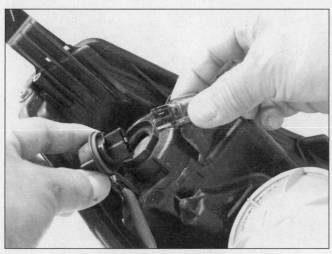

19.3c Pull the bulb out of the socket to remove it

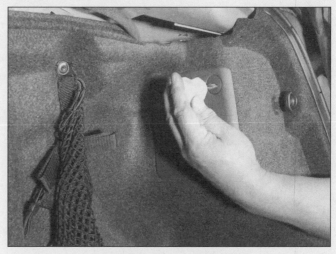

19.5 Remove the access panel

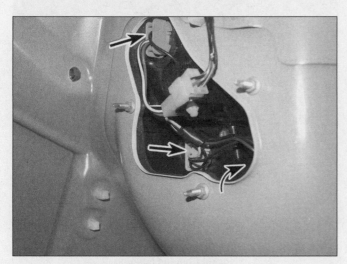

19.6a Bulb locations

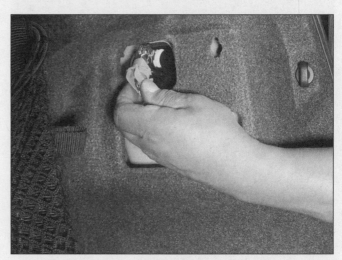

19.6b Twist the bulb holder counterclockwise to remove it from the housing

Rear side marker/brake/turn signal lights

Legacy models

5   Open the trunk lid and remove the rear combination light cover if applicable (see illustration).

6   Turn the bulb holder counterclockwise and remove it from the housing (see illustrations). To remove the bulb, pull the bulb straight out of the socket.

7   Installation is the reverse of removal.

Trunk lid lighting

8   Use a flat-bladed screwdriver to pry open the access panel.

9   Disconnect the electrical connector to the bulb socket (see illustration).

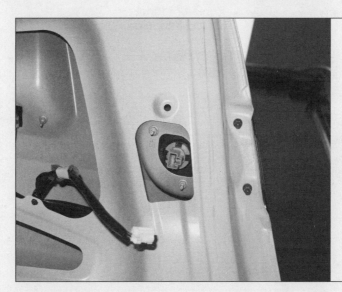

19.9 Disconnect the electrical connector

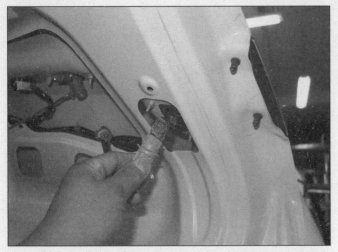

19.10 Rotate the socket to remove the bulb and socket

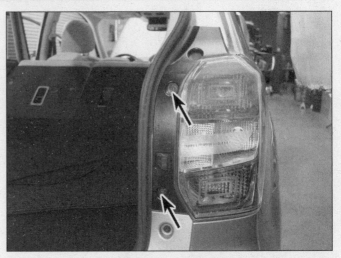

19.13 Screw locations

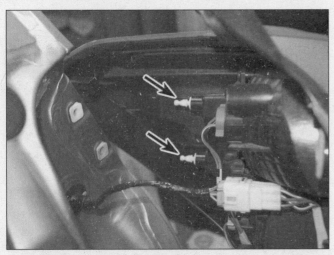

19.14 Pull straight out to free the ballstuds that secure the light housing

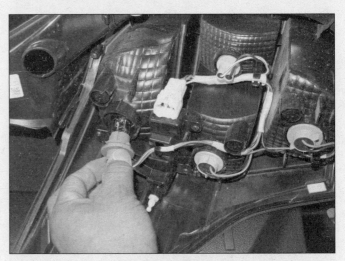

19.15 Twist the bulb socket counterclockwise to remove the socket from the housing

10   Rotate the socket counterclockwise to remove the bulb socket, then pull the bulb straight out of the socket to replace it (see illustration).

11   Installation is the reverse of removal.

Forester models
12   Open the litgate.

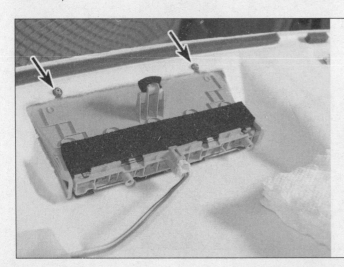

19.17 High-mount brake light fixture speed-nuts (these must be pried off)

13   Remove the two screws securing the light fixture to the vehicle (see illustration).
14   Pull the light housing straight out to release the two pressure clips on the outside edges, then disconnect the electrical connector (see illustration).
15   Twist the bulb socket to remove, then pull the bulb straight out to replace them (see illustration).

High-mount brake lights
Note: *The high-mount brake light is an LED type bulb. Bulbs are not serviced, only the entire fixture.*

Legacy models
16   Remove the rear parcel shelf (see Chapter 11).
17   Disconnect the high-mount brake light electrical connector and remove the speed-nuts (see illustration).
18   Installation is the reverse of removal.

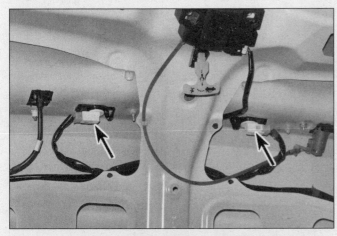

19.30a License plate light socket locations

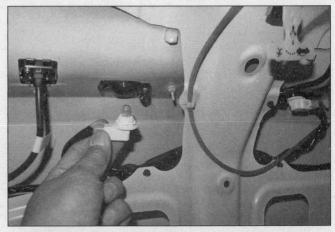

19.30b Pull the bulb straight out of the bulb socket to remove the bulb

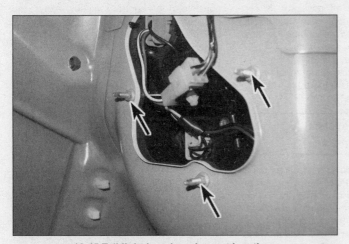

19.45 Tail light lens housing nut locations

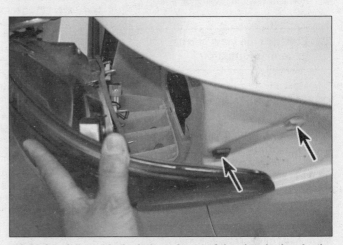

19.46 Carefully guide the bolt studs out of the slots in the plastic clips and remove the housing

Forester models

2013 and earlier models

19   Pry off the screw covers and remove the screws, then detach the high-mount brake light and disconnect the electrical connector.
20   Installation is the reverse of removal.

2014 and later models

Roof spoiler type

21   Open the liftgate and remove the trim (see Chapter 11).
22   Unbolt the roof spoiler.
23   Remove the screws and separate the high-mount brake light assembly from its mounting plate.
24   Installation is the reverse of removal

Liftgate mounted type

25   Open the liftgate and remove the trim panels (see Chapter 11).
26   Unbolt the high-mounted brake light fixture from the liftgate.
27   Remove the high-mounted brake light assembly and disconnect the electrical connector.
28   Installation is the reverse of removal.

License plate light

Legacy models

29   Open the trunk and remove the trunk lid trim panels (if applicable).
30   Rotate the bulb socket to remove the bulb and socket assembly (see illustrations).
31   Remove the bulb from its socket by pulling it straight out.
32   Installation is the reverse of removal.

Forester models

33   Push the license plate light housing to the left while pulling the end of the housing downwards.
34   Remove the housing from the liftgate.
35   Rotate the socket counterclockwise a quarter turn, then remove the bulb from its socket by pulling it straight out.
36   Installation is the reverse of removal.

Interior lights and dome lights

37   Pry the lens off the interior light housing.
38   Detach the bulb from the terminals. It may be necessary to turn the bulb until the flat surfaces at the ends are aligned vertically.

Pull the bulb straight out.
39   Installation is the reverse of removal.

Fog light bulb replacement

40   Remove the lower mud guard/close out panel (see Chapter 11, illustration 10.2a).
41   Disconnect the electrical connector.
42   Rotate the bulb counterclockwise to remove it.
43   Installation is the reverse of removal.

Tail light lens housing removal and installation

44   Open the trunk and remove the cargo netting and the three cargo net fasteners. Then remove the trunk side liner trim (if applicable).
45   Remove the three nuts securing the housing to the body (see illustration).
46   Pull the housing away from the body (see illustration).
47   Disconnect the electrical connections (if you haven't already from the inside of the trunk) then remove the lens.
48   Installation is the reverse of removal.

20 Horn - replacement

1   The low tone horn is located in front of the radiator, while the high tone horn is located behind the mud guard/close out panel just in front of the right wheel well area (see illustration).

2   For the low-tone horn, remove the intake duct and upper radiator to grille close out panel.

3   For the high-tone horn, remove the lower right hand mud guard/close out panel to reach the horn bracket and electrical connection (see Chapter 11, illustration 10.2a).

4   To replace either horn, depress the release tab and disconnect the electrical connector, then remove the bracket bolt.

5   Detach the horn from its mounting bracket.

6   Installation is the reverse of removal.

21 Electric side view mirrors - general information

1   Most electric rear view mirrors use two motors to move the glass; one for up and down adjustments and one for left-right adjustments.

2   The control switch has a selector portion that sends voltage to the left or right side mirror. With the ignition ON but the engine OFF, roll down the windows and operate the mirror control switch through all functions (left-right and up-down) for both the left and right side mirrors.

3   Listen carefully for the sound of the electric motors running in the mirrors.

4   If the motors can be heard but the mirror glass doesn't move, there's probably a problem with the drive mechanism inside the mirror.

5   If the mirrors don't operate and no sound comes from the mirrors, check the fuse.

6   If the fuse is OK, remove the mirror control switch from its mounting without disconnecting the wires attached to it. Turn the ignition ON and check for voltage at the switch. There should be voltage at one terminal. If there's no voltage at the switch, check for an open or short in the circuit between the fuse panel and the switch.

7   If there's voltage at the switch, disconnect it. Check the switch for continuity in all its operating positions. If the switch does not have continuity, replace it.

8   Re-connect the switch. Locate the wire going from the switch to ground. Leaving the switch connected, connect a jumper wire between this wire and ground. If the mirror works normally with this wire in place, repair the faulty ground connection.

9   If the mirror still doesn't work, remove the mirror (see Chapter 11) and check the wires at the mirror for voltage. Check with ignition ON and the mirror selector switch on the appropriate side. Operate the mirror switch in all its positions. There should be voltage at one of

20.1 Typically, the horns are located on small mounting brackets that are bolted to the vertical support in front of the radiator and air conditioner condenser. The high tone horn is below the right hand headlamp area behind the close out panel.

the switch-to-mirror wires in each switch position (except the neutral "off" position).

10   If there's not voltage in each switch position, check the circuit between the mirror and control switch for opens and shorts.

11   If there's voltage, remove the mirror and test it off the vehicle with jumper wires. Replace the mirror if it fails this test.

22 Cruise control system - general information

1   The cruise control system maintains vehicle speed with a PCM-controlled servo located in the engine compartment, which is connected to the throttle body by a cable. The system consists of the cruise control unit, brake switch, control switches, vacuum hose and vehicle speed sensor. Some features of the system require special testers and diagnostic procedures that are beyond the scope of this manual. Listed below are some general procedures that may be used to locate common problems. 2006 and later models have an electronic throttle body and do not use a cruise control cable (the PCM is in direct control of the electronic throttle body).

2   Locate and check the fuses (see Section 3).

3   Check the brake light switch (see Chapter 9).

4   Visually inspect the control cable between the actuator assembly and throttle body for free movement, replace it if necessary.

5   Check for trouble codes (see Chapter 6).

6   Test drive the vehicle to determine if the cruise control is now working. If it isn't, take it to an automotive electrical specialist for further diagnosis.

23 Power window system - general information

1   The power window system operates electric motors, mounted in the doors, which

lower and raise the windows. The system consists of the control switches, relays, the motors, regulators and associated wiring.

2   The power windows can be lowered and raised from the master control switch by the driver or by remote switches located at the individual windows. Each window has a separate motor that is reversible. The position of the control switch determines the polarity and therefore the direction of operation.

3   The circuit is protected by a fuse and a circuit breaker. Each motor is also equipped with an internal circuit breaker; this prevents one stuck window from disabling the whole system.

4   The power window system will only operate when the ignition switch is ON. In addition, many models have a window lockout switch at the master control switch which, when activated, disables the switches at the rear windows and, sometimes, the switch at the passenger's window also. Always check these items before troubleshooting a window problem.

5   These procedures are general in nature, so if you can't find the problem using them, take the vehicle to a dealer service department or other properly equipped repair facility.

6   If the power windows won't operate, always check the fuse and circuit breaker first.

7   If only the rear windows are inoperative, or if the windows only operate from the master control switch, check the rear window lockout switch for continuity in the unlocked position. Replace it if it doesn't have continuity.

8   Check the wiring between the switches and fuse panel for continuity. Repair the wiring, if necessary.

9   If only one window is inoperative from the master control switch, try the other control switch at the window.

Note: *This doesn't apply to the driver's door window.*

10   If the same window works from one switch, but not the other, check the switch for continuity. If the continuity is not as specified, replace the switch.

11   If the switch tests OK, check for a short

or open in the circuit between the affected switch and the window motor.

12   If one window is inoperative from both switches, remove the trim panel from the affected door and check for voltage at the switch and at the motor while the switch is operated.

13   If voltage is reaching the motor, disconnect the glass from the regulator (see Chapter 11). Move the window up and down by hand while checking for binding and damage. Also check for binding and damage to the regulator. If the regulator is not damaged and the window moves up and down smoothly, replace the motor. If there's binding or damage, lubricate, repair or replace parts, as necessary.

14   If voltage isn't reaching the motor, check the wiring in the circuit for continuity between the switches and motors. You'll need to consult the wiring diagram for the vehicle. If the circuit is equipped with a relay, check that the relay is grounded properly and receiving voltage.

15   Test the windows after you are done to confirm proper repairs.

24   Power door lock system - general information

1   The power door lock system operates the door lock actuators mounted in each door. The system consists of the switches, actuators, a control unit and associated wiring. Diagnosis can usually be limited to simple checks of the wiring connections and actuators for minor faults that can be easily repaired. The system uses an electronic control unit; in-depth diagnosis should be left to a dealership service department. The door lock control unit is located behind the instrument panel, to the right of the fuse box.

2   Power door lock systems are operated by bi-directional solenoids located in the doors. The lock switches have two operating positions: Lock and Unlock. When activated, the switch sends a ground signal to the door lock control unit to lock or unlock the doors. Depending on which way the switch is activated, the control unit reverses polarity to the solenoids, allowing the two sides of the circuit to be used alternately as the feed (positive) and ground side.

3   Some vehicles may have an anti-theft systems incorporated into the power locks. If you are unable to locate the trouble using the following general Steps, consult a dealer service department.

4   Always check the circuit protection first. Some vehicles use a combination of circuit breakers and fuses.

5   Operate the door lock switches in both directions (Lock and Unlock) with the engine off. Listen for the click of the solenoids operating.

6   Test the switches for continuity. Replace the switch if there's not continuity in both switch positions.

7   Check the wiring between the switches,

control unit and solenoids for continuity. Repair the wiring if there's no continuity.

8   Check for a bad ground at the switches or the control unit.

9   If all but one lock solenoids operate, remove the trim panel from the affected door (see Chapter 11) and check for voltage at the solenoid while the lock switch is operated. One of the wires should have voltage in the Lock position; the other should have voltage in the Unlock position.

10   If the inoperative solenoid is receiving voltage, replace the solenoid.

11   If the inoperative solenoid isn't receiving voltage, check the relay or for an open or short in the wire between the lock solenoid and the control unit.

Note: *It's common for wires to break in the portion of the harness between the body and door (opening and closing the door fatigues and eventually breaks the wires).*

25   Daytime Running Lights (DRL) - general information

1   The Daytime Running Lights (DRL) system illuminates the headlights when the engine is running. The DRL system supplies reduced power to the headlights so they won't be too bright for daytime use, which also prolongs headlight life.

Daytime running light resistor - removal and installation

Legacy

2   Remove the front bumper cover (see Chapter 11).

3   On the left side of the engine compartment, just below the left headlamp assembly, remove the fasteners securing the daytime running light resistor.

4   Disconnect the electrical connections and remove the resistor.

5   Installation is the reverse of removal.

Forester

6   Remove the lower mud guard/close out panel (see Chapter 11, illustration 10.2a).

7   Locate the daytime running light resistor in the area just below the right headlight assembly.

8   Unbolt the resistor, disconnect the electrical connections and remove it.

9   Installation is the reverse of removal.

26   Airbags - general information

1   All models are equipped with a Supplemental Restraint System (SRS), more commonly known as airbags. This system is designed to protect the driver and front seat passenger from serious injury in the event of a head-on or frontal collision. It consists of an airbag module in the center of the steering wheel and, if equipped, another airbag inside the instrument panel, above the glove

compartment. Additionally, some models are equipped with side-impact airbags, side curtain airbags and seat belt pre-tensioners (which are pyrotechnic devices that reduce the slack in the front seat belts during an impact of sufficient force to trigger the airbags).

Airbags

Driver's side

2   The airbag inflator module contains a housing incorporating the cushion (airbag) and inflator unit, mounted in the center of the steering wheel. The inflator assembly is mounted on the back of the housing over a hole through which gas is expelled, inflating the bag almost instantaneously when an electrical signal is sent from the system. The roll connector, generally referred to as the clockspring, on the steering column under the module carries this signal to the module. The clockspring can transmit an electrical signal regardless of steering wheel position. Information about removing the driver's airbag assembly and the clockspring is in Chapter 10, Section 14.

Passenger's side, side impact and side curtain airbags

3   The passenger's side airbag is mounted above the glove compartment and designated by the letters SRS (Supplemental Restraint System). It consists of an inflator containing an igniter, a bag assembly, a housing and a trim cover.

4   To remove passenger's side air bag remove the instrument panel trim (see Chapter 11). With the trim panel removed you can get to the four bolts that secure the passenger air bag to the dash.

5   The passenger's airbag is considerably larger than the steering wheel-mounted unit. The trim cover is textured and painted to match the instrument panel and has a molded seam that splits when the bag inflates.

6   Side impact airbags, if equipped, are located in the outer sides of the front seat backs.

7   Side curtain airbags, if equipped, are mounted along the outer edges of the headliner, above the door opening.

Airbag control module

8   The airbag control module supplies the current to the airbag system in the event of a collision, even if battery power is cut off. It checks this system every time the vehicle is started, causing the airbag warning light on the instrument cluster to go on then off, if the system is operating properly. If there is a fault in the system, the light will go on and stay on, flash, or the dash will make a beeping sound. If this happens, the vehicle should be taken to your dealer immediately for service.

Precautions

Disabling the SRS system

Warning: *Failure to follow these precautions could result in accidental deployment of the airbag and personal injury.*

9   Whenever working in the vicinity of the steering wheel, steering column or any of the other SRS system components, the system must be disarmed. To disarm the system:

 a) *Point the wheels straight ahead and turn the ignition key to the LOCK position.*
 b) *Disconnect the cable from the negative terminal of the battery (see Chapter 5).*
 c) *Wait at least two minutes for the back-up power supply to be drained.*

10   Whenever handling an airbag module, always keep the airbag opening (the trim side) pointed away from your body. Never place the airbag module on a bench of other surface with the airbag opening facing the surface. Always place the airbag module on a flat surface in a safe location with the airbag opening facing up (don't set it in a corner or next to a wall). Never dispose of a live airbag module. Return it to your dealer service department for safe deployment, using special equipment, and disposal.

11   Never measure the resistance of any SRS component. An ohmmeter has a built-in battery supply that could accidentally deploy the airbag. When working around the instrument panel and console, you will see several large yellow connectors; they're the harness connectors for the airbag system. Generally speaking, it's a good idea to avoid unplugging these yellow connectors unless absolutely necessary.

12   Always disable the airbag system when working in the vicinity of the front grille or bumper. Use extreme caution when working around the front impact sensors. Do not remove or unplug them unless absolutely necessary.

13   Never use electrical welding equipment on a vehicle equipped with an airbag without first disconnecting the cables from the battery terminals (negative first, positive last) (see Chapter 5).

27   Wiring diagrams - general information

1   Since it isn't possible to include all wiring diagrams for every year covered by this manual, the following diagrams are those that are typical and most commonly needed.

2   Prior to troubleshooting any circuits, check the fuse and circuit breakers (if equipped) to make sure they're in good condition. Make sure the battery is properly charged and check the cable connections (see Chapter 1).

3   When checking a circuit, make sure that all connectors are clean, with no broken or loose terminals. When unplugging a connector, do not pull on the wires. Pull only on the connector housings themselves.

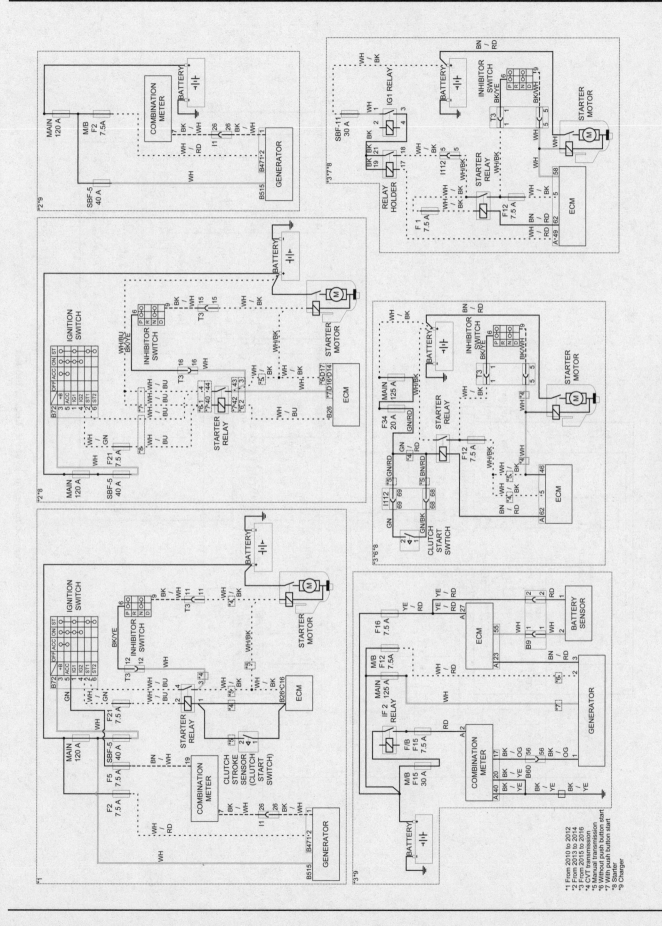

Starting and charging systems - Legacy models

*1 From 2010 to 2012
*2 From 2013 to 2014
*3 From 2015 to 2016
*4 CVT transmission
*5 Manual transmission
*6 Without push button start
*7 With push button start
*8 Starter
*9 Charger

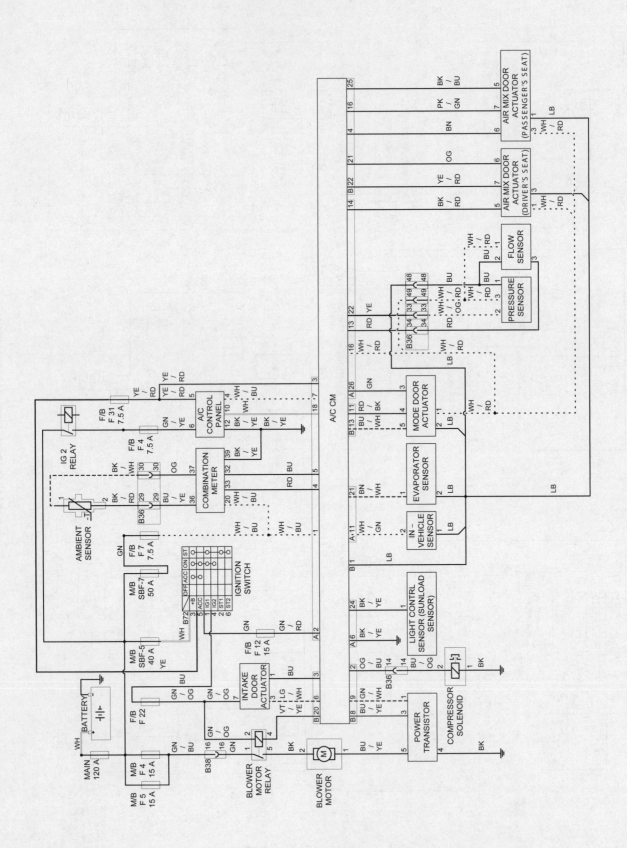

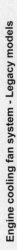

Engine cooling fan system - Legacy models

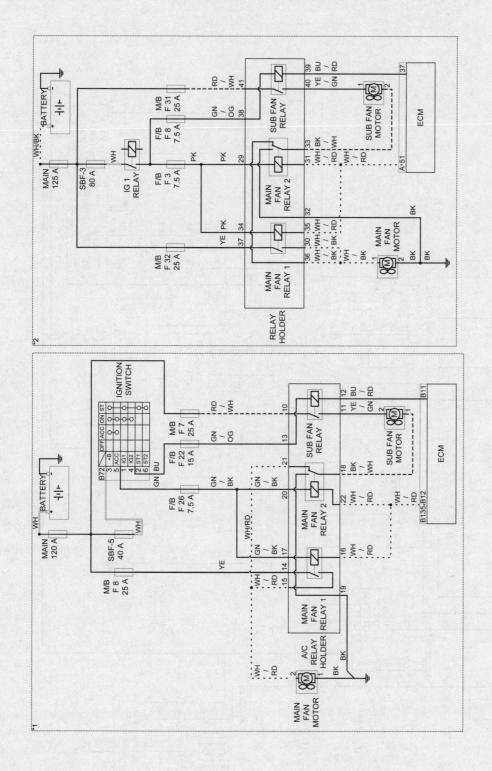

Air conditioning and heating systems (automatic) - 2014 and earlier models

*1 From 2010 to 2014
*2 From 2015 to 2016

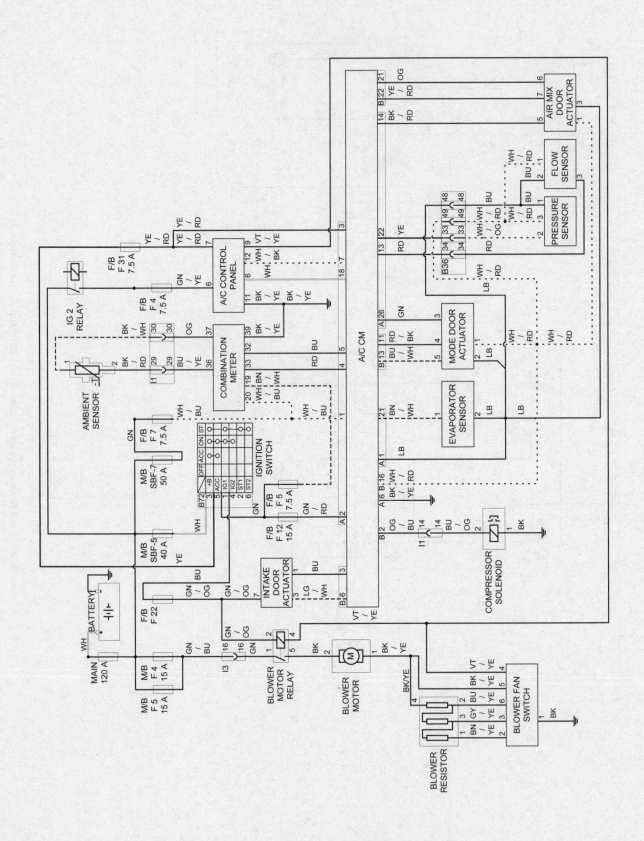

Air conditioning and heating systems (manual) - 2014 and earlier models

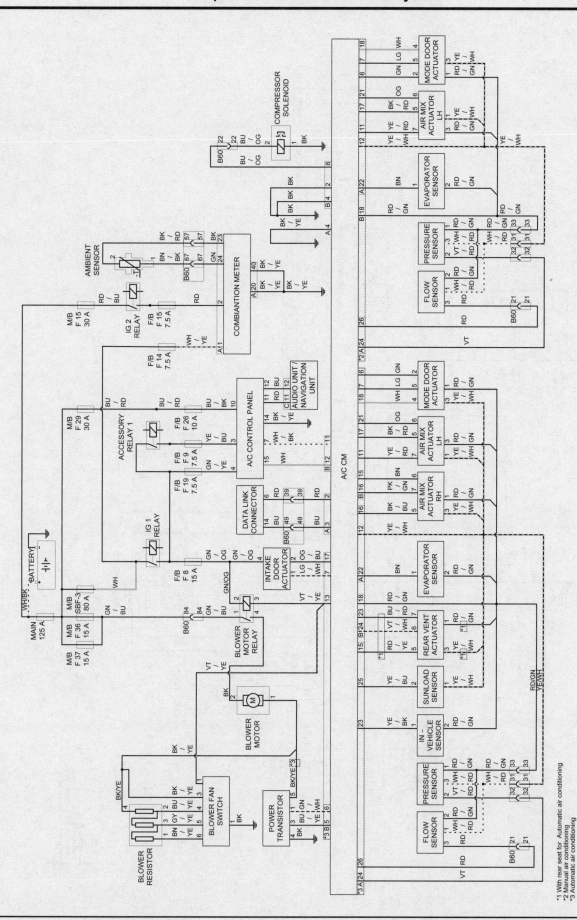

Air conditioning and heating systems - 2015 and later Legacy models

*1 With rear seat for Automatic air conditioning
*2 Manual air conditioning
*3 Automatic air conditioning

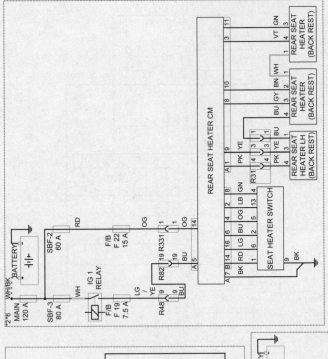

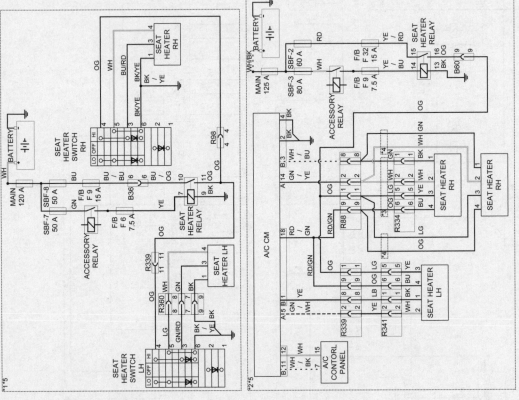

Seat heater system - Legacy models

*1 From 2010 to 2014
*2 From 2015 to 2016
*3 With power seat (passenger's side)
*4 Without power seat (passenger's side)
*5 Front
*6 Rear

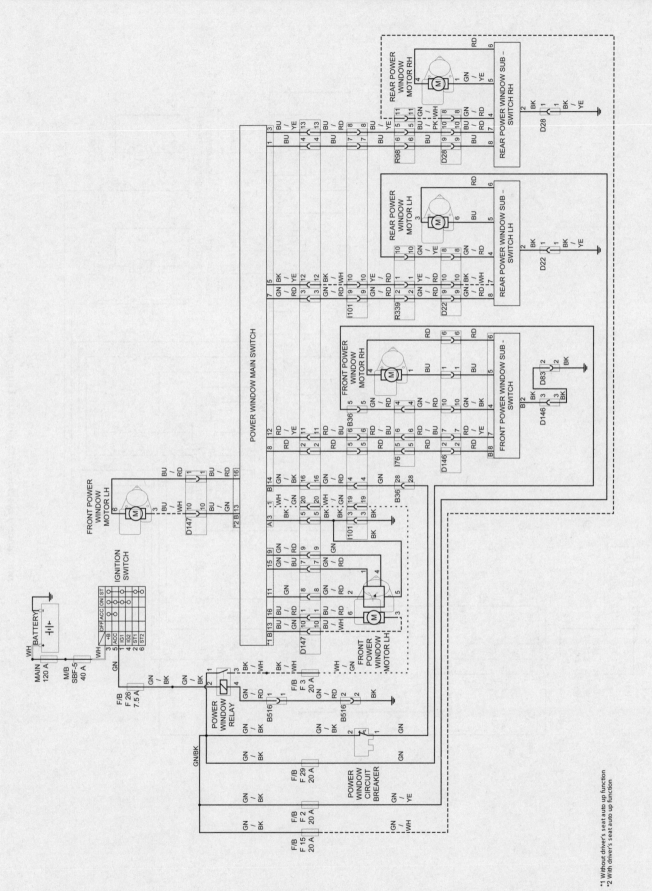

Power window system - 2014 and earlier Legacy models

*1 Without driver's seat auto up function
*2 With driver's seat auto up function

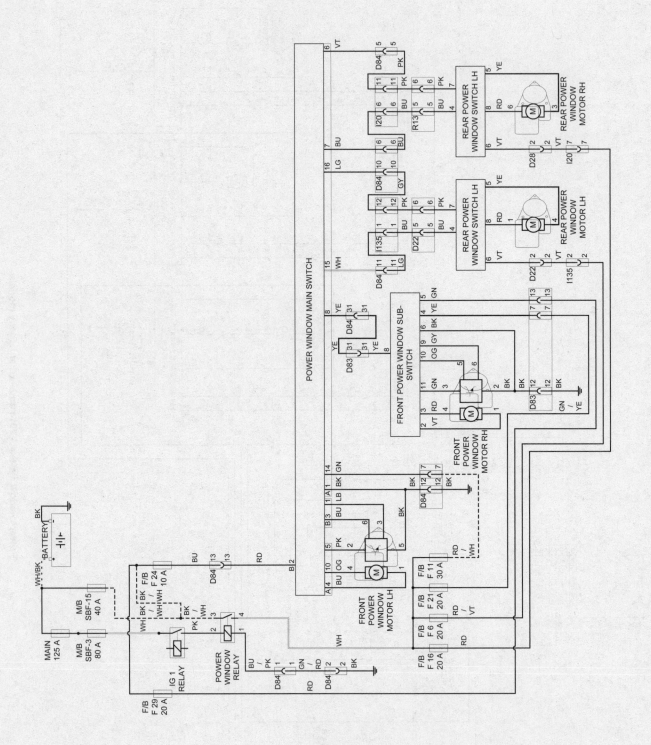

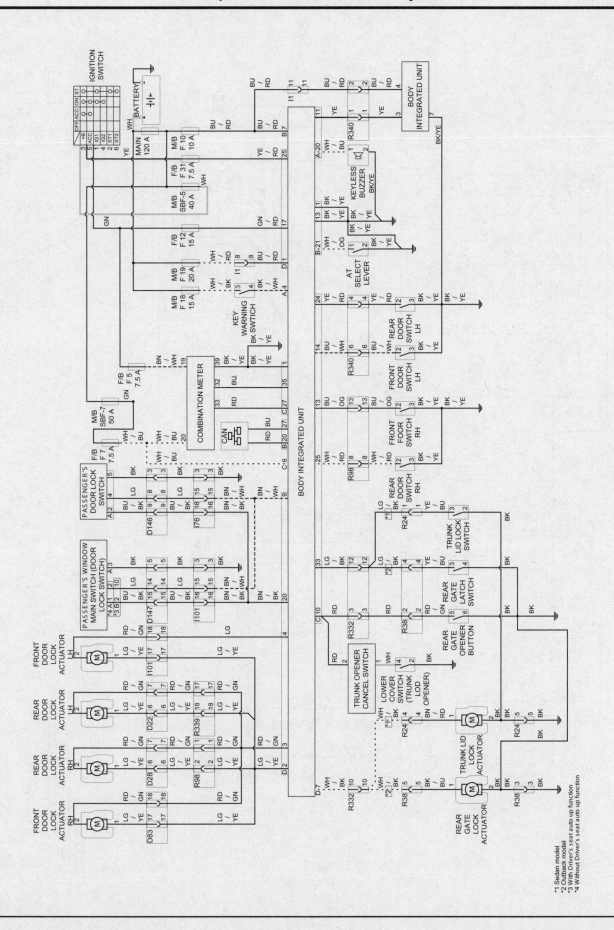

Power door lock system - 2014 and earlier Legacy models

*1 Sedan model
*2 Outback model
*3 With Driver's seat auto up function
*4 Without Driver's seat auto up function

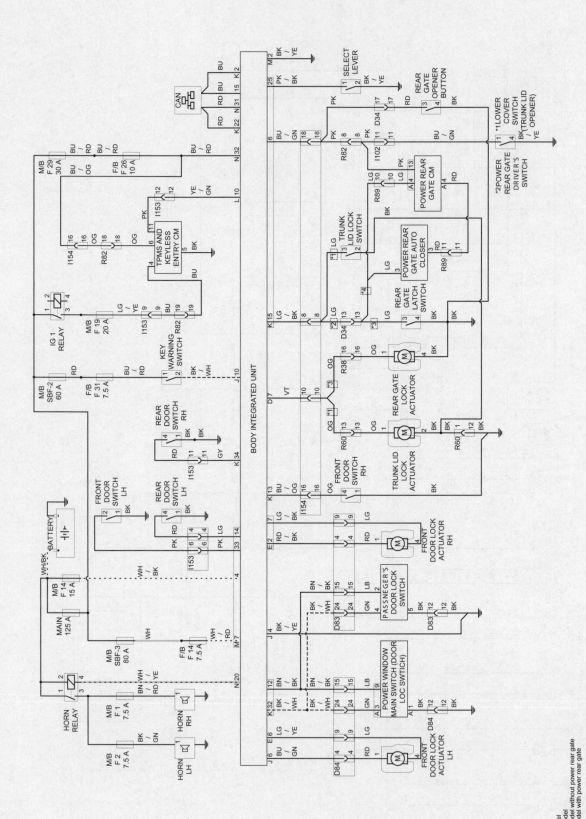

Power door lock system (without keyless entry) - 2015 and later Legacy models

*1 Sedan model
*2 Outback model
*3 Outback model without power rear gate
*4 Outback model with power rear gate

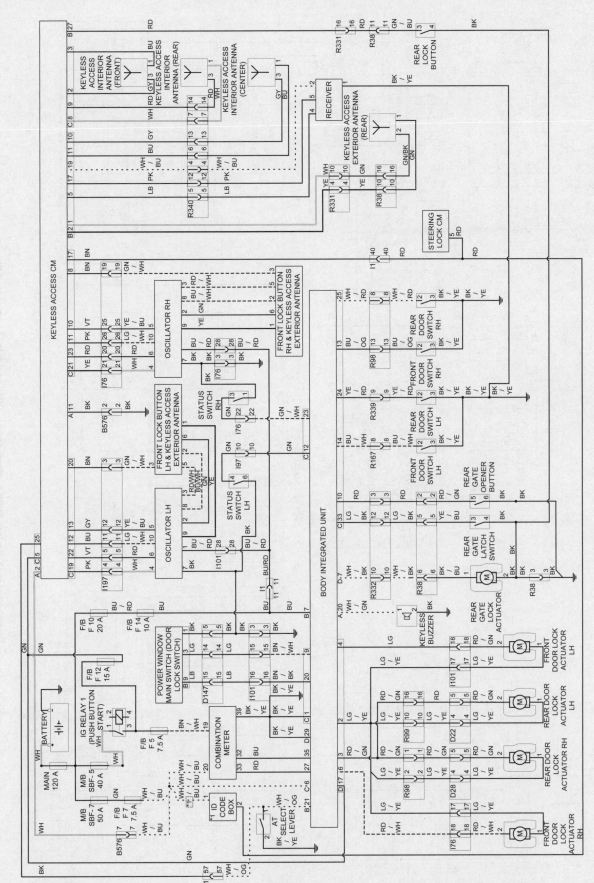

Power door lock system (with keyless entry) - 2013 and 2014 Legacy models

*1 With ID code

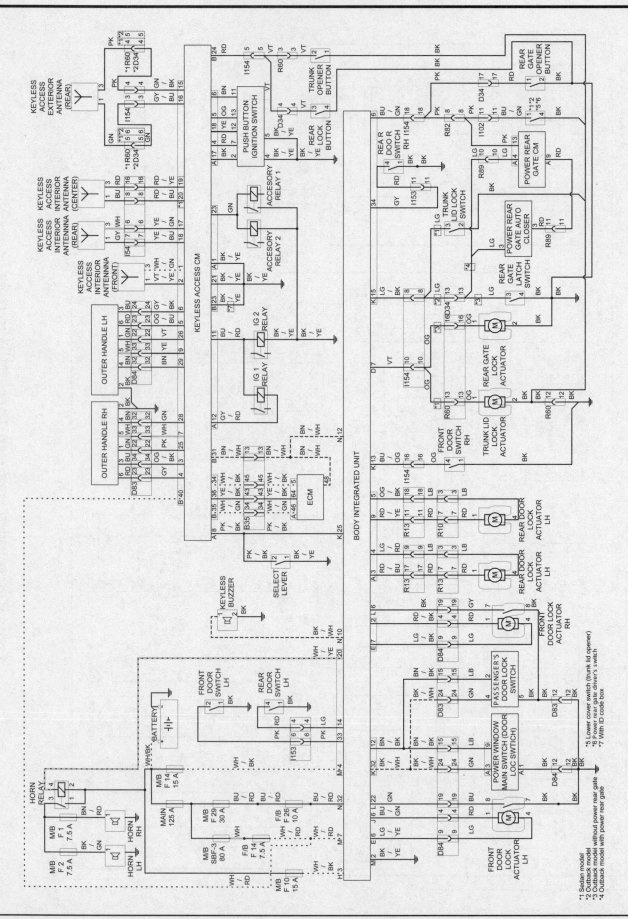

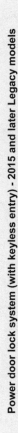

Power door lock system (with keyless entry) - 2015 and later Legacy models

*1 Sedan model
*2 Outback model
*3 Outback model without power rear gate
*4 Outback model with power rear gate
*5 Lower cover switch (trunk lid opener)
*6 Power rear gate driver's switch
*7 With ID code box

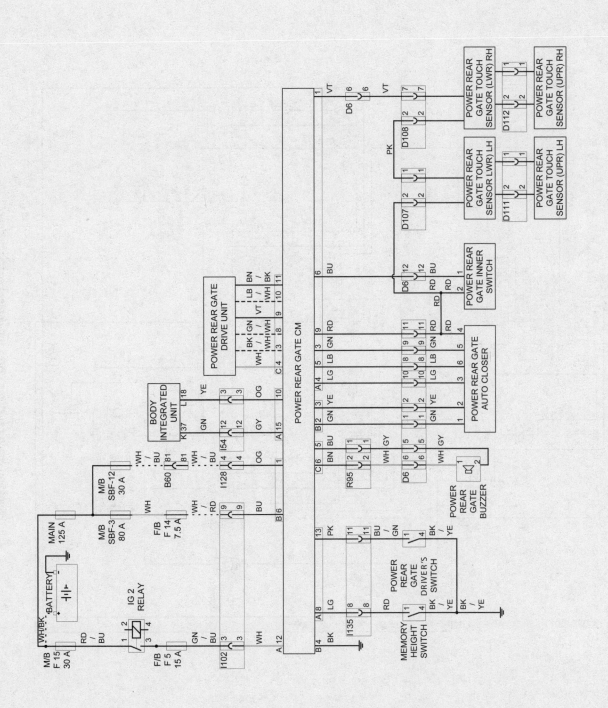

Trunk lock system - 2015 and later Legacy models

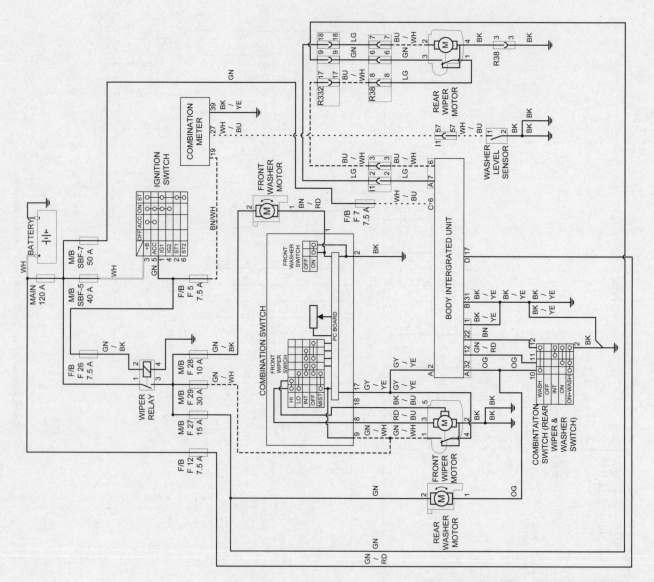

Wiper and washer systems - 2014 and earlier Legacy models

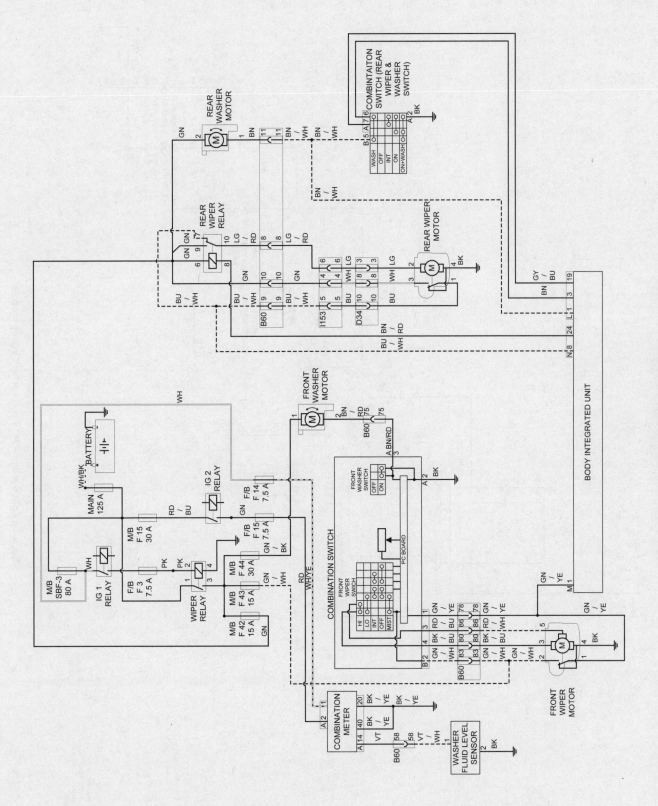

Wiper and washer systems - 2015 and later Legacy models

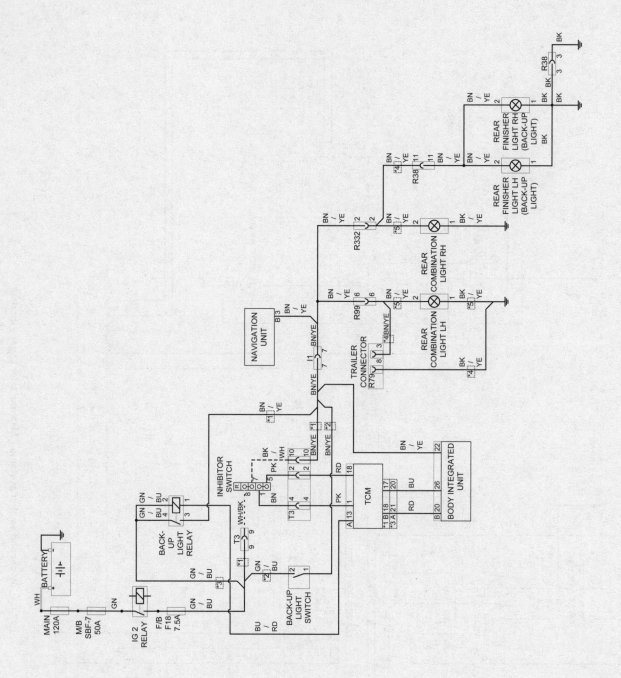

Back-up light system - 2014 and earlier Legacy models

*1 CVT
*2 Manual transmission
*2 Automatic transmission
*3 Outback model
*5 Sedan model

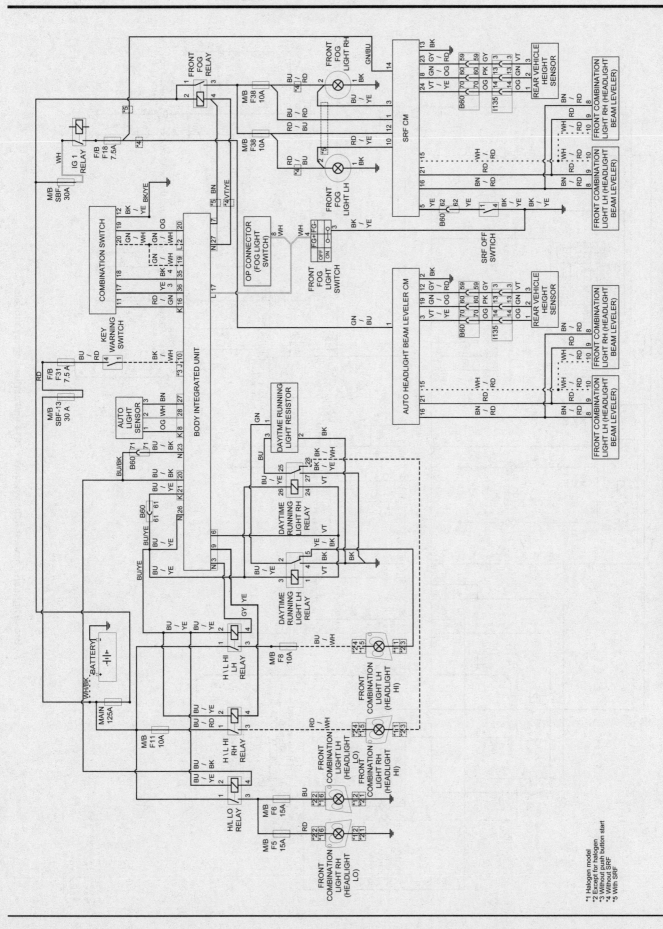

Headlight, fog light and turn signal light systems - 2014 and earlier Legacy models

*1 Halogen model
*2 Except for halogen
*3 Without push button start
*4 Without SRF
*5 With SRF

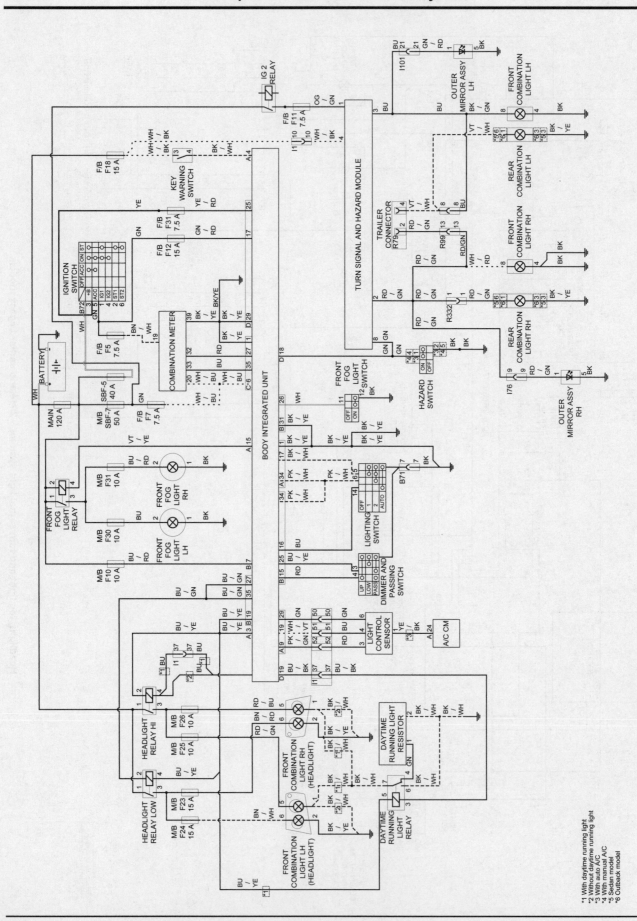

Brake light and marker light systems - 2014 and earlier Legacy models

*1 With daytime running light
*2 Without daytime running light
*3 With auto A/C
*4 With manual A/C
*5 Sedan model
*6 Outback model

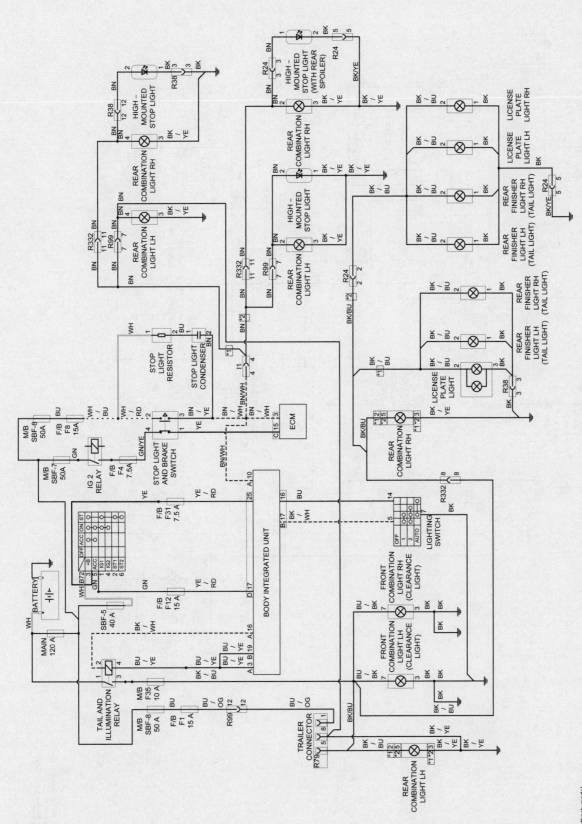

Headlight system - 2015 and later Legacy models

*1 Outback model
*2 Sedan model

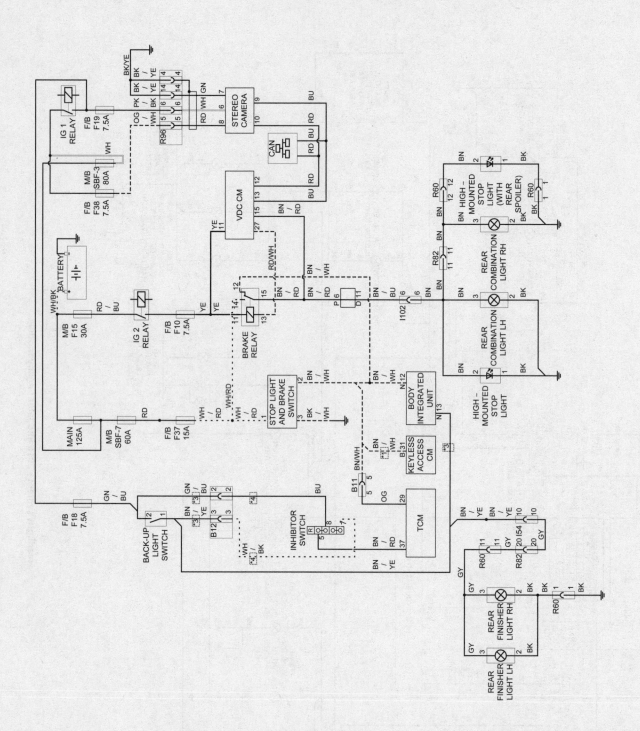

Brake light and back-up light systems - 2015 and later Legacy models

*1 With push button start
*2 With EYESIGHT
*3 Manual transmission
*4 CVT

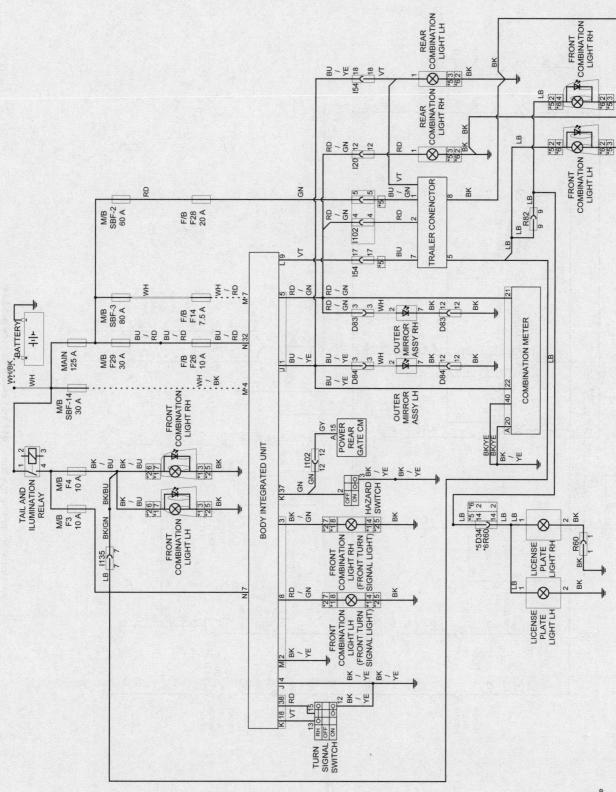

Turn signal and marker light systems - 2015 and later Legacy models

*1 With Halogen
*2 Without halogen
*3 With power rear gate
*4 With mirror turn
*5 Outback
*6 Sedan

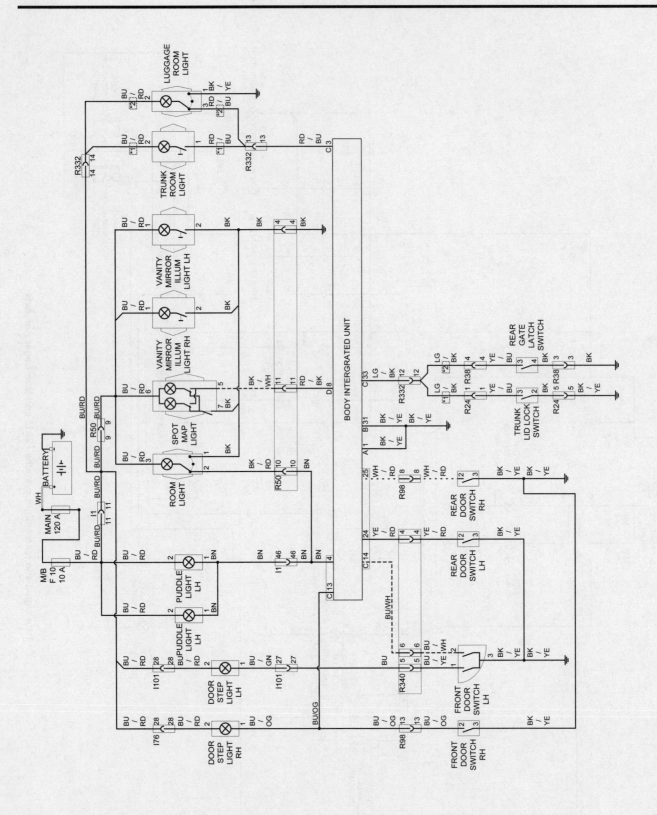

Interior lighting system - 2014 and earlier Legacy models

*1 Sedan model
*2 Outback model

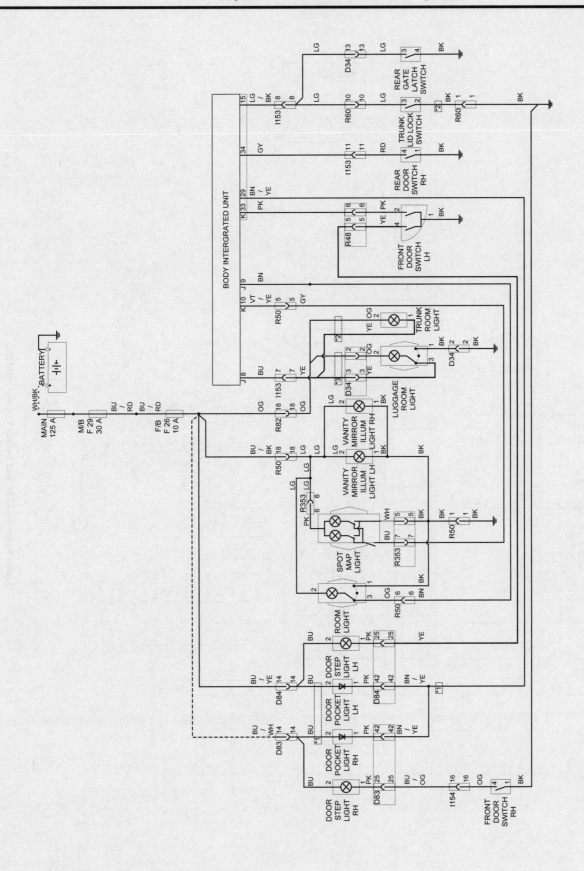

Interior lighting system - 2015 and later Legacy models

*1 With door pocket light
*2 Sedan model
*3 Outback model

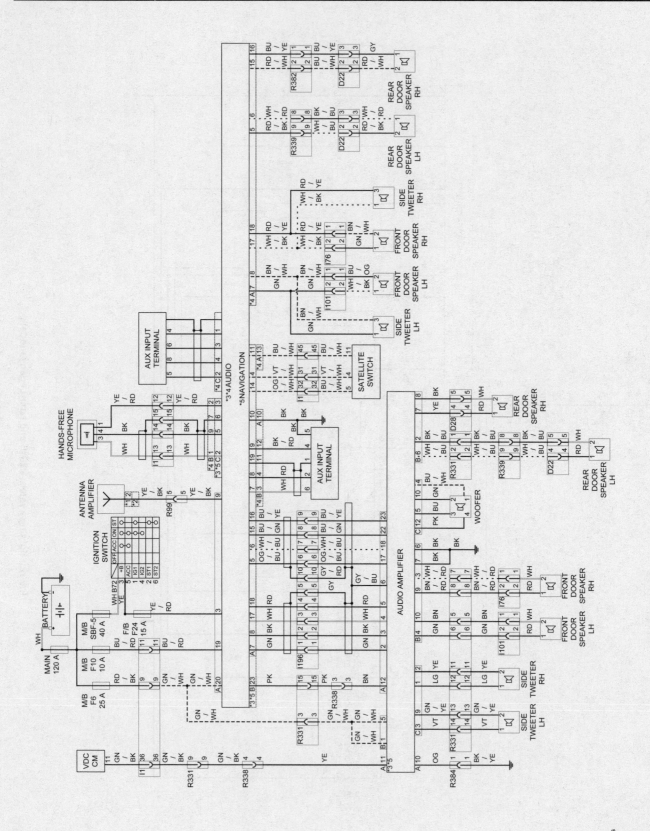

Audio system - 2014 and earlier Legacy models

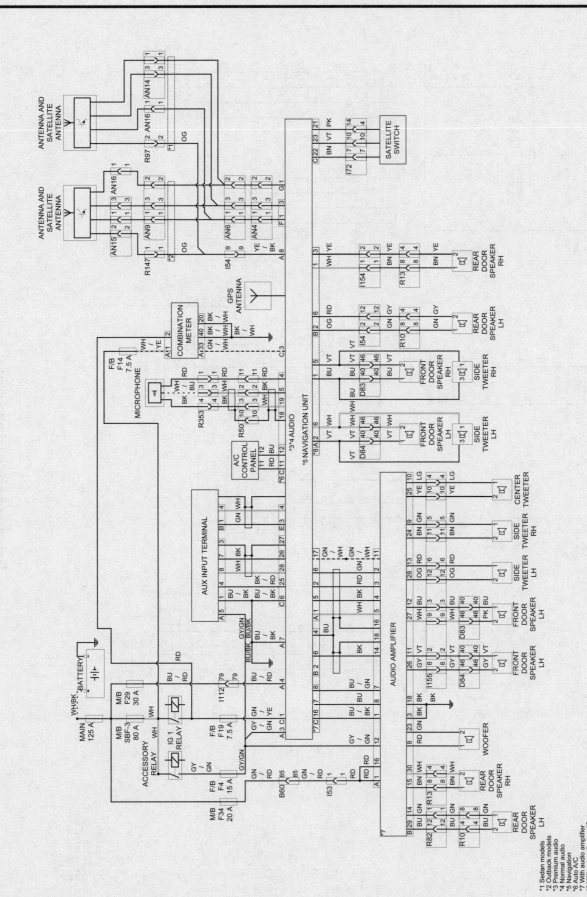

Audio system - 2015 and later Legacy models

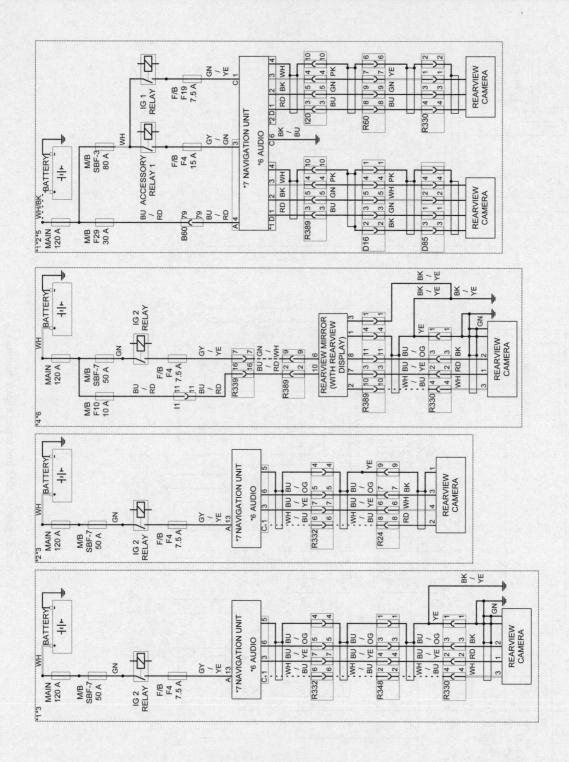

Back-up camera system - Legacy models

*1 Outback model
*2 Sedan model
*3 From 2010 to 2014
*4 From 2011 to 2014
*5 From 2015 to 2016
*6 Audio
*7 Navigation

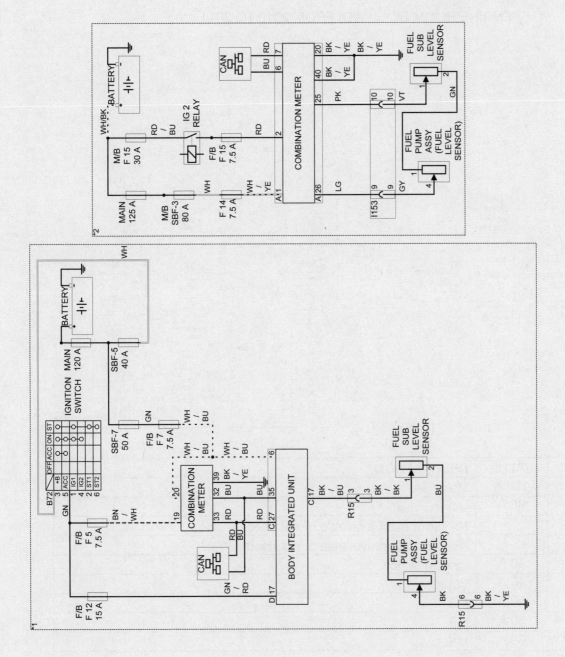

Fuel pump system - Legacy models

*1 From 2010 to 2014
*2 From 2015 to 2016

ENGINE ROOM SIDE (M/B) FROM 2010 TO 2014

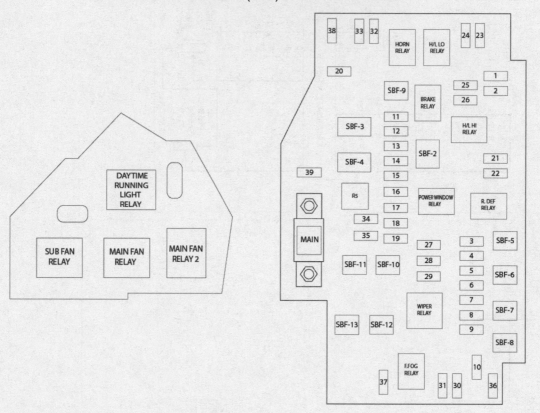

FUSE/RELAY	VALUE	DESCRIPTION
MAIN	120 A	Main fuse
SBF-2	80 A	Main fan relay
SBF-3	-	No information available or not used
SBF-4	-	No information available or not used
SBF-5	40 A	Ignition switch
SBF-6	40 A	VDC CM
SBF-7	50 A	F/B
SBF-8	50 A	F/B
SBF-9	30 A	EPB CM
SBF-10	30 A	
SBF-11	30 A	Power seats
SBF-12	-	No information available or not used
SBF-13	-	No information available or not used
F1	-	No information available or not used
F2	7.5 A	Generator
F3	-	No information available or not used
F4	15 A	Blower motor relay
F5	15 A	Blower motor relay
F6	25 A	Audio, Navigation unit, Audio amplifier

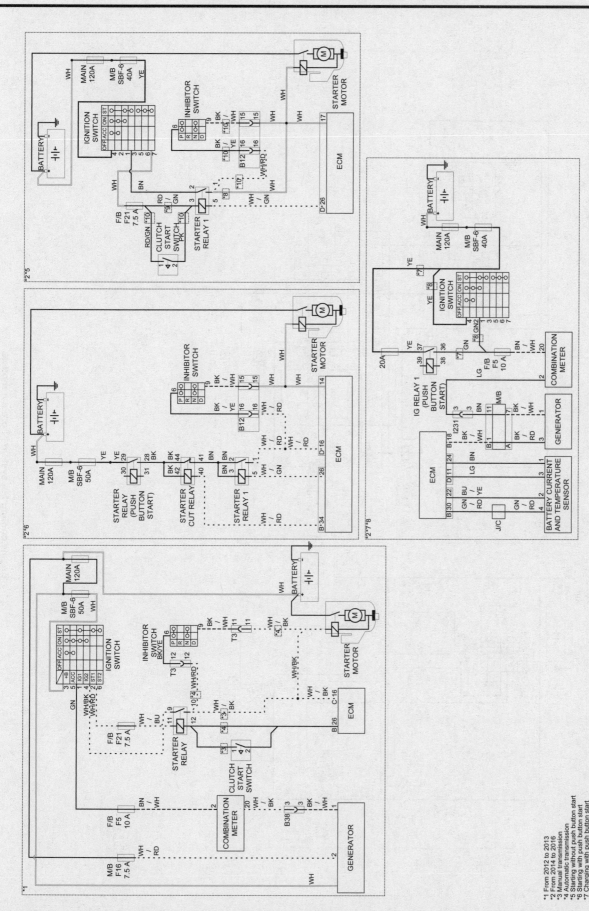

Starting and charging systems - Forester models

*1 From 2012 to 2013
*2 From 2014 to 2016
*3 Manual transmission
*4 Automatic transmission
*5 Starting without push button start
*6 Starting with push button start
*7 Charging with push button start
*8 Charging without push button start
*9 CVT
*10 Manual transmission

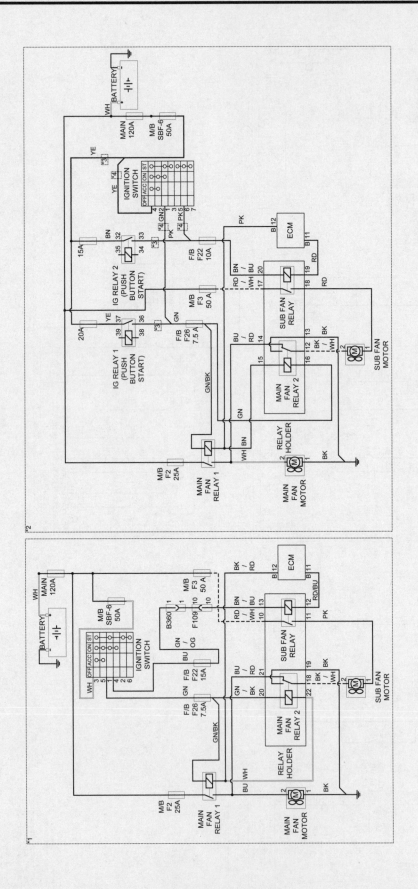

Engine cooling fan system - Forester models

*1 From 2012 to 2013
*2 From 2014 to 2016
*3 With push button start
*4 Without push button start

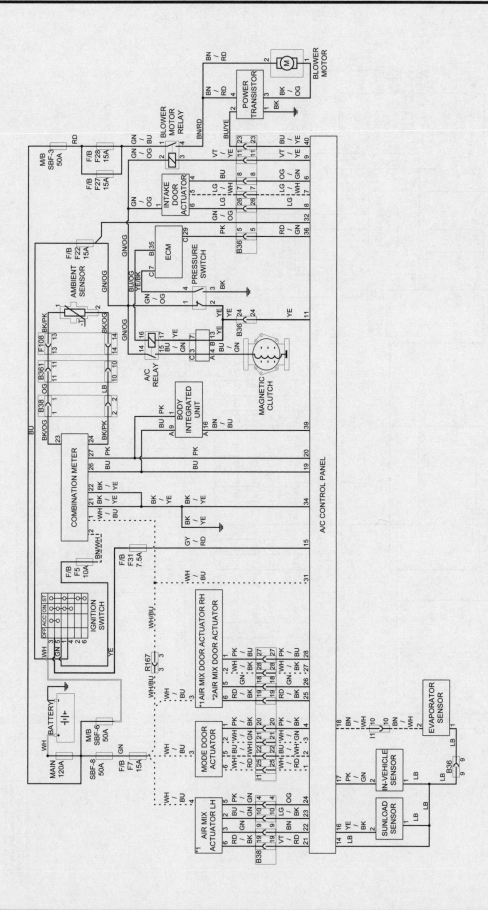

Air conditioning and heating systems - 2013 and earlier Forester models

*1 With independent air conditioner
*2 Without independent air conditioner

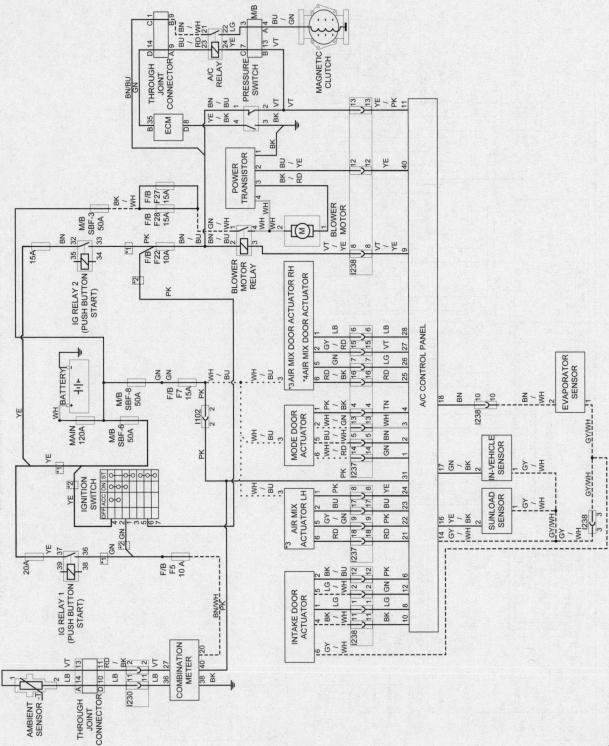

Air conditioning and heating systems - 2014 and later Forester models

*1 With push button start
*2 Without push button start
*3 With independent air conditioner
*4 Without independent air conditioner

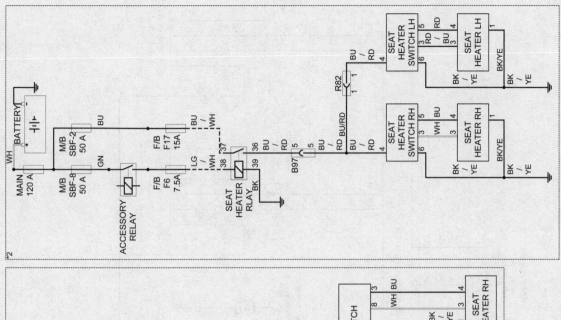

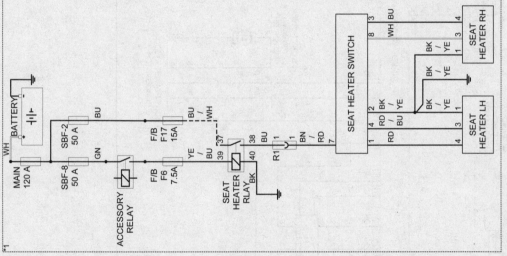

Seat heater system - Forester models

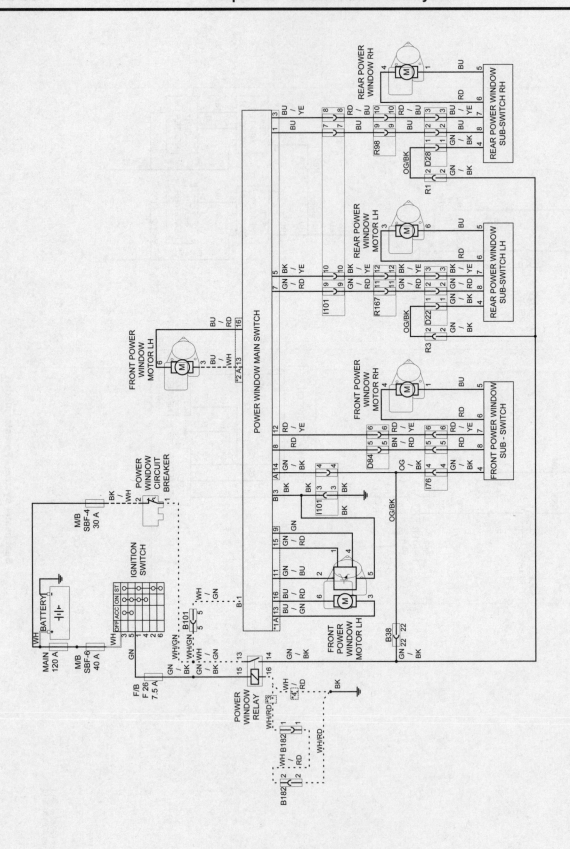

Power window system - 2013 and earlier Forester models

*1 With auto reverse function
*2 Without auto reverse function
*3 With remote engine start system
*4 Without remote engine start system

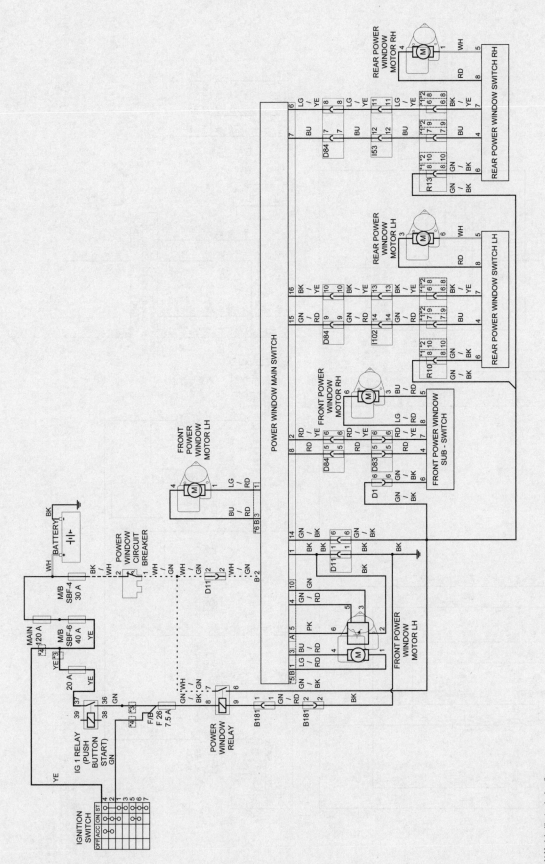

Power window system - 2014 and later Forester models

*1 Model with standard audio
*2 Model with high grade audio
*3 With push button
*4 Without push button
*5 With auto reverse
*6 Without auto reverse

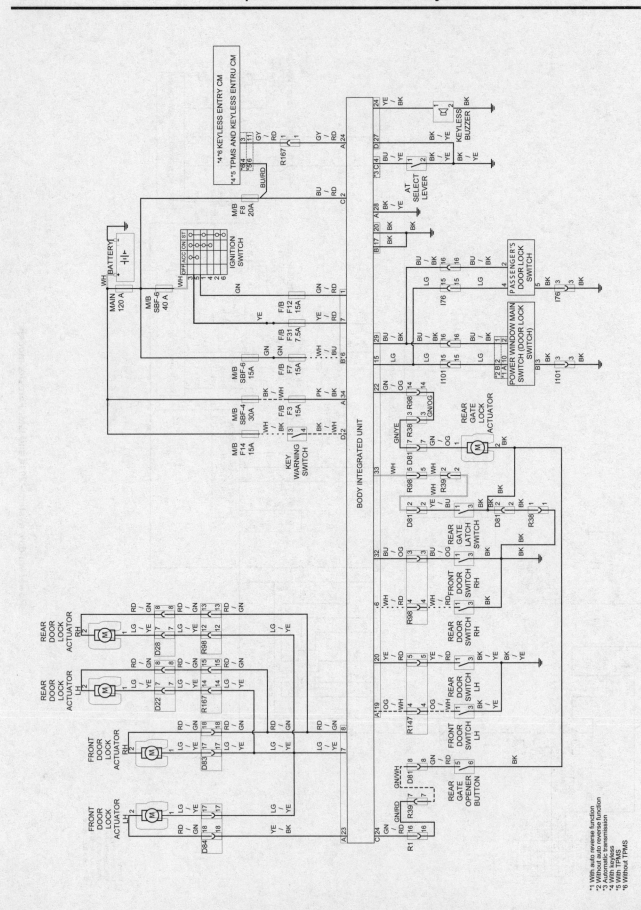

Power door lock system - 2013 and earlier Forester models

*1 With auto reverse function
*2 Without auto reverse function
*3 Automatic transmission
*4 With keyless
*5 With TPMS
*6 Without TPMS

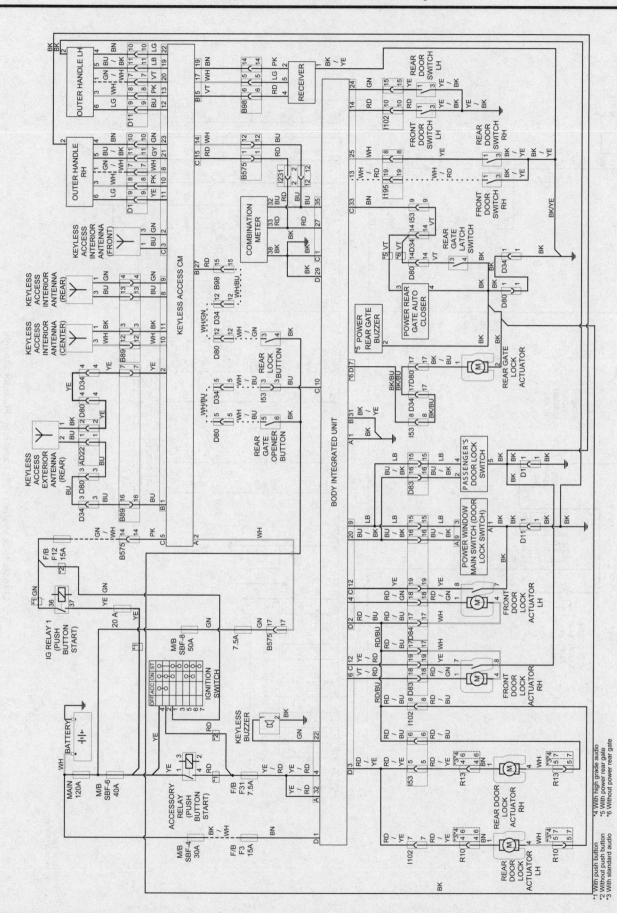

Power door lock system (keyless entry) - 2014 and later Forester models

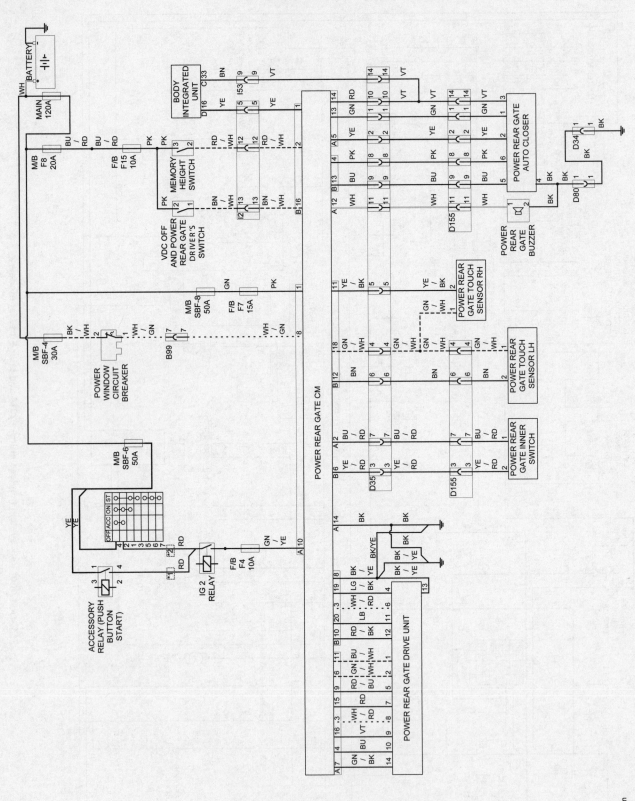

Liftgate lock system - 2014 and later Forester models

*1 With push button
*2 Without push button

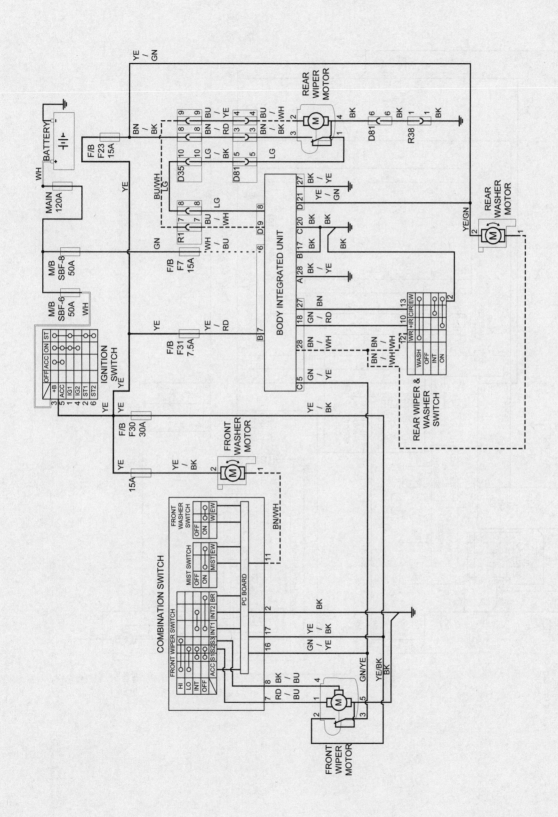

Wiper and washer systems - 2013 and earlier Forester models

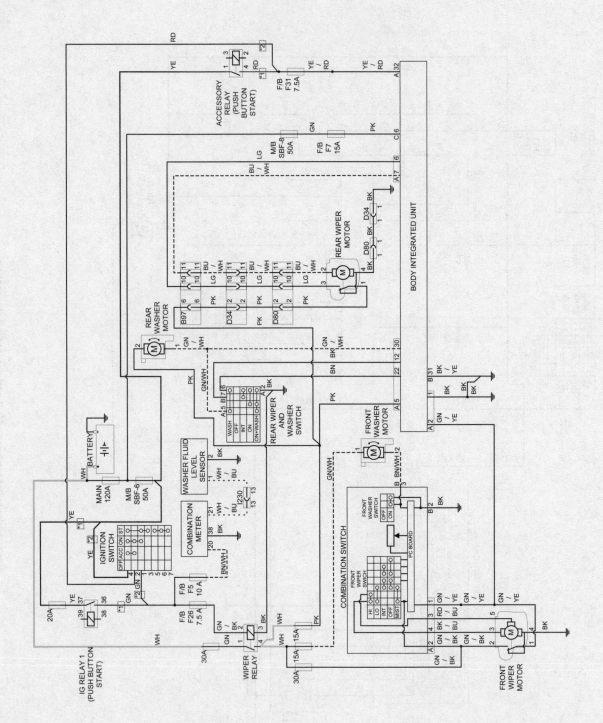

Wiper and washer systems - 2014 and later Forester models

*1 With push button start
*2 Without push button start

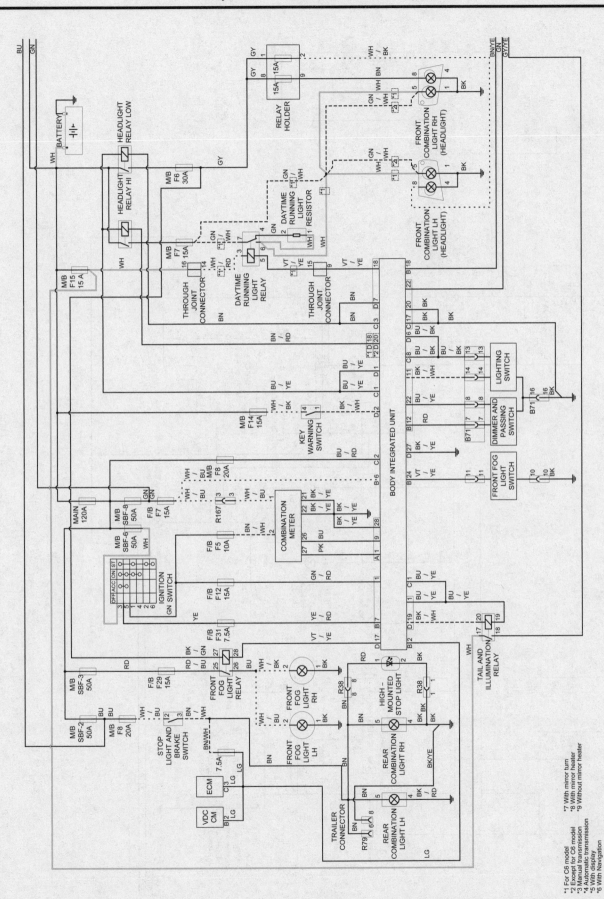

Exterior lighting system - 2013 and earlier Forester models (1 of 2)

*1 For C6 model
*2 Except for C6 model
*3 Manual transmission
*4 Automatic transmission
*5 With display
*6 With Navigation

*7 With mirror turn
*8 With mirror heater
*9 Without mirror heater

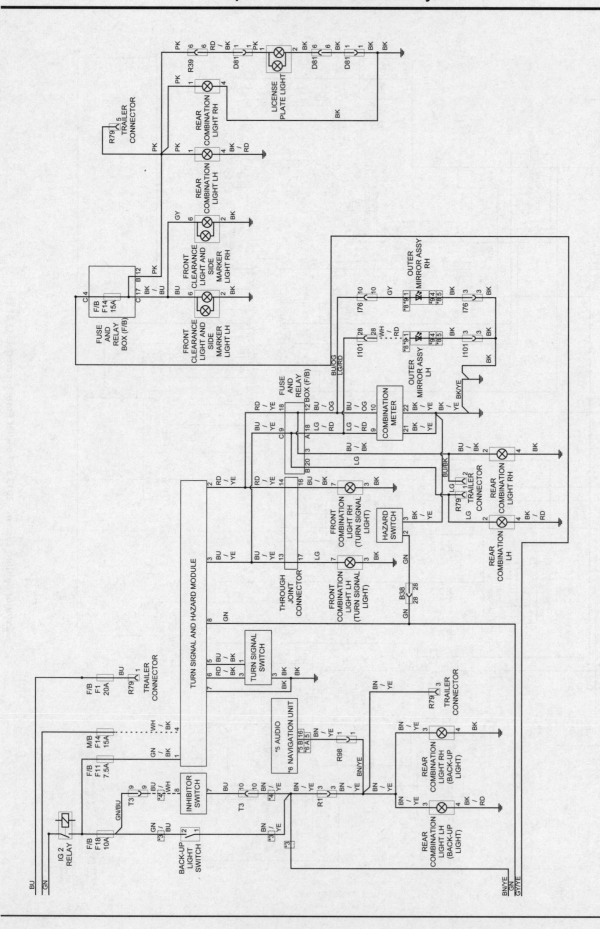

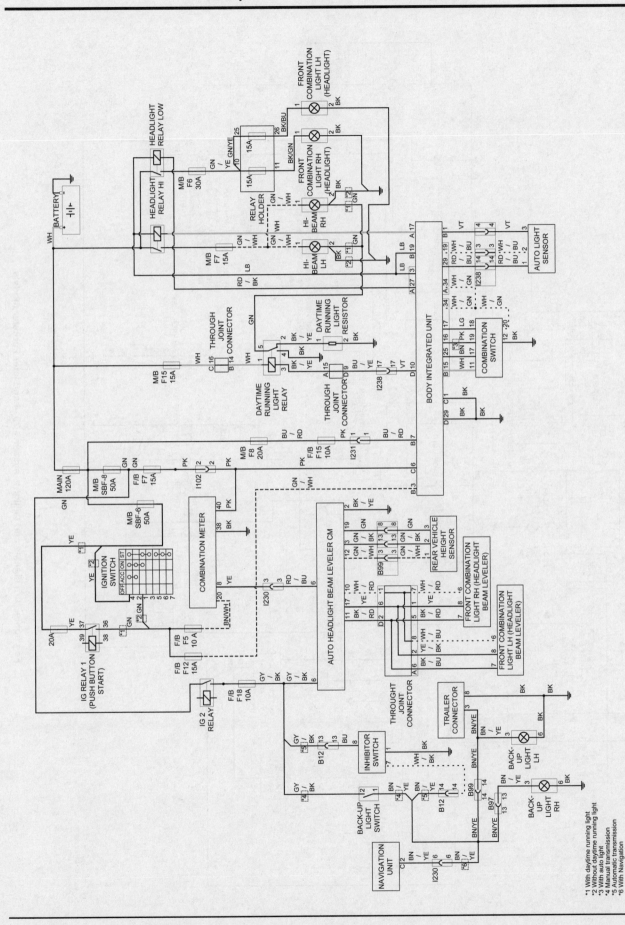

Headlights and back-up lights system - 2014 and later Forester models

*1 With daytime running light
*2 Without daytime running light
*3 With auto light
*4 Manual transmission
*5 Automatic transmission
*6 With Navigation

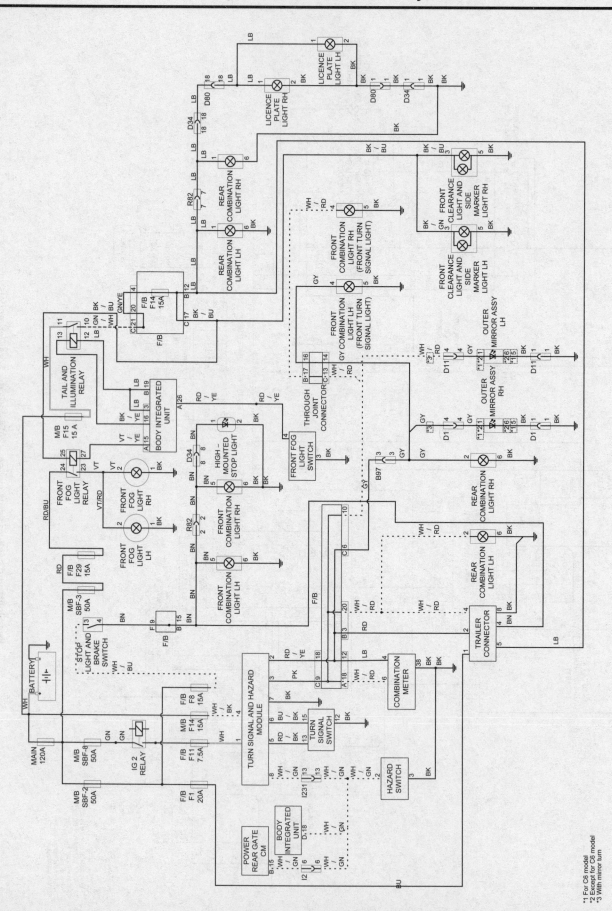

Fog lights, turn signals and taillights system - 2014 and later Forester models

*1 For C6 model
*2 Except for C6 model
*3 With mirror turn

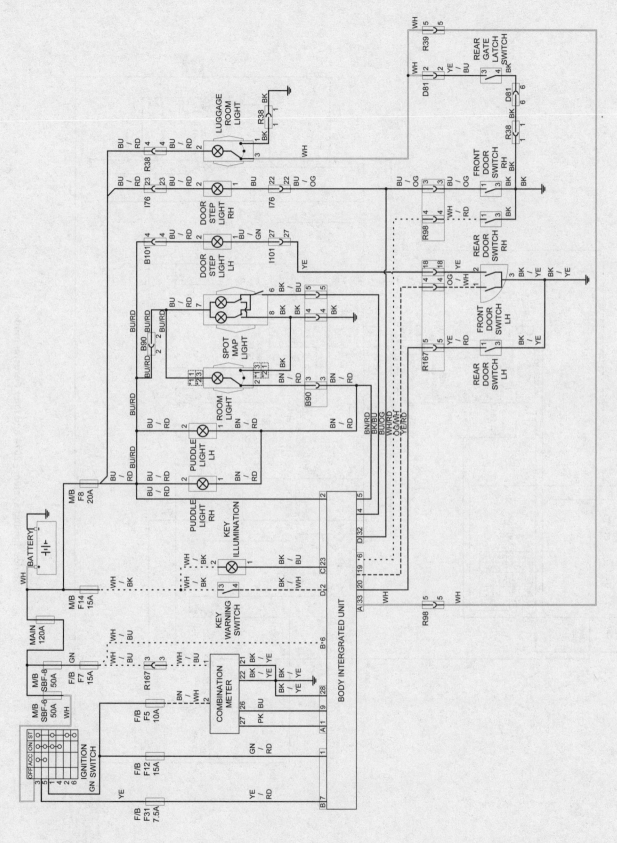

Interior lighting system - 2013 and earlier Forester models

1 With sunroof
2 Without sunroof

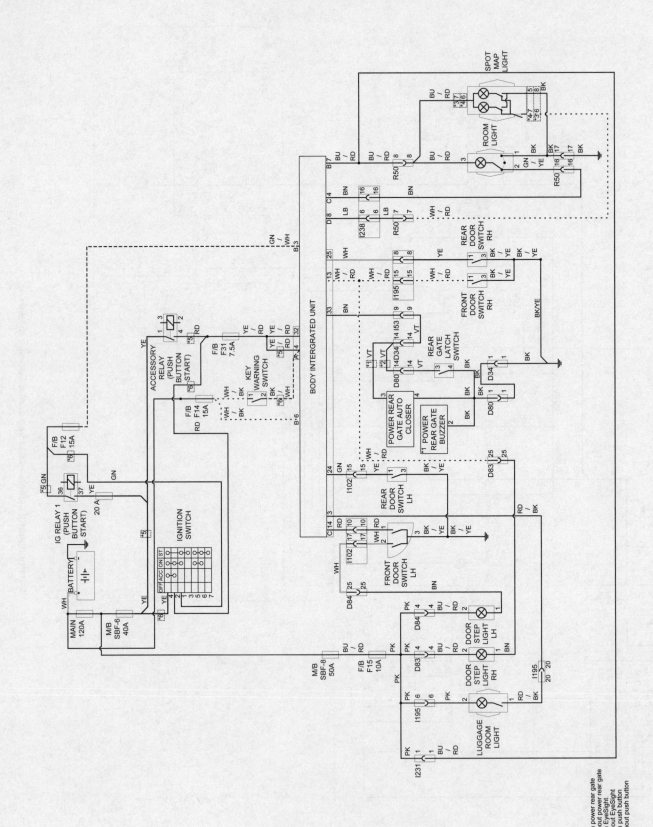

Interior lighting system - 2014 and later Forester models

*1 With power rear gate
*2 Without power rear gate
*3 With EyeSight
*4 Without EyeSight
*5 With push button
*6 Without push button

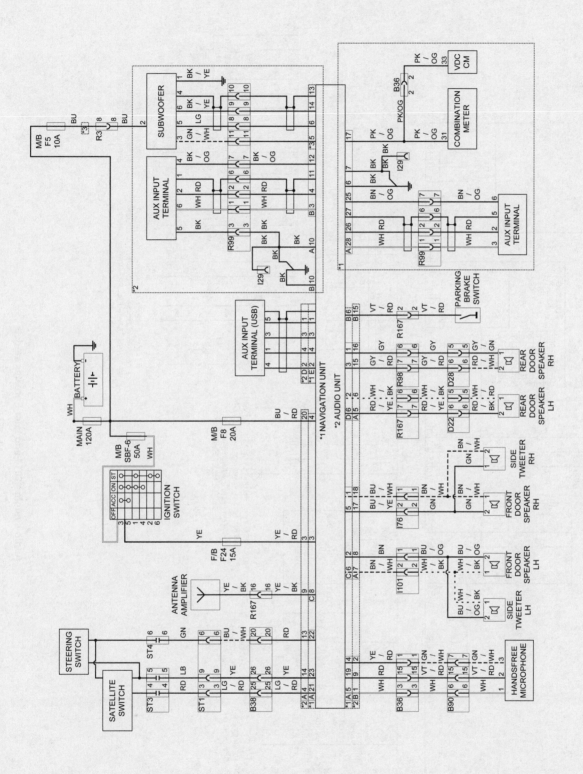

Audio system - 2013 and earlier Forester models

*1 Navigation
*2 Audio
*3 With subwoofer

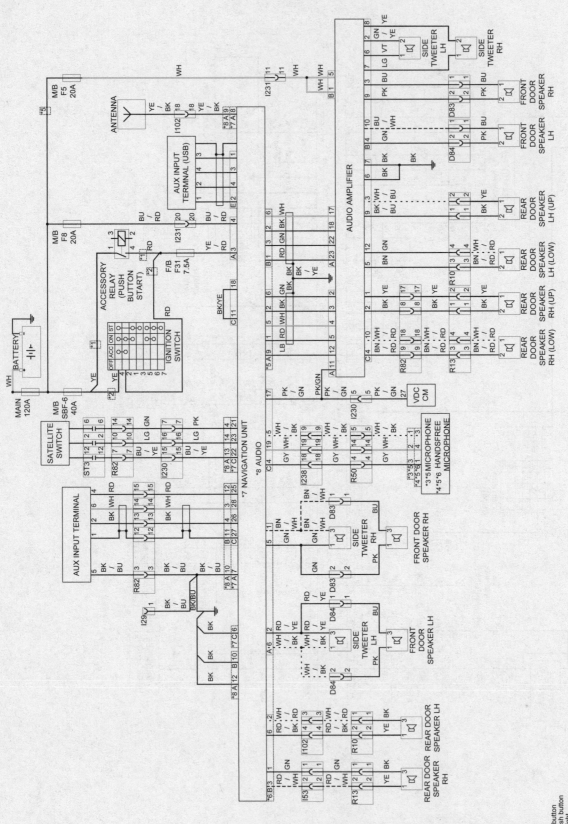

Audio system - 2014 and later Forester models

*1 With push button
*2 Without push button
*3 With EyeSight
*4 Without EyeSight
*5 Premium
*6 Standard
*7 Navigation
*8 Audio

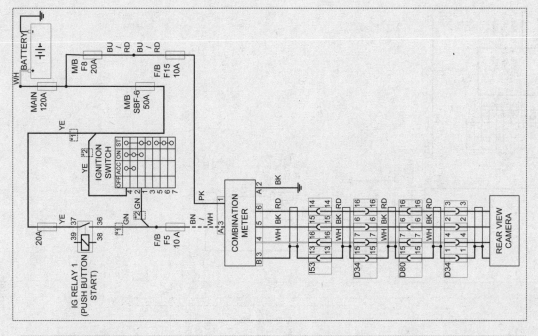

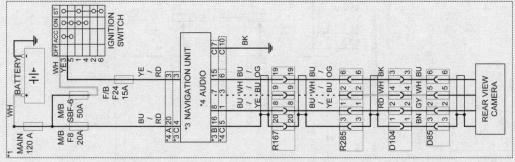

Back-up camera - Forester models

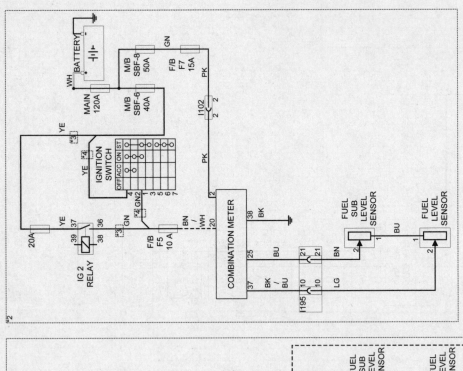

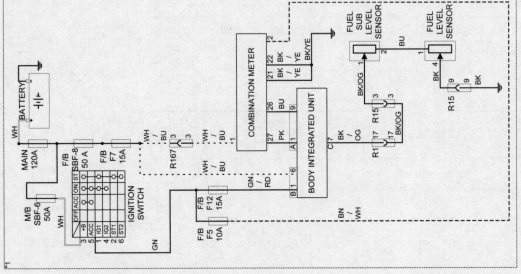

Fuel pump system - Forester models

*1 From 2012 to 2013
*2 From 2014 to 2016
*3 With push button start
*4 Without push button start

ENGINE ROOM SIDE (M/B) FROM 2012 TO 2016

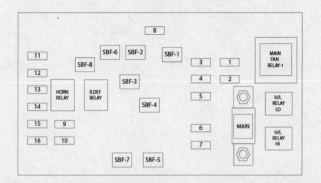

FUSE/RELAY	VALUE	DESCRIPTION
MAIN	120 A	Main fuse
SBF-1	50 A	VDC CM
SBF-2	-	No information available or not used
SBF-3	50 A	F/B
SBF-4	30 A	Power window circuit breaker
SBF-5	30 A	A/F, oxygen sensor relay
SBF-6	50 A	Ignition switch
SBF-7	30 A	Main relay, IG relay, A/F, oxygen sensor relay
SBF-8	50 A	F/B
F 1	30 A	VDC CM
F 2	25 A	Main fan relay 1
F 3	25 A	
F 4	-	Sub fan relay
F 5	10 A	Main fan relay 2
F 6	30 A	Headlight LH, Headlight RH, Front fog light relay
F 7	15 A	Headlight LH and RH (C6 model)
F 8	20 A	Spot map light, Room light, Door step light LH, Puddle lights
F 9	15 A	Horn
F 10	-	No information available or not used
F 11	15 A	Fuel pump relay
F 12	10 A	TCM
F 13	7.5 A	ECM, Data link connector
F 14	15 A	Key illumination, Key warning switch, Turn signal and hazard unit, Body integrated unit
F 15	15 A	Tail and Illumination relay, Daytime running light relay
F 16	7.5 A	Generator

Notes

Index

Strut/coil spring assembly (front) - removal and installation, 10-5
Suspension links and subframe (rear) - removal and installation, 10-10
Tie-rod ends - removal and installation, 10-14
Trailing arm - removal and installation, 10-10
Wheel alignment - general information, 10-17
Wheels and tires - general information, 10-17
Suspension links and subframe (rear) - removal and installation, 10-10
Suspension, steering and driveaxle boot check, 1-20

T

Thermostat replacement, 3-7
Throttle body - removal and installation, 4-8
Tie-rod ends - removal and installation, 10-14
Timing belt and sprockets - removal, inspection and installation, 2A-11
Timing chain cover, timing chains and sprockets - removal, inspection and installation, 2A-15
Tire and tire pressure checks, 1-11
Tire rotation, 1-16
Top Dead Center (TDC) for number one piston - locating, 2A-6
Trailing arm - removal and installation, 10-10
Transaxle mount - check and replacement, 7A-4
Transmission Control Module (TCM) - removal and installation, 7B-5
Transmission Range (TR) sensor - replacement, 6-21
Trunk lid - removal and installation, 11-16
Trunk lid latch and lock cylinder - removal and installation, 11-16
Trunk/liftgate support struts - removal and installation, 11-17
Tumble generator - description and component replacement, 6-29
Tune-up and routine maintenance, 1-0
Air filter check and replacement, 1-21
Automatic transaxle fluid change, 1-26
Battery check, maintenance and charging, 1-14
Brake fluid change, 1-21
Brake system check, 1-19
Cabin air filter - replacement, 1-28
Cooling system check, 1-18
Cooling system servicing, 1-24
Differential lubricant change, 1-27

Drivebelt check, adjustment and replacement, 1-21
Engine oil and filter change, 1-13
Exhaust system check, 1-17
Fluid level checks, 1-8
Fuel filter replacement, 1-24
Fuel system check, 1-18
Ignition coil check, 1-26
Introduction, 1-8
Maintenance schedule, 1-7
Manual transaxle lubricant change, 1-27
Seat belt check, 1-17
Spark plug replacement, 1-25
Spark plug wire check and replacement (2009 SOHC Legacy/2009 and 2010 SOHC Forester models), 1-28
Suspension, steering and driveaxle boot check, 1-20
Tire and tire pressure checks, 1-11
Tire rotation, 1-16
Tune-up general information, 1-8
Underhood hose check and replacement, 1-17
Wheel bearing check, 1-27
Windshield wiper blade inspection and replacement, 1-16
Turbocharger
description and inspection, 4-12
removal and installation, 4-15
Turn signal/hazard flasher - check and replacement, 12-6

U

Underhood hose check and replacement, 1-17
Upholstery, carpets and vinyl trim - maintenance, 11-5

V

Vacuum gauge diagnostic checks, 2B-6
Valve clearance - check and adjustment, 2A-24
Valve covers - removal and installation, 2A-7
Variable Valve Lift (VVL) system (2012 and earlier models) - component replacement, 6-30
Variable Valve Timing (VVT) system - description and component replacement, 6-31
Vehicle identification numbers, 0-6
Vehicle Speed Sensor (VSS) - replacement, 6-22

W

Haynes Automotive Manuals

NOTE: If you do not see a listing for your vehicle, consult your local Haynes dealer for the latest product information.

ACURA
12020 **Integra** '86 thru '89 **& Legend** '86 thru '90
12021 **Integra** '90 thru '93 **& Legend** '91 thru '95
Integra '94 thru '00 - *see HONDA Civic (42025)*
MDX '01 thru '07 - *see HONDA Pilot (42037)*
12050 **Acura TL** all models '99 thru '08

AMC
Jeep CJ - *see JEEP (50020)*
14020 **Mid-size models** '70 thru '83
14025 **(Renault) Alliance & Encore** '83 thru '87

AUDI
15020 **4000** all models '80 thru '87
15025 **5000** all models '77 thru '83
15026 **5000** all models '84 thru '88
Audi A4 '96 thru '01 - *see VW Passat (96023)*
15030 **Audi A4** '02 thru '08

AUSTIN-HEALEY
Sprite - *see MG Midget (66015)*

BMW
18020 **3/5 Series** '82 thru '92
18021 **3-Series** incl. Z3 models '92 thru '98
18022 **3-Series** incl. Z4 models '99 thru '05
18023 **3-Series** '06 thru '10
18025 **320i all 4 cyl models** '75 thru '83
18050 **1500 thru 2002** except Turbo '59 thru '77

BUICK
19010 **Buick Century** '97 thru '05
Century (front-wheel drive) - *see GM (38005)*
19020 **Buick, Oldsmobile & Pontiac Full-size (Front-wheel drive)** '85 thru '05
Buick Electra, LeSabre and Park Avenue; **Oldsmobile** Delta 88 Royale, Ninety Eight and Regency; **Pontiac** Bonneville
19025 **Buick, Oldsmobile & Pontiac Full-size (Rear wheel drive)** '70 thru '90
Buick Estate, Electra, LeSabre, Limited, **Oldsmobile** Custom Cruiser, Delta 88, Ninety-eight, **Pontiac** Bonneville, Catalina, Grandville, Parisienne
19030 **Mid-size Regal & Century** all rear-drive models with V6, V8 and Turbo '74 thru '87
Regal - *see GENERAL MOTORS (38010)*
Riviera - *see GENERAL MOTORS (38030)*
Roadmaster - *see CHEVROLET (24046)*
Skyhawk - *see GENERAL MOTORS (38015)*
Skylark - *see GM (38020, 38025)*
Somerset - *see GENERAL MOTORS (38025)*

CADILLAC
21015 **CTS & CTS-V** '03 thru '12
21030 **Cadillac Rear Wheel Drive** '70 thru '93
Cimarron - *see GENERAL MOTORS (38015)*
DeVille - *see GM (38031 & 38032)*
Eldorado - *see GM (38030 & 38031)*
Fleetwood - *see GM (38031)*
Seville - *see GM (38030, 38031 & 38032)*

CHEVROLET
10305 **Chevrolet Engine Overhaul Manual**
24010 **Astro & GMC Safari Mini-vans** '85 thru '05
24015 **Camaro V8** all models '70 thru '81
24016 **Camaro** all models '82 thru '92
24017 **Camaro & Firebird** '93 thru '02
Cavalier - *see GENERAL MOTORS (38016)*
Celebrity - *see GENERAL MOTORS (38005)*
24020 **Chevelle, Malibu & El Camino** '69 thru '87
24024 **Chevette & Pontiac T1000** '76 thru '87
Citation - *see GENERAL MOTORS (38020)*
24027 **Colorado & GMC Canyon** '04 thru '10
24032 **Corsica/Beretta** all models '87 thru '96
24040 **Corvette** all V8 models '68 thru '82
24041 **Corvette** all models '84 thru '96
24045 **Full-size Sedans** Caprice, Impala, Biscayne, Bel Air & Wagons '69 thru '90
24046 **Impala SS & Caprice and Buick Roadmaster** '91 thru '96
Impala '00 thru '05 - *see LUMINA (24048)*
24047 **Impala & Monte Carlo** all models '06 thru '11
Lumina '90 thru '94 - *see GM (38010)*
24048 **Lumina & Monte Carlo** '95 thru '05
Lumina APV - *see GM (38035)*
24050 **Luv Pick-up** all 2WD & 4WD '72 thru '82
Malibu '97 thru '00 - *see GM (38026)*
24055 **Monte Carlo** all models '70 thru '88
Monte Carlo '95 thru '01 - *see LUMINA (24048)*
24059 **Nova** all V8 models '69 thru '79
24060 **Nova and Geo Prizm** '85 thru '92
24064 **Pick-ups** '67 thru '87 - Chevrolet & GMC
24065 **Pick-ups** '88 thru '98 - Chevrolet & GMC
24066 **Pick-ups** '99 thru '06 - Chevrolet & GMC
24067 **Chevrolet Silverado & GMC Sierra** '07 thru '12
24070 **S-10 & S-15 Pick-ups** '82 thru '93, **Blazer & Jimmy** '83 thru '94,
24071 **S-10 & Sonoma Pick-ups** '94 thru '04, including **Blazer, Jimmy & Hombre**
24072 **Chevrolet TrailBlazer, GMC Envoy & Oldsmobile Bravada** '02 thru '09
24075 **Sprint** '85 thru '88 **& Geo Metro** '89 thru '01
24080 **Vans - Chevrolet & GMC** '68 thru '96
24081 **Chevrolet Express & GMC Savana** Full-size Vans '96 thru '10

CHRYSLER
10310 **Chrysler Engine Overhaul Manual**
25015 **Chrysler Cirrus, Dodge Stratus, Plymouth Breeze** '95 thru '00
25020 **Full-size Front-Wheel Drive** '88 thru '93
K-Cars - *see DODGE Aries (30008)*
Laser - *see DODGE Daytona (30030)*
25025 **Chrysler LHS, Concorde, New Yorker, Dodge** Intrepid, **Eagle** Vision, '93 thru '97
25026 **Chrysler LHS, Concorde, 300M, Dodge** Intrepid, '98 thru '04
25027 **Chrysler 300, Dodge Charger & Magnum** '05 thru '09
25030 **Chrysler & Plymouth Mid-size** front wheel drive '82 thru '95
Rear-wheel Drive - *see Dodge (30050)*
25035 **PT Cruiser** all models '01 thru '10
25040 **Chrysler** Sebring '95 thru '06, **Dodge** Stratus '01 thru '06, **Dodge** Avenger '95 thru '00

DATSUN
28005 **200SX** all models '80 thru '83
28007 **B-210** all models '73 thru '78
28009 **210** all models '79 thru '82
28012 **240Z, 260Z & 280Z** Coupe '70 thru '78
28014 **280ZX** Coupe & 2+2 '79 thru '83
300ZX - *see NISSAN (72010)*
28018 **510 & PL521 Pick-up** '68 thru '73
28020 **510** all models '78 thru '81
28022 **620 Series Pick-up** all models '73 thru '79
720 Series Pick-up - *see NISSAN (72030)*
28025 **810/Maxima** all gasoline models '77 thru '84

DODGE
400 & 600 - *see CHRYSLER (25030)*
30008 **Aries & Plymouth Reliant** '81 thru '89
30010 **Caravan & Plymouth Voyager** '84 thru '95
30011 **Caravan & Plymouth Voyager** '96 thru '02
30012 **Challenger/Plymouth Saporro** '78 thru '83
30013 **Caravan, Chrysler Voyager, Town & Country** '03 thru '07
30016 **Colt & Plymouth Champ** '78 thru '87
30020 **Dakota Pick-ups** all models '87 thru '96
30021 **Durango** '98 & '99, **Dakota** '97 thru '99
30022 **Durango** '00 thru '03 **Dakota** '00 thru '04
30023 **Durango** '04 thru '09, **Dakota** '05 thru '11
30025 **Dart, Demon, Plymouth Barracuda, Duster & Valiant** 6 cyl models '67 thru '76
30030 **Daytona & Chrysler Laser** '84 thru '89
Intrepid - *see CHRYSLER (25025, 25026)*
30034 **Neon** all models '95 thru '99
30035 **Omni & Plymouth Horizon** '78 thru '90
30036 **Dodge and Plymouth Neon** '00 thru '05
30040 **Pick-ups** all full-size models '74 thru '93
30041 **Pick-ups** all full-size models '94 thru '01
30042 **Pick-ups** full-size models '02 thru '08
30045 **Ram 50/D50 Pick-ups & Raider and Plymouth Arrow Pick-ups** '79 thru '93
30050 **Dodge/Plymouth/Chrysler** RWD '71 thru '89
30055 **Shadow & Plymouth Sundance** '87 thru '94
30060 **Spirit & Plymouth Acclaim** '89 thru '95
30065 **Vans - Dodge & Plymouth** '71 thru '03

EAGLE
Talon - *see MITSUBISHI (68030, 68031)*
Vision - *see CHRYSLER (25025)*

FIAT
34010 **124 Sport Coupe & Spider** '68 thru '78
34025 **X1/9** all models '74 thru '80

FORD
10320 **Ford Engine Overhaul Manual**
10355 **Ford Automatic Transmission Overhaul**
11500 **Mustang '64-1/2 thru '70 Restoration Guide**
36004 **Aerostar Mini-vans** all models '86 thru '97
36006 **Contour & Mercury Mystique** '95 thru '00
36008 **Courier Pick-up** all models '72 thru '82
36012 **Crown Victoria & Mercury Grand Marquis** '88 thru '10
36016 **Escort/Mercury Lynx** all models '81 thru '90
36020 **Escort/Mercury Tracer** '91 thru '02
36022 **Escape & Mazda Tribute** '01 thru '11
36024 **Explorer & Mazda Navajo** '91 thru '01
36025 **Explorer/Mercury Mountaineer** '02 thru '10
36028 **Fairmont & Mercury Zephyr** '78 thru '83
36030 **Festiva & Aspire** '88 thru '97
36032 **Fiesta** all models '77 thru '80
36034 **Focus** all models '00 thru '11
36036 **Ford & Mercury Full-size** '75 thru '87
36044 **Ford & Mercury Mid-size** '75 thru '86
36045 **Fusion & Mercury Milan** '06 thru '10
36048 **Mustang V8** all models '64-1/2 thru '73
36049 **Mustang II** 4 cyl, V6 & V8 models '74 thru '78
36050 **Mustang & Mercury Capri** '79 thru '93
36051 **Mustang** all models '94 thru '04
36052 **Mustang** '05 thru '10
36054 **Pick-ups & Bronco** '73 thru '79
36058 **Pick-ups & Bronco** '80 thru '96
36059 **F-150 & Expedition** '97 thru '09, **F-250** '97 thru '99 **& Lincoln Navigator** '98 thru '09
36060 **Super Duty Pick-ups, Excursion** '99 thru '10
36061 **F-150** full-size '04 thru '10
36062 **Pinto & Mercury Bobcat** '75 thru '80
36066 **Probe** all models '89 thru '92
Probe '93 thru '97 - *see MAZDA 626 (61042)*
36070 **Ranger/Bronco II** gasoline models '83 thru '92
36071 **Ranger** '93 thru '10 & **Mazda Pick-ups** '94 thru '09
36074 **Taurus & Mercury Sable** '86 thru '95
36075 **Taurus & Mercury Sable** '96 thru '05
36078 **Tempo & Mercury Topaz** '84 thru '94
36082 **Thunderbird/Mercury Cougar** '83 thru '88
36086 **Thunderbird/Mercury Cougar** '89 thru '97
36090 **Vans** all V8 Econoline models '69 thru '91
36094 **Vans** full size '92 thru '10
36097 **Windstar Mini-van** '95 thru '07

GENERAL MOTORS
10360 **GM Automatic Transmission Overhaul**
38005 **Buick Century, Chevrolet Celebrity, Oldsmobile Cutlass Ciera & Pontiac 6000** all models '82 thru '96
38010 **Buick Regal, Chevrolet Lumina, Oldsmobile Cutlass Supreme & Pontiac Grand Prix** (FWD) '88 thru '07
38015 **Buick Skyhawk, Cadillac Cimarron, Chevrolet Cavalier, Oldsmobile Firenza & Pontiac J-2000 & Sunbird** '82 thru '94
38016 **Chevrolet Cavalier & Pontiac Sunfire** '95 thru '05
38017 **Chevrolet Cobalt & Pontiac G5** '05 thru '11
38020 **Buick Skylark, Chevrolet Citation, Olds Omega, Pontiac Phoenix** '80 thru '85
38025 **Buick Skylark & Somerset, Oldsmobile Achieva & Calais and Pontiac Grand Am** all models '85 thru '98
38026 **Chevrolet Malibu, Olds Alero & Cutlass, Pontiac Grand Am** '97 thru '03
38027 **Chevrolet Malibu** '04 thru '10
38030 **Cadillac Eldorado, Seville, Oldsmobile Toronado, Buick Riviera** '71 thru '85
38031 **Cadillac Eldorado & Seville, DeVille, Fleetwood & Olds Toronado, Buick Riviera** '86 thru '93
38032 **Cadillac DeVille** '94 thru '05 & **Seville** '92 thru '04 **Cadillac DTS** '06 thru '10
38035 **Chevrolet Lumina APV, Olds Silhouette & Pontiac Trans Sport** all models '90 thru '96
38036 **Chevrolet Venture, Olds Silhouette, Pontiac Trans Sport & Montana** '97 thru '05
General Motors Full-size Rear-wheel Drive - *see BUICK (19025)*
38040 **Chevrolet Equinox** '05 thru '09 **Pontiac Torrent** '06 thru '09
38070 **Chevrolet HHR** '06 thru '11

GEO
Metro - *see CHEVROLET Sprint (24075)*
Prizm - *'85 thru '92 see CHEVY (24060), '93 thru '02 see TOYOTA Corolla (92036)*
40030 **Storm** all models '90 thru '93
Tracker - *see SUZUKI Samurai (90010)*

GMC
Vans & Pick-ups - *see CHEVROLET*

HONDA
42010 **Accord CVCC** all models '76 thru '83
42011 **Accord** all models '84 thru '89
42012 **Accord** all models '90 thru '93
42013 **Accord** all models '94 thru '97
42014 **Accord** all models '98 thru '02
42015 **Accord** '03 thru '07
42020 **Civic 1200** all models '73 thru '79
42021 **Civic 1300 & 1500 CVCC** '80 thru '83
42022 **Civic 1500 CVCC** all models '75 thru '79

(Continued on other side)

NOTE: If you do not see a listing for your vehicle, consult your local Haynes dealer for the latest product information.

42023 **Civic** all models '84 thru '91
42024 **Civic & del Sol** '92 thru '95
42025 **Civic** '96 thru '00, **CR-V** '97 thru '01,
　Acura Integra '94 thru '00
42026 **Civic** '01 thru '10, **CR-V** '02 thru '09
42035 **Odyssey** all models '99 thru '10
　Passport - see ISUZU Rodeo (47017)
42037 **Honda Pilot** '03 thru '07, **Acura MDX** '01 thru '07
42040 **Prelude CVCC** all models '79 thru '89

HYUNDAI
43010 **Elantra** all models '96 thru '10
43015 **Excel & Accent** all models '86 thru '09
43050 **Santa Fe** all models '01 thru '06
43055 **Sonata** all models '99 thru '08

INFINITI
　G35 '03 thru '08 - see NISSAN 350Z (72011)

ISUZU
　Hombre - see CHEVROLET S-10 (24071)
47017 **Rodeo, Amigo & Honda Passport** '89 thru '02
47020 **Trooper & Pick-up** '81 thru '93

JAGUAR
49010 **XJ6** all 6 cyl models '68 thru '86
49011 **XJ6** all models '88 thru '94
49015 **XJ12 & XJS** all 12 cyl models '72 thru '85

JEEP
50010 **Cherokee, Comanche & Wagoneer Limited**
　all models '84 thru '01
50020 **CJ** all models '49 thru '86
50025 **Grand Cherokee** all models '93 thru '04
50026 **Grand Cherokee** '05 thru '09
50029 **Grand Wagoneer & Pick-up** '72 thru '91
　Grand Wagoneer '84 thru '91, Cherokee &
　Wagoneer '72 thru '83, Pick-up '72 thru '88
50030 **Wrangler** all models '87 thru '11
50035 **Liberty** '02 thru '07

KIA
54050 **Optima** '01 thru '10
54070 **Sephia** '94 thru '01, **Spectra** '00 thru '09,
　Sportage '05 thru '10

LEXUS
　ES 300/330 - see TOYOTA Camry (92007) (92008)
　RX 330 - see TOYOTA Highlander (92095)

LINCOLN
　Navigator - see FORD Pick-up (36059)
59010 **Rear-Wheel Drive** all models '70 thru '10

MAZDA
61010 **GLC Hatchback** (rear-wheel drive) '77 thru '83
61011 **GLC** (front-wheel drive) '81 thru '85
61012 **Mazda3** '04 thru '11
61015 **323 & Protegé** '90 thru '03
61016 **MX-5 Miata** '90 thru '09
61020 **MPV** all models '89 thru '98
　Navajo - see Ford Explorer (36024)
61030 **Pick-ups** '72 thru '93
　Pick-ups '94 thru '00 - see Ford Ranger (36071)
61035 **RX-7** all models '79 thru '85
61036 **RX-7** all models '86 thru '91
61040 **626** (rear-wheel drive) all models '79 thru '82
61041 **626/MX-6** (front-wheel drive) '83 thru '92
61042 **626, MX-6/Ford Probe** '93 thru '02
61043 **Mazda6** '03 thru '11

MERCEDES-BENZ
63012 **123 Series Diesel** '76 thru '85
63015 **190 Series** four-cyl gas models, '84 thru '88
63020 **230/250/280** 6 cyl sohc models '68 thru '72
63025 **280 123 Series** gasoline models '77 thru '81
63030 **350 & 450** all models '71 thru '80
63040 **C-Class:** C230/C240/C280/C320/C350 '01 thru '07

MERCURY
64200 **Villager & Nissan Quest** '93 thru '01
　All other titles, see FORD Listing.

MG
66010 **MGB** Roadster & GT Coupe '62 thru '80
66015 **MG Midget, Austin Healey Sprite** '58 thru '80

MINI
67020 **Mini** '02 thru '11

MITSUBISHI
68020 **Cordia, Tredia, Galant, Precis &**
　Mirage '83 thru '93
68030 **Eclipse, Eagle Talon & Ply. Laser** '90 thru '94
68031 **Eclipse** '95 thru '05, **Eagle Talon** '95 thru '98
68035 **Galant** '94 thru '10
68040 **Pick-up** '83 thru '96 & **Montero** '83 thru '93

NISSAN
72010 **300ZX** all models including Turbo '84 thru '89
72011 **350Z & Infiniti G35** all models '03 thru '08
72015 **Altima** all models '93 thru '06
72016 **Altima** '07 thru '10
72020 **Maxima** all models '85 thru '92
72021 **Maxima** all models '93 thru '04
72025 **Murano** '03 thru '10
72030 **Pick-ups** '80 thru '97 **Pathfinder** '87 thru '95
72031 **Frontier Pick-up, Xterra, Pathfinder** '96 thru '04
72032 **Frontier & Xterra** '05 thru '11
72040 **Pulsar** all models '83 thru '86
　Quest - see MERCURY Villager (64200)
72050 **Sentra** all models '82 thru '94
72051 **Sentra & 200SX** all models '95 thru '06
72060 **Stanza** all models '82 thru '90
72070 **Titan pick-ups** '04 thru '10 **Armada** '05 thru '10

OLDSMOBILE
73015 **Cutlass** V6 & V8 gas models '74 thru '88
　For other OLDSMOBILE titles, see BUICK,
　CHEVROLET or GENERAL MOTORS listing.

PLYMOUTH
　For PLYMOUTH titles, see DODGE listing.

PONTIAC
79008 **Fiero** all models '84 thru '88
79018 **Firebird** V8 models except Turbo '70 thru '81
79019 **Firebird** all models '82 thru '92
79025 **G6** all models '05 thru '09
79040 **Mid-size Rear-wheel Drive** '70 thru '87
　Vibe '03 thru '11 - see TOYOTA Matrix (92060)
　For other PONTIAC titles, see BUICK,
　CHEVROLET or GENERAL MOTORS listing.

PORSCHE
80020 **911** except Turbo & Carrera 4 '65 thru '89
80025 **914** all 4 cyl models '69 thru '76
80030 **924** all models including Turbo '76 thru '82
80035 **944** all models including Turbo '83 thru '89

RENAULT
　Alliance & Encore - see AMC (14020)

SAAB
84010 **900** all models including Turbo '79 thru '88

SATURN
87010 **Saturn** all S-series models '91 thru '02
87011 **Saturn Ion** '03 thru '07
87020 **Saturn** all L-series models '00 thru '04
87040 **Saturn VUE** '02 thru '07

SUBARU
89002 **1100, 1300, 1400 & 1600** '71 thru '79
89003 **1600 & 1800** 2WD & 4WD '80 thru '94
89100 **Legacy** all models '90 thru '99
89101 **Legacy & Forester** '00 thru '06

SUZUKI
90010 **Samurai/Sidekick & Geo Tracker** '86 thru '01

TOYOTA
92005 **Camry** all models '83 thru '91
92006 **Camry** all models '92 thru '96
92007 **Camry, Avalon, Solara, Lexus ES 300** '97 thru '01
92008 **Toyota Camry, Avalon and Solara and**
　Lexus ES 300/330 all models '02 thru '06
92009 **Camry** '07 thru '11
92015 **Celica Rear Wheel Drive** '71 thru '85
92020 **Celica Front Wheel Drive** '86 thru '99
92025 **Celica Supra** all models '79 thru '92
92030 **Corolla** all models '75 thru '79
92032 **Corolla** all rear wheel drive models '80 thru '87
92035 **Corolla** all front wheel drive models '84 thru '92
92036 **Corolla & Geo Prizm** '93 thru '02
92037 **Corolla** models '03 thru '11
92040 **Corolla Tercel** all models '80 thru '82
92045 **Corona** all models '74 thru '82
92050 **Cressida** all models '78 thru '82
92055 **Land Cruiser** FJ40, 43, 45, 55 '68 thru '82
92056 **Land Cruiser** FJ60, 62, 80, FZJ80 '80 thru '96
92060 **Matrix & Pontiac Vibe** '03 thru '11
92065 **MR2** all models '85 thru '87
92070 **Pick-up** all models '69 thru '78
92075 **Pick-up** all models '79 thru '95
92076 **Tacoma, 4Runner, & T100** '93 thru '04
92077 **Tacoma** all models '05 thru '09
92078 **Tundra** '00 thru '06 & **Sequoia** '01 thru '07
92079 **4Runner** all models '03 thru '09
92080 **Previa** all models '91 thru '95
92081 **Prius** all models '01 thru '08
92082 **RAV4** all models '96 thru '10
92085 **Tercel** all models '87 thru '94
92090 **Sienna** all models '98 thru '10
92095 **Highlander & Lexus RX-330** '99 thru '07

TRIUMPH
94007 **Spitfire** all models '62 thru '81
94010 **TR7** all models '75 thru '81

VW
96008 **Beetle & Karmann Ghia** '54 thru '79
96009 **New Beetle** '98 thru '11
96016 **Rabbit, Jetta, Scirocco & Pick-up** gas
　models '75 thru '92 & Convertible '80 thru '92
96017 **Golf, GTI & Jetta** '93 thru '98, **Cabrio** '95 thru '02
96018 **Golf, GTI, Jetta** '99 thru '05
96019 **Jetta, Rabbit, GTI & Golf** '05 thru '11
96020 **Rabbit, Jetta & Pick-up** diesel '77 thru '84
96023 **Passat** '98 thru '05, **Audi A4** '96 thru '01
96030 **Transporter 1600** all models '68 thru '79
96035 **Transporter 1700, 1800 & 2000** '72 thru '79
96040 **Type 3 1500 & 1600** all models '63 thru '73
96045 **Vanagon** all air-cooled models '80 thru '83

VOLVO
97010 **120, 130 Series & 1800 Sports** '61 thru '73
97015 **140 Series** all models '66 thru '74
97020 **240 Series** all models '76 thru '93
97040 **740 & 760 Series** all models '82 thru '88
97050 **850 Series** all models '93 thru '97

TECHBOOK MANUALS
10205 **Automotive Computer Codes**
10206 **OBD-II & Electronic Engine Management**
10210 **Automotive Emissions Control Manual**
10215 **Fuel Injection Manual** '78 thru '85
10220 **Fuel Injection Manual** '86 thru '99
10225 **Holley Carburetor Manual**
10230 **Rochester Carburetor Manual**
10240 **Weber/Zenith/Stromberg/SU Carburetors**
10305 **Chevrolet Engine Overhaul Manual**
10310 **Chrysler Engine Overhaul Manual**
10320 **Ford Engine Overhaul Manual**
10330 **GM and Ford Diesel Engine Repair Manual**
10333 **Engine Performance Manual**
10340 **Small Engine Repair Manual**, 5 HP & Less
10341 **Small Engine Repair Manual**, 5.5 - 20 HP
10345 **Suspension, Steering & Driveline Manual**
10355 **Ford Automatic Transmission Overhaul**
10360 **GM Automatic Transmission Overhaul**
10405 **Automotive Body Repair & Painting**
10410 **Automotive Brake Manual**
10411 **Automotive Anti-lock Brake (ABS) Systems**
10415 **Automotive Detailing Manual**
10420 **Automotive Electrical Manual**
10425 **Automotive Heating & Air Conditioning**
10430 **Automotive Reference Manual & Dictionary**
10435 **Automotive Tools Manual**
10440 **Used Car Buying Guide**
10445 **Welding Manual**
10450 **ATV Basics**
10452 **Scooters** 50cc to 250cc

SPANISH MANUALS
98903 **Reparación de Carrocería & Pintura**
98904 **Manual de Carburador Modelos**
　Holley & Rochester
98905 **Códigos Automotrices de la Computadora**
98906 **OBD-II & Sistemas de Control Electrónico**
　del Motor
98910 **Frenos Automotriz**
98913 **Electricidad Automotriz**
98915 **Inyección de Combustible** '86 al '99
99040 **Chevrolet & GMC Camionetas** '67 al '87
99041 **Chevrolet & GMC Camionetas** '88 al '98
99042 **Chevrolet & GMC Camionetas**
　Cerradas '68 al '95
99043 **Chevrolet/GMC Camionetas** '94 al '04
99048 **Chevrolet/GMC Camionetas** '99 al '06
99055 **Dodge Caravan & Plymouth Voyager** '84 al '95
99075 **Ford Camionetas y Bronco** '80 al '94
99076 **Ford F-150** '97 al '09
99077 **Ford Camionetas Cerradas** '69 al '91
99088 **Ford Modelos de Tamaño Mediano** '75 al '86
99089 **Ford Camionetas Ranger** '93 al '10
99091 **Ford Taurus & Mercury Sable** '86 al '95
99095 **GM Modelos de Tamaño Grande** '70 al '90
99100 **GM Modelos de Tamaño Mediano** '70 al '88
99106 **Jeep Cherokee, Wagoneer & Comanche**
　'84 al '00
99110 **Nissan Camioneta** '80 al '96, **Pathfinder** '87 al '95
99118 **Nissan Sentra** '82 al '94
99125 **Toyota Camionetas y 4Runner** '79 al '95

Over 100 Haynes
motorcycle manuals
also available

7-12